Children of Crisis

ALSO BY ROBERT COLES

Bruce Springsteen's America

Lives of Moral Leadership

The Moral Intelligence of Children

The Call of Service: A Witness to Idealism

Their Eyes Meeting the World: The Drawings and Paintings of Children (with Margaret Sartor)

The Call of Stories: Teaching and the Moral Imagination

The Spiritual Life of Children

Rumors of Separate Worlds (poems)

Anna Freud: The Dream of Psychoanalysis

The Child in Our Times: Studies in the Development of Resiliency (edited with Timothy Dugan)

That Red Wheelbarrow: Selected Literary Essays

Harvard Diary: Reflections on the Sacred and the Secular

Times of Surrender: Selected Essays

In the Streets (with Helen Levitt)

Dorothy Day: A Radical Devotion

Simone Weil: A Modern Pilgrimage

The Political Life of Children

The Moral Life of Children

Agee (with Ross Spears)

The Doctor Stories of William Carlos Williams (editor)

Dorothea Lange

Women of Crisis, II: Lives of Work and Dreams (with Jane Coles)

Flannery O'Connor's South

Walker Percy: An American Search

Women of Crisis, I: Lives of Struggle and Hope (with Jane Coles)

The Last and First Eskimos (with Alex Harris)

A Festering Sweetness (poems)

Privileged Ones: The Well-Off and the Rich in America (Volume V of Children of Crisis)

Eskimos, Chicanos, Indians (Volume IV of Children of Crisis)

The Mind's Fate: Ways of Seeing Psychiatry and Psychoanalysis

William Carlos Williams: The Knack of Survival in America

Irony in the Mind's Life: Essays on Novels by James Agee, Elizabeth Bowen, and George Eliot

The Darkness and the Light (with Doris Ulmann)

The Buses Roll (with Carol Baldwin)

The Old Ones of New Mexico (with Alex Harris)

A Spectacle Unto the World: The Catholic Worker Movement (with Jon Erikson)

Twelve to Sixteen: Early Adolescence (with Jerome Kagan)

Farewell to the South

The South Goes North (Volume III of Children of Crisis)

Migrants, Sharecroppers, Mountaineers (Volume II of Children of Crisis)

The Geography of Faith (with Daniel Berrigan)

The Middle Americans (with Jon Erikson)

Erik H. Erikson: The Growth of His Work

Drugs and Youth (with Joseph Brenner and Dermot Meagher)

Wages of Neglect (with Maria Piers)

Teachers and the Children of Poverty

Uprooted Children

The Image Is You

Still Hungry in America

Children of Crisis, Volume I: A Study of Courage and Fear

FOR CHILDREN

Dead End School

The Grass Pipe

Saving Face

Riding Free

Headsparks

Children of Crisis

Selections from the Pulitzer Prize–winning
five-volume Children of Crisis series

With a new introduction by the author

Robert Coles

BACK BAY BOOKS

Little, Brown and Company
Boston   New York   London

First Edition

The author is grateful for permission to reprint as an epigraph the following
previously copyrighted material: excerpt from William Carlos Williams's
Paterson, copyright 1948 by William Carlos Williams. Reprinted by
permission of New Directions Publishing Corp.

Library of Congress Cataloging-in-Publication Data

Coles, Robert.
    Children of crisis : selections from the Pulitzer Prize–winning five-volume
Children of crisis series ; with a new introduction by the author / Robert Coles.
        p. cm.
    Includes index.
    ISBN 0-316-15102-5 (pb)
    1. Poor children — United States.   2. Children — United States.   3. Children
of the rich — United States.   4. Children with social disabilities — United States.
I. Title.
HC110.P6C56 2003
305.23'0973 — dc21   2003047522

10   9   8   7   6   5   4   3   2   1

Q-MART

Printed in the United States of America

*To the children across America who have had so much to teach us —
and whose lives have become our nation's history.*

*In loving memory of Jane, and to our children and grandchildren;
and with grateful thanks to Eric H. Erikson and Anna Freud for
their constant encouragement, instruction.*

*With grateful thanks also to Terry Adams, whose careful interest
and concern very much enabled and gave shape to this book.*

"Outside

        outside myself

                there is a world,

he rumbled, subject to my incursions
— a world

        (to me) at rest,

                which I approach

concretely —"

Book Two,

Paterson

William Carlos Williams

"All that each person is, and experiences, and shall never experience, in body and mind, all these things are differing expressions of himself and of one root, and are identical: and not one of these things nor one of these persons is ever quite to be duplicated, nor replaced, nor has it ever quite had precedent: but each is a new and incommunicably tender life, wounded in every breath and almost as hardly killed as easily wounded: sustaining, for a while, without defense, the enormous assaults of the universe."

Let Us Now Praise Famous Men

James Agee

Contents

Introduction

What follows are words that were meant to give an account of American children of various backgrounds who grew up in the 1960s and 1970s. Those boys and girls became, in their own way, teachers. They sometimes spoke loud and clear about what crossed their minds, or they used crayons or pencils or paintbrushes to show through artistic representation what they saw, experienced, wanted to convey through portraits of themselves, of others, or through the rendering of particular faces, buildings, scenes. Over time the stories of those children, their remarks, as heard by the doctor who came to know them, became the subject matter of a series of five books, each called *Children of Crisis,* with the subtitles spelling out one or another aspect of a nation's social geography: the South's embattled racial climate of opinion and habit during the 1960s; the rural life of Dixie and beyond — up the hollows of Appalachia, and in the farms across the nation that require the traveling hands of laboring men and women (and sometimes children, too) if crops are to be planted, harvested; the cities of the North, which received so many thousands of needy and vulnerable families, eager to try the new kind of life available away from sharecropper cabins, migrant labor settlements, or the mountain hollows of, say, West Virginia, Kentucky; out West, the people who claimed the land, or worked it, now called Native Americans, once described as Indians, or now called Spanish-speaking citizens, once summoned as Chicanos, and up Alaska, those whose Eskimo bearings in distant communities gave way to the accessible life of a far northern state's busy commercial and even industrial life; and finally, those who, across a continent, have risen to the top, acquired money and the privileges that go with it — the not rare sagas of "rags to riches" that a nation has long savored, treasured.

In a sense, then, the *Children of Crisis* books tell a story of a nation's people, whose lives take place under a broad variety of circumstances; but those volumes, published between 1967 and 1977, also tell another story, that of a physician who left the bounds of a particular profession as it once exerted its hold on one of its practitioners — only to find himself taken up in the somewhat different manner that social observers find convenient, useful. Since all stories have their beginnings, perhaps it is best to go way back to the very start of this one — to a time that preceded by almost five years any of the work and writing that would initiate the *Children of Crisis* series. In 1955, I was learning to be a pediatrician at the University of Chicago's Billings Hospital. One of my young patients was dying of leukemia and had no chance of survival. He was ten years old, Jimmie was, a policeman's son, quite lively in nature, and ever ready to converse with his hard-working physician, who was constantly worried about what to do, when, on behalf of a whole ward full of desperately ill youngsters. I can still see his alert, watchful face as it scrutinized my worried effort to hear his heart, elicit the reflexes of his arms, his legs, keep track of his pulse, and his sweaty, blotched skin. Yet for all the exhaustion exacted by his mortal illness, he could be not only friendly, but ever forthcoming in response to my neophyte's questions. Once, as we talked, he asked a favor of me: Would I want to meet his three "best buddies"?

Yes, of course — and soon enough I was sitting with Carl, Johnnie, and Larry, who were asking questions about their pal's medical condition, his prospects, even as they let me know that they understood well what would soon be happening. "He's going to die, Jimmie is," Carl told me — and then, of a sudden, I was shown a picture of Jimmie that this friend had drawn, even as I was offered an explanation: Carl's mother was an elementary schoolteacher, and she encouraged him (as well as her classroom students) to draw pictures. Carl was good at drawing, liked to do it a lot, and had carried with him a large "sketch," he called it, of Jimmie. Now I realized what was in the folder he had in his right hand, and soon enough I was looking at a picture of Jimmie — and hearing this from Carl: "He's a great hitter, and he's always wanted to be a baseball player." Silence, and then a boy's lowered head, after which these words got spoken: "I figure, if Jimmie doesn't get better, I can remember him this way, standing near the base, ready to swing his bat and knock a bases-loaded homer — he's done that, you know."

I remember those words, decades later, because I wrote them

down, so touched was I by them, by the earnest goodwill of the lad who spoke them, and by the large, multicolored picture given me — a solid Jimmie standing with his bat in his hands, and before him a full baseball field, with a pitcher at the ready, and a friendly, cloudless sky above, the sun beaming a smile on all that stretched below it.

Weeks later, Jimmie would be gone from his family, his friends — and his stricken mother would be asking me if I might want to keep Carl's drawing. He'd initially shown it to me; I'd handed it to Jimmie, who had asked his mother to "save" it, at home — and now I was holding it, affecting and compelling both, in my hand for keeps. To this day, I think of that boy, Jimmie, pictured, and I think of his neighborhood friend, Carl — the picture drawn, the words spoken, amidst a tragic time in a child's life, and that of his family and friends. I go back to that early clinical experience in my life, because I learned so much then — a moment when a crisis, this one medical, prompted poignant expression, both verbal and visual.

A year later I was in Boston, working first at the Massachusetts General Hospital, then at the Children's Hospital — learning, in a few years' time, to move from pediatrics to child psychiatry. So doing, I got to know many boys and girls who were having trouble at home or at school or in one or another neighborhood — to the point that they were referred to us at the hospital, in the hope that what prompted their worries or fears or outbursts of anger would somehow yield to the understanding that physicians aim to acquire as they closely attend their patients. In 1956, as I worked with those young people psychiatrically, an epidemic of polio broke out across New England, and soon enough I was working with my fellow doctors to do all we could for youths now paralyzed in one way or another. The Salk vaccine had not yet been developed, and polio was a much and justly feared disease that changed the lives of those it struck. All day, every day, we doctors did the best we could (precious little, alas, so often) on behalf of the children we came to know on wards now all too full of immobilized patients and their frightened, grief-stricken parents.

One day, as I talked with Tim, a fourteen-year-old high schooler, an accomplished student and a fine athlete, I heard him move from a specific discussion of his legs, their sudden seeming lifelessness (for him, a fast runner, an especially disastrous development), to a broader consideration of what had happened, what might be in the offing not only for him, but for others: "My mom says there's always hope — but you have to be realistic. This is a big crisis for all of us in the family, not only me. I got sick, and here I am, trying my best to get better, to get those legs back to where they were; but there's just so much you can do with concentration and determination. Dad would say to us, he taught us: 'Where there's a will, there's a way.' That's true to some extent, I guess — not all the time, though. In a crisis, a real tough one, you find out a lot you never knew. You find out what's true for you, in your situation. Mom is a teacher, and she tells us you learn different things at different times in different ways. I'm going through this crisis, and I hope I get out of it walking — and smarter about life. I heard my mom telling that to one of the doctors — that I'd be a lot smarter when all this is over. She meant that I'd take a lot less for granted, and I'd know when to appreciate the small things in life — that are, really, the rock-bottom big things: your family, your friends, your hometown, and your country, and the sun shining on your green lawn, the birds circling around, for a nibble here and there, and your dog, looking and looking at you, for a bite of food, or for some direction — and don't we all need it, search hard for it!"

I was so fortunate to have a tape recorder at hand as those words came my way. I was trying to document, in a hospital setting, the manner in which young people responded to certain medical problems that beset them — whereas, then and there I was in the presence of something else, something far more precious: a thoughtful person giving voice to impressive, even haunting wisdom. Over and over I played that tape, and as I listened, the word *crisis* kept staying with me — polio was a wide-ranging physical disease, a serious crisis, yes, but it also was an ironically enabling presence of sorts in the minds of those afflicted: an instrument of probing, personal reflection in those unlucky enough to have caught it.

Over a year's time, I got to hear quite a lot from Tim, about his present prospects and future aspirations. I also heard other young patients talk about the dreaded disease, now become for them an aspect of daily living. I heard about the trials and tribulations of children, for sure, but I also heard about the strengths those youngsters found and mobilized mightily: new ways of thinking, of seeing life, its possibilities and opportunities as well as its downsides — all in all, the risks of disease become the daily experience of it, sometimes for the bad, sometimes for the good. Eventually, I got to attend Tim's graduation from college, from law school. He would always have a "weak left leg," he called it; but with the help of daily exercises, he managed to "limp along," then "run, limping," and eventually even think of his "bout with polio" as a "big prod" to his educational and professional life —

he, who would go to college, then law school, and become a defender in courtrooms of individuals injured in accidents, or laid low by life's bad turns.

"I got knocked down by a virus," Tim told me on his fiftieth birthday, "and here I am trying to lend a hand to some folks who can't take very much for granted, and are staring at poverty or illness, and hoping someone will knock on their door, and say, 'You bet, I'll lend a helping hand.'" A lawyer was looking back, was remarking on fate, on "chance and circumstance," as George Eliot put it so succinctly in *Middlemarch*. So it went for Tim — fate tapping him on the shoulder; and so it goes for all of us, to our possible benefit occasionally or, sadly, to our utter detriment.

In 1958, under the old doctors' draft law, I had to put in two years of military service — and, accordingly, ended up in Biloxi, Mississippi, where I helped run a psychiatric service in the hospital of Keesler Air Force Base. When I went down South to start working there, I was not by any means celebrating this new episode in my professional or personal life; soon enough, though, I'd be getting to know an America I'd not before witnessed, never mind had any reason to try to comprehend in its variousness — the ironies and paradoxes of a region's everyday life. Yet such an assignment, reluctantly embraced, with no small amount of melancholy, would become an enormously significant one for me; a whole new education unfolded before my once dismayed eyes (speaking of ironies) — the civil rights struggle that children, among others, steadfastly pioneered: past mobs shouting hate, threatening injury, six-year-old African-American children walked into the school buildings of New Orleans. On my way to a medical meeting I saw one of those children, Ruby Bridges, trying to approach a school's steps, while men and women assailed her with words, waved placards bearing messages of contempt, rage. Even as I heard the voices of ill will, I saw a child forthrightly walking, policemen to her side — and so observing, I heard in my mind the voice, the words, of a Boston boy, Tim: here, too, I realized, was a young one going through a crisis, a nation's lessons become her very own.

Within weeks, my wife, Jane, and I were visiting Ruby Bridges at her home — making our acquaintance with her, and with her mother and father. There were other children initiating school desegregation in New Orleans at that time — encountering mobs in front of a school. Jane and I got to know them as well — all in weekly visits, on occasion biweekly ones. Jane, a high school teacher, spoke at greater length with the parents and teachers of the children. I sat with one child, then another, in their homes — talking and observing the children draw, even as, sometimes, I tried to follow suit. We had a great time with those many crayons, all of us, I think it fair to say: a social and educational crisis become ours to attempt sketching, coloring, getting down to appropriate size, shape. For a while I listened, recalled afterwards; then I began lugging a tape recorder around, much to the amusement of the children, who noted readily my mechanical incompetence, my chronic frustration. Ruby and others would eventually be of more than help — anticipate my inadequacies, more than address them. Later on, Jane and I moved to Atlanta, in hopes of learning from older children, who were initiating high school desegregation; we got plenty of valuable advice there about taping and transcribing interviews from youths avidly able to press the right buttons, replace exhausted tapes — and quite interested in having their say put down on the record, courtesy of a gadget whose workings they had come to know rather well.

By the middle 1970s, a decade after I'd begun talking with Ruby and others in New Orleans, with seven of the "Atlanta ten," as the high schoolers who started desegregation there were called, I'd been all over the United States, become the appreciative student, as it were, of "all sorts and conditions" of a great nation's children — white Southerners as well as their African-American school counterparts in that region's embattled schools, and children whose parents were migrant farm workers, or lived up the hollows of Appalachia, or out West, or way north of the Arctic Circle. All the while I was keeping to a set routine: weekly visits, transcriptions of conversations, editing of them — no mean job for one who was actually trying to learn to write in ordinary language, to do justice, also, to the heart and soul of what he'd heard, observed, concluded. All the while, too, I tried to keep in mind the remarks I'd been fortunate, indeed, to hear spoken by Dr. William Carlos Williams, whose writing I had studied as a college student, and whom I had come to know, emulate as best I could. So often, in medical school, I visited him, went with him on his house visits, his hospital rounds: such a privilege, so much to learn and later keep very much in mind. He was aging and ill as I began the work that would eventually be described in the *Children of Crisis* books, but he certainly was able, as always had been the case, to make bluntly clear his way of working, his manner of connecting with certain individuals, then telling others, as a writing doc, what he had come to know. Here he is once, speaking of the "doctor stories" he wrote, and of so much else (what an observer gets to know through encounters with fellow human beings): "The stories develop their own energy; they take over — leaving me behind. I read them, afterwards, and hope I will forget that it was me, me, me — me going to visit patients, me glad when I could be of help to them, and me driven to write about them and proud that I could. If I've managed to get rid of myself as an annoyance to the reader, but still give the best of myself and what I've experienced to that reader — then the effort has been worth it, and is a success."

By 1977, I felt that I'd given my all to the kind of "effort" Dr. Williams had put on the table for himself and others (his readers) to consider. Perhaps the story of the children whose pictures and words show and tell a good deal in the five volumes of *Children of Crisis* is also the story of a doctor who listened long and hard to a young patient (Tim, in Boston, in 1956) and who found his way to the learning places that homes and schools and city streets and country places can provide. Along the way there were teachers carried within as well as heard in casual talks that became long discussions: Erik Erikson and Anna Freud, very much my instructors (and heroes) in psychoanalytic training, thinking, practice; Robert F. Kennedy, with whom I was so lucky to work, during his memorably intense visits to some of the nation's at-risk children, whose plight (and whose dignity and importance as future American citizens) he recognized and sought earnestly, passionately to address. (He was the one who very much encouraged me to go west, live in New Mexico and elsewhere, so as to observe, learn from the boys and girls out there.)

"It takes two to make a truth," said Nietzsche; and so it can go, our humanity thereby affirmed: the observer and the observed, the child and the parent, the teacher and the student, the attending (and one hopes, attentive) physician and the patient, the speaker and the listener — and the writer and the reader.

I
A Study of Courage and Fear

The South

I came to the South a New Englander, not only by birth but with over a quarter of a century of living and growing up. At the end of a psychiatric residency I was called to Mississippi to serve my required two years in the military as a doctor, in this case as the chief of an Air Force neuropsychiatric hospital. The Air Force is a memory, but the South has become a real, a fresh part of my life. At first it was a region that I cared little to know, in fact it took me from several assignments I would have preferred. It has become one whose continuing pull upon my mind and heart prevents me from staying away for very long.

It is easy to categorize and give names to experiences once we are done with them. It is often sad that we do, because the effort takes away much of their original and spontaneous character. I suppose we need to try — it helps others understand, and makes us feel less anxious because more in control of our fate. As I look back at the past years in the South, I recall how easily I slipped into its very distinctive life and how pleasant I found that life to be. Only now do I stir anxiously at the thought of just how long (weeks turning to months) it took me to develop the dim awareness that became the vague uneasiness which marked a change in my thoughts and habits while living there.

One way of putting it is that I was a white, middle-class professional man, and so I easily fitted into that kind of Southern society. Only gradually did I begin to notice the injustice so close at hand, and as a consequence eventually take up my particular effort against it. (There would be those various categorical "stages" in such a development, ranging from faint glimmers to horrified, full recognition.) In the South, of course, anyone who begins to discover "injustice" in the world is in fact noticing the existence of a caste system wherein Negroes have an inherited position in a social organization which both needs them and yet notices their skin color before any individual attainments or accomplishments.

3

I think the major conclusion that I now draw from my first stay in the South is less one of deliberate accommodation to its social evils than of intense preoccupation with a brief but demanding interlude in my life — a new kind of job in a new location. The world cries out with its innumerable trials and horrors — the betrayal of human life, made cheap and stripped of its dignity, in every nation. The very nature of the human mind forces us to limit our interests and compassion, or else we drown in their diffusion and our own extreme pain.

In any event, toward the end of my second year South I was interrupted one day on a bicycle trip along the shore of the Gulf of Mexico by the sight and sound of a vicious battle. To this day I can remember my mind working its way toward some comprehension of what was happening, fighting its way through its old attitudes for a moment, then slipping back to them in relief. I saw a scuffle, and at first I wondered why people would want to behave that way. For a few seconds, I suppose, my lifetime — and I don't think only mine — was recapitulated: its innocence, its indifference, its ignorance, its sheltered quiet, its half-and-half mixture of moral inertia and well-intentioned effort. For a while I could only see *people* fighting. I heard shouts and cries. Some nasty and vulgar words fell upon my ears. I recall thinking for a moment that it was a Sunday, a beautiful Sunday; and it was a shame that people could be so mean-spirited and irreverent on Sunday, on any day, on such a clear, warm morning in early spring. I pedaled faster; I almost had the scene out of sight; but I can remember today slowing down, hesitating, only able to stop by lifting my body from the seat of the bike, by using my dragging, scuffing feet. I let the bike lie on its side, and stood still.

Not only was there a fight, but among the people I could see several *women*. A woman screamed that a man had smashed her watch and stepped on her glasses. Before I saw that she was a slender, middle-aged *Negro* lady, that he was a young, athletic *white man*, I felt the sympathy and horror that the weak share with the weak against the powerful. With that feeling I also knew for a moment that I would not easily be able to go to the woman's aid. In another flash, however, I realized I could justify my reluctance: it was a *racial* incident; the truth of what was happening was that the people were not simply people, the men and women not simply that.

I can still feel myself standing there, benighted, frightened, seized with curiosity, suddenly quite restless. I was not morally outraged. I did not want to join in the Negroes' protest for equal access to that essentially useless, shallow bit of seashore. Eventually, I simply wanted to go away; and I did. Riding home I condemned *all* the antagonists for fighting, for choosing to fight for such absurd stakes, for being the kind of people who *would* fight. I am not now very proud of those minutes. Yet if I forgot them, I would be even more ashamed.

That night I worked in the emergency ward of the base hospital, a duty which fell on each doctor with unnerving regularity. I had come to know the local police quite well during those evenings; they were on call, too, and we shared the long stretches of dark silence in that small town. The incident I had inadvertently witnessed was very much on the minds of both policemen, and their insistent talk about it made it impossible for me to forget it. We had never before mentioned the subject of race, but not, so far as I know, out of self-conscious or fearful avoidance in any of us. I liked those two policemen. They were kind, polite, and quite intelligent — considerably more so than many I had met in similar situations in certain Northern hospitals.

Like the event itself, I recall the first words: "They'd be dead now if it weren't for the publicity they get these days," followed by an avowal from his companion that "They will be if they try it again. We're never going to have mixing in this state." They had been talking with me; suddenly I felt them talking *to* me — *at* me. Their voices tightened. They spoke as crisply as a Southern drawl will permit — the honey in it had crystallized. They seemed aloof, yet fiercely determined to make their feelings clear to me, to the others nearby — now I realize to themselves. I found myself slipping into a psychiatric posture with them, noticing their defensive anger, their accusations — diffusely directed at history, at Northerners. I decided that *they* were afraid, but I really didn't know why. I said little in reply. I wondered how men so strong, so appealing, so sensible could be aroused by an event I had managed to put out of my mind. Then a patient came in, and I was strangely glad to see him. His minor infection kept me exceptionally busy. If he hadn't been there . . . I remember thinking that I would not have told my friends that I had seen the "swim-in." I saw their mood, observed their tension, felt their resentment, sensed their irritability, and feared my own involvement in any of them. Psychiatrists, of course, learn to watch for the unreasonable, avoid entanglement with the irrational. I imagine it was handy for me to be able to call upon such professional practices.

By morning we had talked of town news, the fishing and shrimping, the new shopping center going up, the meaning to the area of a projected increase in the population of the air base. That dawn we left, friends to one another as before. During the next weeks I continued with my usual tasks of work and play; but something had taken place. I can recollect, for instance, picking up the Jackson and New Orleans papers, reading in them of the coming probability of school desegregation in nearby New Orleans. It was well before the fateful day of its start, but the New Orleans papers were bitter and the Jackson papers almost incredulous. Somehow that news didn't manage to slip by me the way some news does, out of the impossibility of keeping totally abreast. It wasn't simply my reading, however, that was being affected. I started noticing where Negroes lived, where they didn't; where they were in evidence, where they were not; how they behaved with white people, and white people with them.

This new consciousness took root over several months. I find it hard to do justice to whatever growth and consolidation of feeling may have occurred during those months, because to think about that time now often invites in myself a certain scornful disbelief — that I could have lived so long under such a clearly oppressive social, political, and economic system, only to have been so blithely, so very innocently unaware of its nature. Yet I was.

Today there may be other problems than blindness facing many people living in the South. Large numbers of people in the region have awakened to the racial problem, and many of them, like me, must be freshly sensitive to the limitations which all human beings discover in their involvements and sensitivities. As if that were not enough, many probably are also coming to know that strong commitments push and tug at one another with their various demands, so that new kinds of indifference — even arrogance and hate — can follow old blind spots or prejudices. For example, there is the fighter's need to shed himself of much of the ambiguity of life, to sacrifice perspective, kindheartedness, and even, at times, good judgment to the interests of the hard battle. When I look back at my first days there I am glad that I came to know the South as I did; but I also feel torn and paralyzed when I think of those times too long. I enjoyed one kind of life then, and that kind is gone for me.

Of course the South has always had its moments of paralyzed nostalgia. Nostalgia can be for anyone a valuable way to avoid the terrible strain of the present by forsaking its reality in favor of the more pleasant world of memory. There is a painful ambiguity to Southern life: the genuine beauty of the landscape, the very real tradition of generosity and neighborliness, the long-standing sense of persecution, moral as well as economic, at the hands of powerful and hypocritical Americans from other areas. Effective protest, even against many open and declared social evils, does not always easily find a voice; and seg-regation in the South has hardly been considered anything but in-evitable for both whites and Negroes: each in their own way have known for generations the futility or risks of trying to change so awe-some and peculiar a social system.

The protest I witnessed at the seashore in Mississippi showed that whatever balance it had taken to keep a way of life from being seen as a social evil was beginning to be upset. Not only was the protest no accident, but the restraint of the town's police was no acci-dent either — whatever solemn excuses they offered for it. The South was feeling the swift encouragement (and consequent fear) of a chain of events connected to world history as well as our own nation's. My life is no "average white Southerner's" (hopefully none of our lives submit to approximations like that), and I am not sure that sit-ins such as I saw that day affect the majority of the South's white popula-tion as they do many of us who live elsewhere. Yet I think most people of the South — Negroes and whites alike — have experienced some of that same surprise I did, a jolting flash when one kind of world begins to collapse, another begins to appear, and it all becomes *apparent*.

My work of the past years has been to study what happens to people in the midst of such social changes, how they relinquish their old ways and take up new ones, how, that is, they manage the various stresses and exertions of doing so. I shall never know how those Ne-groes and whites felt whom I saw that day on the Gulf Coast of Mis-sissippi, but I think I have some fair notion about how others like them have felt in equally tense if not so vicious encounters — the children in desegregated schools in Louisiana, or in Georgia, where I lived for two years; the sit-in students from all over the South, and the whites who have been confronted by them; some leading segregation-ists, whom I came to know over a good number of months; and most recently, some sharecroppers and migrant workers, the poor of both races whose hands harvest our cotton and food for little enough re-ward indeed.

Doing such work has required so much travel throughout the re-gion that I know much of it better than any part of the North where I have lived. Even before I started studying some of the problems in the South, however, I had become somewhat sensitive to it through the as-tonishing contrast there with all that New England taught me to ex-pect from nature and people. The very names of the towns were surprising. Some were familiar enough, but there are special prefer-ences, too, such as the Greek and Roman names given to town after town in state after state: Rome in Georgia, Mississippi, and Tennessee; or Sparta in Georgia, Tennessee, and North Carolina. The ancient city of Carthage on the Gulf of Tunis is no more, but of fourteen cities which carry on its name over the world, six are in the South. There are other names less classical but in their sum a story of the region: Laurel, Enterprise, Liberty, Eufala, Senatobia, Natchitoches, Yazoo, Magnolia, Opelouses, Amite, and the Fayettevilles and Waynesboros, telling of flowers, ideals, Indians, and the French or English who lived there or came to do so.

The South's difference from the rest of the nation depends upon more than villages named in honor of Indian tribes or patriots to be celebrated. The South is not only its history, of those towns, of slavery, of rebellion. The skin feels the bouts of winter warmth, and must live with the heat in summer, dry in Atlanta, steamy in New Orleans; for heat is the South, and the weather is indeed kinder in winter and fatiguing in the summer. Whole theories of human nature have centered themselves on climate, and most often they seem single-minded or excessive, except for a moment in February when a soft wind rises from the bay and comes into Mobile, and with it a warm sun which brings out azaleas and high spirits both; or a time in midsummer when the damp heat in Louisiana has gone on long enough to make nerves already worn thin become frayed beyond recovery.

The earth, too, is special, much of it red with copper. The growth is different; tropical plants and palm trees, the famous wisteria and symbolic magnolia. The water is particularly abundant and rich in its variety: wide rivers, their tributaries weaving through the entire region, and the still smaller bayous, and canals, and the swamps with the mist over them. Lakes are everywhere, and much of the oceanside shows a tropical green band when it touches the shore.

The people have their own ways, too — their words, their food and stories, their kind of churches and praying. It's been noted so often, but an outsider like me coming from Northern or Western cities is surprised at first by the very few names that are not Anglo-Saxon; those names, of course, shared by Negroes, who are not simply confined to ghettoes as they are so predominantly in the North, but are everywhere. They take care of homes and often live near them; they work in stores, gas stations, office buildings, and on the farms which still dominate the area; they cultivate and harvest crops, sharing in some of the profits in exchange for land and house, or moving from state to state to wait for harvests and gather them.

White and Negro alike, the people are, I suspect, church-going beyond all others in the nation. The land seems covered with churches, and their denominational variety is astonishing. Revivals are common, and strict tithing by no means rare. The Bible is read literally in many towns throughout the section, which is still rural, strong on family and unashamed patriotism. Many whites have not yet surrendered their intensely suspicious regional and national pride, and many Negroes have till now found no reason to let go of the apathy and dependency, the alternation of good-natured frolic and sulky aloofness which characterized for so long their lack of pride in both themselves and their condition. Both races share some of the social form of the society — the expressions like "Y'all come back," said frequently out of meaning as well as ritual, or the food, like pecan pie, grits and okra, which come upon any visitor fairly soon and which one "favors" or is "partial to."

The federal roads are coming in, television with its widespread news and "culture" is everywhere, and national loyalties have always contended with local ones. The region, though, for good and bad has had a stubborn power, not only in its social and economic system, but in its history, its earth, its language and literature. Certainly what I have described about the South's particular nature is familiar to most of us, and has been repeatedly described before. I had read those descriptions and "knew" their message before going to live there. Yet the experience of those differences of living and thinking made for a sharper kind of awareness in me of the very real effect of those differences on the outsider who comes to live there as well as the lifelong inhabitant of the section. Too much can be made of these "local" variations; but then too little significance can be granted them in an age that recognizes perhaps rather exclusively the grossest kinds of political and economic power, or dwells with a certain preoccupation upon the unqualified sovereignty of early childhood experiences.

My work has been concerned with changes in Southern life as it moodily breaks with the past. For well over a generation a "new South" has been anticipated and hailed, but its arrival is now certain. As I walk through Atlanta or Charlotte the people can be seen in all their hurry, dressed out of New York, their office buildings as new, ugly, and efficient as those in other "growing" sections. The airports are the same boxes of never-ending buoyant music, and the runways as hungry for jets as all others. Yet Southerners have resisted as well as yielded to and even welcomed our modern nearness to one another. In studying the adjustment of white and Negro children (and their parents and teachers) to school desegregation I have learned to expect just that unusual blend of affection and reserve, accommodation and resentment which characterizes not only racial relations as they change in form and substance these days, but the South itself — recasting itself, but in its own fashion.

No one interested in the individual as he encounters a society in swift transition will be bored by Mississippi or the Carolinas. Some of the South's people hurt and exploit others, but the region itself has been ruthlessly exploited over the generations. Many of its people are poor, ignorant, and capable of an absurd kind of defensive chauvinism, but many are sturdy, hardworking, and kind people, so that as a whole every bit of Faulkner's vision seems sound. For all the shrill and resentful voices there have been many silent warriors in hopeless causes, many silent sufferers reduced to poverty and defeat; and now their descendants fight against hateful mobs and the mean conditions of life which generate them.

These past one hundred years have not been a pretty story, and distress has not fallen upon one race alone. The kind of political tyranny practiced by whites over Negroes has gained little for large numbers of whites, and the saddest part of studying whites hating Negroes by forming mobs or being nasty to them in schools, or sharing their fate on the collapsing farms of the region or in the flow of migrant farmers which travels through it each year, is how very treacherous that "psychological satisfaction" of racial superiority has really been to the lives of those who have sought nourishment from it, and sometimes almost it alone.

A nation within a nation, emerging from years of exile and hardship, the South's people today are showing individual dignity and courage as well as fear and desperation. Today, when some of us wonder whether our social order is in fact becoming drab and lifeless through its ability to make many of us fearfully similar and compliant, the South still clings to its almost biblical struggles between those willing to risk and dare and those anxious to flee and hide. Perhaps out of no special virtue except its own tragic history, the people there are fighting one another with an intensity and consistency which is rare indeed in our country.

The protagonists have been ordinary people, but all of them have found themselves in a place and a time which have given heroic and symbolic proportions to their struggles. I am thinking, in this connection, of a white woman in New Orleans whose four children, with only a very few others, defied the mobs attempting a total boycott of an elementary school in opposition to one little Negro girl. Why did this woman, deeply of the South, not by any means committed to "integration," hazard her life, the lives of her husband and children? I was in the company of those who tried to find the answer; a reporter, a sociologist, a psychiatrist, each of us worked at our common curiosity about human nature and its motives. I think we were all baffled — perhaps because we were all eager for the categorical solution, afraid of the clumsy, undefined, paradoxical flow of life and its events which may, in fact, be the truth of it.

Again and again — I talked with this woman over a period of two years — she came back to her only reply: she hadn't *planned* to dispute the angry, threatening crowds; she didn't think she was actually in favor of desegregation when all the uproar started; perhaps she was now, though; but she had always believed in education for her children, and she also felt a deep loyalty to the South's tradition, as she put it, "of good manners."

One day she was at her most open, and most persuasive: "My heart is divided, and at the worst of it I thought we'd die, not just from dynamite, but from nervous exhaustion. I wasn't brought up to have nigras at school with me or my children. I just wasn't. . . . If I had to do it over, I wouldn't have made this system, but how many people ever have a say about what kind of world they're going to live in? . . . I guess in a sense I did have my way with those mobs. But I didn't plan to, and we were near scared to death most of the time. . . . People blame the South for the mobs, but that's just part of the South. If I did right, that's part of the South, too. . . . They just don't know how a lot of us down here suffer. We didn't make all this, we just were born to it, and we don't have all the opportunity and money down here that they do in the North. . . . I told my children the other day that we're going to live to see the end of this trouble, and when we do I'll bet both races get on better down here than anywhere else in America. . . . Why? Because I think we're quieter down here, and we respect one another, and if we could clear up the race thing, we really would know one another better. . . . We've lived so *close* for so long. . . ."

A full transcript of what this woman has said at various times tells more than any comments from those who have heard her. She is not alone in her courage. The South is filled with an underground of sly liberals in the midst of situations hardly likely to support their efforts. It is filled with a tradition of solid, dignified Negroes and ashamed, confused whites, enough of both so that it would take a bold man indeed to separate and weigh their respective suffering. It is also, however, filled with bitter, spiteful whites and fearful, apathetic Negroes, some of them capable of exploiting their own people or demeaning them.

Perhaps nowhere in America is there so much that is good and bad about human beings so clearly in evidence. Few would want to keep the region's special virtues at the price of its outrageous faults. Yet, it is a beautiful land to see, and its people in their guilt and distress may have a good deal to teach us all. The United States as a whole has known little frustration and defeat for some time. The South has lived intimately with both, and it may have some wisdom to offer from that experience. This is surely a time in our national life when we need any help we can get about how to live properly and sensibly in the face of prolonged uncertainty, ambiguity, and even the frustrations which come from not winning every battle in every war. The South has not only seen the gloomy and tormented side of man's destiny; it has seen it and known enough of it perhaps to realize also the redemptive promise and power in human suffering. Sorrow may be fated, but to survive it and grow is an achievement all its own.

When I Draw the Lord He'll Be a Real Big Man

In recent years child psychiatrists have steadily increased their ability to understand what is happening in the minds of even their youngest or only remotely communicative patients. When Freud insisted upon the extreme relevance of childhood experiences to the lives of grownups he did so in a middle-class Viennese climate that held children either innocents in need of progressive enlightenment or devilish knaves whose mischief deserved every possible restraint and punishment. On a tide of free associations he and his followers carried virtually an entire culture backward to the life of the child's mind, and as a result the new profession of child psychiatry came into existence.

Within the psychoanalytic tradition his daughter Anna took the lead in giving the profession purpose and competence. In fact she turned the new interest in children to a continuing study of them; to a concern with childhood she added her concern for children. Soon, in the twenties and thirties, the influential pull of psychoanalysis came to be felt by academic psychologists and anthropologists, so that children in all sorts of cultures eventually were watched, while children in the Western world were observed, tested, and measured as carefully as adult ingenuity permitted.

Once children became so significant to doctors or social scientists, ways had to be found to learn what was going on inside them as well as what they could or could not do at various ages. Direct observation was — and still is — championed by Anna Freud. The psychoanalytically sensitive can discover in the "ordinary" or "random" behavior of children, be they in the nursery, classroom, or clinic, a number of patterns and clues to what holds their attention and concerns them, or worse, troubles them. No tests or questionnaires are necessary, only watchful eyes and attentive ears. When such direct observation is coupled with conscientious interviews of parents and teachers, the child's behavior becomes reasonably well understood.

Yet those who treat children have a task rather different from those who study them. They have to not only find out what they can, but so reach and affect the child's mind that he no longer ails. The child must be helped to comprehend what bothers him, and he must then settle the problem so decisively that he no longer feels upset, or indeed shows any signs to the ever-watchful clinician that he may still be troubled "deep down." To accomplish that goal in young children of five or six, to exchange views with them, to learn what they feel, commonly requires in the doctor a willingness to abandon his reliance upon one of his chief assets in his work with grown-ups, or for that matter older boys and girls — the service of the spoken word.

In the case of very young children, say of six months or a year, by the nature of things the child psychiatrist will direct a heavy share of his attention to the parents, or those standing in for them by choice or necessity. Infants and toddlers who refuse food, develop unusually cranky dispositions, and in general show signs of poor emotional or neurological development that cannot be explained by the presence of a physical illness are babies responding to unduly apprehensive care, or worse, to cruel care or no care worthy of the name. As a result a generation of therapists have appreciated the value of holding the baby, playing with him and feeding him, so that what he does not obtain outside the office he at least consistently gets inside. What must be communicated by the doctor at that age is solicitude and affection.

As children go into the third year their interest in play becomes quite reliable and developed, an obvious result of their increasingly organized and purposeful mental life; in brief, they have more going on within them that seeks engagement and expression with the outside world, both of people and things. During the thirties and into the forties child psychiatrists took increasing clinical advantage of that fact, harnessing toys and games to their investigative and therapeutic efforts — a development stimulated by the simple yet revolutionary psychoanalytic tenet that all behavior, however discrete or frivolous, makes sense and is likely to express something more (or other) than what is apparent.

In contrast, much less clinical attention has been given the drawings children so abundantly produce from three and four until adolescence. For that matter, the grown artist has both confused and fascinated psychoanalysts. Freud looked closely at the lives of a number of them, but was careful to acknowledge that what actually makes the artist, what separates him from others (non-artists whose lives and problems resemble his, or would-be artists who never seem to make the grade) is unaccountably nonspecific, i.e., not by itself derived from any necessary, particular — or at least presently obvious — kind of psychological experience or development.

A few psychoanalysts have continued to struggle with the twin problems of what makes for creativity, and what can be learned from artistic productions, be they ordinary or outstanding. Ernst Kris gave close attention to those who paint and what they produce, and particularly demonstrated the revelatory nature of drawings and paintings done by the psychotic: illness finds its way to the canvas in both themes and styles of representation. Henry Murray spent years perfecting the Thematic Apperception Test, an imaginative and practical way to take advantage of our everyday inclination to look at pictures and talk about them in ways that tell some truth about ourselves. With the development of the Children's Apperception Test boys and girls also could be asked to say what a series of pictures — photographs of drawings or paintings — meant to them.

Of course for several decades social, experimental, and educational psychologists, or those interested in measuring neurological development, have used drawings in studying the attitudes children have, how competent and coordinated they are with their hands, or how they see themselves or others. Asking a child to draw himself, his parents, or simply a boy or a girl has become one of a number of ways to appraise growth, development, intelligence, and in some cases a patient's psychological status.

In therapy, however, child psychiatrists often use toys and games rather than crayons and paints. Even in research the significant work done by social scientists on the child's growing sense of racial identity, his awareness of prejudice or his capacity to have it consistently, has involved the use of dolls and other toys coupled with questionnaires or a series of picture cards. Such methods have the advantage of being standard, somewhat measurable ways to evaluate children and compare their feelings on one or another issue.

On the other hand, to ask a child to draw whatever he wishes to draw in order to learn about his racial attitudes, or even to request from a series of children that they each draw the same person, place, or thing for such a purpose, is to court the subjective and the individually variable, usually thought of as the clinician's job. Consequently any "results" that emerge from that sort of endeavor must rest upon the validity of case histories, upon the cumulative insights of a very particular kind those histories may offer. In this regard, I am offering the analysis of many hundred drawings as evidence only of what they suggest to a child psychiatrist who has come to know those who drew them. I value these pictures for what they have told me about individual children, rather than children in general or children of one race or another. The fact that many other children, under certain social and historical circumstances, share feelings that these children have been willing to indicate with crayons and paint is probably a fair assumption. That is as far as I would care to take the matter of what scientific relevance this study has.

The reader is entitled to know why, how, and where these drawings came into being, and who did them. As I have already mentioned, my work in the South studying school desegregation fell into three rather distinct categories: weekly (at a minimum) interviews with high school children of both races; weekly interviews with young children — from five to eleven — of both races; and periodic interviews with the parents and teachers of all these children. I was able to *talk* with the adolescent youths (say, in Atlanta) and the adults who taught them or were their mothers and fathers or grandparents. Young children, however, are often uninterested in conversation. They want to be on the move, and they are often bored at the prospect of hearing words and being expected to use them. It is not that they don't have ideas and feelings, or a need to express them to others. Indeed, their games and play, their drawings and finger paintings are full of energetic symbolization and communication. It is simply that — as one eight-year-old boy once told me — "Talking is okay, but I don't like to do it all the time the way grown-ups do; I guess you have to develop the habit."

Before I ever started my work in the South I had been interested in what the children I treated would tell me with crayons and paints — and chalk, for I always kept a blackboard in my office, and often a child would suddenly want to use it, then just as quickly apply the eraser to it. Because of my own interests I made a point of asking children whether they would like to sketch whatever came to mind, or indeed draw for me their home, school, parents, or friends. Some did so eagerly, some reluctantly; some would have no part of my schemes for a long while, though in the course of treatment those who refused invariably changed their minds, as if they recognized that now they were able to let me know something once unmentionable and as well forbidden to representation.

I kept those files with me when I went South — a stack of drawings made by the middle-class children who make up the major population of a child guidance clinic and a child psychiatrist's private practice. When I started visiting the four little girls in New Orleans whose entry into the first grades of two white schools occasioned the strenuous objection of mobs and a boycott by most white children, I carried with me paper and crayons. From the very beginning I made a point of asking those girls to draw pictures for me: of their school, their teacher or friends, anything they wanted to draw. I also took an interest in the artwork they did in school, always a favorite activity for children in elementary school. There is no doubt about it, they learned that I was interested in their sketches, and without exception they have furnished me an increasing abundance of them over the years.

That same school year (1960–1961) a few white children trickled back to the boycotted schools, in spite of tenacious mobs that in varying strengths constantly besieged the two buildings. I began going to the homes of those children too, and I encouraged those children to draw as well as play games and talk with me. (They were five children from three homes.) During the second year of desegregation, from 1961 to 1962, I continued my studies in New Orleans and expanded them there (while also starting them in Atlanta) just as the city itself, by coming to some terms with its unruly elements, enabled its harassed schools to return gradually to normal. I started interviewing the eight Negro children who were added to the roster of pioneers; they went into three additional elementary schools. (I also expanded the number of white children I was seeing so that I could include their classmates.) All in all in New Orleans I was following up twelve Negro children and twelve white children that second year, as against the four Negro and five white children who in the first year were at one point the entire population of two schools.

In addition to those children I was seeing regularly and continually, I traveled widely in the South, spending a week or two in other villages, towns or cities where younger Negro children were initiating (and white children were experiencing) school desegregation. I lived for a while in Burnsville, North Carolina — a small, rural mountain village — and nearby Asheville, its metropolis. I spent several weeks in Memphis, and later I worked in Birmingham. Finally, in 1964, I divided three months' time between Jackson, Mississippi, and the little farming community of Harmony, near Carthage, Mississippi. In all these instances I tried to gain some impression of how children other than those I knew in New Orleans were managing the social and personal trials of desegregation. At times I felt rude and presumptuous asking children I scarcely knew to draw a picture of their school, a friend, eventually of themselves. Yet these children (and especially their parents) found it easier to draw than to talk; in fact I came to see that they expected me to ask them to *do* something, to test them in some way.

Television reaches across the barriers of race and caste, class and neighborhood, bringing our self-consciousness, our preoccupation with knowing and measuring the "normal" and "timely" in the child's growth and development, into cabins and tenements otherwise far removed from our national life. For example, I was astonished to find the mother of a six-year-old boy in an isolated Mississippi town relax visibly when I took crayons from my pocket, placed them on the paper of my clipboard, and asked her whether her son and I might draw pictures together. "Son, the doctor is going to learn about you and find out how good your thinking is, like they say it has to be done on TV," she told the boy, and they both seemed able, finally, to comprehend my purposes. David drew eagerly, as if taking an examination at school, and his mother no longer worried so openly about just what the white doctor had in mind. "It's testing you're doing," she told me, answering her own silent questions aloud, "and I'm sure grateful for that because David will do better in school if he knows what his mind is about."

In New Orleans, as the months passed by, a firm relationship be-

tween the children and me developed, so that our drawing and painting exercises became more enthusiastic and personal. I encouraged
the children to draw whatever they wished. The troubles and joys of
their lives gradually took on form and color, and so did their shifting
feelings toward me. At times I tried to direct their attention toward
one or another concern I had: how they regarded themselves; how
they felt they were managing at school; what skin color meant to
them, and to others in their neighborhood or the city; why the mobs
formed, and to what purpose; how they saw themselves getting along
with their white or black classmates; how they viewed their teachers,
and how they felt their teachers felt toward them as children, or as representatives of a race or a group of people. (One white child brought
me up short at the very beginning of my work by telling me she thought
her teacher prejudiced toward her: "She wishes my daddy made more
money, so I could dress better. She always talks about the nice kids she
used to teach in the Garden District, and how good they behaved. I
think she minds me as bad as the nigra girl.")

What have these children had to say in the drawings they have
done these past years? Is there any reasonable way to categorize and
classify their pictures so that the individual child's feelings are pre-
served, and yet more general conclusions made possible? I think the
answer to the second question is yes, and I will try to show why by describing the interests and concerns these children reveal when they
take up crayons or a brush.

Drawings and paintings can be compared in a number of ways:
the use of color; the subject matter chosen; the child's command of
form; his desire to approximate the real or his ease with whatever fantasies come to mind; his willingness to talk about what he draws and
explain it, to expand upon its relevance or significance — for his own
life or the lives of others around him. Moreover, anyone who has
worked with children and watched them draw over a period of time
knows how sensitively the child's activity and performance will respond to his various moods. One day's chaos on paper may give way to
another's impressive order and even eloquence. The child's fear and
shyness, his doubts and suspicions about adults, especially doctors or
visitors to his home, are translated onto the canvas: little may be
drawn, mere copying is done, or only "safe" and "neutral" subjects are
selected. Often the child may say that he has absolutely nothing on his
mind, or that in any event he does not know how to draw. Weeks later
that same child may ask for crayons or pick them up quite naturally.
What he said in the past is of little concern to him; at last he feels safe,

or interested in exchanging ideas and feelings with his doctor, that older stranger who keeps returning to his home.

Any discussion of what a given child (or one of his drawings) has to say about racial matters, school problems, or mob scenes must take pains to put the child's social observations, his prejudices and partialities, into the context of his home life. By that I mean to insist upon the young child's strong inclination to reflect his parents' views; but even more, transfer to the neighborhood his personal tensions and struggles, so that other children, not to mention teachers or policemen, take on a meaning to him quite dependent upon how he manages with his parents, brothers, and sisters.

I am saying that each child's particular life — his age, his family, his neighborhood, his medical and psychological past history, his intelligence — influences what and how he draws. I am also saying that the way these children draw is affected by their racial background, and what that "fact" means in their particular world (society) at that particular time (period of history). My task in the analysis of these drawings has been not only to understand them, but to learn to appreciate their significance in clinical work with adults. Over the years I have heard grown-up Southerners of both races recall their childhood experiences, their "old" attitudes; but there may be a distinct difference between the memories we have and the actual feelings we once had (or didn't have but now claim to have had) years ago. For that matter, it is often interesting to obtain the reactions of a parent or a teacher to a given drawing. A mother in New Orleans said to me once: "I looked at Mary's picture and all I could see was that she didn't draw it as good that time as she does others." The girl's teacher had this to say about the same picture: "Mary had trouble keeping the drawing accurate. She must have lost interest in it, and the result is a poor picture." Mary herself had the following appraisal to make: "Maybe I tried too hard, but it's a better picture than the easy ones I do." In point of fact, for the first time she had tried (and struggled) to include herself (and her brown skin) in one of the landscapes she usually did so easily.

The first Southern child to put my crayons and paints to use was Ruby. She and I started talking, playing, and drawing together when she was six years old, and braving daily mobs to attend an almost empty school building. Upon her first meeting I told Ruby of my interest in drawings, and she showed me some she had done at school and brought home to keep. Over the years she has drawn and painted during most of our talks, so that I now have over two hundred of her productions. Many of the topics were her choice, while other pictures were started in response to my specific suggestion or even request. I would ask her to draw a picture of her school, or of her teacher. I would ask her to paint a picture of anyone she knew, or wanted to portray. I might ask her one day to try putting herself, her brother, or her sister on paper, while on another occasion I might ask her to sketch a particular classmate or schoolmate of hers. (For many months there were only two or three of them, the children of the few whites who defied the boycott. We both knew them, and each of us knew that the other spent time with them, Ruby at school and I in visits to their homes.)

For a long time — four months, in fact — Ruby never used brown or black except to indicate soil or the ground; even then she always made sure they were covered by a solid covering of green grass. It was not simply on my account that she abstained from these colors; her school drawings showed a similar pattern. She did, however, distinguish between white and Negro people. She drew white people larger and more lifelike. Negroes were smaller, their bodies less intact. A white girl we both knew to be her own size appeared several times taller. While Ruby's own face (Figure 1) lacked an eye in one drawing, an ear in another, the white girl never lacked any features (Figure 2). Moreover, Ruby drew the white girl's hands and legs carefully, always making sure that they had the proper number of fingers and toes. Not so with her own limbs, or those of any other Negro children she chose (or was asked) to picture. A thumb or forefinger might be missing, or a whole set of toes. The arms were shorter, even absent or truncated.

There were other interesting features to her drawings. The ears of Negroes appeared larger than those of white people. A Negro might not have two ears, but the one he or she did have was large indeed. When both were present, their large size persisted. In contrast, quite often a Negro appeared with no mouth — it would be "forgotten" — or she used a thin line to represent the mouth; whereas a white child or adult was likely to have lips, teeth, and a full, wide-open mouth. With regard to the nose, Ruby often as not omitted it in both races, though interestingly enough, when it appeared it was in her white classmates a thin orange line.

Hair color and texture presented Ruby with the same kind of challenge that skin color did. So long as she kept away from brown and black crayons or paints she had to be very careful about the hair she drew. White children received blond (yellow) hair, or their hair would be the same orange that outlined their face — always the case with Negro children. Many people of both races had no hair. No Negro child had blond hair.

The first change in all this came when Ruby asked me whether she might draw her grandfather — her mother's father. It was not new for her to ask my permission to draw a particular picture, though this was the first time she had chosen someone living outside of New Orleans. (He has a farm in the Mississippi Delta.) With an enthusiasm and determination that struck me as unusual and worth watching she drew an enormous black man, his frame taking up — quite unusually — almost the entire sheet of paper (Figure 3). Not only did she outline his skin as brown; every inch of him was made brown except for a thick black belt across his midriff. His eyes were large, oval lines of black surrounding the brown irises. His mouth was large, and it showed fine, yellow-colored teeth. The ears were normal in size. The arms were long, stretching to the feet, ending in oversize hands; the left one had its normal complement of fingers, but the right was blessed with six. The legs were thick, and ended in heavily sketched black boots (a noticeable shift from the frayed shoes or bare feet hitherto drawn).

Ruby worked intently right to the end, then instantly told me what her grandfather was doing, and what he had to say. (Often I would ask her what was happening in the place she drew or what the person she painted was thinking.) "That's my momma's daddy and he has a farm that's his and no one else's; and he has just come home to have his supper. He is tired, but he feels real good and soon he is going to have a big supper and then go to bed."

Ruby's father at that time was unemployed. It was not the first time, though never before had he been fired simply because his daughter was going to one school rather than another. He tended to be morose at home. He sat looking at television, or he sat on the front steps of the house carving a piece of wood, throwing it away, hurling the knife at the house's wood, then fetching a new branch to peel, cut and again discard. He also suffered a noticeable loss of appetite — the entire family knew about it and talked about it. The children tried to coax their father to eat. His wife cooked especially tasty chicken or ribs. I was asked for an appetite stimulant — and prescribed a tonic made up of vitamins and some Dexamyl for his moodiness. I gave him a few sleeping pills because he would toss about by the hour and smoke incessantly. (In a house where eight people slept in two adjoining bedrooms with no door between them it seemed essential to do so not only for his sleep but the children's.)

I asked Ruby whether there was any particular reason why she decided to draw her grandfather that day. She told me she had none by shaking her head. She smiled, then picked up the crayons and started drawing again, this time doing a pastoral landscape (Figure 4). Brown and black were used appropriately and freely. When it was finished she took some of her Coke and a cookie, then spoke: "I like it here, but I wish we could live on a farm, too; and Momma says if it gets real bad we can always go there. She says her daddy is the strongest man you can find. She says his arms are as wide as I am, and he can lick anyone and his brother together. She says not to worry, we have a hiding place and I should remember it every day."

She was having no particularly bad time of it, but she was rather tired that day. By then she also knew me long enough to talk about her fears, her periods of exhaustion, her wish for refuge or escape. Only once before Ruby decided to draw her grandfather and a countryside scene had she mentioned her impatience with the mobs, her weariness at their persistence: "They don't seem to be getting tired, the way we thought. Maybe it'll have to be a race, and I hope we win. Some people sometimes think we won't, and maybe I believe them, but not for too long."

It took Ruby several more months to be able to draw or paint a Negro without hesitation or distortion. From the beginning I wondered whether it all was my fault, whether she was in some way intimidated by the strange white doctor who visited her, with his games and crayons, his persistent curiosity about how she was getting along. Though in fact I am sure she was, there is reason to believe that the pictures she drew reflected a larger truth about her feelings than the undeniable one of my somewhat formidable presence. Her mother had saved many of the drawings she did in Sunday school (all-Negro) before either desegregation or strange visitors came into her life, and the same pattern was to be found in them: whites drawn larger and more intact than Negroes; brown and black used with great restraint, just enough to indicate the person's race but no more. It was as if Ruby started drawing all people as white, then turned some of them into Negroes by depriving them of a limb or coloring a small section of their skin (she preferred the shoulder or the stomach) brown.

It seemed to me, then, that on my account Ruby had merely tightened up a preexisting inclination to be confounded and troubled at the representation of racial differences, not to mention the implications those differences had for how people lived. Eventually I asked her why she thought twice about how much brown she would give to a colored child. She was then eight, and we had known one another for two years. She replied directly: "When I draw a white girl, I know she'll be okay, but with the colored it's not so okay. So I try to give the colored as even a chance as I can, even if that's not the way it will end up being."

Two years later Ruby and I could talk even more openly. At ten she was still the outgoing, winning girl she always had been, though of course each time I saw her she was taller, thinner, a bit more composed, a little less the child. She wasn't very much interested in drawing any more. She preferred to talk. She and I looked over many of her drawings and at various intervals she made comments about them, much as if she were a colleague of mine. Almost in that vein I commented that her most recent work was less prolific but very accomplished indeed: "You didn't draw much this past year, but when you did the people were really alive and very accurately shown, and the buildings look as real as can be." She smiled and answered quickly: "I guess when you grow older you can see better, and so you can draw better. My teacher told me last week that my handwriting was getting better, too." A few minutes went by and I decided to persist with my comments on her artwork, this time with a bluntness I can only justify as feeling quite "right" and appropriate at the time: "Ruby, you know my wife and I were looking at your drawings last night, and we both noticed how differently you draw Negro people now, in contrast to the way you did years ago when we first started coming to see you. Do you think there's any reason for that, apart from the fact that you're now a better artist in every way?"

She paused longer than usual, and I began to feel in error for asking the question and nervous about what she might be feeling. I was scurrying about in my mind for a remark that would change the subject without doing so too abruptly when she looked right at me and spoke out: "Maybe because of all the trouble going to school in the beginning I learned more about my people. Maybe I would have anyway; because when you get older you see yourself and the white kids; and you find out the difference. You try to forget it, and say there is none; and if there is you won't say what it be. Then you say it's my own people, and so I can be proud of them instead of ashamed." When she finished she smiled, as if she had delivered a hard speech and was relieved to have it done. I didn't know what to say. On the one hand she was still the same Ruby I had known all those years; yet she now seemed grown-up. Her arms were folded quietly in her lap; her language was so clear, so pointed; and she somehow seemed both content with herself as she was and determined to make something of herself in the future. "Ruby is an exceptionally alert child," one of her teachers wrote on her report card a few days before Ruby and I had this talk. The teacher realized that her pupil had gone through a lot and had gained an order of understanding, of worldliness, that is perhaps rare in elementary school children, at least in more sheltered ones.

Ruby had for several years a classmate named Jimmie, a lively, agile, particularly freckled boy whose blond hair tended to fall over his forehead. She drew several pictures of him for me; he sat near her and they knew one another rather well. When I first asked Ruby to do a picture of any school chum she wished (there were only three at the time) she obliged with a painted picture of Jimmie that certainly did not ignore his hair and eyes (Figure 5). (I could not help contrasting the painting with one of a Negro boy [Figure 6] Jimmie's age and size she had done the day before.) "He is a good boy, sometimes," she said of Jimmie, adding the last word of qualification after a genuine moment of hesitancy. In point of fact Jimmie's behavior troubled her. One minute he would be attentive and generous, anxious to play games or even share food with her. Yet in a flash he could turn on her, and not just as one child will do with another. Ruby knew why, and could put it into words: "Jimmie plays with me okay, but then he remembers that I'm colored, so he gets bad." I asked whether he was "bad" at other times — fresh or spiteful simply out of a moment's impulse. She handled my question rather forthrightly, even with a touch of impatience: "Well, he's bad sometimes when he wants things his own way and someone won't let him get it; but I mean it's different when he gets bad because I'm colored. He can be my friend and play real nice with me, and suddenly he just runs and says bad things, and he even gets scared of me and says he's going to leave; but he comes back. He forgets, and then he remembers again."

Jimmie's parents had it no easier. Like him they could not establish in their minds a clear-cut set of attitudes toward colored people. When riots made their son's school attendance dangerous they kept him home. As the mobs achieved their purpose, a near-total boycott, the noise they made and the terror they inspired in passersby gradually subsided. A few white families sent their children back to the schools involved, some in direct defiance of the small crowds that persisted, others rather quietly, almost secretly, through rear doors or side doors. Jimmie's parents sent him back as soon as it was safe to do so openly. When I saw him come to the school, neatly dressed, carrying his lunch box, I thought the very spirit of sanity resided in him, and with him was returning to the deserted halls and classrooms of the building he so casually and confidently entered. There was something very open and calm about him as he walked along — and I guessed something refreshing, something unsullied, also.

As I came to know Jimmie and his family I realized how unfair I had been to the boy when I first saw him. I pictured him as Ruby's hope. In fact he returned to school in spite of Ruby because his parents did not want him to waste months of time learning nothing. When he first met Ruby he told her the facts rather explicitly: "My mother told me to stay away from you." Ruby told me what she had been told, then informed me that Jimmie had contradicted his own words only seconds later by asking her to join him in a game. "So I did" was her way of letting the matter drop.

When Jimmie and I started drawing together he made his feelings about Negroes rather clear: either they were in some fashion related to animals, or the color of their skin proved that if they were human they were certainly dirty human beings — and dangerous, too. I don't think Ruby ever knew the fear she inspired in Jimmie, nor did Jimmie have any idea how very much Ruby strived to portray herself with his features and coloring, as if then she could be less afraid of *him*.

When I asked Jimmie to draw his school as it appeared to him the very first day he came to enroll in it — before Ruby's presence caused its various afflictions — he drew a rather conventional brick building; he carefully emphasized its stucco character by covering the bricks with some yellow. There were no chimneys. The grass was uniformly green, and flowers were everywhere. The sun looked down on the almost bucolic scene with a smiling face. I have seen dozens of such drawings by children of Jimmie's age, though I did take note of his definite artistic ability and his very keen, even meticulous powers of observation.

For a while Jimmie drew pictures of his home, his parents, his friends, and himself. He was particularly fond of landscapes, and once did eight of them in two weeks — each surprisingly different, though all dwelling upon trees, grass, and water. When I first asked him to draw a picture of Ruby he looked at me quite in dismay and said he couldn't. I asked why. He now appeared cross: "Because I don't know what she looks like. I don't look at her close if I can help it."

I asked him whether sometimes he couldn't help noticing her. "Accidents happen sometimes, Jimmie, even when we try to do as we feel we should." He nodded, and allowed that he had managed a few glimpses at Ruby, and would try to draw her. He started to do so rather furtively, then somehow lost his nervousness, so that by the end he was the confident and scrupulously attentive craftsman and landscapist he always was — except, that is, for what he had done to Ruby (Figure 7). It was almost as if he had suddenly embraced surrealism. In the midst of a stretch of grass he abruptly placed her, without feet, legs inserted in a piece of land left strangely sandy and barren in contrast to what surrounded it. He made Ruby small, though her arms were larger proportionately than those he usually drew. She had only the thinnest line of a mouth (Jimmie usually was careful to show teeth and indicate lips by double lines) and pinpoint eyes. Her hair was frizzly black, yet curiously and inappropriately long. She was brown-black, much more strikingly so than Ruby's medium-brown complexion justified.

I asked what Ruby was doing in the picture. Jimmie said that he didn't know. I asked whether he could imagine something she might be doing, even if it wasn't apparent from the drawing. He thought about it for a few seconds, looking intently at what he had done and at the crayons. I saw his eyes fall upon a bottle of cola and some crackers. A second later he had his answer: "Maybe she is drinking a Coke and eating candy or something. My mother says niggers eat stuff like that all day long, and their teeth rot away because they're no good for you all the time." The sweet tooth he was learning to master only with difficulty Ruby somehow was permitted to enjoy, though he felt sure her day of suffering would come.

In time Jimmie was able to develop on paper the various (and conflicting) feelings he had toward Ruby and her race. He drew Ruby many times, at intervals upon my request and often because he wanted to do so, or felt that I silently wished him to do so. For many weeks she appeared only as a speck of brown or in caricature, sometimes both in one picture, usually on what he reminded me was *his* street. Jimmie had obvious trouble picturing her at all. He hesitated as he did at no other time. He told me that he didn't know what she looked like: "She's funny. She's not like us, so I can't draw her like my friends. Besides, she hides a lot from us." Whereupon I asked him where she hid. "She doesn't really hide. I mean she stays away sometimes; but if I say something, she answers me all right." I wanted to know whether he had any idea why Ruby might be keeping her distance from him and the others. He knew exactly why: "Well, she's colored, that's why." I reminded Jimmie that colored children lived nearby, and often played with white children. (In New Orleans large areas of the city are thoroughly mixed racially, and have been for generations.) He knew that, too: "That's different. It's on the street not in school. My daddy says that on the street it's for everybody, but inside is where you have to be careful."

In fact he made a distinction at first between the classroom and the school playground. When I asked him whether he would draw a picture of Ruby at school he readily obliged, though invariably he put Ruby in the play area outside the building. Finally I mentioned what I saw him doing, and he scarcely hesitated before replying: "The teacher said it won't be long before we go back to normal. She said that if most kids still stay home and the people still make all the noise in front of the school, then they'll send Ruby away and the trouble will be over; she said Ruby still isn't a regular member of the school, but that we have to be polite, anyway." The yard, for him, was like a waiting room, and in one drawing he put a bench in it — in actuality there was none — and Ruby on the bench.

In time Jimmie took Ruby into the building he drew, and in time he regularly came to see her as an individual. Amorphous spots and smudges of brown slowly took on form and structure. Ruby began to look human every time, rather than, say, a rodent or a fallen leaf one day and a rather deformed human being the next. Eventually she gained eyes and well-formed ears. It took more time for her to obtain a normal mouth; and only after a year of knowing her would Jimmie credit her with the pretty clothes he often gave to other girls. In describing Ruby's speech after he had finished his pictures Jimmie for a long time tried his best to render a Negro dialect (or his version of one). His parents began enjoying such performances, and also hearing from him how "the nigra" was doing in school. *They* were changing, too — from calling Ruby a "nigger" to calling her a "nigra," and from wanting no mention of her at home to insisting upon information about her schoolwork and her general behavior. By the middle of our second year's talks Jimmie was forgetting himself and telling me in his own words and accent what Ruby might be saying in one of his productions.

Jimmie may have tried to ignore Ruby, he may have consigned her to anonymity, even to the indignity of a dot, or an animal-like appearance, but he never really overlooked the difference her presence made to his school. He showed how embattled it was by drawing a policeman here, a picket with a sign there. The demonstrators were drawn big and open-mouthed, their arms unusually beefy, their hands prominent indeed, a child's view of the shrill, stifling, clutching power they exercised over the school's population. As they gradually lost that power and began to disband, Jimmie pictured them as the smaller, less galling irritants they were becoming.

The school building itself took on a variety of shapes in Jimmie's mind and on his paper. At first it was a confusing, almost ramshackle building, its walls as flimsy and unreliable as the school's future seemed at the time. Slowly, though, Jimmie realized that — as he put it — "We're going to make it." Quite casually, without self-consciousness, he showed that he meant what he said. His school grew in size, each time looking sounder and more attractive for all the wear it was taking from its assailants. Eventually he allowed the building to dominate everything around it from the shrubbery to the crowd of human beings who once impressed both him and Ruby with their persistence and assertiveness.

On occasion Jimmie would confine Ruby to her own section of the building (Figure 8), even as Ruby twice drew herself in the middle of a black circle, in turn within the building. Ruby told me each time that she meant to draw her desk, that the circle was her version of a desk. Though I never pressed the matter with her, I felt I could be more curious with Jimmie. I asked him whether he was assigning Ruby a permanent corner of the building. (It was, I thought to myself, always the corner under the chimney, and the chimney was always emitting noticeable — at the very least — or commanding billows of smoke, even on the warm spring days Jimmie did the pictures in question.) On the several occasions I questioned him on the matter he denied any such intention. Then one day he anticipated my renewed interest by letting me know his ideas on why he placed Ruby where he did: "She has to be in the same place, because she always tries to sit near the teacher, and if we take her seat she gets upset and says its hers, and once she cried. So I keep her in the same place, and that's why." Since Jimmie often complained that his teacher talked too much and was moody, perhaps the chimney — in Jimmie's mind — was meant to symbolize his teacher (his disposition black, his talk mainly hot air) rather than racial conflict or the place of the Negro in this world. No matter what the doctor makes of a picture, there are often other possible interpretations. It is only after enough of a particular child's drawings have been seen that certain trends or directions in thinking (and representation) can be reasonably established — for *that* child, of course.

From the very start of our talks I asked Jimmie not only to draw Ruby but her parents and friends as well. He occasionally saw Ruby's mother when she accompanied Ruby to school, though I doubt he would have protested lack of acquaintance as an excuse for not attempting a picture. His first drawings showed that if he had to distort Ruby's appearance somewhat he had to caricature other Negroes far more grotesquely. Ruby's father would appear with enormous teeth and animal-like arms coming down to his feet. Her mother came out equally simian. On several occasions he put both of them in the same picture; they were above the ground and below a tree, a compromise Jimmie never elsewhere felt called upon to make. Quite the contrary, he always started his drawings with broad strokes of brown and green to indicate the land, then firmly placed his people and buildings upon it.

For Jimmie, Ruby's house had to resemble its occupants, even though he knew perfectly well where she lived and what houses looked like on that street (it was not far from his own). He labored long and hard on his own house, or his school, drawing the walls and windows, the doors and chimneys with increasing skill and refinement over the several years we met. For a long while, however, a Negro home had to be clearly seen as just that, some lines hastily sketched perpendicular to one another, always brown, often not quite fitting together, so that the homes seemed irregular and exposed, though always warm, for every one of them had a chimney stack and plentiful black smoke to justify its presence. It is not that Jimmie has a "fixation" upon chimneys or smoke. His own home often as not lacked both. No Negro home he drew lacked either.

He furnished other homes or his school with chairs and tables, even curtains, but not Ruby's house, or those of her neighbors. He piled Ruby's house and those nearby on top of one another, as if they were a jumble rather than a row of buildings. What is more, he denied them grass and for a long time he denied them the sun.

I remember so very well the day Jimmie let the sunshine fall upon those homes. It was, in fact, a rather cloudy and humid day, very much an autumn day in New Orleans. I could tell by the slower speed of his drawing hand that he was paying more attention to the homes he was "building." As we often did, he and I talked as he worked. I was drawing, too; sometimes Jimmie would assign a topic to me in trade for an assignment from me. He told me to draw the Lake Pontchartrain bridge. "You better get a lot of paper, because it's the longest bridge in the world," he warned me as we began. As we proceeded I realized that he himself would require more time than usual. He was doing an exceptionally meticulous job with Ruby's house and a nearby store. He finished the store first, and then told me about it: "Ruby goes there every day after school and gets herself a Coke and some potato chips, and sometimes she gets some extra potato chips to bring to school the next day. She gave us some yesterday; and I like potato chips better than almost anything except maybe dessert and candy, and maybe sometimes ice cream."

From the store Jimmie moved to the houses. Instead of brown he used red, and instead of hasty lines he slowly moved his crayon along, sometimes backtracking to broaden and strengthen what he had done. When the construction proper was over, the decoration began: a door, two carefully drawn windows, one with curtains, a chair, and outside some grass, a tree, three flowers, and finally a blue sky with the sun in it, shining directly over the new building.

When Jimmie had finished he turned to ask me how I was doing. I was still working on the bridge, and he offered to help me. After we had finished that we compared our work. Jimmie said he was tired: "That's a lot we've done. I want a Coke." (We always had one at a nearby stand.) I had noticed his drawing, indeed had watched him draw it. He knew that, yet he wanted to make sure I took note of what he did: "Did you see my picture?" "Yes, Jimmie, I did, and I liked it a lot. You did a real good job with the house." "Well, I tried to make it strong, like you did with the bridge. If a bridge isn't strong it could cave in, and then someone could get hurt. They could drown in the lake. And if a roof fell down in a house it would be the same." At that point we were ready to leave his living room for the street. I let him turn off the tape recorder — always a great pleasure for him — and carry it to my car. When we were outside we felt light rain beginning to fall. Jimmie was annoyed: "Why does it rain every time I go outside? I just drew the sun, but it didn't help any with the weather." Then he wanted to know whether New Orleans had any rivals in America for cloudy, rainy weather. I told him that I didn't know; but I liked the weather there, the semitropical quality of it. He did, too: "It may get cloudy and rain, but the sun comes out a lot, too; and when it does, you like it better, because you've missed it."

What both Ruby and Jimmie chose to draw or paint reflected the particular lives each of them lived. I once asked Jimmie whether he thought his friends saw things the way he did — whether, for instance, any of them might draw his school, his teacher, his classmate Ruby as he did. Once and for all he cautioned me against whatever inclinations I might have to generalize: "I don't know. Which one of them do you mean?"

I followed Jimmie's advice to the best of my ability as a clinician, so that in all I spent four years getting to know two-score children like him and Ruby in New Orleans and other Southern cities. Though each child had his own life — including his own quality of artistic interest and ability — there *were* certain patterns to be discerned in what these children chose to draw. Thus, Jimmie's drawings and Ruby's drawings resemble one another in the way all children's drawings do — the style, the sense of proportion, the preoccupations that change from year to year. If they also differ because Jimmie and Ruby are different artists, different human beings, the racial crisis they both witnessed and experienced served to draw them together by giving them a common experience, a shared number of difficult times together. Eventually that crisis influenced not only what they thought but what they drew. Other children in their school, their city, all over the South, have been similarly aroused and affected.

For the many I have known there can be no question that in the beginning they fear their white-skinned or dark-skinned classmates. Nor can there be any question of the very hard struggle they must contend with inside their minds as they try to sort out the hate and envy they have come prepared to feel toward one another, the curiosity, the interest, the confusion over the whole matter of black and white, bad and good, wrong and right.

The issue of what skin color means is already confronting the child by three, let alone school age. In my interviews with grown-up Negroes and whites their memories hark back to one event or another that marks a first awareness of skin color and its implications. Yet, as I have said, the memories of adults are no substitute for direct observation of what children themselves see and do. Some of the children I have come to know were three when I first started talking with them — they were the nursery school brothers, sisters, and cousins of the older children I was visiting. All in all these children have lived in cities, towns, and the countryside. They have ranged in age from three to ten. They have lived in rather comfortable homes or in very poor ones. They have been both white and Negro children, both boys and girls. What they all have in common is their American citizenship, their Southern residence, and their Southern ancestry. Most were caught up, willingly or otherwise, in school desegregation; but I have worked closely with others, too — Negro and white children *not* going to desegregated schools, though obviously living at a moment in history when the subject has an unprecedented immediacy.

Every Negro child I know has had to take notice in some way of what skin color signifies in our society. If they do not easily — or at all — talk about it, their drawings surely indicate that the subject is on their minds. Like Ruby, many have trouble using black and brown crayons and paints. One three-year-old girl obviously avoided using those two colors in the pictures she made; instead, she used her fingers as if *they* were crayons. After watching her use green and orange, then rub her hand alongside them, I asked her what she was doing. She said, "Nothing, just trying to make a picture." Her mother, however, was nearby, and later she unabashedly explained it all to me: "She has been telling me on and off for weeks that she knows she can rub some of her brown skin off and use it for coloring. My two boys talked like that for a while when they were two or three and then they got over it. So I guess she will, too."

Negro children of elementary school age have not had enough time to set themselves straight about "why" they are colored and what that fact will mean for them in the future. Often they will try to deny the fact, or they will accept it so extravagantly that it is clear they are yet confused and troubled. Ruby abstained from browns and blacks; another girl of six I knew in New Orleans could scarcely use any other color. Her white classmates — like Ruby she was in a desegregated school — were drawn Negro, a touch of yellow here or there sometimes giving me the clue to their racial identity. For a long while I assumed that my whiteness — and my middle-class, professional whiteness at that — in some way made these children reluctant to color themselves brown or made them exceptionally anxious to color everyone brown. When I compared drawings done by the children for me with those they did with others, at Sunday school, even at the request of their older brothers and sisters or parents, I learned that what I found significant and revealing in their drawings had a consistency and persistence quite its own, quite independent of my presence.

Is it true, then, that the words "Negro" and "white" help distinguish the dreams and fantasies of children? That is, do children of each race draw themselves and those of the other race quite differently? At two and three have they very different ideas about who they are, who they will be, all based on a budding sense of racial identity? I would answer yes to those questions. Before he is born the Negro child's color is likely to matter a great deal to his parents. By the third year of life the child is asking the kinds of questions that ultimately will include one about his skin color. A mother of five children in Jackson, Mississippi, described it to me rather explicitly: "When they asks all the questions, they ask about their color, too. They more than not will see a white boy or girl and it makes them stop and think. They gets to wondering, and then first thing you know, they want to know this and that about it, and I never have known what to say, except that the Lord likes everyone because He makes everyone, and nothing is so good it can satisfy Him completely, so He made many kinds of people, and they're all equal before Him. Well, that doesn't always satisfy them; not completely it doesn't. So I have to go on. I tell them that no matter what it's like around us, it may make us feel bad, but it's not the whole picture, because we don't make ourselves. It's up to God, and He can have an idea that will fool us all. He can be trying to test us. It's the favorite child sometimes who you make sure you don't spoil."

I asked her when she found such conversation necessary. "I'd say about two or two and a half," she answered rather quickly. A bit deferentially she turned to me and asked: "Do you think that's too early for children to know?" I said no, I didn't. I said that what she told me confirmed some of my own observations. She smiled, a little proud but still a little nervous. She wanted to pursue the matter further: "I know I'm right on the age; I've gone through it with too many to forget when it happens. But to tell the truth I never have been certain what to say. That's why I try to talk about God. No one knows what color He is. I tell the children that it's a confusing world, and they have to get used to it. You have to try to overcome it, but you can't hide it from the kids. When they ask me why colored people aren't as good as whites, I tell them it's not that they're not as good; it's that they're not as rich. Then I tell them that they should separate being poor and being bad, and not get them mixed up. I read to them from the Bible, and remind them that the Lord is a mighty big man, and what He thinks is not the same as what white folks do, or even black folks. He's bigger than all of us, I tell them, and I hope that makes them feel satisfied, so they don't dislike themselves. That's bad, not liking your own self."

Again and again I have heard mothers talk of similar struggles, and seen their children represent on paper those same struggles (and the "answers" to them they have been given or devised on their own). It is not that Negro and white children in the South have thoughts unlike those of other children. A thematic analysis of the hundreds of drawings and stories they have produced shows their kinship with all children. They draw their mothers and fathers, food and clothes, animals and trees. They show how sensitive they are to people: to what their parents say, or their teachers, or their brothers and sisters. They reveal the affections they have, and they also reveal the tensions, the conflicts and resentments that are inexorable and shifting, part of growing up, part of life ongoing. With only one or two exceptions these children were in no sense "sick." They had no symptoms, gave no clinical evidence of serious trouble with eating and sleeping, with nursery school or regular school, with family and friends. They did not come to see me in a clinic; it was I who sought them out because of their role in a social struggle. I had to remind myself of that fact constantly. (For that matter, even when — years ago — I treated severely disturbed children in a Boston hospital I tried to keep in mind the "healthy" side of their mental life, the strengths and abilities they somehow had mustered and consolidated in spite of the afflictions pulling at them and giving them — or those around them — so much worry.)

Sometimes I erred by becoming too much the investigator. When I did so, when I emphasized racial matters too much, when I seemed to be forcing a point here and there, the child or his mother often managed to bring me up short. One five-year-old colored boy had been unusually explicit in both his talk and pictures: he wished he were white, and that was that. He said so, and he drew himself so. When I asked him whether he thought he *was* so, he said no, he was colored, but there was little harm in wishing otherwise. I asked him whether he thought all colored children shared his views: "I don't know, I only know the ones I play with. We all say let's turn white, then we pretend it's done. But we know it isn't all the while. And a white boy, he told me in school one time that he plays 'nigger' sometimes with his friends, and they say they're black and pretend, and then turn back to being white."

Being black and being white is, however, a long-term affair, regardless of the minds ability to make believe. Thus, while all children draw animals — indeed are quite interested in them — it is the Negro child who is often apt to call himself one of them with exceptional consistency. Negro children usually draw themselves and their friends as smaller than white children. In the stories they tell that involve the two races (based on the pictures they draw) the white child is almost invariably asking the Negro to do something, or having it done. Moreover, again and again I have been assured by Negro children that the Negro in the picture is smiling, or working hard at whatever task he has set upon. That there is anger and spite toward white people burning underneath is also discernible, though by no means are such emotions easily conveyed to other Negroes (even to the child's parent), let alone a white observer like me.

One Negro mother put rather well the feelings I have heard many others express: "I guess we all don't like white people too much deep inside. You could hardly expect us to, after what's happened all these years. It's in our bones to be afraid of them, and bones have a way of staying around even when everything else is gone. But if something is inside of you, it doesn't mean it's there alone. We have to live with one another, black with white I mean. I keep on telling that to the children, and if they don't seem to learn it, like everything else I have to punish them to make sure they do. So I'm not surprised they don't tell me more than you, because they have to obey me; and if I have to obey you and they have to obey me, it's all the same. Just the other day my Laura started getting sassy about white children on the television. My husband told her to hold her tongue and do it fast. It's like with cars and knives, you have to teach your children to know what's dangerous and how to stay away from it or else they sure won't live long. White people are a real danger to us until we learn how to live with them. So if you want your kids to live long, they have to grow up scared of whites; and the way they get scared is through us; and that's why I don't let my kids get fresh about the white man even in their own house. If I do there's liable to be trouble to pay. They'll forget, and they'll say something outside, and that'll be it for them, and us too. So I make them store it in the bones, way inside, and then no one sees it. Maybe in a joke we'll have once in a while, or something like that, you can see what we feel inside, but mostly it's buried. But to answer your question, I don't think it's only from you it gets buried. The colored man I think he has to hide what he really feels even from himself. Otherwise there would be too much pain — too much."

The task, then, is one of making sure the child is afraid: of whites, and of the punishment his parents fearfully inflict upon him whenever he fails to follow their suit. The child's bravado or outrage must be curbed. In my experience even two- and three-year-old Negro children have already learned the indirection, the guile needed for survival. They have also learned their relative weakness, their need to be ready to run fast, to be alert and watchful. They have learned that white children, as well as adults, are big, strong, and powerful; and that such power is specifically related to the colored man's defenselessness.

In drawings such attitudes come up again and again. If the Negro child is alone in a white school his loneliness there is carried over to the other situations he draws. For example, I asked one Negro boy in Asheville, North Carolina, to select a neighborhood chum and any classmate he decided (in his school the child would have to be white), then place them both in a landscape the child was particularly fond of drawing for me. I said to him at the time: "Johnnie, I'd like to see how you fit the boys and girls you know into that countryside you like so much to draw." He obliged, showing a rather robust white boy near the summit of a mountain, and a rather fragile Negro one well below (Figure 9).

What Johnnie told me was happening in the picture he drew shows how a seven-year-old child can summon the sharpest most outspoken fantasy without the slightest embarrassment. "Freddie wishes he were up top, like Billy, but he isn't, because there's not room for both of them up there, at least not now there isn't. They're not talking, they're just there. Freddie would be afraid to be on top. He wouldn't know what to do. He's used to where he is, just like Billy is. Billy is a big eater, and he has to have food with him everywhere he goes. So Freddie is getting some food for him from the farms and maybe he'll carry it up. But he'll come right down. He might get dizzy, and Billy would not like for him to stay there too long, because he might slip and get killed if the two of them were there when there's only room for one."

I wanted to know why Freddie was so small, why his arms were so much less than Billy's arms, and how they managed when they were together, up or down the mountain. "Freddie doesn't get to be so big, because he stoops over. He picks the crops and plows, so his back is bent, that's why; and his arms are bent for the same reason. But Billy, he can stretch when he wants to, and the air up there on top is real healthy for him. When they talk it's real hard, because they are far from one another, so they have to shout."

Did Johnnie think they both did well in school? "Well, I think so," he replied. Then he added: "But I'm not sure. Maybe Billy does better. He can talk better, so he comes out better in school, too."

How do boys like Billy look at boys like Freddie? White children in the South have a virtual field day attributing many of their own problems and struggles to Negro children. The segregated social system comes to bear upon children as well as adults, so that long before a white child goes to school he has learned that good and bad can find very real and convenient expression in black and white skin. Negro children are described as bad, ill-mannered, naughty, disobedient, dirty, careless, in sum everything that the white child struggles so hard *not* to be. Moreover, the white child's sense of his own weakness, loneliness — or angry defiance — are also likely to be acknowledged indirectly by being charged up to the Negro. Nowhere is this more obvious than in the drawings of young white children. While Johnnie was letting me know how he saw the world, a white classmate of his was doing likewise — and with the virtuosity, I felt, of a real draftsman.

Allan liked his ruler. He would never draw without it and when he started he did so by putting the ruler on the empty paper, as if *it* would decide, he merely follow orders. Allan liked order and structure. He used the ruler to make sure that the walls of his buildings were straight, the pathways of his roads were direct, and the mountains undeviating from ground to summit. Even with human forms or trees he would use the ruler, rounding off his lines when necessary. Allan talked more than most children of seven, and one day spoke as follows about Johnnie's presence in school: "I guess he's okay. But if we had a lot more everything would get bad. The teachers wouldn't know what to do, and neither would we. Johnnie, he's not making any trouble, but he's different from the rest of us, and that's important. So he shouldn't be with us, any more than we should be with him; because differences mean something." I asked him what differences meant. "They mean that one thing is one way and another was made different; and if they didn't have differences, then everybody would be confused, and they wouldn't know what's right and what's wrong to do."

Later he drew a picture intended to show me what he meant about Johnnie being different from himself. I asked for just that. I said, "Allan, could you *show* me what you mean? Could you draw a picture that shows how Johnnie is different — or is it because his skin color is different and that's it?" "No," he shook his head, "it's more than skin color, because if I get a sunburn, I get tan, but I'm still not like Johnnie."

In the drawing he decided to do a street scene. He drew a road, then buildings along each side. A few cars appeared. Then he turned his attention to the sky. After that he decided to control the movements of his cars by placing a traffic light prominently on one side of the road. Finally he drew Johnnie, leaning on the post that held up the light, turned red. On the other side of the street he populated the store windows with several white faces, and put one white man on the street opposite Johnnie.

Now some of the details in this drawing were similar to others I have seen white children draw when they have in mind to show their social awareness, their realization that Negro children live a less hopeful or protected life. Thus, the sun was noticeably on the "white" side of the street, a side whose buildings were far bigger and sturdier than those on the "other" side. Red walls, orange windows, green grass and trees contrasted with the makeshift brown and purple lines of the buildings on Johnnie's side of the street. They had no grass or trees nearby. Moreover, clearly Johnnie was the less intact person, his features in less proportion, his body less carefully and sensibly constructed (Figure 10). It was all very familiar.

On the other hand, I thought the use of the traffic light rather unusual. It signaled a definite, commanding red. Allan told me that it was a major road he had drawn, and a dangerous one to cross. The red light was on, a warning to motorists that speed had its dangers. I asked him whether there was a green light sometimes. "No," he said. "This is one of those red lights that goes on and off. It's to warn the cars not to go too fast, but it's a big highway, and *you're not supposed to cross over.*" Did that go for Johnnie as well as the others? Yes, he had no doubt about that. Nor did he think Johnnie in danger of confusion either: "He knows about the light; and he's so close to it that he can't very well forget it, can he?"

Allan is a very orderly boy. He is sensitive to what he may do, to when and where he may do anything, to the "stops" and "goes" of daily life — to be learned (and resisted) by all children. The longer I knew him the more I realized how neatly he had assigned the forbidden to Johnnie and others like Johnnie. *They* were the wrongheaded ones; they were unruly, even messy, disobedient, wild, unpredictable. Allan summarized it all very pointedly one day by telling me what was for him an unforgettable incident: "Johnnie dropped his ruler in class and he didn't even seem to care whether he got it back or not."

Allan and Johnnie, Ruby and Jimmie, the boys and girls I have known these past years have all had in common their childhood, their developing sense of themselves and the world around them. Each of these children has learned to identify himself, somewhat, by his or her skin color — learned so during the first two or three years of life. What they have learned about their skin has been but the beginning of what they will learn. Yet, when they finally know what color they possess and what color they lack, they know something more than a few facts; they know something about their future. As one little Negro girl in Mississippi said after she had drawn a picture of herself; "That's me, and the Lord made me. When I grow up my momma says I may not like how He made me, but I must always remember that He did it, and it's His idea. So when I draw the Lord He'll be a real big man. He has to be to explain about the way things are."

The Students

The Matter of Chocolate

There is more to tell about Ruby, whose drawings we have already discussed. She was born in December 1954. She entered this world in a sharecropper's cabin at the hands of a cousin who in the words of the child's mother "knew about children getting born." She was a warmly welcomed first child. Her father, in his early twenties, had just returned from the Korean War, where for wounds received in combat while risking his life to save a white soldier he received a Purple Heart. Her mother was nineteen when she married, and the same age when she became a mother. The parents had known one another as children, and grown up together, in a hot, sleepy Mississippi town whose existence was confirmed only by several stores, a post office, and a gas station. For miles in all directions from the town the rich soil of the Delta stretched, and both their families had worked its soil, picked its cotton, for generations.

"Farm work is all I knew before I got into the army," was this military hero's summary of his education and occupation. He barely knew how to read and write, had attended school only cursorily until twelve, then simply worked at farming. It was fortunate for him that in the army he learned how to repair automobile engines because on his return home he married and started a family but was quickly confronted with the joblessness of a shrinking rural economy. Some of his brothers took to the nomadic if familiar life of migrant farm-workers. His mechanical skills prompted him to choose New Orleans. ("I figured I knew how to make cars work, so I could take on the city.")

The young couple brought their baby daughter (six months old) to the city, and soon were settled in its eastern industrial slums, an area whose worn shacks on unpaved streets seemed impressive to two people whose rural homes were hardly more than primitive cabins. "I got a good job in a station through a cousin, and we just lived along real quiet like" was the way the father summarized their lives before the crisis of school desegregation. By then, the year 1960, they had two more girls and one son, and Ruby's mother was expecting a fifth child.

The question has often been asked of me, and particularly by my psychiatric colleagues: Why did these parents consent to let their children face the ugliness and danger that occurred in desegregating the New Orleans schools? Ruby's mother at first replied tersely, "We just did." After months of our visits she talked much more openly. Her several answers basically showed that little calculation or sleight-of-hand was involved in the decision. She had no burning ideological zeal, no secret desire for prominence or profit. They had never expected the trouble they met. If they had, they would never have begun. Ruby's father once said, "we agreed to sign for Ruby to go to the white school because we thought it was for all the colored to do, and we never thought Ruby would be alone. . . . We thought she'd be going with hundreds of them."

If they had applied out of naïve faith and quiet hope, their first surprise, that their daughter would be alone, was quickly followed by their second, that she would by her mere presence at the school occasion an uproar which would plague them for months. Indeed, the grim historical facts of the kinds of pressures brought to bear upon this child of six when she started school are a matter of public record. Riots greeted her arrival there, and a boycott soon followed. Daily crowds, abusive and taunting, hailed her for many months. For a long while she had a classroom and teacher to herself. At one point there were only four fellow students, so nearly complete was the white boycott on her account.

I first saw Ruby when she was facing her worst time in the first grade, and I have continued to see her on occasion ever since then. During those years she emerged from anonymity to international notoriety, then slowly saw her fame disappear, so that in one of our recent visits she could talk about my departure this way: "I told my daddy I miss the people from before that came. . . . Are you coming here for my promotion next year, too?"

What she missed was the excitement and attention she had received, which could now perhaps be seen as pleasant. She had never been "sick," no matter how lamentable some of her experiences, but she had become frightened and anxious, and she had suffered private worries unknown to the world which watched her on television and saw her in newspapers. Despite the noise and disorder outside, her work in school was good and her attendance regular. For a while it was her parents who were most severely tested. Her father lost his job, and he and his wife feared for their lives. Their families in Mississippi were afraid of lynching. Yet they were strong and stubborn people — to be alive is an achievement when one grows up in the unspeakable poverty and toil that were theirs — and they managed. The father obtained a new job, not from a white man this time. Neighbors rallied round them and guarded their home. Significantly, they drew close to their children, but not anxiously so.

Ruby slept well, studied well at school, played regularly after school, and developed only one symptom — a puzzling one for her parents, who ate hungrily and heartily if not healthily. One day at the height of the tension her mother described it for me this way: "She doesn't eat the way she used to. Ruby was always a good eater. Now she stays clear of a lot of foods and she won't eat unless we all eat with her." They assumed she had lost a bit of her appetite because of the strain she faced, and in a general sense they were correct. Ruby for a while had to eat alone at school, and she had been leaving her lunches untouched, hiding them in various spots of the near-empty building. When she joined her few white schoolmates at lunch she ate with them hesitantly, enough so that they noticed it. Slowly she relaxed at lunch, but only because she was very careful about what she took to school to eat. At home she ate listlessly, and never alone. Once she had sought snacks constantly and with scant discrimination; now she was fussy.

On several visits I asked Ruby about her appetite, and she replied that it was "good" or "pretty good." She seemed unwilling to pursue the matter, but glad to share a Coke with me. One day I again asked about her appetite. Her mother had been particularly worried — "I went and got her some vitamin pills today to keep her healthy." After being questioned, she was silent for a few seconds, then looked at our doll house nearby. I asked her whether she wanted to play with it. She nodded with obvious relief and enthusiasm. Ruby and I had spent considerable time with this set, or with crayons and paints. The set included Negro and white dolls and a house for them. We were arranging the house's furniture when I asked how her schoolwork was coming along. She replied "okay," then volunteered that "they're still there." They were, I knew, and still pretty nasty. "They tells me I'm going to die, and that it'll be soon. And that one lady tells me every morning I'm getting poisoned soon, when she can fix it." She paused a moment, then added, "Is it *only* my skin?" I wasn't sure what she meant. I asked her, "Is *what* only your skin, Ruby?" She did not answer. She picked up her teacups and asked me whether I wanted some tea. I said yes, and we made some. While brewing it we talked about the kinds of cookies we'd have with it and then she volunteered that her sisters consumed large numbers of cookies each day, but not she. Had this always been the case? No, she told me, and I knew that her parents had said the same. I had known her long enough to recall her sweet tooth on earlier visits, and its indulgence in the very chocolate cookies (Oreos) she now steadfastly refused.

Ruby and I had been talking quite regularly about her school experiences. She told me she had especially disliked eating there alone, although she didn't mind being alone with her teacher. In fact, she regretted in certain ways the slow return of white children to "her" school. On each of my visits she would give me the tally: "Two more came back." Talkative about such matters, Ruby became quite silent about any discussion of her appetite. Her parents were the ones who were concerned, and they described their concern to me one day as follows: "She don't eat the way she used to, and she only eats what's hers alone, and she won't share from our food." Further questioning revealed that the girl was largely rejecting freshly prepared food and favoring packaged and processed food, especially potato chips and Cokes. She had always been drawn to fried and mashed potatoes, pork chops, cookies and ice cream, and now would have none of them. She was reluctant about peanut butter and jelly sandwiches, once her favorite. She shunned greens even though formerly she had not.

Before discussing Ruby's food habits and home life further, we may indicate what happened to her when she left home each morning and approached the school. Anyone who cared to "hear" could learn what this girl was told every day as she approached school. "You little nigger, we'll get you and kill you" was a commonplace. Some of the language is unprintable. But one comment is both printable and important. Spoken in a high-pitched but determined voice, its words were always the same: "We're going to poison you until you choke to death." Its speaker was always the same. In the midst of so much abuse, this threat sounded relatively mild. Watching Ruby coming to school I felt that *all* the rebukes, all the fierce tongue-lashings, were to no avail. She came with federal marshals at first and later with her mother, and would invariably march rather firmly and stolidly right into the building. She rarely looked at her accusers, though even the slightest of hurried, backward glances from her shoulder sent each of them into excited pitches of slander. One seemed to compete with another for the child's attention.

Those backward glances I was to learn in later months were specifically directed and significant. Ruby had been told to ignore the crowd, and she told me for some time that she did: "I pays no attention to them. I just goes in." But she *was* paying attention to the one who threatened her death by poisoning and choking. She had asked her mother whether that lady owned a variety store near her home, the same variety store, white-owned, that had refused to sell Ruby's mother food when the trouble about school desegregation first started. Of course, the woman was not the one who owned the store, but the associations in Ruby's mind might be put together as follows: A woman tells me I'm going to be poisoned. It is dangerous anyway, going to school. I can't get candy and cookies and my family can't buy other food from our old store — we go to a supermarket now. Of course, I'm familiar with threats about food; that is, being told that if I'm bad I'll be punished by missing meals or getting indigestion. My mother has told me I'll choke on some of my bad words, and she has also kept me from certain pleasant foods when I've been fresh or cruel with my sisters and brother. So I'd best be circumspect. And since I'm not sure about how good and how bad I am, and since I seem to be having a rather bad time of it and therefore may well *be* "bad," I'm worried enough to have lost a good deal of my appetite, and to fear punishment — from that lady outside the school building, and from my parents, too, who say they are not worried but must be, what with all those threats.

At first Ruby's food habits changed without her family's knowledge. She simply pretended to eat her lunch, but left most of it untouched, either discarding the food or leaving several days' total in her desk, to be later done away with in secret. By the time this behavior was apparent to her teachers and the few white children in the school, her parents *had* begun to notice a definite fall in her appetite at home. They also found themselves questioned about what poison is and how it works.

"She keeps on asking me, 'Is it only my skin?' and I tells her that if she was white there'd be no crowds there. Then she'll ask if we'll all die if they gets poison to our food, and I tells her that's foolishness . . . I tells her nobody's going to get our food like that, but I can see she don't believe me all the way." These recorded words helped to discover what was happening. They describe Ruby's fears and her mother's awareness of them. Is it *only* my skin?" was a question Ruby asked many times of her parents and of me. The origins of the question are in both public and private matters, a twin derivation that must be emphasized.

What Ruby meant when she asked this question of her family, and of me in our talks and play, was that she comprehended her exposure to harassment and wondered about its causes. She is a Negro; she knows that and could hardly help knowing it during those months. There are restrictions and penalties associated with her racial condition; she knows that and has been taught them. No, she cannot go here or sit there. No, her race's people do not ordinarily appear on television programs or in movies. Yes, she would probably never finish school, because money is short, expenses high, her family large, and opportunities very few. Yes, most of her race are poor, and menially employed. You will remember that Ruby drew white children strong and able-bodied; Negroes undersized, even stunted. Her doll-house play also showed that she knew the facts of her future life: who was always mistress and who had to be servant. Nor was it all sketched and played this way merely for my benefit. Her mother daily confirmed and enforced what her children knew, what they *had* to know as they grew older and left their backyards to face the world of school, buses, and shopping centers.

Yet, Ruby is also a girl in a particular family, and now the eldest of six children. She was a growing girl of six years when she was told every day that she would die from something she ate. Her symptomatic reply of appetite loss and sharp sensitivity to categories of food and food technology reflected her awareness of her social and racial vulnerability. But her question, her play and talk, showed that she vaguely expected *other* punishment or knew of *other* causes for worry or guilt.

Once she told me she had been punished that day for striking her sister hard enough to fell her. Her mother had lost her temper and punished her with a "good" whipping. Ruby told me that her mother had said words to this effect: "We're letting you off easy and often these days, because we know you're under a strain at school; but there are limits." I asked Mrs. Bridges later what had happened and she replied, "Ruby has always got on bad with Melinda [eleven months her junior]. She bosses all the children too much and they gets angry; so I have to punish her — even now when I know she's getting it bad at school . . . but two bads won't make Ruby a good girl."

Ruby, then, was learning to be a good girl, a rather conventional task for one of her age. Her envies, her feelings of rivalry toward others in her family, are not unusual. She is a girl of sound mind and body, a lively, rather perceptive child whose drawings and frolic show imagination even as they indicate the normal anxieties and fears of a growing child. Were it not for the intersection of her childhood with a moment of our country's history, her difficulties at school or with her family would not be under discussion.

Anna Freud's work during the Second World War demonstrated that tensions in the family engage with public tensions; that is, the adjustment of children to the various hardships of war depended to a considerable extent on how they managed with their parents, nurses, or guardians. True terror can invade and destroy the happiest home; but an unhappy home can be crushed by the merest discomfort.

Ruby's home life seemed basically sound, and her family stable. As a girl of six, she was fast learning the rights and wrongs of her world, shaping her conscience to reflect what her family urged. The crisis of school desegregation became involved in this development, its perils and punishments fitting in with her prior guilts. Her mother had threatened her often with no supper if she persisted in wrongdoing — hitting her sister too hard, failing to obey a command or request. Now segregationist mobs were telling her she might be hurt, poisoned, and killed. One member of that mob, impelled by reasons within her own life, kept telling Ruby of poison in her lunch or supper, forging in the child's mind a link between home and school, between the child's personal conflicts and this public struggle which found her a sudden participant.

Small wonder that Ruby developed temporary symptoms and asked her fearful question — one stimulated by racial conflict, but also related to her psychological development and the quality of her family life. Small wonder, also, that with slow improvement in the city's crisis and continued growth on Ruby's part, she is now a normal, even lusty eater. "Lord, she eats the table up now," has been her mother's consistent report to me in recent years. Ruby is now saying goodbye to childhood, and her school is quietly, fully attended on a desegregated basis.

Eventually attending that school with Ruby was the child of a woman who once vowed the contrary, not only for her own child but for all other white children. Mrs. Patterson withdrew her son Paul from the third grade when Ruby entered the school, and he went without schooling the rest of that year. The following year Paul attended a private school specifically, abruptly, and furiously organized for the white children "dispossessed" by the Negro child. The next year the boy's mother bowed to the inevitable. To abide by her principles would cost more money than she could afford. The public school was a better school, a nearer school, a free school, and now hardly boycotted. Her boy wanted to go back there. She agreed, saying like others I was interviewing, "There's only a few of them in our schools now, anyway. The real ruin will be for the next generation, when they flood us unless we get them all to go North."

For that matter, as language went this woman's was mild for a member of the mob that bothered Ruby. Moreover, part of her threat to Ruby was one she hurled at her own children. If they misbehave she threatens to choke them. I have heard her use the expression commonly enough to indicate that for her it has the meaning of a serious spanking. Her children do not seem overly frightened by the threat. She is a cooperative informant and I visited her and her sister and two of their children for the same length of time I saw Ruby. I saw and heard her on the streets, angry and shouting. I was introduced to her there, by a minister who knew her well.

There is no question that this woman fears and hates Negroes, and there is also no question about her generally suspicious personality. She is poor, now in her very late thirties, with little education (eighth-grade) and perhaps too many children as well as a wayward, fickle, heavily drinking husband. Most of all she is tired: "I have enough to do just to keep going and keep us alive without niggers coming around. They're lower than our dog in behavior. At least he knows his place and I can keep him clean. You can't ever do that with them. They're dirty. Have you ever seen the food they eat? They eat pig food, and they eat it just like pigs, too."

When she is weary she becomes surly, and underneath it all very sad and very frightened. She is struggling to manage herself and her large family in the face of poverty, ignorance, social isolation (like Ruby's parents, she comes from a farm in nearby Mississippi), and virtual abandonment by her occasionally employed husband. She herself is an obese woman, plucking candy from cheap assortments during every visit I made. Her five children are as old as nineteen and young as four.

She has had no history of contact with a psychiatric clinic. One of her children is mildly retarded and mildly spastic, and has been followed by one of the free clinics in the city. Her other children are "normal"; that is, they appear to have no symptoms warranting referral to a child-guidance clinic. One boy was a bed wetter until fourteen, but seems without major emotional troubles now. He is rather tough and laconic, very much like his father. Her husband has bouts of heavy drinking, at irregular intervals, which are followed by pious sobriety. He is a guarded, aloof man, possibly very paranoid under his stylized silence or episodic drinking. Yet, he seems less entangled with racism. He will sneer at "niggers," then shrug his shoulders and sit back saying nothing, or very little. His silence is often his wife's cue for a bitter remark about the lowly nature inherently attached to Negro skin. One of her complaints is that her husband cares very little for the education of his children. Another is that he is not suitably aroused by the perils of the Negro advance into the white world. I have never heard her directly attack her husband's character or habits of drink and work.

Mrs. Patterson does, however, complain about her own life, even as she can complain about Negroes. Her life is cheated and impoverished, and she feels at times lonely and hard-worked with little hope of an end to either condition. Her feelings emerge in remarks like this: "I have to do the best I can with little help from anyone, and I'll probably die young doing nothing else."

There is no very special reason why this woman joined a mob and said what she did while its member. When I asked her why she joined she replied with conventional hatred for Negroes, not unlike those of other people who never have joined mobs. She was undoubtedly influenced by the attitude of her city, its hesitant police and politicians; that is, by the fact that there *was* a mob, that one was allowed to form and daily continue its actions. She is not a psychotic woman, and when reality changes, as it has over these past three years, she makes her ideological and practical adjustment to it. She now defends *her* right to *her* school against the claims of "the niggers." The same Negro child no longer bothers her as before.

As for her choice of threats for Ruby, they surely bear some relationship to her own problems. Feeling her own life frustrated and empty, she could only want to poison another's, *but* as a devout Baptist she could only allow herself to express such despair and rage at a Negro. She, who ate chocolates so passionately, who was so lonely herself, would poison a lonely chocolate-brown girl. The need for a public scapegoat could not be more clear. Yet, the history of her life shows that for her, unlike some, the possession of a *public* scapegoat is no compulsion. Deprived of the outlet of the mob, she goes on, her family goes on, strained, tense at times, but law-abiding.

In a sense the chocolates Ruby came to shun and the chocolates one of her hecklers craved were a symbolic link joining their fears.

Ruby once told me I could choose vanilla cookies because I was white. I have often heard Negro children and adults similarly attach importance to the white or brown color of food, clothes, even furniture. Ruby at the height of her difficulties was all *too* Negro. She avoided reminders and "reinforcements" as the poisonous threats she believed them to be.

Her taunter of each morning ate chocolate cake and candy to soften her feelings of desolation. Listening to Mrs. Patterson then and listening to her again and more closely on tapes it becomes clear that Ruby's isolation as a Negro expressed this woman's sense of her own condition. She shouted at the Negro girl because she was moved to cry out and protest her own fate. What she called the Negroes she feared herself to be; what she saw in that Negro child was herself, unhappy and isolated. She wanted that part of herself to die, and in one of those "moments" which allow people like her "expression," she said as much with her threats toward Ruby. Indeed, the transcripts of her associations during our conversations — the trends in our talks — reveal again and again her mind's unwitting connection of frustration and loneliness with chocolates, with worthlessness, with Negroes, with Ruby.

Pioneer Youth: John Washington

"We once were slaves, but now we have to free our country as well as ourselves," said a Negro minister to his flock in the summer of 1961. His church is in Atlanta, Georgia, and in the words of one parishioner, "it is a hard-praying one." It is also an old and a new church: the red-brick building housed a congregation of white Methodists for many years; but the neighborhood around the church had changed recently, and with it the character of worship practiced in it. "We're Baptist sometimes," the minister had explained to me, "but sometimes we're just ourselves. We takes the Bible at its word, and goes off on our own kind of original praying." Most of his flock were new to the city, and their rural ways of worship did indeed persist in that church: passion and severity, heaven and hell, sin denounced ecstatically. It was a hot terribly humid day, but everyone was immaculately dressed in clothes never worn except in church. They listened attentively, nodding often and occasionally shouting their assent to one point or another made in the sermon. It was a sermon meant to bolster the spirit of a community set to accomplish part of its liberation; school desegregation would take effect the coming week. Sitting in the church was John Washington, a youth of fifteen who was to be one of ten students (in a city of a million, a state of several million) to lead his race out of its special schools and into those shared by the rest of the community.

After the church service had ended, I was at a loss to see how John would be able to live up to his avowedly solid faith during the time ahead. For one thing, he himself seemed bored and restless during the rather long time of singing, reading, and listening. Moreover, I had been in Negro churches better led, more neighborly and warm-hearted in atmosphere.

Yet, whatever I felt, in our first interviews John emphasized to me his reliance upon religion, and predicted his ability to survive — through faith — whatever dangers and pressures he was soon to face. "If it gets rough, I can always pray and go to church, and that will calm me down real fast" was the way he once put it. He spoke quietly and slowly, as if he was needing and gaining strength from his own words.

John was born in South Carolina in the early summer of 1946, the fourth child of Joseph and Hattie (Turner) Washington. His grandparents grew up in the homes of people once slaves — all of his ancestors worked on cotton for generations. His parents took pride in telling me that theirs was the first generation free enough to raise children who would never see a slave. John's birth was attended by his aunt, one of the younger sisters of his mother. His parents were sharecroppers, and until the Second World War had been having an exceedingly hard time of it. Their yearly income had never been more than two hundred dollars. They lived in a cabin at the edge of a large plantation; the cabin still stands, occupied by Mr. Washington's younger brother. He now averages about a thousand dollars a year for farming cotton and tobacco. The land is rich and seemingly inexhaustible. Several times I visited the farm with John — after I had known him for two years — and we both noticed the curious presence of shabby, makeshift living quarters amid abundant wild flowers, heavily cultivated land, and well-fed animals — hogs, chickens, even a goat.

John's father never left that farm until he was drafted to fight in the war. He had his basic training in New Jersey, then went to Europe, where he served as a cook for troops fighting in France. He says that he will never be able to forget the sight of men dying in war, but he counts his time in the army as the best and most influential period of his life: "I never had it so good. I ate food I never dreamed I could, even in battle; and I had a good bed and real fine clothes. I saw the world outside, and I figured I wouldn't stay a 'cropper' after that."

He didn't. He came home for a year and tried resuming his earlier life. He had married a nearby girl when she was fourteen, he sixteen. When he was drafted at twenty they had three children. His wife Hattie very much wanted to remain in South Carolina. Her large family lived only a few miles away from his. They were all part of a community. If they were poor beyond description, essentially illiterate and almost totally isolated from the social, cultural, political, and economic life of the nation, at least they knew it in their bones; and so they feared the risks and burdens of leaving one another as well as a life both familiar and communal, whatever else it was not. Some, of course, had left, even before the war. Each family had its son or daughter, cousin or neighbor "abroad," in the Southern or Northern cities.

Hattie finally agreed to leave, to emigrate, but not until John had been born in his grandmother's cabin. Her husband Joseph had agreed to wait for the birth. Hattie had hoped that by the time their new child had arrived, Joseph would change his mind about moving. Instead, he was more determined than ever. Their fourth child was their first son; he was given his paternal grandfather's name. Mr. Washington wanted a job in a city. He wanted schooling for his children, particularly his new son. He wanted to go northward, to Philadelphia or New York. His wife persuaded him to compromise on Atlanta. "I felt safer going to Georgia since we had to go at all," she now recalls, "and if it was to do again, I'd still rather be here than up there North." She didn't like cold weather, snow, distance from her family, large cities or the way people get along in them — shunning one another, making her feel lonely. In Hattie's town white people spoke to her on sight, asked after her. Hattie knew Negroes had a much tougher life to live, but she wasn't sure that moving from one place in America to another would solve *that* problem. To this day she feels this, her own version of the Southerner's pride. She accepts the higher standard of living she now has in the city, and the new-found rights she has there — to vote easily, to ride anywhere on the bus, to walk into any store without worrying whether she will be arrested for doing so. Yet, she also will say nostalgically: "I'd sooner have an outhouse and all the land we had than live like we do here, crowded together, even if the plumbing is good." Another time she remarked that, "We knew white folks by their names and they knew us; and when we met we were real cordial to one another. Now it's everyone strange to everybody else, and it don't make any difference what your color is, people will let you die in the street before helping you. My granddaddy had his life saved by a white man, on a road right near our house. Now fancy that here."

In Atlanta young John began to grow up. Six months after he was born his mother was again pregnant. John eventually was to have seven brothers and sisters. Two brothers followed him, and two sisters followed them. This steadily increasing family settled at first in the outskirts of the city, where Mr. Washington obtained occasional employment as a dishwasher in a restaurant, then as a handyman in a service station. When John was two his parents moved into the neighborhood they now call their own. They have since lived continually in the same apartment, the five sisters in two bedrooms, the three boys in another, the parents in the living room. In addition there is a kitchen. For the entire Washington family — including the relatives in South Carolina and a few north in Chicago — this apartment represents the highest standard of living yet achieved. It is heated, has electricity, is not rat-infested, has running water, and though poorly furnished and crowded in comparison to the way most Americans live, it is by no means unattractive, because Mrs. Washington is a neat housekeeper.

John's childhood, as a matter of fact, was a fairly strict one. His mother, I eventually learned, had a breakdown shortly before the family moved to Atlanta. John was a few weeks old. She became despondent and her mother took care of the baby. She turned to the local minister and to a rather intensive reading of the Bible for support. She recovered upon moving to Atlanta, but since then describes a definite change in her personality: "I used to be easygoing, but since we had to be on our own I've been careful to be good and do things right. I turned to religion so that we would survive, and I've tried to instill the Word of God in all my children, and sometimes I think even my husband may get it."

I found her at times suspicious and preoccupied with religion. As her remark indicated, she and her husband have not always had a good time of it together. He is a very heavy drinker, enough so to be considered an alcoholic: he can't quite live with or without liquor. After two years of visiting the family and interviewing young John, I learned from him what he himself had only recently learned from his oldest sister, that when he was three, following the birth of his youngest brother, their mother had left for several months, hospitalized for "mental troubles." Mrs. Washington later talked very briefly about the episode: "I don't remember much. I know I got low, and they gave me electricity, and I got pulled back."

From what I could observe and gather from her response to my questions, she still has her moody times. How much they influenced John during his childhood is hard to know. He was breast-fed until "over a year" old, even while his mother was upset. His grandmother also cared for him then, in South Carolina, and for a month in Georgia. At about three months his mother was alone with him; she was still shaky psychologically. Later, when his mother's illness required hospitalization, his grandmother again cared for him.

John was rather strictly toilet trained, in contrast to the way his three older sisters were reared. A very interesting change fell upon him and all the other children who followed him; they were rigorously and even punitively made to respect what was essentially a new — and I would imagine fearful — routine for their parents as well as them. In our first discussion of the subject Mrs. Washington noted that, "In the country we didn't much worry, except for the difference between the house and the trees, and that they has to get to know the difference. But in the city we knew we had to watch out in the apartment. The white owns it, and we just made sure the kids took care of theirselves right off."

It became clear to me — though very slowly — that not only plumbing (sink, running water, and radiators) was new to John's parents when they moved with him as a baby to the city. We often forget what a perplexing and intimidating event it may be for people to leave the secluded poverty of sharecropper cabins for city living: its crowded streets, with their cars and rules of traffic, its noisy anonymity. John's strict upbringing reflected in some degree the guarded adjustment his parents were making to Atlanta. His mother put the matter this way to me once: "If we had stayed on the farm, I wouldn't have been so hard on John when he was little; but his daddy and me had to be more careful of what we did and what the children did, living in a new place where the rules are different — and for a long time you don't know what they are."

So far as John's parents, older sisters and past teachers can recall, he was not a particularly outstanding boy, either at home or in school. His appetite as an infant and child was normal. He grew normally, suffered the usual childhood ailments. At school he started out hesitantly and without distinction, but gradually gained ground, so that in the sixth grade he was one of the three or four leading students in his class. He always excelled in sports, whether in his neighborhood or at school. His parents proudly attributed his agile manner, his athletic excellence to the rural, farm boy "soul" in him. "John was born on a farm," his mother once reminded me, "and that's where his soul got fixed. He can run and jump because that's what you do when you live where we did. People say he's so strong, and his muscles are so good, but we're not surprised. He carries my daddy's body, and he'll hand it down, too — if the city don't take it out of him, somehow."

Whatever value both parents put on a limber body, they matched it with emphasis upon the worth of education. Amid the talk we hear these days about "culturally disadvantaged" Negro children, I think we tend to overlook the fact that Negroes — not only those from the skimpy Negro middle class — have had a widespread interest in education, though to be sure it has necessarily been education of a special kind. Negro colleges are scattered all over the South. Negro seminaries seem to be everywhere. Negro boys have aimed for teaching or the ministry as commonly as white boys have hoped to become lawyers, doctors, or businessmen. By Northern white standards many of the schools and seminaries are weak indeed. We may, today, scoff at state-supported A. and M. (agricultural and mechanical) colleges as part of the "Uncle Tom" tradition that started with Booker T. Washington and is only now ending. We may be dubious about the endless educational courses and credits taken and achieved by the thousands of Negro teachers in the South's segregated schools — all leading so often and ironically nowhere but to further spiritless, flawed learning. Yet, such efforts have at least enabled the hopes and ambitions of Negro people to find some outlet, however small, during a period in history when nothing else seemed at all possible.

For example, Mrs. Washington wanted a future for her children, and even though she doubted its realization, she constantly invoked it as a possibility. Not only did she want her first son to be a teacher; she told me that her grandfather had wanted her father to be a teacher. When today we observe the aimlessness and apparent inertia of many Negroes, we may be seeing people who once had ambition, but have forsaken it.

John entered school at six, and for several years was a rather ordinary pupil. His favorite subjects were geography and history, to which he apparently brought considerable imaginative effort. His fifth-grade teacher gave him a book of travel adventures by Richard Halliburton as a reward for excellence in written reports on such subjects as "wheat" and "cotton." Mrs. Washington saved them and I have read them. They are neatly written, with pictures of cotton fields and sharecroppers working in them. As a matter of fact, John as a young boy was once told by his mother that such pictures showed the kind of life he might be living, had his parents not moved to Atlanta: "I told him that he has cousins working at cotton, and would you believe it, he said no, it wasn't so. He was six or so, and he believed we had always been in Atlanta; and every time we took him to see his grandfolks he wanted to know why *they* had left the city to work so hard in the fields."

John had some trouble with arithmetic when first introduced to multiplication and long division, but slowly mastered both. He also tended to talk or whisper in class enough to earn B's and C's in conduct. He was never known to have any psychological troubles. He has always had a lusty appetite ("he'd eat us poor if I didn't tell him there isn't any more left"). He never had trouble sleeping; and generally — from what his parents and former teachers say — he was obedient at home and school without turning obedience into the compulsion of uncritical compliance.

John entered junior high school (and adolescence) at twelve. He took up with a girl in his class, a rather attractive and quiet girl who then dreamed of being a nurse, and afterward became one. John continued to see her over the years, though they became "old friends" rather than courting friends. I noticed that they drew closer together — at his behest — when he faced the ordeal of desegregation.

He became involved in that ordeal quite casually. He was a tenth grader in one of the Negro high schools in Atlanta. He had been thinking of quitting school, as many of his friends had been doing with increasing frequency. He fought with his parents over this, and the considerations at issue tell about his home life. His father, as I mentioned, had been drinking for many years, but until John was about ten had managed to confine his intake to weekend bouts. John remembers as a child that his father would simply disappear, sometimes coming home for brief periods, sometimes lying down to sleep in hallways or alleys and then being picked up by the police and jailed, dried out and returned home, or brought to his family directly. However, he generally kept sober during the week, and kept his job out of jeopardy. About the time John entered high school his father's controls weakened; he insidiously began weekday drinking. Mrs. Washington apparently saw what was coming, and obtained work at a nearby factory where she helped assemble children's toys. She called upon her religious faith more than ever at that time, and attributes her job to divine intervention: "I saw him going for the bottle worse than ever, and I prayed to God for guidance. He told me to go and find a job, and let it be between Him and my husband, what will come from the drinking. So I looked, and I found one, and it's a good job, too."

The older sisters took care of the younger children. John became a kind of father to them, something he himself once readily described: "My sister Mary and I have sort of been mother and father to my younger brothers and sisters, especially the sisters, because they're young enough to need us." With this in mind, John wanted to leave school, find work, and establish his position as the chief breadwinner of the family — its most reliable man. His mother, however, objected. She feared her son would take after his father if he didn't consolidate his own life, educationally and professionally. His father, too, objected to John's leaving school; so much so that he stopped drinking for the few weeks the decision was in balance.

Largely for those reasons — the various fears of his parents — John stayed in high school, and obligingly set to work studying harder than ever before. Listening to him talk about it several years later, I felt he must have been relieved to see his own struggles and decisions act to stabilize his family. In a way, he achieved his purpose without quitting school.

When the city of Atlanta and the state of Georgia yielded to a federal court order requiring a start toward school desegregation, they chose to begin with the last two years of high school. John was a sophomore at this time and like all his classmates was confronted with the choice of applying or not for transfer the next year to a white high school. The school board would then act upon the applications, selecting the children it judged suitable to make the move.

My experience in city after city of the South has taught me to expect no set pattern for the kinds of children who have taken on the leadership in school desegregation, nor any pattern for the criteria imposed by school boards in selecting them. Many Negro parents would not allow their children to face the dangers involved: some because they were poor and afraid that they would lose their jobs; some because they were comfortable and unwilling to risk the loss of that comfort; some because they were (and are) so fearful of whites, or hate them so, that they would not want their children exposed to them even if they were assured it wasn't dangerous.

School boards in Southern states have not always shown a consistent interest in trying to select the students whose abilities would augur well for making desegregation work. In many instances the age of the child and his place of residence were the only considerations observed. Indeed, often the school boards regarded themselves as under legal attack and accommodated themselves minimally, and only under court order. Frequently they would agree to desegregate, and announce that fact publicly; later on they set a time for those who wished to apply for transfer. In Atlanta a large number applied when they learned that the eleventh and twelfth grades of several white schools would be open to them.

John decided on impulse to request a transfer. Like his friends and classmates, he had been paying particular attention to what he once called "race news." He was eleven when the Little Rock crisis occurred, and remembered it vividly. He later told me that he would "never forget that if I live to be one hundred. I was walking every inch with those kids." In 1960, just a year before Atlanta faced its crisis, New Orleans had been the scene of more riots, in a sense worse than any before them in duration and intensity, let alone the vulnerability of the children involved. John had particularly worried for the young children — he had a sister of seven. "I kept on picturing her going through it, and I figured if she did, I'd walk beside her; and just let anyone try anything."

Walking home one day with his friends, he heard some say yes, they would, some say no, they wouldn't think of going through mobs or sitting through insults at a white school. John recalls the atmosphere and conversation as follows: "We were just kidding around, like any other time; only that day it was about integration and what we would do now that it was coming to Atlanta. We kept on daring one another and teasing each other. My friend Kenny said he was going to do it regardless; and the girls let out a big cheer and hugged and kissed him. Then Larry called him a fool. He said we would be giving up the best two years of our lives for nothing but trouble. He meant the end of high school, and the dances and football games — everything you hope for when you're beginning high school. Well, we most of us said we would do it — I think more to be the hero before the girls. Then they fell to arguing just like we did. My best girl then was Betty, and she told me she would sign up if I would, but we had to promise we both meant it to one another. I can still remember the bargain. She said, 'No joking' and I said, 'No joking,' and that was it. A week later we went down singing to get the forms and apply. I didn't even tell my folks until it came time to get their signatures, and that was where the trouble started. They said no, sir. I tried to tell them we were all going to do it, but it didn't cut any ice with them. Momma started praying

out loud, and quoting the Bible to me about getting into heaven by being poor, and if I tried to go to school with whites and rise up, I'll
probably lose my soul. And Daddy told me I'd get myself killed, and
they'd get him to lose his job, one way or another. For a while I
thought I was out of the running before I even started; and a lot of my
friends had the same trouble."

In a sense the week of struggle for his parents' signatures became
a real time of intimacy and discussion between the three of them. It
was also a confrontation of the generations, the past incredulous at
what the present seemed to expect as its due. John heard from his parents stories of experiences which they themselves had long since "forgotten": accounts of terror, humiliation, and repudiation which had
formerly been handed down from parent to child as an inheritance, to
be told and later relived. John was particularly moved by his mother's
insistence that his generation was the first to be spared the worst of
it — the constant possibility of lynching, the near-total lack of hope,
the daily scorn that permitted no reply, no leeway. To be free of that, to
be safe from night riders, to have steady work, to be left mostly alone,
all that seemed enough. "They wanted me to be glad I could walk on
the sidewalk," John summarized their conversations, "because they
used to have to move into the gutter in their town when a white man
approached them. But I told them that once you walk on the sidewalk,
you look in the windows of the stores and restaurants, and you want
to go there, too. They said, maybe *my* children, and I said *me,* so that
my children will be the first really free Negroes. They always told me
that they would try to spare me what they went through; so I told
them I wanted to spare my children going through any mobs. If there
were mobs for us to face, we should do it right now. And besides, I told
them they were contradicting themselves. My mother always brags
about how wonderful the farm life was, and my daddy says he thought
the city would save him, and it drove him to drink, so it's too bad he
ever left South Carolina. Suddenly, though, all the truth was coming
out." When I asked him how *he* explained their opposing sentiments
he replied briefly — and for me his words are unforgettable — "I guess
people can believe different things at different times."

As he persisted they relented. Eventually they gave their reluctant, apprehensive endorsements. They apparently were proud as well
as filled with foreboding as they signed their names, itself not an easy
task for either of them. John must have sensed their pride. He described an unexpected rise of sentiment in himself as he watched his

parents sign their permission: I think I got more emotional over that than anything else that happened; even more than walking in the building the first day."

Before walking into any school building for white children he would have to meet the standards of school officials worried about how to implement an uncongenial court order in the face of an uncertain and fearful population. John expected to be one of hundreds of new Negro students. He may have been dimly aware that no Southern city had yet taken more than a handful of Negro children to start desegregation, but neither he nor his friends ever gave much thought to the likelihood that only a few of them might be chosen. To some extent they believed — and correctly — that their city was determined to secure their safety. That belief, that faith, helped these children forget or "overlook" some of the possible dangers in the future. John put it to me quite concisely one day several weeks before those dangers actually started coming to his attention: "I try not to think about what's going to happen when school starts. I just go from day to day. We never thought it would be a picnic, but we figured we'd just take what comes, and then we could have stories to tell afterward."

John was interviewed, along with many of his friends, by school officials who were trying to make their choices more rationally and thoughtfully than some of their counterparts had done in other Southern cities. John realized during the interviews that a quiet and sincere presence was wanted, that an inflammatory or argumentative one was feared. He was asked by the school system's deputy superintendent how he would manage insults and even attacks upon himself. He replied that he would ignore them. If anyone threatened to injure him or interfere with his activities, he would call for help from others, namely his teachers. He was pointedly asked whether he would strike back if hit. He said he would not. He was asked why. He said he would only be inviting worse injury by doing so; he would, after all, be outnumbered, literally a thousand to one. I asked him, on hearing him tell of this exchange, how he expected to maintain that degree of almost fearless restraint. My question was: "John, in your own mind — apart from what you told them in the interview — do you think you would act that way if one or two boys pushed or shoved you, and called you names?" He replied: "That's where my daddy is right. He told me a long time ago, 'The only way a colored man can win is to fool the white man into thinking he's won.' I don't think that's always right, but it has to be like that until we get strong enough to make it even steven."

John was chosen, one of ten in a city of a million. He was surprised and quite disappointed rather than honored to learn that he and a girl he casually knew would be the only two of their race to enter the large "white" high school near his "old" one. Again he made light of his worries by speculating that since they were so few, none of them would be allowed to enter at all. In fact one of the girls selected for another school soon decided to forgo her chance. She took stock of the threats and dangers about to begin and decided they were too much for her.

John did not seem to falter. I talked with him all that summer, and was myself a bit unnerved at his day-to-day calm in the face of harassment by phone and mail. Unlike the children of New Orleans, Little Rock or Clinton, Tennessee, that year, John would never face a mob. Yet, John could not have known that he would be spared; and so he experienced — somewhere out of sight — a long summer of anxious waiting.

During that time I talked with him two or three times a week, and finished gathering my general medical and psychiatric impressions of him — his past health, his way of getting along with himself and others, the history of his family, his interests and activities, his hopes, any of his difficulties he cared to remember or talk about. John's general health had always been good. His mother recalled that he suffered the usual childhood diseases, including an episode of colicky stomach when he entered school at age six. He had experienced occasional headaches in the past few years, but no other symptoms. John was not reluctant to talk about his father's alcoholism. He did so with a mixture of sympathy and anger. His mother's biblical preoccupations also upset him. As she gave vent to her warnings of sin and redemption, all the children kept a respectful silence until she stopped, then tactfully resumed their activities. In contrast, John himself had no trouble with drinking, no biblical preoccupations. He did not smoke. He had never had any trouble with the law. By his own description, he was "an ordinary teen-ager."

For three summer months he awaited his role in desegregation. He worked at cutting lawns, emptying trash, helping his father by substituting at the gas station, or selling Cokes at local baseball games. I saw very little evidence of anxiety in him. He did become concerned with his "strength," and accordingly set himself a routine of exercise. His sister asked him whether he was worried about trouble in the fall, and he impatiently denied it. He had noticed he was short-winded on occasion, and that alone was the reason for his exercise. I was on the lookout for "trouble," but his appetite held up; he slept well; he seemed to his family quieter and more relaxed than usual.

The week before school started, the threats on his life, on his family's life, reached their terrible and bizarre peak. The telephone calls came in round the clock, angry voices talking of dynamite, alarmed voices talking of "racial amalgamation," plaintive voices urging John to reconsider his ill-advised decision "before it is too late." His parents — and especially his older sisters — wanted the phone changed. A city detective watching their home advised them to change their number. John would not hear of it: "I'm going to have to get used to that, so we might as well start now." Such a response showed how firmly and stubbornly he was girding himself. As I look back — and only in retrospect can I see it and say it — his willingness to take on the constant irritation and heckling of the telephone calls foreshadowed his future capacity to deal with similar episodes in school. At the time I failed to understand why he wouldn't let his family follow their inclinations and the advice of the police department. Oversensitive as I was to the possibility of incipient neurotic illness under stress, I failed to recognize this youth's desire to have his preliminary struggle with the enemy on "home territory," and win it.

On the first day of school he was escorted and driven to school by city detectives. I watched him walk up to the door of the high school, heavily guarded by police, the students and teachers waiting inside for him, and wondered how he felt, what he was thinking, and whether in fact he had any words to describe those seconds. Everybody else seemed to have words: national and local political leaders, reporters, observers, all noted how important it was for a Southern city to initiate school desegregation without violence. There was none.

Certainly the white children and their teachers felt themselves in the presence of history; and so did John. He told his mother later that he said a prayer she long ago taught him as he left the police car; when that was finished, still walking toward the school, he looked quickly at the building and thought of words he had heard from his grandparents as a boy: "It's going to get better for us, don't you ever forget that." Approaching the front door, he thought of the classroom and pictured the students sitting, waiting for him to enter, and then watching him as he did.

They were doing just that, watching closely, and would continue to do so for two years. They stared at him and looked away from him. At the end of the first class some of them heckled him. A few days later he found insulting words scribbled on his books. Some of the students tried very hard to be friendly, though most of them kept an apprehensive distance from him. He, too, watched apprehensively; but he also worked hard in school, studied earnestly at home, and took things as they came each day.

During his two years in a desegregated high school I kept trying to learn how he managed to cope with the constant strains. I kept careful track of his moods, particularly so because I became puzzled at his altogether remarkable composure in the face of various social provocations or intellectual hurdles. In the first place, he was woefully unprepared for the transfer academically. He had prepared himself for unfriendliness, but not for the long hours of homework required to catch up with, not to say keep abreast of, his fellow students. Meeting these problems daily and a host of others he had never expected, he survived and — I came to see — flourished. I had a hard time understanding why.

I did note his increasingly guarded and circumspect behavior as it spilled over from life at school to life elsewhere. Even at home he walked more carefully, spoke a bit more slowly. He seemed less relaxed, less willingly outspoken and humorous. These were times now when his appetite diminished; he picked at meat once gobbled, played with French fries once almost swept into his hungry, growing body. His mother and sister bought steak they couldn't afford to strengthen him, fight his loss of interest in ordinary food. He wanted only to be left alone, to study.

He sought out some academic help; he went to see a professor at the Negro college he would someday attend. He told me then that he was worried about his math and his French. Yet his tutor told him that his math seemed good, that he was doing his homework correctly. His French teacher in his "old" high school made the same observations about his work in French. Still, he did not seem appropriately reassured by them, or by his good grades as they started coming in. I saw that as evidence of tension, of an increasingly brittle determination that was costing him a high price in humorless rigidity and lack of perspective.

He didn't sleep as well as he once had. He had dreams, on occasion remembering fragments of them to tell me because he (and I) thought that studying dreams was my job. He also told me about his ordeal and that of his white classmates; for he saw that they, too, were having difficulty in reconciling their past expectations of Negroes with his particular presence.

There are two special moments worth mention here. In a way, each tells the story of what happened to John during those two years — how, to some extent, he survived as handily as he did. The first involves the one dream he did remember fully; the only one, in fact, he ever related to me in careful detail and worried seriousness: "I was walking to school, and was stopped because some railroad tracks were there and a long train was going by. I tried to get across the train, because it didn't seem to be going too fast; that is, I tried to leap across the connections between the cars. I know you can't, but in the dream I was staring at them as the only hope to get across, because the train seemed to stretch on and on in both directions. Well, finally the train did pass by so that I could get to school; but it stopped, with the last car right near me. I saw a lot of children on the car; it was like a platform, like in a campaign, where speakers speak from. They were colored children; I think they were maybe seven or eight, and I think one might have been my little sister. Then I saw some grown-ups. Then more and more of them came out from the car, and they came off it, toward me. They were colored, too. They had on suits and ties, I think. One of them was my French tutor [from his former Negro high school] and I think I saw my granddaddy, but I'm not sure. Then I got nervous, because I knew I had to get to school, and I was afraid I'd be late. So I started to move on, and suddenly I saw a huge hole in the road; it was a kind of pit, and I could see my momma and daddy in it. It was mainly their faces I saw, as big as life, just staring there. Then I woke up, and I was clutching the sheet. Boy, was I glad to be in bed. I really felt it had all happened. I went to school this morning, and I had to catch hold of myself near the railroad tracks. I thought I'd see that pit and fall into it. I've never had a dream stick with me like that."

The dream had obviously been upsetting to him, though he could make no sense of it. He had the dream several months after school desegregation had begun; indeed, he was well along the year, and well past the worst tension he had experienced in those first few awkward weeks. He had learned "how to behave" — at least his teachers felt so. I realized that he had his own doubts and fears, though at first I didn't know exactly what this dream told about them. About fifteen minutes after he had told me the dream (and I told him that I didn't know what it "meant") he came forth with two details to it that he had forgotten: "There was something else that just came to me. One of the boxcars on the train said Southern and Gulf Limited; and I think I saw Warren Sands near the pit. He seemed to be standing there, smiling. I think I was glad he was there or something — that was just as I woke up. I must have been afraid I would fall in there; and maybe Warren was

there to rescue me." Warren Sands is a white youth. He was a classmate of John's, a friendly boy, active in student government, one of the
first to come greet him and talk openly with him several weeks after
school had begun.

Then I asked John what *he* thought the dream "meant." He
shrugged his shoulders and replied, "Beats me. The only thing I could
make of it was that it showed I'm nervous about getting to school."
His next comment was about Warren: "I don't know how Warren got
into it. He's just a classmate of mine." In point of fact Warren was not
just a classmate, and John himself had made that quite clear to me. I
said nothing, because he wanted to talk next about his troubles with
French, a foreign language which — as he was putting it then —
"must have been invented to give trouble to people studying it." Yet,
his main trouble, from his teacher's viewpoint, was not his ability to
study the language, but his hesitation at speaking it in class. There
were "conversational hours," the one time John was forced into a social setting by an academic routine. He was embarrassed, and very shy
about taking up with anyone in French. Several white boys had tried
talking with him, to no avail. He balked on his words. The teacher had
sensed the awkwardness right off, and had frankly been unable to deal
with it except by talking with John herself. On those occasions his
French came to him easily. It was, however, a weekly ordeal for him
and the whole class.

John and I never talked about his dream that year, though I think
our talks generally helped him — and me — put some of his feelings —
and my own, too — into explicit language. The following summer I
asked him whether he remembered the dream, and he did; it was one
that somehow lingered, stayed in his consciousness. He still couldn't
make much sense of it; he called it "a sign of the strain I was under
then." I had, of course, come to the same conclusion; but a few weeks
after I heard that dream, I saw John face a strain in real life (and talk
about it afterward) that gave me some concrete idea what the dream
may have meant to him.

John and I went to a basketball game at his high school. The opposing team was from a school not yet desegregated. John as the only
Negro in the audience attracted attention from the visitors by his mere
presence. Indeed, a good part of the audience eventually paid more attention to him than the game. After the game, as we started leaving,
one heckler after another confronted us. They had also seen the game,
and now that it was over they turned their attention to John. Their
language was awful, their behavior threatening. Were it not for quick

action by hastily summoned police, there might well have been a riot. I was quite alarmed, and afterward sad and very angry. John was astonishingly steadfast during the episode, and rather composed afterward. I had known him for several months by then, and so I felt free enough to say what I did: "I don't know how you can take that sort of treatment; I really don't." He smiled, and looked at me as if he understood my problems and would try to help me as best he could. In a moment he did. He started with gentle criticism of me: "You don't know how I can take it because you haven't ever *had* to take it." He paused, "You see, when I grew up I had to learn to expect that kind of treatment; and I got it, so many times I hate to remember and count them. Well, now I'm getting it again, but it's sweet pain this time, because whatever they may say to me or however they try to hurt me, I know that just by sticking it out I'm going to help end the whole system of segregation; and that can make you go through anything. Yes, when they get to swearing and start calling me 'nigger' I think of the progress we're making, I'm making, every minute; then I know I can take even worse than we had tonight. I saw much worse happen to my momma and me when I was eight or nine, and we were shopping, and a woman decided she belonged ahead of us in a line in a store downtown. She slapped my momma, and momma didn't do a thing. I got so angry I kicked the lady and shoved her; so she called the police and soon the whole store seemed after us. The worst of it was that I got the beating of my life from my parents for doing that. You see, we just grow up to take it. But not you, you don't have to, and that's the difference."

When John had graduated from high school and I was trying to make sense of his two-year experience, I kept on returning to those two events, his dream and his virtual "speech" to me (and at me) after the basketball game. The dream told of his struggle going to school and being at school, not only with hecklers but with those who became kind to him (like the white boy whom he belatedly remembered to be in the dream) only to make him feel that he was turning his back on his own people. He felt a traitor trusting and accepting the friendliness of white people. Several times he could frankly tell me how hard it was for him to respond to some of the genuine respect and affection shown him by white students at school.

I suspect he also felt accused by his own people for the increasingly conscious desires he felt to leave their company, to spend his time with white people, even to be white. After we had known one another four years he told me that some of his friends in college deny ever having thought of what it was like to be white. I no longer record our talks on tape, but he spoke words to this effect: "I would never have admitted to you two years ago that I wished I was white when I was at school with whites. I never really could admit it to myself. The thought would cross my mind, and I'd try to forget it as quickly as it came."

John could also show signs of exhaustion and depression; he could summon a level of self-criticism far more severe than any censure I ever saw him direct toward others. He did not get depressed that night at the basketball game — I think taking me to task helped prevent it. At other times, however, he became weary, sulky, gloomy, and unable to heed easily what he had assured me was the persuasive voice of his past life, reminding him at all times that he must not retaliate, that he must endure insults in silence.

John was particularly unhappy during the last months of his final year of high school. He knew he had done a good job, but he also knew it was time to say good-bye to friends he wished he had known longer and whom he realized he would never see again. He had studied hard and been rewarded with consistently high marks, despite inadequate preparation for the academic burden. In his senior year he decided to attend a local Negro college. Even though he was tempted mightily by the prospects of going North to an Ivy League school, he was also afraid of the prospect, and he admitted that he was perhaps tired of the strains that go with desegregated education — the self-consciousness and constant girding of oneself. Were "things different," were he from another home, he might have welcomed a continuation in college of such mixed blessings and hurdles. Beneath the surface lay other problems, though — the troubling fragments of his home life and the attention they demanded from him. His older sisters were leaving home for marriage; his father was sick, his mother rather worn. In a sense his crisis had been theirs, and they had all prospered under it; for their lives had found a real, tangible, and significant purpose. That accomplished, John felt he could not simply walk off. Perhaps his family would eventually learn to need him less, but he felt that he and they both were not yet ready for his departure from Georgia.

As it turned out, he was wise to stay in Atlanta. His father's drinking became worse, though it had improved while the family was under the pressures of John's critical situation at school. His mother, too, declined into a condition of chronic, spiritless fatigue. John both studied and looked after his younger brothers and sisters as well as his parents. They had all supported him; he now worked at helping them.

As I have watched John grow from a youth to a young man, and reflected upon his capacity to endure the simple trials not only of growing but of growing in a home such as his, of growing while a student in a white school, while taking a leading part in an important social change, I have found the limits of my own particular professional training rather severely defined.

John, after all, came from a very grim home, psychiatrically speaking. Both parents have serious mental disorders, the father at the very least a heavy drinker, the mother at the very least subject to distracted, suspicious fits of not very coherent religious preoccupations. John's childhood was characterized by poverty and what we now call "cultural disadvantage." He had a mediocre early education. When he decided to apply for an education at a white school he was not deeply or specially involved in the civil rights struggle. He belonged to no organization working for desegregation. He was not "enlisted" or encouraged to seek an application form; it was almost a matter of a moment's whim, a teen-ager's dare, a response to the company he kept, to their collective teasing of one another — fear and desire blended into a challenge.

Yet, this rather "ordinary" youth survived handily two years of an academic schedule far more burdensome and severe than any he had ever been taught to expect or endure. He also survived the daily loneliness and fear of his special position at school. Finally, he survived the ugliness and nastiness of threats, foul language, even some shoves and pokes in the corridors and corners of the school and in the streets nearby.

What accounts for such durability, such a hardy spirit against such odds? Where did John find his strength? Is his case an exception that proves nothing? It certainly is not an unusual story. John's life is not unlike many others I have encountered in Little Rock, Arkansas, in Clinton, Tennessee, in Asheville, North Carolina, in New Orleans, Atlanta and Jackson. Many of these pioneer children have not been hand-picked or particularly able and bright — not natural leaders, chosen for that reason to lead their race into white schools. Whatever has enabled them to get along as well as they have is no mysterious and rare gift of intellect or "personality development."

John's family life — seen by itself — simply does not explain his capacity to deal with the problems confronting him while I knew him. What, after all, in his childhood, in the personality of either of his parents, can account for this boy's sound mind, his strong will, his competence in the face of a stiff academic challenge, his survival in the face of a severe (and threatening) social challenge? His mother received a diagnosis of paranoid schizophrenia when in a mental hospital. His father, as I have said, is an alcoholic. Were John's case presented at a clinical conference, few psychiatrists would deny the ominous quality of a "family history" such as John's — unless, that is, we called upon Erik Erikson's work in showing the many influences, public as well as private, that combine to make us what we are.

In point of fact, John — and his brothers and sisters — had learned both the melancholy and the strength in their mother's personality. She is full of doubt, hesitation, anxiety, vacillation, religious fanaticism — yes, all of it and upon occasion more. She also can be a stern, tough woman, and a very determined one. She can pray and sing; what is more, she can dissolve many of her tensions in prayer and song, in faith and in hard work. When John was under pressure he could fall back on her ability to wave aside pain, concentrate hard on the intense moment — and the distant future's promise.

Likewise John could fall back on some of his father's characteristics as well as find them a burden. His father was more to him than an "alcoholic" or an illiterate, unemployed, "severely disturbed" man — what I regret to say people like me all too often have to say, and *only* to say, about men like him. To weigh the "effects" of Mr. Washington's illiteracy (or alcoholism) on his children, we must concede right off that different effects (from parental behavior) can emerge at different times in a child's life, in anyone's life. I am convinced, for example, that in his worst (that is, most fearful) moments, John drew upon some of his father's capacity to shrug his shoulders at the world, to avoid looking at it too clearly. John shrugged off cannily the useless baggage of anxiety a fear-ridden world gave him. He had *reason* to do so; he had a *chance* — to become more than he ever was by making all that he was somehow work and work not only for himself but for everyone he knew, for history.

Finally, John received attention and honor, from others — and himself, too. The tough side of his personality, the stubborn, crafty, inventive qualities that poor and persecuted people often develop simply to survive, found an event, a challenge that could draw upon them — make them qualities that could guarantee success rather than, as before, keep chaos at arm's length.

John went on to college, to do quite well there. "That high school became my life," John told me the day after he graduated from it. It was his answer to my curiosity about "what enabled him to do it." "That school glued me together; it made me stronger than I ever thought I could be, and so now I don't think I'll be able to forget what happened. I'll probably be different for the rest of my life."

The Teachers

Teaching the Teacher: Miss Lawrence

Alabama is her native state. She is a high school teacher, a middle-aged, buxom woman whose blond hair has effectively concealed some white for several years. She teaches English, and considers herself a hard teacher, determined to enforce grammatical rules and correct imprecise language. Though not very trim, she is neat. With her clear complexion and her hair worn nicely waved and cut fairly short, she presents a fresh appearance. She favors colorful dresses, too; when my wife complimented her on one of them she explained that the world is dreary enough, and so every little bit of "glow" counts. If there is any underlying sadness in her, it is well hidden.

Though she lives alone in Atlanta, she has several brothers in Alabama and a sister in Mississippi, all with children; and she is an adoring aunt. She admits to favorites among her four nephews and three nieces, but she manages to keep all of their pictures in her wallet.

In class she is thoroughly impartial. She combines her harsh demands in composition with a usual willingness to let the children write about anything they desire. She encourages her children to read widely. If her reputation is to be believed, she is popular but strict. A pupil said to me, "Miss Lawrence, she makes everyone work hard, but she's a nice lady, too."

Miss Lawrence went to college, in Atlanta, and started teaching there upon graduating. She liked teaching in high school because she liked awakening minds, with whom she could converse and share many of her own thoughts and feelings. She particularly liked teaching juniors and seniors in high school. She could send young people into the world more sensitive and thoughtful. Sensitivity concerned her; she used the word often. She called it "the chief virtue" and she worked hard for it in all of her pupils by correcting their errors and pointing out the many shades of meaning in the books they read. "This is your last chance," she told every graduating class, "your last chance to learn English well, to be sensitive to its possibilities." As a result, a tradition had grown in the school: she was called "Last Chance Lawrence."

Years ago she had gone North to get some additional education herself. More recently she had studied at a Southern university. In both cases Negro graduate students were in attendance. She never cared much about political affairs. She would scan the paper very lightly, picking up the gist of the news but not getting into it. She preferred to read short stories, even at breakfast. While others became increasingly involved in the issue of desegregation as it was slowly fought for many years of her life, she kept her attention on Galsworthy and Dickens. She was a Southerner, though. She had never liked Northern cities. They were big and rude places, and frankly — she was shy about saying it — she found the Northern Negroes harsh and discourteous, a poor comparison to their Southern relatives. She had gone through a crisis or two in the North about race and she had learned from the experience, but she was grateful for the quiet and civility of the South: "I learned a lot about Negroes while in the North, but I think the South has some lessons in personal dignity to teach the rest of the country."

What she had learned in the North had not come so easily. She left Georgia for the North because she was an educated, sensitive Southern lady who wanted to do graduate work in education. Negroes were her last concern when she arrived in New York City. She was interested in her courses and in the city's cultural life. She lived in a graduate dormitory. She found it convenient and in addition she felt sheltered from the unfamiliar and sometimes overpowering ways of the city. She had her own room and shared a bath with several others on her floor.

"It may seem strange to you," was the way she began to tell me about an episode of her life that had happened long ago, fourteen years to be exact. She paused, then she started again. "It may seem strange to you that a teacher like me would react to a nigra woman like I once did, but since then I've talked with a lot of people about it, and it's a more common occurrence than you'd think. I'll never quite forget the second it took place. It was an ordinary morning and I was coming out of the shower when suddenly I saw that nigra woman.

There were several showers and she was standing there, drying herself. She had just come out herself (I thought about that later, you know) and we were probably taking showers at the same time. Anyway, she came out of hers just a few seconds before I came out of mine. When I saw her I didn't know what to do. It was as if I'd seen the Devil himself, or I was about to face Judgment Day. I felt sick all over, and frightened. What I remember — I'll never forget it — is that horrible feeling of being caught in a terrible trap, and not knowing what to do about it. I thought of running out of the room and screaming, or screaming at the woman to get out, or running back into the shower. My mind was in a terrible panic; I thought of everything I could do at once, but I felt paralyzed. I felt like fainting, and vomiting, too; it was shock, like seasickness; it took hold of me all over and I wondered whether I was about to die. My sense of propriety was with me, though — miraculously — and I didn't want to hurt the woman. It wasn't *her* that was upsetting me. I knew that, even in that moment of sickness and panic. Then I came to my senses. I realized I had to do something; but all I could do was just stare at her. I must have looked as pale as a sheet. It seemed like an eternity, though it probably was only a few awkward seconds. Finally, I jumped back into the shower and stayed there, listening for her to go and thinking about it all where I *could,* because I felt safer. It was awful.

"When I came back to my room I felt as if I had been through a terrible nightmare. I felt exhausted; and then I actually found myself crying. It wasn't the way you cry when you think about something or somebody, and then get sad and cry about it; it was just a flood of tears that suddenly came upon me. I only realized I was crying when I started feeling the tears on my face."

She apparently was shaky for hours after the incident. Even today she can recall the emotions — disgust, anger — she initially felt toward the Negro woman for causing the crisis. Those emotions were soon followed by shame: that she, an educated woman, had behaved so irrationally. She eventually concluded that the reason she didn't say anything to the Negro but fled was that words were irrelevant, whereas action at least extricated her from an "ugly situation." It was an explanation suited to her longstanding belief, held before she ever left Georgia and still very much in her mind, that feelings about race are deep and silent parts of a person. They do not respond to laws, but only to new experiences. "Words and explanations about race don't mean much," she explained to me. "It's what the person's life has been over the years. I was almost trembling then, and nothing a rational mind could offer — to myself or that Negro woman — would really have made sense of it to *either* of us.

"Of course, over the next few days I became more and more ashamed of myself. Finally I tried to put myself back in the shower room, but I promptly became clammy again. I was sure that if that nigra lady came in I would do the same thing again — flee. Mind you, I don't think I was prejudiced then, any more than I really am now. We grow up with certain ideas, and you can't shake them in a second."

Though she found it difficult to go back into the bathroom at all, she did, every day. She found herself dreading the time the Negro would return. She would be washing her face, and might picture the Negro staring at her after she cleared her face of soap. She would be in the toilet closet and think of the Negro opening the door and confronting her. For the first time in her life she found herself looking at Negroes more closely on the street. She noticed the clothes they wore, or whether they appeared in a movie or restaurant. "You never give some things a thought until you've gone through something like that, then you find yourself suddenly aware, even if it's out of fear.

"I can't tell you how much that split second in my life affected me. Sometimes I have to remind myself that it was *only* a split second, because it's lasted forever, in a way." She told me that one day when we decided to resume talking about her experiences in the North. "I didn't actually see the woman so that I could recognize her, though I kept on thinking that she would remember me and somehow catch up with me. I knew I wouldn't be able to pick her out in a crowd. To be honest they all look alike to me, unless I know a particular one. For a while I thought of going to a hotel or getting an apartment, but I knew that was absurd; and besides, I was more ashamed of myself than anything else.

"After a while I realized that there was more than one Negro in that dormitory; and so I'd better gird myself or do *something* to settle the matter once and for all, though I didn't know exactly what. I noticed them in the cafeteria. I looked at each of them — there were five or six, I think — wondering which one was *the* one. Of course, none paid me the slightest attention. I kept waiting for some trouble to happen, some scene to occur suddenly. It was ridiculous, I know. After several days I could sit in the cafeteria and watch them calmly. I seemed to be getting it into my system that they were just like anyone else. I had just about convinced myself of that fact when two of them came from the cafeteria line one day and sat down opposite me. I can remember the meal to this day. I had veal — breaded veal cutlets, some lima beans and mashed potatoes and rice pudding. I looked at them, and I thought I was going to have to get up. I felt sick again, really just like before. I tried to turn away. I was afraid — not only of what I felt, but afraid for them to see me. I don't think they ever had any idea what was happening, and I'm not sure I did for a while. I just sat there for a few minutes. Then I realized I couldn't eat to save myself. So I got up and left. I think I turned and smiled at them, though, almost as if I were excusing myself from the table to them. It was terrible. I was shaking all over inside; and most of all for fear they'd know what was happening. But I knew after I had left that they couldn't have noticed anything. It had all happened inside me."

What she eventually learned to do that summer was sit with Negroes and eat with them, and shower in the full knowledge that next to her, in the very next stall, there might be one. "It was hard for me myself to believe that I'd done it by the end of the summer, but I had. When I came home I wouldn't tell anyone. I didn't think they would understand. At that time people would have thought one of two things: I was crazy (for being so upset and ashamed) or a fool who in a summer had become a dangerous 'race mixer.' (Things may have changed here in the last few years, but it's *only* in the last few years.) When I came back I felt as lonely as I felt up there. Oh, today it's almost fashionable to talk about Negroes, at least among some of the middle-class people here. We've become such a Northern city, with business moving down and all those companies and their employees. In a way this is New York for all the country people who move in here from south Georgia or Alabama. They try to become sophisticated, if they make some money. They try to be like they think 'everyone' is. I don't mean to criticize them too harshly, though it does trouble me at times. I just don't approve of attacking our region, the way some of our own Southerners do now. They all laugh at what they call the 'rednecks' or the 'poor whites.' Well, I think we've *all* shared in this problem and done our share of wrong — so we've all got to take the blame for the wrongs done. I think the way to start is to be positive, accept the best of our Southern kind of relationship with nigras, then work to change all the negative things.

"Most of the children I teach come from well-to-do families, and they've been brought up to say the 'right' things about tolerance, but I wonder if they really believe their own words. I know children in the poor sections of the South who *don't* say the right things, but they are capable of real softness and kindness to nigras when they're not in school with them, in *their* [white] school. I don't mean to be hard on our middle class here, but sometimes I fear we'll lose the best in the South, and end up with another Northern climate, where people don't care about one another, regardless of race. I've seen whites ignore and insult Negroes up North the way many segregationists down here would never think of doing. I know we're paternalistic, but we do care for one another. We'll have to learn to have different kinds of caring, but I hope when we do it will be our very own kind."

When desegregation was imminent she indicated, discreetly but firmly, her interest in teaching a desegregated class. Those who could not do so, who would not do so, had been given a chance to say so. Their superiors did not wish to enforce a collision of reluctant, angry or fearful teachers with nervous children, whites for the first time with Negroes as well as Negroes with whites. "I had my doubts about integration," Miss Lawrence recalled. "Not because I didn't favor it, but I think I tend to be cautious, and I felt that perhaps we should wait a while, and educate our nigras more fully, and prepare our white people, too. I suppose I was still reacting to the experience I had up in New York. I kept on wondering what I would have done had those Negro women I finally got to know been different. What if they had been less tactful and understanding; I could have become annoyed and angry with *them,* instead of being ashamed at *myself.* When people are tense, their minds do funny things. I'm setting up a double standard, I know. I'm asking the nigra to be better than we often are. Isn't that part of the problem, though, to get us to understand one another? We made them worse, and now we expect them to be better. Yet, you have to start with human nature somewhere when you're planning a change like this. I don't think it's realistic to assume that all people are going to be able to deal with their emotions so intelligently that they can cope with some of these things easily. That's why I was so much in favor of going slowly, and carefully educating both us and the nigra for change. On the other hand, once I actually started teaching a desegregated class I wasn't so sure. I came to disagree with my own earlier attitudes." The two Negro children learned from her, one for a year, one for two years. They were the first Georgians of their race to study with a white high school teacher in a white school.

"We were as nervous as they were." I heard several teachers say the words almost as if they had all rehearsed them. Miss Lawrence described the first day of desegregation briefly: "You could hear a pin drop. Those children just sat there and they looked as if at any moment a frightful disaster, a tornado or something, might come upon them. It was obvious that none of them wanted to sit near the Negro child, and yet they were so curious you could read it all over their faces. I'll have to admit it, I was, too. How were we to know what might happen? After a while you realize that we *should* know, because we're the same old people, the same old teacher and children, in the same old room; some scattered dark faces don't make it any different. But you have to go through it to know it, or we did. No one else ever had in Georgia."

She felt that she had never faced so strenuous a year. Before school even opened she found herself aware of the loneliness the Negro children would experience, and the fear and confusion the white children would feel. She briskly started her first class with a firm declaration of her wish for "order"; she would insist upon it in her classroom, and everyone must know that, and not forget that. Then she outlined the year's work before them. She wanted them to realize they had come *together, to work.* She wrote the three words on the blackboard; she then underlined them slowly.

They did work; she made sure of that. She allowed no nonsense. She never had in the past, and this was hardly a year to start doing so. Work, she reasoned, would unite them. It would dampen the tension in them, and thwart the stirrings of hate and violence. She had always watched her students closely. In fact, until this year, she had grown tired of the mechanics of teaching. There was just so much that one could do with the same books, the same stories, year after year. What saved it all was that she had never tired of watching adolescents. They grow in so many different ways. This year she expected to see more growing than she ever had before.

The first weeks were filled with apprehension and uncertainty, with more of both in the teachers than the children; or at least more that she could recognize. "We are so much more fixed than they are. We can't help it, we're older. We've lived with segregation as a fact of our entire lives. Take lynching; lynching was hardly protested when I was a girl. Our children may oppose integration, but it's a fact of their young lives, not something strange and impossible, the way it seemed to me for so long. I really don't think any of our young people will run away nearly screaming from a Negro in a college room the way I did."

Miss Lawrence read constantly. In the early morning she would rise to enjoy the best hours of her day, relaxing over coffee and jellied toast, and reading "Mr. McGill." Often she talked to me of Ralph McGill. "I read Mr. McGill like the word of the Bible. He's not as popular down here, you know, as I think he is in the North. We've been calling him names for years; my closest friend does. She'll read a column of his and then call me up to tell me what a terrible person he is, how he's against all things Southern. In my opinion, Mr. McGill should be declared a college, a one-man fully accredited college, by the Association of American Colleges. I've wanted to write him that for years, but I'm shy at such things. I think all of us have been prodded by him, even those who keep on calling him ugly names. He has courage, and he has a sense of timing. He doesn't say something and then forget it. He knows what a teacher knows, that you have to repeat and repeat, and not despair when your students seem apathetic or even resistant. He's been doing that for years, patiently saying things that the rest of us were afraid to say, and maybe even became angry at him for saying — I suspect as much out of shame as anything else. He never got too far ahead of us — that's what I mean by good timing — and he never left us impatient or in despair. I think all this means that I feel he really is one of us, and he knows what's happening here. I don't resent the Northerners who come down here and preach at us, or write their books after a two-week tour of a couple of Southern cities. I just don't pay any attention to them. People going through what we are going through have to learn from themselves. Mr. McGill is of us, and he writes for us."

All that year she kept watch over what her children learned at school: "I've never kept my eyes so fastened on a class." She kept scrutinizing herself, too. "How can you plan some of these things?" she asked herself and me one day. "You can plan all day and predict until the world ends, but there's no way for anyone to be sure about how children will act. Some of the children I would have thought least likely to approach those nigras have done it so nicely and casually, while others I thought their potential friends are afraid to lift a finger, or risk a shred of their 'reputation.' The first thing I learned was kindness and decency didn't have anything to do with I.Q. scores or grades. There's the matter of heart and compassion, and say what you will about intelligence, I'm not sure it has all that much to do with sensitivity. What I mean is that the very broadest kind of intelligence will include sensitivity; but I'm thinking of a very able student of mine — he gets almost all A's. He cares much more for his own memory and how well he can use it to get a high mark from me than for what is happening around him, to white people or black people, to any fellow human being."

The teachers talked to one another, comparing experiences and attitudes much as their students did. Miss Lawrence did this not only in her own school but with friends she had in other schools. All her friends agreed upon the need for outward calm and firm discipline, regardless of the turmoil in the students. Some wanted to go further, help bridge the silence and hesitation between dark and white students. Yet, any move in this direction required planning. The pulse of the class had to be carefully estimated day by day. The image was Miss Lawrence's and she continued it with the remark, "You can't treat a condition until you take stock of it.

"It's like anything else, what happens in the classroom will depend on us and the children both." She was evaluating the progress of desegregation, and emphasizing some of the variables. "I've been collecting stories this year, because each school is different, and even the classes in them." She gathered obvious pleasure from telling about teachers in one school peeking into a classroom during the first days. "I can just imagine what the parents or children would think if they saw that scene, a group of teachers behaving like children looking in a store window. Well, it was quite a novelty, and we're human like everyone else. Look at all those TV people who came around the first few days, and the reporters, too." Then she liked to mention the incident with the psychological facet to it: "I think you would be particularly interested in what happened to another English teacher. She was no integrationist, just a hard-working teacher. The first week she assigned a theme which was to be titled "My First Week at School," or something like that. She has been assigning that topic for years, and so have I. Would you believe that out of all her classes, with all those children, she received only a small handful of themes which even mentioned desegregation in connection with the first week of school? Imagine that, with all the police and the nationwide publicity, with all the coverage on television, those children were simply afraid to mention the subject. They ignored the most important thing to happen that week, or that year. It shows you what the mind can do. I've often wondered whether it was a deliberate thing, whether they were simply frightened, or whether it was unconscious and they really forgot. I suppose those children reflected the atmosphere around them: everyone was holding out on everyone else; no one really dared to say what he thought, or no one except a very few outspoken segregationists. Even they were quiet at first, at least in school itself. Those were crucial times, those first weeks. All kinds of attitudes were set, or for that matter prevented, by the policies we teachers adopted."

She felt that about her work generally, that teachers can do a lot. She was proud of her profession. "It all depends upon what you want, I mean what the teacher wants. The first thing, as I keep on saying, is that children must learn; nothing must be allowed to interrupt that. After that, it's almost a matter of what the teacher decides to do, of what her goals are. I know two history teachers who teach the same course. One of them sticks to facts and events; the other is concerned with ideas and ideals. Isn't that the same alternative that faces all of us in this situation, too? I teach English — grammar and composition as well as literature. Yet, I don't think a day passes that I don't have some opportunity to draw some moral, some more universal message from our work together in class. I've always done that, telling them how important order is, in punctuation or driving on the road, to preserve us from chaos. Of course, when we read *Macbeth* or any of the novels they select, from Dickens to Conrad, there's unlimited chance for talk about personal freedom, tyranny, and what have you. Sometimes I wish we adults could see things the way some of these youngsters do. My purpose, as I see it, is to encourage the best and curb the worst in every class I teach. I know I can do it. I believe it's as much a matter of the teacher's desire as anything else, at least in a school like this, in what you might call a middle-class area. With very poor children I think it's only natural for teachers to lose a lot of their interest and concern. It's so hard to fight hunger and the bitterness it produces.

"In our school a teacher can play it as safe as she wants. She can let the children know that she cares about facts only, or she can take an interest in them as human beings. It has to be both, I believe. If I see *any* child lonely or terrorized, I feel that if he is going to learn, something must be done about his terror as well as his answers in tests. If I see a brute or bully at work, I've got to help him, too, or he'll flunk more than my examinations. I don't believe in all this psychology, this psychological approach, they call it. I believe in *teaching*. They have fancy new names for all that we do today, but any teacher worth anything always has known a lot of these things intuitively, don't you agree with that?"

She would pause, then launch into examples: about how she helped the two Negro students speak up, by calling upon them firmly but sympathetically; about how she sensed real fear in a white girl and consequently spoke with her after class, telling her that she herself, a grown woman, a school teacher who had traveled far in America, and beyond, too, had gone through some moments like that in the past, moments of tension and irritability and a sense of being *cheated*. "I said to her that she felt tricked, that was the word I used, and I could see her face respond — she knew that I was telling the truth, because I had supplied a word, an accurate word, for her confused feelings."

Miss Lawrence characterized the first two years of desegregation in Atlanta as "the two most exciting years" of her teaching career. "I've never felt so useful, so constantly useful, not just to the children but to our whole society, American as well as Southern. Those children, all of them, have given me more than I've given them. They've helped me realize that some unpleasant times in my own life were not spent in vain. That's a privilege, to be able to have your life tested and found somewhat consistent, at least over the long haul. I guess I grew up there in New York, and used the strength from it down here later on. I was just another teacher up North for the summer, but it made me a better Southerner, a better person, for a long time afterward."

The Protesters

Larry

He thought he might have appendicitis. The pain in his stomach had persisted for a day, then moved vaguely to the right side of his abdomen where he felt it intermittently. He had no appetite, and he thought he might have a fever. He waited for another day, then became worried enough to seek out a doctor. The pain seemed to have settled deep in him, and he feared that the next event would be rupture, and a belly full of poison. "For a while I thought I'd be going to medical school next year," he told me after outlining his symptoms in an orderly and precise fashion. He was then a senior at a first-rate Eastern college. He was bright, well spoken, intensely idealistic, very much determined to reach Mississippi and be of service there. "Even if I do need surgery, I'll be able to get down there within two weeks, won't I?" he both stated to me and asked me as I prepared to examine him.

Though I couldn't be certain, I did not think that he had appendicitis. I told him so, and also told him that we should keep an eye on his pain and his general state of health. Then I asked him how he was managing at the orientation sessions. (It was the summer of 1964 and we were in Oxford, Ohio, for two weeks before going into Mississippi.) He said that things were going well, but his manner — the impatient legs, crossing and recrossing, the averted eyes — told me to let the subject drop. I asked him to come back in twenty-four hours for another examination.

He was back that evening, after a service had been held for the three missing civil rights workers, later found dead in Philadelphia, Mississippi. His stomach seemed better. For the first time in two days he had eaten a full meal. Now that the threat of surgery was gone, he was in good spirits. "I dreaded the idea of spending the summer in the hospital and not in Mississippi," he said almost immediately. I told him that even had the worst been the case, an appendectomy was no longer the serious matter it used to be. "You would have certainly arrived South by mid-July."

For a few moments there was silence. I wanted to ask him, again, how he was feeling, how the orientation sessions were going. He was less restless and apprehensive than he had been, and I decided to ask him how he happened to become involved in the project. He gave me a quick glance, as if to say that he knew who I was and what I had in mind; moreover, knowing it, he was not interested in the kind of casual talk I only *seemed* to have in mind. I expected the awkward spell of quiet that fell upon us to be followed by his departure, when suddenly he spoke: "Do you think it will do any good? I've been asking myself that more and more. I know it's good for us. We'll learn a lot about the South. What about the civil rights movements though? How can a few hundred students change Mississippi?"

The questions were unanswerable at that time. We both knew that only events themselves would provide the answers. I asked him his major and it was history, with a minor in American literature. I suggested that it was hard to evaluate history as it was happening. Inconsequential incidents may be significant beginnings. Elaborately planned uprisings may come to nothing. We talked in such generalities — banal generalities — and he became more relaxed and more talkative, that day and on the other days we met.

"I expected to be in Europe this summer. My cousin and I were going there. My brother is studying at Oxford, and the three of us were to travel in England, then go to France and Italy, and maybe Greece. Then this happened. I wasn't really very interested in civil rights. My parents were always much more involved in that kind of thing than I was. To tell the truth, for a long time I was bored with the whole subject. I remember that a couple of years ago I asked my father why he never seemed to get tired of all those 'causes.' One after another he takes to them, and each time you would think the whole world stands or falls on what happens. We had quite a fight. He said I was pretty casual because we had money and I said he was pretty tense because he didn't trust his own success; he constantly feared someone would take his job away. I suppose I was unfair to him. Actually, I think he's a very sincere man, and wants to help when he can. The only way he really helps, though, is with money. That's what used to bother me. I saw him write the checks, then look satisfied with himself when he was finished. He would tell my mother to be sure to address the envelopes and mail them right off the next day. I could see the look of satisfaction on his face. He had done his generous deed and he wanted my mother to know it. He was almost distrustful of her, as if she might take away his glory by not mailing the check. I had never read Freud then, but I used to wonder why he was so worried that somehow his checks wouldn't be mailed.

"I still don't know exactly when I decided to go South instead of to Europe. I read of the project and heard that students were being recruited. I went to a meeting — a question-and-answer meeting — because there were no movies around that I hadn't seen. I think I really went for the same reason you're probably here: I wanted to find out what kind of people would be there. I noticed right away that they weren't the ones I expected. I thought they would be the politicians, who always work up a storm over one issue or another. Instead they all seemed to be like me, and more were there than I expected.

"We heard a few speeches. I almost left in the middle of one of them. A Negro kept on telling us how rotten America was; how rotten every white man was. I wanted to stand up and ask him why he was asking for our help if we were so damn 'corrupt' and 'hopeless.' No one dared say anything though. I knew some people felt like speaking out but couldn't. You feel guilty, to blame for it all. You also feel that the man who is talking has been so hurt and beaten down that he's no longer rational. So you excuse him, as you would anyone who has had a rough time.

"I think I first thought of joining up when I heard another Negro talk — this one from Mississippi. Unlike the first Negro, he stumbled and paused; at times it was even hard to understand him. He was the real article, though, as genuine a person as I had ever seen. He really got to me — standing there and asking us so politely to come down for the summer, as though we were future guests of his. He offered to put all of us up, even if he and his neighbors slept in the woods. Someone finally had the nerve to ask him what we would do. I wondered about that, too, but I was afraid to ask. I thought it might offend him.

"He didn't hesitate for a second. He knew exactly what we could do. 'You can live with us and give us some of your strength, and maybe then the white people of Mississippi will stop and take a look and remember that colored people aren't alone any more.'

"I remember feeling that I *had* to go shake his hand. All I could do was look at it — a huge, big black hand it was — and they were lined up shaking it. I left after my turn — I wanted to get some distance on my emotions. If I had stayed I would have joined, because of that man.

"It wasn't easy to forget him. A few days later I still found myself thinking of him. I could hear his deep, strong voice. I pictured him standing there, all that way from home, and in an Ivy League college. He was the first person I ever met who made Faulkner seem real to me; I used to think he was just a romantic writer. Now I had met the kind of real person who inspired him.

"Two of my friends decided to go down there, and I began to feel that if I didn't go I would feel lousy all summer. I pictured myself going through a museum in London or Paris and feeling like a worthless coward. I talked to my parents about it, and they said I should go to Europe; there would always be summers to spend on civil rights. (What do you think of *that* for a long-range view of things?)

"They were trying to be helpful, I know. They sensed that I *did* want to go to Europe, but that I didn't want to admit it to them. I also sensed that they were really afraid of what would happen to me if I went South. I asked them whether that wasn't true. No, not at all; they wanted anything I wanted, so long as I turned out to have a 'happy' summer. I work hard at college, they reminded me. I deserved a rest. Each person makes his own contribution toward a better world. You can't compare lives. I could do a lot for civil rights just by doing well at school, then going to law school and doing well there. Eventually I would be able to help as a lawyer with civil rights cases. That's where the real victories would be won, anyway. And so it went, one argument after another. I kept on wondering what that poor Negro farmer would make of us: my father trying to have it both ways by giving money but taking no risks and preventing me from taking any either; my mother always ready with an excuse in the form of a reminder that there are many roads to Rome. For my own part, I was excited less about civil rights than a particular Negro who makes Faulkner's writing come alive.

"I didn't *decide* to go South. I simply couldn't get myself to buy that ticket to Europe. When I finally called my parents to tell them that I was going South, they said no. Since I was under twenty-one, I had to get their written approval. They refused it, and we had the fight of our lives at home.

"I've never seen more truth come out in a shorter time. My father tried several strategies. First he told me that he was sympathetic to the project's aim, but opposed to *my* involvement. To that I didn't even have to reply. With a look I confronted him with his hypocrisy. Then my mother tried another tack. She wanted me to wait a year, '*just* a year.' My father agreed. They insisted that I would 'have more to offer.' I told them they were trying to buy time, on the assumption that in a year I would lose interest; and I admitted that I might. Yet, the more I heard them talk, the more I wanted to go, then and there. My father's temper eventually got the better of him, a good thing in a way, because he is always more honest when that happens. He shouted, 'You can't go, period.' He paced the room, and in a few minutes it all came out: we were fools; the Negroes in Mississippi should leave and come North; a few hundred college students can't fight a whole state, with the police and the courts against them; they would jeopardize the Negroes and risk their own lives, all to no avail; it is selfish and romantic to try being a hero when a complicated political problem requires — as he put it — 'other approaches.'

"I knew there was no point continuing the argument that day. I also knew that if I were going to get any place, it would be through my mother. She didn't say much after my father exploded. She just mentioned that she was afraid for my safety — and I respected her for saying so. It was the one honest moment we had.

"I let a few days go by, and then I asked my mother very casually one day whether she would give her permission. I had the form with me, and a pen. I said, 'Mother, just sign. I won't get hurt. If you don't let me go, we'll fight all summer, and we'll all be hurt worse than anybody in Mississippi will be.' She looked at me for a second, and said she thought I was right; then she signed.

"For weeks my father refused to talk to me when I came home. He flushed, or gave me a look that meant he was arguing with me inside himself. He's a lawyer. It's his job to argue. He does it all day, and half the night. He doesn't know when to stop.

"I made my plans as if he had given his approval. I went to the preliminary meetings, and my mother's signature was accepted as sufficient by the leaders of the project. Meanwhile, Mother slowly worked on my father, without telling me what she was doing. She bought a few books on the South, and read them. She left them around for my father to see: Lillian Smith's book, *Killers of the Dream; Segregation* by Robert Penn Warren; and Ralph Ellison's *Invisible Man*. He read them — I later found out — in that order. It was a good way to get into the problem — reading what two white Southerners had to say, then a Negro who lived in the South.

"Lillian Smith really moved him. He broke his silence on the subject by asking me questions about her and her book. Was it all true, or was she a writer, someone who exaggerates or is always dramatic? Why did Negroes stand for the treatment they received? (While you may think some of his questions naïve, they show how hard it is — even for someone who is *trying* — to understand what is happening down there.) In a few weeks he was no longer curious. He talked as if he had lived in the South for years. He insisted that there had to be change down there, fast change. He signed my application without a word of protest — and here I am. I'm not sure now that my father isn't more confident than I am about what this project will accomplish. It's going to be a harder summer than I thought."

During those days of orientation I saw the fear in Larry. I also realized how unwilling he was to talk about his fears. "Sometimes it's best not to think," I heard Larry — and many others — say as the orientation period ended.

During the summer I met Larry several times. We spent a week together when I had occasion to stop traveling about Mississippi and stay in the "Freedom House" he and eight others occupied. All along, from June to September, I tried to learn how he was adjusting to the rather special kind of life he was living. By the end of the summer it was quite clear that he had survived a difficult time rather well. As I proceeded to take stock of my observations — and his, as we recorded them on tape — I realized how various his moods and feelings had been during that relatively short, if eventful, span of time.

Two days after he arrived in the rural cabin that was to be his summer home I found him more confident and unafraid than he would ever again be in the South. He was staying with a large farming family. He was determined to be open and friendly, and immediately so. He saw in his hosts his own attitudes: they were warm, indeed more hospitable than any people he had ever known.

On the day of his arrival he started teaching, concentrating particularly on elementary schoolchildren and their reading problems. He
wanted the twenty or so children in his class to have a summer rich
with words and stories. Three of his students came from the home
where he stayed. Their mother packed lunches for them and for him.
She herself ate at her "white lady's place," where she had spent time
and worked since she herself was a child, at her mother's side: "Then
we didn't much go to school. We learned about life tagging after our
mother, and if the white folks were good, they would teach us something now and then. My mother can't believe it, the children going
to school so regularly, and now a white man from the North staying
with us."

The second time I saw Larry he had been ten days with her and
her children, but felt much worse about matters. He had tried very
hard to be friendly, so hard that he could not very well recognize the
nervousness and fear he inspired in the Negro family — and felt himself. He could, however, acknowledge that he didn't like the food
served him, and often found talking with Mississippi Negroes awkward: "I try and try to get them to call me by my first name, but either
they won't, or they get around it by not using my name at all. I'll work
up a sweat making conversation, but it's hard to keep it going. I'm
used to talking about ideas and events, or about people, writers or
politicians, men in the news or in history. They talk about what's happened during the day, or what they're going to do in the next few minutes. I know they want me with them and like me, just as I want to be
here and like them; but it's difficult being together — I know that, too.
It's not only the race barrier that gets in our way; it's the social differences, from the world of upper-middle-class New England to the poor
South."

What kept him going, indeed kept his spirits high, was is work.
He was so obviously doing so very much, and so very much that was
worthwhile. The children adored him, he could see that: "They may
find it hard having us around them at home, but they love coming by
our school, and they at least relax *here*." In the beginning he was appalled by the children's faulty grammar. Sometimes he had trouble understanding them at all. After a few weeks he decided that the problem
was his as much as theirs. Many of the children spoke the strong,
forceful, active language of the Negro farmer. Perhaps he should let
that be, rather than fight it; perhaps — instead of dwelling on the grim
history of slavery — he should try to teach the children pride in their
race's history, in its survival against odds no other people in America

have faced, in its ability, despite everything, to produce a distinctive culture: "I think it's important for these kids to know what is really outstanding about Negro life, its writers, singers, and artists; its men of science and learning. I didn't know about those people myself until I got involved in this project. All I knew was that the Negro has been nearly destroyed by slavery and persecution. It never occurred to me that he had really built a very significant culture of his own here, even in the South. I owe the fact that I did learn such things to the people who got this project going. They made sure right away that we didn't try to turn these children into pre–Ivy League types. Despite their warnings, it took me a few weeks to appreciate the more positive forces working in the lives of these boys and girls."

A week later — his fourth in Mississippi — I found him relaxed with the Negro community but increasingly concerned with the white people of the county, of the entire South. Until then he had hardly noticed them; suddenly they were on his mind every day. He went to several church services and coffees, only to find himself ostracized. Instead of welcoming him, people glared at him. The only words he could elicit from people were harsh and critical ones. Twice he was asked to leave the church. He refused. He never before had found it necessary to defy others in front of a church, to claim (against their wishes) his right to worship. When he went to the drugstore or the post office he met up with the same opposition, so much so that he found ordinary tasks like mailing a letter or buying razor blades and toothpaste extremely difficult: "I'm *afraid* in the evening; they might dynamite us or snipe at us; but it's shopping I *hate* — meeting the whites and seeing the murder in their eyes."

As he talked one could feel how lonely he was, and conflicted. He was sensible enough to see that the white townspeople he dreaded — but was drawn to — were not mad, not especially evil: "They make me wonder what I would do if I were in their shoes. I've never been in a situation where I would be ruined socially and economically for trying to live up to my moral code. Their code is supposed to be like mine, Christian; but I guess we just don't read those words in the Bible the same way."

At times he simply wanted to see white people, to be with them rather than argue with them or speculate about their predicament. "A day will pass — or two and three — and I won't see a white face. I even forget for a while that I'm white. I'll see another white person and register shock. Then I'll go downtown and feel like an explorer who has been away a long time and finally has returned."

The split between the Negro and white world that he was noticing every day became a decisive emotional experience for him, marking off in his thinking the past from the present and future. He felt that
he never again would be able to take certain things for granted. In a
sense he felt a break with his earlier life; something had started in
Mississippi that was destined to affect him long after he left the state:
"I feel I'm taking advantage of these people in a way. I'm living with
them and being fed by them; and even if I'm teaching their kids,
they're teaching me much more. I'll never again be able to take even
the ordinary things of life for granted. It took coming down here to
realize how privileged my life has been. I knew it in the abstract, from
reading books and taking sociology courses, but now I've learned lessons about people and their problems that a million books and
courses couldn't get across to me. In fact, I'm afraid to go back to those
books and courses."

That last sentence, spoken in the middle of the summer, would
be repeated by him again and again. He found himself thinking of his
return to school with mixed pleasure and dread. He missed the
movies, the dormitory and its comforts, the social life of college. He
wanted to swim, play tennis, or simply take a drink without worrying
about sheriffs and dynamite. "I have to admit, every once in a while I
just want to fly away from here. I picture myself stretched out on a
sandy beach, sipping a gin and tonic. A few seconds of that and I feel
ashamed. It's the truth, though, not an idle daydream: we can always
leave here when we wish. We know it, and I'm starting to realize that
the people in the town do, too — both Negro and white."

He spoke like that to me during the week I spent doing medical
examinations on the children in his class. While the summer was far
enough advanced to justify a return North, he now found the possibility of that return both haunting and ironic: "So long as I can go. I've
never *really* settled in here."

We spent long hours that week talking about degrees of "involvement" and "commitment." How fair is it to come down, spend two
months, then depart? How hard should one like Larry try to commu-
nicate with white people? Is there really the trust between him and his
Negro schoolchildren that he hopes for, or imagines to be? How well,
deep down, was he getting along with his "family," the Johnsons?
What would happen when he came home, when he saw his parents,
his friends, their style of life, their concerns that were once — still
are? — his concerns? Could he take memorizing and studying for
multiple-choice exams in order to get good enough marks for law

school? (More and more he thought of being a lawyer rather than a doctor.) Apart from an occasional moment of nostalgic, boastful recall would he forget the whole summer within a year, perhaps even less?

He was gloomy as well as fearful of the future, or at the very least speculative about it. He felt like a frivolous, privileged intruder upon the lives of the Negro children he taught, and certainly upon those in the civil rights movement who were giving the struggle more than a summer of their time. While he was angry at the state's white people, he also was newly sensitive to the charges they had leveled at him and his kind. What he imagined the Negroes thought about him confirmed what he had heard angry whites say, and what he now — in his cheerless, doubtful spells — believed to be true: he *was* an outsider; it was indeed only a summer's effort for him; in a few weeks there would be the same old and terrible confrontation of impoverished dependent Negroes and whites with at least power if not widespread affluence; and, above all, he knew that he wanted to leave, even as he wanted to stay. He knew that even were he to stay a year or two more he would still have his departure in mind upon occasion. That fact, that option if no other one, made him a privileged person among the needy.

One night we talked through to dawn, and I heard him express a good deal of his guilt and confusion. If he felt a bit easier for having done so, I was more than a little troubled when we had finished. True, some of what he said was familiar to me before I ever set out for Mississippi that summer: as a psychiatrist I knew the strains felt by many youths as they obsessively wrestled with questions of freedom, authority and social customs. Yet, the conflicts Larry now had were grounded in the harsh truths of a political and historical struggle. They were not primarily private conflicts. Nor were they simply personal tensions masked by participation in a social cause, or finding symbolic expression in that cause. Before Larry ever became involved in the civil rights struggle he felt both loyalty and defiance toward a number of people, from his parents and teachers to his friends. He was unsure of his major, unsure of what profession he would choose, unsure of his standing with girls he successively dated, even unsure which friends were in fact his close and lasting friends. His uncertainty was not, however, asserted by "symptoms," by the various disorders of thought, mood, or body that bring some youths to psychiatrists. It took a summer in Mississippi for him to become enough upset and alarmed about his torn feelings — his doubts and misgivings — to want to talk with me about them.

Regardless of how appropriate I thought his nervousness to be, he had his doubts: "I wonder what's coming over me. I used to be pretty calm about life. I knew what was going on; I always read the papers and magazines. But I never let current events rub off on my *personality*. I never became tense, just because the world is tense. Now it's different. I wonder whether I'm becoming sick. Everything that goes on here bothers me inside — makes me sweat, or makes me lose my appetite, or get a headache, or lose sleep. Sometimes I think I'm going nuts, but then I see it happen to others too, and I figure that it's not imaginary things getting to me, not in the least. So I talk to myself. I say, 'Larry, it's right to get worked up. If you didn't you'd be a fool, or a louse; if you didn't *then* you'd be sick.' That helps — while I'm here. What about when I go back though? What will happen then? Will I just forget the whole thing, chalk it up to a nightmare, or even worse, a kind of summer-camp experience — exciting, even dangerous, but no longer a part of my real life? That's the kind of possibility that scares me more than the segregationists do; because if that happens I will really have become one of them — in my own New England way, one of them."

We had our last talk in Mississippi two days before he left for home, then school: "I can't believe I'm still here, when I think back to my first few hours in the town. I was so scared I couldn't even allow myself to know I was scared at all. I kept on telling myself how wonderful everything was, the people, their attitude, their life. When you asked me how we were getting along, I said, 'Great.' I can remember saying it — exactly where we were when I said it. The answer stuck in my throat, but I didn't know why. It took time for me to see how scared I was and how scared the Johnsons have been all their lives, and how scared a lot of white people are down here, including the sheriffs, who have guns."

Larry's departure from Mississippi was as touching an episode as I saw in my work in the South. As at graduation time in high school or college, there was a succession of events — suppers, informal picnics, and dances — to mark the occasion. On one evening Mr. and Mrs. Johnson made a large supper for Larry and his students, for neighbors and other civil rights workers, and for a few visitors — a lawyer, a minister, myself — whom they called the "older generation of Northern help." It was actually a community celebration, and was held in the Baptist church. Larry had been arrested twice during the summer, once for "speeding," once for failing to halt (at least long enough to satisfy a waiting policeman) at a stop sign. Each time they had emptied his pockets, removed his watch, and held him in jail for what they

called "the processing" of his violation. Each time his watch was returned damaged. The second time he refused to take it back. Before
supper the Johnsons gave him a watch. Mr. Johnson said very little:
"Larry, this is for you from us. We're proud to know you, and we thank
you. I don't know what more to say, except God bless you."

A year afterward he would still recall the event as if both he and I
had not been there, and needed a detailed description of what happened. "It was late afternoon, not evening. They eat early, because
they rise early and work long hours. (It took me time to get back into
the swing of things up here, supper at seven instead of five.) They
came together quietly, in the church. They don't talk too much. They
can be silent without feeling nervous or inadequate. They handed me
the watch and thanked me for being with them, and for doing what I
could that summer. Mr. Johnson handed me the watch. Then Mrs.
Johnson asked me if she could help me put it on — and that about
broke me up. There wasn't a dishonest moment the entire time. She
wound up the watch and strapped it down on my wrist. They clapped,
but only for a second or two. Mrs. Johnson announced that she had
made some delicious fried chicken. She asked us all to eat it before she
had a chance to get at it; if we didn't do so, her hands would pick up
one piece after another, her dress would stretch and then split, and
that would be more than she could bear, or afford either. I never ate so
much in my life, and I never felt so good. I told the Johnsons that
since many people work fifty years for a watch, I was getting away
with a lot. Mrs. Johnson didn't wait a second to reply to that: 'We're
giving you a freedom watch, not a slavery watch.'"

Larry left very early in the morning, and he left quickly. The
good-byes were kept down to a minimum. They all pretended — or
believed — he would soon be back. As he drove North he never
doubted that he would see the Johnsons again, but he did doubt his
capacity to resume life at college. "I kept on wondering how I could
face it: the silliness and emptiness; the instructors who think they're
God because they've read a few books and can sit and talk about
'ideas'; the ivy that doesn't only climb the buildings but grows up the
legs and into the brains of both teachers and students. What would a
football game mean to me? A spring riot over nothing? A rule about
wearing a tie at breakfast? I could hear all those instructors telling me
how 'complicated' everything is, and how 'practical' you have to be,
and how more 'research' has to be done; and I knew I would do one of
three things: cry to myself, scream at them, or just smile."

After he had returned and settled into his studies some but not all of his bitterness left him. He began to realize that it was not very sensible to compare school in the North and life in Mississippi. They were different, almost incomparably so. He kept up a continual and spirited correspondence with the Johnsons, and with several of his students. At Christmas he returned to see them. The more he realized that he could keep in touch with the South and with his friends there, the less he had to insist upon confronting his college with Mississippi at every possible turn. Just before he went South a second time he had this to say: "I'm settled back here, I guess. I'll never be settled back the way I was before, but I'll stay and graduate. I don't hate college the way I did when I first came back; I think I really appreciate it more. I want my friends in the South to have what we have here. They even have a chance to have more than we have here, by avoiding some of the mistakes we've made.

"Anyway, I think I'm going to law school. Whatever I decide to do I'll never forget the civil rights issue, and its meaning — for me as much as the Johnsons. That's what happened last summer; I learned that the struggle was mine as much as theirs. I told them so just before I left, and they laughed. They apologized for 'giving me trouble.' I said, 'That kind of trouble I need.'"

After Joe Holmes

I was born in Reform, Alabama; that's between Birmingham and Columbus, Mississippi. My daddy worked on shares — cotton and some tobacco. We had our own garden, too. (I can remember the first time I ate tomatoes from a store, and corn from the can. I thought they tasted real strange.) There were us seven children who lived (we lost some before they were born and some after they were born) and my mother took care of everyone, including keeping my daddy going in the fields, and keeping an eye on his mother and her own mother; though, naturally, both grandmothers helped out a lot around the house.

It wasn't so bad growing up as some in the movement like to picture it. They don't know what hurts you and what doesn't. To listen to some of them you'd think a colored boy in the South is born in hell, and when he grows up he's entitled to get a diploma that says he's been there. I'd as soon live on an Alabama farm as be in New York or Chicago. As a result of being in the movement I've got to both places, on fund-raising trips, and it's really like hell up there: cold, so cold no one can relax his limbs; and the way people live there, it makes a coffin in a cemetery down South seem like a mansion.

Back home we had our bad times and our good ones, but I never used to divide them like that: it was just life, moving along, and me, living. You know how it is: you're not like the trees or the rocks, so you keep doing things and more things, and you know you're "you" even if most all the time there's no reason to think about things that way. When I was eight or nine I once asked my mother about that; I said, "Momma, tell me how it was decided I would be me, and someone else would be them, like Mr. Jameson's boy Andrew." You know who Andrew Jameson was? He was the mayor's son, and my age. He's become a lawyer now, like his daddy. My mother used to go help there sometime, not regular though — if they had extra laundry, or a party to give. ("He's the bossman of the whole county, Mr. Jameson is," my daddy would say proudly, "and your mother has gone to work for him.") Well, anyway, my mother didn't have a very good answer to my question. She said, "Son, you can't know about things like that. The Lord, He's the only one who knows, and He don't tell until we gets to meet Him, which is you know when." I hadn't given up on my mother's Bible faith then, so not only did I hear her, I was satisfied with her explanation.

Looking back, I was satisfied with everything in my life until in church one day a man stood up and said we were going to rewrite the history books in our lifetime. There are always a few people to speak out on Sunday, but mostly it's Scripture they will read, or a lesson from it they have received that they feel the urge to tell. Suddenly Joe Holmes, he just stood up and said his television set was speaking the Lord's will. Every day it showed pictures of what the colored man was doing, and how he was coming into something, at last. "It must be God's desire," Joe said, and then he wanted to know if we were all ready. "Are you ready for the Day?"

I thought he meant Judgment Day, just the way it's always meant that; but he was talking of something else. He must have known we were confused, because he explained himself before we could ask him to: "There'll come a time not too much away when we'll have to say to the white man that it's over, treating us bad, and we are as much citizens of the country as everyone else has been all along." I remember him talking as if that day was tomorrow, or next week at the latest. I never had heard anything like it.

We just didn't ever think like that, let alone speak aloud such thoughts. You grow up and take things for granted the way they are. If the rich take them for granted, so do poor folks. Why should they think it will ever change, the world where colored people have to be below the white man? My daddy's reaction was to say that poor Joe Holmes was always funny in the head, and now he had gone and lost his head. My mother said his head wasn't bad and it wasn't lost; it was just that he didn't know when to keep his mouth shut. He kept on saying out loud things no one can say, unless he's bound straight for the penitentiary — and plenty of us go there every year. "You just forget that kind of talk." I recall those words from my daddy. But my mother said, "Don't forget them, but don't let them fasten on to your tongue, or there'll be no end for you but the chain gang."

I forgot about Joe Holmes and his speech until a few weeks later I heard that Joe Holmes was beaten up near to death by the police. Some students in the Birmingham civil rights movement were going from county to county trying to get us all organized, to start school desegregation and get better streets for us, with lights, and get us some jobs maybe. Joe went to a meeting they had, and they started coming to see him at home. We heard that he said they could even use his house, come live there. I guess the sheriff heard the same thing. One night they were waiting for Joe on his way home from town. We knew they were watching him. ("It's a matter of time, only time," my daddy kept on saying.) They must have followed him until they could get him in secret, on the long, empty stretch of road going North. He was beat so bad they must have thought he was dead when they left him. It was a white man who saw him, lying near the road, and he drove to our cousin Mac's house to tell him that a nigger was sick on the road and needed help fast. Mac said he knew what it was that happened even before he started his car to go find Joe. The white man said it looked from the distance like a stroke or something, there being blood; but he must have been a stranger, a salesman or something. Mac knew, and any *white* man from Reform would have known, too.

Mac and two others, they drove Joe to Birmingham. They called the civil rights people to tell them ahead what was coming. They had people waiting outside the city on the main highway, and they worked a long time on Joe, the best doctors they could find. It took a week, but Joe died. His head was hurt so bad he never woke up, and probably without the doctors he would have been gone in a few hours.

We heard the news right off, as soon as Mac heard. His wife sent word over with Jean — she's their little girl. My mother started crying. She and Joe grew up together, and she used to kid daddy that Joe was too much like a brother for her to marry, but if not she would have. My daddy was upset, too. He started to say that Joe got what he deserved for being so bold, but he thought better. He looked at my mother and I guess he changed his thinking. He said that the time was when colored people could be killed to suit the whites, but no longer. Then he got nervous, for having said what he did; he warned us kids not to let it happen to us, not to become like Joe Holmes. I could see that he was afraid, and that he was mad, both at the same time. He kept on repeating that colored people used to be murdered all the time, but that it was different now. I wasn't sure he *believed* it was different, any more than I was sure that I did, either. My mother, she didn't say anything; she just cried, then she stopped, then she started again and stopped.

Whenever she cried I felt like crying, too; they're like an alarm clock in you, your mother's tears. I didn't cry though. I felt too old to cry, being a man. (I was fifteen then). Anyway, a few days later I found something better to do. The civil rights people came to town, and they came to our door, asking if we would help them. They said we couldn't let Joe Holmes die for nothing, not in 1961 we couldn't. They said they were going to hold a meeting in a church if they could get one, or outside Joe Holmes's house if they couldn't get one, and would we come. My father said he couldn't; it wasn't safe. He said there was no point making extra trouble, and causing more people like Joe Holmes to die. He said they didn't know what it's like in Reform, Alabama, the civil rights people didn't. "This isn't Atlanta, nor even Montgomery, and don't you forget it," he told them. They had an answer for him right away: "We know. But they talked like you in Atlanta for a long time, and in Montgomery a lot of people still do talk that way; it isn't until they stop talking defeat and start acting victory that there is any change."

My mother didn't say anything until they were about to leave. She asked them how we could find where the meeting would be. They said they would come back with slips of paper that would tell us. My daddy said not to bother. My mother said nothing. After the civil rights people were gone my mother and daddy took to fighting, as much as they ever did in their lives. Daddy said we weren't going to get into any trouble. My mother said she agreed, only you can't blame someone for wishing it was a fair world, and not so hard on us, and trying to bring things about so that we always aren't so down on our luck. There wasn't more to speak about after that. Daddy asked us all to forget the whole thing. He said Joe Holmes would ask the same thing, after what happened, because Joe didn't believe in people getting killed for nothing, himself included.

I kept on thinking maybe I should do something more, being younger. At school the teachers said we shouldn't talk about it, even if it was the only thing on our minds. They said we had learning to do, and that was that. When they buried Joe, a lot of people must have said the same thing. They just didn't show up. I know, because I went without telling anyone. My father would have punished me good if he knew.

I couldn't get Joe's wife and his kids out of my mind, nor what the minister said at his funeral. He said that it wasn't only the Lord who wouldn't turn his back on Joe; *we* had to keep him in mind, too. No one said anything about the white people that killed him, but the minister did say that as bad as everything all was, a lot more people were joining our side than ever before had, and Joe Holmes was probably the most famous man in our county now.

When we left the church the rights workers were there, handing out slips of paper, to announce the rally they were having the next day. They were holding it in a field near the church, and we were all invited to come. Some were burying the paper in their pockets, and others were throwing the paper away, as if someone were watching them. I decided I would throw mine away, so my daddy wouldn't even see it, and then go to the meeting anyway.

And that was how it got to me, finally. I heard people my age, or not much older, speaking up the way I used to think and not ever dare tell my own mother and my own father that I was thinking. They said we have taken it long enough, being killed and killed and killed, after being worked like horses and beaten like dogs, and everything bad. "Amen," we all said, and "Amen" I said to my taking it any more. I signed up with them, even though I knew it would cause trouble for me.

I went home and told my mother what happened. She told me to keep it quiet for a while until I was able to finish my schooling and maybe get a job someplace else. She was afraid for my father, and what would happen to us. She was afraid for me, too. She told me I was right though, right as could be; only you have to be careful to stay alive.

Things happened so quick though. The civil rights people didn't up and leave us, the way we thought. They opened up an office and moved in with us. They started holding classes for those who wanted to learn more, and they started visiting us at home, even if some were afraid to have them come. Then everything changed, all over the county, so that we knew we had more friends than ever before. Every night you could see on television that it was all changing, even in Alabama. So after a time my daddy said I could stay and not leave town, and work in the movement. "You can even keep the rights people here if you want," he told me, and then he said that he wished he could have had the chance when he was my age; but he hoped I wouldn't think he could have done anything then, no matter how hard he would have tried: "They killed us all the time then."

That's how I became one of the leaders here in Reform, and how I got to go to Selma, and up to Washington. It was Joe Holmes who did it, and the students who came here and stood by him at the grave and stayed with us. Sure, the sheriff gave us a lot of trouble, but he never dared beat anyone else, let alone kill anybody, and now with us getting the vote and all, they say he will retire when his time is up. But how it got to me, finally, was hearing a colored boy my age speaking better than any white man I ever heard. I told myself that's no boy, he's a man, and since he's about your age, you can be just like him, which after a while I did become.

The Integrationist South

"I'm the True Southerner": Mrs. Trumbull

In many respects she is the most explicitly Southern person I know. Her name is Southern, Flora (Searcy) Trumbull. Her speech is as soft, her accent as honeyed as any in the South. In her bones — they are slight and she is a thin and small woman — she is the delicate Southern lady the region continues to venerate and make a show of defending. Her family background is unblemished: in the early eighteenth century her ancestors came to Virginia, then moved down to South Carolina, to Charleston. "That's where they were during the

American Revolution," she once told me. In that same conversation she rather quietly and wryly reminded me that she was a daughter of both that revolution and a later one: "Sometimes I tell my own daughters they're going to have to choose when they're twenty-one — either they'll be a Daughter of the American Revolution or a Daughter of the Confederacy."

Mrs. Trumbull lives in Mississippi on a plantation, "a smaller one," she apologetically says. Her husband was a lawyer as well as a farmer, and his death, in 1957, revealed to her how very much she had become a Mississippian, and a planter's wife.

"I was born in South Carolina, and I expected to die there. Do you know that both my parents made a point of telling my brother and me that they never had put a foot out of that state. They claimed distinction for that, and even said that their parents hadn't either — though I think each of them had something on the other in that respect. I later found out what: both sets of grandparents had traveled out West, and my father's father had gone to Washington, even to New York — 'on business,' he insisted when I confronted him with what I had discovered."

She knew that laughable as the determined and boastful parochialism of her parents was, they were living quite intimately with history, with the temper and style of their generation's South. "It was fashionable for Southerners to stay home then, or travel only to Europe. They would even justify their travel to London or Paris by reminding themselves of the great sympathy felt for the Confederacy in London or Paris. It may seem absurd to you, but that's the way many of our present-day leaders were brought up to think. I don't frankly know how I managed to free myself of such blindness. In a way, it was coming to Mississippi with my husband that did it. I realized that after he died. I went back to Charleston on a visit — alone this time, and so more exposed to people and their views. I found old friends of my age still talking about the wonderful, mystical South, unblemished by Negroes except in the cotton fields or our kitchens. Those friends are young, too, if you think being forty-five is young.

"One evening I went to a party, filled with youthful conservative segregationists. They knew the South they wanted was gone forever. (I don't believe it ever existed.) Four years after 1954 they must have known history was moving in the opposite direction. Yet, there they were, talking like my parents, only sounding harsher and more absurd. Suddenly I understood what had happened to me. When, as my mother put it, I went 'West' to Mississippi I went from the frying pan to the fire; but I also went away, to a different state with different customs, even if staunchly segregationist ones. (People forget how very different each Southern state's history is.) It was geographic distance and a new social situation that gave me a real chance to see what nonsense and cruelty I had overlooked all my life — indeed even accepted as fair and honorable."

I first met her in 1958, shortly after her husband had died. I was living in Mississippi at the time, and a doctor I knew told me I should go see her: "Mrs. Trumbull is the most outspoken integrationist who has ever managed to stay alive in this state. She's a well-to-do white lady, unquestionably a Southern lady, and the mother of four daughters. She has gray hair, and she's a churchwoman, a devout Methodist. Maybe for all those reasons no one has shot her yet. One thing I know, there isn't anyone else in the state — white or Negro — who would dare talk the way she does — without expecting to die in twenty-four hours."

When I approached her house I felt disrespectful for doing so in a car. The home, the trees, shrubbery, and flowerbeds around it, the cotton fields nearby all suggested an earlier, quieter age: columns in front of the fine, white plantation manor; high ceilings and antique furniture bought in the shops of Royal Street in New Orleans; delicately scented rooms where one is sent to be "refreshed"; warm air that must not be cooled, as Mrs. Trumbull puts it derisively, "artificially"; fragile china and carefully brewed tea served by the strong hands of a tall, confident young Negro servant; a sense of timelessness. We sometimes take authors to task for being "romantics" when in fact they do literal justice in describing people like Mrs. Trumbull and homes like hers.

During the two years I lived in Mississippi I gradually came to appreciate how astonishing her leadership was. In subsequent years, while living in Louisiana and Georgia, I continued to visit her, or watch her in action at a committee organized to insure peaceful desegregation of schools, or at meetings of human relations councils — groups dedicated to what Mrs. Trumbull delicately called "improvement for all the people of the South." Her voice would ever so gently yet firmly emphasize the word "all." As she put it once: "You have to pay respect to the possibilities in language. Perhaps we in the South have produced so many writers because everyone, from the intellectuals to the ungifted, has to learn the subtleties and indirections of what my husband used to call 'race talk.' Even outspoken segregationists who seem capable of nothing that is refined so far as the Negro is concerned will resort to euphemisms and pretense under certain circumstances.

"I remember a friend of ours who screamed 'treason' just because I used the word 'Negro' instead of 'nigger.' (I think I was probably the first friend he ever heard do so; and he took a long time to get used to it.) Yet, when he went hunting he wanted company, and the company he most wanted and enjoyed was that of his 'nigger boy,' James. They were friends, anyone who cared to look closely could see that. They enjoyed talking about work to be done on the plantation, about everything from the weather and the state of the crops to hunting. They hunted together, too; only the Negro had to go as 'help.'

"Well, I saw them going and coming back, and they were companions. They even drank together. The Negro was his boss's age, and they had known one another since they were both children. They had grown up together. For a while when boys they called one another Jimmie and Ted; but soon Jimmie became James, and Ted had to be called Mr. Theodore, which still makes James privileged, a 'house nigger,' as men like him are called — in 1960, mind you. The others, field hands or more remote servants, have to say Mr. Stanton.

"Anyway, one Sunday I saw Ted Stanton and James coming back; half drunk they were, and as happy and familiar with one another as could be. I asked my husband how Ted could do it, do it in his mind so that James and he got along the way they did. I'll never forget what he said: 'There's not very much logic to human emotions. People do contradictory things, and there's no explaining why. It's just in their nature to do so.'

"I disagreed with him then, and I do now. It's the one thing we never agreed on, to his last day. I believe that when Ted Stanton talks about needing 'help' from James he is behaving in a very logical, predictable way. When I first asked my husband how Ted could do it, I meant that I was surprised at the man's ability to miss the logic of his own behavior. Ted wants a friend's company, but he has to call for his 'help.' That means Ted, despite all his money and influence in our community, follows the rules rather than makes them. He thinks of himself as a leader, but he talks like a follower. It's not that his actions are illogical, it's that he protects himself from the truth that would explain them."

Mrs. Trumbull willingly talked with me about her reasons for being extraordinarily committed to so unpopular a cause. She, like Ted Stanton, had grown up close to Negroes, had been cared for and "helped" by them. Her mother had been a sick woman, intermittently confined to bed with tuberculosis while her three children were growing up. Mrs. Trumbull has two older brothers, both lawyers, both in Charleston, both in her words "conservative and segregationist, but not indecorously so."

"Why you and not them?" I asked her — and, as we got to know one another, she asked herself out loud. If she had been a boy she would now have the same social and political attitudes her brothers have, or so she was inclined to speculate: "I've thought about all this vaguely. You have to think about what you're doing when it's so unpopular. It's hard to do it though. You don't want to discuss your motives too much with those who are taking the same risks you are — if you start doing that, you'll soon stop doing anything else. So you talk to yourself sometimes, in front of the mirror while dressing; or when you should be reading and your mind drifts; or after one of those calls, telling you your life is about to end.

"I never come up with a real answer. Right now I'm 'too far gone,' as my friends tell me rather angrily at times. To them I'm sick, mentally ill. They wouldn't even believe *you* if you told them I was sane. They would say you're crazy, too. That's how they dismiss anyone whose thinking they don't like, or they fear. They call the person insane, or they say the ideas he advocates are crazy ideas. Sometimes I find myself going along with them, thinking just as they do — about myself. I'll remember the quiet life I lived as a child in South Carolina, and ask myself what in those years ever made me the way I am now. (Isn't that what you're trying to find out?)"

"To some extent," I replied. "Though I don't think we can fully 'explain' someone's contemporary behavior on the basis of specific childhood experiences. I think we can look back at a life and see trends in it — of cruelty or kindness, of concern for others or self-absorption, of indifference or continuing involvement in one or another problem or activity. Yet, such trends — they are patterns of thinking or acting — come about for many reasons, some of them apparently innocuous, or inconsistent with one another. There may have been a cruel parent who inspired compassion in a suffering son; or a kind parent whose child for one or another cause grew to confuse easy-going toleration with indifference, or gentleness with weakness. Then, as you know, events in the world, and in one's later life, bring out things in people, or for that matter, prevent people from being the kind of people they perfectly well might have been. So, I think a lot happens in childhood that either helps make us what we are, or prevents us from becoming what others are; but each person's life — entire life — has to be considered very carefully before 'explanations' are offered for his or her willingness to take an unpopular, a very dangerously unpopular stand in full public."

Once she gave me a long letter she had written to herself. She had been told by the sheriff of the county that he could not be responsible for her safety, for her life, if she continued her advocacy of "race-mixing." This time he not only said so, but wrote her a letter telling her so. She started her letter of reply in direct response to his, but soon felt impelled to wander through her past.

"Of course I have always known that one day a vulgar threat on my life, or my family's safety, might become much more, a nightmare become real. I have discussed the dangers with my daughters, and though they are more fearful than I — they have more living ahead of them, more to lose — they support my position.

"What is my position, according to you so likely to cause me 'serious harm'? I simply believe in the law of the land, in the obligation that every American citizen must assume to obey the courts and the decisions of Congress.

"You, sir, may find me simple-minded for insisting that Mississippi is one state in the United States, and as much subject to the Constitution and its spirit as any other state. You address me as if I were in peril. You write to me as if I were a confused outcast, causing trouble, but also deeply in trouble with herself, and in need of what you call 'wise counsel' before it is too late. My 'eccentric position,' you tell me, will 'ruin' me and my children. We might very well die, you say; or at a minimum, we will be destroyed socially and psychologically. Fortunately I have enough money to resist economic pressure. If I didn't have enough I am sure you would have mentioned the likelihood of *that* ruin, too.

"I want you to know why I'm doing what I am; why I am 'risking my life,' as you have described it, 'in order to get a few niggers into a school, and change everything around against the will of the people.' Until you understand that fellow Southerners, and not simply 'outside agitators,' want to abandon segregation as both criminal and wrong, you will be as confused about me as your letter was insulting to me.

"As you know, I am from South Carolina, and I dare say as Southern as you or anyone else in this town. Perhaps it is because I am a woman that I feel the way I do, a woman who grew up with two brothers who constantly made light of what I could do or be. Instead of being their pet younger sister, I became someone they could bully, and call weak. My mother and I were close, though, and in her eyes she was weak, too. She believed that all women were weak because she believed my father, and he said so — often. He was a rich man, partly through money he inherited and partly through money he made in law and investments. My brothers worshiped him, and my mother obeyed him. She was the 'Southern woman' you sheriffs are always talking about; the one who is so wonderful and beautiful and fragile and delicate and in need of your brute force to protect her against — of all things — the nigger-lust in every Negro's body and soul.

"Actually my mother was silently strong; and my father was noisily weak, so weak that he had to scare everyone around him to compliance, submission, agreement, or at least a pretense of such behavior. Thus, neither of my brothers ever had a chance to be anything but lawyers, and anything but intolerant — about the poor, the North, Negroes, foreigners, and in a way, women.

"My mother and I were supposed to mind the house, the garden, and ourselves. I remember my mother waiting until my father left the house to read his newspapers and magazines. She used to go to the library to read books — there. 'Your father wants us to breed and decorate the world, but when someone is lynched I feel a child of God has been killed against His will, and my instinct as a mother is aroused.' She told me that when I was about ten or twelve. I suppose I must remember that women then had only recently been able to vote, let alone object to murder.

"When I was a teen-ager my mother wanted to join a group of Southern churchwomen who had organized to protest the wave of lynchings that periodically took place over the South. My father absolutely forbade it, and she gave in immediately to his decision. At least she pretended to do so. That's where she and I have always differed. I believe that women and men have to respect one another. When I was engaged to my husband he promised me that he would never treat me as a child because I was a woman. He never did, and I will never be able to forget his kindness and fairness. To my mind, the Negro is treated like a child by nervous white people, who feel safe so long as they have someone to step on and generally abuse — women and Negroes, not to mention children! When I was fifteen I told my mother that — long before I read books by historians or psychologists. She smiled at me and told me not to get too 'thoughtful,' as she

put it. That was her way of admitting how impossible it was sometimes to look at certain problems. Of course, I think my mother would
be different now. Women have become much more independent, even
among the sheltered rich or middle class.

"I came here to Mississippi because it was my husband's home.
His family has been here for a long time, and they are fine people.
They are now troubled and frightened by my stand. They worry for
my life and even for their own, since the Klan does not discriminate in
its hate; a family is a family to them. I don't say my in-laws go as far as
I do, even when we talk in the privacy of our own homes. They try to
make up for the historical record, for the cruelty that the Negro race as
a whole has suffered in the South, by being unusually generous with
their tenant farmers and household help. They have even offered to
help them go North, and pay them a yearly wage *there* until they feel
settled. None of the Negroes want to leave though; they are as devoted
to my husband's family as they were ten or twenty years ago.

"I argue that it's still paternalism. My sister-in-law and my two
brothers-in-law say that *their* generosity is not paternalistic. It's hard
to settle the point, but I think we all agree that the *system,* apart from
exceptions, is paternalistic, at best. I would rather have a few favored
Negroes on their own but poorer, and the rest finally free. My husband
always agreed, but he never would say so out loud, and his brothers
and sister are like him today, silent about what they think.

"Since he died I've been the one who has taken the risks, gone
out on a limb by writing letters and helping form committees, in order
to *declare* what some know in their hearts is right — and others feel is
dead wrong. For doing that, speaking my mind, I have been ostracized
and threatened as if I were a murderer, or a foreign agent. Even those
who agree with me think I am crazy — "emotionally disturbed," one
of them told me after two martinis. Those who disagree with me are
trying to find out how much I'm paid by Northern emissaries, or government people. It would all be funny if it weren't done at the expense
of a whole race of people, who have about lost their patience with
such antics all over the world.

"People have asked me to wait. 'This thing will take generations.
Why do you want to take the whole burden on yourself — and your
children?' (They always wait before they add the last few words; and
they smile, so as to conceal their nastiness with a veneer of friendliness.) Of course I thank them for their concern — especially for my
children — and tell them the simple truth: they want nothing done; I
want to do something; that is that.

"'Are you afraid?' they ask. There would be something wrong with me if I weren't. But I'm no more afraid than they are. At least I know why I'm afraid, and what I fear. They're so frightened and suspicious they've lost their common sense. They talk of 'conspiracies' and the like. They get nervous at every whisper, every news story, every rumor, every hate-mongering voice they meet up with. Yes, I'm afraid that one day I'll be shot at. I've settled my affairs in case it happens, and I'm ready to go. Meanwhile, I live every day as my conscience tells me to do, and as a result I feel content with myself, if scared at times. What about my friends, who wish me so well and keep on telling me to talk with a doctor or minister for 'counsel'? They're angry, distrustful, shrill, and hateful — and getting worse in all those respects every day. Most of all, they're guilty, and they don't know it. Who needs the 'counsel,' I ask you?

"There is one more matter I would like to bring up. I have been asked by everyone from the police to members of my family why I have 'chosen' (as they put it) to be so 'different.' The truth is that I was brought up to feel as I do. My mother taught me most of what I say. She may have feared saying it in public — and sometimes even at home when my father was present — but if she were alive today she would be proud of me for doing so. My husband might have disagreed with me, but he never would have tried to silence me. We would have talked it all out — and perhaps changed one another a bit in doing so. Now he is gone, and I must do what I feel is right, without his advice or views. I miss him when some of those threatening calls come, but I can't dishonor his memory by buckling under to those calls because he isn't here to protect us. I told my daughter the other day that we owe it to his memory to be strong — to prove that he truly *gave* us his strength, that we have it in us, to use and rely upon. So long as I can think back and see my mother and my husband, I think I'll be able to keep my courage up. I know they would be happy for what I'm doing. They would be afraid, too; I know that. If they were alive they might be so afraid that they wouldn't do what I'm doing. I know that, too. But they are gone, and I am here. Perhaps I'm too loyal to them — still — but I feel somehow I can make the best of them live on, in honor."

Mrs. Trumbull never mailed that letter to the sheriff. Instead she sent him yet another curt note, reproving him for his "illegal, unconstitutional manner of law enforcement." She had kept a diary for years, and told me she intended to make the letter a part of it.

I felt lucky to have a chance to read the letter, but at a loss to answer her question after I had finished. "Does this explain anything to you, about why I've taken the stand I have?" I said yes, it did; as much as such things could be explained. Her reply to that was quick in coming and a surprise to me: "I think explanations don't settle an issue, they only make way for more questions. I've asked myself a lot of the questions you've asked me, directly or indirectly, these past years. After I answer them I still don't feel at rest. There are other women who have had mothers like mine, and have lost husbands like mine. I could have done other things with my memories, or my loneliness. It seems that I couldn't though. That's the only explanation I've ever been able to find for myself that sets my mind to rest."

Stay Home or Go to School?

The first children I came to know in New Orleans were Negro children, and for a while it appeared that they would be the only children in the two schools the four little girls were attending. As one of them reminded me in a talk we had after her first few days of school: "I don't see anyone but the teacher all day. They said I would be seeing the white kids, but none have come yet, and the teacher, she says they may never come — all on account of me. But I told her they will."

In point of fact several white children were almost always at school during her long ordeal, though it took her time to become aware of their presence. For a time she *was* the first grade of a fairly large school, while a fluctuating handful of white children constituted the remnants of the other grades, the second through the sixth.

Two of these white children came from minister's homes, one Baptist and the other Methodist. Four of them, two boys and two girls, came from a third home, a Catholic one with five other children, headed by an accountant.

"We are eleven, so we're a mob, too," the wife of the accountant and the mother of their nine children once told me as we stood in her kitchen and looked at an angry crowd outside and not far away. She was counting those on her side because she knew those on the other side had become her enemies.

She lived near the school, near enough to see it from her backyard; near enough to see and hear the crowds from her front window. She was born in Louisiana, as were her parents, and their parents. She and her husband were "ordinary" people, or at least so it would once have seemed. That is to say, they lived with their children in a small, lower-middle-class area, their home like thousands about it, their life distinguished by little except its daily routine of care for one another and the children. They were both high school graduates.

Just before the crisis which came upon their city they had no interest in politics and were against school desegregation. "We never really thought they would do it, and then we found that not only did they mean to go ahead, but ours was slated to be one of the schools." That was the way she summarized her surprise, her previous attitude of mild or unexcited opposition to what the newspapers less indifferently called "mixing."

In a matter of weeks this mother and her children were being subjected to a degree of danger and intimidation which rivals for violence any I've seen in the South. Her house was assaulted, its windows broken, its walls stained with foul inscriptions. Her husband's place of work was threatened and picketed. It became necessary for the police to protect her children as well as the little Negro girl whose lone entrance precipitated disorder in the streets and sporadic violence destined to last for months. In watching this Southern white lady walk through those mobs with her small children, one could not but wonder why she persisted. Why did she take on that challenge, and how did she endure it?

After years of interviews with her, I have had to guard against tampering with my recollection of this woman, against making her into someone she wasn't at the time she made the various choices — choices which in turn helped make her into the person she is *now*. This is a problem psychiatrists must always keep in mind. It is possible to forget the truth of the past when the present, with its visions and formulations, is the vantage point from which the conclusive determination is being made.

Here is how — word for word — she once described her attitude when the conflict of school desegregation, hovering over the city for months, settled upon her children's school.

"I couldn't believe it. First I became angry at the nigras. I figured, why don't they leave well enough alone and tend to their own problems. Lord knows they have enough of them. Then, I thought I just couldn't keep four children out of school; not on one little nigra girl's account. So I thought I'd just send them and see what happens. Well, the next thing I knew, mothers were rushing in and taking their children out; and every time they did it, they would get cheered. The end of the first day of it there wasn't much of a school left.

"The next day I decided to give it one more try. I was going to stay away, keep my children away, but to tell the truth the idea of having four children home with me, squabbling and making noise and getting into trouble, was too much for me. So I thought I'd just stick it out and maybe things would quiet down, and then we'd all forget one little nigra and our children would go on with school.

"The crowd was there the next day and they were more of one mind now. They started shouting at each white mother that came to the building, and one by one they pulled back. It was as if the building was surrounded and only the police could get through, and *they* weren't doing anything. The mob let Ruby (the Negro girl) through, because they said they wanted her to be there alone. They screamed when the minister brought his girl, and I decided to withdraw. Well, I was walking back home, and I saw the back door to the building. They were so busy with the minister and shouting at the reporters, they weren't looking at the rear. So I just took the children there and let them go in. At that moment I thought, 'It's better than their being at home, and better than their listening to those people scream all day from our porch.' It was bad enough *I* had to hear it, and my baby too young for school.

"The *next* day I really decided to join the boycott. I couldn't see fighting them, and they weren't going away like I thought. Well, my husband stayed home a little later than usual, and we talked. I said no, no school for the kids, and he agreed. Then he said maybe we should try to move to another part of the city, so that the kids could continue their schooling. Then I said I'd try *one more day*. Maybe the mob would get tired and go away. After all, they had their way — there was only the children of a minister or two left out of five hundred families. I snuck the kids in, and later that day one of the *teachers* called, to ask me if I was sure I wanted to do it. She sounded almost as scared as me, and I think she would just as soon have had the whole school closed, so she could be spared listening to that noise and that filthy language.

"That night, I think, was the turning point. A few of the mob saw me leaving with the children, and started calling me the worst things I'd ever heard. They followed me home and continued. Thank God the police kept them away from the house, but I had the sickening feeling on the way home that I was *in* something, unless I got out real fast. In the morning I couldn't send them, and I couldn't *not*. One woman came here instead of to the school, to swear at me just in case I tried sending the children off. I guess she thought that just her being there would take care of me. Well, it did. I became furious; and I just dressed those children as fast as I could and marched them off. Later that day those women from the Garden District came, and they said they'd stand by me and help me and even drive the children the one block, and I guess I soon was a key person in breaking the boycott.

"But I didn't *mean* to. It was mostly, I think, their language, and attacking me so quickly. I didn't feel any freer than the nigra. I think I gained my strength each day, so that I was pretty tough in a few months. After a while they didn't scare me one bit. I wouldn't call it brave; it was becoming *determined*. That's what happened, really. We all of us — my children, my husband, and me — became determined."

Of course I am giving you one section from hours of taped conversations. I knew her quite well when we had that talk, and it was not the first time she had given me an account of those experiences. When I listen to her voice today I can almost feel her drifting — precisely that — drifting — and then coming to terms not only with her past but with history itself. Choice was required: at some point her children either had to stay home or go to school. Each alternative had its advantages: a home without restless children, or a home unbothered by restless and angry outsiders — calling at midnight to predict death and destruction, shouting similar forecasts in the daytime.

We are still left with the matter of why this woman chose as she did, and how she managed the strength to make her choice stick fast so long.

Surely we may call that unassuming strength her courage. Not everyone, even among the so-called mature, will take on the possibility of death day after day with evident calm. In this woman's case her commitment, her course of courageous action developed through a series of "moments" or "accidents." Step by step she became an important participant in a critical struggle. Indeed, in looking back at her life and the situation she faced we may forget that a historical event was once a crisis by no means settled. Had the boycott in New Orleans held fast, the forces at work there for segregation would have become stronger, perhaps decisively so for a long time. That is what I heard from people on both sides of the struggle as it was occurring.

Our "Southern lady," like Conrad's Lord Jim, slipped into an important moment that became a determining force in her life as well as her country's history. Not only her views on segregation but her participation in community affairs and the goals she has for herself and her children are far different now than they "ordinarily" would have been. "I met people I never would have," she said to me recently, "and my sights have become higher. I think more about what's important, not just for me but for others; and my children do better at school because they're more serious about education."

What can one say about this woman's choice? Certainly there was no one reason that prompted it. I have talked with enough of her neighbors to realize the dangers of saying that her past actions or beliefs might easily differentiate her from others. Many of her nearby friends are decent, likable people. Before a mob they simply withdrew themselves and their children. This woman had also planned to do so. Yet she never did, or she never did for long or for good. She drifted. She tried to resolve the mixed feelings in her mind. She weighed her fear of a mob against her annoyance at her children's loss of schooling and their bothersome presence in the home. She was a hopeful person and she assumed — wrongly indeed — that the riots would end quickly. She is a sound, stable person, and once under fire she did not waver. She is the first one to remind me that her husband's employers stood by him. Had *they* wavered, she is certain that she would have quickly withdrawn her children from the school. For that matter, were her husband different — that is, more of a segregationist, or generally more nervous and anxious — she might never have dared stand up to a mob's anger.

In sum, there were a number of reasons which helped this woman's courage unfold, each of them, perhaps, only a small part of the explanation, though each necessary. I suppose we could call her — in the fashion of the day — "latently" courageous. A crisis found her strong, and in possession of certain ideals. Those ideals gained power through a cumulative series of events which eventually became for one person's life a "point of no return." She puts it this way: "After a few days I knew I was going to fight those people and their foul tongues with every ounce of strength I had. I knew I had no choice but that one. At least that's how I see it now." It was an impressive experience listening to her tell her story, and watching her realize — often only in the telling — what had actually happened to her feelings and her goals.

Lookers-On and the Last Ditch

Even when an entire social system is in convulsive transition there are many who neither try hard to resist change nor lift a willing finger to bring about a new kind of life. From people on both sides of the struggle one hears summoned the "ordinary" man, the "average guy," the "typical person" as potentially friendly, vaguely supportive, fitfully antagonistic, or somewhat — but only somewhat — alarmed. Such descriptions, inevitably tentative, ambiguous, or open-ended, reflect the uneasy truth known to ideologues and just plain idealists of all persuasions: many people, perhaps most people, are content to live in society rather than commit themselves to its alteration, let alone transformation. Among those so content are numbered the discontented as well as the reasonably well-to-do. Just as I have found all classes represented in both the sit-in movement and the various segregationist organizations, I have found among a wide range of people in both races an essential determination that their lives — in the words of one (Negro) citizen of Georgia — "not be bothered by all the trouble around."

A Store Is a Store

The more I watched sit-ins and other demonstrations over the South the more interested I became in the specific psychological effect they exerted. What happened to white people (or Negroes) as youths or ministers quietly, solemnly marched before them, or toward them? During a long — perhaps too long — interview with a tired, angry, still nonviolent Negro youth in Atlanta I heard him suggest an end to our talks, and a beginning for another series of conversations.

"I can see how you might want to know how someone like me keeps his head from splitting in all directions, but I think you're losing a real opportunity. You should go speak with those white folks — the ones who look at us, and stare, just stare without giving a clue what's going on in their minds. Or you could go talk to the store owners we picket. Some of them look as if they're ready to go mad, not get mad. One came out yesterday and begged us to leave him alone. He said he didn't care one way or the other what happened. He just wanted to make a living and mind his own business — I mean *really* mind his own business, without us bothering him. We told him he could. All we wanted was to help him make *more* money, by serving us. But no. He said the white people would stop coming, and he'd go broke or have to move to a Negro neighborhood.

"To tell the truth, I felt sorry for the guy. I don't know how he feels about segregation and integration, but he didn't strike me as very different from my own parents. They want to stay alive, and when given half a chance, they'll keep quiet and do just that, stay alive. Now the trouble is, a lot more Negroes have trouble staying alive than whites, so a lot more of us are moved — moved to *do* something, get involved in the *movement*. But there are plenty of Negroes, even the poorest — maybe especially the poorest in some towns — who don't want to get involved. They say leave me alone, and after you've tried to get them to join you, and they've said leave me alone again, only louder, you know they mean it."

I went to talk with the very storekeeper he mentioned, and eventually came to know him rather well. The Negro student knew him only as a demonstrator does a man of property who repeatedly refuses what is asked of him. I soon learned, however, that the nonviolent student was a shrewd — and in a way compassionate — judge of human nature. Eventually I was able to tell the middle-aged merchant how the Negro youth had appraised his position and his attitude.

"He's right. I want peace and quiet, and I want to go on making a living. If he knows that, he knows that he's wasting his time trying to preach to me or demonstrate. The way I see it, he and I are together. Neither one of us made the world the way it is; and all I want is to stay alive in it, just as he does. At the rate he's going, he'll spend most of his life in jail, and I'll go broke. What does *that* solve for either of us?"

I found him to be a stubborn but pleasant man, a native-born Georgian, in turn a high school graduate, a soldier in the Second World War, and the recipient of a degree in pharmacy. He bought his drugstore with a large loan, and worked for years to own, really own, his business, located in a small town that is really a suburb of Atlanta.

He and his wife grew up together, and fitted together very well. He tended to be serious, even somber. She had a light touch to her voice and her everyday mood. He worried about money and the marks each of their three children brought home from school. She was a devout Baptist and *believed* in faith: "I tell my husband and my children both that it matters not what things of this world we have, so long as we pray for God's grace." (She would often exalt her sentence structure when reproving what she called "the excessive worldliness about us.") They received me cordially into their home, and talked as openly with me — I became convinced — as they did with their neighbors or, for that matter, between themselves.

Sometimes, particularly when under pressure, her husband fell back upon her outlook. Indeed, one day I heard him, and not her, talk of God with such feeling that I at once sensed I was hearing not only his strongly held opinion but perhaps the (hitherto secret) inspiration for his wife's piety.

"Who ever stops to figure out why we live the way we do? Those nigra students come and try to talk with me and the other businessmen on the block. They tell us they're going to sit in, they're going to picket, they're going to do this and that to embarrass us, and shame us, and make us lose money, until finally we surrender to them. They ask me: don't you feel guilty, don't you feel ashamed for all you've done, all your people have done to us? They say if I don't give in, they'll *make* me — by marching up and down, and being nonviolent, and letting people spit on them, and shout at them, or getting the police to arrest them.

"For a long time I tried to ignore them. First I thought they would get tired and go away; then I thought the police would take care of them, or my customers. But they didn't get tired, and it seems that the more they're arrested, the more they want to come back.

"My customers were the ones that became tired. They told me they just couldn't keep on coming in and out of the store, past those nigra students, with their signs and their songs and their slogans. Some of them made a point of shopping downtown, though the drugstores and restaurants there are being picketed, too. Some tried to cut down on their shopping trips. They would save up things to buy, and come here once instead of twice a week.

"I had to close the counter. Who wants to eat with those people trying to move in and eat beside you? I lost money that way, but there wasn't any choice. Every customer I had would have left me if I hadn't done it. White people won't eat with nigras, and the sooner those students find that out, the better it will be for everyone."

I asked him at that time what he felt about the students. Did they bother him as little as he had been saying, or was he trying to "forget" — at least in our conversations — how troublesome they actually were to him?

Yes, it was true they bothered him, though he wanted very much not to take their actions personally. That was the clue to survival, he felt: "I've seen other businessmen knuckle under. They get so angry at the nigras that they close their stores or they start fighting them, and make all their white customers afraid to come near, for fear of violence. Or they try to make a settlement with the nigras, and lose all their white customers that way."

Why did those customers leave — out of fear, distaste, outrage, resentment, shame? Again and again we came back to that issue; he was obviously interested in discussing it, and I felt that the more he talked about his "average" customer, the more I came to know the contradictory substance of *his* views, not to mention the customer's. They were earnestly held views, but easily abandoned ones. Over several years I watched a changing social and political situation utterly undermine some of those views, and make others seem antique or irrelevant even to the man who once proclaimed them. Yet again and again he did come back to certain principles that *were* consistent.

"Say what you will, people run a store to make money. You offer things to the customers, and you hope they'll buy what you have to sell. Now this race thing has suddenly come up; I don't know from where. All my life I've lived with nigras, and not treated them bad, nor them me bad. We've got along — and recently a lot of them have come to me and told me how sorry they are for what I've gone through. Like with most white folks, a lot of the colored just want to live and let live.

"That's my philosophy: live and let live. You can't make a rich man the equal of a poor man. Even in Russia that guy Khrushchev has villas and big cars and all that, while the peasants live the way our tenant farmers do, or worse. The same holds with race. The white man is different from the nigra, all over the world he is. They say we in the South are unfair to colored people. All I want to know is where do they really give a nigra the same acceptance a white man gets? In Boston, or New York? In England? (I've been reading how they have their problems there, the same ones we do.)

"You go into a nigra's home in Atlanta and you'll see them eating well, and wearing good clothes. They have cars, bigger ones than I would ever buy. They have radio and television, and everything else. I've seen their drugstores. They sell the same things I do. They have what the country has to offer. Isn't that enough?

"They try to tell me no — that they're treated inferior. They try to make me feel as if I'm persecuting them, as though I've done something wrong to hurt them. One of them said to me the other day: 'Don't you feel that in turning us away you're being un-Christian?'

"I say no to them every time. I don't see what Christianity has to do with politics or the customs we have. I don't want to hurt them, and I don't want them to hurt me. It's as simple as that. They're trying to make me into a slave owner, or something. I can see that, and I told them that once. I told them they weren't going to get me angry or excited, the way some people get. They want that to happen. It gives them satisfaction. It makes them think that they're right — that we'll lose control and give in after a while.

"I went to see my minister and talked with him about this. He said that I had to examine my conscience and pray. I told him I have, and that I can't see why I should have to make up for whatever troubles the colored man has in Georgia. I'm just an ordinary person. I can barely depend on enough money to pay my bills. I can't subsidize an integrated cafeteria in my drugstore. Soon it will be segregated again — all black.

"The minister told me that the problem was larger than both of us. (Our church has no colored in it.) He said we both faced a lot of trouble these coming years, through no fault of our own, but because the society is changing and the average man has to adjust himself to it. I told him I was as flexible as anyone — I'm just waiting to see every other drugstore — and church — in Georgia 'adjust.'"

A year later (1963) he was no longer the besieged storekeeper. He had won his battle, and kept his store white. The Negroes eventually tired of demonstrating in front of his store. He continued to fear their renewed interest and attention, and out of his experience he developed an interest in what they were doing elsewhere. He often talked with his customers — and his minister — about "the problem."

"You know, it is our number-one problem today, *the problem*. I'm like you — I have to be in my business. I want to know what people think, where they're headed in their thinking. To be truthful, I think we're slowly going to settle this thing. We already have nigra children in the schools, and it's only a matter of time before they'll be back here asking me for coffee and Cokes. I ask some of my customers what they think, and I can hear them being as annoyed with the whole thing as I am. They're no longer as shocked though — any more than I am. When those colored boys first came here last year I thought they were crazy. Then I thought they were hoodlums pretending to be nice and

Christianlike. Now, from what I see on television, they're the younger generation of nigras, or at least they're *some* of the younger generation. I still think a lot of nigras don't care one way or the other. Like most of us whites, they want calm. You only live once, and you don't want to spend your days fighting."

His drugstore was desegregated in 1965, after the Civil Rights Bill was passed. He was nervous and fearful when it happened, but also relieved: "They finally got around to me. To tell the truth, I thought they were overlooking me as not worth their while. I told my wife I felt hurt. When I saw them come in I shuddered again, just like before. They weren't the same nigras, and I thought they might get tough or violent. But they didn't. They just moved in on those counter chairs and asked for coffee. My countergirl looked scared, and confused. She turned to me and asked me with a look what she should do. I didn't say a word. I just nodded to her. She knew what I meant. She started pouring. They didn't seem to want to stay long. They drank a bit, then they got up and left. The three white people at the counter just sat there. They had stopped drinking *their* coffee out of curiosity. We all looked at one another, then one of the customers said to me: 'A store is a store, I guess; and you have to serve whatever walks in from the street.'

"That wasn't the way he talked last year, I remember. But I guess it wasn't the way I did either. It's changing down here, that's what's happening, and the man in the street, he has to keep up with it, even if he doesn't always go along with it. I suppose that comes later, agreeing with what's already happened. Some of my friends say that if we had fought this battle harder, the integration people never would have won. I tell them that we did fight once, and lost. No one ever let us vote on this. We're all segregationists, the white people of Georgia; or most of us are. But we've got caught up in something that's bigger than us, and we've got to live with it, the way I see it. There's no choice. When I say that to them, they agree with me, no matter how much they talk of killing every nigger in sight. So I guess most people make their peace with things as they are."

The Last Ditch

On August 5, 1964, a press service story quoted an FBI agent who was working in the area of Neshoba County, Mississippi, where the remains of three civil rights workers were found: "I wish I could have a psychiatrist examine whoever did this right now and see what they'd be thinking now that we've got the bodies."

I had heard a similar remark several weeks earlier from an agent in McComb, Mississippi. A house occupied by several "integrationists" had just been badly damaged by dynamite, and while I was looking into some of the medical problems — two students were injured — the officer was trying to find out who was responsible for the explosion. Standing near the debris with soda pop in our hands we talked about the details of the incident. The officer assured me that it was a serious attempt at murder rather than a mere effort to warn and frighten, and then he turned his attention to explanations. Why would people want to do this? He asked it, then I asked it, both of us less curious than appalled. Yet, slowly the curiosity rose in him, and well after we had finished our talk he came back to the question. Why would anyone have nothing better to do in the middle of the night than plant dynamite? He was clearly suggesting that only an unhappy, a disturbed person would be awake so late, preparing that kind of deed. Perhaps, he suggested, I had some thoughts on that matter.

We each returned to our work, though I found myself ruminating about how indeed I might have explained to him exactly what my thoughts were. As I tried to lay that challenge to rest I kept on coming back to the chief capability we have in psychiatry, the case history. Perhaps if we had had the time I would have been able to show him what I felt to be the answer to his question by telling him about a particular segregationist's life, including of course the life of his mind.

This man did not murder the three civil rights workers, or plant dynamite in that home in the terror-stricken McComb area of Mississippi; but he has committed appallingly similar acts, in company with many others. He has been in mobs and will not deny having seen Negroes assaulted and killed as a result. I am sure he would satisfy those agents and all of us as a prototype of the bigot who is a potential killer. I thought of him immediately that morning in McComb, and again when I read the report of the government agent's dismayed call for psychiatric help in Philadelphia.

I first met John, as I shall call him, while he was protesting the archbishop's decision to admit some children who were Negro but also Catholic to the parochial schools of New Orleans. It was a warm, faintly humid early spring day, a Saturday too, and the next year's school opening hardly seemed a timely worry. Up and down he walked, picketing, tall, husky from the rear, an incipient paunch in front. He wore a brown suit, slightly frayed at the cuffs, and on its right shoulder rested his sign, wrought and lettered by himself: "Fight Integration. Communists Want Negroes With Whites." His shirt was starched and he wore a tie. He had brown eyes. He was bald but for the most meager line of black hair on his neck — baldness must have happened early and fast. His face was fleshy and largely unlined, and I thought, "Forty or forty-five."

Several of those in the picket line seemed unaware of the gazes they attracted. John, however, was the most engaging and communicative. Looking at people directly, he would talk with them if they showed the tiniest interest. He moved faster than the others, and seemed to be in charge, now signaling a new direction for walking, later approving or suggesting luncheon shifts.

We moved along the pavement side by side, he and I. Would I want a sign — he had several in reserve? I would rather talk with him; I was very much interested in his opinions. I felt it important that he, that they, not be misunderstood, and I would do my best to record fairly what he thought and wanted. I am a physician, I told him, a research physician specializing in problems of human adjustment under stress. A little amplification of this, and he laughed — it *was* a strain, the police and the scoffing people, and those reporters with the sly, obviously unfriendly questions. He would talk with reporters, any of them, so long as they were not niggers, not Communists, because he wanted to be heard. It was important to be heard or nothing could be accomplished. He wanted to do something, not merely have his say, and so he would surely talk with me if I were a teacher, if I wanted to report the truth to the educated. They needed the truth. I agreed. He was visibly impressed with certain credentials which, in my nervousness, I had offered: cards, pieces of paper which I now know were unnecessary for his cooperation. We began that day, later in the afternoon, signs put aside, over coffee. I arranged to meet him regularly, weekly, for several months at his home, or over coffee in a diner. He gradually told me about himself and his life, about what he believed and how he came to see things as he does.

He is a passionate segregationist ("you can put down the strongest, the strongest it's possible to be"). He has plans. He would like to exile most Negroes to Africa, perhaps sterilize a few quiet ones who would work at certain jobs fitting their animal nature, itself the work of God, he would emphasize. He would strip Jews of their fearful power, sending them off also, but to Russia, where they came from and yearn to return. There are other suspicious groups, Greeks, Lebanese — New Orleans is a port city, and he has worried about them leaving their boats. Do they try to *stay* on land? Unlike the niggers and Jews, whose clear danger to his city he had formulated for some time, he had not determined his exact position on such people, or his solution for them.

He was born in central Louisiana, say for example a town like Acme in Concordia Parish. The state is split into its southern, Catholic and French area and a northern section, basically Protestant and Anglo-Saxon. Typically, his father was the former and his mother Scotch-Irish, a wayward Baptist who embraced the Roman Church (the only term used for the Catholic Church in certain areas of the so-called Bible Belt) a few weeks before her marriage. Born their second child in the month America entered the First World War, he was sickly and fatherless his first year of life. While his father fought in Europe the boy was taken with what we now call "allergies," a timid stomach which mostly rejected milk, a cranky skin which periodically exploded red, raw, itchy, and was often infected by his responsive scratches. His sister was five years older, and she remembered all this. She and her mother, still alive, have told him about his fretful infancy, and he knew it well enough to be able to pass on their memories. *His* first memory was a whipping from his father's strap. With his father home from war, a second son and last child was born. John was three. He had pinched the infant, done enough wrong to the child's skin to cause a cry and attract his father's punishing attention. That was to happen many times, though he held a special place in his mind for this earliest occasion: "My brother and I started off on the wrong track, and we've never got along with one another."

His brother is tall and thin, ruddy-faced and blue-eyed like his mother, wears a white shirt to a bank teller's job near their hometown. John, dark and short like his father, has several "blue-shirt" skills which at various times he has used. "I can build a house myself" was his way of summarizing them: carpentry, electric work, plumbing, even bricklaying.

The childhood development of the boys forked: one neat, precise, his mother's favorite as well as her physical reflection; the other, by his own description, naughty, often idle or busy being scrappy. John in short was an overlooked and troubled middle child. He resembled his father, yet had hated him for as long as he can remember. Oddly, though, his manner, his temperament sound like the father's as he describes the man and shows pictures of him, now ten years dead, a large blustery fellow, open, opinionated, rumpled, a mechanic preoccupied with automobiles — under them daily, reading magazines about them by night. He had storms within him, and they fell upon his middle child, alone and arbitrarily, the boy felt.

Once John and I had talked long and hard — it seemed like a whole day. I noticed it had actually been three hours. The length of time measured a certain trust, a certain understanding that was developing between us. I found myself knowing him, recognizing some of the hardships he had endured, not just psychological ones, but the hunger and jobless panic which must have entered so many homes in a decade when I was scarcely born and he yet a child. I felt guilty for a moment, torn between him and the simple but of course complicated facts and experiences of his life, and him as he now is, a shabby fanatic. He was feeling his own opening toward me, and with considerable emotion in his voice, lifting his right hand in a gesture which might well have been his father's, he interrupted our talk of Huey Long's racial attitudes and how they compared with those of his family: "Daddy [Southern fathers can be "daddy" to their children forever without embarrassment] had a bad temper, and I took it all myself. We had never had much money and bills would set him going, but he wouldn't touch my mother, or my brother or sister either. Yes" (I had asked), "my sister and brother both favored Ma, and Daddy, he'd feel no good because he couldn't get a week's pay, so he had to hit someone. Oh, he was for Huey boy all the way, except Huey was soft on niggers, but I think Daddy was, too. He used to say they were children, and we should protect them. But if they're like kids, they're like bad ones, and just like animals, so they've got to be watched over. You wouldn't let a wild animal go free in your home or in school with your kids, would you? It's right crazy how we forget that sometimes. Look at Harlem, and what happens when they let them go. They rape and kill our women and dirty the whole city up. I've been there and seen it. No" (prodded again), "I don't blame Daddy, because, you see, in those days we had them firm under our grip, so it was different and you didn't have to worry about them. But look at now." We did talk about current events for a few minutes, but each of us tired suddenly, and hardened.

Of course, from those old times to the present had been an eventful period for him as well as for the Negro race. He almost died twice. At seven he had a serious bout of pneumonia which — with no help from antibiotics — almost killed him. He recalled gratefully a Negro maid who cared for him through this, one of those (few now) who knew and willingly lived in her "place." She died shortly after he recovered. Abruptly and looking still young ("I think she was around forty, but you can't tell with niggers"), she collapsed before his very eyes while preparing supper for him. It was by his description probably a stroke that took her, and she proved irreplaceable. They had paid her a pittance, but she had stayed with them for lack of better. About that time several Negro families started moving North, while others trekked south to New Orleans. Though his father had not really been able to pay Willi-Jean her established wages for many months, only death ended her loyalty and their comfort. "I got pneumonia again when I was twelve, and so did my brother. It nearly killed Ma taking care of us. She used to try to keep everything in its place, I think that's why it was so hard without Willi-Jean. With us sick on top of it, she almost didn't get through it all, she got so nervous."

In telling him of my interest in his medical history, I asked him several times to describe in further detail his fits of illness, and the care given him during those times. It seemed clear that he had, in fact, suffered badly at his mother's hands, neglected by her for his sister or brother, blamed by her for getting sick. The Negro woman's sudden death was actually a severe and deeply resented blow to him. His affections for her were hastily buried with her. He had to keep on his guard against his mother's personality, now no longer buffered by Willi-Jean. During one of our last talks he said, "You know, Doc, I think I *did* have a bad time with sickness when I was a kid. When I was twelve I almost died of pneumonia, and then I broke my leg a few weeks after that and lost that year of school." He had tried to run away from home before he contracted pneumonia, and after his recovery, too, until his lame leg made such attempts impossible for a while.

If his mother was nervous, oppressively ritualistic, and hardly his advocate, his father was a heavy drinker, temper-ridden, and fearfully unpredictable. When drunk he was moody. He also became brutal, and his middle son was his customary target. Declaring a truth whose painful implications he could not look at too closely, John once reflected, "I never figured why Daddy picked on me. We got along fine when he was sober, but when he got liquored up, I got it first and hardest. I looked like him and helped him most in fixing things around the house, but he never remembered things like that when he was drunk." Not that his parents weren't "the nicest parents anyone could ever want." Any vision into their shortcomings, any criticism of them, had to be followed eventually by the atonement of heavy sentiment. He had long ago learned how dangerous it was to speak his mind. Perhaps his life, as we now see it, has been a quest for that very possibility. "I used to be afraid to say anything for fear it would get someone upset at home, so I just kept quiet and ran my trains." Trains were his chief hobby for a little longer than is usual, well into the early teens. He warmed while telling me about his empire of them, and he became wistful afterward. I wanted to hear of his childhood interests, and in speaking of them, he said ambiguously, "I knew trains better than anyone in town."

By the last two years of high school he had found an easier time. His mother reached menopause, surrendered in her war against dust and for order, and became cheerless and distant. His father now drank less, but had to struggle hard with another form of depression, an economic one which he shared with his country. Amid all this John strangely enough prospered. His sister married poorly, a marginal farmer soon dispossessed of his land. Slothful and malignant, he beat her regularly, fathered two children by her, and left shortly thereafter. She never remarried and has had to work hard to keep her two children fed and clothed. John's brother had trouble with learning. He left high school after one year, and for a time, nearly penniless, he drew food and small coin from government relief programs. Recently he has managed a job in a bank, but his wife is a heavy drinker, maybe worse, and they have five children. John says they "live like pigs," and apparently this state of decay set in very rapidly after their marriage. His brother's cleanest, most organized moments are at his job.

John, however, graduated from high school, the first in his family to do so, and went beyond that by securing a coveted job in the local hardware store. He had come to know its owner and his daughter, too. Always interested in fixing things — bicycles, injured cars, faltering plumbing, stray wires — he began in the hardware store as a willing and unpaid helper. The radio, new and mysterious, was his love, and he tinkered endlessly with the various models. The store had many other gadgets, and it also had his girl friend, the owner's daughter. He determined at about fifteen to marry her and did so at twenty. At the time of his marriage he was a relatively prosperous man, now wearing a white collar, regularly paid in dollars increasingly powerful out of their scarcity. ("My folks said I married real well, especially for those days.")

To hear him talk, the twelve months before and the twelve months after his wedding day were his best time. He remembers the pleasure and hope; but his nostalgia is brief, and is always tinctured with the bitterness which soon followed. His father-in-law's business collapsed, to be foreclosed by the handful of creditors who seemed to be gathering the entire countryside into their control. These provincial financiers, with their small banks all over the state, were controlled by Big Power and Big Money, both in New Orleans. Governor Huey had said so, and they killed him. John, with a wife and a boy of three months, had no choice but to try Huey's gambit — follow the Power, follow the Money. "We just up and moved. An uncle of my wife's thought he could get me work repairing radios. They were like TV today. No matter how poor you were, you needed some relaxation." John got a job and held it. He started by going into homes to repair wires or replace tubes. Soon he was selling radios themselves, all shapes and sizes on all kinds of payment plans. He was an exceptional salesman, seeing the radio as a box of easily summoned distraction for weary, uncertain people. He aimed at first not to sell but to explain, tracing with the future customer the webs and tangles of copper, informing his listener of their connections and rationale, pressing hard only at the end their whetted appetite, their need. ("Mostly they were people without cash.")

However, by the time a second world war was underway most Americans had radios, and his work slackened. In early 1942 he was the father of a four-year-old son, a two-year-old daughter. He owned a comfortable home in a distinctly middle-class area of white frame houses, each bulky, yet each a bit different. Most, though, had green shutters, high ceilings, thick walls, large, long windows, but no garage, all expressions of a warm, wet climate. More likely than not every residence had a single car so that the streets, palmy, well-paved, were lined on both sides just as from a plane's view the roofs asserted rows of radio antennae.

He still lives there, though many of his former neighbors have moved. For some the neighborhood was out of keeping with what they had recently become. They left for one-storied new houses in sprawling developments outside the city. The emigrants were replaced by others for whom the same neighborhood's value was defined by what they had just left. There are, however, a few who still prize those old houses, see their faintly shabby gentility and cherish their age and the memories they inspire. For John it is this way: "Those ranch houses are too expensive. Funny thing with a lot of the nigger lovers, they move out into the suburbs and then tell us how we should open our streets to them. I won't leave and I'd shoot to kill if they ever tried to buy a house nearby." (He cannot afford to leave. "They" are 2.4 miles away at their nearest.)

The war came as a relief. The economy was stagnant, floundering with too many unemployed. Poor people had bought their radios, and he was beginning to feel the pinch. ("Even the niggers had them. Some of them even had two.") Actually, he had sold many to Negroes in his years of salesmanship. He had collected money from them and taken showers after he came from their houses. Outweighing such services for Negroes was his participation in lynchings. He's been in two. His words: "We'd go home to see our folks, and you know in the country things are more direct, and there's no busybody reporters around. Once I heard one being organized, so I dropped by to see it." The other time was a rather spontaneous and informal affair. He noted that they "did it real quick like, the way you should. When you draw them out it makes it hard because you might get bad publicity. There are still lynchings around in farm country, I don't care what they tell you in the papers. We know how to take care of them when they get wise. We don't use rope, it's true, and get the crowds up we used to get. We may not always kill them, but we scare the Jesus out of them. You know the buckshot shootings you read about every now and then, it's the same thing as rope or fire. They know what'll happen if they get smart." Did he object at all to this? "Hell, no."

The Negroes were working for the Communists, any he would want to kill; I must know that. Had there been Communists in his town when he was a boy, during the twenties and thirties when lynchings were more public and common, some of them seen by him as a youth? Of course. The Communists took over in 1917, he knew the autumn month, but some of them had been working in this country even before that. He wasn't sure how far back, but he thought maybe twenty or thirty years, and they wanted to take this country, its free economy, for their prize. John was capable of broad, apocalyptic strokes: "This is a war between God and His Commandments and the Devil, and we may lose." I broached the subject of loss. How could God lose? "To punish us." Why would he want to do that? "We disobeyed him." Just an example or two — I was interested in them. "Nigger-loving."

In any case, he was glad to go to war in 1942, for he was accumulating unpaid bills. He yearned for the East — he wanted to go fight the Japs. He wasn't so sure about why we were fighting the Germans, who were combating the Reds, and might be our allies if we would have them. Hitler's enemies were his enemies: the Jews, moneyed, slyly alien, and the main support of the Negroes, inferior lackeys who did their bidding for small reward. This was all communism, personified in those hundreds of thousands of hook-nosed or black-skinned natives who lived in New York, in Hollywood. They were the capitalists, too; they controlled publishing houses, banks, and the stock exchanges. Their voices commanded a crippled, traitorous President's ear, bought the votes of errant, susceptible congressmen. "I was never against the Germans. I was proven right. Look at us now. They're our best protection against the Commies." Still, he added, the Germans would be of small help if the UN and integration took over America.

He never fought, though he helped others fight. He did his service at an army camp in New Jersey, a very small distance from Manhattan's subversion, perversion — and fascination. He went to New York all the time, to look, to see his enemy. He would always tell his friends how well he knew his New York enemies, and his friends, from what I could see, always seemed interested and stimulated by the details he supplied.

From all those furloughs to Union Square, Harlem, and Greenwich Village he managed to return home alive, heavier by fifteen pounds, his balding completed. He worried about work after his discharge, with good reason. He came home to children grown older, a wife with moderate rheumatoid arthritis ("her joints are stiff all the time"). He was now irascible and sullen. His wife usually wanted to stay away from him — out of pain, out of lack of response. She was withdrawing into her narrowing world of routine care of the home and the symptoms of a chronic, slowly crippling disease. To help her she had a young Negro, a high school girl, not very experienced, but not very expensive. (The price of Negroes was rising, along with other postwar costs.) A mulatto, as thin and lissome — I gathered from pictures I saw of her with his children — as her mistress was fattening and severe, she stayed with them for three years, five part-time days a week, until her marriage bore unexpectedly heavy demands of her own in twin sons.

During those years right after the war John found life confusing and hard; and he became bitter. He tried television-repair work, but couldn't "connect with it" as with radio. He drew unemployment relief for a while, short rations in the face of consuming inflation. Finally, nearly drowning in doctor's bills, in debt even for essentials like food and the most urgently needed clothing, his home heavily mortgaged, he found rescue in the state government, a clerk's job in a motor vehicle registration office. Now barely secure, in his mid-thirties, he was free to settle into concentrated, serious suspicion and hate. It was, after all, the decade of the fifties, when many of our countrymen would seek far and wide for subversives — and when the Supreme Court would declare segregated schools unconstitutional.

I met him, of course, well ripened in such zeal and involved in actions based upon it. From our first meeting it was clear that he relished talking, and talked well. He had found comfort for his views from his employer, a Louisiana state government whose legislature, in its very chambers, had carried on a mock funeral of a federal judge, a native son who had ordered four Negro girls into two elementary schools in New Orleans. The governor was a man whose chief merit seemed to be as a banjo player and singer whose theme song (composed by himself) was "You Are My Sunshine."

John dips constantly into the literature of segregation for support. It ranges all the way from the remarks of a scattering of biologists about a purported inferiority of the Negro on the basis of a supposedly lighter, smoother brain (fewer lines on the all-important frontal lobes) to the pathetic gibberish of the insane. He reads in such allied fields as the frantic anticommunism which holds the President and Supreme Court contaminated victims, even agents. There are always such diversions from the mainstream as the menacing ability fluorides have to erode America's freedom.

One of the first questions he had hurled at me, in our early tentative moments, was about his son. The young man was contemplating marriage and, a loyal Catholic, was about to attend a pre-marriage instruction course offered by their local church. The church was hell-bent on integration, however, and John feared the worst for and of his son. Did I believe "in integrated marriage courses"? I wanted to know more about this. Well, he would kill his son if a Negro came into such a class and he, John Junior, remained. His customary composure cracked (one of the few times I was ever to see this, even when I knew him much better) and he shouted at me. I began to doubt whether he was "reasonable enough" for me ever to get to know "reasonably well." Yes, he'd kill his own son, he shouted. Would I? I thought not. Still, I told him I wanted to hear more about integrated marriage classes. Well, if I wanted to hear more, he would oblige.

The real truth was that he and his son hadn't been able to get along for many years, and for that matter he and his wife weren't now "together" as they used to be. Menopause along with arthritis had come to his wife, heightening with its flashing signals her sense of decline, pulling her from her husband into a separate bed. (He still remembered his mother's menopausal depression, and he mentioned it when talking about his wife's health.) Once scornful of even an aspirin, she now juggled and swallowed seven separate encapsulated remedies. Their daughter, *his* daughter, his great delight for years, had rewarded him with excellent school work and high achievement in pre-college tests. Yet her success in the form of a full scholarship had eventually transported her away from home. Now it was their son, an office worker by day and part-time college student by night, who was about to leave. His family was dissolving, his marriage disintegrating. He was lonely.

"My boy is a fool, and he always has been." He became angry at first, but later appeared to regret his own remark. His son, it seems, cared little about Negroes and their threatening postures. He and his son had fought about ways of dressing, table manners, and hobbies; had fought all along as the boy tried his own ways and John resisted, tried to pinion the lad, fashion him in his father's image. Murderous thoughts by a father at the shameful possibility of his son's "church marriage class" becoming desegregated were but a final expression of long-standing turmoil.

It was against a background of such family problems that John ardently pursued a world as white and shadowless as possible. His work for most of the fifteen-odd years since the war had been uncertain or dull. He tired of temporary jobs selling in stores, then became bored with the security but confinement and meager pay of his state position. About a year before I met him he had run for a significant political office, claiming he would ferret out Communists in his district, export Negroes North or across the Atlantic, deprive Jews of any local if hidden sovereignty, and keep a careful, alert eye upon Washington and New York. He lost, but polled a good vote. In the course of the campaign he met a man who shared his ideals. The man owned gas stations, more of them than he could operate by himself. ("He liked to watch the help, just like me. You can't trust a nigger out of the reach of your eye.") John, priding himself on his sharp vision, purchased one of the stations, mortgaging his house further. His wife was enraged; her arthritis worsened, a coincidence he noticed and wanted me to know about. Selling fuel was a tough but slimly profitable venture; a fortunate arrangement in some ways, however, because he was able to inform a fellow gasoline vendor, fast and angrily, about a Negro employee working for him whose child was one of the handful to initiate school desegregation. John helped organize the mobs around the city's desegregated schools. He was noisily attentive to those buildings, those nearly deserted and embattled buildings where a few Negro and white children stubbornly persisted in getting educated together. To enable the Negro attendant to lose his job was actually as heartening an experience as John had enjoyed in a long time, and he referred back to this accomplishment frequently. He liked disorder in the streets, but he was not one to pass up private spite or intrigue either.

In time, we began to understand the design of his life, how old threads appear in apparently new patterns. Remember John while very young: a dark and sulky boy whose black-haired, ill-humored father preferred his fair wife, daughter, and younger son. John understood all too well arbitrary discrimination, the kind that appearances (height, build, complexion) stimulate. He was born in a state split among many lines — northern, Anglo-Saxon, light-skinned, Protestant country farmers on the one hand; southern, Catholic, Mediterranean types on the other, many of the thousands who lived in a wicked, international port city. His parents brought these different traditions together in an uneasy marriage, and the boy grew up a victim of this delicate arrangement. How accidental is it to find him years later moodily resenting dark people?

A psychiatric evaluation finds him oriented and alert, in no trouble about who or where he is — his name, the date and place of our talks. His mind works in understandable fashion. He does not hallucinate, and though we may consider his beliefs delusional, they are held in common with thousands of others, and do not seem insistently private or as incomprehensible as those in schizophrenic delusional systems. His thinking is not psychotic; it flows in orderly and logical steps, given certain assumptions that are shared by many others and thus have social rather than idiosyncratic sources.

He is intelligent, beyond question so. He grasps issues, relates them to others, takes stock of problems and tries to solve them. He has read widely and deeply, if with self-imposed restrictions. Much of what he reads gives him real encouragement. Full of references to God and country, encouraging virulent racism, recommending violence as possibly necessary in some future Armageddon of white versus black, Gentile versus Jew, biblical patriotism versus atheistic internationalism, this "literature" seeks an America which we hope will never exist, but it also collects its readers into a fellowship. One can call all these people crazy, but it is a shared insanity not an individual one. John works; he has a family and friends. He is fitful, alternately cheerless and buoyant. He is not shy or withdrawn; and he is in definite contact with many people, and responds to their feelings. Can we call him "sick"?

In one of those compact appraisals of an individual person we might say that John is not insane, not psychotic in any operational sense of the word; neither retarded nor delinquent. He has no police record, has committed no crimes as his society defines them, is even careful to obey laws on picketing or demonstrations where they exist or are enforced. (*His* kind of demonstration has often been encouraged by some officials of his state.) Absurdly xenophobic, an anti-Semitic, anti-Negro "paranoiac"? Yes, along with many, many thousands in his region. A frustrated, defeated man, a sometime political candidate, a feckless sidewalk crank, occasionally irritable and only rarely dangerous? Yes, but far from alone.

Born in a region long poor and defeated, into a family itself humble and moneyless, often at the mercy of capricious economic, social or political forces, the boy at home faced those first insecurities, those early rivalries, hates, and struggles which often set the pattern for later ones. White man against black embodied all those childhood hatreds, all those desperate, anxious attempts children make to locate themselves and their identities amid the strivings of siblings, amid the conscious and unconscious smiles and grudges, animosities and predilections of their parents. He was an active child, a fighter who managed to survive perilous disease and hard times. When grown he had some initial modest success at home and at work, only to return from war into a sliding, middle-aged depression, a personal one, but one that plagued his family, and some of his friends, too. (The papers talked of a "dislocated, postwar economy.") Individual psychopathology, social conflict and economic instability, each has its separate causes. On the other hand the mind can connect them together, and for many people they are keenly felt as three aspects of one unhappy, unpredictable life.

I looked first to "psychopathology" for the answer to the riddle of John, and those like him; for an explanation of their frightful actions. Rather than seek after political, social, or economic ills, I chose medical or psychiatric ones, the kind that seemed "real" to me. John's life shows that it can be understood best by looking at it in several ways, and *one* of them is certainly psychiatric. Yet I have to keep on reminding myself that I have seen mobs such as he joined collect in one city while in another they were nowhere to be found. While the incidence of individual psychopathology probably is relatively constant in all Southern cities, the quality of police forces and politicians has varied, and so have their ideas about what constituted law and order. I have seen avowed segregationists — some of them unstable individuals in addition — submit quietly to the most radical kinds of integrated society because they worked on a federal air base. American laws and jobs seemed curiously more influential than "deep-rooted" attitudes.

The FBI agent who spoke to me in McComb was standing in front of a dynamited house in the very heart of the most oppressive area in the South. James Silver's "closed society," the state of Mississippi, has a long history to fall back upon, one enforced by social, economic, and political power; no corner of the state had been more loyal to its past. Certainly I and others with me were frightened, though perhaps the FBI agent was not, by the hateful, suspicious attitude we were meeting at the hands of many of the townspeople. The Negroes were scared, and many of the whites had a kind of murder in their eyes. In the face of all that, the agent posed a question only in terms of illness, of individual eccentricity.

In McComb, in Mississippi, at that time, a dynamited house and even three murdered youths were not unique. There were klans, councils, and societies there whose daily words or deeds encouraged the burning of churches, the dynamiting of houses, the beating, ambushing, and killing of men. A few weeks after the "incident" in McComb I examined a minister brutally beaten in a doctor's office in Leake County, Mississippi. The doctor — no redneck, not "ignorant" — had literally pushed the minister and a young student with him into the hands of a gang *in his own office*. Every bit of evidence suggests a plot arranged by that doctor — he knew in advance the two men were coming because they had telephoned to ask for medical help. Shall we suggest psychiatric examinations for him and for all the others in the state — businessmen, newspaper editors, lawyers — who ignore, condone, encourage, or fail to conceal their pleasure at such episodes?

I wonder about the eager emphasis given private, aberrant motives by some in our society. Many ignore crying, horrible, concrete social and political realities whose effects — as a matter of fact — might lead us to understand how John and others like him continue to plague us. It is easier, I suppose, to look for the madman's impulse and make explaining it the doctor's task.

The bestiality I have seen in the South cannot be attributed only to its psychotic and ignorant people. Once and for all, in the face of what we have seen this century, we must all know that the animal in us can be elaborately rationalized in a society until an act of murder is seen as self-defense and dynamited houses become evidence of moral courage. Nor is the confused, damaged South the only region of this country in need of that particular knowledge.

II
Migrants, Sharecroppers, Mountaineers

The Land

I am writing about the land. I am writing about people, of course, about fellow citizens, and particularly about children, who live uprooted lives, who have been stranded, who are hidden from the rest of us. Nevertheless, I am writing about the land, miles and miles of it, the rich American earth. I am also writing about *a* land, the United States of America, some country that is hilly and rocky and often windswept or fog-covered, some that is a plateau, high and leveled-off and dry, some that is low and flat and at the water's edge. More precisely, I suppose, I am trying to approach the lives of certain individuals who may in various ways differ, as members or representatives of this or that "group" of people, but who for all of that share something hard to define exactly or label with a few long and authoritative words, something that has to do with the way people, however unlike in appearance or background, manage to live on the land and come to terms with it, every day of their lives.

The men and women whose lives, I repeat, I can only approach, do not live in cities (though their children and grandchildren may or perhaps will someday) and certainly do not live in the prosperous suburbs that hug those cities so rigidly. People who are called migrant farmers or sharecroppers or tenant farmers or mountaineers or hillbillies are not to be found in the small towns and villages that often are taken to be the repositories of America's rural heritage — by those who live in large, metropolitan centers and are willing to go just so far afield, so far toward the "country" in search of anything, including their nation's history. It can be said that migrants and sharecroppers and mountaineers live both nowhere and everywhere. Their homes, their houses, their cabins (which I fear all too commonly can be appropriately called shacks or huts) are scattered all over. They defy the dots and circles that, with names beside them, appear on maps. I can pick up one of those maps and point my finger at the smallest towns in, say, a county of the Mississippi Delta, or one of Florida's south-central counties or Kentucky's eastern counties, and still know that however large the atlas and however tiny, even microscopic, the places shown, I will not find large numbers of tenant farmers, migrants, or mountaineers, respectively, in any of them, be they county seats or the remotest of hamlets.

It is outside the town limits, in between one town and another, straddling county lines, even state lines, that they can be found — settlements of families, as I have come to think of them in my mind. Their cabins, with a protective coloration like that of animals, have almost invariably become part of the land: the wood and metal walls turn rusty brown and dull gray and blend into everything else and successfully camouflage entire settlements. They are often nameless settlements, or if they do have a name it is to set people apart from others, and just as important, attach them to the land's contours, to this particular field or creek or that hollow or bend in a river or valley.

Some of the settlements, of course, move across the land — a caravan of trucks, a few buses, a single car or maybe two, all filled to the brim with migrants. Yet, when the vehicles are brought to a stop it is done beside bushes and under trees. The point is to be inconspicuous, to hide, to disappear from sight; and so a number of families disperse, become little knots of people here and there, anxious for the ground as a resting-place and anxious to blend into things, merge with them, and thereby hide away from the rest of us, from the world that gazetteers and atlases and census bureaus take note of, from the world of the police and the government, but also from the merely curious and even the openly concerned.

The next day, when light comes, the trek is to be resumed and the risks of travel have to be taken. So, they emerge, the migrant settlers. They assemble and move on, and again they are wanderers whose chief purpose is an accommodation of their energies to the earth's needs. If the earth is ready, about to bear its fruits, the migrants try to be there, do their work, then slip away. As some of them have said to me, and will say in these pages, a whole life can be lived away from almost everyone but oneself and one's immediate relatives and companions. One knows hundreds of acres of land well — byroads and side roads and dirt roads and asphalt roads. One recognizes familiar terrain in a dozen states, in places all over. Yet, one is no one: frequently unregistered at birth, ineligible to vote, unprotected by laws that apply to others, often unrecorded as having died, and all during life an actual resident of no municipality or township or state — even stateless in the larger sense of being decidedly unwanted and spurned by a whole nation.

Surely it must be different with sharecroppers and mountaineers, though. If migrants cover the land, cover a virtual continent in search of work, sharecroppers or tenant farmers are by definition rooted to a specific piece of land, as are mountaineers, who after all live up along the sides of particular Appalachian hills. A dazed, rootless itinerant field hand does not to all appearances live like a sharecropper, who may never have left a particular plantation, or like a mountaineer, who stubbornly stays up his hollow, come what may. Yet, for all three the land means everything, the land and what grows on it, what can be found under it, what the seasons do to it, and what man does to it, and indeed what long ago was done to it by a mysterious Nature, or an equally baffling, chronicle of events called History, or finally what it was made by God, like the other two inscrutable, but unlike them, at least for the people we are to meet and try to know here, very much present and listening and in fact a person, *the* person: He Who listens and remembers — and Whose land it all really is, something plantation owners and growers and county officials may forget for a while, but will ultimately discover at a given point in eternity's scheme of things, so thousands of harvesters believe.

I am not saying that all these people, so scattered and so different and so removed from one another (but so very much alike) do not share man's general need to confine his fellow man, give him a name, call a certain stretch of territory his, pinpoint him in time and space. The title of this part of the book right away declares that my concern is with people who migrate from one place to another, and people who work the land that ostensibly belongs to others, in exchange for a share of the profits, and people who cling hard indeed to a mighty and prominent range of mountains. And the first pages in this section declare the migrants to be Americans, the sharecroppers to be Americans, and the mountaineers to be perhaps the most typically American of Americans — in the old-fashioned, conventional sense of what has constituted an American for the longest period of time. (Indians and blacks, also here when the Republic was founded, would not become Americans until much later.)

Indeed, it is possible to get quite precise; a variety of names and phrases, like nets, can pull in just about all these people. They live in the "Black Belt" of the South, from Georgia to Louisiana, or near Lake Okeechobee and the Everglades in Florida; or they live on the edge of the Cumberlands, the Alleghenys, the Blue Ridge mountains; or they spend time in the lowlands of the Carolinas, in Virginia's tidewater area, all along a stretch of Long Island, in upstate New York, downstate New Jersey, or in New England, where tobacco grows (in Connecticut) and apples fall from trees (in Massachusetts, for instance) and potatoes cover the ground (Maine's far north Aroostook county). Still, when all that is said, we have only begun. These twentieth-century people, living in the world's richest, strongest twentieth-century nation, are to some extent obeying rituals and commands, are responding to urges and demonstrating rhythms that defy (as well as yield to) the influence of contemporary American life — again, as we the majority know and experience that life. The "migrants, sharecroppers, and mountaineers" who are gathered collectively together in this book live not only *on* the land, but *in* a land, one in certain respects all their own. The land all these people know so well has physical boundaries that can be traced out, if we have a mind to do so; but it is just as important for us to know about those psychological boundaries, within which a certain kind of encounter takes place between human hands and the earth; the boundaries between all those fields and meadows and clearings and forests and all those people bent on eating and sleeping and amusing themselves and staking out things for themselves and finding things for themselves.

I would like to begin, in other words, by describing the land and what it is like, what is *there* for men and women to work on, to handle every day. And it should be emphasized that the men and women and children whom we are trying to know here do indeed "handle" the land, do so quite stubbornly and successfully and patiently and cleverly and at times fearfully, but at other times fearlessly and casually and yes almost brazenly, in view of all the threats and the misfortunes, the never-ending dangers and obstacles.

What *is* the land like? To migrants the land is not "like" anything; rather, it never stops appearing, waiting, calling, needing, summoning, urging, and then disappearing. To sharecroppers the land is more familiar, but not all that familiar, because it belongs to someone else, and always what is to be done must be settled with that stranger, that boss. To mountaineers the land is almost anything and everything: a neighbor, a friend, a part of the family, handed down and talked about and loved, loved dearly — loved and treasured and obeyed, it can be said, as we agree to do when we get married.

Yet, once more, for all those differences, the three kinds of people are one people; and it is what they do that makes them one. Together they grapple and fight the land, dig into it, try to tame it, exploit it, even plunder it; together they placate the land, bring water to it, spread nourishing substances over it, and in many ways curry its favor. They appeal to it, both openly and more slyly, with rakes that brush and stroke and caress and with hands that pick and pluck, and with words and songs, too — prayers and pleas and cries and requests and petitions. High up the hills of West Virginia men petition for sun; they live nearer the sun than most people, but they can be denied the sun by clouds that hang to the hilltops. In the "Black Belt" men petition for rain; the land is rich and the sun plentiful, but water is needed, and not everywhere has man had the money and ingenuity to bring that water in and keep it at hand, ready and waiting — "the irrigation" as a sharecropper calls it, the pipes and way yonder the dams and artificial lakes he may have heard a plantation owner or his foreman talk about. In southern Florida men petition for peace and quiet of sorts: for an autumn without hurricanes; for a winter that brings no icy blasts, no ruinous frosts; for a spring and summer that offer rain, but not too much rain — though if a choice has to be made, for more rather than less rain, because the droughts are the greatest danger, are a calamity all too familiar in and near the Everglades.

Much of that petitioning takes place right out in the fields themselves, and is done by tenants or itinerant field hands or proud landowners of small plots up in the hills. As with many things that happen in the world, the cliché holds: one has to see something to believe it. In this case one has to hear as well as see: hear the nervous statements and observations, the speculations and predictions, has to hear the doubts and the exasperated, anguished cries which express a sense of futility, foreboding, or distress, a desperate suspicion that all is lost, perhaps only for this year, perhaps even for good. Alternatively, there are the good moments, the occasions when the petitions have been answered, when grateful men and women and children can say thank you or thank You, Almighty God, for befriending us through yet another stretch of time — from planting to plowing to harvesting, from spring through summer and into the autumn, or way down in Florida, from autumn through the winter and into the spring.

The seasons at their worst can bring all but certain defeat, or at their kindest the seasons can offer the distinct likelihood of victory; but most of the time the seasons only begin to influence the land — do so decisively, but not conclusively. Men, men and their wives, parents helped by their children, can through work, hard and tough and backbreaking work, manage to get a reward for their efforts: "crops" or "produce" or "a harvest," the reward is called. Their work is called menial; such efforts are considered automatic and stereotyped — but by whom? Nature is a formidable adversary, most of us will acknowledge in an offhand way, but we who spend most of our lives in the cities have no reason to understand just how formidable Nature can be — and therefore cannot know how shrewd and inventive a field hand, yes a common, ordinary, badly paid, poorly educated field hand has to be, faced as he is with land that must be coaxed, persuaded and prompted, aroused and inspired, however much richness and fertility it possesses.

I have seen those field hands walking the flat land, climbing patches of hilly land under cultivation, talking to themselves as they sow seeds, calculating the moment to take it all in, what they have planted and managed to grow. Later on I will hope to give some indication of what is thought and said by sowers and reapers, planters and harvesters, but as a start the majesty of the challenge to be faced by men who would tame the land had better be acknowledged. Modestly the men themselves admit that "it is no mean job," and if they will not advertise the cleverness and ingenuity required, they will most certainly let you know how fickle spring can be, how disappointing summer sometimes is, how overly prompt and forbidding a particular autumn's appearance was, and how utterly devastating it turned out, that last winter.

Joys are to be had, though; and keenly appreciated, too — a magnificent rural landscape, much of it semitropical, which still exists, miraculously enough, in this giant of an industrial country. In winter Alabama's mean temperature is 48 degrees Fahrenheit and in summer 79 degrees Fahrenheit. On the average, less than thirty-five days witness temperatures below the freezing point. Snow falls once or twice a year, and then only in the northern part of the state. The prevailing winds come from the south. Rain is generally plentiful, amounting to over fifty inches a year. In West Virginia, for all the timber-cutting and the depredations of insects, substantial remnants remain of a vast, primeval forest, a blanket of hardwoods and pines that once completely covered the state. Hemlocks, chestnuts, and oaks are to be found in abundance. Some tulip poplars stand two hundred feet tall. Some sugar maples stand one hundred feet tall. And there are others: ash trees, whose wood is used in baseball bats, tennis rackets, and hockey sticks; or the buckeye; or sourwood trees that supply the sourwood honey that is much loved up the hollows; or those holly trees, the Christmas holly and the mountain holly; or the black cherry tree, whose bark is used in making cough syrup; or the black walnut; or the silver bell; or the spruces so thick, clothing one ridge after another; or the lindens, which stand more alone, and can go dozens and dozens of feet into the air.

What air it is, too! The air up those hills and mountains can be so clear and dry and bracing that the lungs shudder, the head feels much more invigorated than it wants to be. The air can also be raw and wet, or heavy and clammy. Rain is plentiful, at times more than plentiful. Some regions receive seventy or eighty inches a year. Needless to say, trees flourish under such conditions, but incredibly, so do people — the kind who find the brisk winds, the chilly weather, the continual dampness appetizing, and even intoxicating. For such people clouds are no dreaded stranger, thunder and lightning are music, and fog an amusing, welcome visitor. There is enough sun to grow a few vegetables, and the forests — why, without the water, without the mist and the dew and the long "downfalls" and the sudden cloudbursts, there would be no forest worth the name up the side of those hills, only fires and the burned remains that fires leave. Instead, those trees continue to stand; and also around are plants and flowers, hundreds of different kinds, all very much known to mountaineers as well as botanists. The forests are filled with shrubs, lovely ones like azaleas and rhododendrons and wisteria and laurel. A man looking for berries finds huckleberries and strawberries and raspberries. A man wanting to take a look at flowers finds lilies and bloodroot and phlox and the colorfully named lady slipper or bleeding heart or Indian paintbrush or Devil's walking stick or bee balm. On the other hand, a man who has more serious things (or simply fauna instead of flora) on his mind can find foxes, skunks, opossums, raccoons, rabbits, beavers — or frogs and toads and turtles and snakes, plenty of all of them, and up in the sky, plenty of birds, some that stay year round, and many that come and stop and leave during and in between the seasons.

Men who till the soil, who live intimately with a given kind of terrain, whatever its features, are men who share more than their particular "culture" or "life-style" may at first glance seem to indicate. Perhaps most of all there is the vastness of the land, its size, its expanse, its ability to seem limitless and all-powerful. The sun rises out of the land tentatively, then with increasing assurance and influence; the sun goes down into the same land flaming, even if weak enough, at last, to be stared at. The days and seasons come and go, but the land stands firm. Snow may cover the land, water drench it, wind dust it off or try to carry it off, lightning seem to jab at it, tornadoes bear down on it mightily and fearfully, the sun warm it up, draw it out, excite it; whatever happens, the land remains, survives, *is*. Yes, in the thirties America had its "dust bowl," and its earth still shows the ravages of man; but by and large the people in this book, plundered and needy though they may also be, live on rich, fertile land, yielding and boun- tiful, so blessed as to be for decades and decades almost defiantly pro- ductive, even in the face of predatory man's greed and carelessness, which have been compensated for only recently and in certain places by chemicals and water pumped in from afar.

Most of Appalachia and the rural South and for that matter the rural North is graced with a wonderful, life-giving, utterly reassuring abundance of water, so that the irrigating canals and pipes that mi- grants know in central Florida are not part of a desperate, do-or-die stand, such as a farmer might have to take in Alabama or parts of Cali- fornia. Water beats down upon the Appalachian mountains, and all over them one sees the result: gorges and ravines and passageways pouring forth that water; rivers never very low and in spring almost invariably flooded; rivers that compete with one another, join and sep- arate, fight for streams and draw competitively upon tributaries. Wa- ter comes to Mississippi and Louisiana from the greatest of American rivers, but water comes openly and secretly even to Florida, whose land stretches further south than any other state, whose land also can experience seasons of bad, worrisome drought. As is the case with the Carolinas, sand reefs and generally narrow, elongated islands hug both of Florida's shores, thus making for a whole series of lakes, lagoons, bays, and splendid, restful harbors. The state is laced with rivers and lakes, including the very large Lake Okeechobee, near which thou- sands of migrant farmers spend their winters at work with the crops. The lakes are frequently connected by subterranean channels, and for that matter isolated subterranean springs and streams can be found all over the state. The springs and streams eventually become rivers, and through a system of man-made canals farmers try hard to exert a de- gree of control over the natural largesse.

More often than not, mountaineers and tenant farmers and mi- grants can be found living near that water, near creeks and not far from lakes and quite close to the waters of any number of rivers. The mountain settlements are squeezed into a valley a river has carved out, or pressed close to a creek whose banks actually provide a clearing, a way down, a road out of the wilderness; or settlements are crammed near a lake, where a hungry migrant or tenant farmer can search for fish, which is one thing that costs nothing. "We never lose sight of water, and we never lose sight of the sky, and we never lose sight of the land, that's how we live," I was told by a tenant farmer who lives in what history books variously call the Black Belt, the Black Prairie, the Cotton Belt. He actually lives in Alabama, whose land is several colors; black yes, but also red and sand-brown and mixed with green moss and the whiteness of chalk. Along the Gulf of Mexico and some miles north — a so-called timber belt — the land is sandy but quite responsive to fertilizers. Then comes the famous black soil: laced with limestone and marl formations; essentially devoid of sand; especially suited to the production of cotton and grains. A little farther north one finds land rich in minerals, rich for instance in the iron that makes Birmingham a steel city. And, finally, Alabama's land becomes part of the Tennessee valley, and there contains red clays and dark loams which, again, can nourish grains and vegetables.

It is, of course, easy for a visitor like me to work himself up into a lather about such things, to become almost euphoric at the variety of trees or birds or types of soil; about striking waterfalls and rapid streams and sluggish rivers and wide estuaries and bayous dripping with Spanish moss; about lonely herons that rise out of mist only to fall quickly and just as quickly disappear. All of that is the heady and maybe corrupt stuff of southern nostalgia or Appalachian romanticism. All of that would seem to border on the bizarre or the Gothic and even the outrageous when it is made to accompany a discussion of how, for example, an extremely poor migrant, most of the time hungry, and without money and maybe even a roof of any kind over his head, manages barely to stay alive. Tourists may hear about those plateaus and mountaintops, those headwaters and ebb tides, those rich clays and silts and peats and gravelly or sandy spots, and all the lovely flowers and shrubs they bear. Tourists, too, may hear about soft white sands and a coast's shallow indentations, which become inviting bays; and tourists love to hear about mild, equable weather or low, marshy tracts that offer surprisingly good fishing. All the while terribly forsaken and just about indigent families live nearby, nearer-by in fact than most tourists will ever realize; and those families have little time to care about such matters, such attractions, or so we might reasonably believe.

Certainly it is true that migrant farm workers don't look upon their experiences the way casual travelers might. Nor do sharecroppers wax lyrical about the South, that haunting, mysterious, strangely uncommon region which has both defied and invited descriptions all through American history. Mountaineers have their ballads to sing, their guitars to "pick" away at, but they don't stand on ridges or the edges of plateaus or way up on peaks in order to get breathtaking views, which are then photographed and thereby carried home, to be shown one evening after another. No, in Logan County, West Virginia, mountaineers don't find themselves quaint; and in Adams County, Mississippi, tenant farmers don't burble about those antebellum homes, or gush in pride and awe at the river, the great god of a river; and in Collier County, Florida, or Palm Beach County, Florida, migrant workers don't join hands with conservationists and worry about wildlife in the beautiful, ever spectacular Everglades.

And yet, I have, I think, learned a few things from these people. I have learned something more than how they live and scarcely stay alive. I have learned what little margin, what little leeway I was prepared to give them. I came ready to comprehend their suffering, their misery, the injustice of their position in our society, and I came prepared to write down my indignation and rage and horror. But I am not sure I was prepared to ask myself a single thing that would upset the central beliefs I brought with me to the "Black Belt" and those migrant camps and the Cumberland Mountains. I believed that these groups are the poorest of our poor, the most overcome, the most broken, the most bowed down; that they are sunk, lost, tired, discouraged; that they are faced every day with dreary work, if indeed any work, and with miserable living conditions and with varying degrees and kinds of hunger, malnutrition, and illness; that they are at the mercy of things, compelled to face life passively, fearfully, even automatically; and that finally, if they deserve sympathy and concern and the conscientious efforts of the rest of the nation in their behalf, they also have to be looked at directly and without illusions, for their own sake. There is no use trying to fool ourselves about the seriousness of their problems or the damage done to them over the generations by the circumstances that not only surround but utterly envelop their lives, and there is no use, either, indulging ourselves, by turning such people into storybook characters, full of nobility and interesting, intriguing passions and charming or innocent (hence particularly enviable) virtues.

And yet — I have to say that again — a good portion of this book will, I hope, spell out what goes, what has to go, after "and yet," even as still other parts of the book will confirm quite grimly what has just preceded those two words — confirm human misery, confirm the waste, the outrageous and unconscionable waste of lives, and particularly of the energy and talent and spirit that these lives have to offer.

Still, right here in the beginning of this part of the book I want to quote the words of a man who understands a lot about the land and a lot about his life — a lot that I found (and maybe still find) hard to fathom and comprehend, but even harder to accept and fit into my scheme of things, my political ideas, my psychological theories, and my social values. He works on the land in between what I suppose could be called the rural South and Appalachia, in a broad valley at the foot of the hill country of Tennessee. Although no one man can speak for the three groups I am concerned with here, this man comes as close as any in combining elements that belong to all of these groups. He is a tenant farmer; he practices a kind of sharecropping, by no means the worst, most exploitative kind, and finally, not uncommonly, he has two close relatives who have joined the eastern migrant "stream." The man I call a yeoman, a sturdy and almost fierce small farmer, talks about matters other than his "problems," and those other matters, I would argue, ought to get recorded at the very start of things — much earlier, alas, than I came to grasp them in the course of my work.

I approach his land (*his* it is, because he so feels it to be) on a dusty path rather than a road. I get annoyed, because the path is winding, a bit wind-raked, pitted, and creviced. I look for shade; it is warm and very muggy. I have been there before, but now that all the crops are "down" — which means all the seeds are in the earth, the weeds have yet to appear, and time seems a little more available — there is every hope of the "big talk" the yeoman himself had once promised we would one day have. This was the day, and he was ready. He is especially talkative compared to others who do his kind of work, and for that I am grateful, though a little suspicious. Maybe silence is all that can be trusted by me — one who is so at the mercy of words. I am just starting out, and I have, after all, been warned again and again that this man should be glum, burdened, restrained, anything but generous with his thoughts. Instead he seems unexpectedly plainspoken and outgoing. I have noticed that he drinks rather copiously, and in ostensible jest but out of genuine candor and friendliness, he had offered to take me to a still, a place where moonshine is made, "the first one you'll find upon leaving Alabama and coming up the road into the hills of Tennessee, yes sir." Perhaps the drink explains it, then, his voluble, blustery, open, giving manner.

So, as I listened over a long day and several others to the yeoman talking, I wondered: what drives him on, this expansive man, who has so much to be sad about, but insists, protests, protests *too much*, his pleasure in taking on — all of nature, it would seem? And why does he not face up to the substance of his life, the social and economic vulnerability that he experiences, the overwhelming difficulties that drag on, that will not, maybe never can, let go of him? In the next chapter (and perhaps all through this part of the book) I shall discuss some of that; but now is the time to let him talk about what he gets out of life, rather than what he wants out of it or what monstrous evils it most assuredly does visit upon him.

"I can't say I'm pleased with everything," he will say and repeat from time to time. "And yet," he adds and will stubbornly add from time to time — until at last, years after this first conversation, I will have finally been stopped in my tracks and made to hear, made to realize. "And yet, even if you're not pleased, you can still be glad for what you have to be glad for, not much that's big and important, I know, but there's something, there's something good we can tell you we have." Later on he became a little less "defensive," a little less boastful; but now, almost a decade since we first met, I have yet to hear him go back on that kind of affirmation — only progressively expand on it, while at the same time admitting to the obstacles he has to contend with every day of his life.

"I can't say it's not a struggle; it is, a bad one. If I had to choose, I'd not choose this life — maybe another one that's easier. I only know this one here, though. How can you go picking out another kind of life if you only can have the one you have? I can't say I'm a happy man here; we have it bad a lot. I can't say I mind my work, though, and if I had to choose, like I say, I don't think I'd know what to do but tell the Lord that I'll take this one, this life, all over again, with the pain and all. Every morning I wake up and I'm thinking to myself, what should I do today? We have the few chickens and I go and check on them and see if they've given us a few eggs, and I feed them of course. There will be a day or two, and more sometimes, when it's a lot easier to feed the chickens than us.

"I have to get the water, and that comes next. I take my oldest boy with me. He talks about going to a city one day, but I have an answer for him. I say: go, go North, go to Chicago or a place like that, and you'll see, oh will you, and you may not come back here, and you may find yourself a job with good money, but you'll pine for it here and you'll be sorry and you'll ache; you'll hurt, real bad it'll be. I'm not trying to scare him. It sounds like I am, but I'm not. We're born to this land here, and it's no good when you leave. I did once; I was in the Army. I know what I could have done. I know how I could have stayed there, in the state of Indiana, up toward Chicago. But I asked myself if I wanted to be in a place I didn't want to be in — even with a check from the welfare people, or a job if I could get one — or if I wanted to be back here, doing what I was taught by my daddy to do. You can see how I answered myself.

"Now I have the same kind of talks with my boy, especially in the early morning. We're out there walking over to the pump before the sun is all the way up. He'll say to me — he's tired and just waking up, I know — that if we lived in a city, someplace big you know, there would be water there to turn on and we'd be able to sleep later. Yes, true; I admit to him when he's right. I tell him that he's right. But I say, look Jimmy, there are some places where you like to get up, or at least it's not so bad, and there are other places where you could sleep all morning and have a million dollars lying near you, and still you wouldn't want to go out and take a walk there. Maybe with a million dollars I would go anywhere. Jimmy told me I was sure wrong saying I'd turn my back on a million dollars. But he knows what I'm telling him: for us it's a choice we have, between going away or else staying here and not seeing much money at all, but working on the land, like we know how to do, and living here, where you can feel you're you, and no one else, and there isn't the next guy pushing on you and kicking you and calling you every bad name there ever was. If you go, that's what you go to. If you go you can't hardly breathe, there are so many people, and you never see the sun, you *never* do. I used to wake up, when I was in the city on leave, military leave, and I'd ask myself, where is that sun, where does it hide itself from you?

"I've noticed that by the time we're on the way back from the well, Jimmy is persuaded, yes sir. He'll agree with me; he'll say he likes it, going out into the air, first thing in the morning, and toting the water. By the time we've done that, the chickens have eaten up everything and they hear us and they cackle away for more, but they're not going to get it. Momma is all waken up, and she's working to do the best she can for us, for breakfast; and there'll be days when we have eggs and toast and grits and everything, and there'll be other days when it's coffee, thin as can be, and nothing in it, even for the baby. Yes, it gets bad — in winter especially. We make enough to get by, but there's no spare, and if there's an extra expense, then we don't have a single thing to fall back upon. I can't ask for anything. I can't call on anyone — except for God, and sometimes He'll answer. He'll send the minister over with a package for us.

"No matter, though. I always have my work. You can feed off that, you know. In the winter it's the chickens and keeping us supplied with wood and water and all like that. The rest of the year it's much more; it's doing everything, practically anything you could think of. After breakfast I go out and start with the planting, or the weeding or the harvesting; it depends on what season you're in. I know my land, I'll say I do. I know the weather, too. When I've come back with the water I can tell my wife and children what the day will be like. I can say it's going to be a day of sun, all the way; or I can say the clouds are there, thick as can be, but don't be fooled, because they're going to be burned right up, sent running like a pack of squirrels by that foxy old sun; or I can say we're in for it, a heavy day of clouds, or the good rain, lots of it I hope, or maybe just a few drops that won't add up to anything.

"The weather helps make the land what it is, you see. Good weather, any farming man needs that. But to begin with he'll need soil he can work on; and you stop anybody within a hundred or two miles of this place and they'll all agree that hereabouts we've been blessed by Almighty God with good farmland. I talk to my land, you know. I ask it to be good; each year at the start I do. And each year at the end I say, thank you and amen. It's like being in church and talking with God. It's His land, anyway, and I do believe if we could ask Him He'd be in favor of us thanking Him — thanking Him through a little whisper or two while we're out there doing the work. If God sends sun and rain and He's already given you your land that's good, then there's just one more thing needed, and it's not hard to guess what it is: work. Jimmy laughs when I tell him we've got to go and see if we're up to God, if we can do the work He'd expect from us. Jimmy thinks his old daddy is starting to get *real* old, and be like his granddaddy was when he was at the end and ready to pass on. But I've always believed that when we leave our house and start in out there on the land, we're meeting God and doing all we can to show Him we can hear Him and we can believe in Him; and the proof is that He's there, helping us with the gift of His land, you see, and His sun you see, and His good, good rain, His precious rain that He sends us just when we need it and sometimes in-between and to spare. It's up to us to go out and do our best by Him, and work on His land, and take good care that we get everything we can out of it, all the vegetables and the cotton, and the flowers — I'm not forgetting them. My wife takes them over to town and we sell them. We get a good price on them. I hear they go to some man in Birmingham, maybe it is, and he sells them again to anyone who wants to have flowers and likes flowers — and the man who buys them and takes them home probably wishes he was out here and growing them and not in Birmingham, Alabama, paying his dollar for having a look at them, a little look, before the poor flowers go and die.

"When I come home it's a tired man that walks in that door. I'm hungry, because I don't eat all day. It doesn't go down good in my stomach, food doesn't, when I'm sweating and bending and my back is bent over and my front is all caved in. I get pains, bad ones all across my middle and up to my chest. We don't have a doctor near here, and I'm not one to feel sorry for myself. I told my wife I'd stop having food during the day, and I'd feel better; she said I was dead wrong, but I wasn't. It's been two years or so, two summers, since I went back in the middle of the day for some of her soup that she makes, or the potatoes. She holds it all for me, and then I'll eat and eat at the end of the day, and it's like I say, I don't get the pains then, nor at the start of the day, with breakfast.

"I'll stop when it's hot, bad hot, in the summer. I'll stop around the middle of the day, when the sun is high — maybe going down some, but only a little. I have my tree, my favorite tree. It's my bed away from bed, my wife says; that's what she calls it, my bed away from bed. And she's all correct, every word. I can doze off. I can lie there and look up to the sky and have my talk with God, just like I was in church, or just like I was up there, and taken in to see Him and hear His judgment, like we all will, one day. I can lie there and ask myself: James, what have you done this morning? Then I can say: James, you've done what's waiting out there for you to do, which is all anyone could have told you to do and expect it to be finished. The next thing, I can ask: what is ahead for the afternoon? And you know, I'll have it running through my mind, as if I had a television camera in my head, and it could take pictures of what is *going* to happen, way before a man gets himself up and lifts his arms to start. Lying on my back over there I have the tree over me, better than any curtain you'll ever buy, and when I want to turn off what crosses through my own head, and listen in to someone else, I just do. I say: James, I'm real tired of you and all the thoughts that's going through you to worry you. I say: James, there are others in God's Kingdom. The next thing you know, I hear a bird up there, talking to another bird, and they're just going and going, maybe arguing or maybe telling each other that it's a good day, and to be glad for it.

"We have good soil here, and the birds know it; just like you and

I, they try to find the best places to stop and rest. It's fine, hard soil, but not too hard. There are plenty of worms, and birds like them and I like them too, because I need worms for fishing. That's what I do when I have time; and we need those fish. My wife some of the time says that if it wasn't for the fish I catch, we'd all be gone by now. She's wrong, but it helps to bring her home a good catch. There's hunting a little way north of here in some woods, but I don't have the time. I don't have a car, either. With a car I could go hunting up in the hills. But I put all my time and energy into this land that I've got to use, that's mine to use, and I'm not ready to feel sorry for myself, no I'm not.

"I don't like feeling sorry for myself, and I don't like my wife to get doing that, nor my children. Nor do I like others, anyone else, to say: isn't it sad, how bad off they are out on that farm. We have people who will come by and try to get you feeling all bad about yourself and how you live. I don't like it, not having much money, and being a lot down and out half the year — that's through the winter and the first part of the spring — but I get by, and I'd like to keep trying to get by. I'd like help, of course. I admit to that. I'd like the government people to help the poor, small man, and not only the big boys, the big farmers, who own the Agricultural Department, there in Washington, yes they do. One of the people here, an agricultural agent we have, told me that it's true, that they have a big Agricultural Department in Washington, and it gives men with plantations, the real large ones, lots and lots of money for *not* planting their crops. I came home and told all my family that there might be a lot of hope for us: one day someone out of Washington will discover us, here in Tennessee, and he'll say that we can have plenty of money, the green bills, all we need to live on, if we just sit here and don't lift a finger, just look at the land and don't plant crops in it. But I'll tell you something: I couldn't do it, be here and not do my growing. I'd have to leave here, I would. I'd leave so fast no one would believe I was gone; that's what I'd do if I was told I shouldn't plant, I shouldn't work on my land, and if I don't then I'll be paid for doing nothing.

"I'd about die if I didn't have my work. I wouldn't know what to do with the time; the hours would pass by, one after the next, and I'd be here, sitting and looking at my land with my legs still and my arms just hanging down and I'd be staring — I would be like a scarecrow, that's what. I wouldn't have any life in me left. The money would be welcome, but I know I'd soon die. And the worst of it, the real worst of it, would be knowing that the land is just sitting there, lying out there, not being touched, not being asked to do anything, not being planted, not coming up with the shoots — just those weeds, that are always there. I wouldn't be pushing the shoots along; I wouldn't be telling them to grow and get bigger and try the world out, because it's not bad, what with sun to keep you warm and a good shower you get every once in a while. There will be days when I can almost see my little shoots growing and they're weak and tender, but they're strong, too. It won't be long, I know, before they'll be hardier; they'll be tough, and no weeds can get them, not then. No weeds ever win out around here — not with me around to look at things and do what has to be done. There are times when I wish the good Lord would say to Himself that He should treat us all like we're in His Garden, and He should help the good people along, and take up the bad people, the weeds, and put them someplace else — maybe up on one of the stars, way away. Then the weeds could have another chance there, to start over and not turn into weeds, you might say. I don't want people to be killed, as if they could *only* be weeds and nothing else!"

He doesn't want to harm anyone, not even people who have no great respect for him, and indeed do him and his kind no good, perhaps a lot of harm. "His kind" belongs to the South and to Appalachia both, to a whole half of a nation, really. It so happens that on several counts he is rather in between: he lives at the edge of the rural South, but at the edge of Appalachia; not far from two good-sized cities yet very much in a rural setting; he is a light-skinned black man who appears to be a nicely tanned white man — and, finally, his speech includes elements of the mountaineer's language, of the white yeoman's, and of the black tenant farmer's. Those who have spent any length of time in counties like Buncombe County or Yancey County in North Carolina (to move a little east from Tennessee) will know what I mean.

Certainly he is not Everyman; in this instance, though, I believe a particular person comes rather close to speaking for three large and scattered "groups," which are different in many respects but also alike in many ways. Among migrants, sharecroppers, and mountaineers one finds black people and white people — and various shades of both. They are people who stay put in the South with a vengeance, or they wander without respite over a whole wide expanse of this nation. For all the distinctions to be made, the classifications and comparisons, the "cross-cultural" similarities or the psychological and sociological differences, what is shared among these people might be called something of the spirit: a closeness to the land, a familiarity with it, and despite the suffering and sacrifice and rage and hurt and pain, a constant regard for that land, an attachment to that land, a kind of love.

For years I have heard that love emerge, even in the midst of bitterness and frustration. I have watched migrants try to stop being migrants, become instead city folk; and I have watched sharecroppers head joyfully and eagerly North, glad to be rid of plantation owners and foremen and sheriffs, the whole miserable, mean lot of them. I have watched mountaineers slip through mountain passes and valleys toward Dayton, say, or Chicago — all too willingly, because work and the food money can buy is far better than constant and unappeased hunger. As they get ready to leave, those many men and women and children, they deny having any regrets. *And yet* they do: they are losing something; they feel low and sad; more precisely, they anticipate the yearning they may later have, the homesickness, the lovesickness, the sense of bereavement. Dispossessed, they have to leave; they ought to leave. It was an awful life. *And yet* — one more time: "If I don't have to go, maybe it'll be my sons. They'll be the ones to cry and not me. They'll be happy, I know. They'll be looking ahead, I know. But it'll be a shame for us to leave, my family; it's a shame when you leave the only thing you've known, your land — and remember, it's land that's seen you trying and that's tried back, tried to give you all it could. There's no land up there, just people and buildings. I know that. That's too bad. That's the way it has to be; I know it. I do. But I don't have to like it. I don't. I never will, even if I have to say good-bye and go on up the road myself, away from here, from my land."

So far he and hundreds of thousands of others are still there, still migrant farmers, still sharecroppers or tenant farmers, still living up those mountain hollows. They all look for changes, hope for them, dream of them — and at the same time stand their ground, and more literally, walk it, walk that ground and work it, and stay with it and stay on it, and know it as a friend, a giver, a lover, a great protagonist that is ready to bargain, that is ready to resist, that is *there*. The American land.

The Children

Uprooted Children

For nine months the infant grows and grows in the womb. The quarters are extremely limited; at the end an X-ray shows the small yet developed body quite bent over on itself and cramped; yet a whole new life has come into being. For some hundreds of thousands of American migrant children that stretch of time, those months, represent the longest rest ever to be had, the longest stay in any one place. From birth on, moves and more moves take place, quick trips and drawn-out journeys. From birth on for such children, it is travel and all that goes with travel — forced travel, by migrant farm workers who roam the American land in search of crops to harvest and enough dollars to stay alive — "to live half right."

How in fact do such children live, the boys and girls who are born to migrant farmers? What do they gradually and eventually learn — and what do they have to teach us, the homeowners and apartment dwellers, the residents of villages and towns and cities and states? To begin with, many migrant children are not born in hospitals, not delivered by physicians, or even carefully trained midwives like those who work with the Frontier Nursing Service in eastern Kentucky. Again and again the migrant mother will casually describe the work she does in the field all during her pregnancy, the travel she undertakes during that same period of time, and finally the delivery itself: done in the rural cabin, or yes, done "on the road" or even in the fields. However indifferent one may be to the cause of such people, it is hard to accept the fact that in the second half of the twentieth century, in the United States of America, women bear their children on the side of a road, or in a one-room house that lacks running water and electricity — in either case, attended by a friend or neighbor or relative, who is able to offer affection and sympathy, but not medical help. Here is how a rather conservative grower both confirms the existence of and objects to a state of affairs: "Sure, some of them have their babies away from hospitals. I know that. We'd never turn them away from a hospital, here or anyplace. But they have their own life, you know, and they don't do things the way we do. It's ignorance; and it's superstition. A lot of them, they don't know where the hospital is, and they don't want to go there; and some of them, they just want to be with their mother or their aunt, or someone, and they'll scream out there. I've even heard them a couple of times by the side of my fields, and the best thing you can do is leave them alone. Once one of my men went over and tried to take them to the hospital, but they screamed even louder, and he thought they believed he was going to arrest them, or something. It's awful, how ignorant people can be."

Yes, people can be very ignorant. One migrant woman I have come to know is a mother of four children. She attended school for three, maybe four years, and then only "now and then." She admits to knowing very little about any number of things, though she does claim a certain kind of awareness of herself: "Yes sir, I've always had my mother with me, come the time to have the child, except for once, and then my sister, she was real good with me, yes sir. I have them real easy, and it's bad for a little while, but then something happens, and the next thing you know, the baby is crying. I bleed for a week, and I have to keep washing myself, but soon you're not doing so bad, no sir, you're not. The first time and the second time my momma tried to take me to the hospital, you know. She comes from Sylvester, Georgia, yes sir, and she never went to any hospital herself, to have us; but she said I deserved better, and she tried. She just told me when the pains started that I had to come with her, and we went to the hospital, and I got scared, but I went in, and I was shaking real bad, not because of the baby, but I thought they'd arrest us, and I'd end up having the child, my first one, in a jail.

"When we asked to see a doctor and I said I was hurting, and there'd be a baby soon, the way it looked, the nurse said who was my doctor, and my momma she said there wasn't any. Then the nurse said that was too bad, and did we have a deposit for a bed, and it was a lot, more than we ever see, and we said no, but we'd try to pay any bills we ran up, and as fast as possible. Then she shook her head, and she said it was too bad, but we should hurry on up to the other side of the county, to the county hospital, and that was where we might get in, though she wasn't sure, but her hospital, it was an all-private one, and you couldn't come there except if a doctor brought you in, or if there was the money, and only then could she call up a doctor and ask him if he could come over and take the case.

"So that's what happened, and we went back, and it was good that

I had my girl real easy-like, my momma said. The next time we tried another hospital, but it was the same thing. So, after that, we knew what to expect, yes sir. You get to know about things after a while."

She had learned something, learned a lot actually. Ignorant, barely able to write her name, never a reader, without a diploma of any kind, even one from a secondary or elementary school, she yet had figured out how certain private hospitals are run, what "criteria" they demand before a potential patient, however much in pain and in serious medical difficulty, becomes an actual patient. She needed no teacher, no social scientist to tell her the economic and political facts of life, of *her* life. I was gently reprimanded when I asked her whether she might not have been helped by a policeman or a fireman, who traditionally (so I thought from my work as a doctor in northern cities) respond to the pleas of women about to deliver babies: "You couldn't be *too* serious, I don't believe, because you must know, you must, that if we ever go near the police, or the fire people, or like that, the sheriff, then it's like asking for trouble, and a lot, too, because they'll tell you, if you pick the crops, they'll tell you to stay away, and if you go asking them for anything, then it won't be but a few seconds, and they'll have you locked up, oh will they."

She has never been locked up, nor does she believe in keeping her children locked up — watched over, carefully controlled, trained to do all sorts of things. "I lets them be," she says when asked how she spends her day with them. In point of fact, like all mothers, she constantly makes choices, or has no choice but to make a particular choice. For instance, I have watched her and other migrant mothers begin to breast-feed their children as a matter of course. For some months I assumed they naturally *had* to do so, because bottled milk is expensive, and certainly there are no physicians around to prescribe this formula and that one, and all the rest of the things American mothers of the middle class come to take for granted. Finally I began to notice how much she enjoyed suckling her child, and how long she went on doing it, and how sad, very sad she became when at a year and a half or so the time came to stop (for what reason, even then, I began to ask myself). So, I went ahead one day and made an observation: "If you had a lot of money, and could buy a lot of milk at the store, would you want to feed your small babies that way, with the bottle?"

She knew exactly what I was getting at, knew it in a sure, self-confident way that did not have to reduce itself into a barrage of nervous, anxious, wordy statements and counter-questions and explanations: "Yes sir, I know what you means. There are times when I find myself wondering if I'll ever get a chance to try one of those bottles out. I'd like to, but you have to keep going to the store then, for the milk, and then I'd run dry — and what if I started with the bottle and I couldn't buy any more milk, because there was no crops, you know, and then I'd be dry, and the baby would be suffering real bad, she would. If I had all that money, like you say, I'd try it, though. But I don't think I'd want to keep away from my baby all the time, like that, and so I don't think I'd try it for so long that I'd run dry, no sir, because I like being near to the baby. It's the best time you ever have with your child, if you ask me. That's right, it's the best time."

She holds the child firmly and fondles her lavishly as she feeds her. She makes no effort to cover her breasts, not before me or her fellow workers. Many times she has carried her infant to a field, done picking, stopped to go to the edge of the field, fed the child, left the child to itself or the care of its grandmother or older sister, and returned to the tomatoes or beans or cucumbers. Many times, too, she has reminded me that picking crops can be boring and repetitive and laborious, and so made very much more tolerable by the presence of good, clean, cool water to drink, and a good meal at lunchtime and best of all, a child to feed lying nearby. She knows that the chances are that good water and food will not be available, but an infant — yes, the presence of an infant is much more likely: "To tell the truth, I do better in the field, when I know my baby is waiting there for me, and soon I'll be able to go see her and do what I can for her. It gives you something to look ahead to."

She plans then. She plans her days around the crops and around the care of her children — she and her mother do that. Sometimes they both pick the crops, and nearby the children play, and indeed upon occasion the oldest child, nine years old, helps out not only with the younger children but the beans or tomatoes also. Sometimes the mother works on her knees, up and down the planted rows, and *her* mother stays with the children, on the edge of the farm or back in the cabin. Sometimes, too, there is no work to be had, and "we stays still and lets the children do their running about."

To my eye, migrant children begin a migrant life very, very early. By and large they are allowed rather free rein as soon as they can begin to crawl. Even before that they do not usually have cribs, and often enough they lack clothes and usually toys of any sort. Put differently, the migrant child learns right off that he has no particular possessions of his own, no place that is his to use for rest and sleep, no objects that are his to look at and touch and move about and come to recognize as familiar. He does not find out that the feet get covered with socks, the body with diapers and shirts and pants. He does not find out that there is music in the air, from mysterious boxes, nor does he wake up to find bears and bunnies at hand to touch and fondle. In sum, he does not get a sense of *his* space, *his* things, or a rhythm that is *his*. He sleeps with his mother at first, and in a few months, with his brothers and sisters. Sometimes he sleeps on a bed, sometimes on the floor, sometimes on the back seat of a car, or on the floor of a truck, and sometimes on the ground. If the locations vary, and the company, so do other things. Unlike middle-class children, the migrant child cannot assume that internal pains will soon bring some kind of relief, or that external nuisances (and worse) will be quickly done away with after a shout, a cry, a scream. One migrant mother described her own feelings of helplessness and eventually indifference in the face of such circumstances: "My children, they suffer. I know. They hurts and I can't stop it. I just have to pray that they'll stay alive, somehow. They gets the colic, and I don't know what to do. One of them, he can't breathe right and his chest, it's in trouble. I can hear the noise inside when he takes his breaths. The worst thing, if you ask me, is the bites they get. It makes them unhappy, real unhappy. They itches and scratches and bleeds, and oh, it's the worst. They must want to tear all their skin off, but you can't do that. There'd still be moquitoes and ants and rats and like that around, and they'd be after your insides then, if the skin was all gone. That's what would happen then. But I say to myself it's life, the way living is, and there's not much to do but accept what happens. Do you have a choice but to accept? That's what I'd like to ask you, yes sir. Once, when I was little, I seem to recall asking my uncle if there wasn't something you could do, but he said no, there wasn't and to hush up. So I did. Now I have to tell my kids the same, that you don't go around complaining — you just don't."

She doesn't, and a lot of mothers like her don't; and their children don't either. The infants don't cry as much as ours do; or at least the infants have learned not to cry. They are lovingly breast-fed, then put aside, for work or because there is travel to do or chores or whatever. The babies lie about and move about and crawl about, likely as not nude all day and all night. A piece of cloth may be put under them, "to catch their stuff," but not always, and in the outdoors, in the fields, usually not.

As for "their stuff," what we call "toilet training," migrant children on the whole never, never get to see a full-fledged bathroom. They never take a bath or a shower. Sometimes they see their parents use an outhouse; and sometimes they see them use the fields. The children are taught to leave a cabin or car or truck for those outhouses and fields, but the learning takes place relatively slowly and casually, at least to this observer's eye. What takes place rather more quickly has to do with the cabin itself and the car: at about the age of two the child learns he must respect both those places, though not very much else, including the immediate territory around the house — all of which can be understood by anyone who has seen the condition of some outhouses migrants are supposed to use, or the distance between the cabins migrants inhabit and those outhouses, or for that matter, a good serviceable stretch of woods.

They can be active, darting children, many migrant children; and they don't make the mistake of getting attached to a lot of places and possessions. They move around a lot, and they move together, even as they sleep together. They are not afraid to touch one another; in fact, they seek one another out, reach for one another, even seem lost without one another. They don't fight over who owns what, nor do they insist that this is mine and that belongs to someone else. They don't try to shout one another down, for the sake of their mother's attention or for any other reason. At times I have felt them as one — three or four or five or six children, brothers and sisters who feel very much joined and seem very much ready to take almost anything that might come their way. Some might say the children clutch at one another nervously. Some might say they huddle together, rather as Daumier or Käthe Kollwitz showed the poor doing. Some might say they belong to a "community," get along better than middle-class children, grow up without much of the "sibling rivalry" that plagues those more comfortable and fortunate children. Some might say they "adapt" to their lot, "cope" with the severe poverty and disorganization that goes with a migrant life. I find it very hard to say *any one* such thing. At times I see migrant children very close together, it's true, but much too quiet, much too withdrawn from the world. At times I see children together but terribly alone — because they are tired and sick, feverish and hungry, in pain but resigned to pain. Nor does that kind of observation go unnoticed by their mothers, those weary, uneducated, unsophisticated women — who have trouble with words and grammar, who are shy for a long time, then fearfully talkative, then outspoken beyond, at times, the outsider's capacity to do much but listen in confusion and sympathy and anger: "It's hard with the children, because I have to work, and so does my husband, because when the crops are there, you try to make the money you can. So I gets them to be good to one another, and watch out for each other. But a lot of the time, they're not feeling good. I know. They've just run down, the way you get, you know. They don't feel very good. There'll be a pain and something bothering them, and they all look after each other, yes they do. But it's hard, especially when they all goes and gets sick at the same time, and that happens a lot, I'll admit.

"I guess I could be better for them, if I had more to give them, more food and like that, and if I could be a better mother to them, I guess it is. But I try my best, and there's all we have to do, with the crops to work on, and we have to keep on the move, from place to place it is, you know, and there's never much left over, I'll say that, neither money nor food nor anything else. So you have to say to yourself that the little ones will take care of themselves. It's not just you; it's them, and they can be there, to wait on one another. But I'll admit, I don't believe it's the right thing, for them to be waiting on one another so much that — well, there will be sometimes when I tell their father that they're already grown up, the kids, and it's too bad they have to worry so much for each other, because that's hard on a girl of seven or eight, worrying after the little ones, and each of them, looking after the smaller one. Sometimes I think it would be better if we didn't have to keep moving, but it's what we've been doing all these years, and it's the only thing we know, and it's better than starving to death, I tell myself. So I hope and pray my kids won't have to do the same. I tell them that, and I hope they're listening!"

She tells her children a lot, as a matter of fact. She does not spoil them, let them get their way, indulge them, allow them to boss her around and get fresh with her and become loudmouthed and noisy and full of themselves. She can be very stern and very insistent with them. She doesn't really speak to them very much, explain this and that to them, go into details, offer reasons, appeal to all sorts of ideas and ideals and convictions. She doesn't coax them or persuade them or argue them down. She doesn't beat them up either, or threaten to do so. It is hard to *say* what she does, because words are shunned by her and anyway don't quite convey her sad, silent willfulness, a mixture of self-command and self-restraint; and it is hard to *describe* what she does, because whatever happens manages to happen swiftly and abruptly and without a lot of gestures and movements and steps and countersteps. There will be a word like "here" or "there" or "OK" or "now" or "it's time," and there will be an arm raised, a finger pointed, and most of all a look, a fierce look or a summoning look or a steady, knowing look — and the children stir and move and do. They come over and eat what there is to eat. They get ready to leave for the fields. They get ready to come home. They prepare to leave for yet another county, town, cabin, series of fields. They may be sad or afraid. They may be annoyed or angry. They may be troubled; but I have never seen any evidence that they are afraid of being left behind. They may be feeling good, very good — glad to be leaving or arriving. Whatever the mood and occasion, they have learned to take their cues from their mother, and one another, and hurry on. I suppose I am saying that they tend to be rather obedient — out of fear, out of hunger, out of love, it is hard to separate the reasons, the reasons for the obedience or the reasons we also learn to be compliant. I hear just that from the owners of farms and the foremen who manage them — that migrant children are "a pretty good bunch." Well, if the people who employ migrants by the thousands find them "lazy" or "careless" or "shiftless" or "irresponsible" or "ignorant" or "wild" or "animallike," then how is it that their children manage so well, even earn a bit of praise and respect here and there? "I know what you mean," the owner of a very large farm in central Florida says in initial response to the essence of that question. Then he pauses for a minute and struggles with the irony and finally seems to have his answer to it, which is a very good half question indeed: "Well, I don't know, you take children anywhere, and they're not what their parents are, are they?" Then he amplifies: "Sometimes they're better than their parents and sometimes they're worse. You'll find good parents and bad kids and vice versa. As for these migrants, if you ask me, it's the parents who have never amounted to much and maybe they try to do better with their kids, though they're certainly not very ambitious, those parents, so I don't think they push their kids to be successful, the way we might. Maybe it's just they're good and strict with their kids, and if that's the way they treat them, then the kids learn to behave. Of course, they can't really spoil their kids, I'll admit. They don't have much to spoil them with; and what they have, they tend to be wasteful about, you know."

Life is, as the man said, lean and bare for migrant farm workers, and their children find that out rather quickly. Hunger pangs don't always become appeased, however loud and long the child cries. Pain persists, injuries go unattended. The heat does not get cooled down by air conditioners or even fans, and cold air is not warmed by radiators. Always there is the next town, the next county, the next state, and at every stop those cabins — almost windowless, unadorned and undecorated, full of cracks, nearly empty, there as the merest of shelters, there to be left all too soon, something that both parents and children know.

How does such knowledge come alive — that is, get turned into the ways parents treat children, the ways children act, behave, think, get along, grow up? How consciously does a migrant mother transmit her fears to her children, or her weariness, or her sense of exhaustion and defeat, or her raging disappointment that life somehow cannot be better — for her and for the children who confront her every day with requests, questions, demands, or perhaps only their forlorn and all too hushed and restrained presence? I have watched these mothers "interact" with their children, "rear" them, demonstrate this or that "attitude" toward them or "pattern of behavior." Always I have wondered what is *really* going on, what unspoken assumptions work their way continually into acts, deeds, and even occasionally into words — some of them surprisingly and embarrassingly eloquent, to the point that what is revealed has to do not only with their assumptions, but mine, too. For instance, I had known one migrant farm worker, a mother of seven children, a black lady from Arkansas, two years before I finally asked her what she hopes for her children as she brings them up. She smiled, appeared not at all brought up short or puzzled or annoyed. She did hesitate for a few seconds, then began to talk as she glanced at the hot plate in the cabin: "Well, I hope each one of them, my three girls and four boys, each one of them has a hot plate like that one over there, and some food to put on it, and I mean every day. I'd like them to know that wherever they go, there'll be food and the hot plate to cook it. When I was their age, there wasn't those hot plates, and most of the places, they didn't have electricity in them, no sir. We'd travel from one place to the next, picking, taking in the crops, and there'd be a cabin — a lot of the times they'd make the chicken coops bigger to hold us — and the bossman, he'd give you your food, and charge you so much for it that you'd be lucky if you didn't owe him money after a day's work. There'd be hash and hash, and the potatoes, and bread, and I guess that's all, except for the soda pop. There'd be nothing to start the day with, but around the middle they'd come to give you something and at the end, too. A lot of the time we'd get sick from what they'd bring, but you had to keep on picking away or they'd stop feeding you altogether, and then you'd starve to death, and my daddy, he'd say that it's better to eat bad food than no food at all, yes sir. Now no one can deny that, I do believe.

"But now it's changed for the better, the last ten years, I guess, it has. They've put the electricity into some of the cabins — no, not all, but a lot — and they've stopped giving you the food, in return for the deductions. You can get a meal ticket, and keep on eating that way, and they'll give you a sandwich and pop for lunch for a dollar or more, sometimes two, but there's no obligation, and if you save up the money you can get a hot plate and cook your own, and carry the plate up North and back down here and all over the state of Florida, yes sir. And it's better for the children, I think, my cooking. It's much, much better.

"Now, I'd like them to amount to something, my children. I don't know what, but something that would help them to settle down and stop the moving, stop it for good. It's hard, though. They gets used to it, and when I tell them they should one day plan to stop, and find work someplace, in a city or someplace like that — well, then, they'll say that they like the trips we take to here and there and everywhere, and why can't they keep going, like we do. So, I try to tell them that I don't mean they should leave me, and I should leave them, but that maybe one day, when they're real big, and I'm too old to get down on my knees and pick those beans, maybe one day they'll be able to stop, stop and never start again — oh, would that be good for all of us, a home we'd never, never leave.

"You know, when they're real small, it's hard, because as soon as they start talking, they'll want to know why we have to go, and why can't we stay, and why, why, why. *Then* they'd be happy if I didn't get them in the car to move on. But later, I'd say by the time they're maybe five or six, like that, they've got the bug in them; they've got used to moving on, and you can't tell them no, that someday if God is good to us, we'll be able to stop and stay stopped for good. You see, I do believe that a child can get in the traveling habit, and he'll never stop himself and try to get out of it. That's what worries me, I'll admit. I'll hear my oldest one, he's eleven, talk, and he says he thinks he can pick a lot faster than me or anyone else, and he'll one day go farther North than we do, and he'll make more money out of it, and I think to myself that there's nothing I can do but let him do it, and hope one of us, one of the girls maybe, if she meets a good man, will find a home, a real home, and live in it and never leave it.

"We tried three times, you know. My husband and me, we tried to stay there in Arkansas and work on his place, the bossman's, and we couldn't, because he said we were to stay if we liked, but he couldn't pay us nothing from now on, because of the machinery he'd bought himself. Then we tried Little Rock, and there wasn't a job you could find, and people said go North, but my sister went to Chicago and died there, a year after she came. They said she had bad blood and her lungs were all no good, and maybe it was the city that killed her, my Uncle James said. So, we decided we'd just stay away from there, the city, and then the man came through, from one of the big farms down here, and he said we could make money, big money, if we just went along with him and went down to Florida and worked on the crops, just the way we always did, and that seemed like a good idea, so we did. And with the kids, one after the other, and with needing to have someplace to stay and some food and money, we've been moving along ever since, and it's been a lot of moving, I'll say that, and I wish one day we'd find there was nothing for us to do but stop, except that if we did, there might not be much food for that hot plate, that's what worries me, and I'll tell you, it's what my boy will say and my girl — they tell me that if we didn't keep on picking the crops, well then we'd have nothing to eat, and that wouldn't be worth it, sitting around and going hungry all the time. And I agree with them on that.

"So, we keep going, yes sir, we do. I try to keep everyone in good shape, the best I can. I tell them that it'll be nice, where we're going to, and there will be a lot to see on the road, and there's no telling what kind of harvest there will be, but we might make a lot of money if there's a real good one. I don't believe I should hold out those promises, though — because they believe you, the kids, I know that now, and it just makes them good, happy children, moving along with you, and helping you with the crops. They do a lot, and I'd rather they could be working at something else, later, like I said before, but I doubt they will."

Her children, like others I have seen and like those already described, are in a sense little wanderers from the very start. They are allowed to roam cabins, roam fields, roam along the side of the road, into thickets and bushes and trees. They follow one another around, even as their parents follow the crops, follow the sun, follow the roads. Nor does all that go unnoticed, except by the likes of me: "I lets them have the run of the place, because we'll soon be gone, and they might as well have all the fun they can. They want to go with us and help us with the picking, and they do sometimes, and they learn how to pick themselves, and that's what they say they'll be doing when they get big and grown up, and one will say I'll cut the most celery, and one will say I'll pick more beans than you, and one will say tomatoes are for me, and soon they've got all the crops divided up for themselves, and my husband and me, we say that if the life was better then we wouldn't mind, but you know it's a real hard life, going on the road, and we don't know what to do, whether to tell them, the kids, that it's a bad time they have in store for themselves — and you don't have the heart to do that, say that — or tell them to go ahead and plan on the picking, the harvesting, and tell them it'll be good, just like you kids think. Except that my husband and I, we know it's just not true that it's good. So there it is, we're not telling them the truth, that's a fact."

She does tell them the truth, of course. She tells them that life is hard, unpredictable, uncertain, never to be taken for granted, and in fact rather dangerous. She tells them whom to fear: policemen, firemen, sheriffs, people who wear business shirts, people who are called owners or bossmen or foremen or managers. She tells them that no, the rest rooms in the gas stations are not to be used; better the fields or the woods. She tells them to watch out, watch out for just about anyone who is not a picker, a harvester, a farmhand, a migrant worker. She tells them why they can't stop here, or go there, or enter this place or try that one's food. She tells them why sometimes, when they are driving North with others in other cars, the state police meet them at the state line and warn them to move, move fast, move without stopping, move on side roads, move preferably by night. She tells them that no, there aren't any second helpings; no, we don't dress the way those people do, walking on that sidewalk; no, we can't live in a house like that; no, we can't live in any one house, period; no, we can't stay, however nice it is here, however much you want to stay, however much it would help everyone if we did; and no, there isn't much we can do, to stop the pain, or make things more comfortable or give life a little softness, a little excitement, a little humor and richness.

Still, the children find that excitement or humor, if not softness and richness; to the surprise of their parents they make do, they improvise, they make the best of a bad lot and do things — with sticks and stones, with cattails, with leaves, with a few of the vegetables their parents pick, with mud and sand and wild flowers. They build the only world they can, not with blocks and wagons and cars and balloons and railroad tracks, but with the earth, the earth whose products their parents harvest, the earth whose products become, for those particular children, toys, weapons, things of a moment's joy. "They have their good times, I know that," says a mother, "and sometimes I say to myself that if only it could last forever; but it can't, I know. Soon they'll be on their knees like me, and it won't be fun no more, no it won't."

The "soon" that she mentioned is not figured out in years, months, or weeks. In fact, migrant children learn to live by the sun and the moon, by day and by night, by a rhythm that has little to do with days and hours and minutes and seconds. There are no clocks around, nor calendars. Today is not this day, of this month, nor do the years get mentioned. The child does not hear that it is so-and-so time — time to do one or another thing. Even Sundays seem to come naturally, as if from Heaven; and during the height of the harvest season they, too, go unobserved. As a matter of fact, the arrival of Sunday, its recognition and its observance, can be a striking thing to see and hear: "I never know what day it is — what difference does it make? — but it gets in my bones that it's Sunday. Well, to be honest, we let each other know, and there's the minister, he's the one who keeps his eye on the days, and waits until the day before Sunday, and then he'll go and let one of us know, that tomorrow we should try to stop, even if it's just for a few hours, and pray and ask God to smile down on us and make it better for us, later on up there, if not down here. Then, you know, we talk to one another, and the word passes along, yes it does. I'll be pulling my haul of beans toward the end of the row, to store them, and someone will come to me and say, tomorrow is Sunday, and the reverend, he said we should all be there first thing in the morning, and if we do, then we can be through in time to go to the fields. Now, a lot of the time there's nothing to do in the fields, and then it's a different thing, yes it is; because then we can look forward to Sunday, and know it's going to be a full day, whether in the church, or if the minister comes here, to this camp, and we meets outside and he talks to us and we sing — and afterwards you feel better."

Does she actually forget the days, or not know them, by name or number or whatever? No, she "kind of keeps track" and "yes, I know if it's around Monday or Tuesday, or if it's getting to be Saturday." She went to school, on and off, for three or four years, and she is proud that she knows how to sign her name, though she hasn't done it often, and she is ashamed to do it when anyone is watching. Yet, for her children she wants a different kind of education, even as she doubts that her desires will be fulfilled: "I'd like them all, my five kids, to learn everything there is to be learned in the world. I'd like for them to read books and to write as much as they can, and to count way up to the big numbers. I'd like for them to finish with their schooling. I tell them that the only way they'll ever do better than us, their daddy and me, is to get all the learning they can. But it's hard, you know, it's very hard, because we have to keep going along — there's always a farm up the road that needs some picking, and right away; and if we stay still, we'll soon have none of us, because there won't be a thing to eat, and we'll just go down and down until we're all bones and no flesh — that's what my daddy used to tell me might happen to us one day, and that's what I have to tell my kids, too. Then, they'll ask you why is it that the other kids, they just stay and stay and never move, and why is it that we have to move, and I don't hardly know what to say, then, so I tells them that they mustn't ask those questions, because there's no answer to them, and then the kids, they'll soon be laughing, and they'll come over and tell me that they're real glad that we were going up the road, and to the next place, because they got to see everything in the world, and those other kids — well, they're just stuck there in the same old place."

Space, time, and movement, to become conceptual, mean very special things to a migrant child, and so does food, which can never be taken for granted. Many of the children I have studied these past years — in various parts of Florida and all along the eastern seaboard — view life as a constant series of trips, undertaken rather desperately in a seemingly endless expanse of time. Those same children are both active and fearful, full of initiative and desperately forlorn, driven to a wide range of ingenious and resourceful deeds and terribly paralyzed by all sorts of things: the weakness and lethargy that go with hunger and malnutrition, and the sadness and hopelessness that I suppose can be called part of their "preschool education." Indeed the ironies mount the more time one spends with the children, the more one sees them take care of one another, pick crops fast, go fetch water and food at the age of two or three *and* know what size coins or how many dollar bills must be brought back home, talk about the police, listen to a car engine and comment on its strengths or weaknesses, discuss the advantages and disadvantages of harvesting various crops, speak about the way property owners profit from the high rents they charge for their cabins. At the same time, of course, those same children can be observed in different moods, heard making other statements — about how tired they are, about how foolish it is to spend a week in school here and another few days there, and then a couple of weeks "up yonder," about how difficult it is to make sense of people and places and customs and attitudes, about life itself, and yes, about how human beings on this planet treat one another. One of the mothers I came to know best over a period of three years let me know exactly what her children thought and said about such matters. "They'll ask you something sometimes, and you don't know how to answer them. I scratch my head and try to figure out what to say, but I can't. Then I'll ask someone, and there's no good answer that anyone has for you. I mean, if my child looks right up at me and says he thinks we live a bad life, and he thinks just about every other child in the country is doing better than he is — I mean, has a better life — then I don't know what to say, except that we're hardworking, and we do what we can, and it's true we're not doing too well, that I admit. Then my girl, she's very smart, and she'll tell me that sometimes she'll be riding along with us, there in the back seat, and she'll see those houses we pass, and the kids playing, and she'll feel like crying, because we don't have a house to stay in, and we're always going from one place to another, and we don't live so good, compared to others. But I try to tell her that God isn't going to let everything be like it is, and someday the real poor people, they'll be a lot better off, and anyway, there's no point to feeling sorry for yourself, because you can't change things, no you can't, and all you can do is say to yourself that it's true, that we've got a long, hard row to hoe, and the Lord sometimes seems to have other, more important things to do, than look after us, but you have to keep going, or else you want to go and die by the side of the road, and someday that will happen, too, but there's no point in making it happen sooner rather than later — that's what I think, and that's what I tell my girls and my boys, yes sir I do.

"Now, they'll come back at me, oh do they, with first one question and then another, until I don't know what to say, and I tell them to stop. Sometimes I have to hit them, yes sir, I'll admit it. They'll be asking about why, why, why, and I don't have the answers and I'm tired out, and I figure sooner or later they'll have to stop asking and just be glad they're alive. Once I told my girl that, and then she said we *wasn't* alive, and we was dead, and I thought she was trying to be funny, but she wasn't, and she started crying. Then I told her she was being foolish, and of course we're alive, and she said that all we do is move and move, and most of the time she's not sure where we're going to be, and if there'll be enough to eat. That's true, but you're still alive, I said to her, and so am I, and I'm older than you by a long time, and why don't you have faith in God, and maybe do good in your learning, in those schools, and then maybe you could get yourself a home someday, and stay in it, and you'd be a lot better off, I know it, and I wish we all of us could — I mean, could have a home."

The mother mentions schools, not *a* school, not two or three, but "*those* schools." She knows that her children have attended school, at various times, in Florida, Virginia, Delaware, New York, New Jersey, and Connecticut. She may not list those states very easily or confidently, but she knows they exist, and she knows she visits them, among others, every year, and she knows that upon occasion her daughter and her sons have gone to elementary schools in those states, and stayed in those schools maybe a few weeks, maybe only a few days, then moved on — to another school, or to no school "for a while," even though during the period of time called "for a while" other children all over the country are at school. What happens to her children in "those schools"? What do they expect to learn when they arrive? What do they actually learn, and how long do they actually stay in school? Rather obviously, migrant children spend relatively little time in classrooms, in comparison to other American children, and learn very little while there. During the two years I worked most closely and methodically with migrant families who belong to the "eastern stream," I had occasion to check on the children's school attendance for ten families. I found that each child put in, on the average, about a week and a half of school, that is, eight days, during the month. Often the children had colds, stomachaches, asthma, skin infections and anemia, and so had to stay home "to rest." Often the children lacked clothes, and so had to await their "turn" to put on the shoes and socks and pants or dresses that were, in fact, shared by, say, three or four children. Often the parents had no real confidence in the value of education, at least the kind they knew their children had to get, in view of the nature of the migrant life, and in view, for that matter, of the demands put upon the migrant farmer who lives that kind of life. Nor did the children usually feel that what they had already learned — rather a lot, if outside the schools — ought to be forsaken in favor of the values and standards and habits encouraged within schools often enough attended, at best, on the sufferance of the teachers and the other children.

Rather obviously, migrancy makes regular school attendance, even if very much desired by a particular set of parents for their children, next to impossible. The most ambitious and articulate migrant farmer I have ever met, a black man originally from northern Louisiana, describes all too precisely the dilemma he must face as a parent, a worker, an American citizen: "You don't realize how hard it is, trying to make sure your kids get a little learning, just a little. I don't expect my oldest boy — he's named after me — to go on and finish school. The little schooling he'll get, it's no good, because he's been in and out of so many of them, the schools, and he gets confused, and it's no good. You'll go from one state to the next, and sometimes the school will remember Peter, and they'll try to pick right up with him, where he left off, and give him special teaching, so he doesn't lose all his time just finding out what's going on, and where the other kids are. But, in a lot of schools, they don't seem even to want you, your kids. They'll give you and them those sour looks when you come in, and they'll act toward you as if you're dirty — you know what I mean? — as if, well, as if you're just no good, and that's that. My boy, he sees it, just like me, even if he's only nine, he does. I try to tell him not to pay attention, but he knows, and he tries to be as quiet and good as he can, but I can see him getting upset, only hiding it, and I don't know what to say. So I just try to make the best of it, and tell him that no matter what, even if it's a little bit here and a little bit there, he's got to learn how to read and how to write and how to know what's happening, not just to himself, but to everyone in the world, wherever they all are. But the boy is right clever, and he says, Daddy, you're not talking the truth at all, no sir; and it don't make any difference, he says, if you get your schooling, because the people who don't want you in school, and don't pay you any attention there, and only smile when you tell them you're sorry, but you won't be there come next week, because you've got to move on with your family — well, those people will be everywhere, no matter where you want to go, and what you want to do, so there's no getting away from them and why even try, if you know you're not going to win much."

Yet his son Peter does try, and his failure to get a decent education, an even halfway adequate one, tells us, if nothing else, that earnestness and persistence, even on the part of a rather bright child, can only go so far. Peter has always been the quietest of his parents' children, the most anxious to learn things and do things and question things. His younger brothers and sisters tend to be more active, less curious, more impulsive, less contemplative. From the very start Peter wanted to attend school, and worked hard while there. His efforts caught the attention of several teachers, one in Florida and one in Virginia. He has always asked why and indeed proposed answers to his own questions — all of which can annoy his parents, and apparently his teachers, too, upon occasion. I have spent an unusually long period of time with Peter, not only because he and his family have had a lot to teach me, but because sometimes the exceptional child (perhaps like the very sick patient) can demonstrate rather dramatically what others also go through or experience or endure more tamely and less ostentatiously but no less convincingly.

It so happens that I knew Peter before he went to school, and talked with him many times after he had spent a day "in the big room," which is what he often called his classroom when he was six or seven years old. To a boy like Peter a school building, even an old and not very attractively furnished one, is a new world — of large windows and solid floor and doors and plastered ceilings and walls with pictures on them, and a seat that one has, that one is given, that one is supposed to own, or virtually own, for day after day, almost as a right of some sort. After his first week in the first grade Peter said this: "They told me I could sit in that chair and they said the desk, it was for me, and that every day I should come to the same place, to the chair she said was mine for as long as I'm there, in that school — that's what they say, the teachers, anyway."

So, they told him he could not only sit someplace, but he could have something — for himself; and they told him that the next day he would continue to have what was formerly (the previous day) had — and indeed the same would go for the next day after that, until there were no more days to be spent at the school. I believe Peter's remarks indicated he was not quite sure that what he heard would actually and reliably take place. I believe Peter wondered how he could possibly find himself in possession of something and keep it day after day. Peter and I talked at great length about that school, and by bringing together his various remarks made over many weeks, it is possible to sense a little of what school meant to him, a little of what that abstraction "life" meant (and continually means) to him: "I was pretty scared, going in there. I never saw such a big door. I was scared I couldn't open it, and then I was scared I wouldn't be able to get out, because maybe the second time it would be too hard. The teacher, she kept on pulling the things up and down over the windows — yes, a kid told me they're 'blinds,' and they have them to let the sun in and keep the sun out. A lot of the time the teacher would try to help us out. She'd want to know if anyone had anything to ask, or what we wanted to do next. But she seemed to know what she was going to do, and I'd just wait and hope she didn't catch me not knowing the answer to one of her questions. She said to me that I had to pay attention, even if I wasn't going to be there for very long, and I said I would, and I've tried to do the best I can, and I've tried to be as good as I can. She asked me as I was leaving the other day if I would be staying long, and I said I didn't know, and she said I should ask my daddy, and he'd know, but when I did, he said he didn't know, and it all depended on the crops and what the crew man said, because he's the one who takes us to the farms. Then I told the teacher that, and she said yes, she knew what it was like, but that I should forget I'm anywhere else while I'm in school and get the most I can learned.

"I try to remember everything she says, the teacher. She's real smart, and dresses good, a different dress every day, I think. She told us we should watch how we wear our clothes, and try to wash ourselves every day and use brushes on our teeth and eat all these different things on the chart she has. I told my momma, and she said yes, what the teacher says is correct, yes it is, but you can't always go along, because there's no time, what with work and like that, if you haven't got the shower, you can't take it, and maybe someday it will be different. I asked her if we could get some chairs, like in school, and we could carry them where we go, and they'd be better than now, because you sit on the floor where we're staying, and the teacher said a good chair helps your back grow up straight, if you know how to sit in it right. But there's not the money, my daddy said, and it's hard enough *us* moving, never mind a lot of furniture, he said. When I get big, I'll find a chair that's good — but it can fold up. The teacher said you can fold up a lot of things and just carry them with you, so there's no excuse for us not having a lot of things, even if we're moving a lot, that's what she said, and one of the kids, he said his father was a salesman and traveled all over the country — and he said, the kid, that his father had a suitcase full of things you could fold up and unfold and they were all very light and you could hold the suitcase up with one finger if you wanted, that's how light. My daddy said it wasn't the same, the traveling we do, and going around selling a lot of things. He said you could make big money that way, but you couldn't do it unless you were a big shot in the first place, and with us, it's no use but to do what you know to do, and try to get by the best you can, and that's very hard, he says.

"I like going into the school, because it's really, really nice in there, and you can be sure no bugs will be biting you, and the sun doesn't make you too hot, and they have the water that's really cold and it tastes good. They'll give you cookies and milk, and it's a lot of fun sitting on your chair and talking with the other kids. One boy wanted to know why I was going soon — I told him the other day, and he thought I was trying to fool him, I think — and I said I didn't know why, but I had to go because my daddy picks the crops and we moves along, and we have to. The boy, he thought I was trying to be funny, that's what he said first, and then the next time he came over and he said that he'd talked with his daddy and the daddy said that there was a lot of us, the migrant people, and it was true that we're in one city and out, and on to the next, and so I had to go, it's true, if that's what my daddy does. Then he said, the boy said, that his daddy told him to stay clear of me, because I might be carrying a lot of sickness around, and dirt, and like that; but he said, his name is Jimmy, he said I was OK and he wasn't going to tell his father, but we should be friends in the yard during the playtime, and besides he heard his mother say it was too bad everyone didn't have a home and stay there from when he's born until he's all grown up, and then it would be better for everyone.

"I thought I might never see Jimmy again, or the school either, when we drove away, but I thought I might get to see another school, and my momma said that Jimmy wasn't the only boy in the world, and there'd be plenty like him up North, and they might even be better to us up there while we're there, though she wasn't too sure. Then I was getting ready to say we shouldn't go at all, and my daddy told me to shut up, because it's hard enough to keep going without us talking about this friend and the school and the teacher and how we want to stay; so he said if I said another word I'd soon be sorry, and I didn't. Then I forgot — we were way up there, a long way from Florida, I think, and I said something Jimmy said, and they told me I'd better watch out, so I stopped and just looked out the window, and that's when I thought it would be good, like Jimmy said his mother said, if one day we stopped and we never, never went up the road again to the next farm, and after that, the next one, until you can't remember if you're going to leave or you've just come.

"That's what my momma will say sometimes, that she just can't remember, and she'll ask us, and we're not always a help, because we'll just be going along, and not knowing why they want to leave and then stop, because it seems they could just stop and never leave, and maybe someone could find them a job where they'd never have to leave, and maybe then I could stay in the same school and I'd make a lot of friends and I'd keep them until when I was grown up. Then I'd have the friends and I wouldn't always be moving, because they'd help me, and that's what it means to be a friend, the teacher said, and Jimmy told me that if I'd be staying around, he'd ask his mother if I could come over, and he thought that if I came during the day, and his father wasn't home, then it would be all right, because his mother says she's in favor of helping us out, my people, Jimmy says, and she said if she

had the money she'd buy houses for all of us, and she said there must
be a way we could stay in one place, but Jimmy said he told her what
I said: if we don't keep moving, we don't eat. That's what my daddy
says, and I told Jimmy. It's all right to go to school, my daddy says, but
they won't feed you in school, and they won't give you a place to sleep,
so first you have to stay alive, and then comes school. Jimmy said my
daddy was right, but he was making a mistake, too — because his
daddy says that if you don't finish school, you'll have nothing to do
and you'll starve to death, so it's best to go to school and learn whatever the teacher says, even if you don't like to."

Peter has come to know several Jimmys in his short life, and he
has left several schools reluctantly, sadly, even bitterly. On the other
hand, he has also been glad to leave many schools. He feels he has
been ignored or scorned. He feels different from other schoolchildren —
and has felt that one or another teacher emphasizes those differences,
makes them explicit, speaks them out, and in a way makes him feel
thoroughly unwanted. I knew him long enough and followed his family's travels far enough to get a fairly quick response from him after his
first day in a particular school. The experience invariably would either
be good or bad, or so Peter judged. He would talk about what he saw
and felt, and in so doing reveal himself to be, I thought, remarkably
intuitive and perceptive. Yet, he insisted to me on numerous occasions
that what he noticed other migrant children also notice, and no less
rapidly than he. "I'm a big talker" he told me after one of our "big
talks." His younger brother, Tom, would see the same things, though,
when he went to school; he might not put what he sees into words, or
even be fully aware of what he senses happening, but he would know
it all, know the hurt and loneliness and isolation and sadness, know it
all in the bones, in the heart, in the back of his mind — wherever such
knowledge is stored by human beings. So Peter believed, or so I believe he believed, on the basis of his observations and remarks and
complaints and questions, all shared with me during the two years we
conversed — in Florida and North Carolina and Virginia and upstate
New York, each of which claims to offer children like Peter what every
American child presumably is entitled to as a birthright, a free public
education: "I always am a *little* scared when I try a new school, yes;
but I try to remember that I won't be there long, and if it's no good, I'm
not stuck there, like the kids who live there. We'll come in and they'll
tell you you're special, and they'll do what they can to make you good,
to clean you up, they'll say, and to give you better habits, they'll say. I
don't like those kinds of teachers and schools that they're in.

"Yes, I met one today. She wasn't worse than the last one, but she wasn't better, either. We could tell. She started in with what we had on, and how we could at least clean our shoes, even if they weren't good, and all that; and I said in my mind that I wish I was outside, fishing maybe, or doing anything but listening to her. Then I recalled my daddy saying it would only be two or three weeks, so I didn't get bothered, no. She asked me my name, and I told her, and she asked me where I was from, and I told her, and she asked me what I was going to school for, and I told her — that it was because I *had* to — and she smiled. (I think it was because I said what she was thinking, and she was glad, so she smiled.) I told myself later that if I'd gone and told her that I was there at school because I wanted to be a teacher, like her, or even the principal, then she'd have come after me with the ruler or the pointer she has in her hand all the time. Well, I figure we'll get a good rest there, and the chairs are good, and they give you the milk and cookies, and my momma says that's worth the whole day, regardless of what they say, but I think she's wrong, real wrong.

"To me a good school is one where the teacher is friendly, and she wants to be on your side, and she'll ask you to tell the other kids some of the things you can do, and all you've done — you know, about the crops, and like that. There was one teacher like that, and I think it was up North, in New York it was. She said that so long as we were there in the class she was going to ask everyone to join us, that's what she said, and we could teach the other kids what we know and they could do the same with us. She showed the class where we traveled, on the map, and I told my daddy that I never before knew how far we went each year, and he said he couldn't understand why I didn't know, because I did the traveling all right, with him, and so I should know. But when you look on the map, and hear the other kids say they've never been that far, and they wish someday they could, then you think you've done something good, too — and they'll tell you in the recess that they've only seen where they live and we've been all over. I told my daddy what they said, and he said it sure was true, that we've been all over, and he hopes the day will come when we'll be in one place, but he sure doubts it, and if I wanted I could tell the teacher he said so — but I didn't. I don't think she'd know how to answer Daddy, except to say she's sorry, and she's already told us that, yes she did, right before the whole class. She said we had a hard life, that's what, the people who do the picking of the crops, and she wanted us to know that she was on our side, and she wanted to help us learn all we could, because it would be better for us later, the more we knew, and maybe most of us would find a job and keep it, and there'd be no more people following the crops all over, from place to place, and it would be better for America, she said. Then she asked if I agreed, and I didn't say one way or the other, and she asked me to just say what I thought, and I did. I said I'd been doing enough of traveling, and I'd seen a lot of places, and I wouldn't mind stopping for a change, no ma'am, and if we just stayed there, in that town, and I could go to school there — well, that would be all right by me, and it would be better than some of the other places we stop, I could say that right off, a real lot better.

"There'll be times when I wish I'd have been born one of the other kids, yes sir; that's how I sometimes think, yes. Mostly, it's when the teacher is good to you — then you think you'd like to stay. If the teacher is bad, and the kids don't speak to you, then you want to go away and never come back, and you're glad that you won't stay there too long. Now school is good, because it's a good school and they pays attention to you; most of the time though, in other schools, you just sit there, and you want to sleep. Suddenly the teacher will ask you what you're thinking, and you tell her the truth, that you don't know. Then she'll ask you what you want to be, and I don't know what to answer, so I say I'd like to work like my daddy at the crops, and maybe one day get a job in the city, and stay there. Then they'll tell you to study hard, the teachers, but they don't give you much to do, and they'll keep on asking you how the crops are coming, and how long you'll be there, and when are you going to be going, and like that. Sometimes I won't go to school. I tell my momma that I'm not going and can I help take care of my brothers and can I help in the field, or anything, and she'll say yes, mostly, unless she thinks the police will be getting after me, for not being in school — but most of the time they don't care, and they'll tell you you're doing good to be caring for your brother and working. Yes sir, they'll drive by and wave and they don't seem to mind if you're not in school. Once a policeman asked me if I liked school and I said sometimes I did and then he said I was wasting my time there, because you don't need a lot of reading and writing to pick the crops, and if you get too much of schooling, he said, you start getting too big for your shoes, and cause a lot of trouble, and then you'll end up in jail pretty fast and never get out if you don't watch your step — never get out."

Peter seeks consolation from such a future; and he often finds it by looking back to earlier years and occasions. In his own brief life as a young child, a young migrant, a young boy of, say, eight or nine or ten, he has begun to find that the one possession he has and cannot

lose is yesterday, the old days, the experiences that have gone but remain — and remain not only in the mind's memories and dreams, but
in the lives of others, those brothers or sisters who are younger and
who present a child like Peter with themselves, which means all the
things they do that remind Peter of what he once did and indeed can
continue to do as the older brother becomes a companion of younger
children. I found myself concluding and in my notes emphasizing all
of that, Peter's tendency to *go back,* to flee the present for the sake of
the past. After all, I had to repeat to myself again and again, Peter finds
school useless or worse. He finds his parents tired and distracted or
worse. He finds himself at loose ends: I am a child, yet today I can
work, tomorrow I may be told I'm to attend school, the next day I'll be
on the road again and unsure where I shall soon be, when I shall again
be still for a while — sitting on the ground, that is, or in a cabin,
rather than upon the seat of a car or a bus. In the face of such uncer-
tainties, earlier moments and ways and feelings become things (if such
is the word) to be tenaciously grasped and held. And so, Peter will
help pick beans, and do a very good job at moving up and down the
rows, but soon thereafter be playing on his hands and knees with his
younger brothers, and sucking lollipops with them and lying under a
tree and crawling about and laughing with them. His mother in her
own way takes note of what happens, and needs no prodding from any
observer to describe the sequence of events: "I think stooping for
those beans can go to your head. You get dizzy after a day of it, and
you want to go down on your back and stretch yourself all you can
and try to feel like yourself again, and not all curled up on yourself. If
Peter goes along with his daddy and me and does the stooping and
picking, then he'll be real tired at the end of the day, and it seems he
wants to be like my little ones — and I say to myself if it'll help him
feel any better, after all that work, then Lord he can do what he likes,
and if I had it in me to keep them all little babies, then I'd do it, because that's when they're truly happiest, yes sir."

Yet, it turns out that her children and thousands of other migrant
children are not very happy for very long; actually, many of those children have a hard time understanding the many contradictions that
plague their lives. For one thing, as already indicated, migrant children of two or three are allowed, in some respects, a good deal of active, assertive freedom. They are encouraged to care for one another,
but also encouraged to fend for themselves — go exploring in the
woods or the fields, play games almost anywhere and anytime, feel
easy and relaxed about time, about schedules, about places where

things are done and routines that give order to the doing of those things. Again and again I have seen migrant children leave their cabins for the day and return anytime, when and if they pleased — to get themselves a bottle of pop and make for themselves a meal of "luncheon meat" and bread and potato chips, or often enough, potato chips and potato salad and Coke, period. At the same time, however, those very children are also taught obedience and a real and powerful kind of fatalism: one can only go here, do that, and most of all, submit to the rigors and demands and confusion and sadness of travel — always the travel, inevitably the travel, endlessly the travel, all of which can amount to a rather inert and compliant and passive life. Put differently, the child is told the grim facts of his particular life, but also given dozens of stories and excuses and explanations and promises whose collective function, quite naturally and humanly, is to blunt the awful, painful edges of that very life. It can even be said that migrant children obtain and learn to live with an almost uncanny mixture of realism and mysticism. It is as if they must discover how difficult their years will be, but also acquire certain places of psychological and spiritual refuge. Naturally, each family has its own particular mixture of sentiment and hard facts to offer and emphasize, even as each child makes for himself his very own nature; he becomes a blend of the assertive and the quiet, the forceful and the subdued, the utterly realistic and the strangely fanciful. What I am saying, of course, goes for all children, but at the same time I must insist that migrant children have a very special psychological fate — and one that is unusually hard for them to endure.

For example, I mentioned earlier that migrant children tend to be close to one another, tend to care very much for one another, tend almost to absorb themselves in one another, and certainly — the first observation one like me makes when he comes to know them — tend to touch one another, constantly and reassuringly and unselfconsciously and most of the time rather tenderly. At the same time those same children, so literally touching to each other, can appear more and more untouched — indifferent, tired, bored, listless, apathetic, and finally, most ironically, isolated physically as well as psychologically. Many of them, unlike the boy Peter, just discussed, abandon themselves to a private world that is very hard for any outsiders to comprehend, even a mother or father. School means nothing, is often forsaken completely, even the pretense of going. Friends are an affair of the moment, to be forsaken and lost amid all the disorder and turmoil and instability that goes with one move after another. Sports, or-

ganized and progressively challenging sports, are unknown. Needless
to say, the migrant child does not go to restaurants, theaters, movies,
museums, zoos, and concerts; nor do those television sets he watches
work very well; they are old and half broken to start with, purchased
secondhand (with a bit of luck) on a never-ending installment basis,
and in addition, as Peter's mother puts it, "way out in the country you
can't pick up the pictures," particularly when there is no antenna, and
the set has been bouncing around for miles and miles, as indeed have
its owners.

It is hard to convey such experiences, such a world, to those who
don't see it and feel it and smell it and hear it. It is even harder to describe that world as it is met and apprehended and suffered by hundreds of thousands of parents and children. I say this not as a
preliminary exercise in self-congratulation — what is hard is being
done and therefore deserves admiration — but to warn myself and the
reader alike, particularly at this point, against the temptation of psychological categorization, the temptation to say that migrant children
are this or that, are "active" or "passive," resort to excessive "denial"
and too many "rationalizations" and "projections" or resort to an almost brutal kind of realism, a kind of self-confrontation so devoid of
humor and guile and hope and patience as to be a caricature of the
analysis the rest of us value, be it psychological or political or philosophical. I am saying that migrant children are many things, and do
many things with their brief and relatively sad lives. They can be ingenious and foolish. They can have all sorts of illusions, and they can
speak about themselves with almost unbearable candor and severity
and gloom. They can feel disgusted with their lot, or they can pay no
attention to it, simply endure what has to be; or they can romp and
laugh and shout, even though their observer knows how close to the
surface are the tears (and fears) and how overworked even the fun
seems at times — the kind of thing, of course, that can happen to all
of us.

In a sense, as I write about these young children I am lost. How
literally extraordinary, and in fact how extraordinarily cruel their lives
are: the constant mobility, the leave-takings and the fearful arrivals,
the demanding work they often manage to do, the extreme hardship
that goes with a meager (at best) income, the need always to gird oneself for the next slur, the next sharp rebuke, the next reminder that
one is different and distinctly unwanted, except, naturally, for the
work that has to be done in the fields. I also want to emphasize that

extremely hard-pressed people can find their own painful, heavy-hearted way, can learn to make that way as bearable as possible and can laugh not only because they want to cry and not only in bitter, ironic resignation (the kind melancholy philosophers allow themselves to express with a wan smile) but because it has been possible, after all the misery and chaos, to carve a little joy out of the world. That is to say, they make do, however sullenly and desperately and wildly and innocently and shrewdly, and they teach their children unsystematically but persistently that they, too, must survive — somehow, some way, against whatever odds.

Peter's mother, over the years, has essentially told me about that, about the facts of survival, not because I asked her what she has in mind when she punishes or praises her children, or tells them one or another thing, but because she constantly does things — for, with, to — her children. In a moment of quiet conversation her deeds, thousands of them done over many, many years, sort themselves out and find their own pattern, their own sense, their own words — oh, not perfect or eminently logical or completely consistent words, but words that offer vision and suggest blindness and offer confidence and suggest anxiety, the responses of a hardworking and God-fearing mother who won't quite surrender but also fears she won't quite avoid a terrible and early death: "I worry every day — it'll be a second sometime in the morning or in the afternoon or most likely before I drop off to sleep. I worry that my children will wake up one time and find I'm gone. It might be the bus will go crashing, or the car or the truck on the way to the farm, or it might be I've just been called away from this bad world by God, because He's decided I ought to have a long, long rest, yes sir. Then I'll stop and remind myself that I can't die, not just yet, because there's the children, and it's hard enough for them, yes it is — too hard, if you ask me. Sometimes I'll ask myself why it has to be so hard, and why can't we just live like other people you see from the road, near their houses, you know. But who can question the Lord, that's what I think. The way I see it, I've got to do the best I can for my children, all of them. So, I keep on telling them they've got to be good, and take care of each other, and mind me and do what I says. And I tell them I don't want them getting smart ideas, and trying to be wild and getting into any trouble, because you know — well, the way I sees the world, if you're born on the road, you'll most likely have to stay with it, and they're not going to let go of you, the crew man and the sheriff and like that, and if they did, we'd be at a loss, because you go into the city, I hear, and it's worse than anything that ever was, that's what we hear all the time.

"I'm trying to make my children into good children, that's what. I'm trying to make them believe in God, and listen to Him and obey His Commandments. I'm trying to have them pay me attention, and my husband, their daddy, pay him attention, and I'd like for all of them to know what they can, and grow into good people, yes, and be a credit to their daddy and me. I knows it's going to be hard for them, real bad at times, it gets. I tell them that, and I tell them not to be too set on things, not to expect that life is going to be easy. But I tell them that every man, he's entitled to rest and quiet some of the time, and we all can pray and hope it'll get better. And I tell them it used to be we never saw any money at all, and they'd send you up in those small trucks, but now they'll pay you some, and we most often have a car — we lose it, yes sir, when there's no work for a few weeks and then we're really in trouble — and we have more clothes now than we ever before had, much more, because most of my children, they have their shoes now, and clothes good enough for church, most of the time. So you can't just feel sorry about things, because if you do, then you'll just be sitting there and not doing anything — and crying, I guess. Sometimes I do; I'll wake up and I'll find my eyes are filled up with tears, and I can't figure out why, no sir. I'll be getting up, and I'll have to wipe away my eyes, and try to stop it, so the children don't think something is wrong, and then, you know, they'll start in, too. Yes, that has happened a few times, until I tell us all to go about and do something, and stop, stop the crying right away.

"You can't spend your one and only life wishing you had another life instead of the one you've got. I tell myself that, and then the tears stop; and if the children are complaining about this or that — well, I tell them that, too. I tell them it's no use complaining, and we've got to go on, and hope the day will come when it's better for us, and maybe we'll have a place to rest, and never again have to 'go on the season' and move and keep on moving and get ourselves so tired that we start the day in with the crying. Yes sir, I believe I cry when I'm just so tired there isn't anything else to do but cry. Or else it's because I'll be waking up and I know what's facing us, oh I do, and it just will be too much for me to think about, so I guess I go and get upset, before I even know it, and then I have to pinch myself, the way my own momma used to do, and talk to myself the way she would, and say just like her: 'There's no use but to go on, and someday we'll have our long, good rest.' Yes sir, that's what she used to say, and that's what I'll be saying on those bad mornings; and you know, I'll sometimes hear my girl telling herself the same thing, and I'll say to myself that it's good she can do it now, because later on she'll find herself feeling low, and then she'll have to have a message to tell herself, or else she'll be in real bad trouble, real bad trouble."

Mothers like her possess an almost uncanny mixture of willfulness and sadness. Sometimes they seem to do their work almost in spite of themselves; yet at other times they seem to take the sad and burdensome things of life quite in stride. As they themselves ask, what else can they do? The answer, of course, is that complete disintegration can always be an alternative — helped along by cheap wine, and the hot sun and the dark, damp corners of those cabins, where one can curl up and for all practical purposes die. Migrant mothers know all that, know the choices they have, the possibilities that life presents. Migrant mothers also know what has to be done — so that the children, those many, many children will at least eat something, will somehow get collected and moved and brought safely to the new place, the new quarters, the next stop or spot or farm or camp or field, to name a few destinations such mothers commonly mention when they talk to me about what keeps them in half-good spirits. I will, that is, ask how they feel, and how they and their children are getting along, and they will answer me with something like this: "I'm not too bad, no sir, I'm not. We keeps going, yes sir, we do. If you don't keep going, you're gone, I say. You have to keep moving and so you don't have time to stop and get upset about things. There's always another spot to get to, and no sooner do you get there — well, then you have to get yourself settled. There'll be yourself to settle and there'll be the kids and their daddy, too, and right off the work will be there for you to do, in the fields and with the kids, too. So, the way I see it, a mother can't let herself be discouraged. She's got to keep herself in good spirits, so her children, they'll be doing fine; because if I'm going to get all bothered, then sure enough my kids will, and that won't be good for them or me neither, I'll tell you. That's why I never lets myself get into a bad spell."

Actually, she does indeed get into bad spells, spells of moodiness and suspicion and petulance and rage, and so do her children from time to time, particularly as they grow older and approach the end of childhood. By definition, life for migrants is a matter of travel, of movement; and their children soon enough come to know that fact, which means they get to feel tentative about people and places and things. Anything around is only precariously theirs. Anything soon to come will just as soon disappear. Anything left just had to be left. As a matter of fact, life itself moves, moves fast and without those occasions or ceremonies that give the rest of us a few footholds. The many young migrant children I have observed and described to myself as agile, curious, and inventive are, by the age of seven or eight, far too composed, restrained, stiff and sullen. They know even then exactly where they must go, exactly what they must do. They no longer like to wander in the woods, or poke about near swamps. When other children are just beginning to come into their own, just beginning to explore and search and take over a little of the earth, migrant children begin to lose interest in the world outside them. They stop noticing animals or plants or trees or flowers. They don't seem to hear the world's noises. To an outside observer they might seem inward, morose, drawn and tired. Certainly some of those qualities of mind and appearance have to do with the poor food migrant children have had, with the accumulation of diseases that day after day cause migrant children pain and weakness. Yet, in addition, there is a speed, a real swiftness to migrant living that cannot be overlooked, and among migrant children particularly, the whole business of growing up goes fast, surprisingly fast, awfully fast, grimly and decisively fast. At two or three, migrant children see their parents hurry, work against time, step on it, get a move on. At three or four, those same children can often be impulsive, boisterous, eager, impatient in fact, and constantly ready — miraculously so, an observer like me feels — to lose no time, to make short work of what is and turn to the next task, the next ride.

However, at six or eight or ten, something else has begun to happen; children formerly willing to make haste and take on things energetically, if not enthusiastically, now seem harried as they hurry, breathless and abrupt as they press on. I do not think I am becoming dramatic when I say that for a few (first) feverish years migrant children are hard-pressed but still (and obviously) quick, animated — tenacious of life is perhaps a way to say it. Between five and ten, though, those same children experience an ebb of life, even a loss of life. They keep moving along; they pick themselves up again and again, as indeed they were brought up to do, as their parents continue to do, as they will soon (all too soon) be doing with their own children. They get where they're going, and to a casual eye they seem active enough, strenuous workers in the field, on their toes when asked something, called to do something. Still, their mothers know different; their mothers know that a change is taking place, has taken place, has to take place; their mothers know that life is short and brutish, that one is lucky to live and have the privilege of becoming a parent, that on the road the days merge terribly, that it is a matter of rolling on, always rolling on. So they go headlong into the days and nights, obey the commands of the seasons and pursue the crops; and meanwhile, somewhere inside themselves, they make their observations and their analyses, they take note of what happens to themselves and their children: "My little ones, they'll be spry and smart, yes they will be; but when they're older — I guess you'd say school age, but they're not all the time in school, I'll have to admit — then they're different, that's what I'd say. They'll be drowsy, or they won't be running around much. They'll take their time and they'll slouch, you know. They'll loaf around and do only what they think they've got to do. I guess — well, actually, I suppose they're just getting grown, that's what it is. My boy, he's the one just nine this season, he used to be up and doing things before I even knew what he was aiming to do; but now he'll let no one push him, except if he's afraid, and even then, he'll be pulling back all he can, just doing enough to get by. The crew leader, he said the boy will be 'another lazy picker' and I stood up and spoke back. I said we gets them in, the beans, don't we and what more can he want, for all he pays us? I'll ask you? I guess he wants our blood. That's what I think it is he wants, and if he sees my children trying to keep some of their blood to themselves, then he gets spiteful about them and calls them all his names like that; and there isn't anything you can do but listen and try to go on and forget."

She tries to go on and forget. So do her children, the older they get. Once wide awake, even enterprising, they slowly become dilatory, leaden, slow, laggard, and lumpish. Necessarily on the move a lot, they yet appear motionless. Put to work in the fields, they seem curiously unoccupied. The work gets done (and by them) yet they do not seem to work. I suppose I am saying that older migrant children begin to labor, to do what they must do if they are not to be without a little money, a little food; but at the same time the work is not done in a diligent, painstaking and spirited way. Again, it is done, all that hard, demanding work; the crops get taken in. What one fails to see, however, is a sense of real purpose and conviction in the older children who, like their parents, have learned that their fate is of no real concern to others. The point is survival: mere survival at best; survival against great odds; survival that never is assured and that quite apparently exacts its costs. If I had to sum up those costs in a few words I would probably say: care is lost; the child stops caring, hardens himself or herself to the coming battle, as it is gradually but definitely comprehended, and tries to hold on, persist, make it through the next trip, the next day, the next row of crops.

So, all year round, all day long, hour after hour, migrants stoop or reach for vegetables and fruit, which they pull and pick and cut and at the same time those migrants settle into one place or prepare the move to another; and at the same time those migrants try to be parents, try stubbornly to do what has to be done — feed the children and get them to listen and respond and do this rather than that, do it now rather than later. I have described the determination that goes into such a life — of travel and fear and impoverishment and uncertainty. I have described the first and desperate intimacy many migrant children experience with their mothers. I have described the migrant child's developing sense of his particular world — its occasional pleasures, its severe restrictions, its constant flux, its essential sameness. To do so I have drawn upon what can actually be considered the best, the most intact, of the people I have seen and heard. After all, when parents and children together live the kind of life most migrants do, it seems a little miraculous that they even halfway escape the misery and wretchedness — that is, manage to continue and remain and last, last over the generations, last long enough to work and be observed by me or anyone else.

There is, though, the misery; and it cannot be denied its importance, because not only bodies but minds suffer out of hunger and untreated illness; and that kind of psychological suffering also needs to be documented. Nor can an observer like me allow his shame, outrage, and compassion to turn exhausted, suffering people into courageous heroes who, though badly down on their luck, nevertheless manage to win a spiritual victory. I fear that rather another kind of applause is in order, the kind that celebrates the struggle that a doomed man tries to put up. Migrant parents and even migrant children do indeed become what some of their harshest and least forgiving critics call them: listless, apathetic, hard to understand, disorderly, subject to outbursts of self-injury and destructive violence toward others. It is no small thing, a disaster almost beyond repair, when children grow up adrift the land, when they learn as a birthright the disorder and early sorrow that goes with peonage, with an unsettled, vagabond life. We are describing millions of psychological catastrophes, the nature of which has been spelled out to me by both migrant parents and migrant children. The father of six of those children — a hard worker but a beaten man — talks and talks about his failures and his sense of defeat, about his sense of ruin at the hands of a relentless fate whose judgment upon him and those near him and like him simply cannot be stayed: "There will be a time, you know, when I'll ask myself what I ever did — maybe in some other life — to deserve this kind of deal. You know what I mean? I mean I feel there must be someone who's decided you should live like this, for something wrong that's been done. I don't know. I can't say it any other way. All I know is that it's no life, trying to pick beans on fifty farms all over the country, and trying to make sure your kids don't die, one after the other. Sometimes we'll be driving along and I say to myself that there's one thing I can do to end all of this for good, and it would save not only me but the children a lot of hardship, a lot. But you can't do that; I can't, at least. So, instead I go and lose my mind. You've seen me, yes you have; and I know I'm going to do it. I start with the wine, when I'm working, just so the hours will go faster, and I won't mind bending over — the pain to my back — and I won't mind the heat. There'll be days when I work right through, and there'll be days when I stop in the middle of the day, because I don't want to get sick. But there will be other days when I hear myself saying that I've got to let go, I've just got to. I've got to get so drunk that I'm dead, dead in my mind, and then if I live after it, that's fine, and if I never wake up, that's fine, too. It's not for me to decide, you see. We can't decide on anything, being on the road, and owing everything to the crew leaders and people like that. The only thing we can decide, my daddy used to tell me, is whether we'll stay alive or whether we won't. He said no matter what, we should keep going; but he got killed when the bus that was taking him and a lot of others got stalled right on a railroad track and it was crushed into little pieces by the train. I'll think of him, you know, when I get full of wine. I'll think of him telling me that you can't figure out what's the reason the world is like it is; you can only try to keep from dying, and it may take you your entire life to do that — and I guess he didn't expect that suddenly he'd be gone, after all the work he put in, just to stay alive."

His wife has some observations to make about him and the effort he makes to stay alive: "My husband, he's a good man a lot of the time. He never talks about the children, not even to me, but he loves them, I know he does. Once he told me that it hurts him every time one of our children is born, because he knows what's ahead for them. You know something? Each time, with each child, he's gone and got worse drunk than any other time. I don't know why, just that it's happened. He almost killed me and all the children the last time. He had a knife and he said he might use it. Then he took us all in the car; he made us get in, and he said if I didn't go along with him, he'd kill me, and if I did, there was a chance I'd live, and the children, too. So, I did, and he drove with his foot pressing on the gas all the way down. I could hear him trying to go faster, pushing on the pedal and trying to force it, and thank God the floor of the car wouldn't let him have his way. Well, he cursed us all, but most of all himself. He was after himself. He was chasing himself. He kept on saying that he had to catch himself and he had to get a hold on himself, and if he didn't, then he might as well die. In between, he'd tell us we were all going to die, and the sooner the better, because the only way for us to have peace, to have rest, was to die. There was no other way, he kept on shouting that to us.

"Then I must have lost my mind, like he had lost his. I started crying, and I can remember screaming to God please to turn my husband and me and the children away from Him, because it wasn't time yet, no it wasn't, for us to see Him. Then I crawled down, I reached down, I don't remember how I did, and pulled his foot away from the gas, and he didn't try to put it back, no he didn't; and the car went on and on, and then it began to slow down, and then it stopped, and then before he had a change of mind, I got out and I got all of us out, all except him, and we didn't leave him, though. Where could we go? I didn't know where we were, and it was dark. We spread ourselves down nearby to the car, and we tried to rest. I looked up at the sky and I couldn't forget it for the rest of my life, what I saw then and what I thought, no sir, I couldn't. When I die I know I'll be thinking like that and I'll be seeing like that: there was the sky, and it was dark, but the moon was there, almost round, and it hung low, real low, and it was colored funny, orange I guess; and all the stars were there, all over, everywhere it seemed. I'd never looked long enough to see so many stars, even though we do a lot of traveling, and we're up through the night, and you might have thought I'd have noticed them, all the stars, before. But moving across the country, you forget about the sky, I guess. I told my boy that, a few days later I did, that we shouldn't forget the sky, because we're going along underneath it a lot of the time, and he said that maybe we forget it because it's like a roof to us, and that if you're under a roof, you never look at it.

"While I was staring up there at the sky, I thought I heard something, a noise. It was the wind, I know, but to me it was God, it was God as well as the wind, and He was there, speaking right into both my ears, telling me to stay where I was, with the children, and near my husband, and He was looking over us, yes, and He'd see that the day would come when we'd have a home — a home that was ours, and that we'd never leave, and that we'd have for as long as God Himself is with us, and that's forever, you know. Maybe it would be up in one of those stars, one of the bright ones, one of the bright stars, maybe the home would be there, I thought — and then I saw one, a real bright star, and I said that's it, that's maybe where we would all go, but not until it's the right time, not a second before, and I was glad then that we stayed around, and didn't all die, and I'm still glad.

"Oh, not all the time, I'm not all the time glad, I'll admit that. I was glad then, when my husband woke up, and he said he was sorry and he was glad, and he'd try to be good and not lose himself on account of wine. I was glad later, too. Most of the time I'm glad, actually. It's just sometimes I don't feel glad. I don't feel glad at all. Like my husband, I sometimes feel myself going to pieces; yes sir, that's how it feels, like you're going to pieces. Once I was real bad — real, real bad — and I thought I'd die because I was in such a bad way. I recall I'd have the same dream every single night, even every time I put my head down, it seemed. It got so that I was scared to sleep, real scared. I'd try sitting up and resting, but not closing my eyes. After a while they'd close, though, and then it would come again, and the next thing I'd know I'd be waking up and shouting and crying and screaming, and sometimes I'd be standing up and even I'd be running around wherever we were staying, and my husband would be shaking me, or my children, they'd be crying and telling me no, no, no it wasn't so and don't be scared, Momma, and it'll be all right, they'd say. But I never believed them when I first woke up, it would take me an hour or so, I'd guess, to shake myself free of that dream, and I'd never really forget it, even when I'd be working. I'd be pulling the beans and putting them in the hamper, and I'd feel myself shaking, and there'd be someone nearby and she'd say, "Martha, you took too much of that wine last night"; and I'd say no, I didn't touch a single drop, not last night or any other night for a long, long time. I wouldn't tell nobody, except my husband, but it was this dream I was having, and thank God now it's left me, but I can still see it, if I want to.

"There was a road, that's how the dream started, and it was all smoothed out and kept clean, and if you looked down on it you'd see yourself, like it was a mirror or something placed on the top of the road. I'd be standing there, and all of a sudden I'd see one car after the other coming, and inside the car would be one of my little ones, then there'd be the next child, and the next one, and each one had a car all to himself, and they'd be going down the road, almost as though they were going to go racing one another or something. But all of a sudden they'd explode, the cars would, one and then another, and soon they'd all be gone, and I couldn't find the sight of my children, and I'd still be standing there, where I was all the time, and I'd be shaking, whether in the dream or when I was waking up, I don't know. More than anything else, what hurt me was that the last thing that happened in the dream was that I'd see myself, standing on the road. I'd be looking down, and I could see my new child — yes, there'd be one I'd be carrying, and I'd be near the time to have the baby, and I'd be big and I'd be seeing myself, like in a mirror, like I said. But I'd have no other of my children left. They'd all be gone; and my husband, he'd be gone; and there'd be me, and my baby, not born yet, and that would be all. No, there'd be no cars, either. They'd all have gone and exploded, I guess."

How is such a dream to be analyzed or interpreted or made to explain something about her, about her wishes and fears and worries, about those things the rest of us would call her "psychological problems"? Why did the dream plague her then, seize control of her mind for those few weeks, then leave her, never to return? For all the world that separates her from me, for all her naïveté (as it is put by people like me when we talk about certain other people) and my sophistication (as it is also put by people like me when we talk about ourselves) we could pursue the meaning of her dream without too much self-consciousness, and with a minimum of theoretical contrivance, density or speculation. For several years, on and off, I had been telling her that I wanted to know how her children *felt,* how their spirits held up (or didn't) and she knew — right from the start, really — what I meant. In fact, once she told me what I meant: "I know. You want to see if they're scared, or if they're not. You want to see if they feel good, or if they feel lousy, real lousy — the way I guess their mother does a lot of the time!" So, the dream did not puzzle her all that much, only frighten her a lot, make her tremble, because at night she couldn't escape what by day she knew, could not help knowing — in every "level" of her mind, in her unconscious and in her subconscious and in her preconscious and in the thoroughly conscious part of her mind and yes, in her bones and her heart: "I'm always thinking, when I get ready to have another baby, that I wish I could be a better mother to them, and give them a better life to be born into than the one they're going to get on account of being my children, and not some other mother's. It's the worst of being a mother, knowing you can't offer your babies much, knowing there isn't much to offer them — there's really nothing, to be honest, but the little milk you have and the love you can give them, to start them off with. I know it's going to be bad for them when they grow up, and sometimes I wonder why God sends us here, all of us, if He knows how bad it's to be.

"There'll be a moment when I'll look at my children, and I'll wonder if they hold it against me for bringing them into this world, to live like we do, and not the others, with the money you know, and with the places where they can stay and not be always moving. The only rest we'll get, I'm afraid, the only rest we'll get is in the grave. Once, a long time ago, I said so, to my oldest boy, and he'll now and then repeat it to the younger ones. I want to tell him to stop, but I know he's right, and they don't get too upset with what he says, even if it's bad, like that. I think they sometimes don't really mind dying. God knows, they talk about it enough. Maybe it's what they hear from the minister. He's always telling us that everyone has to die, and that if you suffer here on earth you live longer in Heaven; and one of my girls, she said if that was the way, then maybe it was all right to be sick, but when you get to die, then is the time you're going to feel better, and not before then, no matter what you try to do."

Her children see no doctors for their various illnesses, and they don't actually "try to do" (as she put it) very much at all for themselves when they fall sick. They wait. They hope. Sometimes they say their prayers. Their mother also waits and hopes and prays, and apparently worries, too — and dreams and forgets her dreams and once, for a number of days, couldn't quite forget them, the terrible, terrible dreams that reflect in detail and in symbol the hard, hard life migrants live themselves, and see their children also as a matter of course begin to pursue. "I wouldn't mind it for myself," says the mother whose dream stayed with her so long, "but it's not good for the children, being 'on the road,' and when we're moving along I'll catch myself thinking I did wrong to bring all of them into the world — yes sir, I did wrong. But you can't think like that for too long, no sir, you can't; and I do believe the children, if they had their choice between not being born at all and being born and living with us — well, they'd choose to be themselves, to be with us, even it it's not easy for them and us, even so."

Sometimes when a mother like the one just quoted made an assertion like that to me, affirmed herself in spite of everything, said that there was after all a point to it all, a point to life, to life pure (and swift and unlucky) if not so simple, I felt in her the same questions I could not avoid asking myself. What *do* they think, those migrant children — about "life" and its hardships, about the reasons they must constantly travel, about the special future that more than likely faces them, in contrast to other American children? Does a migrant child of, say, seven or eight blame his parents for the pain he continues to experience, day after day, and for the hunger? Does that child see his later life as likely to be very much like his father's, or are there other alternatives and possibilities that occur to him as he goes about the business of getting bigger and working more and more in the fields? "What do *you* think?" I have heard from the mother who was once dream possessed and from other mothers like her; and there does come a time when people like me ought to stop throwing questions like that back at the people who ask them (as if we have some royal privilege that grants us the right to do so) and spell out what exactly (if anything) we do think.

Fortunately, migrant children have been quite willing to let me know what *they* see and think, what *they* believe about a number of matters. Like all children, they don't necessarily get into extended conversations; they don't say a lot, go into wordy descriptions of their moods and fantasies and desires and feelings. They do, however, throw out hints; they use their faces and their hands; they make gestures and grimaces; they speak out, with a phrase here and a series of sentences there. Moreover, it has been my experience that they will also use crayons and paints to great advantage, so that given enough time and trust the observer (become viewer) can see on paper, in outline and in colors and shapes, all sorts of suggestive, provocative, and instructive things. When the migrant child *then* is asked a question or two, about this or that he has portrayed, pictured, given form, and made light or dark — well, I believe there is a lot to be heard in those moments, moments in a sense after the deed of creation has been finished, moments when thoughts and (more assertively) opinions can emerge from something concrete, something done, even something achieved, in this case achieved by children not always used to that kind of effort.

So, the children have drawn pictures, dozens and dozens of pictures; particular migrant children whom I came to know for two, maybe three, sometimes four years, and whom, at times, I asked to use paper and pencils and crayons and paints. I might, for instance, want to see a favorite "spot" drawn, a place the child especially liked, a house he might like or a camp he didn't like at all. I might want to know about all those schools, about how they looked and how they seemed from the inside and how they can be compared, one to the other, the good and the bad, the pleasant and the very unpleasant. I might be interested in the crops, in which ones are good and bad to harvest, and how they look, the beans or the tomatoes or the celery or the cucumbers, when they are there, ready and waiting. I might ask about the essence of migratory life, about the way the road appears to the child, about what there is to be seen and avoided and enjoyed on those roads, about what remains in a given child's mind when all the memories are sorted out, and one of them is left — to be chosen, to be drawn, and then reluctantly or shyly or cautiously or openly or even insistently handed to me as "it," the thing that was suggested as a possible subject by me, and therefore to be drawn as a favor or in fear, or resisted out of fear or anger, or refused out of fear or confusion or resentment.

What do they see, then — see in their mind's eye, see casually or intensely, see and through pictures enable others to see? Certain themes do come up repeatedly, no doubt because migrant children share a number of concerns. Tom, for instance, was a seven-year-old boy when he drew for me a rather formless and chaotic and dreary picture (Figure 11) of the fields he already knew as a helper to his parents, a harvester really. When he was five I had seen him race along those rows of beans — picking, picking, picking. Once in a while he would show his age by shouting out his achievements, by pointing to anyone near at hand how much he had just done, how experienced he had become. Children are often like that, a little enthusiastic and a little boastful. They will learn, we tell ourselves, they will learn to take their own abilities for granted, to deal less ostentatiously and noisily with themselves and the world. I knew Tom between the ages of five, when he started working in the fields, and seven, when he still worked at harvesting crops. I spent a lot of time with him and his family during those two years, and since then have made a point of seeing him at least several times each year. (At this writing, he is no longer a child; he is fourteen and he lives with a woman and he is a father and like his parents he is a migrant farm worker — but that will have to be told elsewhere, when I describe the lives of grown-up, yes, at fourteen, grown-up migrants.)

Tom always liked to draw pictures, and in fact knew enough about what some people would call "the problems of representation" to appreciate his own failings: "I'm no good. I'll bet some kids can really do a good picture for you. Each time I try, but when it's done I can't say it looks the way I'd like it to look. It's not like it should be — real, I mean. I know you said it doesn't have to be, but is it a good picture if you have to tell someone what you've tried to draw?" Of course

I reassured him. I gave him my prepared speech, full of encourage-ment and friendliness and praise, all of which, I have to add, I very much meant — because he did try hard, and his mind had a lot going on "inside" or "deep down," all of which he very much wanted to put on paper and afterwards talk about.

The fields, the dark, jumbled, confusing, sunless fields — guarded, be it noted, by a black fence and the outlines of some dark faceless men — were nearby when Tom drew the picture. They were not in sight, those fields, because a strip of pines intervened — none of which appears on the paper — but as Tom used his crayons he could hear all sorts of sounds from the migrants, who were eating their lunches and talking and arguing. One man was singing. Tom worked on the grass, used a wooden board I carried around, talked as he drew, interrupted his work to eat *his* lunch. This is perhaps the mo-ment for me to mention something about migrant children: in con-trast to all other children I have observed and worked with, migrant boys and girls are quite willing to interrupt their particular tasks — for instance, drawing a picture or playing various games with me — for any number of reasons. It is not that they are agitated or anxious or unable to concentrate and finish what they start. It is not that they run about helter-skelter because they are confused or alarmed or afraid. It is not that they don't understand what we are attempting, and have to move on rather than reveal their lack of comprehension. Yes, some of them, like many other children, do have some of the difficulties I have just listed; but I emphatically do not have such essentially psycho-pathological matters in mind. The habits of children are vastly re-sponsive to the habits of their parents. If parents accept (because they have learned they must) the necessity of constantly moving from one field to another, from one responsibility to another, each of which can only be partially fulfilled by any given person and indeed requires a whole field of people, then it is only natural that their children will ex-perience no great need to stick at things stubbornly or indeed consis-tently. The child has learned that there is always the next place, the next journey, the next occasion. The fields are there, being worked on when the child arrives with his parents. The fields are still there, and often enough still being worked on when the child with his family leaves — for another location, another cycle of arrival and initiative and involvement and exhaustion and departure, a cycle that, in the words of the Bible, words that in my opinion convey exactly what thousands of children feel, is a "world without end."

If Tom can distract himself, say, for candy and Coke, yet return and finish what he has started, he can also do a quick turn of drawing or sketching and pause for discussion, which itself can be a pleasant distraction to a child not made anxious at the prospect of a change of direction or action: "I'd like to stop for a second, because when we're traveling on a road like that one, we'll have to stop, you know. My daddy, he says that a field isn't so bad when you're resting on it; it's only when you're picking that a field is so bad. No, most of the time we don't stop by the road. My daddy, he says you can get into a lot of trouble that way, because the police are always looking to see if we're not keeping moving, and if they catch you sitting by the road, they'll take you to jail and they won't let you out so easy, either. They'll make you promise to get away and never come back. They'll tell you that if you're going to be picking, you've got to go ahead and pick, and then you've got to get away, fast. That's why you have to watch where you're going when you're on the way to a farm, and you're not sure where it is. You've got to be careful, and the best thing is to follow someone who can lead you there, that's what my daddy says. Then, if you have to stop, you can find a path and go down it, and you'll be safe, and you won't end up being caught."

He does not seem to regard the fields as very safe or pleasant places to be. The more he works on his drawing, the more he seems compelled to talk about the subject: "I like to be moving along. If you keep moving you're safer than if you just stop in a field, and someone comes by, and they can ask you what you're doing, and they can tell you to get back in the car and go away as fast as the motor will go. Once I was really scared, and so was everyone else. We went way down a road that we thought was safe, and there was a little pond there, and we went and played in it, because they said we could, Mommy and Daddy did. Then the man came, he was a foreman my daddy told me afterwards. Then he said we would all be arrested and we were no good, and we should be in jail and stay there forever. My daddy said we'd go right away, and we did, and he said — the rest of the day he said it over and over — that you're in trouble moving from one state to the other, because the state police, they don't like you, and the sheriffs, they don't like you, and you know the foremen, they have badges, and they can arrest you, and they have men with guns and they'll come along and hold one right to your ears and your head, and they'll tell you that either you work or you move on up the road, and if you sit there and try to eat something, or like that, then you'll get yourself in jail, and it won't be easy to get out, no sir. That's why it's bad luck to stop and rest in a field, and if you see one that has crops, then it's bad luck, too — because you're lucky if you'll have any money left, for all the work you do. I don't like fields, that's what I think."

What else is there to say about Tom's drawing, about the migrant life he has already become part of? Tom looks upon the fields and roads, the fields and roads that never really end for families like his, as both fearful and redemptive: "One thing I'll tell you, if it's real bad on a farm, if they're watching you too close and they don't pay you what they should, then you can sneak away in the middle of the night. Even if they have their guards looking over where you're staying, the guards will fall asleep, and before they wake up, you can be on your way, and then you've got a chance to find a better place to work. That's why you have to keep your eye on the road, and when you leave it to stay in a cabin near a field, or in a tent like we were in the last time, then you should always remember the fastest way to the main road, and you should point the car so it's ready to go and all you have to do is get in the car and start the driving. It wasn't long ago that we did that, just packed up and left. We pretended we were asleep for a while, in case anyone was looking, and then in the middle of the night we up and went, and they probably didn't find out until it was morning, and by then we were a long way and my daddy and the others, they checked in with this man they knew, and he gave them all work to do, picking beans, and he said he was glad to have them, and he'd give them every penny they earned, and not to worry — but my daddy says you never know if you should believe them or not, and a lot of the time they'll just double-cross you and go back on their promise, and you're left with almost nothing, and there isn't much you can do, so you move on and hope it won't keep happening like that, no sir; and sometimes it won't either, because you'll work, and then they'll pay you right what you deserve, and that makes it much better."

Does Tom wonder where it will all end, the travel and the new places to occupy for ever so short a time? Does he dream of some road that will lead to some other way of life? Does the continual motion make him grow weary and resentful, in spite of his own words to the contrary? Does he think about other children, who live not far from the roads he knows so well, children he occasionally, sporadically meets in this school, where he attended classes for a month, and that one, which he liked, but had to leave after two weeks? I have asked him questions like those, but often he condenses his answers in a particular drawing — such as this one (Figure 12): "I don't know where that road is going; I mean, no, I didn't have a road I was thinking of when I drew. I just made the road, and it probably keeps going until it hits the icebergs, I guess. I put some little roads in, but you shouldn't leave the road you're going on. I remember I asked my daddy once if he knew where the highway ends, the one we take North, and he said it probably ended where you get as far North as you can get — and there aren't any crops there, he said, so we'll never see the place, but it's very cold there, and maybe a lot of it has no people, because it's better to live where it's warmer. I said I'd like for us one time to keep going and see an iceberg and see what it's like there. My daddy said maybe we would, but he didn't mean it, I could tell. A lot of the time I'll ask him if we could go down a road further, and see some places, and he says yes, we can, but he doesn't want to — my momma says we've got to be careful and we can't keep asking to go here and there, because we're not supposed to and we'll get in trouble. She says we should close our eyes and imagine that there's a big fence on each side of the road, and that we can't get off, even if we wanted to and tried to, because of the fence. That's why I put the fence in, a little, to keep the car there from getting in trouble with the police.

"No, I didn't mean for there to be a crash, no. It would be bad if one happened. My daddy's brothers, three of them got killed in a crash. They were coming back to Florida from up North, from New Jersey it was, and the bus, it just hit a truck and a lot of people got killed. They say the bus was old, and once down here the brakes stopped working, but the crew leader had it fixed, and it was supposed to be safe. They were younger than my daddy, yes sir, and he said he didn't see how it could be anything but God's desire, that they should all, all of them, be saved forevermore from going up and down through the states and never being paid enough, except for some food and a place to sleep, and after that, they don't give you much money for anything else. I figured that if I was picturing the road and me in the car, I'd put a truck there, too; because, you know, we see a lot of trucks and the buses, too, when we go through Florida and then up North. But I hope the car and the bus in the picture don't crash like they do a lot of the time.

"Sometimes — yes, sometimes I think to myself when we're passing a town, that I'd like to look through the place and maybe stay there — I mean live there, and not go right on to the next place. I used to ask why, I'd ask my momma and my daddy and my uncles, but they all said I should stop with the questions, and stop trying to get a lot of reasons for things, and like that. In school once, in Florida it was, there was a real nice teacher (it was last year) and she said to the class that they should all be nice to me and the rest of us, because if people like us didn't go around doing the picking, then there'd be no food for everyone to eat — the fruit and vegetables. A girl laughed and said that was a big joke, because her daddy had a big farm, and he didn't use any people, just machines. I nearly asked her what her daddy was growing, but I didn't. I guess I was scared. The teacher didn't do anything. She just said we should go on and do our work, and the less trouble in the class the better it would be all the way around. I thought afterwards that I'd like to follow her home, the girl, and see if she was telling the truth; because I didn't believe her.

"I asked my daddy, and he said there are some farms like that, but not many in Florida, because the farmers need us to pick beans and tomatoes, and the machines cost a lot, and you can't get a second crop from the plants after the machine. No, I didn't speak to her, and I didn't follow her either. I mean, I did for a little while, but I got scared, and my friend, he said we'd better turn around or we'd be in jail, and we wouldn't get out of there for a long, long time. Then we did, we turned around, and when I told my sister — she's ten — she said we were lucky we're not there now, in jail, because the police, they keep their eyes on us all the time, if we leave the camps or the fields, to go shopping or to school or like that. I said one of these days I'd slip by. I'd get me a suit or something, and a real shiny pair of shoes, and I'd just walk down the street until I came to where they live, the kids that go to that school, and if someone came up to me and tried to stop me and if he asked me what I was doing, then I'd say I was just looking, and I thought I'd go get some ice cream, and I'd have the money and I'd show it to the policeman, and they couldn't say I was trying to steal something, or I was hiding from them, the policemen and like that. But my sister said they'd just laugh and pick me up, like I was a bean or a tomato, and the next thing I'd know I'd be there, in jail, and they might never let me out, except if one of the growers comes, and he would say it was OK if they let me out, and he'd pay the fine, but then I'd have to work for him.

"That's how you end up, I hear. They never do anything a lot of people, but work for the same man, because they always are owing him money, the grower, and he is always getting them out of jail, and then they owe him more money. My daddy says, and my sister, she says that the grower keeps on giving them the wine, and they drink it, and they'll be drunk, and the police will be called, and arrest them, and then the grower will come, one of his men mostly, and pay to get people out, and then they'll have to work some more — until they get killed. I hope it'll never happen like that to me. I'd like someday, I'll be honest, I'd like to go to the city, and I could get a job there. Once there was a nice boy who sat beside me — not long ago, I think it was this same year — and I was going to ask him if I could get a job from his father. No, I didn't want to ask him what his father's job was, but he seemed like he was real rich, the boy, and I thought maybe I could get a job, and I could maybe live there, in the house there, you know, where the boy does, and then I wouldn't have to be going North later this year."

Would he miss his mother and father? "No — I mean, yes. But I think they could come and see me sometimes. If the people let me live in their house, maybe they would let my daddy come and see me, and my mother could come, and they wouldn't stay too long, I know."

Migrant children see everything as temporary. Places come and go; and people and schools and fields. The children don't know what it is, in Tom's words, to "stay too long"; rather, they live in a world that lacks holidays and trips to department stores and libraries. Children like Tom, for example, don't see any mail, because their parents lack an address, a place from which letters are sent and to which letters come. Children like Tom don't know about bookshelves and walls with pictures on them and comfortable chairs in cozy living rooms and telephones (which are put by telephone companies into *residences*) and cabinets full of glassware or serving dishes or stacks of canned goods. A suitcase hardly seems like a very important thing to any of us, yet migrant children have dreamed of having one, dreamed and dreamed and can say why after they draw a picture, as a girl of nine named Doris did: "I was smaller when I saw a store, and it had big suitcases and little ones; they all were made of leather, I think. I asked my mother if she could please, one day, get one for me; not a big one, because I know they must cost more money than we could ever have, but a small one. She said why did I want one, and I said it was because I could keep all my things together, and they'd never get lost, wherever we go. I have a few things that are mine — the comb, the rabbit's tail my daddy gave me before he died, the lipstick and the fan, and like that — and I don't want to go and lose them, and I've already lost a lot of things. I had a luck bracelet and I left it someplace, and I had a scarf, a real pretty one, and it got lost, and a mirror, too. That's why if I could have a place to put my things, my special things, then I'd have them and if we went all the way across the country and back, I'd still have them, and I'd keep them."

She still doesn't have her suitcase. In fact, Doris doesn't have very much of anything, so that when I asked her to draw whatever she wished, she answered as follows: "I don't know if there's anything I can draw." I suggested something from the countryside — she seemed sad, after all, and in no mood for my kind of clever silences, meant to prod children like her into this or that psychological initiative (and revelation). She said no, the countryside was the countryside, and she sees quite enough of it, so there is no need to give those trees and fields and roads any additional permanence. Rather, she said this: "I see a lot of the trees and farms. I'd like to draw a picture I could like, and I could look at it, and it would be nice to look at, and I could take it with me. But I don't know what to draw." Her judgment on the countryside was fairly clear and emphatic, but so was her sense of confusion. She knew what she didn't want to do, but she was at loose ends, too. She seemed to be asking herself some questions. What do I want to see, and carry with me through all those dismal trips and rides and detours and long, long, oh so long journeys? Where can I find a little beauty in the world, a touch of joy, a bit of refreshment and en- couragement — and self-supplied at that, through crayons I have my- self wielded on paper? Is there anything worth remembering, worth keeping, worth holding onto tenaciously, without any letup whatso- ever? Perhaps I am forcing melodrama on Doris's mind, which cer- tainly needs no more worries or fears. Perhaps, for her life is a matter of getting up and working in the fields and eating what there is to eat and sleeping and moving on, moving here and there and always, al- ways moving. I don't think so, though. For all the fancy words I use, and all the ambiguities and ironies I hunger after, the little girl Doris has insisted that I also listen to her. She has even made me realize I must do more than listen and observe and collect my "data" and, like her, move on: "If I draw a picture, a good one, I want to keep it. The last time you said you wanted it, and I told my mother I liked it and I wanted to keep it. I asked my mother if I could get some glue and put it on the window of the car, but she said no. She said we'd get stopped and arrested."

So, Doris did two pictures at each sitting, one for herself and an- other one, as similar as possible, for me — all of which leads me to state another thing I have noticed especially among migrant children: unlike other children I have come to know, girls like Doris and boys like Tom don't want to give up drawings they make, not to me and not even to others in their family or to neighbors. It is not a matter of property; nor does the child cling to the picture because he feels "realized" at last through something artistically done. Nor is he drawn irresistibly to the form and symmetry he has wrought, to all those colors at last made accessible to himself. Doris one day told me why she wouldn't let go, and I will let her explanation — unadorned by my translations and interpretations — stand as quite good enough: "I just want it — because it's good to look at, and it may not be as good as it could be, but it was the best I could do, and I can take it and look at it, and it will be along with me up North, and I can think of being back here where I drew it, and then I'll know we'll be coming back here where I drew it, and I can look ahead to that, you see." Doris did a second drawing, essentially the same, which she gave to me, then put the first version away — with her rabbit tail and other belongings. She had done many other drawings for me, but somehow this one, a picture of the few things she owned, meant more to her than any of the others. It was as if she had finally found some kind of permanence for her meager possessions, and also a talisman of sorts. So long as her things had a new and separate life of their own, in the picture, they would all be collected together, her little world of possessions, as they could not be in the suitcase that has never come. Now she could look ahead and look back and have some sense of direction, some idea of a destination, some feeling that life has its rhythms and sequences and purposes. But I said I would not do what I have just done, speak for her, be her interpreter.

We are all compelled whether we know it or not, and the well-educated and well-analyzed are not the only ones who comprehend the mind's constraints. I have to make my little and not so little remarks, and Doris has to carry a few personal effects all over America. Another child known to me, whom I will call Larry, can paint the necessities that govern his particular life (Figure 13). What would he like to draw above all else, he was asked, and he said in reply that he didn't want to draw at all this time. He wanted to paint. Well, why did he want to paint this time? (We had together been using crayons for over a year.) "Oh, I don't know — except that tomorrow is my birthday." He was to be nine. Half because I wasn't actually sure what day "tomorrow" was, and half because, I suppose, I knew the *reason* why time had become blurred for me during the weeks I had moved about with Larry and his family, I asked him what day his birthday was: "It's in the middle of the summer, on the hottest day." He was dead serious, and I was both puzzled and embarrassed, a condition of my mind which he noticed.

He was moved to explain things, to help me — to do what I am trained to do, formulate and soothe and heal or whatever. "I don't know the day. The teacher in one of the schools kept saying I had to bring in a certificate that said where I was born and gave the day and like that. I asked my mother and she said there wasn't any. I told the teacher, and she said that was bad, and to check again. I checked, and my mother said no, and so did my daddy, and so did the crew leader. He said I should tell the teacher to shut up, and if she didn't I could just walk out of school and they wouldn't go after me or give me any trouble at all. No, I didn't leave, no sir; I stayed there for as long as we did in the camp. It was the best school I'd ever seen. They had cold air all the time, no matter how hot it got. I wanted to stay there all night. They gave you good cookies all the time, and milk; and the teacher, she said she wanted to buy us some clothes and pay for it herself. She said I should tell my mother to come to school and they would have a talk; and she said I should get my birth certificate and hold on to it. Then one day she brought in hers and showed it to us; and she said we all should stand up and say to the class where we were born and on what day of the year; but I didn't know. She said we should ask where our mothers were born and our fathers. So I did and I told her. I was born here in Florida, and my mother in Georgia and my father there, too; and my mother said it was a hot, hot day, and she thought it was right in the middle of the summer, July it must be, she said, around about there, but she wasn't sure. Then I asked her if she'd go register me, like the teacher said, and she said I'd better stay home and help out with the picking, if I was going to go listening to everything and then getting the funny ideas and trying to get us all in trouble, because the crew man, he said if we started going over to the courthouse and asking one thing of them, and then another — well, they'd soon have us all in jail, my mother said."

He painted a picture of his certificate, and thus showed both me and himself that he could persist with an idea, an intention. Paint to him meant a more worthy and lasting commitment. To paint is to emphasize, to declare out loud and for all to hear — or so he feels: "If you paint a certificate it won't rub away, like with the crayons. I don't know how they make the real ones, but they have big black letters and one of them, it has a red circle — and the teacher, she said it was a *seal*, and it belonged to a city and it was put on a lot of important papers." If he had his certificate what would he do with it, once he had shown it to his teacher? He would keep it, treasure it, fasten it to himself in some foolproof way that he himself could only vaguely suggest rather than spell out: "I'd never lose it, like I did my belt. My daddy gave me a belt, and I was afraid if I put it on all the time, it wouldn't look so good after a while; so I kept it with me, and put it with my shoes and when we went to church I'd have on my shoes and my belt. But once in a camp there was a fire, and I lost my belt and my shoes; and I should have worn the belt, my mother said, or carried it with me wherever I went, even to the field. But I didn't, and too bad."

Shoes cannot be taken for granted by children like him, nor belts, nor socks; nor (so it seems) birth certificates, which presumably everyone in America has. Since I know that children like Larry are born in cabins or even in the fields, with no doctors around to help, and since I know that they move all over and have no official address, no place of residence, I should not have been surprised that those same children lack birth certificates — yet, I was indeed surprised. Who am I? Where do I come from? When did it really happen, my entrance into this world? Those are questions which, after all, the rest of us never stop asking, in one form or another; and they are questions Larry asks himself in a specially grim and stark fashion, because he really doesn't have the usual, concrete answers, let alone all the fancy symbolic or metaphysical ones. Since he is, I believe, a bright and shrewd child, he won't quite let the matter drop, as many migrant children seem to do. I'm not at all convinced they actually *do* let "the matter" drop. Given a little acquaintance and the right conversational opening, I have heard other migrant children tell me what Larry has told me: it is hard to settle for near answers and half answers when the issue is *yourself*, your origins as a person and as a citizen.

Put a little differently, it is hard to be an exile, to be sent packing all the time, to be banished, to be turned out and shown the door. In the drawings of migrant children I constantly see, at no one's behest but their own, roads and fields (quite naturally) but also (and a little more significantly) those souvenirs and reminders of other places and times — when a comb was given as a present, when something that at least looked precious was found; and finally other drawings show even more mysterious objects, such as windows that are attached to no buildings, and doors that likewise seem suspended in space. Why, exactly why, should a number of migrant children flex their artistic muscles over windows and doors, over sandboxes, or more literally, over a series of quadrangles? I cannot speak for all the migrant children I know, even as many of them can only stumble upon their words, only stand mute, only look and grimace and smile and frown, only ask questions in reply to questions. Yet, a few of those children eventually and often unexpectedly have managed to have their say, managed to let me know what they're getting at, and by implication, what is preventing me from recognizing the obvious concerns of their lives. I have in mind a girl of eight who spends most of her time in Collier County, Florida, and Palm Beach County, Florida, but manages a yearly trek north to upstate New York and New Jersey and into New England, to the farms of Connecticut. As I became a regular visitor of her family, she above all the other children expressed an interest in the paints and crayons I brought along, as well as the various games. She loved a top I had, and a Yo-Yo. She loved the toy cars and trucks and tractors: "I know about all of those. I know my trucks. I know my tractors. I know the cars, and I've been in a lot of them." She once asked me how fast I've driven. She once asked me what it was like to be on an airplane. She once asked me if an airplane could just take off — and land on the moon or the stars or the sun. She once asked me why there are always clouds up North — and why down South the sun is so mean and hot, so pitiless to people who don't own air conditioners or screens or even mosquito repellents or lotions to soothe burned and blistered skin.

She was, in fact, always asking me questions and making sly, provocative, even enigmatic remarks. "I love the Yo-Yo" she told me, "because it keeps going, up and down, and that's what I do." What did she mean? "Well, we don't stay in one camp too long. When the crops are in, you have to move." As for the pictures she did, she liked to put a Yo-Yo or two in them ("for fun") but most of all she liked to make sure the sun was blocked out by clouds that loomed large over the sketched or painted scene — which frequently would have a door or a window or both, along with, say, a lone tree or some disorganized shrubbery. In one picture (Figure 14) she allowed a door to dominate the paper. I expected her to *do* something with the door, to attach it or use it in some way, but she simply let it be and went on to other things, to the sun and its grim face, to the clouds, those sad, inevitable clouds of hers, and to a sandbox and a Yo-Yo, and finally, to a tall plant which I thought might be a small tree. I asked her about that — the pine tree, as I saw it: "No, no, it's a big, tall corn. We pick a lot of corn up North." She was, in other words, getting ready to go North. It was early May, and soon they would all be on the road. What does that mean, though, to *her?* I've asked her that question in various ways and she in her own ways has replied — through her drawings and paintings, and in the games we've played and finally, with these words: "I hate to go, yes sir, I do. I found some sand over there, and my brother Billy and my brother Eddie and me, we like to go and make things there. Soon we'll be going, I know. I can tell when it's happening. First we move our things into the car, and then we go in, and then we go away and I don't know if we'll come back here or not. Maybe, my mother says — all depending, you know. I try to remember everything, so I won't leave anything behind. Every time we go, my daddy, he gets sore at me, because at the last second I'll be runing out of the car and checking on whether I've left any of my things there. I'll go inside and come out and then I know I haven't left something."

Twice I watched her do just that, watched her enter the cabin, look around and leave, watched *her* watch — look and stare and most of all touch, as if by putting her hands on walls and floors and doors and windows she could absorb them, keep them, make them more a part of her. She is a touching girl. She touches. In a minute or two, while the rest of her family frets and adjusts themselves, one to the other and all to the car which they more than fill up, this little girl of theirs scurries about — inspecting, scanning, brushing her body and especially her hands and most especially her fingers on a broken-down shack she is about to leave. When I saw her look out of the window (no screens) and open and close the door several times (it didn't quite open or quite close) I realized at last what all those windows and doors she drew might have meant, and the sandboxes and the corn up North, the corn that was waiting for her, summoning her family, drawing them all from the cabins, making an uproar out of their lives: up and down, to and fro, in and out, here and there, they would go — hence the Yo-Yo and the windows from which one looks out to say good-bye and the doors which lead in and out, in and out, over and over again.

It is hard, very hard to do justice to the lives of such children with words; and I say that because I have tried and feel decidedly inadequate to the job — of all the jobs I have had, to this one I feel particularly inadequate. I do not wish to deny these American children the efforts they make every day — to live, to make sense of the world, to get along with one another and all sorts of grown-up people, to find a little pleasure and fun and laughs in a world that clearly has not seen fit to smile very generously upon them. Nor do I wish to deny these children their awful struggles, which in sum amount to a kind of continuing, indeed endless chaos. It is all too easy, as I must keep on saying, for a doctor like me to do either — see only ruined lives or see only the courageous and the heroic in these children. I am tempted to do the former because for one thing there is a lot of misery to see, and for another I have been trained to look for that misery, see it, assess it, make a judgment about its extent and severity; and I want to praise their courage as an act, perhaps, of reparation — because I frankly have often felt overwhelmed by the conditions I have witnessed during seven years of work with migrant farm families: social conditions, medical conditions, but above all a special and extraordinary kind of human condition, a fate really, and one that is terrible almost beyond description.

What Conrad, in "Heart of Darkness," called "the horror, the horror" eventually has its effect on the observer as well as the observed, particularly when children are the observed and a professional observer of children does the observing. "The horror, the horror" refers to man's inhumanity to man, the brutality that civilized people somehow manage to allow in their midst. The crucial word is "somehow"; because in one way or another all of us, certainly including myself, have to live with, contend with even, the lives of migrant children — those I have just attempted to describe and hundreds of thousands of others — who live (it turns out, when we take the trouble to inquire) just about everywhere in the United States: North and South, East and West, in between, near towns or cities and also out of almost everyone's sight.

Somehow, then, we come to terms with them, the wretched of the American earth. We do so each in his or her own way. We ignore them. We shun them. We claim ignorance of them. We declare ourselves helpless before their problems. We say they deserve what they get, or don't deserve better, or do deserve better — if only they would go demand it. We say things are complicated, hard to change, stubbornly unyielding. We say progress is coming, has even come, will come in the future. We say (in a pinch) that yes, it *is* awful — but so have others found life: awful, mean, harsh, cruel, and a lot of other words. Finally, we say yes it *is* awful — but so awful that those who live under such circumstances are redeemed, not later in Heaven, as many of them believe, but right here on this earth, where they become by virtue of extreme hardship and suffering a kind of elect: hard and tough and shrewd and canny and undeluded; open and honest and decent and self-sacrificing; hauntingly, accusingly hardworking. I have many times extolled these children and their people — extolled them all almost to Heaven, where I suppose I also believe they will eventually and at last get their reward, and where, by the way, they will be out of my way, out of my mind, which balks at saying what it nevertheless knows must be said about how utterly, perhaps unspeakably devastating a migrant life can be for children.

I am talking about what I imagine can loosely be called psychological issues, but I do not mean to ignore the bodily ills of these children: the hunger and the chronic malnutrition that they learn to accept as unavoidable; the diseases that one by one crop up as the first ten years of life go by, diseases that go undiagnosed and untreated, diseases of the skin and the muscles and the bones and the vital organs, vitamin- and mineral-deficiency diseases and untreated congenital diseases and infectious diseases and parasitic diseases and in the words of one migrant mother, "all the sicknesses that ever was." She goes on: "I believe our children get them, the sicknesses, and there isn't anything for us to do but pray, because I've never seen a doctor in my life, except once, when he delivered my oldest girl; the rest, they was just born, yes sir, and I was lucky to have my sister near me, and that's the way, you know." She has some idea about other things, too. She thinks her children are living in Hell, literally that. She is a fierce, biblical woman when she gets going — when, that is, she is talking about her children. I have heard the sermons, many of them from her, and I see no reason, after these years of work with mothers like her and children like hers, to refuse her a place in the last, sad summing up that mercifully allows an observer to go on to other matters while the observed, in this instance, pursue the most they can possibly hope for — the barest, most meager fragments of what can only ironically be called *a life.*

"This life," says the mother, "it's no good on me and my husband, but it's much worse than no good on the children we have, much worse than it can be for any of God's children, that's what I believe. I'll ask myself a lot of the time why a child should be born, if this is the life for him; but you can't make it that we have no children, can you? — because it's the child that gives you the hope. I say to myself that maybe I can't get out of this, but if just one, just one and no more of my children gets out, then I'd be happy and I'd die happy. Sometimes I dream of my girl or one of my boys, that they've left us and found a home, and it has a backyard, and we all were there and eating in the backyard, and no one could come along and tell us to get out, because we could tell *them* to get out, because it's our land, and we own it, and no one can shout at us and tell us to keep moving, keep moving. That's the life we live — moving and moving and moving. I asked the minister a little while ago; I asked him why do we have to always move and move, just to stay alive, and not have no money and die, and he said we're seeking God, maybe, and that's why we keep moving, because God, He traveled, you know, all over the Holy Land, and He kept on trying to convert people to be good to Him, you know, but they weren't, oh no they weren't, and He was rebuked, and He was scorned (remember those words?) and He couldn't stay anyplace, because they were always after Him, always, and they didn't want Him here and they didn't want Him there, and all like that, and all during His life, until they punished Him so bad, so bad it was.

"The minister, he said if you suffer — well, you're God's people, and that's what it's about. I told him that once he preached to us and told us all morning that it was God who was supposed to suffer, and He did. Now it shouldn't be us who's going from place to place and, you know, nobody will let us stop and live with them, except if we go to those camps, and they'll take all your money away, that you must know, because they deduct for the food and the transporting, they tell you. Pretty soon they'll give you a slip of paper and it says you've worked and picked all the beans there are, and all the tomatoes, and the field is empty, and you've made your money, but you've been eating, and they took you up from Florida to where you are, and it cost them money to transport you, so it's all even, and they don't owe you and you don't owe them, except that you've got to get back, and that means you'll be working on the crops to get back South, and it never seems to stop, that's what. Like I said, should we be doing it, the crops every last place, and without anything to have when it's over? They'll come and round you up and tell you it can be jail or the fields, that's what they will tell you, if you get a bad crew leader, that's what. Once we had a nice one, and he was always trying to help us, and he wanted us to make some money and save it, and one day we could stop picking and our children, they could just be, in one place they could be, and they wouldn't always be crying when we leave. But he died, the good crew man, and it's been bad since. You know, there comes a time, yes sir, there does, when the child, he'll stop crying, and then he doesn't care much, one way or the other. I guess he's figured out that we've got to go, and it's bad all the time, and there's no getting around it."

That is what the migrant child eventually learns about "life," and once learned finds hard to forget. He learns that each day brings toil for his parents, backbreaking toil: bending and stooping and reaching and carrying. He learns that each day means a trip: to the fields and back from the fields, to a new county or on to another state, another region of the country. He learns that each day means not aimlessness and not purposeless motion, but compelled, directed (some would even say utterly *forced*) travel. He learns, quite literally, that the wages of work is *more* work. He learns that wherever he goes he is both wanted and unwanted, and that in any case, soon there will be another place and another and another. I must to some extent repeat and repeat the essence of such migrancy (the wandering, the disapproval and ostracism, the extreme and unyielding poverty) because children learn that way, learn by repetition, learn by going through something ten times and a hundred times and a thousand times, until finally it is there, up in their minds in the form of what me and my kind call an "image," a "self image," a *notion*, that is, of life's hurts and life's drawbacks, of life's calamities — which in this case are inescapable, relentless, unremitting.

By the time migrant children are nine and ten and eleven they have had their education, learned their lessons. In many cases they have long since stopped even the pretense of school. They are working, or helping out with younger children, or playing and getting ready to go out on dates and love and become parents and follow their parents' footsteps. As for their emotions, they are, to my eye, an increasingly sad group of children. They have their fun, their outbursts of games and jokes and teasing and taunting and laughing; but they are for too long stretches of time downcast and tired and bored and indifferent and to themselves very unkind. They feel worthless, blamed, frowned upon, spoken ill of. Life itself, the world around them, even their own parents, everything that is, seems to brand them, stigmatize them, view them with disfavor, and in a million ways call them to account — lace into them, pick on them, tell them off, dress them down. The only answer to such a fate is sex, when it becomes possible, and drink, when it is available, and always the old, familiar answers — travel, work, rest when that can be had, and occasionally during the year a moment in church, where forgiveness can be asked, where the promise of salvation can be heard, where some wild, screaming, frantic, angry, frightened, nervous, half-mad cry for help can be put into words and songs and really given the body's expression: turns and twists and grimaces and arms raised and trunks bent and legs spread and pulled together and feet used to stamp and kick and move — always that, move.

"I do a lot of walking and my feet are always tired, but in church I can walk up and down, but not too far; and my feet feel better, you know. It's because God must be near." So she believes — that God is not far off. So her children believe, too. What is life like? One keeps on asking those children that question — for the tenth or so time (or is it the hundredth time?) in the last year or two, because they do seem to want to talk about what is ahead for them, and *that,* one believes, is a good sign for them and a helpful thing (it must be acknowledged) for anyone who wants to find out about such matters, about what people see their life to be, their future to be, their destiny I suppose it could be called. "Well, I'll tell you," the girl says gravely in answer to the question. Then she doesn't say anything for a long time and the observer and listener gets nervous and starts rummaging for another question, another remark, to lighten the atmosphere, to keep things going, to prevent all that awkwardness, a sign no doubt of mistrust or suspicion or a poor "relationship." Yet, once in a while there does come an answer, in fits and starts, in poor language that has to be a little corrected later, but an answer it is — and a question, too, at the very beginning a question: "Well, I'll tell you, I don't know how it'll be ahead for me, but do you think my people, all of us here, will ever be able to stop and live like they do, the rest of the people?" No one knows the answer to that, one says, but hopefully such a day will come, and soon. "No, I don't think so. I think a lot of people, they don't want us to be with them, and all they want is for us to do their work, and then good-bye, they say, and don't come back until the next time, when there's more work and then we'll have you around to do it, and then good-bye again."

There is another pause, another flurry of remarks, then this: "I'd like to have a home, and children, maybe three or four, two boys and two girls. They could all be nice children, and they wouldn't get sick and die, not one. We would have a house and it would have all the things, television and good furniture, not secondhand. If we wanted to work the crops, we'd plant them for ourselves, because the house and the land we'd have would be ours and no one could come and take us away and take the house away, either. I'd make us all go to school, even me; because if you don't learn things, then you'll be easy to fool, and you'll never be able to hold on to anything, my daddy says. He says he tries, and he doesn't get tricked *all* the time, but a lot of the time he does, and he can't help it, and he's sorry we don't just stay in a place and he's sorry my sisters and brothers and me don't go to school until we're as smart as the crew men and the foremen and the owners and the police and everyone. Then we could stop them from always pushing on us and not letting us do anything they don't want us to do. That's why, if I could, I'd like to be in school at the same time my kids would be there, and we'd be getting our education.

"I do believe we could have it better; because if we could get a job in one of the towns, then we could get a house and keep it and not leave and then if I broke my arm, like I did, they would take care of it in the hospital and not send you from one to the other until you pass out because you're dizzy and the blood is all over, and it hurts and like that, yes sir. Also, we could go and buy things in the stores — if we had the money and if they knew you lived there and weren't just passing through. All the time they'll tell you that, they'll say that you're just passing through and not to bother people, and they don't want you to come in and mess things up. But I could have a baby carriage and take my babies to the shopping stores, like you see people do, and we could go into all of them and it would be fun. I'd like that. I'd love it. I'd love to go and shop and bring a lot of things home and they'd be mine and I could keep them and I could fix up the house and if I didn't like the way it looks I could change things and it would look different, and it would be better.

"My mother, she always says it don't make any difference how we live in a place, it don't, because we'll soon be leaving. If it's a real bad place, she'll say, 'Don't worry, because we'll soon be leaving,' and if it's a better one, then she'll say, 'Don't fuss around and try to get everything all fixed up, because we'll soon be leaving.' Once when I was real little, I remember, I asked her why we couldn't stop our leaving and stay where we are, and she slapped me and told me to stop bothering her; and my daddy said if I could find a better way to make some money, then he'd like to know it. But I don't know how he could do any better, and he's the hardest-working picker there is, the crew man told him, and we all heard. My daddy said if he would ever stop picking, he'd never, never miss doing it, but he can't, and maybe I'll never be able to, either. Maybe I'll just dream about a house and living in it. My mother says she dreams a lot about it, having a house, but she says it's only natural we would wish for things, even if you can't have them. But, if you're asking what it'll really be like when I'm much older, then I can tell you it'll be just like now. Maybe it'll be much better for us, but I don't think so. I think maybe it won't be too different, because my daddy says if you're doing the kind of work we do, they need you, and they're not going to let you go, and besides there isn't much else for us to do but what we're already doing. My brother, he thinks maybe he could learn to drive a tractor and he'd just go up and down the same fields and a few others, and he'd never have to go on the road like we do now and he says when I think of going with a boy, I should ask him if he's going to go on the road, or if he's going to stay some-place, where he is, and get himself some kind of work that will let him settle down. But every time you try, they have no work but picking, they say, and the foremen, they're around and soon the sheriff and likely as not they'll arrest you for owing them something. If you get away, though, then you have to go someplace, and if you go to a city, then it's no good there, either, from what you hear, and you can't even work there, either; and it's real bad, the living, even if you don't have to be moving on up the road all the time.

"To me it would be the happiest day in the world if one day I woke up and I had a bed, and there was just me and a real nice man, my husband, there; and I could hear my children, and they would all be next door to us, in another room, all their own; and they would have a bed, each one of them would, and we would just be there, and people would come by and they'd say that's where they live, and that's where they'll always be, and they'll never be moving, no, and they won't have to, because they'll own the house, like the foremen do and the crew men and everyone else does, except us. Then we won't be with the migrant people anymore, and we'll be with everyone else, and it'll be real different."

So, it would be, vastly different. She and children like her would see a different world. Unlike migrant children, other children like to draw pastoral landscapes, like to drench them in sun, fill them with flowers, render them anything but bleak. Unlike migrant children, other children don't draw roads that are fenced in and blocked off or lead nowhere and everywhere and never end. Unlike migrant chil-dren, most children don't worry about birth certificates, or doors and more doors and always doors — that belong, even in a few years of ex-perience, to half a hundred or more houses. So again, it would be dif-ferent if the little girl just quoted could have a solid, permanent home. Her drawings would not be like the ones I have selected, or like dozens of others very similar. The themes would be different, because her life would be different. Her days and months and years would have a cer-tain kind of continuity, a kind we all don't think about, because some things are so very important, so intimate to life's meaning and nature that we really cannot bear to think about them; and indeed if we *were* thinking about them we would for some reason have come upon seri-ous trouble.

Even many animals define themselves by where they live, by the territory they possess or covet or choose to forsake in order to find new land, a new sense of control and self-sufficiency, a new dominion.

It is utterly part of our nature to want roots, to need roots, to struggle for roots, for a sense of belonging, for some place that is recognized as *mine,* as *yours,* as *ours.* Nations, regions, states, counties, cities, towns — all of them have to do with politics and geography and history; but they are more than that, they somehow reflect man's humanity, his need to stay someplace and live there and get to know something — a lot, actually: other people, and what I suppose can be called a particular environment, or space or neighborhood or world, or set of circumstances. It is bad enough that thousands of us, thousands of American children, still go hungry and sick and are ignored and spurned — every day and constantly and just about from birth to death. It is quite another thing, a lower order of human degradation, that we also have thousands of boys and girls who live utterly uprooted lives, who wander the American earth, who even as children enable us to eat by harvesting our crops but who never, never can think of anyplace as home, of themselves as anything but homeless. There are moments, and I believe this is one of them, when, whoever we are, observers or no, we have to throw up our hands in heaviness of heart and dismay and disgust and say, in desperation: God save them, those children; and for allowing such a state of affairs to continue, God save us, too.

Stranded Children

The cabins; they stand off the highways, way off them, up the dirt roads — and almost always the children linger around those cabins. They sit and play or they run all over and play or they linger about and seem not to be doing much of anything — those boys and girls of, say, Tunica County, Mississippi, or Clarke County, Alabama, or McCormick County, South Carolina. In books read by second- or third-grade students, such children are called "country boys" or "farm girls." In textbooks, such boys and girls are called sharecropper children or the children of tenant farmers or field hands. I suppose, as we now seem to insist, it is a state of mind, a quality of upbringing that characterizes those children: they are seriously "deprived" and "disadvantaged" — "backward," it once was put — and they need so very much that perhaps the easiest way to start is to say they need just about everything.

Many of the cabins have been abandoned, but thousands and thousands of them remain inhabited, and the people who live inside know that. They know they have been left behind; know they often have chosen to be left behind, chosen to remain and feel — perhaps the word is *stranded:* "I don't know why we're still here, but we are; and I guess we always will be, yes sir. There comes a time when you say to yourself that the only thing you can do is whatever there is to do, and if there's nothing more, then there isn't. But a lot of them, a lot of our people, they've left, you know. They'll still be doing it, too — a family here and one over there, and mostly by night. That's the time. It'll be around midnight or into the morning, and you can almost hear them. I *do* sometimes. I'll be turning over in my sleep, and suddenly I'll hear a car coming, or there'll be one over the other side of the plantation, a car being started, and I'll scratch myself and ask if it's a dream I'm having, or if it's another family going up there — to Chicago, likely. That's where I think most of us from here go, if they get there; and you wonder sometimes if they don't get lost or give up and stop someplace by the road and settle into raising some food. But like down here, the people up North whose land it is, they probably don't want us growing a lot of food ourselves there, either. They just want us to sweat for them, grow for them."

So, she is resigned to staying put; she is resigned even though her older sister and her two younger sisters and her brother have left the state of Mississippi and even though they all have at one time or another come back and told her to leave, to leave for good and take their mother along so that none of them would ever again live in or return to the plantation every one of them calls "the place." She is resigned to the kind of life her mother had — though she wonders whether even that kind of life will be permitted: "They said we could stay, especially my mother, but if she goes, then they might make me and my family leave here, and they'll burn down the house, like they've been doing, and like they'd really have done already if it wasn't that my mother waited on them for years and years, and the bossman, his wife said no, they should let us alone. You know she came over here, the missus; she drove up one day. She got out of her car and she started looking around, and we got scared, because from the look on her face we thought she was real sore at us, and she was going to take after us and tell us we were in the wrong for something.

"We just waited, and after a while she came over and she said she was real sorry that we didn't have a better place to live, but it was going to be machines now that harvest the crops, and there wasn't much we could do anymore. She went over and looked my mother straight into her eyes and told her she sure was grateful for all she'd done; and it was too bad about her arthritis and the pain she was having and how sad it was to see her bent over like that, but not to worry, because she can stay here for as long as she wants, my mother can, and not to worry about the house (the big house she meant, yes she did) because there was this nice young girl, and she was working out fine, and they had some other help, too — for the heavy work, a boy I believe she said. Then she turned around fast, all of a sudden, and she just marched out and drove off, and she didn't say good-bye — not until she was in the car. Then she waved, but I don't believe there was a smile on her face, no sir; and my mother, it was she that was smiling, and afterwards saying how nice it was for her, the missus, to come up here."

I described the daughter as resigned, yet her words also convey a certain sense of annoyance, however restrained; or perhaps what I notice is a wry or sardonic quality mixed with an earnest and forthright manner that tempers the underlying resignation. The resignation emerges when least expected: "To be telling you the truth, I'm not sure it's going to be any better for my children, not than it was for me or for my mother, and maybe even for my grandmother, and I can remember a little of her. Sometimes I'll be wondering if maybe I should have said to my mother that we've *got* to go up there to Chicago, and then she would have gone; but I never tried it, and I'm just as glad, actually. The way I see it, my little ones wouldn't have been any better off in the city, and worse, maybe — it might be much worse up there. A nephew of mine, he's my sister's boy, I hear he's in jail, someplace near Chicago. Now, the sheriff, he doesn't put us in jail, so long as we don't bother anyone — yes, I mean the white folks. And you'd be crazy, you'd have to be, to go bothering them, don't you know.

"I tell my boys and I tell my girls that they should stay clear of the white man, unless he beckons you, and then try to be nice and polite and do what he's asking if it's possible to do, and if it's not, then always apologize and say you'll do the best you can, and you'll be sorry if it's not enough. They say up North the colored man doesn't have to be afraid of the white no more, and the colored children, they speak up and say as they please before the white man. But there's my nephew — they put him right into jail. And I'll bet there's a lot more of us in jail up there than down here, though I *do* know we've got plenty of us put away down here. The reason is, a lot of the colored people have gone into the Mississippi towns, don't you know, since they can't stay here on the farms and work for the white people, and so they go to a place like Greenville, and some even to Jackson, and that's where they get into trouble with the law, they sure do. So, I'm afraid to leave and I'm

afraid to stay, and whichever I do, I think it might be real bad for my
boys and girls — real bad."

She has five children, or five that have so far stayed alive. She has
had "three or four" miscarriages and two of her children died, one at
seven months, "suddenly and for no reason" and one at age four "of a
real bad cold, it seemed like." Over the years I have come to know her
as well as someone like me will ever really understand someone like
her — which is to say that I do indeed believe that I have learned a lot
about her and her family. Yet I worry about those often discussed
(maybe too much discussed) barriers that separate observers like me
from sharecropper families like hers — and for all their present difficulties, she and her husband and their children are precisely that,
sharecroppers, or so they think themselves to be: "We've been on
shares to the mister and his daddy and before him the old, old gentle-
man, and I do believe it goes back to when we were all slaves, yes sir.
Today there isn't much for my husband to do, except for errands here
and there. But until a couple of years ago, we'd work our land, the part
the bossman gave to us, and at the end of the year he'd come over and
he'd settle up with us. No, there wasn't too much money we'd get; but
you now he'd be giving us the house, this one, all along, and they'd
supply us our food and like that, and if anything special comes up,
something real bad, they're good people, and we could go over there
and ask them, and they'd be glad to help. Of course, we don't ask anything big of them, and we never did. It worked out OK, being on
shares with him, because he's a fair person, and he'd tell me and my
husband to stop standing and sit down, and he'd open his book and
point to the page and tell us it was the one with our name on it, and all
the figures were there, and that's how it all added up — and he never
would be like some of the others. They'll give you nothing, or close to
it, and they'll say you're lucky to be getting the food all along, and lucky
to have a roof over your head."

They do not feel too lucky these days. They worry about their
children, yet don't know how to make those worries less necessary.
They care about their children, yet have no conviction that such love
and concern will matter. Most of the time they simply go about the
business of living, or trying to live, or just barely staying alive: "I'm
afraid we're sick a lot of the time, me and my children are. If it's not
one thing, it's something else, and according to the minister, we're all
of us just as likely to die sooner than later, because God might be waiting on us — you never know. I tell my children, each one of them,
that it's better they be good and obey me and do as I say, because they

can go fast, just like the older people, and it's a long time to spend in Hell, if they're no good and God turns His back on them.

"They're good, though, my boys — the two of them — and my three girls. They like to go along and help me, and most of the time they don't give me trouble. I try to do the best I can for them, and I tell them they've got to look after one another, because their daddy and me might die one day, and then they'd be alone, except for my mother, and she's sick. Then they'll ask about their cousins, and I'll tell them it's a long way from here to Chicago, and I hope it stays that way, because as bad as it is here, it'll be only worse someplace else; and I say it twice, and sometimes more, so they'll hear and they won't forget. Then, of course, they'll ask why it is that the people are leaving, and I say some are, but some aren't, and we aren't, and that's the answer, and there'll be no other answer, and stop asking. But they do, a little later on, and I'll be repeating the same thing. And you know, a while back my boy Henry, he's seven, wanted to know if there wasn't some chance we'd leave here, and I told him no, and why was he keeping on asking me, and he said that if someday *we* didn't go, then maybe *he* would, but I told him how bad it would be if he was up North, and he listened. I could tell he got scared by what I was saying, and he said maybe I was right and it was bad here, and maybe we could die all of a sudden — like I keep on telling him — but from now on he was going to be happy we're here, and from now on he promised he'd stop talking about the North. Like I said, as bad as it is, there's always worse trouble you can get into."

Such children, sharecropper children, learn that particular kind of self-satisfaction rather early. A child born of a sharecropper or a tenant farmer gradually gets a sense of things, a sense of who he is and where he is and what his life is likely to be like. I cannot emphasize strongly enough how early it is that such a "sense of things," complicated and subtle, yet ultimately all too brutal and clear, begins to develop. For example, the mother I have just quoted has what I suppose can be called an "attitude" toward her children, an attitude that begins to take shape well before the boy or girl is born, and an attitude that upon analysis reveals all sorts of things not only about a particular kind of "child-rearing," but also about a whole region, a whole way of life. At different times the mother and I have talked about her children and her hopes for them and her fears about them and her view of what they will have to learn. Any one conversation has its limits, but over the years particular things occur and occur, are stated and stated; and finally one can somewhat reliably feel certain words and sentiments "coming," or "near expression" in the course of a given talk — in which case the observer feels that he, like the children in question, has a little of that "sense of things" just mentioned. Perhaps I am merely saying that the wife of a sharecropper, like the wife of a lawyer or a businessman or a psychiatrist, needs time and various kinds of occasions if she is ever going to get across either to herself or some observer what can so glibly be called her "philosophy," or again, her "attitudes." A sharecropper's wife does not use those words, but she knows what they are meant to mean, and she has her own words that are not exactly vague or pretentious or incomprehensible: "To me, if you ask me what I believe, it's that God wants us to have children, and not only because without them we'd soon disappear, but because as long as boys and girls keep coming, you know the world might one day get better. I get to feeling better when I'm carrying, yes I do. You know something else — each time I'm carrying, the missus up there will be a little nicer to me, all during the time she will. She'll ask me how I'm getting on; and she'll ask me if it's a boy or a girl I want; and she'll ask me if my legs are swelling up, like the last time, or not; and toward the end, if I don't lose the child, like I have, you know, she'll come over sometime, when I'm working up there for her — in the house, yes sir — and she'll tell me not to be in a hurry and to share my work with Alice and with Lucy, because they're helping her a lot, too.

"She's the one, the missus, who gets us the midwife. They say it's better having a midwife than a doctor — the missus told me that the first time, when she brought the woman over and told me she wasn't going to have any of us delivering without someone who's trained and knows all about things. Then the woman kept on coming back every few weeks — it was for my first one — and when I felt the baby asking to be born, moving hard at me, I did what the missus said and told my husband to go up there to the house, and tell her, the missus, that it was the time. And you know what? Well, it didn't take the missus long to get the midwife, and when she came she stayed with me, and she delivered my Martha, and since then she has delivered my other ones, too — except for the ones I lost, and for James, because he came too quick for anyone to get here.

"I love having the midwife woman come, and my mother says it's a miracle, what a colored lady can learn how to do — just about be a doctor, yes sir. I've never gone to a doctor's place, no I haven't, not for myself. But once I went with the missus, because she was in a bad state. Her head was aching, and she couldn't keep her food down, and she kept on having dizzy spells. She called the doctor, and she called her husband, he was up in Memphis; and then she said I should go with her to the doctor, and if she had trouble in the car, then she could stop and I was to go get help. She lasted through the ride, though; and when we got to the doctor's she had me come in with her, and I've never seen such a place in all my life: there was the desk he had, and a table he had her sit on, and he had the books, and he had medicines and he had things to use on you, every kind you can think of, and soon he was listening to her heart, he said, and her lungs, and he'd test her with one thing and another until she must have had every test there was, and then he wrote her out something, and she got the pills at the store, and later on she said, I heard her tell her husband, that the doctor had helped and made her better, he had. Now, the midwife, she's not like the doctor, because she hasn't got her an office. She's not white, either — and I should say that, I guess — and I don't believe she can get you better so fast, the way the doctors can. But if you're like us, the doctors don't see you, because they're not for the colored. I hear say that even our leading people, the leading colored folks here, they'll be real lucky if the doctor will see them, no matter if they have the money to pay or not. The good doctors, they say, will build themselves a special door for us to use, and they'll be real nice to you, if you can pay them; but there will be others, and they tell you that they're only for the white people, yes sir, and we should try to find someone else.

"I once said to the midwife that she should learn other things besides delivering — that way she could help us all the time. But she said she had all she could do to keep up with the babies, as they come; and even so, with her around for us, a lot of colored people just go and have their babies by themselves, one after the other. It's too bad because women can suffer, they can suffer a lot having a child, and it's bad when there's no one to help them — and that's how it was with my mother, and my mother says that she believes we're lucky to have a missus like we do, who will go and get the midwife and pay for her and like that. My mother admits that's one of the best reasons to leave, to go North. I mean, people say that it can be bad up there, but there are the hospitals and doctors, and they'll take care of a colored person, the doctors, and you have a better chance — I mean with delivering and if your baby gets sick and all the rest, you know. Anyway, if the missus becomes nicer to you when you become heavy, that's a good reason to become heavy! Even if she didn't change her attitude, I'd still be wanting my children. Wouldn't any mother?

"One reason I go along with my mother and agree with her — I mean about staying here and not leaving, like people do — well, it's because even if we have it bad here, it's still what we know, and I'm afraid from what I hear — my sister writes me — that we'd be losing if we left, even if we'd be gaining. Yes sir, that's how I'd add it up. That's what my mother says. She'll say to me: 'Ella, sure we could go up there, but I don't want to go. If I thought it was good for *you,* never mind me, I'd go anyway. But there's a good chance it won't be better — for any of us. Maybe the hospitals are good up there, but I'll bet colored people are pushed around in those hospitals, even if they do take us in and listen to our troubles.' That's what she'll say, my mother. Now, I'll tell you, I feel the same way. My little girl, she'll ask me why so many people keep leaving here, the colored people, and when are *we* going; but I say to her there's a lot of colored people left down here, you bet. And there's a good reason why: they know, we do, that it's no good for us anyplace, and before you go changing one sickness for another, then you stop and think — that's what the midwife says about going to Chicago.

"A lot of what she says, the midwife, I agree with. She'll tell you when she hands you your baby that you can't build Heaven for your child here on earth, here in Mississippi; but you can try your best, and make your child feel he belongs here, belongs to you, even if it's not the best life he's been born to have, and even if he would have been better off to have been born somewhere else to someone else. So, that's what I try to do. I whisper to my little baby that it sure is hot here, and we sure don't have all the good food we should have, and sometimes we don't have a single thing good for them to wear — nothing at all — but it could be worse, and at least we're alive, and we do the best we can. The way I see it, a child is lucky to get born in the first place. Like the midwife will tell you, and I know it, oh do I: a lot just die before ever seeing the sun or the sky or the trees. They die inside you, before they're much of anything, and that's a shame. That's what you have to keep reminding yourself, and that's what you have to tell your children, or else they'll grow up and they'll feel sorry for themselves — and you should never let yourself get in low spirits, never."

Does she, in fact, ever get moody and sad and fearful — for all her protests that one must not let such things happen? Do her children, too, begin to wonder just what she means when she tells them they are lucky — of all ironic things (so people like me think) *lucky*? Put differently, is such talk from her an effort to whistle in the dark, an effort to deny or rationalize away the obvious pain and sorrow and bitterness that must in some way plague such impoverished sharecropper women? If so, exactly how long are children, however young and ignorant and naïve, deceived by such obvious (if necessary, some of us hasten nervously to add) psychological maneuvers? I ask those questions not in order to answer them flatly and unequivocally. I think I am in fact recording something when I include the questions in the midst of a particular limited psychological chronicle, when I spell out some of the doubts and confusions and misgivings I happened to have felt and tried to resolve as I listened to people trying to settle and explain a few things for themselves rather than for me.

To start dealing with — not answering — some questions, I had better say yes, she and other mothers like her do indeed become unhappy; they get to feeling "blue," and can be heard saying they feel "bluer than blue." So it goes, too, with the children — the thousands of boys and girls who still live in the rural South, despite all the migration to all the cities all over the North and way out in the West. They try, those parents and those children; they try and try not to "get low in spirits." Sadness among the sharecroppers or tenant farmers or field hands I have met has a peculiar and intense kind of life — and emotions like sadness *do* have a life, one characterized by growth, change, development, and above all, it seems, persistence. When, for example, I speak of sadness, I have in mind a number of ways children or mothers or fathers give expression to what is "inside." Moreover, with the families I am now discussing, the issue of sadness — to be more specific, of abandonment — is significant or important enough, I believe, to stand as the central theme of at least this particular descriptive and analytic effort.

To begin with, there is the rather striking and thoroughly open or explicit *clinging* that mothers such as the one I have already quoted demonstrate toward their infants. Of course, almost all mothers cling to their babies, and I have already described how migrant mothers attach themselves with great intensity to their newborn sons and daughters. In this regard there are differences, though; differences between migrant mothers and sharecropper mothers and differences between both of them on the one hand and many other American mothers, whose position in society goes under the name of middle class. Here, for example, is another mother speaking about her children. She was born a few miles from North Carolina's Atlantic coast, and she expects to die there. She might have been the mother of five, had she not already known a miscarriage and struggled with a dying child: "I did lose my little girl, I did; but you have to expect things like that, you just have to. I recall when I was little, and I'd cry about something, then my mother would get ahold of me and she'd tell me off, she would. She'd say as long as you're going to be living and not dead, you're going to be fighting the tears away, and I'd better start learning right away about how to go ahead and do my work and wipe those tears away. She'd take my hand and make me clear my eyes, and usually, when I think back, I recall her telling me one bad story or another — about how they used to treat us colored people back in the past, and how we didn't disappear from God's earth, even so we didn't, and how I should never forget that for all the bad times there are good times, and it tastes better, something good and juicy, when you've been hungry for a long time.

"When you lose faith in things, you should stop yourself and re-member God and remember that there's always hope. That's what my mother always told me. I think I must have listened to her, because most of the time I keep my spirits up, and I'm now telling my children exactly as she told me, even if she is gone — it's now five years I think. Yes, that's right, I start whispering the words to my little baby, the first thing after they're born — because it's not too early, I don't believe. The reason is they've got to know that we may not have a lot of the things they need, but we have each other, that's what I tell them. Bad as it can get, so long as we keep together with each other, then we'll get by, yes I believe we will. Sometimes a child of mine, she'll get to crying real bad, and I know she's hurting and I know she needs some-thing I can't give her; but I'll come over and I'll hold her and I'll hold her and I'll hold her, and I'll tell her, right into her ear, that if she hasn't got anything — nothing to wear and the sicknesses and the food that isn't what she should be having — then even so there's me, and I'll never leave my children, never. If we're to die, we'll all go together, and that is how it has to be.

"I think my children do pay attention. I try to make sure they'll listen to me and do what's right. My mother used to hit me when I was in the wrong, but afterwards she'd draw me to her and she'd tell me she didn't want to hurt me, but the world is full of a lot of trouble for us, that's the truth, and if we made trouble for each other, on top of all the trouble there is — well, then, we sure couldn't expect to last very long. Even so, no matter how much my mother tried, I guess I failed her some of the time; and now I see it in my own kids: they'll go ahead and forget everything I say to them. I don't know how to explain why they do, but if you ask me, I think they're themselves and not me, and I really think they sometimes don't want to hear what I tell them. They don't want to hear that they can't have what they'd like, and what others have. They'll go around hitting at the door and kicking at a pail, and like that, and they'll ask why can't it be this way and the other way and not like it is. And I ask, too. And I lose my temper, too. I'll be holding my little baby as close as can be and all of a sudden I can feel myself getting full of the devil, and I want to say that I shouldn't be saying yes to the bossman, and my baby should be having this and my baby should be having that — and everything, everything a baby needs. But I know I can't get a doctor and I know I can't get the best food and I know I can't dress my children up like the white folks do — nor like some colored, a few, that do good and I hear make as much money as a lot of the whites. That's why for one like me, you have to talk with yourself as much as with your child. You have to keep yourself quiet and pinch yourself so you don't go crying as bad as your little girl will; and your little boy, he will cry just as much. You see, you're being crossed all the time: there's something else you mustn't do, and there's a reason why you have to stop here and stay away from the next thing. There'll come a time, there'll come a day, when you're ready to shout at God Himself and ask Him why we're on this earth, people like us, if every time we turn there's a sign that says 'Watch Out' or 'Not For You' or — oh, like that, I guess!"

She is plagued by frustrations. I declare her frustrated and emphasize the assertion not because I have any idea that an interpretation of mine is needed after her perfectly clear remarks. As for sadness, she denies feeling it when she describes her various frustrations. She has told me a number of times what makes her feel sad — feel "low" or feel "bad" — and never does she consider her intense attachment to her infant child to be evidence of such a state of mind. Nor does she affirm her sadness when she indicates how baffled she feels, how undermined by the world, how cramped in style and thwarted and deterred and blocked and inconvenienced and restrained and restricted. All the time the world stands in her way and undoes in fact what she might think about or dream of. All the time she fights back, holds and hugs and kisses her children, tells them to submit, to go along with what simply must be. All the time, as I see it, she acknowledges in one way or another, with one phrase or another, her sense of frustration. Willingly or reluctantly (or really, in both ways) she accommodates. She tries to warn her children and herself; she tries to speak out the discontent she feels; more than that, she tries to live the discontent out. That is to say, she draws as close as she can to her children, and she makes them right off partners in frustration — and in that way, I believe, she makes a little less oppressive the very substantial sadness she somehow must find a way to keep under control.

Once I asked her whether she did in fact get "unhappy" when one or another frustration came up. She answered me quickly and with a look that seemed to say that she more or less expected me eventually to get around to such matters: "No, no I don't let these things get me down. I don't. You can't. My mother said you can't, and I believed her when she said it, and now that I have my own kids I believe her more. I try to forget the misery we have, because if you don't you're lost, and you can feel yourself going down — way under the water it is. I try to be as good as I can, and if there's something I can't do, and something my little girl can't do, then I get us to go and forget and turn our minds elsewhere. There's always the jobs you've *got* to do, and you have to tell your kids that they have eyes so they can look ahead, so that even if there's something stopping you, they can look over it and there must be, there just *must* be a way you can get around trouble and get yourself to where you're going — though, I'll admit, there will be some days when I just can't figure out where we're going and how we'll ever get there or anyplace else."

Frustration, frustration mingled with resignation, can turn to other moods, as we all know. The mothers quoted here often enough become irritable, sullen, annoyed, and snappish. They strike out at their children, at their husbands, at themselves. When they do so they describe themselves rather freely as "upset" or "fed up" or "angry," but again, not sad and not overwhelmed or in danger of giving up — and indeed they are not about to surrender, though they may well fear that possibility more than they can bear to realize. I am not at this point trying to get categorical, or make those generalizations that allow us to feel conveniently in control of a bothersome and troubling "problem." Nor do I wish to submit the many and various lives I have met in those rural cabins to a lot of fancy, self-important theoretical language — about the last thing an already burdened and restricted people need. Rather I hope to do whatever justice I possibly can to their lives — and I hesitate to use the word "justice" in this or any other context that has to do with sharecroppers and tenant farmers. I have really wanted the people I have observed to let me know, given enough time and a little trust, how they see their lives unfold or work out or develop.

Sharecroppers, like the rest of us, have an idea about the *trends* in their lives — something that may be obvious, but also something easily forgotten by one like me. If I have ideas about what sharecroppers do with their children, and what they go through in their minds and hearts as their children grow up, then so does a woman like this — who repeatedly objected to remarks I made, remarks full of *my* notions about *her* feelings, and who may well be responsible for this overly long and apologetic preamble: "No sir. No. I'm not going to go along with you on that, no sir. I don't think you've got it right. Maybe I'm just being cross with you because it's a bad day. I have them, you know. I just wake up with the day staring at me and no matter how good I know I should try to feel, all I can say to myself is that it's going to be a bad day. But when you ask me if it bothers me when the little ones get bigger and start running around, then I have to tell you no, it doesn't. A mother, she knows; she'll be giving birth to her little child, and before her eyes she'll be picturing her or him; and if it's a girl the mother will see her when she's little and when she gets bigger, and still bigger, and finally she's all grown up and that's the end of the child. Each time I'll be lying on that bed about to have my child it'll happen like that — with my mind giving me those pictures. When I told my mother, the first time, she said of course I would do that, because when a mother is bringing a baby into the world, she's naturally going to stop and look ahead.

"Now to me it's been good when my girls and my little boy started leaving me. I mean, you can't be together all the time, and after a while you can feel them wanting to get away — in their legs and arms you can. They'll be crawling on you and you know they want to go all over and find out where the floor begins and where it ends and what it's like over there where the crops are, and the pine trees — and you know, like that. I'm happy when they're off looking around for themselves. Yes, I truly am. It's more trouble for me, I'll admit. But I can be free of them longer, and that's good. They'll do a lot of crying, of course, and they'll want to come back to you; but I try to tell them that they should sit over there, in front of the house, and enjoy themselves, because a little later on, it won't be so much fun for them, no sir, it won't. A lot of the time, when they're crawling and when they're learning to stand on their feet and move along, I'll pretend to be busy fixing up something — frying up some grits, or straightening up the room — and I'll follow them with my ears. They'll be fighting and screaming and they'll be teaching the smallest one, and she'll be catching on, and I'll tell myself it's not so bad for the kids, it's not so bad. But I know they're not getting the best there is — for food and like that — and there's not much future here, that's what the bossman says, and he's the one who should know. Then I'll slip, and I'll wonder if maybe we shouldn't have left here, so that my kids could be growing up some-where that *has* a future to give them. But from what you hear, it's not so good up there, even if they do have a future to offer you, because the kids don't have room to play or hardly to breathe; and I heard from the lady down the road after her daughter came home for a visit that there are no sheriffs around to push on you up there, but you can't let your kids go anyplace, because they'll get killed on the streets. The streets are real mean up there, she told me.

"That's why we can be happy here, because for my little girl there's land outside, and she can't hurt herself too much there, I know that. There'll be times I feel myself getting mad at her and the other kids, I'll admit it, and my mother will see me letting my temper go and she'll tell me that's how she'd be sometimes. First there'll be an irrita-tion, and then all of a sudden, I'm shouting and screaming and I don't know what's come over me. Later on I'll recall bits and pieces of what I said and what happened. My mother says we all have to fall to pieces sometimes, or else we couldn't go on.

"When you ask what I say to the kids during a temper, it's hard to tell, except that I'll say things I never should, and sometimes it's like I'm doing the exact same thing I tell my kids *not* to do, and I should be punished like them — as the minister says, with soap on my tongue, ex-cept we don't have soap, no sir, because it costs a lot, and you need a lot of water for it, like she has, the bossman's wife. My husband went in her house once — they'd asked him to carry some furniture down. He said the bossman and his wife and kids leave the water running, and there was soap thrown out in a trash can, and it was a piece you could have used and used.

"I guess the main thing is I tell the kids to stop with their fighting and pushing all over one another. I tell them — I'll be real mad and shouting, yes sir — that they'd better watch out, because it won't be long before they'll be big and grown, and if they start getting fresh then, they'll end up in jail as fast as can be, and that will be the end of them, oh will it. Then I'll speak to them like the sheriff would, I guess, and I'll be telling them what the minister will say — and you know, they've got to learn to pay me attention and obey, and if they don't, they'll suffer for it even more than I tell them they will. And the way I see it, I've got to suffer for them right now. I mean, if they see me get-ting upset and bothered then they'll stop in their ways and get to be-having themselves, you know. It's too bad, that's what I believe, that I can't have a lot to give them. Maybe if we'd gone North I could be shopping and buying things for them; but we're here, and they'll have to like it. They'll ask me those questions, the children do, and it shows you they peek in on what my mother will be saying, or me. They'll bother you with all the whys, until you're ready to go kill them to stop them from talking, yes sir — and I'm not ashamed to admit it. My mother says they're just learning things and having their fun by teasing me, and that's the way a child will be. They'll be upset by you, and they'll want to get even, so they'll go and upset you right back. My boy used to tell me he was going to go shoot the sheriff, and the bossman too, and take over his plantation and live up there in his house, and he wouldn't let me come in because I was bad, and so was the minister. Then he'd say it over and over again, how bad, bad, bad I was, until I had to shout him down, and I'd be telling him he was bad and he'd be telling me the same thing right back and it'd be a fight we'd have — until I just came and grabbed him and made him stop. I'd put my hand over his mouth, yes that was how.

"Maybe if my children were up North, they'd be out fighting the police, the way they tell me they will when they are little. I don't know. Here, you have to watch your step. Here you have to hit a colored man if you're going to hit someone, and that's the truth. I don't let my children go hitting one another too much. They might get ideas in their heads about a white man, and that would be the end for all of us. I teach them to be quiet, and they get to be quiet, and that's good. Sometimes I think they'd like to be doing more talking and playing, but I don't have the time to be with them and also help in the field sometimes and also go work for the bossman, cleaning up his office; and besides, I have my stomach pains, and there must be something wrong in there, and my legs are bad, the veins. There'll be one day I'm feeling pretty good, then the next I feel as bad as can be, so bad I can't describe it. I take to crying and I don't know why. My head will be aching, and all of a sudden there'll be the tears, and I have to wipe them away, and then there'll be more after those I cleared off. It's my older children, I sometimes think. They don't have much hope, and when they lose it, I lose it with them. I'll tell them that it may get better here, you know, but they don't listen much, and I'll wonder if they're asking themselves why it was we stayed here — being colored for one thing, and not getting much that you can call your own, except the cabin they give us.

"We get enough from work and the 'loans against the crops,' the bossman calls them, to keep from dying. But you feel disappointed sometimes, even if you can scrape up some food; and that's how the kids, my children, they get to be — sort of disappointed. And so am I, except that I can't spend my days feeling I've lost all my hope, and it's never going to get better. So, I'll tell the kids to go outside there and sit under a tree and play and don't just stare and stare, unless they want to be resting. I know they're tired a lot, because it's hot, and the bugs, they eat on them and itch them and it wears them down. If they're staring here, near me, and then they start talking and making me feel I was real bad not to have a better life waiting on them when they got born, then I'll be all upset, and one minute I'll want to sit with them and say yes, you're right, you are; but the next I'll want them to stop with their complaining and leave me alone and stop making them-selves upset, and like that. If their daddy comes by, then I'll tell him, and he's very good with them, because he'll just go out after them, and he'll tell them we can't sit back and feel bad, because the only way the colored man has ever amounted to something, it's because he keeps himself going, and you just *have* to, and that's all there is to say, and nothing more."

So she insisted then and so she has many times insisted. Yet, over the years I have learned to doubt her silences and her claims that this or that word (or long speech) represents her final position on a given subject. For a long time she almost literally had nothing to say. She sat out my visits or stood watching me as I anxiously and indeed some-what desperately tried to talk with and play with her children, who be-gan to take me for a strange white fool — first to be feared, then to be suspected, and finally to be indulged and flattered and really helped along in whatever fuzzy and persistent schemes he had in mind. It took their mother much longer to take my presence for granted, then to as-sume my presence as in essence a friendly one, and at last to forget my presence for a minute here and for considerably longer than a minute there — or even *use* my presence, apologetically in the beginning and forthrightly later on, three years later on, when a thought or a ques-tion or a reminiscence would simply be spoken. Those were the mo-ments I remember best, and they were almost always moments when *she* was remembering something. I think I am being true to the occa-sions when I say they were almost invariably (I began to feel *inevitably*) nostalgic.

In her own way she, too, felt the persistent force of past events. Both of us knew that she had found in me a listener, and that I was not by any means the first one. There had been her mother, and there was "the reverend." She shouted and "hollered" at them, too — and some-times, like the rest of us, she stopped in the middle, seized by a moment of self-consciousness, worried by a glimpse of her own petulance, which we all have and which only some people manage to acknowledge. A few times I also raised my voice — I thought because I wanted to get through, be heard by her. She was so absorbed in putting her thoughts to word that I feared she would not hear my remarks, my objections or observations or pleas that one thing or another be considered.

Afterwards, of course, I would have second thoughts about everything said. I would think about our talks, or play them back and try to hear again exactly who said what and when. I would try to figure out why she got so excited and why I did. I would, in fact, be "home," because I was doing what my life had somehow brought me to do: analyzing things and finding reasons and explanations for them or trends and patterns in them. It was a comfortable feeling I had in those small, uncrowded motels — "rural" as the terrain they serve and different indeed from the large noisy motels one finds elsewhere. It was comfortable because I was surrounded by comfort: air conditioning and running water and a bathroom and a good bed and nearby a restaurant that served a reasonable variety of reasonably good food. I was also comfortable because I was now doing something that had continuity.

After all, years of my life had been given over to listening and coming up with interpretations, and in those motel rooms I could sit back and listen to a machine and write things down on sheets of white paper — and do it all under reasonably decent physical circumstances. But I had my doubts in those motel rooms. Should I actually be there at all? Should I be spending all those hours with that woman and her family? Shouldn't I rather be some other place doing some other kind of work? And she had her doubts, too. Although excitement can mask beliefs, it can also make possible their expression — like this: "I've been saying not one good word today, that's what I just realized. I'd better stop. I guess this isn't one of my happy days — but they can't come all the time. I feel happiest after I've gone and spoken my troubles in church. I'm sorry I was having you hear me, but it's no easy time we all have here, and there'll be a minute once or twice a day that I can't be sure I'll last — because there's too much we don't have that we need, and there's not enough of what we do have.

"I get to the point I'm ready to die; I'm ready to say I can't do it any longer, oh Lord, I can't, so You'll have to come and take me, and if it means I'm going to go to Hell, because I can't wait until it's my time to be called, then I guess it'll have to be Hell for me. And you know, sometimes I'll be carrying on a talk with Him, with God, and all of a sudden I'll feel better, like the reverend said I should. The only trouble is I never do let Him know how really bad it can get for us — and the reverend said I don't have to, because He knows anyway. But when I was hollering just now, that's the same thing my kids will hear sometimes, and they know not to speak back, just listen. Their daddy can holler, too; he'll get all upset, and he'll talk and talk and talk, and you can't follow his every word, and sometimes he'll go outside and start kicking things around, but other times he just stops, and I think maybe he'll begin to cry, but he never does. He just sits there, and after a while he'll shrug his shoulders and go back to doing what he was doing before. Then there will be a time when we both start complaining, but soon we decide, most of the time we do, that if there's trouble we have — well, there's also a lot we can recall that wasn't so bad, no sir. And most of all, you have to remember, like we say to ourselves: here we are. That's what my husband will say, and so will I: *here we are.*

"I guess we mean if we're *here,* then how could it be so bad — because if it had been even worse, then we wouldn't still be here. Then we'll get to thinking, and we'll recall a good time we had once, and then another time — how the girls were born, and the boys, and how my mother has been good to us, and how the bossman came over and said there was nothing to be afraid of, because if the civil rights people or the Klan started getting after us, they wouldn't get on his property. He said he'd go and shoot them himself, if he had to, if they didn't leave. He said he knew we didn't have anything to do with the civil rights people, and that's why we shouldn't be scared. So we weren't, and nothing happened.

"You know, there are more happy times than you might think — once you start looking for them. You have to be in the right mind to go look. That's what I'll say or my husband will say — when we're feeling good. There was a Christmastime a few years back, when my brother sent us more money than we'd ever seen, and I went down to the store and the man, he thought I was losing my mind, because I asked for one thing, and then another, and pretty soon I had a big pile of things, and in the beginning he went along and got them, but after a little, he stared at me and he asked me what I'd been having to drink, and he said if I didn't get out fast, he'd have the sheriff out there, and that would be some Christmas I'd have — in jail. Then I naturally decided to show him the bills, and I did, and he looked at them real long and he asked me — yes, he was getting a little more respectful, he was — if he could just take ahold of one of the ten-dollar bills and see if it was OK. After he saw it was real money I had, then he told me I was the luckiest woman in Tunica County, and maybe the luckiest one in the whole state of Mississippi, and if there was anything he could do to be of help, then he'd go over and deliver and he'd even drive me along, because it sure would be heavy, toting along the packages and more packages, and he could understand I'd be fearful of buying things if I didn't know how I'd get them back to the place.

"Yes, I said, he could drive me and my packages and that would be a relief. So, I bought and I bought. I'd see this and that, and I'd ask for the candy and the cookies and the cheese and the meats, you know, and I knew I was going to have me a time, telling my kids that they should eat the new food and it would be good for them and make them grow bigger. They like Kool-Aid, and it isn't often they can have milk for themselves and there we were, having a chicken on Christmas. I had to tell my kids that you may get used to Kool-Aid and like it, but if you have good luck, like we did that Christmas — well, then you can drink milk and eat the better things and they'll taste just as good and even better, once you get used to them. Of course, one of my girls went and spoiled things; she said we weren't going to be having that food again, so why should we try eating it, just for Christmas. Then, I didn't know what to say. It was my husband who answered; he said we should just forget all we ever ate before and all we'll ever eat later on, and just have ourselves a good Christmas — and you know, we did. It was the best day ever in the world, yes it was."

As a matter of fact there have been other good days, too. The memory of one would trigger the memory of another, and on a few such occasions she allowed herself to get dangerously full of them all, to the point that she would appear euphoric (which I suppose was as "inappropriate" in her as in anyone else) or almost bizarrely contented with her life, her lot, her future as she saw it. I am not necessarily referring to a sort of "religious fugue," as I found myself calling some of the vehement joy, the biblically suffused, highly oratorical transport she could manage. On the contrary, it was nostalgia, pure if not so simple, that would come over her and make her feel quiet and pleased with things, but sad, very sad in a reflective way, sad without hysteria and without desperation.

Maybe I am talking about the kind of sadness the rest of us have heard in the blues and "work songs" and "field songs," an almost distilled sadness that defies the outsider's comprehension and sometimes prompts him to think of Kierkegaard's "resignation" or Buber's "acceptance." There is a passion and a biblical quality to the expression of that sadness — though "the reverend" himself comes in for some fairly sharp if forgiving criticism, which would be retracted, I noticed, not immediately but several days later, when one of his sermons (which I would have heard in church) would be repeated as if in repentance by a parishioner who had listened carefully indeed when she was in church. As a matter of fact, during those nostalgic moments "the reverend" is not really condemned as a person. Once, when the story of the lavish Christmas was fondly recalled for me (the third time it was, in three years), "the reverend" more or less served as a link between that particular memory and the larger mood that was to be expressed: "I don't mean to jump on the reverend, but he was down to see us as soon as we got home. No sooner had the grocery man left, than the reverend was there, and it was the first time I ever saw him bend over and lift his hat and treat us like we were — I guess you'd have to say he was looking at us as though we'd become white folks. Yes, the word spreads fast around here, and I'll tell you what must have happened. The colored people in the store were watching, and when they saw the man, the white man, carry our packages and drive us home, they must have gone running home themselves, and I'll bet everyone a hundred miles around knew what happened, and the reverend included.

"He came, like I said, and he was nice and polite, and he didn't have a cross word to say to us, and he was real obliging and asked if we wanted him to come back later, because he could see how busy we were, and with all those groceries and things — well, it might take a day or two to unload them. So, I told him that there wouldn't be no difference; now or later was all right, and we're always glad to have him around, including that time. Then he said he was always glad to come around and that time especially, because he could see we were really happy and in good luck, he said, and that was how it was meant for us to be around Christmastime, because it was a joyful day, Christ being born and like that. Then I said he was right, and we sure felt glad and pleased by our good luck, and we wanted him to know we would pray and thank the Lord. Then he said he was glad of that, and you mustn't take anything for granted in this world, no sir, and the Lord provides, and now we had proof. So, I said yes, I was sure he was right about the Lord and His providing — but this time it wasn't Him, it was from our family up North, and they'd sent us a lot of money, more than we ever before had seen. As if he didn't know from what he heard!

"Well, he didn't have much more to say, the reverend. My mother asked him if he wanted to come and eat with us on Christmas, and he said no, that he liked to eat with his family, and they would be cooking in their home, and everyone should be in his own place on Christmas.

Then he told us again how lucky it was, what happened, and we agreed, and he got up and he was getting ready to go, I thought, except that he wasn't. Instead he walked over and he stared right at me, he did, and then he asked: 'If you have some money left, you can believe that I'll be glad to have it, and I would try to do God's Will with it, and there sure are a lot of people who won't be having the Christmas you're going to have.' It was like that, only he went on and on, and while he was speaking I was thinking and deciding. He'd been staring at me, and the way I figured it, if I stopped staring back, he'd walk away with everything we had, the few dollars left, and all the groceries and everything. But if I just kept on looking right into his eyes, then he wouldn't have me bowing down before him, and he'd stop and leave us be — and it wasn't as if we'd had Christmases like that one every year.

"So, I kept hearing him and looking upon him, and he kept talking and looking upon me, and then he finished with his talk, and I didn't say a word, and then I did. I said, 'Yes sir,' that's what I said. Then I said: 'I know what you mean,' that's what I said. Then I asked him again if he wouldn't like to come and eat some of the food we'd got, and he said no, he had a lot waiting for him over there at home, and then I said the same thing again: '*I know what you mean.*' In a second he was at the door leaving us and you know what, he didn't even remember to wish us a Merry Christmas. I guess he was in a hurry, and people forget a lot when they've got to rush on.

"The reverend, he's no different than anyone else. I mean, he is, because he's God's minister; but he's one of us, that's for sure, and the way I see it, even Jesus had His trouble in the Temple, so you can't trust ministers any more than the rest of us people. Remember what happened to Jesus? He ran into enemies all over, and it was with ministers just like with the other people who didn't like Him. I guess you're pretty lucky in this world if you stay alive long enough — I mean so you can grow up, and not die the first thing when you're born. When you're little and you don't know much except that you're you, and you've been born, all you want is to stay here as long as you can, even if the reverend does say it's better up there in Heaven. I recall when I became a woman and I went and told my mother, she started to cry, and I didn't know why. She said she was glad I'd lived as long as that, so that I could become a woman; and maybe I could go and live longer and have children and like that. Then she told me about all the people that died, her sisters and her brothers and a lot of them before they were ever born in the first place — and now I know what she was telling me about!

"Most of the time you just go along and you don't think back; but my little girl — she isn't little any more — came to me a couple of months back, and told me she was bleeding and what did she do wrong, and I said nothing, and I told her why she was bleeding. I tried to recall what my mother said to me, and I did; and we both sat and talked, and yes sir, we were all filled up with tears, we were. But if you didn't have times like that, then you'd never know you was even living. That's what my mother said when I told her I was bleeding. She said you can't just go along and never have something real important happen.

"Here it's quiet compared to the city, I know. I've never been to a real big city. My uncle, he's been to Jackson and Birmingham and Memphis, because they had him in the Army, you know; and he was up there in New York and then he never did come back. The next thing we knew, he was dead. We got a telegram from a veterans' department of the government, saying he'd been in the hospital and he died there. It was he who was the one that told us all about going to the cities, and that's how my sister and brother happened to leave; in the same year they both left for the North. I thought of going myself, and so did my husband, but why should we, I asked myself. Even if there wasn't my mother or the reverend or the bossman telling you it was no good up there — even so, I would have been smart enough to know it. I mean, is there anyplace on God's earth where a colored man is going to have a real easy time? Is there? I'd like to know where, I would. As I see it, you'll be here or someplace else and it's the same; and you know, I'll picture us all leaving here, and traveling up the road, like the others have done, and I can't see us going too far before I'll want to turn around and get back — because we won't have what we've got and there won't be anything better in its place.

"I recall I went over to Greenville once, with my grandma it was, because she had a sister there. It took the whole day, with the bus late, and we sure had a long walk after the bus. All the time I was missing my home, and I wished I was back there. I'd think of our bed, and my daddy telling us before we fell asleep that we should be good and mind ourselves and not get fresh and if we did he'd hit us bad. I told Grandma I wanted to go home, and she said she did, too, but let's go visit her sister first. Then we did, and her sister said she wished she could go back up with us, but she had to stay, because she came there, to Greenville, with her husband; and he was there because he had a brother who learned to fix automobiles in the Army, and now he wasn't doing so bad, after all.

"That's me, I guess; I'm always looking back on things and recalling them and trying to forget something if it isn't any good. Every time a bad thing happens, I'll try to push myself to think of a good one. Mostly there'll be the Christmastime I told you about, and the times I've been with my grandma — like on the bus, with her looking out of the window and telling me it was real beautiful to look at, the state of Mississippi, even if it didn't treat us the best. That's what I say, too. That's how I believe. I'd be sad if I didn't have those sunflowers around and the pine trees, you know; and even in Greenville, Mississippi, I'll bet we'd have to give up on the flowers we have, and we couldn't have a chicken or two. We bought the chickens with the money we got from Chicago. They sent us a card with the money, and they said they didn't want us eating up everything at once, and we should go buy some chickens, and we did. Then the teacher helped me and my kids write back and thank them; and we couldn't help but add how good the chickens were and wasn't it too bad that they couldn't have them up there in Chicago. And you know, it's not as bad here all the time as it is some of the time, and you have to remember that. We have the seasons, and they change; and so does your luck."

She was smiling when she said that, and she went on in a more or less circular fashion — remembering that Christmas again, not because she was rambling or "senile" or provocative or at loose ends for conversation, but because she wanted to fall back on a few things in her life as long as the spirit moved her to do so. At the same time, I began to realize, she was responding to a moment not only in her life, but her daughter's — a second daughter who had also "become a woman" a little while ago. Sharecropper children, then, like children all over the world, stir their parents, and particularly their mothers, to a variety of responses and states of mind. Sharecropper children can make their parents smile and laugh. Sharecropper children can inspire self-congratulation in their parents. Sharecropper children can cause their parents worry or melancholy. The mood that dominates among those sharecropper children is one of mixed sadness and doubtfulness. I say that not only because I have subjected miles of tapes to something I dubiously call "thematic analysis"; but because I have myself seen what cannot be recorded on a tape recorder, seen gestures and looks and moves and responses to moves and signals made and nods given and arms raised — to express frustration, rage, confusion, hopelessness.

In South Carolina it was once put this way: "I hope maybe you could go tell a lot of people that we never stop trying. I don't have much to offer my kids, but I tell them I'm here and they're here, and it won't be long before we're gone, so the best thing to do is go ahead each day and say thank you, sun, for rising, and good-bye, sun, when it goes down, and I hope to see you tomorrow, and if I don't, then be good to those who stay after me. I do believe the sun must be part of God, because if we didn't have the sun we'd have no crops at all, and then we'd be dead and it's bad enough now even with the sun. All I know is that you can't worry more than from day to day. There'll be times when I start, but I say to myself that I should live by the sun, and not look ahead more than each day, because if I did, I believe my tears would come and they'd come and they'd wash us all away, they would. There'll be sometimes when I recall my mother saying that the sun is meant to dry up all your tears from the night before, that's what — besides making the land grow the crops. So, you see, we'd have a bad time without the sun. If you ask me, we just plain have a bad time all the time. But at least the sun is there, thank God, to help us out. There's just so much helping out that we ever get, and it's not enough; no, it isn't."

For such mothers life has an undeniable sadness to it — interrupted, though, by periods of earnest faith or gaiety or hard work that forces a suspension of all feelings. "When I'm helping out with the cotton and tobacco," says that mother, "I don't keep track of anything, not my kids or the time of day it is or even if I hurt or I don't. It's like you'll be dead for a while — just going along, up and down, doing what you have to do; and then, when you stop, you all of a sudden say to yourself that you're the same old you again, and you have to do this and that, and there's an ache you have, or an errand to get over with. There'll be some afternoons, I'll say so, when I feel real bad, and it's like the whole world has come crashing down on me. But I soon catch my breath and go about my business. I thank God for sparing me trouble while I have to be busy working, and I thank Him for keeping me alive. If I died, there'd be no mother for the kids — my mother died when I was little, and I know — and they'd be even worse off than they already are, and it's pretty bad for them each day, you know."

When I hear sadness expressed, I often hear something else, something that the children I am describing in this chapter begin to convey almost as soon as they can talk and draw and paint. I am speaking of something that the word "stranded" conveys. It is as if the child right off knows (or comes to know or is taught or learns) that he and his family have little future, no prospects, hardly anything ahead but a mean, even cruel struggle for that very minimum of things, mere existence itself. It is as if the child realizes full well that others by the thousands, even by the millions, have left rather than face what is ahead of him or her. A child of ten managed to tell me about himself and his coming fate: "I don't think it'll be much different, my life and my daddy's; I mean, what he's doing and I will do. The trouble is, Daddy says it may be worse for us. My momma says no, it won't, because it can't be, because we're already as bad off as it can get. I'd like to find me a job that I could keep, and it would be a good one, and near here; but you hear there's no work, except helping with the crops, like my daddy does, and he says that's all I can expect is to do that, unless there's *more* machines, so that the bossman won't need but two or three men. Daddy says the bossman told him that it's still cheaper to have us than the machines, and that's why we're here, I guess.

"Yes, I'll ask my daddy sometimes why we don't just up and leave, like a lot of people have been doing. He says that there's no reason to; and if we did, we'd be going from out of one mess into another one. My brother Billy and me, and my sister Alice, we all asked him once, and when he said the same old thing to us, we said that we heard the bossman kept telling the foreman that the colored people would leave Mississippi, every one of them, and Alabama too, if they know what's best for them, but since they don't then they'd better obey and do what they're told. Daddy didn't say anything back. He nodded his head and he went back to cutting the trees, and we were about to go away, and then he said we should stay right where we are, and listen to him, and he told us if we'd all gone up to Chicago or New York, then we might be dead from some accident or poison or all the things they have up there. He said to grow up in those cities is the worst possible thing that can happen to you, even including Mississippi and Alabama. So that's why he stayed, he said; and he's going to stay until the day he dies, and he told us to watch out and not get a lot of ideas, because the next thing you know we'll be all grown up, and we shouldn't have the idea we can go someplace and it'll be better there. That's a wrong idea.

"No, I haven't been to school this year, because of my momma being sick and then my grandma died; and we don't have the clothes. I help my daddy with the planting and I do errands for the foreman and I help with my little brothers. I'd like to go to a big city, even just to visit. I'd like to go to Birmingham, Alabama. I know a kid, his uncle lives there. He works in a big factory, I think. But he came back last year, the uncle did; and he told my friend there wasn't much reason now to go to Birmingham, because they're cutting back on people unless they've gone to school half their life, almost, and have the papers, you know, to prove it. I hope maybe I can go into the Army. I hear say if they consent to take you, they give you all the clothes you'll ever need in your whole life, and they feed you all the time, with the best food in the whole world and all you want of it, and they'll train you for working in a good job. They say it's hard to get yourself accepted, though, because you can't have any sickness, and they check up on you, how big and strong you are. I have some trouble with breathing, and the man in the grocery store, he said it was probably that my heart didn't grow to the right size and I guess it'll never go away. I asked my momma if it could be cleared away somehow, so that my heart could grow, and she said she didn't think so, because it's too late now. But I hear they may be opening some factories right down here. The minister said they might one day, but you can't be sure when; and he said if we pray, then maybe it'll be sooner and not later. Sometimes all of us try to pray at the same time; my momma makes us. I pray the factories will come down here real soon, when I'll be old enough to go and work in them.

"There'll be times when I hear my daddy say that soon there'll be nothing for us to do here, but there still won't be any point going to another place. So we'll be lost, he says, and left with only this roof to cover us — as long as the bossman says it's OK to stay here. I have my friend Tom, and he says he's going to catch a ride on a freight train one of these days, and he'll end up there, in the North; and then he says he'll go to a policeman and tell him he's lost and do they know where you can get a job and something to eat. It's better up North for the colored people, and there you can go ask for help, that's what Tom says. Tom asked if I wanted to go with him, and I said I'll think about it and make up my mind. I didn't ask my daddy, because I know what he'd say, right away. I asked Mr. Robinson, the funeral man, and he said I would be a fool not to go, because you can always get a meal up there, through welfare, but you can't down here. But then he turned around and said I should be careful, because it was real bad up there, real bad, and getting worse all the time. He said if you went up there around ten or twenty years ago, the colored man, then you were all right; but now it's a different picture. He said you end up all the way across the country, up North, and it can be better than here and it can be worse than here, all depending on a lot of things. You can freeze up there, I know. And my daddy says you live in a room or two, and you see no land. All you can see is the rats; they hide way down under the buildings and they crawl up at night and bite you. But they'll give you good welfare money up North, except that you have to pay most of it for the building you live in. I guess we're just going to stay here, and there's nothing else to do: each way, you've got your troubles, everyone says. My daddy always tells us we're just stuck here, and we'd better stay, because we should have left, maybe, a long time ago; and now if we leave it's like asking for trouble, and there's no guarantee it won't be worse than what we've already got, yes sir."

That is what it feels like to be stranded. The word has come back from the North, the word that lets those hundreds of thousands who are still Southerners know how things have changed, say, since 1940 or 1950. And yet, people continue to leave, but often with grave doubts and fears, and with few illusions about the freedom and wealth of those beckoning cities — which of course, always seemed to promise more than they actually delivered, or so many of those who have stayed behind also somehow knew and insisted, perhaps to make themselves feel better. Even those children who definitely plan one day to leave the countryside and go to a city nearby or far away, have their doubts and can talk about them, as did one girl of nine, alternately naïve and cynical, trusting and suspicious, grave and optimistic: "If you're a girl, I believe you can get yourself a job better, whether you're down here or up North. So, I hope to do that, and maybe if I'm married, my husband will be able to find a job, too — though it's not so easy, I know, for the man. When you ask me what I'll be doing later, and where I'll be living, I don't know the answer. From as far back as I can think, I used to tell my mother that we ought to leave here, and not be always doing what they tell you to do, the people that run this place. My mother used to say that one day we'd leave, but we owed all this money, from borrowing until the crops would come in. Then my aunt and uncle, they owed a lot of money and they came over last year, I think it was, and said we should all just up and leave one night, and the money we owed, we more than made up for with work, and the debt was just the bossman's way of keeping us doing whatever he wants. But we stayed and my aunt and uncle left the state.

"Everyone says I can be a maid and wash dishes, but I'd like to be a teacher, if I could. I don't go to school all the time, but when I do I find myself liking some of the teachers, how they dress up and know what to say. One of them is real nice, and she drives a new car to school, and she'll talk to you about going to a meeting in Memphis, and then there was another meeting in Atlanta, and she's been around and all over and everywhere. I did real good in school, and the teacher said I was coming along fine and I should go there more, and she'd teach me more — but we have to take turns. There's my other sisters and my brother, and we go one after the other to school and to church, and maybe one day we'll all have the right clothes, but until then we just have to go by turns.

"Once another teacher gave me a ride and she wanted to know what I was thinking of, for my future; and I said I don't know, and she said I should get on it, and start thinking. I told my mother what the teacher said, and my mother asked what the teacher expected us to do, since we're not getting all that money from the state of Alabama, like teachers do. When I next went to school, I asked that teacher if she could figure out how me and my sisters and my brother could go ahead and amount to something, like she said we should, if there wasn't a nickel or dime in the place, never mind any dollar bills. Yes sir, that's what I said, and it was just what my mother said. The teacher told me I was getting fresh. But I told her right back. I said it was all right for her telling us what to do, but meanwhile we were out there and we didn't hardly see any money, and it was real bad for my mother, trying to figure if we'd be getting what we should to eat every day. Then the teacher said I was beginning to talk like I was from the civil rights people and to shut my mouth or go and leave, and the next day it wasn't my turn to come there anyway, and I gave the shoes to my sister Mary Jean, and I told her to give the worst look she could to her, Miss Holmes. Mary Jean promised she would, and she did; and I never went back for a long time, and when I did she paid me no attention, Miss Holmes did, but I believe Mary Jean went up and asked if she could speak to the teacher, and she explained that none of us has ever seen a civil rights person hereabouts — never; and we just try to work the land and mind our own business, and they would all testify to it, the foreman and the bossman. My mother wanted the school people to know the truth, so she had Mary Jean tell the teacher.

"I don't trust no one, especially most of the teachers, and the big important people. Once the sheriff came to school, and the teacher told us we'd better not make a single sound, or he'd hear us, and he'd send us right to jail. Then one boy raised his hand, and she called on him, and he asked if it was right that they can put us in jail anytime they please, no matter what we say. Well, the next thing the teacher did was tell us that we should get those silly questions out of our heads, or else we would really end up there, in jail. Then the girl near me raised her hand, and she asked the teacher if it wasn't so, that we should all go away from here because there was nothing to keep us. The teacher said again that we should stop the questions and she was sorry she mentioned the sheriff and let's go back to learning arithmetic. There was a girl who was nodding and saying yes, we should go back to the arithmetic, and you know who she was: Caroline Jones, and her daddy is the richest colored man between here and Chicago, my daddy says. He owns funeral parlors and an insurance company, and if you have a complaint, you're supposed to see him, and then he'll tell you if he's going to talk to the white people about it, or if he won't. His girl, Caroline, comes to school with all different kinds of dresses and shoes, and she walks around as if she owns the school. The teachers, I believe they're scared of her, because if her daddy really wanted to, he could probably get them fired, any teacher that crossed Caroline. The other day I asked Caroline if she really planned to be a teacher, because the teacher told her she'd make a good one. Caroline said no, she'd like to go to Hollywood and get a job in the movies. I said that would be what I'd like, too, but I haven't seen many movies. She said her daddy drives her up to Memphis, I think, and they see them there. A while ago we had a television set, and we'd see movies on it; but it wasn't a good set when we got it, and soon it broke down for good. The man at the store said there was no point trying to fix it. Oh, it was left by a family when they went North.

"If I really could choose, I'd leave here, yes sir, and never come back. I'd try to get my whole family to go with me, though. If they wouldn't leave, I don't know if I could. I'm sure if I stay I'll get some job cleaning up for the white folks, and if you get a good woman to work for, she'll be nice to you and slip you a dress or something, before she throws it out. Maybe I could marry Caroline's brother, except she says he's going to Atlanta to college, and she thinks he'll never come back. If he did, and I married him, I'd be rich! Then we'd have a television that works real good, and I wouldn't need dresses from the white folks, no I wouldn't. I could go and get my own, and I'd wear shoes all the time, like the teachers do — and Caroline."

Such children, like all other children, have their dreams; but sharecropper children also have their doubts, very concrete ones, perhaps more of them than most boys and girls do. The younger sharecropper children I have met and observed can draw or paint pictures that express those doubts, and incidentally, a whole range of other feelings, which in sum constitute, I suppose, a "world view" — though the children themselves might wonder, were they to hear that expres-

sion, why I make so much of their halting or casual or eager and enthusiastic efforts. Yet, they *do* manage to "say" a lot in those drawings;
and since children of poor, southern rural families are likely to be even
more silent (at five or six, for instance) than other children in the
presence of someone like me, the use of crayons and paints becomes
particularly important and instructive — I believe for them as well as
their observer. In any event, Lawrence kept on telling me — briefly,
but to the point — that he enjoyed the artwork he was doing, but he
also hoped that I would like what I saw and *keep* it, so I "could show
all the pictures to the other doctors, and they could see if they are correct."

What does the boy mean by "correct"? Well, of course if asked,
he doesn't really know how to answer, or so he says at first. Then he
acknowledges he had wondered whether (as in school) someone is
grading his work: "I've not been to school much, but my sister has,
and she said if you draw something the teacher tells you later if it's
good or bad." He is seven, and actually he has been to school for a
couple of years — though he does miss many days because he is sick,
or because he doesn't have warm enough clothes, or any suitable
clothes at all. (Like others who live nearby, he shares a particular set
of shoes and a pair of pants with his brothers. They rotate the use of
the clothes, and by the same token rotate their attendance at school.)
Finally, he lets me know something else: "The best thing would be if
you kept the pictures, all the pictures I'm making; and even if they're
not so good, they could remind you of the place here, after you go
away."

Lawrence always liked to draw "the place," by which he meant
the cabin in which he was born and now lives, and the land around it,
some of which has pine trees, some of which is planted in cotton,
some of which boasts a few flowers grown by his mother — who, incidentally, is not allowed to grow vegetables anywhere on that land. I
asked Lawrence about that one day, because he put a few tomato
plants and a few pieces of corn near the sunflowers he drew: "Well, it's
not our land, except to grow cotton and corn and then share with the
bossman, if we make money. The bossman says he doesn't want us using his land to grow a lot of food we could use for ourselves, so he said
no to my daddy, and we're only allowed the flowers. My mother likes
the flowers, and she grows them, and when the bossman comes by
every once in a while, he'll tell us they are real pretty, the flowers she
grows, and aren't we glad she's growing them, because they're as good

as can be to look at. My mother doesn't answer him, and later she says he is the meanest man who ever smiled — and he's always smiling at us and telling us we're real good colored people, and he wishes everyone else colored was as good as we are, even half as good, he says.

"That's why, in the picture I tried to fool him and put the corn there and the tomato plants. It used to be that my granddaddy grew a little of each, and he'd go and bring some to the missus and she always said his was the best she ever tasted. But after she died and her husband got sick, the son took over, Junior they used to call him — that's what my daddy told me — and he's tough, real bad tough. He comes around on his inspection, that's what he calls it, and wants to make sure we're all being good and not 'sitting in the sun,' he says, and being 'lazy,' he says, and my daddy says he's scared to tell him to leave us alone, because it's his, the land, but if we didn't do anything but sit under the sun, then it would be *us* who'd suffer the worst — that's what my daddy said he'd like to tell him, Mr. Junior, the bossman. But my mother laughs and says he comes around here because he likes to feel big and important, and he likes to feel like his daddy, 'inspecting' us. Each time he comes he'll take and pick one of my mother's little flowers and put it on his jacket, and he won't even thank her. Then the next thing, he'll be sending the maid they have, Ruth, to come over and pick a whole bunch for the house. Once he sent us a dollar, but most of the time he sends us nothing, and there's not a thing we can do, no sir, that's what my daddy says.

"There was a time we might have gone away from here, but my daddy said no, and I'm glad. I sure know a lot of places here, and I'd hate to leave now. I like the woods the best, and next best the road down beside the big house; it goes near the pond, and there's a well there, and I get the water. The teacher told us if you go to a big city, likely as not you'll have water right in your house, and all you do is turn it on and turn it off, and it's always there, and it's as clean as can be. But she says it's real bad up there, and better to stay here; and my daddy says she's right. He says that here you don't have much except plenty of land, and the little you can get from working it, and up there you get your money, but you're like in jail, from all you hear; and that's no place to be."

He has drawn dozens of pastoral scenes, all of them evidence of his familiarity with the land he and his father and indeed everyone in their family knows so well. He has his very own way of approaching the paper, using the crayons, and in general doing his work. Like many sharecropper children I have met, he has done more drawing in school than anything else, and he could even (toward the very end of the time I spent with him and his family) tell me why: "The teacher said the other day that none of us talk right, and we should be ashamed of ourselves, and how could we ever amount to anything if that's how we're going to be speaking later on. That's why she has us make pictures, she said. Then she told us we'll be hopeless on the rest of the lessons, too — the writing and numbers — so maybe we should just wear the crayons down every day."

Actually, Lawrence does rather like drawing, though he does not wear his crayons down in a blind and obliging way. After all the experience he's had with those crayons, he still seems to value the magic they possess, their constant readiness to offer up a variety of colors. For Lawrence it can apparently be remarkable that something in this world is thoroughly reliable, and almost always *there,* to be called upon and applied. On several occasions, as he prepared to work, Lawrence made remarks similar to this: "Don't those crayons lose their color sometime? I mean, you use them and you use them, and they have the same color always. I thought after you used them a while they wouldn't be so red and blue and green and yellow. My daddy says that anything you own gives out after long, and he says that goes for the land we have here to plant. Daddy says we're lucky, because the land is good here, and it's still got a lot of life in it — but one day the life will go away. Maybe that will happen after I'm gone, he says; but a lot of land, it gives out fast, and there isn't anything you can do. Daddy said we're losing our woods, too — and the bossman isn't stopping it, because they cut down the pine trees, and then they send them away, and before you know it the logs get to be paper, I don't know how. And the bossman makes some money. Up the road they came and put stakes on a big piece of land, and said we were to stay off it, because they'll be planting pine trees and growing them, only to cut them down. The first I heard of it — they were talking at the store, some white men from the city — I came and told my daddy, and he said I make up things in my mind, but they came and did what I heard, and my daddy told me later I was telling the truth, he could see."

Lawrence often begins a drawing with a tree, maybe two of them. Then he moves to the land, the earth he knows so well, the earth he never stops seeing. In the morning, he wakes up and looks through the wide cracks on the floor of the two-room cabin he and his three brothers and two sisters and parents and one aunt and three fatherless cousins and grandmother call home. All during the day he sees the earth as he goes to get water or goes to "help with the planting" or "work on the crops"; and in the evening he finds himself lying on a mattress with two of his brothers and staring down at the darkness of the ground. So, he draws that ground, that earth, that land; and he puts a little grass on it, and some cotton and some corn, and some tomatoes, and sometimes his mother's flowers. He makes the earth prominent, substantial, thick with layers and at times several shades — light brown and dark brown and gray and black. He brings out the consistency of things — the sandiness, the lumps and clods. He brings out the interruptions that rocks make and the intrusions that roots make. He brings out man's artifacts, the ditches that irrigate, the tidy furrows that have to do with cultivation and planting. He brings out the land's larger hospitality to chipmunks and ants and worms as well as to human beings.

While he draws a picture — say, this one (Figure 15) — he is willing to talk about the land he knows so well. That land is all the picture shows, except for a thin blue sky, put in last, and a red-hot sun, which marks the end of a day. There are no people around, no buildings, no evidence of anything human. Or, in fact, is Lawrence there, somewhere — and his family, and his neighbors and his father's bosses and just about everyone in the whole Mississippi Delta? Here is what Lawrence at various times said about that drawing and several others almost exactly like it, a "series" I suppose they could be called: "I guess I always draw the same thing. Maybe you draw what you really know, what you know the best. I know this land best, because my daddy started me out from as far back as I can remember helping him do the chores; and he would tell me there's one thing I'll have to know all my life, as long as we stay here, and that's what to do on the land we have to use. The bossman gives it to us, and it's ours, and he doesn't care what we do, so long as we raise what he wants and do it right and bring it all in; and then he takes care of everything, and tells us how we made out. Daddy says you can't but pray, and no matter what happens, the bossman will say that we could have done better, but we can stay through and try again next year, and he'll help us right through, like he always does, and we won't be without food and we can stay where we are. My daddy says it could be worse for us than it is, and we owe what we have each day to the land; and my mother says we should be thanking God for the good land He gave us around — here in this county.

"I'm always asking my daddy something and he's always giving me the right answer — about the land. He'll do a lot of explaining to us while we take the wagon and go for the water. He'll be telling us about how when he was a boy they didn't have the motors and the engines, and the cotton was a lot harder to take in. Now we have other crops, and it's hard with them, Daddy says, but not as bad as it used to be with the cotton; and we have good water for the land — the irrigation, you know. Daddy says he can remember when they came around from Washington or someplace up North and told us how to plant trees and keep the wind from blowing all the good land away, and the bossman's daddy came over and explained everything to my granddaddy and all the others, and my daddy was there. According to what you hear the white people say — the foreman and his helper and like that — we'll be all right here and there's still profits to make. I heard the foreman say in the store last winter that they still needed the niggers in Mississippi to work in the fields and help out with other work, and since a lot of colored people have gone, that's better. But there still are a lot of the colored people here, and we're going to stay for a long time, the foreman said, and we'll help out with the planting and the caring for the crops and getting them in on time, you know. And if you don't get them in real fast, everything is lost.

"My daddy says he'll never leave here, but I don't know if I'll be here all my life. My mother says maybe I will and maybe I won't, when I ask her. She says some go and some stay, and if a lot of us are up there and away, in the North, a lot of us are still here, where we've always been, and it's bad all around, yes sir. If I could have anything I wanted — like you say — I wouldn't know what I'd do. I'd sit down under that tree — it's my favorite place to sit — and I'd try to decide, and then I'd ask everyone I could, and then I'd make a choice. Sometimes I'll go to school, and the teacher will tell us to keep on wishing we'll be big and rich someday, and the minister, he says some people, they're just chosen by God to have a lot of money, and live real good. Maybe that's what I wish: some money to have, so I could go and buy everything in the store — cans of food and a lot of candy and the curtains my mother has been hoping for, if we ever get the money. My daddy says the biggest time in the world would be if we could get some money and we could fix up where we live to be better, like they did with the church. The lady — she's the bossman's wife and Daddy says her folks own a real big place, a plantation, not far away — every time come Christmas, around then, just before Christmas it is, she'll show up and give us a ham. She'll do it for a lot of people. She used to have a chicken to bring us, my daddy says, and then she thought the hams in the tin can, they're better, so we get them. I wouldn't mind having them all the time, and maybe that's what I should wish for, if I could get my wish come true. Last time, I can remember, she drove up and she told us here we are, a nice ham, and my mother said thank you, and my daddy and all of us, we had to say thank you, and she said we were real good, and she was glad to come by and wish us a merry Christmas, and she hoped we'd be going to church and praying, and my mother said yes, we would, that's for sure, and she said that was real good, and as long as you pray, you'll stay clear of trouble, and that's the truth. Just before she went back into her car she asked my mother if everything was going fine, and my mother said, 'Yes, ma'am,' it was, and she got in and drove off, but before that she said, 'Good.' I heard her. Afterwards, my mother said it was too bad she didn't offer us some things, and we could have said yes. My mother said she hears they're always throwing food away up there at the House, and throwing away clothes, and maybe there would be a few curtains they could give us. But Daddy said if they gave to us, there's all the other tenants, and pretty soon they'd be in trouble with the other white folks for 'pampering the niggers,' that's how they say it. I heard it said once myself in the store that time, like I told you."

Lawrence shows no signs of being pampered. Like everyone else in his family he gets up at sunrise and goes to bed at sunset. There are no clocks to bother him and in general his sense of time has little to do with minutes and hours. He mostly works. He walks for several miles to a pond and fills up with water two buckets he has brought along, all before breakfast. While he is walking he relieves himself. He has never brushed his teeth in his life. There are no toothbrushes in his family's cabin, nor toothpaste. There is one mirror there, a small one, used by Lawrence's mother on Sunday when she "fixes up" herself and "really gets dressed." Lawrence does not regularly wash himself. Sometimes he takes a bar of soap to the pond and washes his hands there. It is a small pond, a shallow pond, and he does not swim in it. I do not believe he should drink the pond's water, but he does drink it; and so does everyone else in his family. For breakfast Lawrence has coffee or Coke and grits, prepared by his mother who is also up at dawn. He has never in his life had bacon and eggs for breakfast; when there are eggs, usually on holidays, they are for dinner, which is the midday meal, and the main one. Usually dinner consists of a glass of Kool-Aid (first) followed by bread spread with margarine, grits again, some greens, and by no means always, a pork chop — or more likely fatback or "streak-meat," which are both more fat than anything else. (The "streak-meat," like the "streak-o-lean" I have noticed particularly among migrants is exactly what the name implies: a hunk of fat streaked occasionally by meat.)

Then comes work for Lawrence, or on relatively rare days, school. There is planting to be done, or chores up where the cattle are. There is fishing, which means food for dinner. There are crops to take in. On school days there are shoes to put on, and the good clothes, which are also worn on Sundays by Lawrence or his brothers, who may be of different ages and sizes, but manage to share clothes without embarrassment or difficulty. I have never seen them talk or act as if something doesn't fit, and their mother hasn't either. Actually, Lawrence's mother keeps her eyes on her children and would certainly know what they do or say, though not very much conversation goes on in the cabin each morning. It is mostly quiet: "A lot of the time it's hot, you know, or it's cold here in the winter; and when the weather doesn't favor you, there's no reason why you should make it worse by talking a lot — that's what I tell my family. My husband, he's not one for talking, anyhow. He just gets up and tries to forget his aches and pains by going to work. Most of the time he'll miss his breakfast, yes sir, and that gives more for the children; and I do the same. With Lawrence, we don't have much to worry about. He's not as sickly as Ronald, and he'll do almost anything we ask. I don't have to say a word to him, you know. I'll catch myself thinking of something and he'll pick up what's in my mind and go do it, and there's never a word spoken between us. Yes, maybe it *is* in my eyes, that he'll see something. I don't know. Lawrence is a good boy. I only hope he stays good. It gets harder to be good the older you get, that's what I believe. Right now Lawrence is below ten, and he helps us out. Soon he'll be over ten, and getting to be grown up, and he'll be asking all those questions, and I'll be quiet like always, but it won't be because there's no reason to say anything. It'll be because I won't know what to say — because, you know, they'll ask you things, like why should they stay here, and that kind of question, and the best thing is to keep your peace and hope they hear from others that if you go and leave for the North there'll be trouble for you up there."

The silence in the cabin occasionally gets interrupted early in the morning. Birds start their talk and seem to be ignored by Lawrence and everyone else in his family. A few miles away a big truck or two can be heard passing, though the road is no major one and few automobiles use it. Families like Lawrence's make up most of the people nearby, and they don't own cars. Eventually the foreman and one of his assistants arrive; the point, of course, is to see how everything is going. Lawrence, like his father, says little to them, but knows why they have come and what he must do: "Daddy told me when I was little to go call him when they came — when it's the bossman himself or the people who work for him, like the foreman. Now I don't go running for him, because Daddy can hear their car, he says. They used to ride up on a horse. They'll just ask if we're taking care of everything, and I'll say, 'Yes, sir, we are, as best we can.' Then they'll look around and drive off. Daddy says he's not sure how they've got the plantation divided up — and how many of us are working the land for them, but it's big, this plantation. The teacher, she said it's 'real big,' and she said she doesn't like to tell stories, so it's true what she says. I heard her tell my mother that the sun could rise and fall on all the land on the plantation, and you would still have land left over."

Lawrence is quite aware of the sun; indeed, it enables him to keep time. He watches the sun every hour or so, and he makes predictions about the weather by judging the sun's heat, its intensity, its degree of control over the sky. Somehow he seems to know whether an early morning haze or the clouds of breakfast time will be burned away or remain; and his description can be a military one: "The sun wins a lot, but sometimes it just can't. The clouds, they're just too strong, I guess. The sun will go after them, but no use. Other days, you can tell that nothing is going to get in the way of that Mr. Sun for too long, no sir. Even the night before you can tell those days, because the sun, he'll go down real slow-like, and he's as red as can be; then he'll settle over there on to the other side of the plantation, and it'll be light so long that you know there can't be a cloud the next day, not one cloud in the whole sky."

Lawrence liked to draw the sun for me, and the moon, too. Both of them have a magic for him, the sun because it makes everything grow and the moon because it stands out so prominently in the otherwise rather dark sky. Millions of men, women, and children have felt the same way about both of those celestial bodies, but I doubt whether many American children who live in the suburbs or the cities spend much time thinking about the sun or the moon. A child like Lawrence lives by the sun in the day and the moon at night; that is, he is helped to tell time, figure out what he should be doing and where, and yes, he is helped psychologically, too.

*   *   *

Another child I have come to know, the nine-year-old daughter of a tenant farmer in Jones County, North Carolina, talks even more than Lawrence about the sky, the moon, the stars, the sun. Like him, she is moved constantly to draw all of them, so removed in space yet so close to her life. Jeannette is the girl's name; and a smart, winning child she is, full of imagination and wonder and humor — but also confusion and gloom. I had to spend more time than usual with her before I found out a little of what her almost frozen appearance managed to conceal. Eventually I had to face the fact that a girl I initially considered distinctly retarded turned out to be perhaps the brightest of all the so-called stranded children I am now trying to describe — children whose fathers, like Jeannette's, still work as sharecroppers or tenant farmers or field hands.

For months Jeannette seemed not only quieter than others in her family, but I have to confess, a little odd. She had a habit of moving near me as I entered the cabin — it can tactfully be called an extremely fragile and vulnerable building, lacking in the appointments Americans usually take for granted. Like a fly or mosquito, I once thought, she would draw close, breathe just hard enough to make a little noise, then withdraw to a distant corner of that one room which eight human beings call "home." Her eyes never stop staring at the visitor. While other eyes, her mother's, say, or those that belong to her sisters or brother or father usually looked down or up or in any direction that amounted to *away*, Jeannette's eyes held fast. Perhaps it was my own nervousness that made me pin words like "retarded" or "inappropriate" or "eccentric" on a girl's open and direct curiosity. In any event, I gradually began to appreciate Jeannette's perceptiveness and the intensity as well as generosity of her mind. She missed little and gave "life" and "nature" the very definite benefit of the doubt. "I know it's not so good for us," she once declared, "but there's never a day I don't see something I like."

Perhaps she is naïve — a child and so childlike. Perhaps "underneath" she is more in despair than she knows or can admit. Perhaps she will soon change her mind, lose what older people like me call her innocence, her exceptionally trusting or confident nature. Yet, I doubt it. After a while one sees how, in the face of great difficulties and recurrent fits of discouragement, a "trait" like Jeannette's optimism has its roots in a long tradition. For example, Jeannette's grandmother, her mother's mother, is the one who inspires the child's spirit of enthusiasm, her sense of expectation about the world. Jeannette's mother, however, is tired and often despondent; like me, I suppose, she finds Jeannette a little unnerving. She once tried to bring alive the child's special qualities: "She's a strange child, my Jeannette is; and I don't know why. I had trouble bearing her, but that's been the case with all my children. She was strong most of the time when she was little, and she was always wanting to eat more and more and more. You have to stop them. You have to tell them you just don't have anything more for them to eat, even if they're as hungry as can be. With Jeannette, I'll say this about her, she was always wondering why — why this and why that. All your kids will do that, but she was worse than the rest of them, yes she was. She'd point to everything and ask me how it all came and from where, and I'd tell her to stop and she didn't. Instead she'd go over to my mother and start talking with her, and my mother was over there on the bed, lying there sick, and she'd try to answer the child, but no one could, I don't believe, with all the learning in the world.

"If you ask me, my mother fell to listening to Jeannette and going along with her. Jeannette would tell her that God was up there in the sun, looking down on us and making the grass grow, and in the night He is in the moon, so we won't be without Him, and my mother would say, 'Yes, child,' and 'You're right, child,' and there wasn't a thing I could say to change their minds, either of them. By now we just know that Jeannette is Jeannette, and she doesn't go to school all the time, but when she does she's good, the teachers say, real good, and why doesn't she come there more, they ask, but they know the answer, I know they do. I haven't clothes for all of them at the same time. And Jeannette isn't that interested in school, because she says she looks around and she sees things, and she learns that way. I guess I see what she means, though I doubt there is much you can see that'll teach you any more than you know already. But you can go ask Jeannette, and she'll one day talk your ear off. She's got a whole lot to say, that girl; I only tell her that me and her daddy and other people, they can't sit and listen all day, not with the chores you have from the first thing you get up to the last second before you fall into bed, and you're as tired as can be, and you're asleep before you know it."

Jeannette has done what her mother predicted, talked and talked with me and asked questions and gladly done drawings and paintings. Her landscapes are her pride, full of trees and flowers. She loves to start with the sky, then come down toward the earth, through trees that are drawn from their top branches first, followed by a sturdy trunk and at last the roots. Most children I know, regardless of race, class, family background or region, begin such drawings the other way around, from the ground on up, with the blue sky and the sun commonly a near afterthought. Eventually, after two pictures were done during the same visit, one with crayons and one with paints, one a daytime scene and one set in the evening (Figure 16), I felt able to ask Jeannette why she liked to start things up in the sky and work downward. That question marked the beginning of a certain frankness she and I shared with one another, one of the most important, instructive and above all touching experiences I've ever had with any child, any human being anywhere. As I get ready to set forth some of the highlights of Jeannette's remarks, made to me over a period of many months, I wonder how any words can quite convey the liveliness in her, *not* (I must say) easily visible in her face, but in her voice itself. Perhaps the best word is *vibrant;* Jeannette has a vibrant personality, which her voice especially gets across to people.

Jeannette's suns and moons are also particularly alive — full, as a matter of fact, of her own animated self. Certainly she means those suns and moons to be something awesome: "The sun, it's hot, but it's real good. I'll be going outside in the morning and I'll wave to the sun and I'll be glad when he comes to visit us, because if he didn't we'd be in trouble. There wouldn't be the crops, and we'd have no place to live; they'd tell us to leave, and Daddy says we'd probably go to Washington, up there, but he doesn't want for us to go there or anyplace else. I don't like the days when there will only be the clouds all day long. I like it when the sun will break through and start shining down on us, but I like it best of all when there's not a cloud in the sky, and just the sun, and you feel real warm because you're right under it, and you sure know.

"I don't know why I start with the sun up there. I like the colors blue and yellow; maybe that's why. I like to look up at the sky. Grandma says it's where we're all going — sooner or later, she says. If you look at the clouds, you can see they look like people a lot of the time. Sometimes there'll be no clouds; maybe that's when the Lord God has called everyone together and they're out of sight, far away from us, maybe right in the sun. I know it must be really hot there, in the sun, but it doesn't matter when you're dead. Then all that matters is whether the Lord is smiling on you or frowning on you. With the moon it's different. You don't want it so dark that there's no light to see by, and the moon carries you through the night, most nights, if you get scared; that's what Grandma told me and she's right. She said if I wake up and I get to shaking and I'm real scared, then go quietly to the door and find the moon and she'll smile on you and everything will be fine. But if the moon isn't there, don't worry either; because it'll be back real soon, and it's never away for more than a few days. Then try to find a good star, and if you can't because of the clouds, then go wake Grandma — but I've never done that.

"When I get big I'd like to go on one of those big airplanes you see passing over. Grandma said they don't reach the top of the sky, just part of the way. She doesn't know where they're going, just to some cities, she thinks, but which ones you can't tell. The first time I thought they might be some bird, but I don't know what the name would be. Then when I went to school the teacher said maybe I was thinking of an eagle when I saw the airplane. She said she was going to write a letter to some people, the ones that own the plane and fly it, and ask them for a picture postcard — I guess it will show what you'd find it like if you went and got in and went right along with the plane through the sky. Once I was up a tree and I thought I'd try to be a plane, and I did, but I fell down. No, I didn't hurt myself. I just kept on wishing I didn't fall. I wished I was still up there, flying and flying, flying way high and away.

"Grandma told me that the only way for us folks is to go up. If you go sideways, you just end up in another county, and it's no different. If you go down, you're on your way to Hell, like Mr. Sam Pierce, the reverend says. He says you have to lower everybody into the ground after they die, but you should really pray that they never go lower than the hole that's been dug, because then they're really headed for trouble. Way down in the middle of the ground, there's no sun you can see, nor the moon; that's what I hear. It's no good. Grandma will say sometimes that it's just as bad up here in Jones County as down underground, but I can't go along with her on that. Like you hear in church: you mustn't go along and give up and look on only the wrong side of things. If the sun comes up in the morning, it means you have the day coming around the turn, and you can be glad."

Yes, she can get a little maudlin, a little rhetorical; and at nine she is clearly not inventing a great and original vision of things. Yet, Jeannette's world — at least the one outside her mind — is a terribly harsh and bare one, which she is earnestly trying to find at least passably comprehensible. In her own family, in other families a few miles this or that way, one can meet children who are not making the kind of effort Jeannette demonstrates. Her sister, the one nearest in age to her, wonders why Jeannette "troubles" about so much: "I'm older by a year, I believe, and I never have worried like Jeannette. She troubles herself, and she goes to Grandma, and they'll get talking, and we don't know what keeps them together so long. Once my momma said she thinks there's a ghost or something that got stuck in Jeannette, and it makes her do a lot of the talking she does; and she's always asking about something, too. She'll wake up and want you to go looking out there, and when she'll hear a noise she'll know what it is, which of the animals. It doesn't make any difference to me. I guess I'd rather be back to sleep. I'll wake and hear her talking in her sleep; but Grandma says we all talk in the middle of the night, only we don't know it. But I'll bet Jeannette talks more than I do."

Jeannette does indeed talk more than her older sister or her younger ones. She also thinks more about the next few years of life than they do. She has thoughts and wishes and daydreams about those years, even as she spends a lot of time playing in the fields or the woods and helping her mother get the younger children into the house in order to eat or go to bed. She imagines herself living somewhere else, living a life thoroughly different from the one she knows she will actually have. Here is how her mind wonders and wanders and hopes and then gives up hoping and in a flash of bitter irony, a child's kind of "black humor," yields to what psychiatrists call "reality": "I'll be walking sometimes and I say something to myself. I say that maybe one day later on I'll be far away from here, and I'll be a singer or I'll have a job on the radio or the television, and I'll live nice, as nice as you'd like to. I could bring everyone in my whole family to live near me, and they wouldn't always be thinking there's no next meal, and they wouldn't be scared all the time of the bossman and his people; and all of us, we'd be happy, like my grandma says God meant for us to be.

"If I had a good job, and I liked it, I'd have clothes and shoes, so I'd never hurt my feet walking, and they wouldn't get hot and burned, you know, in the summer. I'd have a room and it would be like you see in the stores when you go into New Bern: there would be the rugs and the television and a big mirror and you could see yourself, and anytime you wanted to find out how you are looking, you could just go over and there you'd be, right before yourself, and you could fix yourself up and be real nice. You know what I'd like a lot, too? I'd like a plant and some flowers, like the teacher, Miss Johnson, has on her desk; and I'd like to have a car, and then I'd learn how to drive it, and I could get inside and start the motor and wherever I'd want to go, I could get there, pretty soon. The other thing I could do would be find me someone who could fix my leg, so it doesn't hurt, and fix my teeth, because they're bad, and I'll wake up in the night, and the tooth will really be giving me a lot of pain. I'd drive from town to town until I met a nice man, a doctor, and he'd give me medicines for all the troubles.

"If I was feeling real good, and if I still could keep on wishing things, then I'd ask how you get to go onto those planes, and I'd go. You can fly all around to everywhere, the teacher said, and I sure would. Before long I'd be seeing the whole world, all the places and the cities, and somewhere there'd be a lot of water and somewhere deserts and no rain. Then I'd come home and I'd tell my sisters and everyone what I saw and how you can do things — if you're not here and instead you're away, and if you've got some money, you know, and if there's no bossman pushing on you, and there aren't a lot of people around, telling you to do what they say."

Who are "they," the oppressors? Are they white only, or only certain whites? Is there any hope right there in North Carolina or in other such states, or must girls like Jeannette go far away if they are to live even half comfortably, and even a little without aches and pain? One thinks about such matters as a Jeannette talks, and sooner or later she provides an answer: "Maybe we could stay here and I could have my house and I would be in a real nice place, but I don't think the white people will let us — let us live so it's real good for us. My daddy says it's the colored people, too; they'll sit on top of one another, and some will take a lot of money from the white man, so they can boss us around worse than the white man does himself. I think if you're going to find something better — I mean, a good house and some money — then like you hear, you've got to leave here. The trouble is, most of the time they'll tell you that after you go away you don't find much that's good, so you might just as well stay, until you know where to go. My grandma says I'll probably be here all my life, like her, and maybe she's right.

"You know what? You know what I'd like to be, if I'm going to be in Jones County all my life? I'd like to be a scarecrow. Yes sir, if I got to be a scarecrow, I'd have the easiest life. I'd just be standing there, and they wouldn't be pushing on me, like they do, and calling me bad names, whispering them, in the store, when I go there. The lady, she said I was an 'uppity little nigger,' I heard her, because of how I look, how I carry my head, or something. I was outside, and she didn't know and she couldn't see me, and I listened to her talking, and I listened until I heard what she said, the whole of it, and then I went away as fast as I could, and she didn't know I was there. If I was a scarecrow, then maybe I could scare all those white people away; if they said something bad, I could be there and they'd want to run. The only thing is, I'd like to be alive and to fly, not just be standing there you know, like scarecrows do. I could be there in the field for some of the time and keep the birds away, but I could be a bird myself and fly around, all over. But I'd always come back here, because my grandma says they don't like blackbirds in the city."

She drew a picture of a scarecrow for me one afternoon and then added those birds a scarecrow is supposed to keep away — blackbirds among others (Figure 17). All her birds were blackbirds, and so I asked her whether other birds threaten the crops, too. Yes, they do; but mostly it's the blackbirds. Then she added the reason: "They're hungry, and they don't get much to eat, and they have to try. You can't blame them. A long time ago, I recall, my daddy was fixing the scarecrow, so it would stand straight and keep up and not fall down, and he said he feels bad for the birds, for the blackbirds, because all they're trying to do is get the same thing as we are — food; and it's too bad, but if the birds get all they want, then we'll be on the losing side, and so they have to be scared away, or else we'll starve to death ourselves."

Jeannette's drawing of the scarecrow meant a lot to her. Months later she would mention the drawing, ask me if I still had it, ask me whether anyone else had ever drawn a scarecrow for me. I said no, she was the only one, though other parts of the drawing — the sky and sun and earth and blackbirds — had been done at one time or another by a good number of children I have known. She could understand that. She was glad, though, that she alone had thought to draw a scare-crow. When she was a very little girl she had seen a scarecrow and asked her father whether it talked, and if so, to whom. Well, of course, her father had told her that scarecrows don't talk, though she doubted him at the time and in a way she still does. Oh, she *knows* in her mind that they don't, the scarecrows of Jones County and all the others, all over America; but she would like for them to have a say about various matters and through her (perhaps it can be put like that) they *do* have a say — those lonely, ragged, and forlorn things who themselves look scared, who appear more frightened than the birds that fly by and only occasionally ignore the surrounding crops.

"It's talking, the scarecrow," Jeannette told me when I asked the same old question I had asked her so many times: is there anything happening there, in the place you've just drawn? Some children don't like to be bothered with that kind of prodding. They know the inquiry for what it is, an effort to get them to talk about what they have put into a picture, and by doing so reveal a bit of what is on the very young artist's mind. In contrast, Jeannette has never needed much encouragement to set her imagination afire; indeed she welcomes questions — the more the better, it seems. She likes to tell stories. I believe that she was almost waiting for me to be intrigued with her scarecrow. Within seconds of my question she was off running with a story, a reporter's account it almost was: "The scarecrow likes to talk. He talks to the corn and the trees and he talks real loud when the wind comes and blows right through him and shakes him; and then all the birds fly away as fast as they can. A lot of the time the scarecrow wishes there'd be other scarecrows around, and then they could all talk together and have themselves a good time. But there aren't the other scarecrows, so this one talks to himself, and he sings a lot, and that way he doesn't feel too bad. A lot of the time he's hungry, but he doesn't eat the corn, because he's not supposed to. I don't know how he eats. Maybe he doesn't have to. Everyone has to eat, though. Don't they?"

Jeannette doesn't eat too well. Nor do many, many other children like her. I still find myself surprised and dismayed by a child's drawing in which there is a table but no food, or a plate but no food, a bowl but no food. Unlike other boys and girls, sharecropper children do not draw strong kitchen tables or dining room tables, bedecked with flowers and dishes and fruit and vegetables. Sharecropper children don't supply colorful tablecloths and vases and tall glasses with straws inside, and they don't paint or sketch a refrigerator nearby, full of good things to eat, or a stove where all of that is being prepared. When a sharecropper boy draws a home, it is small and inconsequential in appearance, a mere spot on the thick, powerful earth, and all too faithfully his home. When a sharecropper girl draws a kitchen at mealtime or any other moment of the day it is her kitchen and none other (Figure 18).

A boy of eight who lives in McCormick County, South Carolina, drew the home, and a girl of seven who lives in Holmes County, Mississippi, drew the kitchen — which means in this case the entire house, all of its one room. The boy knew what he was doing, and so did the girl. The boy had this to say: "It's what we have. It's not the best place in the world to live, my mother says so, and if we looked far enough, we might find a better place, but it's ours, and so long as we're here, there's no reason to leave, because before we'd be long on the road, looking for something better, we'd probably get put in jail or get real bad sick, and there'd be no one to help us. Our place — you know, my daddy says he thinks it was built by slaves. All the houses around here, they were all built by the slaves. The Mister, his family has owned most of the county, a lot of it, since before we were freed, the colored; and afterwards, we stayed here, and if it hadn't been for them, the Mister and his family, we'd all have had no place to be, and Lord knows, my mother says, if any of us would be alive today. My brother — he's a couple of years older than me — thinks he could build us a better place than this one, but it's not our land, and we're lucky to have what we have. The Mister says we're doing good work with the crops, and we can stay here, and if he can help us during the winter, he will. He lets us charge up the groceries, and then when the crops are in he deducts. Last winter it was so cold my daddy said we might as well be up North. The Mister came over and went from place to place, and he said if we needed paper to fill in the cracks we could come over and get the paper, and he would get some more if it ran out; and he told us to sleep right close to the stove, but we knew how to, anyway."

The girl had this to say: "I did my best to make it look good, the table we have. I can't draw good, but I can draw some things better than others. My favorite is to draw a dress, the one that was sent down for us, my sister and me, from Toledo — no sir, I don't know where Toledo is, except that it's far, far off and my aunt is there, and my cousins, too. They all used to live here, you know, and they left. We got the table from them. They took it and brought it here; the day before they left, they did. No, we didn't have our own before then. We had the bed, and we'd eat there. It was better sitting on the bed, but now that we have the table and the two chairs there, we use them sometimes. We put things on the table, the pot with the soup or the grits, and we get our servings from the table, and Daddy will sit there on the chair and rest himself. He says he doesn't want to go to bed just as soon as the sun goes down, and he gets a good rest on the chair. That's why we're glad to have the table and the chairs. Now I have a good dress I can use for church, thanks to our aunt. Daddy says he doesn't think he'll go up to Toledo, though. You have to get a car, and a car can break down, and then you're lost as can be. My aunt saved the fare for a long time and took the bus, but it was because her husband died that they let her go, the bossman did. He said they couldn't be of use to him anymore, so they should leave when they could, but he wouldn't push on them for when. Then my aunt collected on the insurance. It was supposed to be five hundred dollars, the man told her a long time ago, but he came and gave her two hundred. He said the value of insurance policies was going down, and there wasn't anything he could do. My aunt said he must be the richest nigger in America, from all the insurance he collects every time someone dies. He has a big car and it's got the air-cool in it. He keeps the windows closed all the time. My daddy says he comes by all the houses, and like he did with my uncle before he passed, he collects a quarter from you a couple of times in the month. Then, if you die he brings your wife the cash, but not what he told you. He brings something, though, so at least my aunt and my cousins had their bus fare."

In Washington County, Alabama, some white children could tell that black girl how mean and devious white insurance agents and bossmen can be — to the families of white tenant farmers, who by no means are a numerical match for their black counterparts, but who still exist (and suffer terribly) in parts of the South. Tim is six years old. He is thin and tall for his age. He has hazel eyes and light brown hair. He is far from an open, affable boy, but over the years he gets more and more talkative. His schoolteacher thinks he "may be a little smarter than some like him." What does she mean by that? She, too, doesn't talk very much at first, but eventually she lets me know that she simply assumed that I was aware, as she is, that Alabama has its "poor white people" and "they're low on intelligence, a lot of them." Not that she is prejudiced against her own people; and not that she would ever want to use seriously that term "poor white trash"; and not that she doesn't fully understand why things are as they are: "I know why a boy like Tim doesn't take to school and never will. They're dirt poor, and they have no education, his parents, and they live off of Mr. Williams's land. They work it, and they give him a share of what they make and they keep the rest for themselves. It's pitiful, if you ask me — how they live."

I do not believe the word "pitiful" quite describes Tim and his family. They are poor, as "dirt poor" as can be, which they say themselves. They lack good food and decent shelter. They see little that is promising "up ahead," in the years to come. White though they are, there is little reason for them to be grateful for Alabama's agricultural economy, all of which Tim's parents know. So, while we talked about Tim, his father could interrupt this way: "Tim hasn't got a great future, any more than I did. In every county of this state you'll find your rich men, and the few that do well by serving them. I mean, they'll hire their foremen and they'll have their lawyers and the men who do the insuring and the county agents, the agricultural agents, and the sheriff — they all work for Mr. Williams, you know, one way or the other they do, just like me. The only difference is that I *really* work for him, from the first of the sunlight to the last; the rest, they'll be in the town, in the Donut Shoppe there, sitting and figuring how they can get some more money out of old man Williams and his boy, Sonny Williams. Tim asked me the other day why I didn't have a job like that, with a necktie and a big new car, and I told him there's the rich and the poor in this county, and only a few in-between, and most of us, we're just poor.

"We're not niggers, though; I'll tell you that. I feel sorry for them. They can't read nor write, and as bad as it is for the white, it's worse for the colored. Old man Williams, he has the colored working on his land, too — on the other side of the county. I hear they have it bad, real bad. My wife says they can't be much worse off than we have it, but I reminded her — they'd be killed if they tried to step in the Donut Shoppe or our church or like that, and we're not going to let one of them in our school, no matter what they try to do up there in Washington, D.C. Sonny Williams, he's my age, born the same year, my mother told me, and he's good and polite and respectful to all of us white men who work his daddy's land; and I hear he hates the niggers and wants to drive them all up North. He says they just live for the next meal, and they've got no ambition in them. I don't see how he can go and get rid of all his colored, though; not with all the land under cultivation. They're still needed around here, yes sir — niggers are. But if they want to go up North, I'm in favor of it. I'd never leave here, but I could understand them leaving. Maybe if they went, there'd be more machines the old man Williams would have to buy, and I could learn to drive one, and he'd pay me. I guess he'd have to be real nice to the white, if more of the colored left.

"Maybe Timmie will keep on going in school, and maybe he can get a job there in town, and he could live better. I always tell my children that they're not me, nor their mother, and they can go and find a better life, maybe; and they're not niggers, either — I tell them that. They should keep their eyes open, and there's no telling what comes up, sometimes — I mean a job or a chance to make some money. I'm afraid I don't see much of that — money."

He doesn't see money at all for weeks at a time. Like black tenant farmers or sharecroppers, Tim's father is part of a virtual barter economy. He seeds the black earth, cares for and harvests cotton and a variety of vegetables, and in exchange he gets a rather broken-down cabin (which has electricity but no running water and no heat except for what a coal stove provides) and a share of the profits, a share of what is sold to a nearby "wholesale produce company" — owned and run, it turns out, by the same family that lets Tim (for the boy at six already knows how to pick weeds and later picks the crops themselves) and his father work their "parcel" of land. Tim knows all of that, at age six knows who he is and who his father is and who the colored man is and who old man Williams is and who Sonny Williams is. Shyly, yet with obvious relish he draws a picture (Figure 19) of a great big hulk of a man, and tells me very explicitly what that man is like: "He's the richest man I'll ever see, my daddy says, unless I go a long way from here. He owns the county, just about, and into the next one, too — they say. Daddy says there could be worse, but sometimes he'll change his mind and say no, there can't be worse — not worse than old man Williams.

Now Mr. Williams does indeed appear threatening and even grotesque when compared to Tim's sketches of his dad (Figure 20) or those the boy did of a black "handyman" — which is what Tim and his father both choose to call a man who in fact does exactly what they do, work Alabama's generous land for the very ungenerous old man Williams. Tim might be tempted to be as rich and powerful as Mr. Williams, but Tim at six has some ethical concern inside that literally childish and immature and undeveloped mind of his: "I don't know. I'd like to be like old man Williams, but if I had all he does, I'd want to give some of it away. I mean, I could give some of it to my daddy, and I wouldn't stop there, no. I'd go and give some to Mr. Howe and Mr. Gurney and Mr. Wallace and Mr. McKeon and — maybe everyone old man Williams has working for him. I'd go and give some to his niggers, too; yes, I would. He has those handymen, you know, and they help him and they are in the worst shape in the whole world, and if I had the money they have in the Williams family, I'd share it, that's what I think.

"Daddy says once you get money, you think different; you just want to hold on to what you have. But if you remember your own troubles, then you'll be nicer to other people, that's what he said in his sermon, the minister, and I would, if I became rich. My brother Richard, he says he would, too; and Daddy agreed. He said that the trouble is that Mr. Williams has never been poor a day in his life, and he's never been without anything, so you can't expect him to think as we do. Then my mother said maybe they should start rotating around the money, to more and more people, rather than one man and his family having it, and then there'd be more people with money, and some of them might be willing to go and give a little money to others, especially to the people who work so hard for practically nothing. Then we'd have a better state of Alabama than we do right now. My brother Richard must have told the teacher that — she's Miss Wilson, and she's got the fourth grade all to herself, yes she does — and she got real upset with him and said to him, 'Richard, you've got some crazy ideas in your head and where did you get them?' And my brother didn't lay it on anyone, the blame. My mother said they'll let us talk like that, because we're in school, but not when we get to be a man or a woman — then there'd be the sheriff out after us, and the next thing we'd know, we'd be run out of the county and maybe the next one, too."

So, Tim's view of the world turns out not to be so different from that of other children, who, though black, share much of Tim's experience: with the land, with the bosses and their agents, with parents who feel hurt and used and put upon and cheated, yet also feel unable and afraid to do anything but submit and complain and grumble and fret and murmur and at times shout and cry and scream — all that to themselves or among others like themselves. In the end, however strong the protest, there seems no choice but, once again, to submit, to acquiesce, to go along and hope that somehow and in some way there will come an end to it — an end to the hard, mean toil, barely rewarded and performed for the gain of others. Tim's father speaks, I believe, for this nation's thousands of sharecroppers and tenant farmers, men who keep on working and working, compliantly it seems, but feel worried and victimized and ill-used and, during bad moments, broken in mind and spirit: "I'm all right a lot of days. I just do the work that has to be done. There'll be a day or two out of the month, though, that I get wondering too much about things, and I feel I'm slipping into trouble; yes, I do, I'll admit it. I was born and brought up here, and before me there was my daddy and before him there was his daddy, and way back we go. We love Alabama, and I'd never leave, not for anything. I'm a Southerner, I guess you'd say. But there's a lot of unfairness around here, and I don't think it's right. I'll be plowing or picking and I'll say to myself that it's not right for some of us to have almost nothing, and there'll be others who own everything there is to be owned. But you can't think like that, because then you're getting to be dangerous. That's what the teachers will tell your kids when they go repeating you in school, and I guess the teachers are right, because they know a lot more than someone like me does, I'll admit to that. But they've got their salaries, you know, and they live as good as anyone does here, except for Mr. Williams and his people that run things for him. I guess I run things for him, too — just like his foreman Mr. Graves says *he* does; only I get nothing and Graves gets his big fat check. It's enough to break me up sometimes, but you can't let that happen. You'll become someone for the doctor then, and you don't want that. So you go on and work the next mile of land, that's what."

It is always there for them, Tim's father and all the fathers like him, the next mile of land; and for Tim and all the children like him the land also figures prominently — in their words and thoughts and dreams and drawings and paintings. In contrast to migrant children, who also know the land and work on the land but see it as the cause of their confusing, irregular kind of life, sharecropper children view the fields and the crops as life's one reliable element. When will it all end, migrant children ask in any number of implicit and explicit ways. At least we have the fields out there and what they bring us, sharecropper children feel and often enough even say. Migrant children know that the crops mean money, meager though the amount is, even as share-cropper children associate a harvest with a few if not many meals. On the other hand, the migrant child knows one farm will lead to another, and all of those farms mean, finally, the dazed and bewildered state of mind that goes with such living; whereas sharecropper children have roots — if nothing else, roots. The world may be unfair, the bossman stingy, the children themselves half starved, but at least there is that particular stretch of land out there, familiar and unchanging and yes, full of the miraculous fertility that children like poets can celebrate. The ten-year-old daughter of a Mississippi tenant farmer put what I am trying to say into words a few weeks before her family was to leave for Chicago: "Everyone says you should leave here, but I don't want to. I know all the people around, and I know all the roads and the fields, and I told my daddy that when we get up there we won't know anyone and it'll be strange as can be up there, and we shouldn't go. But he said we have to, and that's that, and for me to stop bothering him and upsetting myself. But I think he'll change his mind when we leave, and we're far away, and then it'll be too late, that's what I think."

She does indeed know "the roads and the fields." She knows the best spot to be cool and the best spot to see the sunrise and the best spot to see the sunset and the best spot to hide and watch rabbits or skunks and the best spot to hide and listen to them talking, the boss-man and the foreman and the assistant foreman — as they are walking along and laughing and kicking stones or smoking or chewing on a piece of grass and saying something like, "The nigger's doing fine, ain't he." She knows where to find water and where to find a soft bed of pine needles and where to find pieces of old, abandoned machinery which are the best playthings she and her brothers have. She knows how "the irrigation" works and how the pesticides work and why the soil needs fertilizer. Put differently, she is informed about things agricultural, and she is protective about the land, her land psychologically if the bossman's legally. Again the contrast has to be made with migrant children, who never really get to know a particular piece of property, but instead experience fields as places that offer a few days of work, but then must be left, and quickly, too.

If migrant children and sharecropper children are alike in being poor and scorned and thoroughly ignored by the rest of us, childhood is different among, on the one hand, a white boy like Tim or the little black girl just quoted, and on the other hand, those migrant children described in the previous chapter. Sharecropper children experience hardships, but they are surrounded by things that give them a tangible refuge, however unpleasant and even stomach-turning some of those cabins can be. In Holmes County, Mississippi, a mother said what I am trying to say: "The kids know everything that goes on you know. Anytime I want to hear about something, I ask them. They sneak around and listen to people, and they're always poking around outside. They'll come in and tell me that the first leaf has turned, and we'll be having cooler weather. They'll come in and tell me that they've seen a little flower sticking its head up from the ground. They'll come in and tell me that the water is beginning to run low or that way over on the other side of the place the crops need more weeding than we thought, or that we forgot to spray a corner of the land, and all like that. You can walk around here and you'll see their marks on the trees and the rocks and you'll see all the huts they've put up and torn down and the other things they've made with the branches and the grass and — well, they've walked over every inch of the farm, yes sir, and probably a million times, I'll bet. If I had to know where the best worms are, I'd go ask them, just like their daddy does. They'll tell you where the best fishing is, and the bossman, you know he takes along one of my kids every time he goes fishing. My boy says the bossman will say it right to him: 'You little nigras, you sure know your fish.' And he'll give them a quarter, if there's a good catch they get. If the fish aren't so good, he'll turn them over to my boy, and then we eat them up for supper, and they always taste good to us, I'll say that.

"If you drove in your car for miles around, my children could show you every bird's nest there is here, and where they're all living, the animals. They keep their eyes on the crops, too. The foreman will always ask them how is everything doing, just like he'll ask me or my husband, and I do believe the children know better than we do. That's why they hate to go over to that school. They'll be sitting there all day, and the teacher will be pushing things on them, the letters and the numbers and like that, and she'll call them the same things the white people do, just as bad, and they'll come home and say they *are* dumb — for going over there and listening to her. They'll tell me they'd rather go out and listen to the animals make noise and help their daddy, if they can, and keep themselves busy and not bother me, than go off there to school and be told all the time that the colored people are no good, and they'll always be like that, because we're working on the land and we're so poor and we don't know how to be clean with ourselves and behave the way we should. Sure enough, it's not a life I'd like for my children, the kind I've had; but if we could make half a living — which we can't, and that's the trouble — then I wouldn't be so sad about anything, and I'd never leave here. You know why? My kids wouldn't let me. Even now they don't want to go — except around mealtime, when I don't give them all they want, because I haven't got it to give, and then they'll change their minds and start telling me we should leave here and go someplace else, where we won't always be afraid there won't be another thing to eat, and come the next time we're supposed to eat, and come the next time after that — until we're so weak we'll never be able to leave here, and that would be the end of us, I guess."

It haunts them, the questions that pose the great alternative. Shall we stay or shall we leave? Shall we keep on fighting a terribly grim and losing battle, in the hope that at least the few years we live on this planet will be spent on familiar and friendly ground, however cold and unfriendly and worse the people are who own that ground, and all the other ground nearby and far away? Shall we, rather, gird ourselves and go — leave as others have left, fearfully, and with all sorts of hopes and expectations? The land restricts and denies. The land awaits and offers up things. The land is someone else's to profit by, but ours to use. The land makes others rich and does little to keep us from extreme and unrelenting hardship. The land is everything we know. The land is, in a way, the source of all our misery. We will miss the land, miss it more than we can ever know — except that even here we *do* know how much our lives are tied to the rhythm of planting and growing and harvesting. We will leave and indeed forget the constant fear, the insults, the hopelessness; we will forget and start again up North, even as our ancestors did centuries ago, when, carried here in chains, they learned how to master the land and make it produce and produce — until white men became rich and proud and cultured and in the end died fighting to keep their land and keep us, their property.

So it goes, I believe, in thousands of minds as men and women mull things over and try to decide whether to continue being sharecroppers and tenant farmers and field hands or whether to make what so often is a fearful and sad as well as a necessary and hopeful break with the past. Sometimes the decision hinges on the children, on how strongly attached they feel to what they already know, on how sick and hungry and tired they are — and in need of help they will never get "nearabouts," as those rural counties are sometimes described. In any event, however the early lives of sharecropper and migrant children differ, one from the other, by the time the children described here and the children described in the previous chapter become eleven or twelve a common fate awaits them, a fate that distinctly overshadows all the differences I have just taken such pains to describe. I am talking about the swift decline of childhood, the abrupt beginning of a working and loving life — all in a matter of months. Then come the responsibilities that go with hard toil and the presence of a woman to feed or a man to cook for and soon, very soon, the arrival of children. At twelve or thirteen, the light and tender moments begin to wane, the world begins to shrink and toughen. Then the wisdom and humor get curbed. Then a kind of battle is joined, and under such circumstances a lot has to be forgotten or taken for granted, rather than enjoyed: the pathways that lead nowhere and everywhere, the rocks hidden all over, the large holes in the ground that indicate rabbits are living nearby, the buttons on the scarecrow, all four of them loose and ready to fall at the slightest provocation, the soil with black ants and toads and caterpillars, and the soil with abundant worms swimming in it, the cool, dry, shaded, restful soil under a pine tree. "You live fast," I often heard from young migrant couples, young migrant parents. Suddenly they were no longer children and all too much the burdened, troubled grown-ups their parents had always been. One can hear the same surprised, puzzled, disappointed remarks from young tenant farmers: "I don't know; it seems yesterday I was just helping out, and now it's all on me, life. My daddy said it was just in time because he fell down and he can't move his left side much, and he came over, the bossman, and said I could take over, if I was planning to stay here, and even if my daddy hadn't gone and fallen sick, I was working along with him, he noticed, and now that I had my woman and all, he thought he might give me a little to do, on top of what Daddy does — some more land to work — and besides that, I can help with driving the truck, if I can learn to tame it. And I can work over in his place where they sort the vegetables and pack them. They pay good there, but it's only a few weeks from the year.

"There was a time I thought I'd never stay here when I got big and could leave, but I guess I'll stay for a little, and see if I like it, now that I'm grown. In a few years they might take me in the Army, and then I'd be able to look over other places to live. Of course, the bossman can tell the Army not to take you, if he wants, because he needs us. He told me if I wanted to go North, he'd let me, but we're to have a child soon, and I have trouble with my eyes, seeing. The bossman said there'd be doctors working for the Army, and they wouldn't let me in. He said one of these days he was going to take me over to his doctor and have him fix up all my ailments, and especially fix my eyes. I said thank you; and I'm still waiting on him, and he's never yet repeated himself or took me over there. But I'll be fine, I hope."

One can only hope, as he does. One can only hope that he will be fine, and his family will be fine and other such families will be fine. One can only hope that his nation keeps on being "fine" — the envy of the world, the pride of the West, the home for hundreds of years, it has turned out, of loyal and resigned young sharecropper men who say that all will go well with them, but know how wicked and cursed the order of things is, know it in ways people like me — however earnest and prolonged our scrutiny — can never really know.

Hidden Children

They live up alongside the hills, in hollow after hollow. They live in eastern Kentucky and eastern Tennessee and in the western part of North Carolina and the western part of Virginia and in just about the whole state of West Virginia. They live close to the land; they farm it and some of them go down into it to extract its coal. Their ancestors, a century or two ago, fought their way westward from the Atlantic seaboard, came up on the mountains, penetrated the valleys, and moved stubbornly up the creeks for room, for privacy, for a view, for a domain of sorts. They are Appalachian people, mountain people, hill people. They are white yeomen, or miners, or hollow folk, or subsistence farmers. They are part of something called "the rural poor"; they are sometimes called "hillbillies." They are people who live in a "depressed area"; and they have been called part of a "subculture." They have also been called "backward," and more inscrutably, "privatistic." They are known as balladeers and they are thought to have a tradition of music and poems and stories that is "pure" — right from old England and old Scotland and early if not old America.

As for the minds of those mountaineers, the rest of us outside their region are not supposed to have any way of really getting around certain traits that (so it is claimed) make the inhabitants of the hollows hard to reach psychologically, even as their territory and their cabins can be virtually unapproachable. Up in the hollows, the story goes, one finds sullen, fearful, withdrawn men and women who distrust outsiders, shun much of the twentieth century, cling to old and anomalous customs, take to liquor rather freely, and in general show themselves to be survivors of a rural, pioneer America for the most part long since gone. Up in the hollows, one is also told, the worst poverty in the nation exists, with hundreds of thousands of people condemned to a life of idleness, meager employment, long, snowbound winters and summers that can be of limited help to a man who has only an acre or two for planting on the side of a steep, rocky hill. Finally, up in the hollows history's cruel lessons are supposed to be unmistakably apparent: an ignored and exploited people have become a tired people, a worn-out people, a frivolous or unresponsive people, the best of whom, the ones with any life at all in them, continue to leave, thereby making an already dismal situation an almost impossible one.

No one, least of all the people in or near the hollows themselves, would want to deny all of that. Appalachia is indeed cut off in some respects from the rest of us; and the region's people are indeed quiet and reserved and often enough full of misgivings about "city people" and "outsiders," and the declarations of concern and the offers of help that have lately come from "them," whom one mountaineer I have known since 1964 goes on to describe as follows: "They're full of sugar when they come, and they say they want to do something for you; but I can't stand the sight of them, not one of them, because they're two-faced and wanting to treat you like you are dumb, a fool, and someone that needs to be told everything he should do and can't figure anything out for himself."

Yet, that same man, who lives way up one of those hollows (in Swain County, North Carolina) has other things to say about visitors and tourists, and by implication, other things to say about himself and his own kind of people: "A lot of cars come riding through here, you know. Everyone wants to look at the hills, and the bigger the waterfall you have to show, the better. They'll stop their driving and ask you directions to things, if you're down there on the main road, and I always try to help. You see, we're not against those people. It's beautiful here, right beautiful. You couldn't make it better if you could sit down and try to start all over and do anything you want. If they come here from clear across the country and tell you how they love what they've seen and they want to see more, I'm ready to help them, and I always act as polite as I can, and so do they, for the most part. The ones I don't like one bit are different. They don't want to look and enjoy your land, like you do yourself; no sir, they want to come and sit down and tell you how sorry you are, real sorry, and if something isn't done soon, you're going to 'die out,' that's what one of them said. I wasn't there, but I heard he came from Asheville, or from some big city, maybe not in North Carolina; and he was supposed to get us meeting together, and if we did there'd be some money in it for us, and he kept saying we're in bad shape, they tell me he did, and worst of all are the kids, he said, and didn't we know that.

"I didn't hear him or his exact words, of course, but it's not the first time it's happened like that, because a year ago I heard someone talk the very same. He came to the church and we all listened. He said we should have a program here, and the kids should go to it before they start school. He said the government would pay for it, from Washington. He said they'd be teaching the kids a lot, and checking up on their health, and it would be the best thing in the world. Well, I didn't see anything wrong with the idea. It seemed like a good idea to me. But I didn't like the way he kept repeating how bad off our kids are, and how they need one thing and another thing. Finally I was about ready to tell him to go home, mister, and leave us alone, because our kids are way better than you'll ever know, and we don't need you and your kind around here with nothing good to say, and all the bad names we're getting called. I didn't say a word, though. No, I sat through to the end, and I went home. I was too shy to talk at the meeting, and so were a lot of the others. Our minister was there, and he kept on telling us to give the man a break, because he'd come to help us. Now, I'm the first to admit we could stand some help around here, but I'm not going to have someone just coming around here and looking down on us, that's all, just plain looking down on us — and our kids, that's the worst of it, when they look down on your own kids.

"My kids, they're good; each of them is. They're good kids, and they don't make for trouble, and you couldn't ask for them any better. If he had asked me, the man out of the East, Washington or some-place, I would have told him that, too. We all would have. But he didn't want to ask us anything. All he wanted was to tell us he had this idea and this money, and we should go ahead and get our little kids to-gether and they would go to the church during the summer and get their first learning, and they would be needing it, because they're bad off, that's what he must have said a hundred times, how bad off our kids are, and how the President of the United States wants for them to get their teeth fixed and to see a doctor and to learn as much as they can. You know what my wife whispered to me? She said, he doesn't know what our kids have learned, and still he's telling us they haven't learned a thing and they won't. And who does he think he is anyway? I told her it's best to sit him out and we could laugh out loud later when we left the church."

Later, when they left the church, they went home to their chil-dren, who were rather curious about the reason their parents had seen fit to go out to a meeting after supper in the middle of the week. There are five of those children and they range from four months to nine years. All the children were born in Swain County, North Carolina, as were their parents and grandparents and great-grandparents going back a century and more. Nor does Mrs. Allen want her children to be born anyplace else, or for that matter, under any other circumstances: "This is good country, as anybody will likely admit once he's seen it, and there's no reason to leave that I can see. You ask about the children I've borne; well, they're all good children, I believe they are. I've lost two, one from pneumonia we thought, and one had trouble from the moment he was alive. He was the only child that ever saw a doctor. We brought him down to Bryson City and there was a doctor there, waiting to see him. The Reverend Mason had called over, and he went with us.

"The doctor looked over the child real good, and I kept on fearing the news was going to be bad, the longer he looked and the more tests he did. Then he said he'd need extra tests, even beyond what he did, and we would have to come back. Of course I told him we'd try, but it's real hard on us to get a ride, and there's the other children I have, and my mother's gone, so they have to be left with one another the whole day, and there's a baby that needs me for feeding. The doctor said he could understand, but he needed those tests, and he was going to have to call some other doctor way over in Asheville or someplace and ask him some things. Mr. Mason said he'd drive us again, and we'd better do what the doctor said. Mr. Mason asked the doctor if there was much hope, even if we did everything and kept on coming back, so long as we had to, and the doctor shook his head, but he didn't say anything, one way or the other. But then my husband, Mr. Allen, he decided we'd better ask right there and then what was happening, and he did. He told the doctor that we're not much used to going to see doctors, and we'd like to know where we stand — it's just as plain and simple as that. The doctor asked if he could talk to Mr. Mason alone, and we said yes, that would be fine by us, but please couldn't they decide between themselves and then come and tell us something before we go back. And they did. They didn't talk too long before they came out, and said they would be honest with us, like we wanted, and the problem was with little Edward's muscles, and they weren't good from the start, and chances are they'd never be much good, and if we come back for the tests we might find out the exact disease, but he was pretty sure, even right then the doctor was, that Edward had a lot of bad trouble, and there wasn't much that could be done for him, and we might as well know it, that he'd not live to be grown up, and maybe not more than a year was the best we could hope for.

"I was real upset, but I was relieved to be told; I was thankful as can be for that. I guess Jim and I just nodded our heads and since we didn't say a word, and it was getting along, the time, the doctor came over and he asked if we had any questions to ask of him. I looked at Jim and he looked at me, and we didn't think of anything, and then Mr. Mason said it was all right, because if we did think of something later, we could always tell him and he could tell the doctor. The doctor said yes, and he said we were good people, and he liked us for being quiet and he wished he could do more. Jim said thank you, and we were glad he tried to help, and to be truthful we knew that there was something real bad wrong, and to us, if there isn't anything we can do, then chances are there isn't anything that anyone can do, even including a doctor, if he didn't mind us saying so. Mr. Mason said he wasn't sure we were in the right, and I said we could be wrong, and maybe they could have saved little Anne from her fever that burned her up — it was the pneumonia, we were sure. The doctor said there wasn't much use going back to what was over and done with, and I agreed. When we left, Mr. Mason said we could take the child back to the doctor anytime and he would drive us, and the doctor told the reverend he wouldn't charge us, not a penny. But Edward died a few weeks later. He couldn't breathe very good, like the doctor explained to us, because of his muscles, and the strain got to be more than he could take, so he stopped breathing, the little fellow did, right there in my arms. He could have lived longer, they said, if we'd have let them take him and put him in a hospital, you know, and they have motors and machines, to work on you. But I don't believe the Lord meant for Edward to go like that, in a hospital. I don't."

Her words read sadder than they sounded. She is tall, thin, but a forceful and composed woman, not given to self-pity. She has delicate bones, narrow wrists, thin ankles, decidedly pale blue eyes, and a bit surprisingly, a very strong, almost aquiline nose. She was thirty and, I thought, both young and old. Her brown hair was heavily streaked with gray, and her skin was more wrinkled than is the case with many women who are forty or even fifty, let alone thirty. Most noticeable were her teeth; the ones left were in extremely bad repair, and many had long since fallen out — something that she is quite willing to talk about, once her guest has lost *his* embarrassment and asked her a question, like whether she had ever seen a dentist about her teeth. No, she had never done anything like that. What could a dentist do, but take out one's teeth; and eventually they fall out if they are really no good. Well, of course, there *are* things a dentist can do — and she quickly says she knows there must be, though she still isn't quite sure what they are, "those things." For a second her tact dominates the room, which is one of two the cabin possesses. Then she demonstrates her sense of humor, her openness, her surprising and almost awesome mixture of modesty and pride: "If you want to keep your teeth, you shouldn't have children. I know that from my life. I started losing my teeth when I started bringing children into the world. They take your strength, your babies do, while you're carrying them, and that's as it should be, except if I had more strength left for myself after the baby comes, I might be more patient with them. If you're tired you get sharp all the time with your children.

"The worst tooth to lose is your first one, after that you get used to having them go, one by one. We don't have a mirror here, except a very small one and it's cracked. My mother gave it to me. When I pick it up to catch a look at myself I always fix it so that I don't see my teeth. I have them in front of the crack instead of the glass. I'd like to have the teeth back, because I know I'd look better, but you can't keep yourself looking good after you start a family, not if you've got to be on the move from the first second you get up until right before you go to sleep. When I lie down on the bed, it's to fall asleep. I never remember thinking about anything. I'm too tired. So is Jim; he's always out there working on something; and so are the kids, they're real full of spirits.

No wonder I lost so many teeth. When you have kids that are as rowdy and noisy as mine, they must need everything a mother's got even before they're born. Of course, even now Jim and I will sacrifice on their account, though they'll never know it.

"I always serve myself last, you know. I serve Jim first, and he's entitled to take everything we have, if he wants to, because he's the father, and it's his work that has brought us what we have, all of it. But Jim will stop himself, and say he's not so hungry, and nod toward the kids, and that means to give them the seconds before him. We don't always have seconds, of course, but we do the best we can. I make corn bread every day, and that's filling. There's nothing I hate more than a child crying at you and crying at you for food, and you standing there and knowing you can't give them much of anything, for all their tears. It's unnatural. That's what I say; it's just unnatural for a mother to be standing in her own house, and her children near her, and they're hungry and there isn't the food to feed them. It's just not right. It happens, though — and I'll tell you, now that you asked, my girl Sara, she's a few times told me that if we all somehow could eat more, then she wouldn't be having trouble like me with her teeth, later on. That's what the teacher told them, over there in the school.

"Well, I told Sara the only thing I could tell her. I told her that we do the best we can, and that's all anyone put here on this earth can ever do. I told her that her father has worked his entire life, since he was a boy, and so have I, and we're hoping for our kids that they may have it a lot better than us. But this isn't the place to be, not in Swain County here, up in this hollow, if you want to sit back and say I'd like this and I'd like that, and you'd better have this and something else, because the teacher says you should. I told Sara there's that one teacher, and maybe a couple more, and they get their salaries every week, and do you know who the teacher's uncle is — he's the sheriff over there in Needmore. Now, if Sara's daddy made half that teacher's salary in cash every week, he'd be a rich man, and I'd be able to do plenty about more food. But Sara's daddy doesn't get a salary from no one, no one, you hear! That's what I said to her, word for word it was. And she sat up and took notice of me, I'll tell you. I made sure she did. I looked her right in the eyes, and I never stopped looking until I was through with what I had to say. Then she said, 'Yes, ma'am,' and I said that I didn't want any grudges between us, and let's go right back to being friends, like before, but I wanted her to know what the truth was, to the best of my knowledge, and nothing more. She said she knew, and that was all that was said between us."

   In point of fact Mrs. Allen is usually rather silent with her children. She almost uncannily signals them with a look on her face, a motion of her hand, a gesture or turn of her body. She doesn't seem to have to talk, the way so many mothers elsewhere do, particularly in our suburbs. It is not that she is grim or glum or morose or withdrawn or stern or ungiving or austere; it is that she doesn't need words to give and acknowledge the receipt of messages. The messages are constantly being sent, but the children, rather like their mother, do things in a restrained, hushed manner — with smiles or frowns, or if necessary, laughs and groans doing the service of words. Yet, there are times when that cabin on the side of a mountain will become a place where songs are sung and eloquent words are spoken. Once, after a series of winter storms had worn them all down, Mr. Allen spoke to his wife and children, at first tentatively and apologetically and then firmly: "It's been a tough winter, this one, but they all are until they're over, and then you kind of miss them. You don't get a thing free in this world, that's what was handed down to me by my father. He said if I knew that, I knew all I'd ever have to know. I heard some of you kids the other day wondering if we couldn't go and live someplace else, where maybe there wouldn't be so much snow and ice, and us shivering even under every blanket your mother made and her mother and my mother, and that's a lot of blankets we're lucky to have. I'm sure there's better land than this, better counties to live in. You could probably find a house way off far from here, where they never get any snow, not once in the winter, and where there's more money around for everyone. Don't ask me where, or how you'll get there. I don't know.

   "I was out of here, this county, only once, and it was the longest three years of my life. They took me over to Asheville, and then to Atlanta, Georgia, and then to Fort Benning, and then to Korea. Now, that was the worst time I ever had, and when I came back, I'll tell you what I did. I swore on my Bible to my mother and my father, in front of both of them, that never again would I leave this county, and maybe not even this hollow. My daddy said I shouldn't be so positive, because you never can tell what might happen — like another war — and I said they'd have to come up here and drag me off, and I'd have my gun out, and I couldn't truthfully say right now if I'd use it on them or not, but I believe the word would get down to them that they'd better think it over very carefully, if they decide to come another time and take me and others who've given them three years already. Why do they always want us to go and fight those wars? It wasn't only the fighting, though. It was leaving here; and once you're over there, you never see this hollow for months and months and then you sure do know what you're missing, Oh, do you!

"When you ask me to say it, what we have here that you can't find anyplace else, I can't find the words. When I'd be in Georgia and over in Korea my buddies would always be asking me why I was more homesick than everyone in the whole Army put together. I couldn't really answer them, but I tried. I told them we have the best people in the world here, and they'd claim everyone says that about his hometown folks. Then I'd tell them we take care of each other, and we've been here from as far back almost as the country, and we know every inch of the hollow, and it's the greatest place in the world, with the hills and the streams and the fish you can get. And anyone who cared to come and visit us would see what I mean, because we'd be friendly and they'd eat until they're full, even if we had to go hungry, and they'd never stop looking around, and especially up to the hills over there, and soon they'd take to wishing they could have been borned here, too."

Mr. Allen never stops saying such things. That is, every week or so, sometimes every day or so, he rises to the occasion — when his visitor is still recognized as just that, a visitor. A year or more later Mr. Allen still will talk affectionately of the hollow he loves, the county he loves, the region whose hills must be, so he once told me, "the most beautiful things God ever made"; still, he has his rough times, and if he bears them most of the time in silence and even pretended joy, he can slip and come out with urgent and plaintive exclamations, once he knows a visitor reasonably well: "Why can't we have a little more money come into these hills? I don't mean a lot of tourists coming around and prying, like you hear some people say we need. I mean some work we could get, to tide us over the winter. That's the worst time. You start running out of the food you've stored, and there's nothing you can do but hope you make it until the warm weather. We all help each other out, of course; but there'll come times when we none of us has much of anything left, and then it's up to the church, and the next hollow. Once they had to fly in food, it was so bad, because of the snow and the floods we had. I can't find the littlest bit of work, and it makes you wonder sometimes. They move factories into every other part of the country, but not here. I guess it's hard, because of the hills. We'd be good workers, though. I was taught to work from sunrise to sunset by my folks. You might think this little farm we've got is all that we need, but it isn't. We'd have nothing to eat without the land we plant, but it's money we lack, that's for sure, and you can't grow that.

You can pick up a little money here and there — for instance they'll come and recruit you to do work for the county on the roads or cleaning things up. But it's not very much money you ever make, and if we didn't really love it here, we might have left a long time ago. I've been all set to — but then I can't do it. When my kids will ask me if I ever thought of leaving, I'll say no, and why should they ask, I say to them. I guess they know I don't want much to talk about some things, so they never push me too much. I wouldn't let them. They'll find out soon enough — about the misery in this world. The way I see it, life's never easy, and you just have to choose whether you'll stay here and live where it's best to live — or go someplace else, where you're feeling sad and homesick all the time, but they've got a lot of jobs, and you can make good money. I hope my kids think it over real hard before they decide — when they get older."

His children love the hollow, and maybe they too will never really be able to leave. They are unmistakably poor children, and they need all sorts of things, from medical and dental care to better and more food; but they love the land near their cabin, and they know that land almost inch by inch. Indeed, from the first days of life many of the Appalachian children I have observed are almost symbolically or ritualistically given over to the land. One morning I watched Mrs. Allen come out from the cabin in order, presumably, to enjoy the sun and the warm, clear air of a May day. Her boy had just been breast-fed and was in her arms. Suddenly the mother put the child down on the ground, and gently fondled him and moved him a bit with her feet, which are not usually covered with shoes or socks. The child did not cry. The mother seemed to have almost exquisite control over her toes. It all seemed very nice, but I had no idea what Mrs. Allen really had in mind until she leaned over and spoke very gravely to her child: "This is your land, and it's about time you started getting to know it."

What am I to make of that? Not too much, I hope. I was, though, seeing how a particular mother played with her child, how from the very start she began to make the outside world part of her little boy's experience. What she did and said one time she has done and said again and again in that way and in other ways. All of her children, as one might expect, come to regard the land near their cabin as something theirs, something also kind and generous and important. In my conversations with Mrs. Allen I gradually realized just how important the land was to her and her children. I could argue that the land around the cabin helped her mind achieve a certain order or pattern to what I suppose could be called motherhood. From the first months of her child's life right on through the years, she as a mother never lets it be forgotten what makes for survival, what has to be respected and cared for and worked over if life is to continue. And so more than once she fondles her little boy on the hill's earth and tells him how familiar he should get to feel about the little farm, and on other occasions, how fine it is to be where they are and have what they have.

Are such gestures or words nonsense, in view of the hard life the Allens live? Is a mother like her whistling in the dark, and trying to teach her children to do the same? "The first thing I can remember in my whole life was my mother telling me I should be proud of myself. I recollect her telling me we had all the land, clear up to a line that she kept on pointing out. I mean, I don't know what she said to me, not the words, but I can see her pointing up the hill and down toward the road, and there was once when she stepped hard on the earth, near the corn they were growing, I think it was, and told me and my sister that we didn't have everything we might want and we might need, but what we did have, it was nothing to look down on; no, it was the best place in the whole world to be born — and there wasn't anyplace prettier and nicer anywhere.

"To me, your children have to respect you, and look up to you. My daddy never let me talk back and get fresh. My mother was easier with us, but you could go so far and not a step further. She would tell us that we come from Scotland, way back, and we should be proud that our name was McIntosh, and she was one of the McIntoshs too, and we might be having poor times, but we were a large family, and we had neighbors and uncles and aunts and cousins, and we'd stand up for each other. Most of all she'd tell us about the hollow, and who came there first, and who lives in this house and the next one. That was the first learning I got — how to leave the house and walk down the hollow a bit and come back. We were high up, and a little further along there was no more hollow, just woods and the hills. I guess they go on for miles. Once I must have gone in the wrong direction, because I was going higher up and suddenly I could see more than I ever saw before in my life. Now I know what I'd done. I'd gone clear to the top of that hill, and there I was, in that little bit of meadowland there, looking over toward the other hills. The first thing that came to me was that God must be someplace near, and I looked and looked and right then, you know — I'd say I was four — I was sure all I had to do was call on Him, like we're told to do in church, and there He'd be. Instead, a big bird came down, right near me. Oh, it was probably a crow, but to this day I can hear the 'caw-caw-caw,' and he come right at me. He'd probably never seen a child like me wandering up there by herself.

"I guess I thought the bird was preparing the way for God himself, because I got down on my knees and I said, 'Please God, be good to me,' just like I have my kids say now, every evening they do. Well, when nothing happened after a few minutes, I must have figured that something was wrong. I started crying for my mother and my daddy, and when they didn't come I started crying even more. But near the side of the meadow — I'll never forget — I saw a large rock, and I went and sat down beside it, and then I climbed on to it. I must have climbed down and fallen asleep, because the next thing I remembered, my daddy was standing over me, and I was waking up. I thought he was going to be real cross at me, but he wasn't. He said I was a good little girl for not going real wild-like and wandering all over and getting so far away they never could have found me. He carried me home on his shoulders and I can see me now, riding high on him — he was about six foot four, I think. And I can see my mother coming out to ask me if I was fine or if I was hurting anyplace. After I told her I didn't hurt in a single place, and I just wanted to have a Coke, because I was thirsty, she said I'd been real good and learned my lessons. 'Trust the woods and the paths there. If you ever get lost again, sit someplace, just like you did, in an open spot, and we'll get to you.' She must have said something like that, because that's what I seem to hear her telling me even now.

"I think I try to go along with my folks, the way they used to look at things when we were kids. My daddy, he's seventy and as strong as can be, even if he gets his dizzy spells. My mother died a long time ago, giving birth to my youngest brother — yes, right here in this very room it was. She started bleeding real bad, and it just never stopped. My folks taught us all to be respectful to them and to anyone else we met who was grown up, and I hope my kids will always be like that. I never try to fool myself or the kids, though. I tell them there's a lot of bad people in the world, some of them right here in this county. I don't believe anyone living up this hollow is bad, no sir; but I know for sure some of the people we see in church, they're crooked as the day is long — and that's what my father would say, and he'd point them out to us. I tell the kids they've got to know that the world's not so good, and there's a lot of trouble going on, and you can't be sure of someone until you know him pretty good. But you *can* be polite, and you should be, that's how I feel. You ought to behave yourself with someone, even if you don't much like him. The other thing is, never forget who's your kin, and who you always can trust. When one of my kids starts getting all teary, and there's something bothering him, you know — then is the time for me to help as best I can; and there's nothing that'll work better than getting a child to see if the chickens have laid any new eggs, or to count how many tomatoes there are hanging on the plants, ready for us to pick. I'll take the child up the path and we'll pick a few berries, or do something; it don't make a difference what, so long as I can say how lucky we are to be here, with the land we have. And God forbid a son of mine will be taken overseas to fight like my husband was. But he saw the world, all over he did; and he couldn't get back here too soon, that's for sure."

She loves her children and she loves her property. When she holds an infant in her arms she often will sing. She sings songs about hunting and fighting and struggling, songs that almost invariably express the proud, defiant spirit of people who may lack many things, but know very clearly what they *don't* lack: "I tell the kids there's more to life than having a lot of money and a big brick house, like some of them have down towards town. Here we've got our chickens and we've got good land; oh, it's not the best there ever was, and we could use twice its size, but we get all you can from it, the vegetables, and with the preserves I put up, I make sure we have something right through most of the year. The other day I was trying to get my oldest boy to help me, and he was getting more stubborn by the minute. I wanted him to clean up some of the mess the chickens make, and all he could tell me was that they'll make the same mess again. I told him to stop making up excuses and help me right this minute, and he did. While we were working, I told him that the only thing we had was the house and the land, and if we didn't learn to take care of what we have, we'd soon have nothing, and how would he like that. He went along with me, of course. But you have to keep after the child, until he knows what's important for him to do."

Mrs. Allen's attitude toward the land is by no means rare among the families I have worked with in the Appalachian Mountains. In fact, an observer can make some generalizations about how children are brought up in, say, western North Carolina or eastern Kentucky and West Virginia if he looks at the land as a sort of unifying theme. From the first months of childhood to later years, the land and the woods and the hills figure prominently in the lives of mountain children, not to mention their parents. As a result, the tasks and struggles that confront all children take on a particular and characteristic quality among Appalachian children, a quality that has to do with learning about one's roots, one's place, one's territory, as a central fact, perhaps *the* central fact of existence.

In Wolfe County, Kentucky, I became rather friendly with a whole hollow of Workmans and Taylors, all related to one another. There were one or two other families, whose names sounded different; yet, I came to find out that the wife, in each case, was also a Workman or a Taylor. The Workmans had followed a stream up a hill well over a century ago and are still there, in cabins all along Deep Hollow, so named because it is one of the steepest hollows around. They were the family I lived with the longest there and observed more intensely and casually — in a mixture I can't quantify — than any other. All the time I was there Mr. and Mrs. Kenneth Workman wanted me to be doing something, to be a worker — true to their name — as are all Workmans in that hollow. They asked *me* how things were going, how I felt about the mountains, and how my spirits were now that I was so high up and so near to God. They wanted to know whether one day I might move nearby and give my wife and children "a taste of good living." Yet, I had come to Deep Hollow warned about suspicious, withdrawn people who wanted no part of strangers.

Kenneth Workman is forty as I write this. He is now a small farmer. He used to dig for coal in the mines down in Harlan County, Kentucky, but he was lucky enough to lose his job in 1954. Many of the older men he worked with also lost their jobs around that time, when the mines were becoming increasingly automated, but they came back to Wolfe County sick, injured, often near death. Their lungs were eaten up with "black lung," with pneumoconiosis as doctors call it when coal dust gets into the sensitive fragile organ and progressively kills one section after another. The men were sick on other counts too: their backs had been injured in mine accidents, or their necks, or the muscles and bones of their legs and arms. Some of them had not only "black lung" but tuberculosis too; and years of fear and anxiety while working underground had taken a heavy toll on their minds. Kenneth Workman talks with little prodding about the mines and his fellow miners and Harlan County and Wolfe County — and also about his children, especially if he has a shot or two of the moonshine that he and his brothers and uncles and cousins make out of the corn they all grow: "I never made so much money in my life and I never will again, I'm sure of that. I'd stay there all week in Harlan County, and then I'd drive home to be with Laura and the babies. I was twenty when I got the job; it was in 1950 I believe. They suddenly needed all the men they could get, because the government was building up the

Army again, to go fight in Korea, and there was a big demand on the coal mines. The draft people called me, and they said I'd be doing Wolfe County and the United States a bigger favor if I stayed a miner and not go into the Army, and I said that was all right by me — yes sir, it was. My daddy said he was real sorry to see me go down into the mines, but up this hollow we don't see much money. We keep going, and we're not going to be pushed out of here by anyone; but when you get a chance to bring in some money, a lot of it, and regular, each week, you don't mind leaving — and I came back every Friday night. I got a car and paid for it, and I got us things, like the radio and the furniture and the television and the refrigerator. If it hadn't been for those four years, we'd be living a lot poorer, Laura and me and the children.

"I went down the mines for them, for the children, I think I could say that. We had two when I went, and five when I came home. Then came the trouble Laura had, the bleeding, and we lost a baby and then we lost another one and more bleeding and I thought we'd never have a child again. But a few years ago something must have happened inside her, you never know what, and here we are with babies again, and it's like having two families, the older family first, and then we had a little rest, and now the younger one. Maybe if I'd kept on working in the mines, I could have taken Laura to a doctor someplace, and he would have figured out what there was wrong and what we should do. Around here there's no doctor, and who can get up the money they ask, even if we could find one. I saw the first doctor of my life down there in Harlan County. The coal companies have them around, and the union has some of its own, you know. They gave me a going-over before I started working, and they said I needed a dentist, and I had some trouble with my bones here and there, I guess; but I was all right for work, they said.

"As I see it, if I'd stayed in the mines we could have gotten Laura to a doctor, maybe in Harlan County. But I might have had to go to one first. The men I worked with, a lot of them had been down those mines longer than me, and it was a terrible sight to see them — working so hard, and they knew — oh did they! — that they were getting killed by the work they were doing, but they had to do it, because there wasn't any other choice. I'd come back and tell my daddy about what the mines do to you, and he'd say I should stop it and stay here in Deep Hollow. He'd say you can't win everything, that's the most important thing to know, and never forget. If I was to stay a miner, he'd tell me, we'd all be living better, and Laura might see a doctor; but I'd be dead just like those miners are dying. If I was to stop and come back, then we'd be in a lot worse shape about owning what we want to own; but I'd be around to enjoy what we do have.

"Now you ask me what we have. I'd answer you this way: the nicest land in the world, and the nicest people in the world to live on it. That's a lot to have, I tell my kids, when they start crying and belly-aching about something, and they'll ask me why it is the people on the television programs live so rich, and we're not living very good up here — well, it's then I'll tell them they're not seeing the half of it. They're not seeing all the bad things about those cities, and all the meanness you'll find out there. Some of the older miners, they'd been in the war against the Germans and the Japs, and they can tell you and so can my daddy and my older brothers. They've been to those cities. I'll tell my kids that if they don't believe me or anyone in Deep Hollow, then by God I'll take that car sitting out there and somehow I'll make it work again, and we'll get ourselves over to Harlan County. There still are some miners there, and I'll let my kids talk with them and let my kids see how they live, the people who do make a lot of money! Sure, they have nicer houses than we do, but the coughing they do, and the spitting up of the black stuff — knowing every second that the coal dust is in you, eating up your lungs — it's all enough to make you want to turn right around and come back here, yes sir; and stay here until your last breath and be glad to be buried right over there."

He would point dramatically when he said something like that, point with his arm not his finger, with his whole body in fact; he would even get up and start walking toward the area where genera-tions of Workmans have been buried by their kin, in simple caskets made out of wood from Deep Hollow. He never would go more than a couple of steps, however. In a few seconds he would be right back in his chair, talking with me and having himself "one or two more" and insisting that his guest do the same: "I guess you'd like to know if we raise up our kids some way that's different from the way other people do. Isn't that it? If you ask me, I'd say that Laura is real good to the kids and I try to be, too. We want them to remember their first years later on as a real good time — when they had a lot of fun, and when they learned all about the hollow and how to take care of themselves and go and do things out there up the hill and in the woods and down by the stream. We want them to be able to say when they're grown up that they're proud they were born to us, and they're proud they're liv-ing right here in Deep Hollow, Kentucky, yes sir. And if we're going to be good parents, we've got to teach our kids a lot about Deep Hollow, so they can find their way around and know everything they've got to know. It's their home, the hollow is. People who come here from out-side are not likely to figure out that we've got a lot of teaching to do for our kids outside of school, and it's not the kind they'll get in books. My boy Danny has got to *master the hollow;* that's what my dad used to say to me, all the time he would tell me and tell me and then I'd be in good shape for the rest of my life."

How does Danny get to master the hollow? For one thing, he was born there, and his very survival augurs well for his future mastery. Laura received no medical care while she carried Danny; the boy was delivered by his two aunts, who also live in Deep Hollow. Danny's first encounter with the Appalachian land took place minutes after he was taken, breathing and screaming, from his mother. Laura describes what happened, and in time goes on to talk about a number of related matters: "Well, as I can recall, my sister Dorothy came over and showed him to me, and then he was making so much noise we knew he was all right. His birthday is July tenth, you see, and it was a real nice day. I'll never forget, because that morning, while I was in pain and hoping the sooner the better, my sister said there wasn't a cloud in the sky, and that meant everything would be fine, and besides she saw two foxes and they were playing nice, and she must have been walking quiet because they didn't pay her any attention, and she said it was good luck when you can just come upon them and they don't get away so fast. She brought me a pail of blackberries that she'd picked and she said they were for later. When Danny was born Dorothy took him over and showed him the blackberries and said it won't be long before he'll be eating them, but first he'll have to learn to pick them, and that will be real soon. Then he was still crying, and she asked me if I didn't think he ought to go outside and see his daddy's corn growing up there, good and tall, and the chickens we have and Spot and Tan, be-cause they're going to be his dogs, just like everyone else's. I said to go ahead, and my sister Anne held me up a little. She lifted up my head so I could see, and the next thing I knew the baby was out there near Ken's corn, crying as loud as he could, bless him, in Dorothy's arms.

"Of course everyone came around to see the child. Dorothy told them all to go back down to her house, but even while I was being de-livered they must have been out in the woods, waiting to see what would happen. When she came out with Danny, all my children showed up, and my husband and Dorothy's husband and her children and Anne's husband and her children. They stood around and they said Danny was a red-haired one, like me, and wasn't it good how loud he was with his crying. Ken held him high over his head and pointed him around like he was one of the guns being aimed. I heard him telling the baby that here was the corn, there was the beets, and there was cucumbers, and here was the lettuce, and there was the best laying chicken we've got. Next thing he told the baby to stop the crying and he did, he just did. Ken has a way with kids, even as soon as they're born. He told him to shush up, and he did, and then he just took him and put him down over there, near the corn, and the other kids and my sisters all stood and looked. Dorothy was going to pick him up and bring him back to me, but Ken said he was fast asleep and quiet, and let him just lie there and we should all go and leave things be for a while. So they did; and Ken came in and told me I'd done real well, and he was glad to have a red-haired son, at last, what with two girls that have red hair but all the boys with brown hair. He said did I mind the little fellow lying out there near his daddy's farm, getting to know Deep Hollow, and I said no, why should I, and he's better off there than in here with me, what with being tired and the blood we have to clear away and it was too early for him to touch me, because you know they don't eat too good at first, and only after a week or so do you feel like they're really drawing on you and getting something for themselves, like they should.

"I don't like to feed my baby inside, if the weather holds good on the outside. I'll just go over there under that hickory and sit and rest and the baby will sit and rest and there's a good wind that cools us off. Of course in the winter that's different. In the winter if you go more than a few steps away from our stove, you're likely to get a bad case of the shivers. I sleep near the stove, the baby right beside me. I have him all wrapped up in his daddy's shirt. Yes, I'll put paper around his bottom, to keep the shirts as clean as can be. I have the rope to the paper good and tight, and it's all right on the child, not too tight. It's better in the warm weather. You can just let the child be; you can let him lie in the sun, or so he won't get burned up, you can put him under that hickory — the largest one right over there. A little of the sun dries him out, and the shade of the tree soothes him."

She was talking about Danny, but she was also talking more generally; for instance, she can remember similar events in the early life of "little Dorothy," who is a year and a half younger than Danny. I have watched her with both Danny and "little Dorothy" or Dottie, named for the aunt who has delivered all Mr. and Mrs. Kenneth Workman's children. I have watched her sun the little boy and soothe him, sun Dottie and soothe her. I have sat nearby as she breast-fed her child quietly, calmly, neither proudly and ostentatiously nor with any shame or worry. Shortly after each child of hers is born, the boy or girl is set down on the land, and within a few months he is peering out at that land, moving on it, turning over on it, clutching at wild mountain flowers or a slingshot, a present from an older brother, or a spoon, a present from an older sister. Next comes crawling; and mountain children do indeed crawl. They are encouraged to crawl. They take to crawling and turning over and rolling down the grass and weeds. They take to pushing their heads against bushes and picking up stones and rocks. They take to following sounds, moving toward a bird's call or a frog's. I have rarely seen mothers like Laura Workman lift up babies like Danny or Dottie and try to make them walk by holding them and pulling them along. No books are read to determine which week or which month should find the baby doing this or that. Life in Deep Hollow and in other such hollows is not lived by the clock or the calendar, by comparisons, by competition, by repeated resort to "authorities" who have something to say about everything. Danny crawled until he stopped crawling and that was that. I happened to watch him stop crawling, start standing himself up in order to walk, and I am sure that I was more moved by these events than his parents — which is emphatically not to say that they had become bored or indifferent. As for Dottie, I saw her begin to crawl, and that evidence of progress *did* get a reaction from her mother: "It's good, because now she'll get to know her daddy's land — where he does his growing and where he keeps his baskets and his tools, and the bushes over there, they'll stop her from getting into anything too steep."

When Danny one day stood up and looked around and plopped himself right down again, his mother said nothing, and when I brought the matter up again, by remarking to Danny's father later that day how sturdy his boy appeared on his two feet, there was only a smile in reply. On other occasions Mrs. Workman did talk about such matters, about the way her children learn to move about: "I guess maybe when they start walking I know they're more on their own. I always hope that by then they've found out all they want to know by peeking into all the places — you know, when they crawl all over and try to see where everything leads to. Yes, if I had to choose a time I like best for them, it might be when they're crawling. That's a good time. I like them up and walking too; but they don't get as much fun out of it themselves, I don't think, as they do when they use their arms and legs like that and just drag themselves here and yonder all day long. When they're starting to walk, they seem to have lost all they've learned while crawling, if you ask me. They'll be walking, and they'll forget about the big rock and fall, and they'll forget the land is on a slope, and they'll forget about the ditches we have near the crops. My husband won't be too patient, either. He'll wish they were either back crawling or up to running all over, that's what you'll hear him say. He doesn't like hearing them cry when they keep on falling, and he thinks they're happiest either crawling or when they're older and free to be on their own. When they're starting to walk they get more scared than any other time, and they'll be slower to move. But I never hurry a child. The Lord made them the way He did, and when they're going to do something they're going to, and that's what you have to know."

Certainly she does know that; and she also knows that the chances are her children will leave her very early to wander far over the hills — and in so doing stay close to what she considers "home." When her children grow up, however, she expects they will have little interest in going any farther away than they have already been — even as many other American children, kept relatively close to their parents' small front yard or backyard during early childhood, begin to leave home almost with a vengeance when older. At three Danny had been all over his father's land, and up and down the hollow. He would roam about with his older brother or sister, tagging after them, trying to join in with their work or play. He had learned how to hold on to things and ascend an incline. He had learned how to pick crops and throw a line into a stream and catch a fish. He knew his way down the creek and up the hill that leads to the meadow. He knew about spiders and butterflies and nuts and minnows and all sorts of bugs and beetles and lizards and worms and moles and mice — and those crickets making their noise. He went after caterpillars. He collected rocks of all sizes and shapes; they were in fact his toys. He knew which branches of which trees were hard or soft, unbending or wonderfully pliable. He knew how to cool himself off and wash himself off and fill himself up — all with the water of a high stream. At three he had been learning all that for about a year. He didn't stop crawling and start walking "for serious" until he was two. Once he started walking he was brought to the Workman's outhouse and told what it is for. He was told to use the woods if he had to, but if he could, to wait for the outhouse. Actually, I was present while both Danny and Dottie were being toilet-trained, as we put it, and what they really had to learn quite thoroughly was the importance of *not* "going" in the cabin.

The Workmans, needless to say, have no medical education; they are not aware of the neurophysiological or psychological facts that pediatricians rely upon when they tell mothers how to start "training" their children. Of course in recent decades pediatricians and child psychiatrists have not always been consistent and sensible; they have at one time advocated training children at a year or a year and six months, and more recently relaxed by suggesting parents might wait a year or more longer. Through it all, the shifting currents of "enlightened" middle-class opinion, the Workmans held fast to their old family traditions, the myths and superstitions of their kinfolk. They emerge as rather interesting indeed. Mrs. Workman does not talk easily or at length about such matters, but eventually her remarks tell exactly what she has in mind: "I do with them what my mother told me, and I guess she did like her mother told her. That's what she said to me when she helped me with Alan, our first. She said I should just not fret over him. There's no point doing much until he's old enough to walk and keep walking, that was her advice. The reason is if they can't walk, they can't really take care of themselves that way. She said it was natural for a child who's lying around and crawling around to be messing around, too. Just cover them with paper, or keep them outside where you don't care. That's all. Now, when they start standing up and carrying themselves here and there on their legs, then they're moving on their own, you see, and you can just take them by the hand — their hands at last are free! — and say look child, here's where you do it and there and there and there, but *not here* — you hear? — *not here!*"

She had raised her voice, and she was certainly emphatic as she spoke those last words, so they deserve that exclamation mark. Yet, I also sensed a tone that was remarkably even or flat, remarkably without the veiled anxiety and even hysteria one senses in most mothers elsewhere, particularly, I suppose, those who come to see a child psychiatrist for advice. Moreover, children like Danny and little Dorothy seem to pick up the meaning of that tone rather well, because I watched both of them listen and hear and finally, heed what they were told; and at no time did they or their mother get into states of high tension or alarm. For one thing, as mentioned, the children were old enough to understand what their mother wanted; and beyond that, their mother's requests were rather modest. While they were learning to accede to those requests by day they were given the protection of an old piece of cloth on their bed: "I've used that cloth with all of them. I've washed it and washed it, and still it's good to use. With the small babies, when they're crawling around the house I've tried covering them with paper, so I don't have to keep putting clothes on them, and then they dirty them, and I have to wash them, and then the clothes wear out — and we don't have the money to buy a lot of new clothes, and especially all those clothes they have for babies, and like that. My mother would tell me that when kids are real young it's hard to dress them and maybe it's wise never to dress them at all, except to keep them warm in winter. Even then you're running a risk, you are, with whatever you use, be it a blanket to wrap them, or anything else. I guess I just try to do the best I can, and sometimes I'll do what my mother said, and sometimes what my sister Dorothy says, and sometimes I just go and act on my own hunch — and let me tell you, the children get on all right, and they grow, you know, and before long it's all something that happened back in the past, because they're walking and they're on their own a lot, and they can take care of themselves, yes they can, and there's no trouble with messing or like that. The woods up there is our biggest help, much more than the outhouse, and that's as it should be."

The woods, its earth and its bushes and its grassland were meant to grow things and receive things, she believes, and there is no reason to become worried and self-conscious and fussy. Yet, I do not mean to imply that a mother like Laura Workman doesn't have some very definite and explicit ideas about cleanliness and order and personal neatness, about the way a day should go and the way a child should look and arrange his things and the way, for that matter, a whole hollow should appear: "I try to teach my children to be good to each other and to anyone they meet. They shouldn't be fresh; and they shouldn't speak unless spoken to, not when there are grown-ups around. By themselves, that is different. The important thing for a child to know is that he's reflecting on his mother and his daddy and himself, too; I mean, if he's a mean one, and he doesn't act to help the next person, then it's all of us — the Workman family and the Taylor family, I guess — who's going to pay for it. The minister says the Lord sort of keeps his accounts on how we're behaving, yes; and if we think we can slip by His big net, then we're kidding ourselves real, real bad. I told Danny the other day that there's no reason for him to spill his food on his shirt, and he shrugged back at me. Then I told him it was going to mean that the shirt would look bad on him, and soon I'd be washing it again, and each time, you know, the poor shirt gets fainter and fainter, and pretty soon you won't be seeing the colors, and it'll be thinner, and the holes will come.

"Now Danny's daddy is no millionaire, and he's got to know he can't be causing us to go down to that store and be buying extra shirts, more than is necessary, and trading off the jars of food I've put up. In February we'll miss that food bad, real bad, and they'll be eating it,

Mrs. Campbell and her brood at the store, and Danny will be hungry. I'm not going to let all that happen, because if the child learns to mind you, then he'll be doing right, and none of us will be suffering. Every day I have to tell the children that if they don't act more careful about something — there's always temptation around here, like in the Bible — then they're going to pay for it later on, because you just can't help suffering if you go and make mistakes.

"There's a God in Heaven, and He gave us this hollow, and it's the nicest place in His Kingdom, it must be. I want the children to re-member that in addition to us owning this, it's God's, so they must not misbehave. Their daddy makes them help with the weeding and we make sure they carry all they pick over to the pile over there. A lot of the trash we'll bury or burn right up and there's no problem. I'll admit the creek down below looks awful bad. The kids will throw things in, and they expect the water to carry everything away. I tell them no un-til I've about lost my voice, but it's hard; they see the mess all over, and they see the other kids adding to it, and I'll be honest with you, their own kin, right down that hollow, they do the same. Mr. Workman went and spoke to his brother, and they agreed, but his wife, my sister-in-law, she's — well, she's no good at keeping her kids in line, she just can't do it. She'll raise her voice on them, and they'll turn and laugh. Their daddy, that's a different story. One look from him and anyone, no matter the age, would go along and do what he wants. The trouble there is he drinks up too much of his corn liquor, Ken's brother does, instead of selling it, like he ought to do. If we didn't sell what we make, there'd be all that less money and it would be harder than it al-ready is.

"If I was to compare my kids against others in the hollow, like you say, then I'd have to call mine more of their own mind than a lot of the others. Maybe it's because we're just about the last one up here, before the hill reaches the top, so we do things more by ourselves than some below, lower down there in the hollow. Maybe it's me. I think most of the kids in the hollow are God-fearing boys and girls, and if there's differences, they don't amount to much, because we're more alike on most things, I'd say. You go and ask any mother in this hollow, or any of the others in Wolfe County, how their kids are turning out, and they'll say, 'Pretty good!' That's what I'd say about mine. I like for them to obey, and when they're called to do something, to snap right to it, and go ahead. A lot of the time I'm too busy, or I'm not feeling good, and they go ahead and slip up, and they make their mistakes, I know; but I guess we all do. I try to teach Danny to wash his face when he goes swimming in the creek. He'll forget, though. It's only natural. I try to tell little Dorothy that she should act like a lady, and not be always fighting, but I did the same when I was her age — I can even remember doing like her, fighting and raising Hell all day long, to be honest about it. I'd never admit that to her! Most of all I want for my children to be good, and work hard, and like I said before, they should be God-fearing.

"I've sent a lot of children down to our school, and they may not always have the best clothes on, and they may behave real foolish-like some of the time, but I think the teacher would tell you that every one of them is proud of his mother and his father, and proud to be born here in Deep Hollow, and proud of what they've tried to do, small though they are, to be of help to us all — even if they've each given us trouble, as a child always will. Don't you believe they all do, when they're growing up? A child who doesn't give you trouble, there's really something wrong with that child. I think, to be real open now with you, I really think I could have been stricter sometimes with them. I'll talk as strict as I can, but I'm not doing like I preach, and our minister says that's the worst a person can do. Their father, he's as bad. He'll go and tell them to do things for him, then he'll forget, and sometimes he'll ask them why they're doing a chore, when it was *he* that told them to go do it. Another thing: he's been too quick to give the boys that whiskey they make. Our son Alan and his wife — she comes from right near the store, a mile or so, and there's a little money in her family — they both are too independent and full of themselves, and it's telling on their babies, if you ask me. She keeps a poor house, she does. She's spoiled; and he makes it worse with the liquor he takes, and he feeds it to her.

"There will be a time I take some liquor, to ease the pains I get. I get them all over — my chest and my shoulder and my knees and my fingers. I'm getting old, it must be that. But I've got my children to raise up, the last of them, and I don't want them to turn out bad. I'd like them to be sober and know how to take their liquor, so they don't go falling all over and forget the things they're supposed to do. I'd like them to learn the most they can in school, even if there's not much point in spending too much time there, you know, because if you keep your eyes open and your ears, too — well, then, you'll learn most of what you have to know right here, doing the work that you should. My son Tim — you've only met him a couple of times — is probably the best of the children; I mean he turned out best. He has a good job working in a garage over in Campton. It's hard not having him here with us, but he has a car, and it's a good one, and he drives over with his family a few times a week. They have a good place to live, right outside of Campton. He learned how to work on those cars from when he was a boy; I never could figure out how he learned it all so fast. No, he never went beyond the school there near the hollow, but the teacher had him fix her car, and she recommended him to the garage in Campton, and I let him go. He said they'd give him a place to stay a few days of the week, and he could come over and work for them. Then he met a girl over there and the next thing we know that was our second son married, and now we've got grandchildren and they're nice to have, just like your own are.

"Tim disappointed a lot of his kin here in the Hollow. They kept on asking him why did he want to leave us, and aren't we good enough for him. I told them to stop, but I'll admit it, I miss him, too. We can't drive over there to Campton, but he's here in half an hour — maybe less, I think. He's a loyal son, don't get me wrong, but he always was the one who wanted things his way, and not ours, and I had a real fight with him more than one time, oh did I! I told him to stop being so all-certain of himself and listen to me and his daddy. He said I was always telling them, the children, to be sure of themselves, and don't let a soul turn your mind around from what you've made it up to be — so that's what he was trying to do; but you can carry a thing too far, that's what. But he's all right, and we're proud of him. He'll often bring us some money we sorely need, too; and we sure have to be grateful for that. We don't get all that much money, and when your son comes over and gives you five dollars and says there it is, all for you, and not to pay any back — that's a day to go and celebrate, you bet.

"I think we find our times to celebrate anyways, yes. You can't just sit and stare and worry, even if you know you have plenty of reasons to. I'll wake up some of the time, and I'll be scratching myself, asking myself what am I going to give those children when they come and expect a good breakfast, and we don't have the eggs, because there's a limit to what even good chickens can lay, and we're down to the last of the bread and I just don't have one single penny in my house, not one, and I need the biscuits for later, because there's two more meals coming up that day, not to mention the next one. I can't go and catch a little liquor, like Ken does. I have to do the best I can. Most of the time I'll persuade everyone to have some coffee we have and wait until the sun is in the middle of the sky and they're all *really* hungry. You see what I'm doing, don't you? I'm fooling them and I'm coaxing them to be nice and help me and not ask for breakfast; and they know it, but they'll never say they do. The only one that did — I guess it's true — was Tim; he would get himself worked up and tell his father we ought to go and see the county people and demand our rights. Well, *what* rights, their father would say.

"Then they'd start their fighting — Tim would be ten or more, I guess. Tim would tell his father we could do something, and his father would tell Tim to stop looking for trouble, and besides we have the best place in the world up here in Deep Hollow. Ken sometimes would say to Tim that he has a real bad disposition, and he always looks at the black side of the world, like the minister will describe, and that's bad, because you lose your faith that way — in God — and you get sour with people, and Tim could be that a lot, sour. I was fearful for his wife, how she would find him, but she says he's always in real good spirits, and maybe it's because he's got that job he likes so much, over there in Campton. He told his brother Alan to come on over and maybe he could learn to do the work, too; but Alan said no sir, you can have your job, because who wants to go and live in Campton, even if it is in Wolfe County, like you say. So, they never agree with each other. I guess everyone has his different moods, and people see things different, real different, and that's always the case, I believe that — though I think all of us here in this family, and the others in the hollow see eye to eye on most things, if you get right down to it. I'll bet there's not one person here who wouldn't walk up the hill there and look as far as he could and come back and say we're the luckiest people that ever was, to be here; and yes, I'm including Tim, him too."

Everyone in the Workman family, including Tim, does indeed love Deep Hollow; but they all have their doubts and misgivings about the hollow, too — and they naturally would, because they have a tough life, a fact they both recognize and strongly deny. I am not writing about the Workmans in order to show how hurt and impoverished they are, nor to prove them the strongest, proudest, most self-reliant and self-possessed of people. The truth of their lives, as the flow of Mrs. Workman's remarks suggested, can only be found in a mixture. Families like the Workmans are proud, yet feel weak and vulnerable. Such families can be faultlessly neat, yet succumb to disorder and even chaos as they try hard to deal with very concrete and painful circumstances, like hunger that goes unappeased by food, and freezing temperatures that enter and take over a house with only one fireplace and no heating system.

People like Kenneth and Laura Workman struggle with other contradictions, too. They struggle to affirm themselves and not fall victim to despair. Put a little differently, they feel at times energetically ambitious and anxious to accomplish this or that; at other times they feel defeated, so that there seems no point to much of anything. Within the same day, even the same hour, I have heard one or another member of the Workman family insist upon the urgent need to do something, and do it right away; but then declare in a tired voice that whatever is done really means very little, not only in the long but even the short run of things. Then, there is always the hollow, and the dozens and dozens of kin who live in it. One moment I will hear a mother like Mrs. Workman compare what she thinks and does with what others think and do, those relatives (primarily) and neighbors who may live even miles away, yet breathe heavily on each other and make for a collective social conformity, easily noticed by an outsider and stoutly defended by mountaineers themselves. At other times, she and other Appalachian mothers and fathers sound very much like po-litical anarchists or rebels of a more individualistic or idiosyncratic kind.

Even more striking with these individuals is the fluctuation in mood or outlook between seriousness and cheerfulness. I refer not to something called "manic-depressive" swings, nor indeed to anything psychopathological. Nor do I simply mean that the Workmans and others in places like Deep Hollow, Wolfe County, Kentucky have their ups and downs; of course they all to, and of course *we* all do. I want to point out that in Appalachia a certain kind of living generates a partic-ular kind of grim but also lighthearted frame of mind that comes to expression again and again in the speech and habits of the people. By the same token, Appalachian mothers demonstrate, as a result of a cer-tain sensibility one meets in those hollows, an equally ironic and at times unnerving mixture of firmness, even sternness with children, which is tempered with a generosity that borders, occasionally more than borders, on indulgence — all logically incompatible, all of it seemingly inconsistent, but all of it still there, to be figured out, I sup-pose, by those whose fate it is to do so.

Again, I have not set up six polarities, six sets of opposing traits to deny each mountaineer his or her particular fate, which is to recon-cile the conflicts in his or her life — and do so in his own way, in her own way. These contradictions or ambiguities are concretely and specifically rooted in Appalachian life and in the traditions that moun-tain people call their own. They assert themselves consistently, per-sistently and confusingly — to a visitor, and maybe even to people like the Workmans themselves. Perhaps the word is themes, ones tied to a special history, a very definite kind of experience within and outside of the family. I believe Mrs. Workman's remarks reveal those themes; and I believe those themes go to distinguish the Workmans and other mountaineers described in this book, from the sharecropper families and migrant farm families that also live close to the land, yet under rather different circumstances.

In the case of the Workmans, none of all this was ever explicitly stated or discussed by them, and when I spent time with them I was in fact not myself of a mind to analyze what they said, to break it down into ideas voiced or assumptions held or whatever. I do believe, however, that I can now listen on my tapes to Kenneth Workman or Laura Workman, or I can read the notes and questions to myself written down years ago and see the point of having those themes around in my mind: they help make a little sense of matters that do indeed seem puzzling. Thus, when Mrs. Workman at the end of the long passage above talks about her son Tim's psychological characteristics she is talking about more than one apparently different or unusual child, who has left Deep Hollow, but also comes back. Tim, as presented by her, is only a slightly exaggerated version of everyone else in Deep Hollow. His preferences are theirs; his values theirs; his purposes or goals certainly very much theirs. Often it takes a generalization or a slight overstatement to make the ordinary or the usual a little clearer. Freud knew that patients mirror the rest of us, a bit sharply and even bizarrely, but still recognizably. What they visibly suffer with and from, the rest of us (to varying degrees and in varying ways) manage to hide from others and of course ourselves, too; all of which is necessary — and hardly surprising. An analysis of Tim's struggle to be loyal to his family, yet to remain his own man, should be offered as an effort to understand Tim and others like him as somewhat different from other Americans of their age, but also somewhat the same. No doubt as the "variables" or polarities or ambiguities pile up, we begin to recognize a distinct kind of person, a member of one or another "culture" or "subculture." But there is a danger that we may become so intoxicated with our theoretical exuberance that we allow our formulations to become islands, upon which we settle and isolate a given "group" of people.

At the edge of Logan County, West Virginia, I stayed with and worked with a family whose head, Paul Evans, was by no means "sick" in any psychiatric sense. He did have a noticeably vulnerable quality to him, though; and he had, in his own words, "more of a restless nature than anyone else around." Like Mr. Workman, he had worked in the mines for a while, then left because he was short of breath, coughing, plagued with chest pains, and afraid he might die were he to continue digging coal. He returned to the little town where he and his family have lived for many generations, and for a while he found odd jobs to keep him busy and provide his wife and two sons and three daughters with money. He worked in a gas station. He worked on the roads, digging and helping pave or even rake leaves. He drove a truck. He swept floors, in the grocery store and in several of the churches near the town. Finally he went back home — that is, back up Rocky Creek, so called, I suppose, because there is one patch of fairly large rocks there, some of them half submerged in the shallow water, along with a substantial amount of garbage that also sinks a little and floats a little. Once Paul Evans and I talked about the garbage, and perhaps that point in our conversation is a good one to begin with: "It's no good, all the paper and cans in the creek. A man came from Holden and told us we should clean up every time, and if we did and came together and made ourselves into some kind of organization, or something, then we could get a little money out of those county people over there in Logan. Have you ever been there, in the town, and talked with them? They'll say that we're lazy, that's why there's no work for us — because we don't go and find jobs. Well, I'd like them to come here and find a job. They could look for a million years, and none would come up. If you're going to find a job, you have to know where they're hiring people, and there's no businesses and factories here, no sir — just us and a lot like us up the hollows and the creeks. They'll go on to tell you how dirty you are, and why don't you go and clean up after yourself. The answer is I've been burying our leftovers all my life. My place is covered with garbage that I've put into the land. We have these homes here, there must be ten, I'd say, and we're all burying our garbage and trying to be as clean as we can, and we'll come to church and nobody can say we're not as spotless as can be. My wife is always telling the kids they should look as good and bright as a brand-new penny some of the time, even if they mess around a lot — and messing around is all right too, you know.

"There'll be times, I admit it, when we all lose our patience here in Rocky Creek, and then we'll just go heave something down that stream. It's natural a person will have his temper and then he'll decide there's no use trying to keep the creek in good shape, because there's hardly a dollar that comes in here to any of us, from week to week. We don't *think* like that, though — no, we don't; it just happens, if you ask me. We'll be sitting here on the porch and there's some stuff the wife has for you to go and bury; and you're in a sour mood; and you say to yourself, what the hell difference does it make. Now, that's wrong, I know it. I don't need a minister to tell me that Eternal Damnation business. I was told a long time ago by my daddy to obey the law, and do what's right, even if it's not written up into the law. But Daddy would admit to us that a lot of things just don't make much sense. You want to work all you can, but there's not the work for you to do, except keeping up the place. I take care of my land like it was a baby of mine. I plant the good part and grow enough to keep us out of the cemetery down there in Holden. I have a couple of pigs and the chickens and I make sure they don't go wandering all over. But sometimes I get tired and I'll sit here and rock myself and take a little of those good spirits we make, and before long I'm either all fixed up to go and shoot someone real big and important that's sitting on top of people like us, or I'm ready to go and sleep right through until the next week or the next year or sometime like that. It's then that I'll be seen throwing our stuff into the creek; and of course the kids will take after me and throw their Coke bottles down there, and it all adds up, I guess. If you ask me, one of those county people should go and do something worthwhile; they all get paid more money than you can imagine, and they're supposed to be working for all the people in Logan County. But they're really out for themselves, and if you cross them, you're in real trouble. The bus will stop coming to pick up your kids, and they'll start breathing down your back about the school lunches your kids get, and it becomes so bad, like I say, you want to go and kill them over in the courthouse.

"Most of the time I'm all right; I mean I figure we're better off here than in some big city, where you never lay your eyes on a piece of land, and you're lucky if you see a bird flying. I tell my kids that this is a good place to be born, and not to worry because somehow they'll make it through, like I did. But there will be a minute now and then that I don't believe myself, listening to myself talk, I just don't believe my own words. It's then that I figure it's real bad here, and the only way we can change anything is to go and take away the mines from the owners, and the courthouse from all those people that are running it. Then my wife will tell me to cool off, and she'll say there's no use sounding like some crank who's going to try to take over the government, and like that. She's a hard-praying woman, you know, and she'll start reading the Bible to me, and she'll get my brothers to come on over and tell me to get to my senses. Well, I've half talked them into admitting I'm right in what I say, but I usually agree with them, in that sometimes you may have the right idea, but you can't just go and do what you say you should do, if all that'll happen is you'll go to jail for the rest of your life, and you know that in advance. So, we'll go up the hill there, my three brothers and me, and we'll start shooting, and the one who hits the targets we choose the most, he's the one to pull out some beer for the rest.

"I worry about my kids, I'll be honest and tell you. I'd like for them to have a better life than I ever had, but I don't believe they ever will, and it's too bad. That's why I tell my wife that we can't be too good to them; even when we do have something they want, we've got to let them know that here in West Virginia, in this county, it's not like they see on that television set. Back a while I was making money, you know, in the mines, and I figured we could have all the gadgets we want, and keep on replacing them with new ones, too, like those store people tell you that you should. Then the money stopped, you bet it did. They admitted I should be getting some compensation, because my lungs were starting to go bad, but I wasn't eligible, because neither the company nor the state allows you any money for that. They just tell you it's too bad what you got in your lungs, but don't come to the state of West Virginia; and the companies, well you know them — if they had their way the whole state of West Virginia would be turned into a big strip mine, so they could take out every piece of coal in these hills and make their money. Then, they'd leave and say, so long buddies, nice knowing you, but we've got to go to the next state, and squeeze it dry like we did yours. That's why I tell my kids that they can't have it easy in this world, no matter how nice those hills look, and even though we do have the woods they play in and a lot of other things around here we all would die for, if they tried to come and take them away. A little ways up in that hollow where they did try and take away some people's land the strip mine people started dumping their dirt, and there was a landslide onto a couple of houses, and they were lucky no one was killed. That's where I'd draw the line. That's where I'd take out my gun and use it. I don't care what they'd charge me with later.

"Sometimes when we're arguing I tell my brothers that they're wrong to keep on bragging how lucky a man is to pick his guitar and be living here, where we have some land to our name and crops that we can grow to feed us. That's good, but it's hard to tell your boy, when he asks you why we don't live better — it's hard to tell him that we're living better than anyone in the United States of America, when we damn well aren't. That's what my brothers will tell their kids — that they should be smiling more and not talking about going over to Cleveland or someplace for jobs when they get bigger. Let me tell you, I don't want my kids going over to Cleveland if they could help it, but if they're smart enough to *talk* about going there, then that teacher must be teaching them something smart over there in school. They'll leave for school in the morning and we haven't had enough to give them for breakfast, and thank God they have the hot lunches for them — we had to fight for that, fight and fight — and for supper we're lucky to have good food. When they leave to wait for the bus they'll be nodding to me and their mother, and my little girl — she's in the first grade — she'll be smiling and all. When I feel real down and low, I'll ask my wife why our child smiles like that, the way things are, and she'll say that a mother wants her children to smile, even if there isn't so much to smile about, so the child obliges. I guess that's the correct thing for the child to do, but you're pretty lucky, if you ask me, if your kids believe you, what you say about staying here and being happy in Rocky Creek. We're all happy in Rocky Creek and we love Rocky Creek more than anything. But we're always worrying about the troubles we have, and there'll be a lot of days that I never feel my face smile, not once. That's the truth, yes it is."

The truth Paul Evans tries to spell out for a visiting observer is indeed contradictory, and he has to make sure I realize that. He himself for a long time has struggled with all those contradictions, and expects to continue the struggle until he dies: "I can see myself there on my deathbed: in one breath I'll be telling my family that we've got the best world there can ever be right here in Rocky Creek, and in the next breath I'll be asking each of my kids to promise me that they get out of here, even though it's only for a few years, to make the money they'll need if they're going to come back — and have enough for their kids to eat. I guess what I say with my *last* breath will decide what I believe; but you have to believe what you know is right, and if there's a lot of argument between you and yourself, then that's the way it goes. I once talked to our minister and told him I only half believed what he said, and he smiled and said he was doing pretty good, for me to be going that far along with him. Ever since then I've really liked the way he speaks. I believe that he is as humble as he keeps telling us to be — as if we're not anyway. Once even my older brother lost his patience with a sermon — and of all of us, he's the one who has most of it, patience. After church he went over and told the minister to stop telling us all the time how the poor are going to inherit the world. *Which* world, he asked the minister, and how humble did he want us to be — *us*, of all the people on God's earth! The minister didn't know what to say. Then my brother really spoiled it; he said he was sorry, and he didn't mean to go and get him upset after his sermon — and of course the minister said thank you, and he was sure my brother meant no harm.

"Now what do you think of that for getting scared at the last second? Of course, it's not the minister's fault; he's only doing what he's supposed to do. Still, he ought to use his common sense. Once he came to visit us, and he asked me what I thought he should be talking more about on Sunday, and I said about the troubles a lot of us are having in Rocky Creek and other places, just making everything hold together from today until tomorrow. Well, you know he got nervous, I could see, and he said he had to go on to the next house. The poor guy, he's no better off than the rest of us, I guess. And I'll say this to you, he's a fine man, he really is. I'll bet he's better than a lot of ministers. He puts his heart into the job, and he loves us, and we love him. He comes from Logan County, only the city of Logan it is. He's had offers to go to other places, but he wants to stay here in the county, and I don't blame him. I wouldn't go out of this county for a big pile of money; not if they came and put it right before me on this table. I believe that if I left, I'd soon be sick and die. How could I sleep, away from that hill over there? And what would there be to do that would be half the fun of hunting in these woods?"

Like all of us, Paul Evans switches back and forth with respect to a number of "attitudes" he has or "issues" he thinks about. He doesn't give names to his ideas, to his moments of anger or deep and proud enjoyment; he doesn't call what goes through his mind or impels him to speak out (and sometimes, scream out) a "thought" or a "position" or an "opinion." He does, though, recognize some of his own inconsistencies, and he talks about them. Again and again those inconsistencies have to do with Rocky Creek and the Appalachian kind of life — its hardships and its real virtues. Again and again the importance of order and cleanliness is emphasized and the presence of disorder and confusion acknowledged — and stream garbage is perhaps a concrete form of disarray that reflects a much larger uproar and agitation, a social and political rough-and-tumble which a plundered region has to live with, now that so much of its wealth has gone elsewhere. Again and again the questions are raised: should we stay or leave? Should we try to shelter our children as best we can, or speak to them about the especially hard fate that awaits them? Should we teach

them the pride we feel in this creek, this county, this state, these familiar, peaceful, lovely hills, or should we come right out with it and
admit how fragile is our hold on these hills, in fact on life itself? Finally, ought we tell them how sad and grim all these alternatives are,
as they bear down on us, or ought we smile and insist that others before us have survived, so we will, too? Those are the questions and
perhaps they are really one question. As Paul Evans sees it — perhaps
more clearly than some mountaineers — all those dilemmas lead to
this: will life in the Appalachian Mountains ever change so that the
thousands and thousands of people who love those mountains, who
were born to be part of them, can at last find it possible to keep the
homes they love and stay on the land they never, never want to stop
loving?

What Paul Evans feels, what Kenneth and Laura Workman feel,
their children also feel; more than that, like children anywhere, they
face the added struggle that goes with assuming for themselves their
parents' struggles. In the case of Appalachian children, the particular
tensions and ambiguities that go with a frequently hard but also satisfying mountain life come across repeatedly in the words those children speak and (with unusual, even dramatic clarity) in the drawings
and paintings they choose to do. For instance, in Rocky Creek, but a
half mile or so away from Paul Evans's house live some of his kin. Paul
Evans's mother was a Potter, and her brother is John Potter, a man very
much like his nephew, though less fiery and given to speeches. He
sulks and broods and then suddenly stops all that and goes hunting
and feels better and plays his guitar and feels even better and gets
country music blasting loud over the radio and then will even talk
about how he feels: "A good hour of music from that little radio and
I'm feeling as good as those birds over there, soaring over us and saying to us: catch us if you can, but you won't." John Potter manages as
best he can, manages without doctors and psychiatrists and pills of
one kind or another; and manages despite a case of "black lung" that
makes him suffer much more than Paul Evans does. John suffers
silently for the most part. When he is low in spirits he sits and cuts
wood and listens to his "hillbilly music" — which at such times
doesn't seem to help him feel any better — and stares out at the hills;
or he goes to his crops and looks at them and decides what they need
and asks his son Billy, aged eight, to "come on over here and lend me
a hand."

Billy does just that, and expertly. Billy is tall for his age, with blue
eyes and black hair. He has a strong face. His forehead is broad, his

nose substantial and sharp, his chin long. Billy is large-boned and already broad-shouldered. He is thin, much thinner than he was meant
to be. His teeth are in fearful condition, but his cheeks are red and he
looks to be the very picture of good health. His mother knows what
ails him though, and she worries: "Billy is a sturdy lad a lot of the
time, but he'll fall sick and it's hard to know what's ailing him. He gets
pains in his mouth, from the teeth I guess, and his stomach hurts. He
has his share of sores, but they don't trouble him any more than they
do the rest of us. I worry because he'll be so good and helpful, and you
know, I think he's the smartest of my children, I believe he is, and the
teacher goes along with me on that; but suddenly he says he's dizzy
and he's afraid he's going to pass out, and a couple of times he has. I
was afraid he might be having a fit or something like that, you know,
but it doesn't last too long — and no, he's never shook, that I could
see, or bitten his tongue, no sir. The teacher says he could go on and
be good in the regional high school they've built, and even beyond
that, but where's the money I asked her, and she shook her head and
said yes, she knew. She said it's terrible the way West Virginia's best
sons aren't getting all they should be. Billy will be all right, though,
even if he doesn't go on in school. He has a good head on his shoulders, and he's nice with the other kids, and he gives his father a big lift,
I'll tell you that. His father will take to feeling sorry for himself and for
me and for just about everyone in Rocky Creek, and then Billy will
come over and practically order his daddy around: tell him to come on
outside and help with the corn and the peas, or see if there should be
more sawing of the wood, or go see the new litter of dogs we have —
it's those things that help snap his dad into a better turn of mind."

Billy is exactly what his mother describes him to be, inventive,
imaginative, intelligent, industrious. Perhaps most wonderful of all,
he is a truly generous boy. He is generous to his father when he clearly
isn't feeling too good about the world, and he is generous to his brothers and sisters and cousins and friends — not *too* generous, not fearfully obliging or nervously amiable, not ingratiating, just directly,
openly, unselfconsciously kind, or perhaps thoughtful in the several
senses of the word, because he does indeed do a lot of thinking in and
around the house as well as at school. Billy has some of his ancestors'
fondness for talking, for telling stories — or singing those stories,
reciting them in the form of long, drawn-out ballads. Billy can also be
stubbornly silent. "It all depends," says his mother, "if he has something that's on his mind, or if he doesn't." Once when Billy and I were
talking about his daily life, about what he had to do around "the

place," and what he did at school, he suddenly stopped himself in the middle of a sentence and asked me if I knew any doctors nearby. No, I didn't, not near Rocky Creek. How does one become a doctor, was his next question, and is there a medical school near Logan County? I told him I had visited the state's medical school in Morgantown, which is clear across the state from Rocky Creek, in Monongalia County. Is that north or south or east or west from where we were? It is north and east, I said. Pennsylvania is nearby, I added. He'd never been to Pennsylvania, he told me, nor to any other state. He'd never been out of Logan County, for that matter; and he wasn't sure he ever would want to go out — except that he had heard a lot of people talk about leaving, and he knew some that have left, though they try to come back as often as they can, he noticed. As for him, he didn't know. Maybe he would someday like to try another county, or even go over to Pennsylvania and see what it is like. His cousin Stephen Potter has tried Ohio, and doesn't like it one bit there, but he sends home those dollars and they certainly are good to receive.

Billy's father has been out of Logan County, has even lived in Beckley, West Virginia, which the teacher has told Billy is in Raleigh County. His mother, like him, has never left Logan County; and she can remember each time in her life she's left the creek and gone more than the few miles it takes to go to church or shop. Billy knows how far his ancestors traveled to get to Logan County — and not because his teacher emphasized subjects like history. The ballads and songs he has heard since he was a baby remind every listener how hard it once was to penetrate those mountains, survive those winters, stick fast and work upon those small plots of land. If Billy went to Ohio like his cousin Steve, or to Pennsylvania, he might forget those songs, and that would be a shame, or as he put it, "no good." On the other hand, he does want to look at the outside world. Right now Rocky Creek is the whole world for him, but he knows there are other worlds. His teacher keeps talking about those worlds and sometimes his father does, too. Billy once asked his teacher where *she* had been, and she listed the cities for the class: Charleston and Morgantown and Pittsburgh and Beckley and over to Washington, D.C. Billy remembers those, and remembers that there were others, though he forgets the names. Billy also remembers what the teacher said after she enumerated the cities. She told the class it wouldn't be a bad idea if they as a class went over to a city like Washington, D.C., and looked around and saw buildings and monuments and statues and all sorts of things like that. Billy feels she was pushing Washington, D.C., too hard on him and his class. West Virginia is a better place than Washington, D.C., he is sure of that.

For the very reason that Presidents have lived and continue to live in Washington, Billy would be less rather than more impressed with the city, if he ever got there and had a chance to look around. Why? Well, because Presidents must be like those people he hears the men of the creek talking about, the county officials and people like that; they're all quite rich and they're all quite crooked. There are a few good people over there in Logan, the capital of Logan County, Billy knows that, and in fact there have been a few good Presidents, "especially John Kennedy." Yet, on the whole it is the same old story: the rich take away from the poor; the mine owners plunder the land and cheat the people; the sheriffs and people like that push around ordinary people and take their orders from a few, a very few, who really run things. Billy has heard all that many times but he wanted me to know that he wasn't simply mouthing things because he had heard them declared by others. How did Billy let me know that he also had been thinking about some of those things? He did so delicately and discreetly and a little indirectly but also by shifting — rather as many of us do in such moments — to a "larger" or more "general" kind of discussion or analysis: "Ben and I — he's my best friend — decided that one day when we're big we'll go to every city our fathers or our mothers or anyone we know have been to; and then we can see what they're like, and if they're better or worse than what you hear people say. We decided we'd include all the states Mrs. Scott says she's traveled through, and especially Washington, D.C., which she keeps on telling us about in school. I'd like to go in the Army when I get big, and maybe that would be the time. Ben says he'd like to join the Navy, because we've neither of us seen the ocean, except on television, and in the pictures of Mrs. Scott's books. If we became sailors on a ship, we'd go all around the world and then when we got back here to Rocky Creek we'd be able to tell everyone what we saw and if they'd ask us whether there's any better part of the world, we'd say no, nowhere.

"If we joined the Army or the Navy we'd see a lot of people, and they'd be different from us, I know that. Mrs. Scott says we came here first, the people in West Virginia, the people in the mountains here, and then came people from the other countries — from France and like that, or Italy, she said. We don't see them here, but they're in Washington, D.C. I guess, and a lot of the colored people, you'll find them there, Mrs. Scott says. I've never seen people like that in my life, but if I did, I wouldn't act surprised. I'd just try to say hello and ask them what they wanted. Sometimes people pass through here, and they come to the beginning of the creek, just off the road there, and they'll want to sell you something, or they'll be checking up on you for the county, to see if you're hiding something they want, that's what my father will say is the reason they come. Last year the sheriff came and he said we were hiding corn liquor, that's what he kept saying, and everyone laughed and told him to go and search the place up and down and every way he wanted and see if he could find it. He didn't find a thing, because it was buried yonder near that tree, and how could he find it, even if he took himself a whole year to go and try.

"I like to see people that I've never seen before. They're people who are not like us; and you can tell they don't live near here, because they'll have on suits and hats, and they'll talk different; yes, even if they come from over in Logan they talk different. The best thing to do is keep quiet and ask them what their business is here and why do they want to come up the creek. If they're looking for trouble they'll soon find out they're wasting their time, but you should be polite and ask them their intention, and it's only if they don't give you a straight answer that you should go and get the gun and let them see they'd better be careful. I told Ben I wouldn't mind working for the county, Logan County, just for a year or two; then I could get those boots that the sheriff has, and his hat and badge and the pistols — he must have three or four — and the belt and bullets. He's got a car with a red light on it that goes around and around, and he can make more noise with that car than you can imagine. He's on the side of the strip miners. My daddy says so; and all you have to do is listen to him and you can tell. Mrs. Scott had him come in one time and tell us we should mind the law and not get fresh, because it doesn't pay, except if you want to end up in his jail over there in Logan. She asked if any of us had questions to ask him, and one of the bigger kids, Larry, raised his hand and asked if he was working for everyone in the county, equal, or if he got his salary from the people who had all the money. Then Mrs. Scott told Larry to stop with that talk, and he was just like his father, and he was always spouting off, Larry's father.

"The sheriff laughed and said he didn't mind answering; and he was working for everyone in Logan County, that's how he saw it, and the best people in the county, he believes, are the people who run the school, because you need the schools if you're going to learn what you should, and if there's grown people ready to spend their lives making sure Logan County has the right kind of schools and teachers, then they're the best people in the world. He was getting red, his face was, the more he talked, and I could see he maybe wasn't sure of what he said — whether he believed it himself, I mean. You can tell when someone is having trouble persuading you and persuading himself, and maybe that's why he's talking in the first place, to make sure he believes what he says. My daddy says it's not so hard to spot bad people, if you remember to keep your eyes open and your ears. I told Ben I didn't think the sheriff was bad, no; he just does what he's told.

"Afterwards, when he left, Mrs. Scott got real mad at Larry — and she said that people blame the wrong men, the sheriff and the school people, when they're only doing the best they know how, and the trouble lies elsewhere, that's what she kept repeating to us. Then I raised my hand and asked her where that was, 'elsewhere.' She got red like the sheriff, and said we're not in school to go blaming everyone on the whole earth, and that was up to God, and we'd better make sure we study our lessons, so there'd be no one blaming *us*. I had on my tongue to ask her if maybe it was Washington, D.C., where all the trouble came from and the crooks and thieves, but she was looking real wild at us, and more me than Ben or the others, and I thought I'd better not say anything for the rest of the day, and I didn't. Afterwards, Larry came up to me and he said I should be promoted ahead of him in the school for saying what I did; and he laughed and said I should even be ahead of that — I should be the teacher, and teach *her*, Mrs. Scott. Larry said the crooks and thieves came from Logan and from Charleston, where the capital of West Virginia is, and out beyond, too — like in Washington, D.C. When I came home and told what happened while we were eating supper, my mother and father laughed themselves so much they said I ruined their supper, but they told me it was worth it.

"I'd like to go see for myself when I get bigger, like I said; I mean, I could go and see what people are like in the cities, over there in Logan. I could get a car, if I went into the Army or the Navy and saved up my money like Steve did. I could drive through, and like Mrs. Scott says, you learn that way, just like from reading the books she has for us. If I could choose, like you say, I think I'd do the traveling and then I'd come back here, and I'd try to work in a store, maybe; that way I'd get some more money, and you see a lot of people in the store, and there's food they have, and they'll give you a good meal, I hear say, if you work for them real faithful, like they need you to do. Then after I'd saved a lot, I'd come back here; yes, I sure would, and by then I'd never want to leave the creek again, and neither would Ben or anyone, once they've gone out and looked around. Steve says you have to look around to know what you've got that's so good, and it's right before your eyes. My daddy says that's only half true; he says we've got a lot good here, but there's a lot we don't have, and it damn well should be that we have some money around here for the men who hurt themselves in the mines. That's what he always says if you tell him there's no place better than Rocky Creek."

Billy's Rocky Creek is a scene he can draw and draw and sometimes paint, too — though he is not usually one for paints because they are messy and he also finds the brush hard to control. Not one picture he did of the creek shows a person in it — and in all he did twelve of them with me. He loves to draw trees on the hills or snow up on the hills, or maybe a cabin or two near some hills, or the sky toward which those hills point. He loves to draw water: the rugged, almost impenetrable land making way for water; or water spilling over the land; or water just sitting there in the form of a lake. In Figure 21 he told me he was going to do the best job possible, "so that Rocky Creek will be there for you, wherever you go, and you can just look at my picture and see it." In Figure 22 he sketched a ravine near the creek and the water that pours out of it — water that often enough has him virtually mesmerized. Billy told me one afternoon that he remembered being very little and asking his dad where that water comes from and how it managed, even over thousands of years, to cut out the ravine — a fact the father had told the son several times, only to be met with a mixture of surprise and disbelief and awe that every parent knows under such circumstances. Apparently, once the question was too much for Mr. Potter, because he told his son God had done it, made the gorge, made the ravine, put the water there, and given it the force it has; whereupon Billy reminded him what he had said, that thousands of years had been required for the slow, erosive process to take place; whereupon the son recalls the father saying, "God sometimes takes it slow in what He does."

The day Billy drew the ravine I asked him, as I have on other occasions, whether he would want to put himself or his father or indeed anyone — say, his dog Speedy — near the ravine, as onlookers perhaps. No he didn't. He just didn't like to draw people or animals he told me, as he had before. He likes to draw the creek and he likes to draw other places he has seen, a nearby hollow, or again, that ravine, or the highest hill he's ever climbed. He likes to draw the moon "almost leaning on a far-off hill." He has seen the moon "leaning" like that from his position on top of a tree halfway up a hill, and it is a scene he likes to see in his mind and reproduce. He wouldn't mind trying to do so with paints, he told me — and in fact a day came when he did (Figure 23).

A little too eager at times, a little unrelaxed when I'm with a child like Billy in a setting like Rocky Creek, I finally did get a picture of the Potter family, or at least some of them, standing near their cabin (Figure 24). I had asked Billy one time too many whether he wouldn't want to show me what his house looks like (as if I didn't know!) or sketch out himself or some of his kin. He had tired of me and my requests — but also tired of saying no. Not that he was seriously annoyed with me; I hadn't been all that forceful or insistent about the matter. I believe now I had simply been unknowing. I hadn't been able to realize what really mattered to Billy, what experiences and images meant everything to him and were used by him to express himself, if not draw himself. When I worked with middle-class suburban children, they always wanted to draw pictures of themselves or their friends or their parents or their teachers. And often I had tried to get them off that track, tried without success to get them to draw a scene of some kind, a building perhaps, or a yard or street they knew. In contrast, Billy never seemed to forget that he was a small part of a much larger scene. At all times he wanted to take on that scene, do justice to it, and like a Chinese or a Japanese painter, smile benevolently and philosophically at man's relative insignificance in the face of the natural world — hence the way he did choose, finally, to portray his house and kin.

Nor ought an observer conclude that the boy was hiding from himself or fleeing into the woods or up a hill. He was not dodging the issue of his future — by telling me, for example, he couldn't draw a picture of himself grown up. Many children I have worked with elsewhere, well-to-do or poor, respond at once tentatively but with surprising eagerness to the opportunity that a drawing about their future gives them. They can be this or that, live here or there, realize one or another dream or fantasy. But Billy knows exactly where he is and where he will most likely be (if *he* has anything to say about it) and he also knows why his future seems so assured, so concretely before him, so definite. He knows that Potters have been in the creek for generations — and that it was no small job in the first place to get there, to dig in and last and last and last over the decades, which have now become centuries. He knows that ravines take an immeasurable, and incomprehensible length of time to come about, and he sees himself and his family and his kin and his friends as also part of something well nigh everlasting, something that continues, goes on, stays, is *there,* however hard and difficult and miserably unfair "life" can get to be.

Am I perhaps speaking wrongly for the boy? I do not think so. Here is what he said to me about Rocky Creek on the last day of a long stay I'd had with him and his family: "When you come back we'll be here, and you'll know the creek, so I won't have to take you around and show you all over, like before. It'll be the same, because it's only the seasons that change the creek. If you come in the spring or the summer, you'll find it's just like it was this spring, or like it is now, in the summer. If I had to choose a time of the year I like best, then I'd choose the winter. It's hard in the winter, and you're cold and you shiver, even near the fire; but the creek looks the best, and we all have the most laughing and fun then. My daddy says he's in a better mood in winter than any other time, because there's no place to go, and we just get buried in Rocky Creek, and we have the big sled we built and we go hunting, and it's a real job you have fooling those animals and catching them, what with the snow and a lot of them hiding and some of them only out for a short time. A lot of time there's no school, because you can't get in here and you can't get out. We play checkers and cards and we take turns picking the guitar and we have the radio with all the music we want, except if there's a bad storm out there. Daddy teaches us how to cut wood and make more things than you can believe. Each winter he has a new plan on what I'm to make out of wood with my knife. He says he's my teacher when there's no school. But it's a little strange about Daddy, our mother says: he begins to feel bad when the sun melts the snow and it's easier on us to leave the creek. He'll go to church and he'll say he's glad the weather is warming up, and we can leave the creek, but then he'll come home from church or the store over there, where we get the provisions, and he'll get real sad and down, and say he wishes we were back in January, and the whole state of West Virginia was covered with snow, and most of all our creek.

"For me, this is the best place to be in the whole world. I've not been to other places, I know; but if you have the best place right around you, before your eyes, you don't have to go looking. Mrs. Scott says they come from all over the country to look at the mountains we have, and Daddy says he wouldn't let one of them, with the cameras and all, into the creek, because they just want to stare and stare, and they don't know what to look for. He says they'll look at a hill, and they won't even stop to think what's on it — the different trees and the animals and birds. The first thing he taught us was what to call the different trees and bushes and vines. He takes us walking and he'll see more than anyone else. He knows where the animals live and where they're going and why they want to go over here and there. He's taking my brother Donald around now and asking him questions; not like Mrs. Scott does. Then he comes home and tells us that Donald is learning — or else he's not learning all he should. If I left here and went to live in a city, I'd be losing everything — that's what I hear said by my father and my uncle and cousins. We've been here so long, it's as long ago as when the country was started. My people came here and they followed the creek up to here and they named it Rocky Creek; they were the ones, that's right. In the Bible we have written down the names of our kin that came before us and when they were born and when they died, and my name is there and I'm not going to leave here, because there'd be no mention of me when I get married and no mention of my children, if I left the creek. The minister says that all over the county people are moving and moving, and they don't know what to call their home, because they'll no sooner get to a place when they'll be planning to leave because of some reason. But us — well, here we are and here we'll be. And that's the big difference, the minister said; and he's right, he sure is.

"I hope when I'm as big as my daddy I'll know the creek like he does. I hope I'll know his shortcuts and I'll be able to use the rifle as good. He's the best in the creek with his rifle, everyone says so. Mrs. Scott asked me a while back what I was going to do with myself later on, because I was doing good on her tests, and I told her I was going to be as good at hunting and fishing as my daddy, and she said what else was I going to do, and I didn't know what to answer, but I said that was enough right there, it sure was. She said she agreed, but she said maybe I could go on with my schooling and all like that, and I said that sounded good, only if I was going to live in Rocky Creek there wasn't much point to doing so, and it's hard, you know, because we don't have the money for the clothes you need and the books. They'll charge for books and for other things, that's what you hear. Mrs. Scott told me to go home and talk to my parents, and she's told me that a few times, to ask my parents, just outright ask them if I can't stay in school all the way through.

"I went and asked them; I asked if I could go to the high school. And then my daddy answered that about once a month Mrs. Scott gets it into her head to send me to a high school or someplace like that and once a month we've got to let her know that there's more to learn right here in Rocky Creek than any other place in the world including a city up North or even a high school down here. All we need is a little work to do, outside the creek, that's what Daddy says, and we'd be all right for as long as we live, and there'd be the Potter family in Rocky Creek until God decides He's going to call the whole human race up to His throne and judge every last man that ever lived — and then maybe He'll tell us we did good to stay in the creek and believe in Him and do all we could to live good lives here."

III
The South Goes North

The Streets

They come to the city streets. They come by car and by truck and by bus and by train. Rarely do they come by plane. They have said good-bye to a little town in the Delta, good-bye to Alabama's "Black Belt" or those towns in south Georgia just north of the Okefenokee Swamp or the lowlands of South Carolina or the eastern shore of North Carolina. Perhaps they have left one of Louisiana's parishes. Perhaps they once lived in Arkansas, near Little Rock or near Pine Bluff. Maybe they are not from the deep South. Maybe they are from Appalachia, from eastern Kentucky or western North Carolina or north central Tennessee or indeed just about all of West Virginia. Maybe they are from no single place; that is, maybe they have been migrant farm workers, who wander and wander, who may once have lived here or there, but now consider no town, no county, no state or even region their "home."

They come to the streets, all of them, from cabins and shacks, flat and rich farmlands or hills that somehow have been made to produce at least something. They come to the streets familiar with a way of life. They have, many of them (though by no means all of them), known the advantages of electricity, of a naked bulb to provide light, of an old refrigerator to keep food from rotting too fast. Good plumbing and heating are rather less familiar to those whom we call sharecroppers or tenant farmers from the rural South, whom we call migrant farm workers, whom we call mountaineers, Appalachia's yeomen from up the hollows. Other things are not familiar at all to such people: well-paid jobs, a sense of political power, a feeling of acceptance from schoolteachers or businessmen or sheriffs or county officials, and in addition, the experience of having a paved road near one's home, or sewer pipes leading to it, or good drinking water nearby.

They have said their good-byes, made their peace with their past, walked away, been driven away, slipped away, been picked up, been sent for. Some may have seen or been in a city before: Greenwood and

307

Greenville in Mississippi, or Selma and Montgomery in Alabama, or Lexington in Kentucky or Charleston in West Virginia or Atlanta and New Orleans, those big, big cities. For many, though, the cities up North are the first cities they have looked at and lived in.

"Lord, I never knew there were so many buildings. Lord, I never knew what a street was, not really, not streets like we have up here, not miles and miles of them." In Tunica County, Mississippi, he had not been totally confined to a plantation, to a sharecropper's cabin and the land nearby that needed his care. He had gone into a town or two, walked down muddy paths along which one home after another stood. And he had even caught a glimpse of Memphis; on his way north he had seen the city he used to hear the Mister talk about, and the Missus, and those laughing, romping children not yet old enough to keep their distance — yes, he'd heard them, too, the little white boys and little white girls, talk on and on about Memphis. But now he is in a city, up North in one. Now he lives there. Now, every single day, there are those streets. And now he is "used to things." What things, though? What up North has he day by day come to accept as the ordinary, the expected? "It started with the sidewalks and the sewers," he will say. He is trying to convey what took him by surprise when he "hit" Chicago, when he entered the city and saw one street and then another. They were beautifully paved. There were sewers. And black people lived all around. He had never before seen so many sewers. He had never before seen so many people, so many black people, and so many sidewalks and paved streets and sewers "that belong to them, the colored man." So it was that a "colored man" like him could at one point talk about "them." So it has been that mountaineers from eastern Kentucky and West Virginia can also feel a sense of detached surprise and wonder when they come to a city like Chicago and see those streets: "Who would ever believe it? Who would ever believe people live like this?" Then one asks what it is that he finds so unbelievable, and one hears again about sidewalks and sewers and firmly paved *roads*. It takes time for a man from a mountain hollow to talk about *streets*.

Yet, eventually they do; those former coal miners or subsistence farmers from Appalachia begin to say a lot about those streets. Friends or relatives come to visit or stay, and they must be shown things. There are lamps for instance, "outdoor lamps." Who would ever have thought that man could so firmly take command of night? A little girl from a place in Kentucky she is rapidly forgetting, but still just about remembers as "Winding Hollow," wants very much to remark upon that light, the light of streetlights: "I wonder how the moon feels? If I was the moon, I'd make a face at all the lamps on all the streets." She used to love the moon, her mother observes. The world seemed safer for the moon's night-light. But now the moon is almost unnecessary, one more faded miracle, one more outworn imperative. The city's streets conquer everything.

A black child in another city uses such military imagery, talks of conquests; he also hasn't been "up North" so long that he can't recall what it was like "back South," but he wants a visitor to know "there isn't any trouble around here you can't conquer, lick it and beat it flat, so long as you know the right person." He has heard that from others on the street, from others his age and older; "street talk" his mother calls the boy's statements — and those streets do indeed define one's sense of space, determine a good deal of how children speak and what they learn. Nor does the child's mother fail to comment on all that and more. The street she lives on is her backyard and front yard; it is the woods and the plantation and the county seat and the long road that leads to it. The street is flat, has no hills and no stream nearby, has no bank to sit on and lie down upon and use to "collect" one's strength. The street is lined with houses; it is "thick with them" — to the point that she and her neighbors sometimes take to wondering. Who in God's world ever had the gall to build so many houses? Where did they come from, all the people who live in those houses now and once lived in them over the years?

Other things inspire comment, too. As a matter of fact, these newcomers to our cities, these émigrés who have never left our own borders, these long-standing American citizens who have fled in desperation from the South to the North, from the quiet and isolated mountains to the crowded flatlands, be they white men or black men, young women or old women, they talk about flights of stairs or door locks or street numbers or mailboxes or light switches. For a while one thinks the problem is that of language; "they" have their words, their dialect, their way of putting things, and it is a matter of time before an outsider will be able to get the point, to understand why those simple, everyday words get mentioned so often — as if they are the keys to some mystery: "I've been here since the war, the Korean War. I came here from South Carolina. My husband was stationed up here, and he sent me a bus ticket. I never went back. I had my first baby inside me. The first surprise I had was the apartment building — I mean all the steps in it, the stairs and more stairs, until you think after climbing so many you'll be seeing the Lord himself." She goes on to remind her listener that in South Carolina there was exactly one step from the ground to the cabin in which she and her parents and her grandparents ("and the others before them") were born. That step was actually a stump of a tree half buried in the ground. The church she went to had "proper steps," two of them. And then suddenly she came to Boston, and encountered steps and steps and steps until she wondered in the beginning whether she could ever survive it all — lifting herself up and taking herself down again, and with no sunlight to help either. As for the hall lights in her "building," as she calls it, "they never have worked, not once."

More than the steps get to her, though. The locks do, the endless numbers of door locks. She was poor in South Carolina and she is poor now. But back South one doesn't have to fasten down one's poverty, defend it fearfully, worry about its vulnerability. Up North it seems nothing can go unguarded, and indeed, "the nothing we have is all locked up." She does, however, lose her keys sometimes — yes, the three keys, to the front door of her apartment and the back door and the street door downstairs. Then she becomes irritated and half amused. She also becomes nostalgic for a minute: "I think to myself that before I came to the city I'd never seen a lock in my life. That was the first thing I told my mother when I went back to see her. I told her they're lock crazy up North. And it isn't as if they're millionaires, our people up there."

She speaks about other matters to her mother. There are, again, those flights of stairs that go round and round and lead from one story to another. In one building she lived on the second story; in another on the fifth, the *fifth* — which means she was so high up she could imagine herself looking down on that small rural church she recalls being so tall. She wonders to this day whether the water tower she used to believe to be the tallest thing in the whole wide world is as tall as her apartment house, which she now certainly knows is far indeed from being the tallest building on her street, let alone other streets. And since she tries to keep in touch with her mother, even though neither of them is very good at writing, there are those numbers to keep in mind. Whoever got *that* idea anyway — of putting numbers on houses? Where do the numbers on her street start? Where does the street start, for that matter? In Dorchester County, South Carolina, so far as she knows, "there's not a number there on any home." She never had a post office box number, nor does her mother even today: "I write her name; I write the town; I write South Carolina — and it gets there faster than letters from her get to me."

Of course she gets her mail put into a mailbox, another one of those newfangled devices that go with city living. Since letter boxes in her building are private but commonly trespassed, she has to have a "mail key," too. For a long while the boxes in her apartment house were hopelessly inadequate — bent and punctured and covered with grime and scrawled words. Finally the postman complained, or higher officials in the post office did, or maybe it was the welfare department, which mails out checks. Someone did, she knows that, because the landlord was compelled to put in new boxes, and a policeman stood there watching while the job was done. It was a mixed blessing, needless to say: "I love the box, but the keys, all the keys you need — just to stay alive up here in the city." She told her mother about her new mailbox. Her mother told the news to the lady who runs the grocery store and gasoline station and post office down in Dorchester County, South Carolina. She is a white woman, and her name is Mrs. Chalmers, and she had a laugh over that. She told her informant to write back to "the poor girl" in Boston and ask how the mailman ever makes sense of them all, the hundreds of boxes he must have to fill up every morning.

People manage to make their adjustments. There are spurts and lags, naturally. Some habits and customs are mastered more quickly than others. Some undreamed-of luxuries try the mind and soul more than others do. In Cleveland a man from "near Beckley," West Virginia, laughs about a few of his recent tribulations and compares them to what his ancestors had to go through — for they were also Americans who moved on (from the East Coast westward) when they had to: "I can't keep up with the light switches in this city. I think it's harder for me to figure out these lights than it was for my kin way back to cut a path through the hills and settle there. Everywhere you go here there's a switch. On and off, that's what you have to think about when you go into a room. Now who's supposed to know every minute of his life where the switch is? I've been up in this place over a year and I forget, and I have my wife on my back, saying, 'The switch is here, don't get dressed in darkness.' Well, what's so damned wrong about darkness when it's early in the morning!"

In the cities late in the afternoon the lights appear, whether he or any other particular person likes it or not, and does or does not join in the act by turning a switch to ON. In the cities people seem to insist that darkness somehow be pushed into corners. There are plenty of those corners, especially in his neighborhood, but never in Ohio has he lived with the kind of darkness he everyday took for granted in

West Virginia. He is the first one to point out that almost every street corner has lights, lights of all colors. There are streetlights — and the stores with their lights, and the gas stations with theirs, and the police cars with lights on their roofs, whirling around and around. And there are those signs, signs full of bulbs, signs that wait on the sun to leave so they can take over and say: look over here, look and remember and buy, and if you do, we'll stay around and get called a success, catchy and clever and able to do our job, which is to light up your mind with desire.

He wants people to know he didn't live so far up a hollow that "this whole electric-light world up here in the city" is in and of itself strange to him. He had sockets with bulbs in them "back home" in his house, and he had television, also — so he really didn't expect to be as surprised as he was when he first came into Cleveland. He used to tighten the bulb in the evening, when he'd sit and smoke his pipe and get drowsy and half watch television. It was his children who often would pay full attention to it, "that picture box." And as a matter of fact, they were the ones who wanted him to loosen that bulb, so they could have the picture and nothing else all to themselves. But he liked to whittle, sometimes. And even if he didn't, the evening is the right time to have a little light around. Mind, he says a *little* light, not so much light that one feels in China during the night — which is where he sometimes thinks he might be as he sits in his Cleveland apartment. China, he learned from a teacher a long time ago, is where the day goes when we have night.

In any event, now his children can't understand why he doesn't switch on all the lights, come dusk. Nor would they think of sitting and watching television in complete darkness. Why do his boys and girls require what they once would have abhorred, glowing lamps? He is quick to note the change and explain it: "It must be they used to want to have our cabin so pitch-black because that way they could lose themselves watching the programs and forget where they were. Now they're gone from there and up here. Now they're in the city, and the television programs are about the city. They don't have to imagine they're someplace else. They don't need it dark, so their minds can wander. *We've* wandered."

For people who come to the city from rural America, there is another irony awaiting them, in the form of cellars. How can it be that these city people — who live so curiously high up in the air, so removed from farms, so oblivious of all that goes into growing food and fetching water and hunting and fishing — how can it be that they have dug themselves so far into the ground? And anyway, what does go on in those cellars? They can be frightening places — dark as can be, low and dank and just plain underneath everything. Heat is made in them, in things called boilers. Pipes and wires go in and out of cellars, or basements, as some call them. And the rats, the rats that are so common, the rats that seem to a mother an inevitable part of her child's life, they also are supposed to come from those cellars: "I'd sooner die than go down into that cellar. I've heard about it. I've heard stories; I've heard there are so many rats down there you can't see anything but them, running all over, faster than squirrels and raccoons and rabbits, much faster. They tell me a city rat is like no other animal. They're in the biggest hurry. They're mean. They don't care about each other and they run and run, on the hunt for scraps of food. They don't know the sun. I do believe rats come into the cellars up from Hell. Hell can't be too far from here, anyway."

She has learned from her neighbor that down in the cellar of her building is a huge boiler, a furnace, "a hot, hot oven." Again she thinks of Hell — and expresses the mixed awe and astonishment and dread she feels, perhaps about a wider range of subjects than the one she mentions: "I never would have believed it until I saw for myself — the heat you can get in this building. You need no fireplaces and no stoves. All you do is turn them on and those radiators start click-clacking, knocking and knocking, *dancing,* my little girl says. Not always, of course; sometimes we don't get any heat — and then the city has to come and scare the landlord. But I still can't get too mad, because back home we'd sit around the stove, and if we went too far away, we'd just have to be cold. It was hard on the children; they didn't have the winter clothes they needed. In the city we get more heat than we ever dreamed we'd have, but my neighbor says they can explode, the boilers. I told her Hell will open up one day, and we'll all sink in — and maybe the boilers are owned by the devil. She thought I was fooling. I was — but maybe it's true. Maybe up here that can happen."

She believes that anything can happen "up here," in the noisy, crowded world of her building, her block, her street. In many northern cities a street contains thousands of people — as many, for instance, as everyone in a whole county of the rural South or Appalachia. And, of course, a street can be a center of commerce, a place where people buy and sell and eat and entertain and are entertained. I have walked a mile on her street with her two sons and seen the stores: the regular grocery stores; the Dignity Grocery, whose owners emphasize their Afro-American spirit; the large drugstore that sells just about anything; the hairdressers, some of whom sell wigs, straighten hair, have white women's faces and hairstyles in the store window, and some of whom say no, no, no — Afros, and nothing else. And there are the funeral parlors and insurance agencies, not unlike those one sees in southern towns. The two boys told me that when their mother came North she went to an undertaker to register with him. I asked them why she would do that, and one of them replied: "My grandma told her to do it, otherwise we could die, one of us, and there'd be no one to bury us, and no place to rest in." They worry about rest, such families do, worry a great deal about what will happen to them, finally, and where they will go next and, most of all, whether always and always they will be tired and unsatisfied and fearful — destined, that is, for "no place to rest in."

On that street there are, in fact, people and places which offer a haven of sorts, if ever so temporary. There are women, mostly, who advertise themselves and their abilities with signs like "Reader-Adviser." There are bars and lounges and coffee shops. There are places that say "Keys Made," but specialize also in taking bets, which means one can sit down, make a telephone call, and have a friendly and informative talk with a broker of sorts, a man familiar with the odds, aware of hot tips, and not always on "the company's side." And there are those pawnbrokers, who are still around, still mostly white, still ready to cash checks and offer money (no questions asked) in return for "goods." But the two boys like most of all a Soul on Wax store. "How Much Can U Stand?" the sign asks, and the boys say there is no limit. Soul pours out of the store. Soul is turned up high inside and demands to be heard outside. "Soul Unlimited," another sign on the window says, and one's ears are inclined to offer no argument to the claim. The boys' mother finds the store an outrage. What right have they to make all that sound, assault one with all that "crazy music"? She loves hymns, passionate hymns. Her sons, though, are really turned on, have a lot of soul in them, and can stop and listen and snap their fingers and move their feet and knees and hips and torso and arms and neck and head in ways I can only marvel at, envy, and (in self-defense) dismiss as "foreign" or "alien" or a touch "wild" and "hysterical."

Among Appalachian whites newly settled in midwestern cities, mothers and children can take me on similar walks. Absent are the many hairdressers and funeral directors. Soul is not there, but God is; and so are country music, hillbilly music, and a gospel music not unlike the kind many blacks find congenial, important, and necessary. Missions are often present, their doors open, their signs prominently displayed and full of urgency. The mountaineer must know that he is not forsaken, that Christ follows His children into the cities, that prayer helps, works, makes a difference, saves. And the mountaineer will need to be saved, too, because those streets of his have stores that are labor agencies of sorts, stores where an earnest, tough, willing, hardworking mountaineer can be guaranteed work all right — hours and hours of it, with very little reward: "They say they'll pay you a couple of dollars an hour, but they take half *and more* out as their fee. I'm left with so little, and it costs so much here, the rent and the food, that I can't keep up with it." So, he goes to the loan company. There are plenty of those, in all the cities, ready with money for the black man, money for the white man, money for anyone prepared to assume undreamed-of debts in the course of paying off other debts.

Once up North, once on those streets and in those buildings, more forms of escape can be sought. Mountaineers like beer and whiskey; so do black men. So, they drink. Do they! One has to add quickly that only some mountaineers get excessively taken up with liquor. One has to add quickly and with particular emphasis (because so many of us are ready to believe otherwise) that only some black men get similarly dependent on liquor — or hooked on God knows what drug. Nevertheless, the streets have their fair share of them, the alcoholics and addicts, as a doctor calls them; the "lost people" one child I know calls them — and then he makes his emphasis: "the *real* lost people."

Does he distinguish "them" in that way from himself and his parents — who presumably are also lost, but by no means *real* lost? "In life some people lose more than others," his mother often says, so perhaps that is just what the boy of nine had in mind. He and his parents are losers, but not driven mad by cravings for shots, shots of whiskey and shots of heroin, which others call "smack" but the child calls "the silent smack." He will tell a listener why he uses that expression, and by the time he has finished he has revealed a lot about a particular child's sensibility and a lot, also, about the streets of a great American city: "I've only been here a year. I'm used to the streets now. You get used to them. I used to wonder if I ever would. I once thought I never would. It hurt my feet to walk on so much sidewalk. Before I came here I never wore shoes. Now I have to wear them all the time, and they hurt. You can't walk on the sidewalk barefoot; glass is everywhere and your feet get cut and bleed. I used to think I might dig up some sidewalk so I could have some earth to rest my feet on, soft earth. My mother says the earth up here must be hard. I asked her how she knew — since we never see any earth here. She said I should stop being smart with her. She says up here if you get too smart, you can get into trouble. I don't want any trouble, not the kind I see hereabouts. Look at those lost people out there; I mean they are *real* lost. I mean, they are gone. They'll never come back. They're on smack. Smack is the end of the road — the last trip, they say. You've arrived when you take it, they say; you can't go any further, they say. They take it and you can see them — going up, up, up. They don't make a sound when they take smack. That's why I say smack is silent — it's the silent smack. You know what? My granddaddy used to say to me: watch out there, you boy, or I'll give you a smack. My mother thought we were trying to be funny when we told her what a smack was up here. Granddaddy would hit us and *his* smack you could hear all over, into the middle of the field. Here I see them taking smack right out in the street, almost; maybe in the hall or in an alley. They don't make any noise, not a sound. When my mother gets mad and shouts about how wild it is here, crazy, she says, and noisy as can be, I'll sometimes argue with her. Some people here never talk, and they're not wild. They're as silent and still as if they're already dead. I do believe if my granddaddy gave them a smack they wouldn't make a sound or a move. I'd wriggle and cry when he hit me, and he'd say, 'Good, it shows you're alive and kicking.' Like I say: on smack, you're dead and gone."

Children like him, black children, or white mountain children newly settled in a northern city, notice all sorts of voices, all sorts of clatter and cries; they are sensitive to noises and curious about where they come from. The streets never seem to quiet down. Even in the middle of the night there are cars moving, people walking, things going on. Why is that? Why is the whole rhythm of life so different in New York or Philadelphia or Boston or Chicago? Why don't people live the same way they did "back South" or "back home" in the mountains? That is to say, why don't they move the way they used to move, and divide up their time in the old ways? What is it about those streets that "gets into you so," to call upon the words I heard one mother use? She was always asking questions like the ones I have just asked. She is utterly convinced that the streets really do change the bodies of those who move into them from the countryside. She would list her reasons rather like a good scientist does, briefly and to the point: "The sun, it's never around. The sky, who sees it? The clouds, they're always over you. The moon, poor thing, fights like Hell to get out from under those clouds; it probably thinks the clouds will get tired, after being there all day. But that's not the way it goes, no sir. They're tricky, those clouds. They let the moon through, then quick as can be, they shut it out again. There are no birds around, except a few pigeons, and they're in a bad state, you can see. They're always at each other. They're not relaxed and easygoing like the birds we had back home in the hills. A day doesn't go by that you're not trying to get something out of your eye. A day doesn't go by that you don't hear the cars hitting into each other, or the fire trucks racing by, or the police and their sirens. Will it be my building next, you wonder? Will it catch on fire or lose its heat? No wonder your body shakes all the time and begins to fall apart. There's just so much a body can take."

Those complaints are by no means the whole story, so far as she is concerned. She simply is not used to the "clock life" of the city. In the country everyone got up when the sun came up, and prepared to go to sleep when the sun left for other places. She and her family lingered, of course. They talked, and after they shared a secondhand television set, they listened to it for a while "into the night." But "come sundown" they withdrew from the outside world into their own world, the world of their cabin — ever so frail, likely as not perched on those cinder blocks, the floors full of holes and cracks, the roof made of rusted tin equally full of leaks. Nor does she fail to notice a bit of a paradox in her current situation: "I used to think to myself that one day I'd go into a city and I'd live better. I'd have a house where I'd be able to close my door and not worry that it's cold outside or raining. Now we have bricks in this building, and it sure is stronger than the cabin we had back there. The cold stays out, and the wind and the rain, but everything else comes in here from outside: the whole street, with its sirens, and the rats, they're always eating their way in, and the bugs and more bugs, and the roaches, huge they are. We had some roaches back home. I'm not denying it. But I kept on top of them. I cleared them out. I kept the mice out, too — field mice, and you'll always have them. But there weren't rats trying to *eat* you, and bugs that *bite* you, and the walls didn't have the lead poison in them that nearly *killed* my girl last year. I used to be afraid of coal. My father was killed down in a mine. Now it's lead you have to fear, around here it's lead."

She is afraid that she and her children will never really accommodate themselves to the "schedule of this place," or as mentioned above, the "clock life." In the city she is supposed to sleep, even though it is light outside early in the morning. In the city she is supposed to ignore dusk, the evening, the night. In the city her husband comes home tired but fretful — when he is lucky enough to have left home and stayed away doing a good day's work. He doesn't carve wood, make things anymore. Where indeed would he get the wood? He doesn't go walking — all the while talking with his dog. ("You'd have to be a murderer to keep a dog up here. Some do, but I can't. I just couldn't.") He doesn't try to fix things, or stand there outside his cabin, lost in his thoughts, alone with his memories, or maybe just still and unbothered and without anything at all on his mind. What he often *does* do is describe those times that are gone and compare them with the "better life" he now has: "I'd get myself in a nice place, where I might hear some birds and listen to some animals sounding off, really sounding off, or where I could look out — no, not at anything special, just at everything, you might say. I'd rest myself standing there. It's hard to explain to you, it is; after being up here a while, it's hard to explain to myself! But we have a better life up here. I don't say it's a happier one. I don't. But it's better, the way we live. Hell, maybe it's happier, too! I always was one to forget the troubles I had and re-member only the good. We had more troubles back in those hills than we do here in this city, living on this street."

And I had better remember those words. More than once he has brought himself up short and let me know how misleading he could be about his own life, about the advantages and disadvantages of one or another part of that life. More than once he and others like him have let me know that I ought be as wary of their words and senti-ments, and above all their nostalgia, as they themselves from time to time become — wary and self-mocking and delightfully clever and shrewdly philosophical: "I'm the kind of man who turns his miseries into a good time — once he's feeling fine. That's when you should turn sweet on the sourness you've been through, when you're through with it, the bad time. When I first came here to the city I used to miss it back there, real bad I did. I'd go to bed thinking of our little house and the hollow and the creek and the trees I'd carved my initials on when I was a boy, and the ones my own boys were starting to carve. Well, I had to stop that. But you know, the thing that made me stop was the minister up here I talked with. He said to me one day: would you go back? Would you really go back? And I came home and I thought, and by God if I didn't decide that a lot of my bellyaches are now gone, and even the worst of what I don't like isn't as bad as some of the troubles we had back there."

He meant "bellyaches" quite specifically and concretely, though he also was speaking symbolically. He and his family are no longer as hungry as they used to be during those long winters, when no money came in, when no work was to be had, when they were denied welfare, when bottled and canned food, grown outside, "up the mountain," and put away for January and February, began to run out, while at the same time the weather remained bitter cold and snow simply would not stop falling. But he used to have other bellyaches, too. Not only could he find no job, not only did he get no help at all from county officials, there was, additionally, the sight of his children. Before his very eyes they were "growing into his shoes," which ironically means growing up to have no shoes, to walk barefoot, to miss school on that account as well as for other reasons, all of them "part of a bundle" he would say: sickness with its attendant weakness; gloominess and self-doubt; and indifference, a child's realization that books don't matter in a neighborhood where very few people, literate or not, can find work.

The streets, then, offer hope. The streets have received, continue to receive, men and women and children who have had to leave their homes elsewhere; they are people driven and forsaken, compelled by fate to seek not merely a new life, but the conditions under which survival is possible. Hard pressed and afraid and tired, they arrive determined to live, anxious to find shelter and food and "something to do, anything that will fill up the hours." Bitter and fatalistic and bewildered, they are also resourceful and canny and inventive. There is the address of a brother to find or the address of kin, not close kin, but above all kin. There is a piece of paper to keep, to show, to look at and use; on it is a telephone number, a contact, the name of a person or an organization. The hand holds on to that paper. The arms lift that paper up again and again so that people of the city can see it. The lips say the word or words one time, two times, ten times. They are tentative hands and arms, and God knows, the voices let out by those lips tremble, falter, are often barely audible. Still, the hands and arms and voices belong to men and women who have picked themselves up and done the moving, the traveling, "the carrying of ourselves"; and once arrived, those men and women persist. Only later will they recall the first moments up North, and reveal why they very much want to stay where they are (even if they at times talk like prisoners condemned). But as they talk they also reveal what it meant to decide upon a departure, to pack up and go off, to get someplace, however far away it may be, however strange and forbidding it may appear to be when reached.

"We got here, we did," a man from Kentucky's mountains could say, three years after he arrived. And then comes, with a shudder one moment, a look of fierce pride the next, an account of what it was like to get there, to see those streets and try to fathom them out, master them: "I near turned back — so near I almost shake thinking about it.

I saw the city from a distance, you know, and I thought I was having myself a dream. I said to my wife, it's not true. She said that it is, and we've seen pictures on television to prove it. I said I never believed those pictures. She said it was true, what we'd seen, and there's the proof over yonder. Well, we got closer and closer, and all I could think was that we were going to die, once we got right in the middle of the city, and probably God Himself would be there, waiting to judge us, like He does. So, I said to myself we'd better just keep right on going, and let what happens happen. And we did. I had a piece of paper with an address written down; it was given to me by our minister. And I had another piece of paper with another address, kin of my wife's. I kept stopping and asking. I asked the police. I asked the people in gas stations. I asked someone walking down the street, and then someone else, and finally we got there. We got to our kin, and we got to the mission, where they helped us find a place to stay and some work for me."

He goes on. He tells about the sad times he had, the low times, and later on the better moments. At one point he thought he might have to move yet again: "I was stalled. I couldn't go back to the mountains, I knew that, and I couldn't stay here and sit around and sit around. Hell, I hate that. I'd die if that's all there was for me, the rest of my life. Maybe there's another city, I thought — where I could work." He found work, though. He didn't have to move. But the point is that he was prepared to do so. At times an observer can find him sullen, morose, resentful. At times he gets irritated, indignant, flushed with anger. He snaps. He looks daggers at people — including his own wife and children. He grinds his teeth. He quivers with rage, and his wife fears he will explode, pack them all up, make for the hills, the hills he loves and talks about and dreams about, the hills whose beauty he cannot get out of his mind, the hills whose praise he sings all the time, it seems — to the point that his younger children get cross and a little contemptuous. "That's silly," says his seven-year-old son, and then he tells why: "We're here. We're living here, and look how we have the food to eat, every day. I have good friends here. I like it. I'd like to go back, but I'd like to stay here until we know if there'll be anything for us back there." And the father nods his head, agrees, even manages a smile for himself and a pat on the head for his seven-year-old son, who is now a Chicagoan.

He has stayed because, as his son points out, there wasn't "anything" back home for his family and many thousands of other families. For all his bitter moments he is a man of moral courage. As he describes himself holding those two pieces of paper and asking, asking again, continuing, following directions, getting more directions, one can sense in him the self-possession, the self-reliance, the self-command he has always had, however petulant and brooding he sometimes is. People like him somehow got to the cities in which they now live. It is less apparent to us that their arrival was preceded by an act of will, by intention become a deed — *and* that to stay meant to resolve something, to settle something in one's mind as well as to settle down in an apartment house. A black man in Harlem describes what he, like the white mountaineer just quoted, went through as he arrived in New York City: "I came by bus. All I had when I got on the bus was a box, a box made of cardboard, and it had a rope around it to hold my things together. I had some socks and underwear, two pairs of each, and a picture of my wife and my kids that we took in a five-and-ten store in Macon, Georgia. I'd only been in Macon two or three times in my life, so New York was more than I could believe. I just couldn't believe it. How could there be a place like that? Of course, I've been here five years, so it's hard to tell you what was on my mind back then, but so far as New York is concerned — how I felt when I saw it for the first time — I *can* tell you, because there are some things in your life that you just don't forget, never. How could you?"

He works himself up to the description of his first thoughts and feelings in New York by doing what a good novelist or historian would do. That is to say, he goes back and makes sure that his listener is thoroughly aware of, reminded of, what preceded that arrival: "Now, you have to picture our place back there in Georgia. Oh, it was something! Today I can't figure out how we did it, live there. It's no paradise up here, but like my wife tells me when I get down in the dumps, a day doesn't go by that we don't take something for granted up here that back there we believed we'd never, never live to have. That's the truth. It was bad for us down South, and getting worse all the time. Some of my family, they went into Atlanta; and even there they couldn't find work. They stood around and sat around. They tried to find jobs. Then they gave up. They came back here and they told me that if I wanted to get out, I'd better go all the way and leave the whole state of Georgia. So, I did. I went to New York because we had an uncle here. Then I sent for my wife and kids, and after a while we sent for my cousins, too. They said they'd been in Atlanta, but compared to New York, the whole state of Georgia was just a little town, that's all it is."

How did he manage, though, during those first minutes and hours of his arrival North? How did he come to terms with Harlem? Where did he go? Whom did he initially see, talk with, ask for help?

No world-shaking psychological and sociological conclusions will come out of whatever answers and thoughts and memories he manages to give to someone like me. Nevertheless, he himself says that he lives to this day with, will always live with "a little bit of that first day in me." Now what does *that* mean? What unforgettable drama unfolded then? The answer is that nothing terribly shocking or melodramatic took place. He simply wants it known that "you don't just move up here and find a room in Harlem and send for your family, no sir." If not that, then what? Oh, a lot, he will say, tossing the ball right back. It is hard for him to put some things into words, and he isn't really interested in doing so. But he has memories, a number of them, and as he keeps on saying, something seems to come up all the time that makes one or another of those memories assert itself in his mind; "I'll be walking down the street and my eye will catch a junkie, and I'll say to myself: Louis, remember the time you saw your first junkie? And then I'll say to myself: Louis, you are here; you're no longer down South; you're here."

With such a remark he can be through with talk, or on his way to a long marathon of it. The fact is that he has become a taxi driver, and so he knows his Harlem. He can take a visitor on a street-by-street tour. He knows that city within a city well enough (if not inside out, which is what he only sometimes claims) to qualify as a guide: "Some people said they wanted a few of us to take the whites on a tour and show them a lot of places. I said sure, sure I would. Maybe it was a mistake, but their white eyes were opened, they were; and you know, that's the same thing that happened to me. My eyes got opened when I came up here."

When he first saw New York he had one thought: how could he get together the money necessary for a return ticket? For one whole week his mind was almost obsessed with that question. He got off the bus and asked the driver if it cost the same fare to go back South. When he got to his uncle's house he asked his uncle if he could loan him the money for the trip back. Yes, but stay, the uncle said repeatedly. No, he would not stay. The city hurt him. His eyes watered when he walked the streets of Harlem — and no, it wasn't because he was crying. Well, maybe "on the inside" he was, but he was *also* crying because things would unaccountably get in his eyes. Things don't get in his eyes now — and that, he says, is because "you learn to close your eyes a little up here, you learn to protect yourself." Nor were his eyes the only problem he had. His ears had never heard so much, so many different kinds of noises. He felt like the squirrels he used to shoot:

"They'd always be sitting and trying to figure out where to go, which tree to climb, which way to turn. The same with me. I'd leave my uncle's place and I'd have my eyes watching all over, and my ears as open as they could be — and the result was I didn't know what to do. It seemed that every direction I would go would only mean trouble, trouble."

He goes on. He describes all the "trouble" he met up with and came to understand — and not to fear quite so much. He describes the things he gradually took for granted: those junkies, the soot in the air, the roar of buses and garbage trucks and freight trucks and the elevated railroad and the machines being used to build or tear down or repair buildings. He describes gutters and hydrants and lampposts and automobile meters; they are all part of the city, part of the streets of Harlem — and it was only when his family did at last come up, and when he saw *them* noticing all those things, and complaining about any number of other things, it was only then that he realized what *he* had gone through: "My boy asked me about the hydrant. After I told him, he wasn't satisfied; he wanted to know where the water comes from. You see, back home we used to walk three or four miles every day to get water and bring it back to the house. We went to a little pond, it was. Don't ask me if the water was clean! I don't want to think about the germs I got into me over all those years. My little girl comes home and talks about vitamins and minerals in her food, how she needs vitamin ABC and XYZ. I tell her: look, Sally Mae, your daddy lived on grits and the water in that pond, back in Peach County, Georgia. He didn't die. He *lived* on it, you hear!"

The little girl is, of course, surprised, and she doesn't really know what to say in reply. All right, *all right,* so he did manage to live on grits and that dirty water. What is *she* supposed to do? She was two when she came to Harlem. She is a New Yorker. Her daddy is no desperate, dispossessed sharecropper. Her daddy is a taxi driver. Her daddy knows a lot; in fact, he knows most everything there is to know about New York City, or at least the only New York City she, Sally Mae, knows about — so why does he every once in a while bring up "all that South business"?

Sally Mae's father agrees with her. Why go back to what is over and done with? Yet he does. He recalls things nostalgically, bitterly, and with a touch of envy directed at others who lack his kind of memories. Most of all he recalls things with decreasing frequency and increasing self-consciousness. And almost invariably he finds that when he lets his mind go back, when he dwells upon the past, he ends up remembering not the South but himself as new to the North, new to New York City and Harlem and those streets he now drives over, all over — to the extent that sometimes his wife will wake up in the middle of the night and hear him reciting them, their numbers, their names, their origins, their endings. During the day he also says a lot of things out loud. Doesn't he have to make himself heard above all those sounds? Doesn't he have to remind himself by talking at the top of his voice that with so many people on those streets, he is himself, a person, and no one else? The time was that he could walk miles and hear no one's voice, see no one's face. He walked on red earth, grew tired, and sat down on that earth, maybe under a tree or beside some bushes or on some grass. The time was that he'd come home and do some more sitting: there was the sun to watch as it slowly seemed to settle itself down from the sky — and then all of a sudden disappear; there were the sunflowers to look at and shower with a little water; there were the dogs to play with, throw sticks toward and away from. Now he never looks at the sky. He just doesn't. He knows about the weather by the feel of things. Is he cold? Is he sweating? Is he getting wet? Does he see whiteness slowly growing and growing, covering up Harlem's streets, making them look different, making them harder to navigate, making his driving more difficult — and more in demand? And now the trees are practically nowhere, sunflowers are unheard-of, and as for dogs, they are around, yes, they are, but he thinks that is rather a shame; "I wouldn't bring a dog into the city, not here anyway. It's unfair to them. We left our dog home. We left her with my sister. The dog is still alive. My sister writes and tells us that Rosemary misses us. I'm sure she does. I miss her. We named her after my younger sister. She got sick and died all of a sudden. She coughed up blood and the next thing she was gone. I wouldn't have named the dog Rosemary, but my mother asked me to. She said she liked hearing the name Rosemary called again. She said she was sure Rosemary was near us and listening and waiting for us to come and join her."

As for his mother, she won't leave Georgia. She wouldn't think of coming to New York. She was born in Peach County and she will die there. Why is that? Why doesn't she follow her brother, follow her son? The son Louis has an answer: "She'd be leaving her child Rosemary, and not only Rosemary. She's lost other children, you know. There's no Harlem Hospital for us in Peach County. There's nothing for us there, the fact is, when you stop and think about it. It was awful for her to see Rosemary die like that. It was awful for her to give us children roots to chew on so we wouldn't get too hungry. But even so, my mother can't leave. She's got to stay. She's got to stay and 'lock up the store.' I hear my customers say, 'I'm glad you came by; I need a taxi; I'm tired.' They've just 'locked up the store' after a long day. I guess the good Lord will send a taxi for my mother one of these days, and when He does she'll get in and be glad. Yes, she will. And you want to know something? She won't turn around, no she won't. There will be no regrets. She'll get in that cab and say, 'My good Lord, how I've been waiting on you! Oh have I!' and then she'll be driven to some city, I guess!"

It is precisely a place like Harlem Hospital that lifts this man's spirit and makes him proud to be living where he is. It isn't that he is completely satisfied with the care his wife and children have received there for a variety of complaints. It isn't that he himself has been showered with love and affection and prompt service there. Still, Harlem Hospital has black doctors and nurses. Once, in an emergency, his girl was treated very well, so well that he could only think, again, of Rosemary — and of what it means to be up North and in a big, modern city, for all its drawbacks and troubles: "I took her there, Sally Mae, and she was coughing bad and wheezing, that's what the doctor told me it was, wheezing. He said her lungs were sick, she had trouble in them, but they had drugs and they'd get her well, they were sure of it. I was reminded of Rosemary, my sister. I thought of her, coughing and coughing, and finally the blood came up, and all of a sudden she was gone. Do you think a poor man down there in Peach County, Georgia, can go to Harlem Hospital and have his daughter fixed up? Do you think even if you're white a doctor down there will see you if you're poor? They wouldn't see a white man's kid, either! I knew a white kid who was sick; I knew his daddy too, because he worked in the gas station near the bossman's house. The doctor saw the white kid once and said he was in *private practice,* that's what the doctor said. He told the man to take his kid up to Atlanta, someplace like that, where they have money and they have 'free hospitals,' something like that. Well, then I could only shrug my shoulders. I thought he was a lucky man, come to think of it! I said to my wife, 'If he was colored, he never would have gotten to that doctor's office in the first place. At least this way he knew where he stood.'"

The long and short of it is that *he* now knows just about where he stands. He lives up North, in America's most populous and richest city, its first city in many respects. Every day he stands there at a corner, waiting for a fare, talking and joking with other cabdrivers. He leans against lampposts. He leans against the walls of buildings. He leans on parked cars. He has his coffee standing up. He can look out at the street that way. For one thing, he can see anyone who might be tempted to get into his cab and drive off, but just as important, he likes to look outside, look at passersby, take in the scene, "watch the world go by," he puts it — by no means with a unique turn of phrase, but with obvious conviction and even a trace of excitement. The streets of that city have caught hold of him, as they have so many others from various classes and races and backgrounds. He is not uncritical of those streets; he sees "a lot of misery every day," and he wants that known. At times he is so critical that if his mind does not seriously take him and his family back to the rural South, it does indeed prompt him to think of other streets, perhaps in smaller towns. But no, that is not for him; maybe for his children but not for him. Nor is the problem only one of race, though God knows "a black man can't just decide to move and expect a big reception out there in the big, fat white suburbs." The fact is that he spends only the very briefest time in the suburbs and he does not know how he would ever get to live in one of them: "Should I take my cab one day and drive out there, over one of the bridges, and go talk to someone about a home? I take fares all over, but I can just imagine what would happen if I tried moving in some of the places I drive through. My kids, they are learning more than I ever dreamed there was to learn in school; so maybe they'll learn how you get to live someplace else. Black people get out of here, I guess, just like I got out of Georgia."

He is optimistic at that moment. Sometimes he sees things far less hopefully. At other times he becomes afraid. He hears talk of violence, of revolution. He sees buildings condemned. He sees fires consume buildings that ought never have been left standing. He sees everything as he drives and stops, picks up people and takes them where they want to go: "I'll hear people talking and I think to myself there won't be a Harlem left. The white man doesn't care about these streets here; some black people do, but some have reached the point that they don't care either." But he does, he very much cares: "I'm not tired of these streets, not yet. If you asked me what I think of my being here, I'd say I'm glad I came. That poor white guy I told you about, the guy who worked in the gas station — well, you know what? He went to the city, too. My mother told us that. She said he up and left. Maybe he went to Atlanta, or maybe he went some other place — up North, maybe. I understand the whites in the South have been going the same way we have. If the land won't take care of but a few rich farmers, and the poor people have got nothing to fall back on, except to sit and starve to death, then they're not going to do that. They're going to leave. They'll come up here."

And so people of both races have; they have left for reasons he knows about, and settled on the streets he virtually hunts along, so agile and forceful a driver is he. In a city people want to get someplace, he reminds his passenger. In a city there's no point lingering and waiting. The streets are there to live on, play on, and ride on. He lives on the streets at night, and his kids play on the streets in the late afternoon, but in those morning hours he's got to ride, ride, ride those streets. The streets will give him money, will take him and his family someplace. He doesn't know exactly where. But who really does? He knows enough to know *that*, though — and so unbothered, unexhausted by large questions, he guns the engine, spots the customer, asks where, and shows what he knows, what he can do: go right to the desired address the fastest way allowed by the city's streets.

Blacks in the City

I Am Black and Nothing Else

He is tall and very thin, so thin that at times I would remember the anatomy I studied in medical school and try to figure out how his lanky, almost threadlike body could possibly hold all those bones and muscles and vital organs I knew must be somewhere under his skin, all inside him. He is fast-moving, too. Long-limbed and lithe, he declares himself able to disappear from anyone's sight "faster than it takes to pronounce my name or where I was born." He laughs when he says that, because he knows he has three names as well as a last name: Thomas James Edward Robinson. His father had three brothers by those names, and they all died before they ever grew up; so, when he was born after four girls, his father decided not to take any chances at all: "He gave me all his brothers' names, and used to tell me that I'd better stay alive, and he meant it." As for Tom's birth-place, it was in Opelousas, in St. Landry Parish, Louisiana, that he was born in 1955. Let people try to say his full name or pronounce "that place" in Louisiana; Tom is sure he can "clear away" before they finish.

Is he a runner? Is he on some track team — perhaps at high school? Is he trying to keep himself in good condition? Three no's and a yes: he doesn't go to school; he would never call himself a runner; and he has never been on any "team," but he very much wants to be in shape. He doesn't exercise formally or methodically. He simply races down the street, "flies down," as the younger children on the block say. He is a hero to them, the seven- and eight- and nine-year-old boys who live in the tenement house he lives in. They are all bunched to-gether, those tenement buildings. They don't stand near one another or lean on one another; they are in fact one thick continuous stretch of brick, and only the end of the block puts an end to them. But as soon as the next block starts one is back with the same problem: which en-trance is what number of what street. Minds like mine for a while can-not stop doing things like that, trying forever to figure out what Tom's *address* is, what number it is — or was, before some "vandal" ripped off all the numbers on the entrances. Finally I did learn to relax. Tom told me to relax. He told me to feel my way down the block. He told me to stop looking lost when I saw each time that there were no num-bers to be found. He told me to stop counting the entrances from the corner until I came to his, near the middle. How did he know I was doing that, counting and counting? I wasn't talking out loud, I knew that, and I wasn't moving my lips. Of course I wasn't; *he* knew that, too. The giveaway was my face; he could tell by the frown on my face: "Your face was just working too hard, man, concentrating too much. That's all." I suppose it is a curse of mine that I couldn't relax then and there and smile and tell him: right, right. Nervous and cerebral, and in a way silently rude, I had to take note of his "intuitive" nature, his dis-like of details like street numbers, his ability to do things without seeming to try.

I did learn eventually to walk down that block somewhat casually and knowingly. I was taught to do so by the boys and girls I came to visit. Another thing I learned from the younger children on that block had to do with Thomas James Edward Robinson, formerly of Opelousas, St. Landry Parish, Louisiana, and now of Roxbury, Suffolk, Massachu-setts. The children call him T.R., sometimes Tom, but never Tommy. He bristles when he hears himself called Tommy, though the teachers used to do it all the time and he never used to mind until he was thirteen or so; until he began to awaken, began to realize what the world is like and what his people are struggling for and what "that name Tom means." He is not, however, without humor when he talks about such matters. He doesn't dislike the name Tom or Tommy in and of itself. He simply feels sensitive about the meaning the name has come to have, especially these days. Actually, he feels sensitive about a lot of things. He doesn't at fifteen know exactly what to do with his feelings.

"I know some of the little kids look up to me," he says, but then he makes a dramatic turn, a reversal in his line of reasoning: "It's not me they turn to, though. It's not. They're no longer Negroes, who find a boss and obey and *obey*. You see that? When you live up here and you're my age, you've been doing some learning, and not in school, and you've been doing some figuring out, and not with the help of any white teacher, or Negro teacher. You've discovered something. You've discovered that either you stand up and think for yourself and be free, or you're a slave, just like we were before, down there in the South. You're either black or you're nothing at all. I am black and nothing else; if I'm not black I'm nothing. You can't be a Negro and be anything but a tool of the white man's. That's what we're learning. That's what we've got to learn, or else it'll be no good, *no good*. They'll just keep on walking all over us. They always have. They still do. Why should they stop, unless we make them stop, *make them stop?*"

He does that often; he says something emphatic, then repeats himself, word for word, even more emphatically, and I am then half ready for a third repetition, but it never comes. He wants me to know that he has his convictions. He wants to know himself that there are convictions he has and will keep and not lose, no matter what the temptation, no matter how sad or lost or grim he might someday feel. And he has seen that in others, in older men — "the defeat in them." He talks about that defeat a lot: "You've got to know that you may never win, not with us outnumbered. If you fight, though, you're winning right there. The only way you can lose is to be an Uncle Tom. That's the way they get you; the way they always have. I used to sit there in school and the teacher would ignore us and be ready to insult us no matter what we said, and I'd take it, man, *I'd take it*. They had me believing I was no good, *no good*. They had me ready to go scrubbing their floors, and opening their doors, and washing their cars. That's what they want us for. They've always needed us to do their dishes and carry their trash away.

"The black man is waking up. I hear my brothers talking all the time. We're brothers and sisters, all black men and all black women.

The kids on this block, they've got to be black, *black*. I laugh with them. I kid them. I say, 'Oh, I think I see a big patch of white on you.' Then they'll laugh back. They'll say they see a little speck of white on me, too — a speck over here, and a spot over there. So, I've got to watch out, too. They're right. You can't just shake off your people's past and start fresh. I heard a man, he knew Malcolm X, say that the other day. He said, 'Brothers, it takes time to get yourself free.' He said, 'You can't free yourself of the white man until you free yourself of the Negro you carry around inside yourself.' Now there's something to remember. I told some kids that; they were playing on the street, and I called them and they came running over. I told them what I'd heard. I told them Malcolm X, he lived right here in Roxbury, and he knew; he knew like no one else has. They all said I was right, but they wanted to get back playing. I can't blame them. I like pool better than anything. I like motorcycles. If I had the money, I'd get on one and I'd never stop. I'd drive until there was no more land left for me to drive on. I'd drive up every road in the world. Do you think anyone has tried it? I'd grab me a sandwich and eat on the bike. I'd sleep by it and keep moving. But you have to have a fortune to own a motorcycle. You have to get rich. And like that man said, the friend of Malcolm X, when you try to get rich you either find you can't, or you start climbing all over your own people and kicking them and shoving them and knocking them down and pushing, *pushing*."

He uses those last two words, that word "pushing," both literally and figuratively. He is speaking of the elbowing that a man on the make, on the rise, can demonstrate. But, of course, he is also talking about drugs, about the pushers he knows and every day watches, sees at work. They do well, make a great deal of money, and tempt him. Nor does he need anyone to point out that last fact, that psychological fact. He knows the facts of envy, rivalry, greed. He knows that people have to deny what at the same time they are drawn to do. He knows the mind's struggles, and in a straightforward and unpretentious manner he can talk about them, even explain the particular ways he has come to deal with such difficulties: "Who can say no to them? The dealers here, the pushers, they've told me I'm a smart boy. That's what they call me, a boy. They say I'm a natural born leader, and there's a place for me in that setup. They say I can be the closest thing to a millionaire I'll ever see. They say I can carry around as much cash as my pockets will hold. They say I should just say yes, and they'll start me out. I can get pants with pockets that stretch down to my shoes, and they can guarantee they'll be filled up with dollar bills, those pockets, before I'm a year older. They're fooling. I know they are. But they make plenty. I would have cash, a lot of cash. We could move to a better building. I could get the bike I want. I could drive up and down this street on the biggest motorcycle you'll ever see.

"I told my dad, and he said he'd kill me first, rather than let me do that. I told him he was a real square guy. He got mad. Then I told him to cool it, *cool it.* I told him I was fooling him, trying to trick him. I just wanted to get his reaction, that's all. I wanted to see what he'd have to say. He didn't believe me at first, though. He thought I was just backing down because he was so mad, and I was scared. He thought I was really trying to con him. But I wasn't, and finally I made him believe me, I made him. I shouted. That's the way he knew I was serious. I told him what I believe. He didn't like what I told him, but he said so long as I don't become a pusher, he won't care what I believe — about being black, you know. I told him he should care, he had to care. I told him the reason I wasn't becoming a pusher. I said if I didn't think it was better to be black, to be a black man, than to be a pusher — well, then I'd go and be a pusher. He couldn't follow me. He kept telling me he couldn't follow me. I didn't know what I could say to him. I thought to myself: it's Louisiana, it's the state of Louisiana that's in his head, and he can't get it out. He'll see a white man and he begins to move out of his way, the Man's way, but he doesn't. He's learned. He's stopped doing what he did down there. But it's in him; I can tell. My grandmother, she says I'm wrong. She says you can't do it, fight the bossman. She still calls them that. I said we have to, or else we'll be slaves. She said she was never a slave. Then I decided I'd better shut up. But she wouldn't stop. She said all I was trying to do was see the bad side, *the bad side.* I said no, that wasn't true. She said I had no faith. I said how could I, looking around and seeing what I did. Then she recited her Bible.

"But my father is glad I'm no pusher, and so is my mother and my grandmother. They don't care whether they're called black or Negro or anything. My father told me I could call him white if I wanted to. He said I could even call him an Uncle Tom. He was setting us up for a fight. He was kidding. He works in a car wash. He hates the white man. Usually he says he doesn't, but once in a while he'll come home dead tired; and then he admits it — that they bleed us, *they bleed us white.* He's bled white, for sure he is, by the time he's ready to go home. All day he's heard his boss tell him to hurry up, move fast, keep on it, stop delaying — and work, work, work. He's the hardest-working man that ever lived. You should see his muscles. When I was a little kid he used to tell me that the colored child, that's what he'd say, the colored child is born with big, big muscles, because there's the cotton to pick and everything else the white man needs doing. You think he was fooling? No sir, he sure wasn't fooling. He'd be serious. He'd be trying to clue me in. He'd be telling me so I wouldn't be surprised later on. I recall asking him about why it is that the white people on television seem to be the big shots, and we have nothing. I asked him if there are a lot of black people with big money, and if there are, why don't we see them on the television. I don't know how old I was then; I know I asked him, I know. And I can tell you what he said. He said white is white and colored is colored, and the whites own the world, most of it, and the colored don't and that's the way it is, and no one can go and do anything about it, and maybe the second time around, in the next world, it'll be the opposite, and won't that be good — a relief, a big relief. My poor dad, and all the poor Negroes, waiting for the second time around, *the second time around!*"

He has gone to work with his father upon occasion, but finds it an impossible job. The whites come in, one after the other in one big new sporty car after the other, and his father washes, washes, washes. He wonders at his father. Where's the man's anger? How can he take it, all day long take it? How can he let himself be ordered around so, treated so abruptly and imperiously? How can he *not* think of becoming a pusher himself? The man must have his secret thoughts, his dreams of triumph and glory. He must — yet he apparently doesn't; or so T.R. believes. And he has indeed tried to find out: "I've asked him, I've said tell me, tell me why you and I and every other black man doesn't go after them, jump them, get them out of our lives for good. He told me to shut my mouth up and not open it again until I got some sense in my head. So, I didn't say anything the rest of the day. Then after we finished supper you know what he said? He asked me if I didn't like what my mother had gone and cooked for us. I said yes I did, I always did. Then he said *that* was why he keeps his cool: if he got wise and started fighting with the white man, he'd soon be out of a job, and we'd have no money, and no food, and we'd starve to death. 'Someday you'll have a family, son. You'll know then; you'll know the difference between a lot of big talk and what you've got to do if you want your wife and kids to eat.' That's what he said, and I didn't even try to answer him. My grandmother was nodding her head off, and I near got sick to my stomach. I wanted to throw up that meal. I really did!"

For money he works in a grocery store, stocks the counters and

Figure 1 Ruby by Ruby at age 6

Figure 2 A white girl by Ruby at age 6

Figure 3 Ruby's grandfather

Figure 4 Ruby's landscape

Figure 5 Jimmie by Ruby at age 6

Figure 6 A Negro boy Jimmie's age by Ruby at age 6

Figure 7 Ruby by Jimmie at age 6

Figure 8 Ruby in school by Jimmie at age 7

Figure 9 Negro friend and white classmate, by Johnnie

Figure 10 Allan draws the difference between Negro and white.

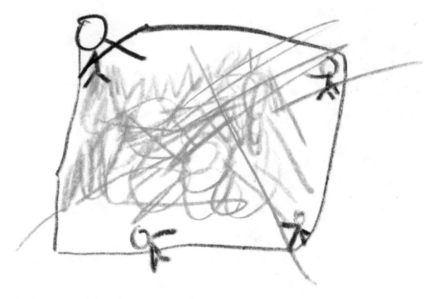

Figure 11 Fields at harvest time by Tom

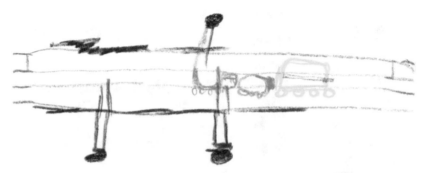

Figure 12 A road by Tom

Figure 13 Larry's birth certificate

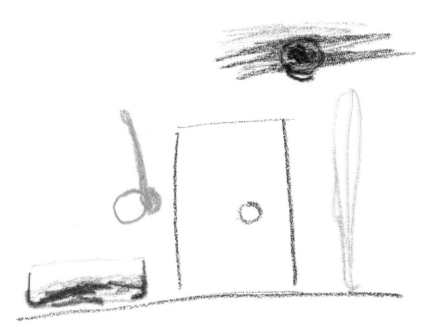

Figure 14 Drawing by 8-year-old migrant girl

Figure 15 A landscape by Lawrence

Figure 16 Jeannette's landscape in crayon

Figure 17 Jeannette's scarecrow with blackbirds

Figure 18 A sharecropper girl's kitchen

Figure 19 Mr. Williams by Tim

Figure 20 Tim's dad

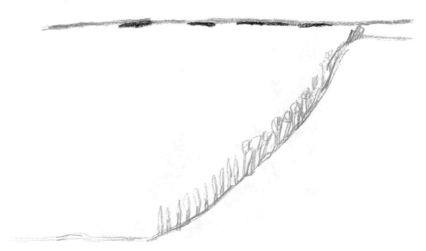

Figure 21 Billy's drawing of Rocky Creek

Figure 22 A ravine near Rocky Creek by Billy

Figure 23 The moon "leaning" on a hill by Billy

Figure 24 Billy's drawing of the Potter family and their cabin

Figure 25 "I can't draw, but I'll try to show you how good a teacher she is — she's with you all the way; you can see it on her face."

Figure 26 "Now a bad teacher — I can't even draw them because they're all alike and they're no good — so, there, the best thing to do is cross them right out, the way they do to us."

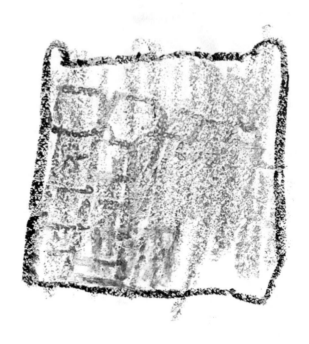

Figures 27 and 28 One house is a grim tenement, and one house, obviously, has a lot to make it pleasant.

Figure 29 A black child shows the teacher with a pointer and on a stool. "She's always over you and on you to do something, and she gets annoyed too quick. She's too nervous about us, I think. She always lectures at us."

Figure 30 A white child says the same teacher is "friendly" and "likes to hug us a lot."

Figure 31 A black child from a ghetto in a northern city draws the school bus (owned, he says, by "white people") that takes him and others like him to a suburban school. His face can be seen amid the dabs of black. The white driver literally blends into the bus, which is the same color as the driver's face.

Figure 32 Another black child draws his bus, and himself and his brother in it, and his (white, suburban, sun-drenched, yellow-colored) school.

Figure 33 "Here I am now. It's raining, and I have an umbrella, but still I get wet."

Figure 34 "Here I am when I'm grown up. That's a cowboy hat. I'm on top of a hill. The school, it's way down there. I could fly in that plane. The kid, he still has to go to school, but I thought I'd give him a cowboy hat, too. That's a crow. She's saying: 'Why don't you kids fly away from school and get yourself a deal someplace.' That's what she's saying."

Figure 35 Betsy's sunless landscape

Figure 36 Hill with pine trees by Betsy

Figure 37 Betsy's snowmobile with bird-filled sky

Figure 38 Village in midwinter by Betsy

Figure 39 Landscape in a winter storm by John

Figure 40 John's landscape with ice floes

Figure 41 Carmen's drawing of her school, teacher, classmate, and (in the background) herself

Figure 42 Self-portrait by Carmen

Figure 43 Painting by Carmen

Figure 44 Woman and gardening girl by Carmen

Figure 45 Sun and cloud in the sky by Rose

Figure 46 Rose's landscape

Figure 47 White man by Rose

Figure 48 Indian man by Rose

Figure 49 Sky by Sam

Figure 50 Sam's evening sky

Figure 51 Miriam's Hopi reservation

Figure 52 Valley landscape by Miriam

Figure 53 Texan traveler by James

Figure 54 James's mob

Figure 55 A policeman by James

Figure 56 A mob assaults James's Garden District home.

Figure 57 Self-portrait by Marjorie

Figure 58 Marjorie's drawing of her sister Susan

Figure 59 Marjorie's Daddy, atop an office building, listens to the wind.

Figure 60 The garden outside Marjorie's house in late summer

Figure 61 Marjorie's grandfather carrying a gun to protect himself

Figure 62 A bus carrying black children arrives at Gordon's school.

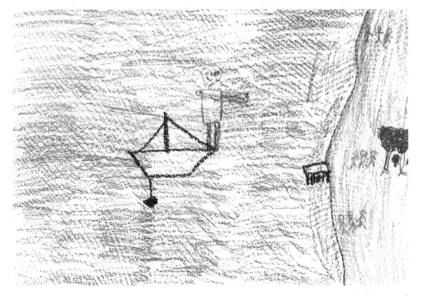

Figure 63 "Sailor, scientist, explorer, and, not least, man removed from others" — by Gordon

Figure 64 Joan's drawing of herself at home

sweeps the floor. At least his immediate superiors are not white, though the store is owned by whites, he knows that. He is tempted to steal from the store. He is tempted to tell his boss — the manager, "the front man," the Negro — to stop it, to stop fooling himself and everyone else. But he is a young man, and jobs for people like him are quite scarce, he knows that. And he is afraid. If he were idle all day and penniless; if he had nothing to do but sit around and stand around and have his dreams of driving around in a motorcycle or a car; if he had to go wash cars and be bossed by a white man and told he was lucky even to have that job; or if he had to go back to school, in the unlikely event a truant officer tracked him down and hauled him into court for being under sixteen and so illegally out of school — if any of those things were to happen he might take to stealing regularly and maybe even pushing, yes maybe even that.

Indeed, he doesn't understand the patience other young men his age show. How can they be so indifferent to the world's injustices? How can they shrug their shoulders and laugh or shake their heads and then forget, all the time forget? Forget it, they tell him. Forget this and forget that he is urged. Why worry, they ask. What's the point, they declare rather than inquire. Why sweat it? Why lose your cool? Why get all hot and bothered and worked up and talkative, "full of speech," his friends will sometimes put it. And more to the point, what can he actually do — that is, besides say all he does, and then repeat himself over and over again? The last question does indeed bother him. He knows that he can right now do very little. He is no Black Muslim, no Black Panther — not yet, anyway. He belongs to no organization, no club, no group or party. He isn't in his own mind agreed upon a course of action, a plan, a way of doing something, anything. He doesn't read much. He hears the radio. He watches television. He listens to records. He listens to older people talk. Then it all goes through his mind, the words and sights; and out of the experiences, the listening and seeing, come *his* idea, *his* viewpoint, *his* words: "I speak for myself and no one else. Can't a black man do that? Can't they let us be different, each one of us? I hear on the television that the black man thinks this way, and he says this, and here's what he believes on that score. I say that's not right; that's not *me* and that's not what I think. They're always trying to corner us, the white man is. But I do believe that today he's worried over us, he surely is.

"I think it was the last day I went to school that I heard my teacher lose his temper and say he was sick of us, sick as he could be and fed up, because he couldn't figure out what it was that we wanted;

and we were driving him crazy, he said. I'm mixed up myself. I mean, I don't know how we can beat him or drive him crazy, Mr. White Man. He's holding all the strings, Whitey is. And he's got a lot of us scared. A Negro is a scared black man. I'm scared but I'm not a Negro. You want to know why? It's because I'm saying it, right here and now: I'm scared, but I'm not going to turn into a Negro over it. I'm going to be black. I'm going to look for ways to outfox Whitey and I'm going to go fight him when I can win. I tell the kids — I say look: don't go fight with those white teachers. They'll come down hard on you. They'll have you over at the police station in five minutes. They have cops right inside the schools now; and those cops are just waiting for the teachers to say go ahead, go ahead and get them. That's why you have to be careful. I agree with my dad on that; you've got to watch your step."

He does watch his step. He keeps an eye out for the police. They make their rounds, drive up and down the street; and all the while he looks at them and mutters or swaggers and smiles in an angry, mocking way. Or he may simply turn his back on them, go inside, get out of their sight. He loves to run and pretend he's on a motorcycle and watch the buildings go by and the street lamps and the people and the stores and buses. But when the police are around he never runs. He stands still, or he quietly and unostentatiously retires into the background. He is convinced that if he were seen running by the police he would be arrested immediately on suspicion of stealing something, doing something wrong. He is convinced that they would not stop him and talk with him and ask him questions. They would grab him and maybe beat him but certainly take him away and hold him and not easily let go of him: "They see a guy like me running, and they go click, click, click in their heads, and I come out a crook, a robber. Where's your knife, they ask. Where's your razor blade, they ask. I see the manager of the store punching that cash register and I think to myself that the police have a cash register in their heads, and there's a button called 'nigger' on it, and every time they see a black man, they push the button and the same answer comes out — go get him, fast. If I had a motorcycle, I'd like to see them go get me. I'd give them a chase."

Until that day comes, he gives others a chase. He runs against anyone who wants to challenge him; and so far no one around has done so successfully. He has speed. He has staying power. He runs effortlessly, too. He seems to be enjoying himself as he moves along, not trying hard, not running out of breath, not running down minute by minute, just running. The children watch, and they run, too. They run to catch him, to be near him when he does stop, so that they can listen to him panting, and no doubt thereby prove to themselves that he is, after all, human and he does tire and he does have to stop and he does need rest. So, they hover close and he laughs and jokes with them and they ask him where his motor is (where *is* it?) and he says he'll be damned if he'll let them in on the secret, no sir. Then they fall to talking about other things: what they did and did not do in school, and what they would like to do "later on" when they get big, and what they think *he* should be doing and what *he* thinks he should be doing.

They are bittersweet conversations, the ones he and his young admirers have. He is struck by the innocence of younger children, the still undampened hopes they have — for him as well as for themselves. He tries to recall whether he was like that, so buoyant and optimistic, so full of gall almost. Yes, he decided, he probably was. He is too young to remember the trip north from Louisiana, but he does have in mind a time when he told his father he wanted to fly airplanes and even make them — have his own factory, so to speak. His father laughed, and he didn't like the way his father laughed. He felt both annoyed and curious. *Couldn't* he someday own an aircraft company? No, he was told, and don't get such silly, crazy ideas anymore.

Soon he stopped having those ideas. Now he tells young boys and girls not to waste their time with idle dreams. They've got to build themselves up, he says. They've got to know how to run, run as fast as they can. They've got to be quick of mind, too. True, he himself falters upon occasion, lapses into reveries: he is a junkie; he has a million dollars; he can run for miles, run until he drops into a pool of his own sweat, and by God, the pool is still on his land, on land he owns outright, on land that stretches as far as the eye can see, as far as his body will go. He will go on further, think of the motorcycles, the cars, the Mustangs and Cougars, and think of the suits and shirts and shoes and coats, think of everything a young *American* thinks of.

I have said so, told him I thought he was more a citizen of this nation than he believed, and in reply he has said I am hopelessly white and he is thoroughly black and that is that. Then I mention television and the radio and how they cultivate common desires in millions of people; I mention the appetites and hopes I feel he shares with many others of his age, not just his race, in this big and rich country. Then he in turn has his say: "Sure I live in this country. They get to me when I see them driving in a car, the junkies do. So do the people on television; they say, go to your nearest dealer and get yourself a big new

Buick, and I want to go. Only the trouble is I don't know that kind of dealer. I know the dealers we have around here: smack, smack, smack — heroin they call it on the TV news. I could be making two hundred a week or more, right now I could. I'm not religious like my grandmother, and I'm not scared like my parents are. I don't know why I hold back. I do, though; *I do*. I don't want to see us killed. You take drugs and you die. I see people sitting around; they're staring off into space and they aren't really alive at all. If I push drugs, I'll be killing them. That's how I see it. I wouldn't be able to run away from that — no matter how fast I run I couldn't.

"You have to believe in yourself. You can't be a pusher and believe in yourself. They have the cars, but they're no good. They're bad people. They're like a lot of your whites. They make a lot of money, and they don't care how, and they don't ask questions. They just go ahead and sell and sell and sell, and spend all they make to live it up. I couldn't do that. If I was arrested by a cop for selling smack, I'd say I should be, and I'd go along and take the prison sentence. A dealer once asked me what I'd do if I was hungry and didn't have a cent to my name. I told him I'd die, I'd sooner die than take his smack. I'd sooner die than sell it. A lot of my friends think the same way. You don't see them all taking drugs, do you? Some do, but a lot don't. It's not fair, the way they say we're all going to go on drugs when we grow up. That's what a teacher told us. That's right; that's what she said. I wanted to shout at her and tell her that I'm a black man, and I'm not going to take drugs, because that's the way we become weaker and weaker, and then the white man can just keep on doing anything he wants to us, anything."

Always the runner, also a fast talker once he gets going, bristling with anger at times, uncertain about his "future," unsure of himself despite all his pointed remarks and cutting observations, he is above all a deeply ethical youth. He is ethical in ways that defy words, his or anyone else's. As he once said: "I do what I do, and I believe my body pulls on me to stay clean and do the right thing. I don't know sometimes which is the right thing and which is the wrong thing, but all of a sudden I find out, and it's because there's something inside me that lets me know. I think it's in my chest, my heart maybe." *What* is in his heart? Why, the voice of his heart is in his heart, he says impatiently — as if an inheritance like that need be mentioned or discussed or asked after or pinned down by someone! And of course his impatience reveals his ignorance; for the fact is these questioners are indeed people who need to ask all sorts of questions and hear all sorts of wordy explanations before they can, finally, catch sight of the most obvious thing in the world, an ethical young man's effort to remain precisely that — no matter what and against all the odds.

To Hell with All of You

Curses, threats, diatribes, oaths, warnings, one indecent or coarse word after another, they all come easily to James Lewis, who is *only* fourteen, someone like me cannot stop thinking to himself. He talks and talks, and if a listener hears him but does not look at the young man's extraordinarily expressive face, the temptation is to surrender or flee immediately to whatever sanctuary can be found. Nor is James (he will not be called Jim) unaware of all that: "I'm a big guy with words, I know. The black man has been listening to the white man's words all his time in this country, so it's good we're finally coming up with our own words. We've got to be rid of Whitey; everything's he's done to us has to be washed away, with the strongest soap we can find. It's the white man who has dirtied up everything: he's ruined the air and the water; he's exploded atomic bombs; he's killed the Indians and made us slaves. He's been murdering and stealing for hundreds of years — and then when we try to stand up for our rights, he calls us thieves and hoodlums and everything else. The white man lives off the black man and the brown man and the red man. That's the truth. I don't hold it against any *one* white man; it's all of them — all of you."

I have to say it again: James Lewis is only fourteen years old, and he goes to school only fitfully. His father is dead. His mother is dead. He has no grandparents alive. He lives with an aunt, his mother's sister. His aunt tells the story directly and to the point: "James was born and a year later his mother died. She had an infection and it hurt her heart, the doctors said. There wasn't anything we could do to save her. They said if we'd brought her to the hospital right away she would have lived, but we had no way of getting her there, and I didn't know then that up here they'll take you even if you don't have any money. In Alabama it sure wasn't like that. They didn't have a 'city hospital' where we lived. James lost his father a year later. He was a young man, but they said he had high blood pressure. He fell dead, yes sir; it happened right in front of the little boy. He was two, yes sir. I lived across the street and the older children came over and told me their father was on the floor asleep, and they couldn't wake him. So, I took them

all in: James and Henry and Lois and Florence. It's only James I have
left of my sister's children. Henry is married. He can't find a good job.
He didn't stay in school, like he should have. He was the only one
born in Alabama. I told him once that he had that lazy South in him
and he'd never amount to anything. Lois and Florence, they're working. I'm proud of them. Lois works downtown. She works an elevator.
Florence works in a candy factory, yes she does. She makes candy all
day! Can you imagine that? And she hasn't put on a pound so far as I
can see, not one!"

As for James she worries about him. He is exceptionally smart,
she knows that; and in fact he has always been a talkative person, a
tough fighter of sorts, a child whom no teacher could ever quite bend
to his or her ways: "They tried to tame him in school, oh did they!
They smacked him and hit him, I know it. I did too; I had to, I just had
to. The teachers called me in, and I did what I could. I tried to explain
that I had my own children and my sister's, and it's been hard on me.
Back South we were close, all of us brothers and sisters, but up here
we've lost touch. My older sister won't take any part in helping out.
She has no children, mind you. She's been married, I think, four or five
times. I've lost track of the men, and I couldn't swear it was ever legal,
the way she lives with those men. I'll get to know the guy, and then the
next thing I'll hear there's a new one. James used to like her when he
was very little. Now he hates her; he hates her so strong that I pray to
God he never sees her. She lives away over from here, and I only see
her when I go to see my brother, who's down the street from her. I
never take James with me. He calls her the worst names. He says she
sleeps with white men all the time — and he's right, I know it. But
she's my sister. We were both born of the same mother and the same
father, and we can remember where we grew up — Beatrice, Alabama;
yes sir, that was the town, and we lived a mile or so down the road
outside.

"I try to tell James about Beatrice and he won't listen. He only listens to the speakers, the people who want to build an army or something. I don't know — black, black, that's all those speakers say. I told
James that in Alabama black was a bad, bad word to us; but it doesn't
register on him, what I say. He likes to talk so much himself that he
hasn't got the time for anyone else. I told my minister we'd better pray
for that boy. He said yes; he said that the Panthers have got him, or
some other people I've never heard of. I asked, what can we do? He
said there wasn't anything we can do, except pray, and the harder the
better, because there's a devil around up here, and he's getting his

hands on our children, and turning them into mean, mean ones. So, every morning I hold up my hands and pray. I even tell James what I'm praying for. He laughs, of course."

James can indeed laugh. For all the strident, stern, unforgiving side to him, the young man also has a light and humorous touch, and it comes across his face rather than out of his mouth. That is to say, he can tell me things I will later think about with a great deal of sadness or apprehension or anger or whatever — while at the time his quick eyes and the sardonic tone of his voice and the smile, at once charming and challenging, all seem to soften somewhat remarks spoken in utter seriousness. "My aunt, she was good to me," he declares with a broad grin of approval. One begins to relax: today will be an easier day; he will be talking about his aunt, and if we can hold to that, have a more personal and warm-hearted conversation, we will not once again end up talking about racist America, racist America — to the point that he himself is exhausted and at a loss to know what can be done, after all his self-described "speeches" have been made. "She was the one who saved my life, I know that." Now the grin leaves his face, but he continues with affection and nostalgia: "She's the nicest woman you could ever want to know. She's my mother, you know. My mother died when I was a baby, and all I remember is my aunt. My father died, too; my aunt tells me I should remember him, because I was two when he passed, but I don't. I've had dreams: I've dreamed I was walking down this street, I don't remember what its name is, and all of a sudden a man comes up to me, he must be ten feet tall, as big as a building, and he says, 'James, I'm your father.' But I tell him I don't have a father. He picks me up, but I fight him off. I get down and run away. I hide, and he's looking for me, but he never finds me. He goes away and I'm glad. Then I wake up. Sometimes in the dream I try to get him arrested. I guess I think he's a crook, some kind of crook. But I don't want to turn him in to the police because they're even worse than any crook. I guess that's why he never gets caught or arrested. I always wake up first."

Then comes the beginning of a switch: "The trouble with my aunt is that she doesn't stop and question herself. She takes everything; she accepts all the troubles she's had, and she never wants to fight back. I've tried to talk to her. I love her. She's my mother, she's my mother. But she'll not listen to you, she really won't. She starts in with her mumbo-jumbo talk, about God and Jesus Christ and being saved, and the next world, and all that. She's drugged up, drugged with religion, don't you see. She's on drugs, just like all the other *Negroes*."

The word gets him going. Like Thomas James Edward Robinson, whose views have just been presented, James Lewis hates the word "Negro." But unlike T.R., who is slightly older, James Lewis has already committed himself to a life of intensely political activity. He does not know T.R.; he lives several miles away. He does know the difference between them, though: "There are a lot of cats around talking black these days. I'm not against them. It's good that we're all waking up. But it's one thing to talk black, and it's another thing to *be* black, and I'll tell you something: I'm not black yet. It'll take me all my life to get black. Do you see?"

I tell him that the answer is no, I don't quite see. All right; he is not in the least set back. Patiently and generously he will try to show me: "I can understand. You're you. I'm me. You try to know the black man, but you're lost before you ever start. You're looking through a white man's eyes. Here in America the black man is just being born. We're all Negroes; we've been Negroes ever since they brought us here. But a lot of us are through being Negroes. No more, no more, we say! And you'll see how we mean it. It takes a lot of time, though, if you're going to walk with your head up. Look at most black people; they walk with their heads down. I never noticed it myself until I heard a man speak and he told us that after we left the place, we should keep our eyes open and see how our people walk. So, I came home and nearly broke into tears right in front of her, my aunt. She goes and cleans up a white woman's house, that's the job she has. She washes the dishes and scrubs the floor and cleans the bathroom and she even has to help her, the bitch, get food ready for supper. What does the white woman do all day, I ask my aunt. Well, she has 'activities,' that's what my aunt says. She doesn't know which 'activities' they are, but she saw some letter and it was about the NAACP, and the woman was giving twenty-five dollars, twenty-five bills. I told my aunt to go and tell her to keep the goddam money. I told her to sit the woman down and say to her, 'To Hell with all of you, to Hell.' My aunt told me to shut up.

"But that's my aunt. She's been brainwashed. You can't change her. She's too old. Like I said, I came home and saw her, all stooped over, and I realized how right that man was: my aunt has been saying, 'Yes, yes' to the white man so long that her whole body now does it, says, 'Yes sir, yes sir.' It hurts me more to see her bending than to hear her talking about 'the good white people.' *Which* good white people!"

He wants to fight a battle someday, take on all those 'good white people' and beat them, beat them decisively, beat them for good. He knows how to fight. He can use a knife, a razor blade, and yes, a gun. The black man has to be armed; he tells me that an unarmed black man is not a black man at all. The white world spends billions of dollars arming itself, but when a black man carries a pistol, everyone shudders, Negro and white alike. So it goes — but so it must no longer be: "We can't always take it; we can't always be on the weak side. We've got to be as strong as the white man — stronger. I can't let the pigs scare me. They're working for whites, every cop is. Sure there are Negro pigs. Who said there aren't? You drive by the police station and you see them, the white pigs and the Negro ones, they're buddies. Do you think that fools us? A man has to be stupid to be taken in by that trick. They hire a few Uncle Toms and march them up and down our streets; then we're supposed to bow down and be good, be real good. All the time my aunt used to say that: be good, be real good. You know what she meant? She meant to do whatever they tell you, the white teachers and the white police and the white landlord and the white store people. Black people live here, but it's the whites who own us. They'll always own us until we stop them — and that means it'll come to a fight. It has to be a fight. I've been fighting for a long time, but that was wasting my time. The whites like it when we have our gangs and beat up on each other: the more we hurt each other the weaker we are, and the stronger they are, and the safer they feel. It's easy to figure that one out!"

He constantly tries to figure things out, and when he does he doesn't hesitate to speak out. If I try to tell him that he sees things in too conspiratorial a fashion, he replies that I can afford not to look underneath and see all the ugliness and meanness and treachery which really do exist in this world. He doesn't quite say it that way; indeed, he speaks eloquently and sharply; "If you have an easy time; if you're rich; if you're on top; if the world is always waiting on you — then sure you can look around and say everything is going fine, and what's the matter with all these people who keep on digging up trouble all the time. But if you're down, way down on the bottom, then you either learn the score or you're a slave. If you want to be a black man, a free man, you have to keep awake, wide awake. You can't miss the tricks. The white man has his tricks, and you can't fall for them."

I do not know how a young man of fourteen whom teachers have described to me as silent, sullen, disobedient, moody, a truant, "up to no good," of "limited intelligence," and yes, "possibly retarded" manages to be so alert, aware, and articulate. He is a very shrewd youth, I can say — and yet somehow those words fail to do justice to him. Perhaps the point is that he has a highly developed political sensibility. He also has a sense of history, a sense of his own personal history and of his people's history. At fourteen many of us are thoroughly self-absorbed, hence indifferent to a host of political and economic "forces" or "pressures" that do indeed exert enormous influence upon everyone. In contrast, James Lewis is jolted out of himself every time he leaves school, leaves his aunt's house, leaves the particular neighborhood in which he grew up — and goes to a store, a clubhouse, a meeting place, where he listens to what most Americans would consider to be revolutionary talk. Yet, even before he became "politicized" (as some would put it, though he doesn't) there were those moments of awareness — and he can remember them and talk about them: "I'd be a kid, a little kid, and I'd look at myself in that old mirror. My aunt, she said she brought it up here from that town of hers in Alabama. I try to forget the name. I don't want to know all about her 'nice times' down there. She'll tell me about them and then she'll tell me that if they hadn't come up here, they all would have 'perished' — that's her talking and not me. So they came up here! A lot it did for them! She has that mirror, but she would often tell me she didn't want to look in it, because she was afraid she'd see her mother, because it was hers, the mirror was, and she used to look into it. You know who gave it to her mother, don't you? A white woman did. I told my aunt it was hers and not her mother's or that white woman's. She said yes, she knew. But she's tired, all the time she is, and she says that she wants to remember herself like she was a long while back and not like she looks now, all old. I'd go and stare at myself and I'd say to myself that no mirror is going to scare me, and I'll never be afraid to look into one, no matter if I live to be one hundred years old.

"I'd look at my skin. I'd look at my nose and my lips and my hair. I'm not ashamed to talk about it; no, I'm glad I can talk about it. Over at the office we make each other talk about how we look. We tell each other how we used to talk and what we used to say to ourselves in front of the mirror and what we say now. I used to think that if I could just hold my nose in, it would look different, thinner. I'd practice, tightening my lips up. My aunt said a lot of women get their hair straightened. She's never done it, but my other aunt, you can bet she does — for the white man! Today I can admit it! I used to think I'd look great if I had straight hair and if I could change my face. I wanted to be white. I didn't dare admit it then, even to myself. Once, though, I did. My friends here really make me admit it every day; but before I joined up, I admitted it to myself for a few minutes. I was in her room, my aunt's. I looked in her mirror. It's the only one we have. She keeps it beside her bed in a drawer. She's even got part of her ticket from Mobile, Alabama, to Boston in that drawer. Can you imagine that? She has a bus ticket from that far back! I looked in the mirror and I saw the same old face, and all of a sudden I thought it would be great if I looked like the kid my aunt talks about — he's in the place she works, the white woman's house. He's the white woman's son, and he's my age. I've never seen him. I've never seen a picture of him. All I know is that she says he's blond; so, when I looked in the mirror I dreamed I was him. I was a white boy with blond hair! I didn't really believe I was, but for a few seconds I almost did convince myself. I tried walking like I thought he would — fancy-like. I swung my hands. I tried to make myself bigger. I tried to talk white. Then I heard my aunt. I put the mirror away. She asked me where I was. I told her I'd been tired and I had gone to sleep on her bed. She said that was OK. She said she was sorry that she had a softer bed than us kids, but she guessed she needed her sleep, because with her husband dead and us to feed, she had to work, and when she came home she was almost as dead as him — but she had to care for us, and cook and all, that's why she needed the best sleep she could get. I told her yes, I was glad she had the soft bed she did, and I left because I wanted to go out and be with my friends. I was glad to see them. I was glad I was right in front of our building and not over in some lousy, rotten white neighborhood; I was glad I was not that white lady's kid and not a damned white cowboy like you see in the movies. The white cowboys almost killed every Indian in America. Didn't they?"

One answers questions like that as faithfully and honestly as one can, but they are, I believe, unanswerable questions. James Lewis knows what he knows, and sees what he sees. I come to hear him, and when we talk I try to tell him what I know, what I see. And he listens as intently as I do. But he continues to say what he believes he ought to say, what he must say, what he wants with all his might to say and to have heard. And I answer back and he looks directly at me and tells me how sorry he is that I am deceived, but how he understands, he understands. And sometimes as I listen to him I remember those moments when I as a doctor, a psychiatrist, have told a troubled, confused patient that yes, I understand, I understand.

Orin

Orin is his name, a name out of Scotland or someplace like that, his father has told him. There were some big, important tobacco people in eastern North Carolina who carried that name, Orin. And as things go in the South, the black man learns from the white man and gets his names from him. So, Orin is eight and black and called Orrie and his father's name is Orin, and he is thirty-three and called Daddy, even by his wife. Orin was born in Old Dock, North Carolina, which is not far from Whiteville, the seat of Columbus County. Orin's daddy once was a field hand, and used to drive a pickup truck; he would also do odd jobs and errands and "everything, you know." At the age of four Orin was brought north to Hartford, and then to Boston. All of which means that he is half a Southerner, half a Northerner — and no kidding: "I'm from North Carolina and I'm from Massachusetts. Four and four make eight, and we've been up here four years and before that I lived four years in Columbus County, North Carolina, my daddy says. No kidding, I'm half-and-half from here and from back home."

He has heard "back home" mentioned and recalled many times. His daddy one day says they'll be going back there soon, and the next day says he won't ever go back. The fact is, though, that every summer for four years in a row Orin has heard his parents debate this question: will we go there to see them or will they come up here — Orin's grandfather and grandmother. Orin's mother has no parents. She was reared by her uncle and aunt. She lost both her parents to pneumonia, she believes. She doesn't know, because no doctor ever got to them. But Orin's father has both parents alive and well. They will live to be a hundred, he hopes and believes, and they are proud and good people, one gathers from listening to their proud and good son. There is only one problem with them; they won't leave that county in North Carolina. They won't go to live in Wilmington or any other city in the state; and they won't go to live in Washington, D.C. — where one of their sons now lives. Nor will they go up to stay in Hartford, Connecticut, where another son lives, or Boston, where their son Orin lives, and where two aunts of Orin's, sisters of his mother's, also live. They will go to those cities to visit, to look around and marvel at what a city can be, but they always want to leave after a week or two; and it seems that if they go North one year, they expect their children to come back South the next year. Young Orin, therefore, has been back to North Carolina twice since he came North to live.

Orin wishes he could live like his grandparents do; but he also is glad to live up North and be with his parents and live the way they do. In Old Dock, Orin loves to go near the mules and the horses and the chickens and the pigs he sees there. He loves to look at fields of tobacco and at the flowers his grandmother grows. He loves to "go exploring": "When I'm in North Carolina I tell my grandfather all about Roxbury. He's been up here, but he says I know a lot more about Roxbury than he does. He says he never hopes to know too much about any city. I told him he was wrong, and he was making a big mistake. He said I should go right ahead and tell him he's wrong; it won't make any difference. He says he's happy where he is and I should be happy where I am."

Orin gets bored with North Carolina after a while. Each time, he has been given a chance to stay longer and return with an older cousin. Each time, he has said no, he will go back with his parents. But it isn't a shy and fearful child, afraid to leave his parents, who refuses to stay longer in Old Dock: "I'd miss my friends. I'd miss the playground. We have a new playground, and all the kids show up there right after breakfast in the summer. We play ball. If I'm going to be a baseball player, I have to practice."

He finds certain things in Old Dock rather hard to accept: the extreme quietness, the flies and mosquitoes that go undeterred by effective window screens or screen doors, the road dust that a car can stir up, the eerie sound of crickets in the early evening, the heat that doesn't come and go but stays and sticks to the body's surfaces and nearly smothers those exposed to it. It can be hot and muggy up in Boston, he knows; and up there one meets plenty of flies and mosquitoes, not to mention mice and rats and cockroaches. Still, there is something nice about a thunderstorm that signals several following days of real cool weather; and most of all, there is something reassuring about all those cars and trucks and buses which ride over smooth, well-paved roads: "When I'm down there I get to wondering if there are more than ten or twenty people anywhere around. That's scary. What if you want to play a good game of baseball? Where would you get the teams from, and would there be anyone to look at the game and be in favor of your side or the other side? I'll go for a walk with my granddaddy and he'll be talking sometimes, but then he stops, and I can't think of anything to say, and there's no one around. He has a dog, but the dog only stays with us in the beginning of the walk. The dog runs and runs, and I'm sure that he's lost, but he shows up at suppertime, and Granddaddy says to me each time that I'm sure from the city, because anyone knows that a dog will find his way back to supper. He's right, I know. It's in the city that you lose your dog. We brought one up here — Beauty. I remember her. She got killed, you know — Dad says it took only two days. I remember my mother crying. She said, 'Now we really are up here, now that Beauty's gone.' My daddy said he'd try to get another dog. But the city is no place for a dog, Momma said, and so we've never had one since."

He doesn't talk about that dog Beauty very much, but over the years he has drawn pictures of her several times — and then gone on to tell me that he can remember Beauty running across a field in North Carolina, and remember Beauty in the car, resting beside him, on the way up North; and he can remember his mother's scream when she heard that Beauty was dead. Beauty was only six when she got killed, two years older than Orin was. A year after Beauty had died, and several months after I first met Orin, he drew Beauty for me and explained to me that the dog was happy, because she was back in North Carolina. About a year after that, Orin was again going to draw Beauty — but suddenly, halfway through, he stopped. He crossed out the picture and nearby started another one: "I want you to see the new swings they put in the playground," he told me, and then he set to work showing me them. I decided to ask him whether he ever saw any dogs in the playground. "Yes, sometimes. But it's not a place for a dog — unless it's a real smart one who knows how to stay clear of the cars." That was all he had to say for a while. He went back to his picture. He had a few finishing touches to do. There was the fence that was being built. There was a street lamp. Finally he handed me the picture and said, "Now, that's it."

I was looking at what he had done, and he was looking at a drawing I did — it was a bargain we had made: if he drew, so did I. Suddenly I heard Orin's words: "I'm just as glad." I didn't know what he meant, and I told him so. He let me know exactly what he meant: "My grandmother told me that Beauty went back to North Carolina. That's silly. She died. But it's just as well she did die. She wouldn't even like our new playground if she was here now. Daddy says a dog born in the city doesn't know any better. But Beauty knew better." And he, does he know better? Would he like to go back there, back to Old Dock — that is, if his parents decided to move back? And if they were undecided, what would he advise them? What is his preference? One wonders about such matters, and stumbles forth with a question like, "Orrie, if you had to choose where you and your whole family would live, where would it be?"

Not for a second does he hesitate: "I like to go visit my grand-parents in North Carolina, but like my daddy says, we can't live there anymore. The white people there don't like us, and they want us to get out fast. Here you never see much of the white people. Daddy says they're no better up here than in Old Dock, but they'll leave you alone more, so long as you leave them alone. They don't want any part of us. I'm glad we're up here. Daddy said if we'd have stayed there we might all be dead. No work means no money and no money means no food — and then you die. Daddy says the rich white people have been feeding a lot of the black people, even if they don't work because of the ma-chines that do the harvesting. I asked him what would happen when the rich white people died. Would all the black people die right after them? My daddy said the rich white people will never die, but he thinks that soon there won't be any black people left in the county down there."

At eight what does Orin see ahead of him? His father was in the Army, and Orin thinks he might also like a few years in the military, "only maybe the Marines." His father learned "about electronics" in the Army, and Orin thinks that kind of work intriguing. In fact, the more one talks to Orin and his parents, the more one sees that the first departure for Orin's father was ordered by the government, and only upon the soldier's return did the second and final departure from North Carolina take place. Orin has heard his father and mother talk about the sequence, and so understands rather a lot about various so-cial and economic and educational issues: "If my daddy hadn't gone into the Army, he thinks he might still be back home, and we'd all be in bad trouble. He doesn't have the kind of job he wants, but he's on the way to getting one. He works in a factory; they make electrical equipment in it. They've promised that they'll keep on teaching him, and that he can be moved up and be over some of the other men one of these days. We're not rich, but we're not poor. My mother says that she'd like to get us out of here, into a better street. I like it here, but she says there are nicer places to live. The white people don't like us moving out to where they live, though; so we may be here for a long time. My dad says that even if he'd gone to school a long time and had the best job he could ever want, we might not be able to live where we'd like. My mother says she can buy us the food we need, and the clothes; and that's more than she ever dreamed she'd be able to do when she was little. She says she likes to look at some of those dollar bills she has and smile and smile. She says when she was my age she'd never seen a dollar bill, never mind anything bigger. Dad gives her five ten-dollar bills every week to spend, and they have more; they're saving some money and they put away some for the rent. Dad says if he could only get some land he could build a house himself. But you can't just go and get land. Back in North Carolina there was plenty of land. The white people would have let us stay on theirs. They even offered to help fix up the place where my dad was born. But they didn't have money to give us, and that's why we're here. My dad says that when you weigh everything, we come out best right where we are — even if the building we live in is falling apart and you pay a fortune to stay in it."

Orin's dad has fixed up his apartment and has even thought of doing repairs in the halls. The trouble is, how far does one go? He laughs when he asks a question like that. He'd like to fix up the entire block, the whole neighborhood, all of the streets his people walk and play on and call theirs. He'd like to help turn what others call a "ghetto" into what he calls "a nice-looking place, where nice-looking houses are." He knows those nice places, those nice houses, exist all over; and he feels that with his job and future he ought to be able to live in such a place, such a house. A day doesn't go by when he fails to mention that hope. The television set brings up close the neighborhood he has in mind, and within seconds he has made his remark. The boy Orin describes what happens: "I can tell when my dad is going to speak. He'll see a program and there's a nice house, and I look over and I see him just staring with all his might. Then he says something. He says he wishes we could live there, in a place like that. He says we could, if we weren't black. My mother always interrupts and says we should be thankful that he's got a good job, and it'll be an even better one soon. She says we've come a long way to be where we are, and you can't have everything. She says when I grow up I'll have it better, and I might even go all the way through school, and I could be high up in a company like the one my dad works for. Dad laughs at that. He says you can't be so sure. True, you have to be thankful for what you have. But who knows if we'll keep on being so lucky? And then he'll say he still wishes we lived in some nice house somewhere."

Once again Orin told me where that somewhere might be: "It would be way out where there are trees and plenty of grass and there would only be black people there — no white people. We would have our own police, and if anyone tried to come and bother us, they'd protect us." He had no more to say on that particular subject. I asked him a question or two, hoping he might go on; but no, at the present time he is content to let the matter drop right there. But not far from his home I have stood with him and other children like him and listened to men talking, men saying more emphatically what Orin said — that the black man has to build his own place, his own home, and by God defend it with drawn guns. Orin's father thinks such talk about guns is "foolish." At eight Orin is not so sure.

The Wanderers

They had almost invariably lived in one place all their lives when they came to the city. They were born where they once lived, and their parents or grandparents or great-grandparents had most likely died there and no place else: a cabin, a shack, a place, or a "spot" on the bossman's property. Suddenly they are no more there. Suddenly they live in a building in a city, far away from "home." And suddenly they are adrift. They do not settle into one building and stay there and stay there, as their sharecropper ancestors did. They move from one address to another. First there is this building, where a brother or sister or cousin or uncle or aunt is staying. Then there is the next building, and the next one, and the next one. Sometimes the buildings are relatively nearby; but a family can just as well hop, skip, and jump all over a city, within the confines of the so-called ghetto, of course. A family can even move from city to city: from Boston to Hartford, or from Harlem to Bedford-Stuyvesant to Newark.

Such families elude creditors, city officials, and, significantly, statisticians who like to know who lives where. Such families can be called all sorts of things: unstable, shiftless, rootless, disorganized. Such families are, to other families in the ghetto, a source of apprehension and surprise and speculation and sadness. For a long time I hesitated to talk about "such families." How did I know that these were in fact a recognizable "group" of people whose "adjustment" to northern cities has been one of continual movement — to the point that within a year or so, four or five apartments are obtained, lived in, then hastily abandoned for the next one. What distinguishes "such families" from other people, who find one building too expensive, a second impossibly infested with rats or cockroaches, a third with no heat, a fourth so full of addicts that "the children stumble all over them, and I'm afraid one day a little child of mine will come here with a needle mark in his arm"?

Over the years I have simply learned to expect that from time to time a family will be pointed out to me as "movers," as people whom

others quickly come to know as "moving, moving, always moving."
Nor is there any one "explanation" for such behavior. Some people
may be fleeing the police, others have no money to pay bills and find a
midnight departure the best way to wipe clean the slate, still others
have less obvious reasons, reasons of the mind and heart, I suppose it
can be said. For example, they can't "take" the city but can't go back
South, either — and so they hope that a new building, a different
street, will perhaps "quiet their nerves down," give them a feeling, at
long last, of the "peace" they openly say they are seeking. Words like
crime, poverty, indebtedness begin to explain something; but again,
for certain people there are ghosts that are to be fled, shadows that
make inexplicable visits, noises that unaccountably are taken to mean
danger, mean the presence of the devil himself.

Here is a woman talking about her own sister: "I can't figure out
what has happened to her and her husband. They're always in trouble.
He's had a few jobs, but in one they closed up the store, and then he
was let off the second time because business is slow and they didn't
even want a man around to clean up. My sister said she had no money,
so I told her to stay with us while she goes on welfare, and then her
husband could come and be with her except for when the welfare lady
shows up. But he wouldn't listen to me, nor she; I couldn't talk with
her, my own sister. They kept on telling us that they were going home,
and they'd rather be in Georgia than up here. Now, can you imagine
that! I reminded them that they shot and killed our brother because he
stared back at a white man and wouldn't apologize to him for saying
something bad under his breath. I reminded them of *everything*. But
they said we had to be real fools to stay in this city. Then, the next
thing I knew they left the building where they'd been a year, and I
thought they'd gone back to Georgia. I was beside myself. One afternoon I'd seen my sister and the next afternoon I went over there and
there was no answer and I thought something was funny, but I went
back to my place and my sewing, and I went over again around suppertime and still there was no answer. Well, I was scared. I scratched my
head and tried to figure out what could have happened. Then I guess I
must have leaned on the door, because it opened — and it was empty.
They never did have much furniture in there. But what there was, it
was all gone. I ran back so fast to my place that I fell. What's the matter, a kid asked me? I wish I knew, I told her. I got upstairs and I told
my husband and he said we should go to the police. But he thought
better, and he decided no, that was the wrong thing to do. We figured
that they must have gone someplace, and we'd hear from them after

they'd settled into their new place. I went over and asked their neighbors, and they said it must have been in the middle of the night that my sister moved, because they don't recall hearing any special noise in the hallway during the day.

"Well, about a week went by and all of a sudden my sister showed up one morning. I pinched myself, and I went over and kissed her, and I wanted to pinch her, too. I asked what happened, and she said nothing, and then I started crying, and then she did. She told me everything. She said they didn't have any money and he didn't know where he could get a job, her husband, and they owed on the rent, three months of it, and the landlord was threatening to kick them out, and they owed other people, and they didn't know what to do. Her husband has a friend who has a car and he said he could come and get them out in an hour, and they could go someplace else, and that way they wouldn't owe anyone a penny anymore, because when you're gone, you're gone, and who's going to go find you out? So, the friend came, and they went to a building way away from here, about two or three miles, my sister figured. Her husband's friend knew a building where they could stay for nothing, because it was closed up by the city, and no one was supposed to be there, but some people were there anyway."

She has a lot more to tell. That move was a mere beginning. The husband got another job, and they moved nearer to their original apartment. He lost the job and they moved to another abandoned building. They have a cousin in a city about one hundred miles away. He thought there was a better chance for both families in his city, so the already wandering family went there. The woman quoted above refused to budge, even though her husband was barely holding on to a low-paying job, and their bills were also mounting. Within six months the sister was back and installed in an apartment not far from the very first one she had upon arrival from Georgia. And there have been three other abrupt moves since that last one just mentioned.

If anyone asks why, why all those moves, there are always thoroughly "objective" reasons. Yet the woman who has not moved once can say this about all those expeditions of her sister's family, which includes three children below the age of five: "I think it's gone to their head, living up here. I've decided that they *should* go back to Georgia, but I know they can't go. They won't go. They'd die down there. They'd starve to death. They might be killed by the sheriff for coming back. He told both of us to 'get the hell out.' But up here, my poor little sister, I don't see how she'll survive this going here and going there.

As soon as they run into any trouble they up and go. They don't seem able to sit back and try to get used to a place, and they can't find help for themselves from their neighbors. My sister was always shy, but now she can't talk to anyone but her husband and her children and me. She says that she'll go to a store and she starts trembling and she can't speak. She's afraid the police will come in and arrest her. She's afraid she'll just start crying and then fall down in a faint. And her husband, when any trouble comes he just stares, and then he starts whispering to her: let's go, let's go, let's move. She says she's glad when they *do* go. She says she feels each time that they may hit upon luck and start a new life and have none of the old trouble. But of course it doesn't take her long to see that it's the same old life, and nothing more."

I realize that the sister and the brother-in-law sound "disturbed," perhaps a little too suspicious, a little too fearful. No doubt they feel sad and bitter also. No doubt they are subject to confusion and spells of disoriented apathy. And I could escalate the language here; I could call them all sorts of psychiatric names. However, I have only met them intermittently; never have they sat down with me and talked about their innermost worries and fears. Their talk has had to do with their struggle for work and a place to stay and a means of obtaining the money they need for themselves and their young children. And it is significant that a sister looks upon them as "different," as badly "upset," as "in trouble" — by which she means psychological trouble. Yet, I have come to know dozens of families whose mode of survival in the city is not unlike the kind just described by this black woman, and I am assured by the people I work with that thousands of families live similarly nomadic and clandestine and hunted and wayward lives. I hesitate to draw upon my clinical vocabulary to describe such people. Their actions obtain from others a degree of social acceptance. There is almost a tradition among some people in our ghettos that under certain circumstances one "picks up and leaves."

Put differently, when a black family comes North and runs into trouble, the husband and wife soon learn that there are indeed dozens of "outs." There is a building here, another one there; they are buildings condemned, abandoned, half torn down, but, most important, rent free. And in those buildings live others — families also on the run, also up against it, also not able to deal with the world as "the rest of people" do. Such troubled, hunted, apprehensive people leave quickly, under cover of night, with a minimum of belongings (not that there is usually an alternative), leave for a friend's house or for a different city, where a relative lives, and perhaps then scatter — a boy here, a girl there, the father in one section of the city and the mother, perhaps with an infant child, way across town. I am trying to emphasize that such practices are not as surprising and shocking as they may seem to outsiders. I am *not* saying that the woman I have already quoted was undismayed at the turn of events in her sister's life. Nor am I denying the obvious torment such nomadic individuals carry around inside themselves, and manage to express by constant change. However, those of us who want to comprehend this way of living must face something that can almost be described as a social custom, an established, widespread manner of attempting to diminish personal fears and anxieties on the one hand and severe social stresses on the other — and surely what is "personal" and what is "social" ought to be categorically distinguished.

I did eventually get to know two such wandering families, and in a sense my efforts to follow them from place to place reminded me of my work among migrant farm workers. I had to attach myself to the children and their parents, and I had to ask them to promise me that when they moved, I would be allowed to follow. They would leave word for me through a mutual friend, however suddenly they decided to depart. And so, we kept up our meetings over three years of time, and I had a chance to get some sense of why it is and how it is that particular families persist in so extraordinarily mobile a life — in the very shadow of slums which can appear to be so solid and impenetrable and unyielding, so static, so unchanging, so *there*. Perhaps I should claim only that I learned what such people *say* about their urban moves, their inner-city travels. For the fact is, a man like James Hudson and his wife Josie Hudson ask the same questions I do, and maybe those questions tell as much as any explanations I can come up with.

"I get to wondering," says Mr. Hudson. Then he stops; indeed, he stops for such a long time that I think to myself that he is confused or troubled. Is he in a daze, in a "state" of some kind? Is he suffering from some injury to his head, some degree of "retardation," some "psychotic process"? Then he brings me up short, and perhaps reveals to me how impatient and how slyly, brazenly condescending one like me can get when he is faced with a person who is different from himself and simply being himself: "I wonder why I brought myself and my wife and my little ones all the way up here. I wonder if there will ever be an end to it, the jobs that don't last. I got a job; they said I should come there at seven in the morning and I'd be washing dishes in the back of the restaurant. They said that in between I could mop the floor. They said I looked strong, and they would pay me fifty-five dollars a week, and I'd go up to sixty if I could prove myself. They said I'd have to come in every day but one, and they'd tell me which day to stay home, and each week it would be different, because they're open all the time. I said good, and I started working. I had to leave way before sunlight to be there at seven. The place is all the way on the other side of the city. If I miss one bus, I'm late. But I never did miss the bus. The bus kept coming late; it was the fault of the bus company. The man who runs the place, he told me I was late three times in a row and I was through, fired. I'd been there on time for two weeks. I was trying to do the best I could. I near cried. I said to him *please*. He said to get out. I tried to tell him about the bus, and he said that everyone always has an excuse, and he wasn't one to be fooled by me or anyone else. Then I came home and I did cry, and so did Josie. My boy asked me why, and I told him not to ask, and soon enough he'd find out.

"I didn't know what to do. I got to wondering. I had the rent to pay, and it's eighty dollars a month, and that's so much money. They collect it, too. They're after you the first day of the month. A man comes and says you've got to pay. If you tell him you can't get heat from the pipes and the rats are all over, he tells you to go find some other place. Well, that's why we moved the first time. I couldn't have two people talk like that to me, not on the same day: the man in the eating place and then the man who works for the landlord, collects his rent. I told the people who live next door that I wish I had a one-way bus ticket back to Echo, Alabama; it's bad there, but it's bad here, and maybe worse if you're me and you grew up down there and not up here. But Josie said she wouldn't go back, even if she had to die up here. She said she missed being down there, but we had nothing down there, *nothing,* and if he hadn't given us some food, the bossman, we would have starved to death every winter.

"I guess you only starve to death once. I guess somehow we made it from year to year back South. But Josie said that the bossman could take a disliking to us, because he has bad digestion one day, and that would be the end of our eating, and we'd all perish. Yes sir, we'd perish, and that's the story. That's why we're here, up here. I had an uncle who said he'd never go North, no matter what. He left Echo a long time ago and went to Birmingham. He said it's better to be in the South, if you have to live in a city. Now he wishes he'd never left Echo. It's worse in Birmingham than here, though. It can't be *too* much worse, I guess. If I took off, my family could get some help from the city. In Birmingham they'd get a lot less than up here. I'm staying here.

Why should we move back there? We'll keep moving up here, if we have to, until I find a job that's going to last. You see, Josie has won, and I believe everything she says. We'll never go back, not with things as they are down there.

"I was telling you something. I know: I was telling you how we moved. We just did. I told the people down the hall I was thinking of going back South, and they said I was as crazy as I could be. I told them, just like I did you, about my uncle in Birmingham, and they said they could suggest something a lot better than going to Birmingham and that way I wouldn't end up in Alabama all over again. And the next thing I knew they were showing us a building where we'd be living more or less like we already were; only there'd be no rent, and no one would know where we were, so they couldn't come and collect on us. So when night came we just slipped out, real fast. It was the same when we left Echo and headed up North to Birmingham and then further up North until we came here, and I guess we can't be any further North than Roxbury.

"We have tried going to other cities. We tried Springfield, Massachusetts, because someone knew people there, and they said you might get a job if you looked real hard. We tried Hartford. I knew enough not to go to Harlem — no sir! I got a job in Springfield, waxing floors. The only thing was, the place closed down. All of a sudden they said we were fired, each one of us. They gave me the cash and said good-bye. I went to three or four eating places and tried to sign up, but they had all they needed; one man said, 'There are plenty of you guys around, and we only need one at a time.' Then he said, 'They come and go, so try again in a few weeks.' I told Josie I was going to ask him if he'd feed us while we waited, but I couldn't say what was on my mind. It's not easy to find yourself work, no sir. Anyway, we left Springfield and came back to Boston. There was nothing else to do. We knew a place to stay — with people, and they were the ones who told us to try Hartford. So, we did. And that was real bad there. I stood in some lines and each time they stopped picking men just a little ahead of me. It was worse on Josie than me. She'd be hoping; then I'd come back and I wouldn't have to say a word, because she could tell on my face what happened. It was good we knew people, and they helped us out. People will do that, you know. It was the same way back in Echo, Alabama."

Eventually he got and held on to a job. He works in a warehouse. He packs boxes of greeting cards and takes what he has done to the post office. He likes his work and likes the money — though it is no great sum in view of the rent he must pay and the price of food and clothing. Still, he has been able to stop wandering, to settle down and stay put. He can now talk about that year of movement, constant movement, as if it were thoroughly a thing of the past. He is a steady worker, and he will stay right where he is and never leave if he can help it. Indeed, one senses again and again the man's strong wish to avoid the unstable, migrant life he lived for those months before he was fortunate enough to find his present job. Yet, one also senses in him a conviction that nothing is to be taken for granted, that anything might happen — which means at some point in the future he and his family may again have to disappear from view: "You lose your job, and they still want your money, and you don't have it, and they say they're going to throw you out of your place anyway, and you owe at the store, and they won't sell to you, so you go away. You find a place where there's no one always trying to collect, collect. When you're living like that — I guess it's hiding — you meet some good people. I never knew that there could be so many real good, nice people. They'll go and take some food from a store, and they'll divide what they got with you. They'll go and take shoes for your kid, not only theirs. I've never done that; I just couldn't get myself to. I'm sure if I had to, I would. I was lucky to know people who would, and then I got myself this job. But if a man sees his kids needing food, is it wrong to steal? I don't believe those store people starve. They drive up in their big cars, I notice. I don't know how we would have eaten if a few of the guys over in those buildings didn't go and get the food — take it. And when I hear they're going to condemn some building, it always makes me feel good, because I say to myself: some people will go and find a rest for themselves in that building, and it won't be the best place in the world, but they'll be able to come there and stay there for a while. Of course, you always hope they'll get a good break and find a place to remain in, and not leave. It's a bad life, always packing up and unpacking, don't you think?"

I told him yes. I also told him how impressed I was with the informal network of friends and relatives and comrades-in-distress he had found all over New England. He said yes, it is true that black men will help other black men, that people in trouble will help other people in trouble. Then he added another "don't you think" — a characteristic flourish of his meant to make his point stronger rather than get a reaction from me. I told him yes again; but I found myself wondering, too, how the kind of "helping" spirit he described might become more widely present in those "better" communities he unquestionably envies and no doubt wishes his children would one day be able to join.

My Room

At least there I have a little home, you know. I have my room. I just stay there. I don't have to do anything else but be in that room. I hate the street. I used to be on the street. I'd stand there and wait. I'd give the man a look. If he looked like he had money and he was shy a little, I'd even follow him a block or so. I'd never do that again. I can't explain to myself how I lasted. I'd rather stand around, but I wanted to run. Once I did. I started running and I didn't stop until I was out of breath. Then I went home. But I didn't have any money the next day, and I said: sister, is it better to eat or to starve? Is it better to have good clothes or be dressed in rags? Do you want to be a washwoman like your mother? She had no hands left after her bosses got through with her. She had no money, either. I put away money. I go to the savings bank every week, and I put in the cash there, and they give me the book with the numbers in it. I have it with me, and it reminds me when I look at it that I'm somebody — because money talks.

I feel sorry for my sisters. There are three of them, and they're all poor as can be. I give them some money every once in a while. They come to me and they say, Jeanne, you've got to help me out. I say, sure I will. Blood is blood. Then they kiss me. They say I'm wonderful. My sister Ann told me once I was a gift from Heaven. Me! I say yes, Ann. I told her I hoped she was right, but I wasn't sure. But *she* was.

I try to live a quiet life. I don't drink. I never have liked the taste of liquor. I smoke, but I could stop if I wanted. It's a habit. My favorite way to spend a day is go looking for a new dress. I love my clothes. I love to buy shoes. I love to buy a pocketbook that goes with a pair of shoes. I have my shoes in the closet, and they're all there when I open it up. I look at them and say, it's a good life if you have the money to own what you like. I counted up fifteen pair. Maybe the day will come when I have a hundred pair. And I could have a different pocketbook to go with each of the shoes.

It used to be I'd take a pocketbook. I'd go into a store and lift one. But I've stopped. Why should you steal if you can afford to pay? I could get caught. I don't want to go to jail. What can you do in jail but sit there? You can't dress up. They push you around. You don't have a penny to your name. It's as bad as the grave, jail is.

My mother is dead. I never saw much of my father. He left when I was little. I remember some men, all right, but none of them was my father. I'm twenty-four. I hope I'll live longer than my mother. She dropped dead right before my eyes. What do you think of that! I was standing in the kitchen and doing the cooking for her because she said she had a headache, a real bad one. I said, Momma, sit down. She did, but the headache didn't go away, so I said, Momma go lie down. She got up to lie down and she fell down, and I heard a big sigh come from her, and her eyes went moving all over the place, and that was the end. She was gone. I didn't know, not then. I ran and got the woman across the hall. She ran and got a policeman, and he came and he was the one who said she wasn't unconscious, she was dead. You know what he asked me, the first thing? Was I fighting with her? He checked her over to see if I cut her up, and he checked me over, and he looked all through the apartment. That's the police for you.

I could tell you a lot about the police. I know them. I know more about the police than anyone does. They collect, you know. They take a cut of everything. The lady I work for, they get money from her. My friend Bill, he always pays the police. Then they get on their high horse and play minister. They preach to you with one hand and take your money with the other. That's the way it is. I know my way around. I know how you go and do your business and how you get in trouble. The secret is money. If you have money, you're doing fine. If you don't, brother, you're in trouble, no matter if you did anything or not, no matter if you're in the right or in the wrong. When I was a little kid my mother would shout at us to be good, be good. A lot of good it does you to be good. And our minister, he'd be shouting at my mother and all the mothers, to make sure we were God-fearing. That's all he ever told us: fear God, fear Him plenty, or you'll sure enough be in a lot of trouble. And he said we should never do anything bad, and we should always obey the Commandments. Well, you know what I found out about him? It took me until I was twenty years old to do it, but I did. I saw him. I saw where he goes. He's no different than me. He's full of talk about God, but he's a man, and he's the same kind of animal he used to tell us we never, never should be. And my poor old momma, she'd listen to him and nod her head and say yes, yes, and believe every word that came out of him, the minister.

I never knew what I wanted to be when I grew up. A teacher once asked me what I'd be doing later, and I felt like sticking my tongue out

at her, but I didn't. I had on the tip of my tongue the words: I won't
end up being like you, sister. I didn't do that, though — tell her off. I
used to dream that maybe one day I'd be rich and I'd have a big house
and servants and all the clothes and shoes I wanted, closets full of
them. I'd even picture the maid being white, and I'd be good to her,
real good. I'd give her days off, and I'd slip her money, and I'd buy her
things, a convertible and some nice clothes. No white woman ever did
that for my mother, or my grandmother. White people are stingy. The
white men that come here to my room, I'll tell you I've had to pull a
knife on some of them. They tell me they don't have the money, after
they've already agreed to pay it. They want to give less, and I tell them
they won't get out of the building alive if they don't give me the money,
all of it we agreed was the price. Then I reach for my knife. And then
every time they come up with the money, every time. What does that
show you about white men?

Look, the black man is no angel, either. I'm not standing up for
black men. I know them. I know them better than anyone else in the
world. *Do* I know them! They're lazy, a lot of them are. It's their wives
and their sisters and their mothers and their grandmothers and their
aunts, it's the black women who keep the men going. Our men are no
good. They've never been any good. But no men are good; that's what
I believe. I know them all. I see them, and I can tell you: they're all out
for themselves and no one else. A man, he's full of himself. He wants
to be satisfied, but he doesn't really care about a woman. They'll say
they do, some of them. But I give them a look-over, and I can tell. One
guy, he was white, and he was crazy; he talked all the time, and he said
he wanted to make me happy, that's all he wanted. I told him, finally,
go ahead, go and see what he could do. Well, he couldn't do a thing,
not a goddam thing. I said to him — since he was talking so much, I
thought I'd join in and talk — that he had the white skin and his hair
was so yellow and his eyes were so blue, so why in Hell couldn't he do
anything he wanted to do. I wasn't kidding. They think they're so wonderful. They're little babies, spoiled children. They don't know what's
going on in the world. They don't know so much that it would take a
year for me to tell what they don't know.

I feel sorry for them, though, the white men. They're scared, and
they're no good, most of them. They'll tell you how excited they get,
on account of my skin being black, and then they don't get excited at
all. It's all talk, a lot of talk. That's the white people: talk and more talk,
until they put you to sleep with their talk. The black men don't talk
much, but some of them are as mean as can be. They're like a German

police dog: their teeth and their noises. I heard a white woman say
that black people are like animals; I was in a shoe store and she didn't
know I was behind her, and I heard her say it to her friend. I had to
think to myself: maybe she's right. Those niggers, I call them, that
come knocking on my door, I hate to let them into the room. But a
man's money is a man's money; and they don't stay too long. I know
how to get rid of them. I give them a look and they leave. I can stare
them down. I can get them so worried that they will go fast, rather
than keep on trying to bother me. Sometimes I will say: mister, you
have had it, and it's time to go — hear! They leave.

I'd like to leave myself one day — and never come back. I'm saving up. I'm putting some cash away, every week I am. I don't put everything away. I have to live. I like to look nice. And I like to have flowers
near me. They're enough to get me through a night. I go into town and
I buy them, then I bring them back to the room. They're all I have to
look at. I need them so bad! In between customers I look at the flowers — roses, red roses — and I picture where they were before someone cut them. They were in a field, don't you know. There must have
been a fence, so the rosebush could lean on it. Sometimes in my mind
I see the sun shining on the roses, and sometimes it's cloudy, and it's
raining, and there's a wind blowing. I take the roses home with me in
the morning and I give them to the kids on the street the next day.

They think I'm a millionaire, the little kids do. They ask me how
I make the money to buy so many flowers, and I tell them I know a
man who sells them, and he gives them to me, gives them away. They
believe me. They say they wished they knew someone, too. I tell them
they will, they will, later on. They're so good, the little kids. It's when
they get to be eight or nine that they turn sour. Oh, they get awful
right before your eyes, and I'm not their mother. I'm glad I'll never be
a mother. I don't want to be. I don't want the heartache. I'd die as soon
as I started seeing my children going bad. What's the use of bringing
them into the world and trying to do everything you can for them?
What's the use if all your work goes down the drain? There's no kid on
my block who's not going to be bad. I just know it. Even the people
who *look* to be good, they're bad underneath. I see them. Every night I
see them. I should know. If anyone knows, it's me. They wear their
nice suits. They have a tie on, a lot of them. They're dressed as if
they're going to church. A lot of the black men, I'll bet they get all
dressed up like that for only two things: the church and me. It's like I
always say: it's a funny world, mister. Sometimes the man, especially if
he's white, starts trying to tell me a story. He wants me to know all

about his life, and I keep on telling him to forget it, just forget it. To get them out, I say to them: it's a funny world, mister, it sure is, and they usually leave right away. If they don't, I go to the door and hold it open. I can't stand the sight of them for longer than I have to.

When I'm not looking at my roses, I close my eyes. I don't like the light on. I like to keep my eyes closed. Then I can picture things. I can go anyplace I want, in my mind. You don't have to travel to get away. You can shut your eyes and use your head! My mother used to tell me when I was real little that the best thing to do when you have a few minutes is to dream, and then the time goes faster. Just close your eyes, she'd tell me, and think of someplace real good and nice. When I've got a lot saved up, five thousand dollars, I'll stop working and go around the world. I'll visit California and Mexico and Africa and Trinidad, those are my favorite places to go visit. I've heard about them.

The only time I talk with a man is if he mentions a foreign country. Then I'll sit down on the bed and ask him all about it. I'll stay a long time with them if they'll tell me something interesting about a place like Mexico. It's when they want to talk about *themselves* that I can't stand them. Why should I listen? They give you a big headache. They don't know there are other people in the world besides them. If you remind them, they look as if you just gave them a spanking, and you were wrong, because they're the nicest one who ever lived. Well, I don't let them get me feeling sorry for them. Their pockets are full of money, aren't they? I should be feeling sorry for the people they got the money from. In this world, if you can make a lot of money, that means someone has lost a lot of money so you can have it. That's my philosophy. Nothing comes easy in this world, nothing.

Let the ministers and teachers preach and tell you to be good; meanwhile, the landlord is squeezing you hard, and so is the grocery man, and so is everyone. I always watch the store people at work in the stores near where I live. They try to get everything they can from their customers. The same goes with the fancy stores downtown. They're just smoother. They put on airs. They try to be so polite with you. White people seem to think that if they can just talk pretty words to each other, and have a big smile, then they can stick the knife in and no one will notice. I hate our black men and their loud mouths; but I hate worse the whispers and the sweet smiles of those white men. And that goes for the women, too — the white women. Black women are mostly too much in pain to be bad; that's what I believe. They're aching and aching all through their lives, they are. I'll be going to my room or coming back home, it doesn't matter which, and I'll see a black woman, a mother, walking down the street, and I'll feel like crying. I admit it. I have to fight back the tears, and sometimes I don't win. I think of my mother. I think of her mother. I think of an old aunt of mine who's still alive, and she's so tired and she thinks she's going to Heaven, so she's so happy. I go visit her once a week. I bring her roses. I bring her money. I give her enough to keep her happy. She thanks me, and she tells me that God is smiling on her through me. I asked her once how she ever got *that* idea. She said she was in church and doing her praying — she prays hard, real hard — and she was answered by the Lord, and He told her yes, I was coming as a favor to Him. *Then* you know what? She went to that minister and told him what she'd heard. She told him I was coming for Him, so as to do His bidding. And he's the one I've seen — he's the minister I mentioned. They almost sent him up to my room by mistake. It's a good thing I told them no in time. But he saw me anyway. And to think: that's what my aunt told him. I asked her what he said back to her. She said he didn't say anything. She said he just nodded his head, and she knew how busy he is, because everybody likes to come and have a word with him, so she just moved away. I told her I was sorry I wasn't there with her. I told her that one of these days I'd like to go there and talk to him myself, that wonderful minister she keeps on mentioning to me.

Yes, I'm sure it would be good for that "man of God" to see my old aunt and me together. He's so convinced he can separate everyone into the saved and the damned, and the good and the bad, that I'd like for him to separate my aunt from me — and himself from me. That's what I'd like. And he could separate some of his deacons from me, too; while he's at it. They own buildings, but they go and visit the building my room is in. The other day a man told me how he liked to travel a lot. I thought to myself that he sure does. People just don't stay at home, like they should. Then they go and call the people they visit bad names. But names don't hurt me. Not while I have a big leather pocketbook and cash inside it and my bankbook. I figure that way I'm as honest as anyone around, as honest as any businessman, as honest as those politicians. You start being a crook and a bum when you don't have money and your clothes are no good. That's what I've learned in my life, and I'm glad I've learned it, let me tell you.

Black Fathers

We have heard so much, and properly so, about the difficulty that black men have obtaining work, hence becoming good providers for their families. Needless to say, a man who cannot bring home money gets discouraged and bitter. Nor can we forget that, until recently, in many cities and counties families became eligible for welfare only when the father was dead or disabled or no longer at home. In thousands of instances, men have left their families for just that purpose. They sneak away when the welfare worker is expected, and return in-between her visits. Or go away and stay away. In Roxbury and Harlem and the Hough section of Cleveland and Chicago's West Side I have over and over again encountered families headed by mothers; and often the various children have different fathers. I have met up also, however, with sturdy, tough, outspoken black fathers, men of astonishing independence and vitality and resourcefulness, for all the burdens they bear, the doubts they have, the fears they fight every day. Somehow, those fathers are less apparent to the outsider than fatherless families, however careful and curious the observer may be. For one thing, they are working, or trying to find work, or off in some corner talking with a friend or two about how hard it is to get a good job and keep it. For another, they frequently are quiet, unassuming, quick to retreat when the children burst forth with remarks or the wife speaks out. But that is not to say a modest and reticent black man (worker, husband, father) needs to be labeled "weak" or "submissive" or "passive" or "dominated" by some "matriarch," some black virago who need only raise her eyebrow to have her way.

During the years that have gone into the work I am trying to report upon here, no individuals have confounded me so persistently as the "black fathers" I have met and spoken with and listened to and for long stretches of time, I believe, sorely misunderstood. Not that I understand black women all that clearly, but I have often found that black mothers can somehow find words for a passionate voice, a cry of mixed despair and hope. I once asked a black mother in Roxbury where, just where, she learned how to give forth so, assert herself, make her wishes and fears so vividly, compellingly known. She had a little trouble putting into words that particular answer, but soon one was forthcoming: "I'm not talking for myself. I'm speaking for Joseph and Sally and Harry and Stevie and Benjie and Mary. I'm speaking for

them, and they push on me until I get the words out, that's what I believe. Because if ever I have trouble saying something, I look at my
boys and girls and the words come to my mouth."

One has to ask how black fathers can talk the way so many of
them do, with their own kind of cleverness, guile, humor, sarcasm, exuberance, and often, in spite of everything, a certain guarded confidence. One such man is Ray Phillips, a cabdriver, a black cabdriver. He
says that, calls himself "a black cabdriver." He still remembers when
many white people wouldn't take a cab driven by a black man, and
when blacks took cabs far less frequently than they do today, and
when white cabdrivers bumped him with their cabs and swore at him,
and when the police were constantly asking him to identify himself
and show cause why he should not be called a liar, a crook, a pre-
tender, a public nuisance or menace. Now, at forty-eight, he is a father,
a grandfather, a fairly good wage earner and, most important, he emphasizes, a husband: "I love my children, but most of all I love my
wife. We've been married for thirty years. Yes, that's right: I was eighteen and so was she when we got married. The minister told us no, because our parents told us no, but then I got my dad to say yes, and
pretty soon we were in the church there, swearing we'd stand by each
other until the end of our lives. Thank God we *did* get married; a year
or so later I was in the Army, the Second World War. My son was born
when I was out in California and then I was sent to the Pacific and I
didn't see him until he was five, I think it was. I'm getting hazy about
all that. He's got two of his own children now. After the war we had a
girl, then another girl, and then I said the time has come to stop. I'm
no millionaire, and three kids is enough. Sometimes I think: I grew up
and there were six of us, and maybe it would have been better with
more children. But I'm glad we stayed at three. My wife would look a
lot older than she does if she'd have had three or four more kids
pulling on her and taking it out of her. A man doesn't know what his
wife goes through all day. All he knows is his own troubles. He forgets
what it means to bring up kids — and I mean *bring* them up, not drag
them up.

"I'll be driving a customer someplace in the city, and if he's a nice,
friendly guy he'll start telling me about all his troubles. He'll tell me
his business is good, but it could be better, then he'll tell me some
other worry he has. Then I'll try to change the subject. I ask if he's
married. Yes, he says. Children? Yes, he says. How's the wife find *her*
work, I say. Oh, fine, fine — that's what they'll say, unless they come at
you with: *what* work? A lot of husbands just don't know what their

wives do all day. I'm the kind of husband who does. I've tried to pitch in and help my wife every way I can. I've tried to be around my kids, too. I was a real father to them, not a man they called father. And I'm a good grandfather, I believe, a very good one. That means I spoil them the way someone should!"

The more he talks the more one forgets that he is anything but an American taxi driver who doesn't make a huge amount of money, who hustles (he puts it) for what he does make, who happens to know just about every street, or so it seems, in Cleveland, Ohio, and who happens also to be close to his wife, devoted to his children, and anxious to be a grandfather about nine or ten times, he says. He never finished high school. He was born in eastern North Carolina, but was brought to Cleveland at age three. His parents were not members of the "black bourgeoisie." His father left North Carolina because he told a white man to go to Hell and was promptly arrested. He escaped from jail, though Ray Phillips was told that the escape was permitted by a deputy sheriff who disliked the man who was insulted and who caused the black man's arrest. How, then, did Ray Phillips manage to do so well, become a successful cabdriver, be so good a husband and father?

Perhaps he has a right to ask me why I have to ask such a question, though God knows even more insulting and patronizing questions are asked these days. However, because Mr. Phillips has a radio in his car and hears a lot of "talk shows" and "call-in" programs, and because he also reads the papers regularly, and because he watches television documentaries, he is prepared for the likes of such questions: "Everyone is looking at the black man today and saying: who is he, and what's on his mind? I know. I flip from one station to another, or I'll meet a real honest fare and he'll say to me: come on, level with me and tell me what you think of all our race problems. Well, I do tell them, even if he's a big, fat white businessman. I say: mister, I'm a citizen of this country, just like you. I was over in the Pacific, fighting to beat Japan and win. I was under MacArthur. I've seen other parts of the world, and I'm glad to be living right here. If the white people would only get off our backs and leave us alone, we'd be the best citizens this country has, and everyone could relax and stop being so damn nervous. That's what I tell people. Sometimes they listen, and sometimes they don't. I can tell. If they want to hear more, I've got through to them. If they shut up and don't say another word, I know I haven't; and I know I'll be getting a real small tip — if I get *any* tip."

The more he talks the more he decides to call himself a teacher. He is only being half humorous. He sees a lot of people in the course of a day, a week, year; and he tries to get the word across, spell out a certain message that he believes, that he considers just and sensible, and that he wants others to hear. He doesn't have the same words for each person. He realizes that many hear nothing, that many are hopeless causes, are unapproachable. He is an observant and intuitive man, a person who can sense what other people are like, can quietly and without a lot of trial-and-error exchanges decide who might and who might not want to hear some of his ideas. And as he gives expression to those ideas, he rather often hears in the casual atmosphere of his cab much the same kind of question I more formally have had in mind over the years, and indeed have just set down above: how is it that this man has become — well, "just like anyone else"? That is the way he finds a lot of white men putting it — tactfully, they believe. He does not get excited or angry with them. He smiles and brings out into the open what they "really" want to say, and thus helps them along, shows them how categorical and indiscriminate they have been: "I say, look: you've met me. Think of the thousands and thousands of guys you haven't met who would talk to you like me, if they had the chance. I happen to like to talk. I've been a cabdriver all these years, and it's an education, and you get to feel comfortable with people, so I can speak up. But I'm just one of about twenty million Negroes. Call me black, call me colored, call me a Negro. I don't care, so long as you see that I'm Ray Phillips — you hear? — and I have my wife and my kids and my grandchildren and I watch the same television shows everyone else does, and when the President said we've got to protect the country from Hitler and the emperor of Japan, he got me to go fight along with everyone else.

"They begin to think by then — the customers who have some sense in them to start with, I guess. You're right, you're right they'll say. Then I look at them through my mirror and I can tell by the look on their face that they *still* think I'm someone special. He's different, their face says. He's a real smart one, they seem to be saying. That's why I can't let it drop there. I have to work. I even have to knock myself a few pegs down. I have to convince them that for every me, there's another me — a million other me's. I have to tell them that my dad was a guy on the run, a 'fugitive from justice,' they called him. I have to let them know that I was born poor and if I'm not poor now, I'm sure a lot poorer than *they* are. Otherwise I keep hearing: you're exceptional, you're an unusual guy. When you hear that you know what that means: he thinks everyone else black is no goddam good. I'm supposed to feel big when someone says to me I'm the greatest person he's met, but I could take the guy to the building we live in and the one next door, and all up and down the street, and there would be men just like me: they're not rich; they work hard and they get by, they *just* get by, and sometimes they *don't,* I'll tell you, with prices going up, up; but most of all, they're like other people in this country. I mean, they try to do the best they can by their wives and their kids, and if they can only come home and be with them, they're willing to work hard, plenty hard, and be glad to have the work. If they don't find work, then that's another story. But so long as a man can get a job, and if he's honest and he's not crazy because of drugs or liquor, then he'll be fine, and if his wife is a good woman, he'll stand by her, I believe, and he'll stand by his children."

Of course, there are exceptions, he reminds himself and me. White fathers betray their children, and so do black fathers. Individual men can be fickle, unreliable, devious, awful examples to their children and harsh and callous men to their wives. Moreover, he repeatedly takes pains to remind me that it is "another story" when a man has no job, or has one but then is laid off and cannot find another one, or finds one but gets little pay and works under demeaning circumstances — all of which causes in husbands and fathers a kind of fearfulness and resentment which wives and children do indeed come to experience. I suppose, in sum, Ray Phillips has this to say: There are plenty of aimless, wandering dazed and ruined black men, even as in America white men by the thousands are alcoholics or philanderers or crooks or loafers or clock-watchers or slowpokes or sleepyheads. Yet, there are among black America's people many millions of men who are faithful husbands, devoted fathers, and hard workers. By and large those men are not as well off as their white counterparts, do not have access to jobs many whites can either take for granted or obtain with relative ease if they so desire. Yet, despite such "facts of life," black men in street after street of our northern cities struggle to find what work they can, and struggle also to maintain intact homes in which children grow up with a sense of continuity and stability in their lives.

None of what I have just written is extraordinary or surprising, but I fear it is quite necessary to bring before the reader a man like Ray Phillips, a man who heads a black family, a workingman who is very much his children's father. No doubt about it, many children (and many white children) don't have fathers like Ray Phillips, but many, many do — and in this last third of the twentieth century, when one slogan after another is fastened upon over twenty million American citizens, it is well to keep a taxi driver in mind as we go rushing on to the next moment of panic and despair.

Who Speaks for Us?

There is in what are called "ghettos" a kind of rage that I fear few of us know about, either because we really don't want to know, or because we simply have no way of hearing the voices of those who feel the rage. I have in mind the thousands and thousands of black people who do not feel themselves to be pathetic and degraded and sick and all eaten up by what is called "social pathology." Nor are many such enraged men and women members of the "black bourgeoisie," unless that phrase is to be ridiculously amplified to include all working people, all men and women who labor hard and are glad to do so and are proud they have done so all their lives. The very word "ghetto," used as it is by white and some black people offends such workers: they feel they live in the *city*, like everyone else, and they do not want their streets talked about as if they are some awful blight upon mankind. Nor do they want their lives characterized in special and near hysterical ways. Nor do they like shifting fads that go from *Negro* to *black* to *Afro-American* — as if whatever a few outspoken men decide is "right" has to be obeyed by everyone, lest he be called an Uncle Tom or racist.

As the reader will notice, many of the people I know, of both races, shift at random from the word "black" to the words "colored" or "Negro"; and the shifts are not always fraught with ideological significance of the kind that is often called "deep-rooted" or "psychological." Sometimes we use words unselfconsciously; they have been used by our parents, and by us over the years, and it requires time and effort to make a shift, to take up new words and feel comfortable with them. Nor does everyone have the inclination to be so concerned with words, phrases, and slogans. Again and again I am reminded in the course of my work that some of the "issues" and "conflicts" and "arguments" that trouble me simply don't vex and hound the people who speak in this book. Why is it that so many of us, who are so concerned about the "true feelings" of others, be they black or red or brown or Appalachian-white or whatever, simply cannot accept on face value some of the things we hear? And why is it so hard for us to believe that sometimes people don't say things or believe things simply because they *don't* — and not because they have some "problem" or are "defensive" about this or "reacting" against that? I have in mind the unwillingness of some black people to demonstrate self-disgust, or to ask white self-proclaimed "sympathizers" for their outrage and pity, or to use some of the fashionable terms such as "cultural disadvantage" that one hears among certain white middle-class citizens? Must it be that those blacks are demonstrating their "pride" in order to conceal their "inner" hurt? Must it be that those blacks are going through some "period of self-assertion," some "stage in their development" as a race or a people?

I believe that thousands and thousands of "ordinary" people feel things in their bones and speak out of their hearts, and often say what to them almost needs no saying, so obvious and concrete and clear-cut are some matters. I cannot claim to have included here every opinion I have come across, every sentiment and allegiance I have heard. I have done my best to indicate the *range* of ideas and activities one like me sees in certain sections of certain cities. I cannot write about what I have not witnessed or heard. I cannot claim access to the words of those who have their own good and wise reasons to stay clear of white middle-class people, or white observers, or white social scientists, or white psychiatrists.

God knows, when I read some of the things I do in various journals, not all of them professional, I wonder what an observer from another planet, even if he had a sense of humor and the longest historical perspective possible, would make of the pompous, muddled language, the self-serving postures, and, worst of all, the narrow-minded arrogance that passes itself off as "science" or "research." If poor people, of whatever race, have been "exploited" by those who make caricatures out of their lives and want only to rip their words and habits out of context so as to make this point or prove that theory, then many readers have been exploited in another way: their hunger for information (one hopes nothing more sinister is at work) has caused them to take in, it seems, almost anything which bears one or another "authoritative" stamp and say to themselves: interesting, interesting. Who is around to shake us and shout: come off it, man? Where are the men ready to demand that we stop being smug, self-centered "benefactors" who secretly or even openly and unashamedly love blood and gore, who enjoy the sight and smell of trouble, who crave objects to pity, groups of people to support faddishly, causes to embrace, then abandon? I fear I have to admit that I have been so shaken and shouted at; and if I cannot accept all the rage I've heard sent in my direction — because what I have seen with my own eyes and come to believe I will hold to and speak about — I can most definitely share much of what I have heard.

I suppose we all worry that our own very special point of view doesn't get understood; but often the loudest complainers are the wordiest and fussiest people. Still, the four words that make up the question *Who speaks for us?* can often be voiced by someone who is simply and directly annoyed and, yes, even wryly amused. Here, for instance, is what I heard in 1969 from a tall, somewhat heavyset worker; that is what he is, and that is what he calls himself and what he wants to make quite sure I call him: "I get sick when I read the papers or the magazines. Mind you, I don't have time to read a lot, but I do my share, and I tell my wife that my stomach turns as a result. I say to myself: who do they think they are, writing all that about us? And on television, those documentaries and talk shows, I don't recognize me or my family or my neighbors; I don't recognize so much that I have to scratch myself and ask whether it *is* my people they're talking about, right?

"I'm thirty-seven years old. I am called a black man. The fact is, mister, I work in a factory, and I have a wife and three children and we live in an apartment. I used to think there were a lot of people like me, thousands and thousands of them. I used to think I'm a worker, and there are a lot of workers like me at the plant, and some happen to be Negroes and some happen to be white, but we'd all been there for years and we knew each other, and when you come right down to it, we're not that different. We spend our days the same way, and when we talk about what we do in the evening and on weekends, it comes out sounding the same then, too. But these days I'm supposed to believe I'm an oddball, a rare bird, you know. I'm supposed to believe I live in a *ghetto,* and all around me are these *diseased* people, and they are *crazy,* and they are *addicts,* and they are *prostitutes,* and they set *fires,* and they think they're in the worst, most terrible situation anyone could be in, and they need everything, man, everything — because the *racial tragedy* has gone to their heads, and they are in a bad way, a real bad way.

"Well, I'll clue you in to something. I'm not rich, and I'm not special. I'm not a doctor or a lawyer. I didn't even finish high school. My mother and father came up here from Virginia — Dinwiddie, Virginia. They didn't have a cent to their name, and no degree either, or rich relative waiting for them. And times weren't so good. It was in the late twenties and early thirties. I was born under Roosevelt, Franklin Delano Roosevelt, and I can recall my father saying it sure was rough trying to make a living. But he got by. He was a janitor. He was a watchman at night. He scraped up enough for us all to live and eat and have a roof over our heads. And when I was sixteen I'd been working three or four years myself, and then I got the job I have now. It's hard work; I have to keep on my toes. But I get a salary that means we all can eat and have clothes to wear and a car and a phone and television and a toaster and a waffler — Hell, what *more* can a guy want! I help make those appliances, so it's only right that I should own them; but I pay, like everyone else.

"They call this a ghetto. Can you beat that? The building is old, and whites used to live in it; but it's a sound building, and we like it here, and we don't want to live with white people, and we're happy with our own people, and that doesn't mean we're Afro-Americans or for black power or any of that. Hell, I work with white people, and I'd like my kids to go to school with them. But I live where I do, and I'm happy living here, and there aren't rats eating up my kids or cockroaches crawling on them. My kids eat good food, and brother, we're not rich, either. I'm just a plain guy — and there are thousands like me right in this section of the city. Why don't people talk about someone like me? Why don't they call me an American citizen, not a black man or Negro or all the other words? I'm not out to tear the society apart. I get up every day and go to work and come home and I'm not on heroin, and I'm not a two-bit drunk, and my kids aren't experimenting with drugs and on the way to being pimps and prostitutes. You know, it's insulting the way people try to create an image of the Negro as some pathetic creature who can't for the life of him take care of himself and has nothing he can really believe in and be proud of. It's bad enough we get that treatment from those white 'bleeders' who just love to find us in bad shape — the worse shape the better they like it. They'll walk by ten blocks of buildings where we live in order to find one that's bad, really bad, so they can start crying and can say: oh, those poor, poor people, they are so low, so down and out. Then they'll go home to their big suburban homes and start crying for us, and they'll take up a collection for us and feel as sorry as they possibly can for us.

"But what about the Negroes who talk like that? It's not just the white ones who bother us, it's our own people who put on a show about how *bad* it is for anyone who isn't white. Their eyes fill up with tears, and they start wringing their hands and say, 'Let's feel sorry for ourselves, brothers; let's feel as sorry for ourselves as we can, because we are the worst-off people you can ever catch sight of, that's for sure.' I have to laugh when I see some white guy and some black guy appear on a talk show, and they tell you that where those Negroes live, it's bad, real bad. After I hear them long enough I start wondering to myself: where are all those bodies lying on the street, and where are all the ruins, and where is the garbage up to your neck, and where are the mice and rats running down your back?"

From a black nurse I hear similar thoughts. She lived for three decades in Harlem, then moved up to Boston's Roxbury section because her brother lives there and she had lost her husband and wanted to be near him and another brother. She has two sons, one a teacher and one an engineer. No doubt about it, they are what some call "middle class"; but there is more to their lives than those words were ever meant to suggest, and even if she is a reasonably well-off person as things go for her people, she is still able to look around and talk: "I sometimes think I'm reading science fiction when I pick up magazines or the papers. When I tell people, white people, I lived in Harlem, their pupils dilate. They give me a look that is supposed to say, I guess: oh, how awful for you; it must have been Hell, a living Hell. People *have* said that to me, word for word. They've practically wanted to give me a medal for bravery and heroism. Then they decide: she's a nurse; she must have been special — you know, the black middle class! Life is easier for them, but it's still no picnic! I've heard that line, too. I've heard black people speak the line and watch their white audience squirm more and more with guilt. It's all very well to laugh and say it won't hurt to make whites squirm; it won't hurt to make them bleed and cough up some cash; it won't hurt to 'mau-mau' them, scare them by telling them we're mad, we're fed up — so unless they do this and they do that we'll explode, we'll burn up the cities, we'll go on a rampage, we'll turn the country over to the Russians by starting a civil war or something. But after a while I think we make fools of ourselves, and the worst of it is we actually start losing our heads and believing all that talk.

"We forget. We forget the ideas people get of us, white people, and the ideas so many of us have about ourselves. Why do my own people, who should know better, parrot the line that goes like this: they are so destroyed and so unable to help themselves that we've got to do something drastic — tear down their ghettos and rehabilitate them. I'm so sick of that word *rehabilitate*. When I was studying to be a nurse, rehabilitation meant getting someone who had been sick back on his feet again and to work and all the rest. Now I hear that Negroes are ruined people, and the ghetto is full of pathology, and only 'massive rehabilitation' will work. And do you know what they want to do? These are our *friends,* so-called, I'm talking about! They want to take our little children and bring them up away from those 'ignorant' mothers of theirs. They want to tear down Harlem and Roxbury. They want to break the 'cycle of poverty,' which I read is 'transmitted from generation to generation.' Why don't more people talk about changing the American business system, which is also transmitted from generation to generation?

"We are called criminals and diseased and addicted, and we are told that the thing to do is build low-cost housing and get some more medical help to the addicts and alcoholics. All the while I see my people leaving their apartments to work, work, work. They teach their children to be good. They save what they can. They go to church and pray as hard as a person can pray. They buy pictures for their walls and records to dance by and listen to and enjoy. They keep the rooms they have as clean as can be, and the hallways, too. They sweep the stairs and make sure the garbage stays in the barrels and gets hauled off on time each week. And no one comes and notices. No one comes and learns that they aren't rich, and they aren't businessmen or professional men, but they aren't exactly poor, either — not the kind of poor who make people weep and want to send off a basket of food. They have jobs and they try hard and they *want* to try hard. They do not want to have their houses and their streets torn down by some white planner — or black planner — who says: Harlem, it's all rats and roaches and dazed people and terrible, terrible tenements.

"I wish, oh how I wish, more people in this world would go and look around a little before they started sounding off. I mean, I know street after street in Harlem and here in Roxbury where black people live exactly like other people do in white neighborhoods — none of which anyone is suggesting need to be razed to the ground, or called 'disaster areas,' or be given 'massive rehabilitation' because the people are so out of it, so deprived and without a culture of any value. I'd like someday to tell people about how *deprived* my childhood was and how *poor* my parents' culture was! I'd like to tell how my father and my mother read from the Bible, and how they read from the history books, and how as children they had taught themselves to read and write, and how they taught us to go and do the same, go and get an education and get ahead. I know, I *do* know, how awful life can be for a black man or a black woman — in the South or up here, too. But it's been pretty awful for all groups, if you go back far enough and see what they faced. I think in America the Negro race had probably had to live with more hardship than any other group of people. But we've come through it, and we're not destroyed by the experience, I don't believe. We are a vital, alive, swinging race.

"Some say it's genocide that America has tried to commit on black people, but if that's been the wish, we've beaten them: we're over twenty million and growing fast. Is that a people facing genocide? And look at those white college kids. They are so 'deprived' culturally that they more and more try to talk like us, dress like us, play our music, dance like us. My God, I hear from my sons that there's no limit to the white man's interest in our habits and our values and our way of doing things! Doesn't that show that we've been busy doing more than feeling sorry for ourselves and complaining that we have nothing? Doesn't that show that we're more than sick, sick, sick? Was it 'sick' of us to learn how to survive and keep our thinking straight and learn how to whistle a good tune and pray plenty and smile and smile and swing, rather than sit and cry all day long? I don't want to hear my mother turned into a huge, smothering dictator and my father into some drunken, doped-up philanderer. Who has come and talked to me, or to my brothers, or to thousands and thousands of others like me in Roxbury and Harlem and any other city? Why don't they know about our good side, our tough side, our damn smart side, our clever-as-can-be side?

"I am a nurse. I've worked in hospitals. I know all the bad side of my people. But is there any group without a bad streak in it? I get sicker by the year of all this propaganda, that's what it is. We're made out to be so bad and so awful and so shiftless that for every white person who cries for us and says give them everything they need, another gets disgusted and says it's hopeless, they're just a bunch of hungry, ignorant animals. We don't need the weepers and we don't need the bigots. We need friends who know that most of us may have our faults, like everyone does, but we're trying, we're working, we're sending our children to school, we're going to church — and you know, we're getting something out of life, too, not just sitting around with our heads in our hands on a drug high. And let any bulldozer come near this street; we'd laugh at the sight of it, and the man driving it would laugh, too. There's not a stockbroker or lawyer on this street, just working people; but we take care of our buildings and our yards like people do everywhere. It's bad on some streets, very bad; but it's bad on plenty of streets where white people live. What I object to is the stories that have all of us at the end of our rope. I don't like our streets thought of as if they were covered with garbage and littered with syringes. The country needs to be more discriminating, that's right! People have got to realize that wholesale words like *ghetto, cultural deprivation, black rage, black despair* — that they can give a completely false impression about twenty million American citizens who are more like their fellow citizens than those fellow citizens may want to believe. But maybe whites have been persuaded to believe what they believe by — of all people! — those who keep on claiming how tolerant they are and progressive and pro-Negro and pro-black and who say how awful it is for us in such a way that everyone begins to believe *we* are awful."

At times I catch myself saying that she and the man I have quoted are lucky; I have with my own eyes for years seen the misery and harshness and meanness and sadness and bitterness of life in Harlem or Roxbury. Yet I think the truth is that those two individuals know full well how far from unique they are, how much they share with others, and how devious and misinformed and sometimes even deluded some of their so-called advocates are. I believe they are onto something about many of us who consider ourselves sensitive and compassionate and interested in serious, thoroughgoing "structural" changes in America's social, political, and economic system. Too often we confuse our aims with those of the people whose "condition" we find so "low" or pitiable. Meanwhile, to our embarrassment, if we even care to look around, some of those people, not a handful by any means but a substantial number, say and do things that announce their lives are not as we say they surely must be, or their hopes are not what we say they ought to be.

To keep our faith in our destiny as the wise ones who know how to distinguish the merely apparent from the real, we ingeniously come up with a series of words: they have all been *brainwashed,* or they have been *co-opted,* or they have been *duped* and *bought out by the power structure.* Poor souls, they want gadgets, while *we* know (we've had them all our lives!) how irrelevant and even obscene those machines and trinkets and diversions can be. And *we* will help *them* — tell them, educate or reeducate them, make them want what we want, make them live the better lives they should have, make them over into people worthy of our dedicated efforts, people whose grim, tragic presence justifies every bit of our rage and despair. Are not we the ones who *know* how all these things work, know how the poor live and how the rich live off them? Are not we the ones who *know* about ghettos and about the black bourgeoisie? As for a man like that factory worker or a woman like that nurse, and as for so many other black (or red or brown or white) people whose vision of their lives and their country doesn't quite fit into ours — we can only shrug our shoulders and remark once again upon the way the oppressed are masked and beaten and fooled. But we will eventually show them, organize them, lead them — until, we always add, they are "ready" to take over for themselves. And if that factory worker has the impression he has been quite "ready" for decades, and indeed has been taking quite good care of himself, as have others like him, then we can only sigh, or these days, grit our teeth and dig in for the long haul.

White Visitors

Law and Order: That's All There Is

He is Irish and he wants everyone to know it. He isn't in the least worried that they may already know and that they may feel he is beating a dead horse, saying the obvious, indulging in a lot of silly, trite, ethnic boasting that these days one would not think was done so openly and loudly — especially by a policeman who works in a completely black neighborhood, and a "tough one at that." For eight years he has worked there, which means for most of his career as a policeman. He is thirty-two and has been on the force for ten years. Edward Herlihy is the name we can appropriately give to him, and with sincerity and conviction he will talk about the Herlihys and Ireland and poverty and the need any society has for a certain degree of conformity, for an ethic of obedience and patriotic loyalty. Eventually he will also make it clear that some of his forceful display of self-confidence, his constant effort to identify himself with a mixture of ironic self-deprecation and fierce pride as "an Irish cop," reflects the fear he has that, quite literally, the United States of America is "going to pieces" and that he and his family are by no means oppressors or agents of oppressors, but rather victims of whatever it is he fears is coming into being — a new kind of country, a new kind of world.

One day, four years after I first met Mr. Herlihy, I sat on his back porch with him. While we both looked at his lovely and nicely tended garden, enjoying the late spring sun and the fresh, brisk air and the peace and quiet of the scene, interrupted only by a noisy, bothersome fly or two, and while we had a cup of coffee and everything seemed reasonably relaxed and casual, he proceeded in an almost offhand way to say things that later, as they are read and considered and analyzed, seem almost apocalyptic in nature. I say all this, in a rather long prelude before drawing upon the man's remarks, because I have had trouble at times reconciling Mr. Herlihy's actual words with his genial, kindly, open manner and also with the circumstances that have surrounded some of our talks — circumstances, if he will forgive the allusion, something like those supposedly to be found in a small English country garden.

"What is to be done?" I am asked, as if I were Lenin himself. (But Mr. Herlihy certainly would not like *that* allusion.) He is tall, thin, blondish, blue-eyed, ruddy. His hands are delicate. His fingers could be those of a pianist. He looks calm always, and I have seen him calm under provocations that would unsettle almost anyone. He never twitches or taps his feet or blinks excessively or stutters or raises his voice too much or gets intense and taut; and only rarely does he become emotional and outraged. He smiles rather often. Occasionally he laughs. He likes to talk, but he does so deliberately, in no rush. He has stories to tell, and he will tell them. At first he can appear to be guarded and tight-lipped, but that is not a fair description. He needs time to know someone, he says; but when he does — well, he *does*. When he asked, "What is to be done?" he was as concerned and forthright and candid a seeker as one could wish. He was referring to the rising unrest he sees about him every day, and he was asking how we as a nation can solve some of the problems he has no doubt most of us have every wish, if not hope, we can somehow learn to deal with successfully: "I was born here, and so was my dad. But my grandfather came here from Ireland, and he used to tell me that compared to Ireland and England and Europe we don't have *any* problems here. I knew he was exaggerating; after all, my father had a terrible time making a living during the depression. He was almost forty when he got married, and my grandfather was over forty when he got married. They both were Irish! I'm the first American in the family. When I got married at thirty, my dad said, 'You're only a boy.' He was only half kidding!

"I wonder sometimes what my old grandfather would think of this country now. I don't believe he ever saw a Negro in his life. How could he have seen them? He came here and settled with a brother who came here before him. They lived among their own people, and they never wanted to see anyone else. They hated the English. *Those* were the people I was taught to hate, not the Negroes. I try to tell some of the black kids that, when they tell me I'm picking on them, but it's no use. They're determined to have everyone hate them, everyone be against them. I've never seen so many bigots in my life; I mean it. A bigot is a person who misjudges another person. Right? Well, that's what the Negroes are like. You come to them and try to be of some help, and they're ready to stab you in the back as their worst enemy. So help me; I mean it. I've given up trying to make sense out of it all. There's no point. You can drive yourself crazy. I take each day by itself, and I try to be a good cop. That's what I am. I'm an Irish cop. I'll say this: I used to think I was a *policeman,* an American citizen who happened to get a job trying to protect other citizens from thieves and crooks and murderers and bullies and liars and all the rest. Lately I hear I'm a pig, and good Lord, a lot of other terrible things. I have to scratch myself and say: is that you, Ed Herlihy? Well, it *is* me: I'm the same, but some of our people, they're going wild, and that's why I say to you: what is to be done?

"One thing you can do is keep your respect for yourself. I'm not a pig or a fascist and all the other things I hear myself called. I've decided I *am* a cop, not a policeman anymore, but a cop. I mean, I *have* to be tough. It's tough where I work, and the people there respect toughness. No, I don't think they respect *me.* They just know that I'm not going to be pushed around — absolutely not. I drive my car through the streets and when they see me, they smile, a lot of the kids. A lot of people won't believe that, especially the loudmouthed white radicals. They want all the Negroes to be fighting with the police. They believe that's all I do, insult people and beat them up. How much more of those lies do we have to hear on television? I am sick and tired of those television programs and those news stories — it's always some screaming white kook or a way-out black militant who is quoted and gets his speech across. What about the hundreds of black people —

they are kids and they are parents and they are old people — who call me Officer Herlihy, that's right. No one asks those people to speak on television. No one runs stories on them in the papers or the magazines. No one asks to talk with me, either — or with the other police who work near the colored people.

"Look, there are some mean, vicious hoodlums around, out to tear down our entire society. To those people I'm a dangerous cop. I've got to be. If I show them I'm the least bit soft, they'll kill me. I've already been fired at four times this year, and it's only May. Once they really meant it; I'd have been dead if I hadn't bent down suddenly. And you know why I bent? All of a sudden I thought I saw a penny. A penny! I figured I might as well pick it up, though it's worthless these days. They didn't know what I was debating in my mind, all those snipers who saw me standing there. Just as they fired, I started to bend, and they missed. I ran for cover. I was taken in by a black man; he owns a little market. You should have heard *him* talk. He called his own people more names than I'd ever dare. I used his phone and we moved in. Did we! We never caught them, though. We arrested a few kids, and we're trying to track the snipers down. But it's slow work. You can't arrest everyone in a building. All you can do is watch people and question them and hope you can trace them to some crazy group.

"It's not really any worse now than it was a few years ago. There *are* these way-out crazy groups, but most of the Negroes are just like they always were. I've been with them for a long time, you know. I'm no college professor, but I think I understand them; they're not bad people, and if they'd be given a chance, they'd be all right. If you ask me, they're being used by those white radical kids. *They* are the enemy. They get their hands on a few Negro kids and teach them the tricks of the agitator, and they hope we'll have a revolution in our cities. But you notice we really don't have one. Sure, we've had riots, but that's not what these agitators are after. They want the black people, the Negroes in the city, to be their stooges; they want to use them to destroy the country. They practically say as much. I have to listen to all that stuff, one hour after another. I stand there and feel like vomiting. They're a bad, bad lot, I'll tell you."

He does indeed tell me. He drinks his coffee and goes on to say, in one breath, that the country is fine, just fine, and in another, that he wonders how much longer we can stave off an utter and complete disaster, in which violence begets violence, and the nation is no longer a stable and strong democracy. And the more he talks, the less hopeful he sounds: "Look, I'm basically optimistic. I have a nice life. I have a good wife and three good kids. I don't make enough to keep up with this inflation, but I'm not starving either. I could sit back and say everything is just wonderful. I've been saving money, and I could dream of the day we all take a trip back to Ireland. Instead, I watch the news when I'm home, and I feel my muscles tense up. I even get a headache. We're miles here from a ghetto, but it's not far enough. The reason is those poor black people, they're sitting ducks for the anarchists and Communists, the crazy, goddam student agitators. I've never felt about Negroes the way I do about these student types. They're a clever and spiteful bunch. The ordinary colored man isn't. He's not so damn brainy, and all filled up with those slogans. He wants a better deal, and I don't begrudge him one, no sir. But he's going to end up getting a worse deal, that's the tragedy. The people of this country, the majority of us, aren't going to put up with violence and anarchy. Without laws you have nothing; I mean, if people don't obey the law, it's not a society any more. We're back in the jungle. You need law and order. Law and order: that's all there is. Without law and order there is chaos and revolution. This is a rich country, and we're strong, and countries all over the world are depending on us. Should we allow a few crazy kids and some kooks in the ghetto to take over our whole nation?

"Some of those television documentary people ought to stop searching all over the place for the craziest, wildest black militants and go and talk to the ordinary man in the street in the colored sections, and they ought to stop broadcasting one speech after another that the college radicals make. I'm sick of hearing about those kids: they're all 'alienated,' you hear. The mayor's office or the governor's office — who knows? — tried to get one of those college people, a sociologist or something, to give us lectures on 'the ghetto mentality,' something like that, and 'the college student and his alienation.' We thought they were kidding. The guy talked and talked. Jesus Christ! He needed three or four shots of rye and a long chaser of beer. The chief said no to any more of that. *He* wants to select the speakers, and why in Hell shouldn't he? They're freaks, some of those intellectuals! Take one look at them and you can tell. They try to talk plain and simple, but they can't do it. They talk down to us. Hell, we know more about 'the society' than they'll ever know!

"But that's the crowd this country has been listening to — for too long. There's just so much patience that the ordinary man has, though. You'll see people expressing themselves more and more. If the Negroes start killing white people, and the college kids dynamite our buildings more and more, you'll see the government step in. If it doesn't, we'll have to vote in a new government. What else can we do? Is this country supposed to turn itself over, lock, stock, and barrel, to its own enemies?"

I find the contrast between those words and his description of his working day rather striking. When he talks about what he does and how he goes about his tour of duty, he speaks with far less rhetoric and terror. Perhaps he can only later, and in the context of a broader, more philosophical discussion, express what he may well actually feel from minute to minute during the course of his car rides through certain streets, or his walks from block to block. Not that he gets half as excited as his words suggest he does, even those strong words just cited. But the calm, matter-of-fact side of his personality most certainly comes across when he talks about "the job, the job."

I have many times, for instance, asked him to tell me what he does; tell me about the small and insignificant things as much as the more dramatic and memorable moments he has experienced — which he naturally enough wants to recount and in a way put to rest within himself. "Well," he begins with a smile, because he is half amused at the remark that is about to follow, "every moment for me is a big moment. It's like you see it on the movies, being a policeman." He knows that I have driven around with him and spent a number of days seeing firsthand what he and others like him do, but he wants to say what I have just quoted for a very shrewd reason: "The public has no idea how hard it is to go down those streets. I think up until very recently a lot of people were inclined to think of us as loafers: we gave people speeding tickets; we were there when there was a parade — that kind of thing. That's why when I saw a movie that showed how dangerous it can be, I thought: good, maybe we'll get some gratitude from people. And I do believe a lot of people are at last beginning to wake up. They're beginning to understand that without the police we'd be back in the Stone Age, and let me tell you, we'd be back there a lot faster than most people would ever believe.

"Every day I have to show myself on every single street I'm in charge of. It's important. They all have to see me. They have to see the car, and they have to see *me*. A lot of people wait for me. They need a ride to the hospital, or they're afraid of someone, or they have a message: a guy is going to beat another guy up, or there's no heat in a building and the people are in real trouble, or there's a hustler or a pimp or a pusher, a dealer who's *bothering* people. Look, I can't go cleaning up a neighborhood like that. All I can do is keep things under control. I can try to make sure little kids aren't being pushed around and scared half out of their minds by the addicts and prostitutes. I can prevent people from killing each other when they're all drugged up and liquored up. I can push the landlords to obey the law and warn the gangs that they can go so far and no further. And every day I have to help a sick lady out, or rescue a kid whose arm is caught on barbed wire, or something like that. And the poor shopkeepers, they want protection! They would have me around all day if they could. The holdups in that neighborhood, the robbery and stealing and breaking and entering — it's unbelievable. We don't report half of it. We couldn't. People wouldn't believe it, and there isn't much we can do about it all, anyway. Like I say, we can try to keep things under control — but only within limits.

"I'm on the scene early, before eight. Walter and I drive around for a few minutes. He's more excitable than I am. He really bleeds for some of the people — and he really would like to throw a lot of the agitators in jail. I keep on telling him: there's just so much we can do. We look at the stores to see if any have been broken into. We check out the hydrants and the street lights. We go see a few of our friends. If I were to tell you that a good policeman knows everything, *everything* that is going on in his district, you would laugh. How can a guy like me keep track of the Negroes in their ghetto? I heard someone on one of those talk shows say that the blacks hate the cops; they hate us and they don't trust us worth a damn, that's what he kept on saying. I had to laugh. I wouldn't be worth anything; I'd be totally useless, if it weren't for some black people. And I don't mean the store owners. I'm talking about young kids and their parents, too — just plain people, like anyone else; people who want to have as much law and order as it's possible for them to have. They know they can't live the way they'd like to. They know they've got to put up with gangs and violence and stealing and drugs and all that, to some extent at least. They want our help, though. They know that if we don't come around and round up a few people and demonstrate that we're ready to take on any really crazy types, then they've all had it, the thousands and thousands of people who live in all those tenement houses.

"Hell, the people in the ghetto are at the mercy of every two-bit thug and gangster around. And when you have poor people like they are, the colored people, and a lot of them just up here from some little town in the South where they lived — I believe it — like animals, then you've got to protect them. And that's exactly what the police of this city do. I could get a thousand signatures of gratitude for all I've done and Walter has done. He's gruff and he doesn't smile much, but he's rescued people from fires and caught kids and made them return what they'd taken — from old ladies and mothers whose husbands have left them, and from some poor kid who suddenly finds a big, tough hoodlum has grabbed a pair of skates his father worked for and saved for and finally bought for him. Why don't the bleeding-heart types worry about that kid? Why don't they worry about the mother who tells us, 'Thank God you're here.' Why don't they worry about the hospitals that serve the poor? Every day some thief tries to break in and steal something and scare the nurses and doctors. If we weren't patrolling the streets nearby, I can tell you what: there wouldn't be a hospital. They'd strip the place bare. They'd strip every store and every building. And it's not the hungry who do it; it's the addicts, who need hundreds of dollars to buy their heroin.

"You know, I'm not the one to tell you what goes on over there in the ghetto. I'm not a crusader, so I'm not so damn sure of myself. I try to do my work, and I'm grateful if I have done just a little bit each day. Walter, my buddy, won't even talk at all. He's so fed up that he's thinking of leaving the force. He'll stay, but it's hard on a man who tries to protect people and be there when they cry for help — it's hard when all he gets from a lot of snotty people is insults and wisecracks and filthy names. Let some of those nice people out in the rich suburbs and the universities come with me for a few days, and see what I see and hear what I hear and do what I have to do. And let them come and talk to the people from my district — the *people,* not the propaganda types, the fast talkers. I give them one day, those nice, kind, sympathetic people who live in quiet streets where everyone has a hundred thousand dollars or so, and they all say hello to each other, and they've got about a hundred or two big, fat books in their houses and plenty of furniture and a car for each kid and summer houses and boats and all the rest. They all don't know what we're protecting *them* from, never mind the poor old colored lady or the young mother I had to rescue yesterday — from her own husband, who came and stole *their own son's bike,* and when she caught him, threw lye at her. That's right! He could have blinded her. He could have killed her. He's no good. He's a pimp and an addict. He's been up before the judge again and again. I'll tell you this: there isn't enough room for them in our jails, and if we doubled, *tripled* the jail space in this country there still wouldn't be enough room to hold all of them. I don't haul a lot of them in. The judge tries to keep a lot of them out on parole, or with their case pending. What else can we do? There aren't enough police, enough judges, enough probation officers — you name it, we don't have it.

"Yesterday I broke up four fights between women and their men. Don't ask me if they were married. I've given up even asking, or God help me, even caring. I told the priest a long time ago: I can't do everything! He smiled, and he told me we'd both have to pray for all of them. I thought for a moment he was kidding, but no, he had a serious look on his face. I couldn't hold my tongue. I said, 'Father Lynch, they don't want our prayers, they really don't. They don't even think they're doing anything bad, living as they do.' He said yes, he knew, but that was all the more reason we had to pray for them. Well, I have! I've been there in church and I've asked our Lord, please, to do something. I sometimes think He's the only one Who ever will, Who *could*. Walt and I agree on that. He's come out of some rough meetings, especially with the addicts when they're desperate for money and they're stealing left and right and they know we're onto them and we're going to take them in, which means they may easily lose the habit once they're in jail. They do smuggle drugs into prisons, I know that. He'll turn to me and say, 'Ed: all we can do is pray to God that a few of the kids will turn out OK.' And I say yes, that's right.

"Neither of us believe one single kid would have a chance, a chance to become a halfway decent person, if the police didn't keep the blocks under some control — at least compared to what the streets would be if we left there for good. And are we tempted! I leave my house in the morning and I ask myself: why should I get the salary I do — barely enough to pay our bills, and plenty of times not enough — in order to risk my life protecting a lot of people from their own kind, their very own 'brothers,' they call each other? And then the college kids call us 'pigs' and 'murderers' and 'oppressors.' Oh, my God, I'd like to lug a few of those kids out to my beat. I'd like them to see what I see and hear what I hear. I'd like them to talk with the people there and hear what they would say about the work I do. Those students, they sit in their campuses and talk, talk, talk. They're full of hate, and if you ask me, they're full of ignorance. They have their ideas, but they don't come out in the world and learn the facts. They insult a man like me, and meanwhile I'm carrying an old Negro lady down five flights of stairs and taking her to a hospital; and I'm protecting a Negro lady from her 'man,' who's drunk and on heroin, *both*; and I'm being rushed to a hospital myself, because I rescued two little Negro babies from a smoke-filled apartment, and they were unconscious and I was also near unconscious.

"Look, I'm not asking to be called a hero. To Hell with that! I'm a cop. I'm nothing more. I'm like thousands of cops all over the country.

I try to do my job the best I can. I make my mistakes. And I admit it, I have my prejudices. Everyone does. But I'll tell you this: I'm out there on the firing line; I'm taking it every day. Because those people got a raw deal a long time ago, they're in a sad way now, a lot of them, and it's left to a guy like me to keep them from killing one another and beating one another. I can't count the number of addicts I've found unconscious; I've had to rush them to a hospital to keep them from dying. Now I don't have the answer to all this. That's not my department. I try to do the best I can. But I don't like being called a pig, and I don't think it's fair to the Negroes themselves if those college kids listen only to the Negroes who attack the police. You know, it's the criminals who always attack us and call us names. Like I keep saying to you: what about the poor people in those buildings, hundreds and hundreds of people in my district alone, who call us up all the time for help and thank us for coming and giving them the help they needed and offer us food and all the rest? Who is telling the American people about that? What do our college students, the radicals among them, know about that? It sickens me, the way the truth gets buried. If I didn't know them better, I'd feel sorry not only for myself but for all the other cops in this country. But Hell, I haven't got time for that!"

A day spent with him would certainly convince his most skeptical listener, even perhaps his most outspoken opponent, that he is at least right on that last count. He is indeed a busy man. He has little free time for much of anything. He is overworked and underpaid. He constantly risks his life, and therefore he is quite naturally afraid. He feels as "rebuked and scorned" as the black people he spends his time with have always known themselves to be. Nor is it only those "college radicals" who trouble him and accuse him so sternly and vehemently. He himself has his misgivings — not so much about anything he personally does as about what he calls "the whole damn business," by which he means, in effect, the train of events that began centuries ago and now has reached a crisis, forcing him to take risks all the time, while the wrongs and injustices (again, centuries of them) persist. For the fact is that he strikes out at "college radicals" for *two* reasons: yes, he believes them to be mean and gratuitously insulting and arrogant and self-centered; but he also considers them privileged, protected, secure, on top of all sorts of ladders — which means, bluntly, that their fathers and grandfathers are so often the ones who own or owned plantations, or real estate, or banks and stores, or whatever. He puts it this way: "Who has to keep the whole country from becoming a big battleground? Who's protecting the wealthy suburbs? Who's keeping the Negroes from killing themselves and killing the white people? The white people who own all those tenement buildings, and the white people who are the lawyers to the landlords, and all the rest? No. It's a guy like me; and I'm not sitting here with stocks and bonds, and my kids off in fancy colleges deciding whether they want to be in the Peace Corps in Africa or maybe spend a year in Europe someplace."

From him I hear angry, brutish, callous remarks, some I don't care to set down here, about black people and college students; but from him I also hear a frustrated kind of indignation that I fear many of us simply do not know about, or do not care to recognize as additional evidence that this nation has a lot of political and economic business left to transact. Presumably, many who consider themselves to have "social consciences" refuse to appreciate one group of people at the expense of another, but prefer to see what is shared among an Edward Herlihy and the people he claims to help and the people he constantly offends. What *do* all of those people share? I believe Mr. Herlihy has himself come very close to an answer. They all, though in different ways, feel themselves now suffering from rather than profiting from all that has gone before them, suffering from the painful and grave part of America's history.

The Welfare Lady

Janet Howe, who is twenty-four and well-educated and articulate and anxious to help "her" families, could surely find other, less strenuous ways to earn the approximately ninety dollars a week she now makes as a welfare worker. Yet, Janet Howe would have it no other way; she likes the families she visits, and for good stretches of time they enjoy her visits. They offer her coffee — not to placate her, appease her, ingratiate themselves with her, but because they like to sit and talk with her; they know she comes to them wanting to do whatever she possibly can. Still, even for her, an obviously able and kind and generous and well-intentioned worker, some sharp and abrasive moments come up, moments in which she is subjected to abuse and bitter invective, moments which she tries hard to "understand" and not so much ignore as "survive." Those are the verbs she often uses as she talks about her work: understand and survive. She must understand the angers and frustrations of her "clients." She must understand the way they take out on her feelings "really" directed toward many other people.

She must understand, too, the fears and resentments, the continuing prickliness of the "political majority" (as she refers to them): the hard-working, also harassed or edgy or worried people who put in long and not always satisfying hours on the job and bring home just enough, just barely enough to pay those mounting bills and make ends meet. They feel threatened or enraged that others should get "for nothing" what they must obtain by working long and hard.

"It is a matter of envy," Miss Howe says. Nor is she being snobbish and coolly analytical when she makes a remark like that. She really does understand how so-called lower-middle-class families feel. She herself came from one of them; her father to this day is a carpenter who is up at six and out of the house at seven and not back home until six or seven in the evening. He works for himself. He is an entrepreneur of sorts who never made a fortune, but also never took a cent of money from anyone, even during the thirties. He detests "freeloaders." He believes that if a man *really* wants to work, *really* is an honest and reliable person, then he will find a job, and "for the life of him," keep it. And he believes in "education," in the importance of saving one's meager dollars so that a girl like Janet Howe can go to college, go to a school of social work, and finally come to be self-supporting. "I hear my father's voice sometimes," Janet Howe says, and then she talks about her own mixed response: "Of course I have a mind of my own, and when his words and philosophy come to me — often it's when I'm driving — I have my answers. I remind myself how fortunate he was. He is white. His family has been around here for a long, long time. He was not a dazed and confused and frightened man from the rural South, or a Puerto Rican never before in an American city and unable to speak English. He was not from a hollow in West Virginia. He went to school; he even graduated from high school. That may not mean a lot now, but it meant a lot forty or fifty years ago. And he has a skill, a 'trade,' as he calls it. He was trained by his uncle; he apprenticed with him, though they never were so formal that they called the work they did together an 'apprenticeship.'

"But I know I could never get away with it; I mean if I said all that to my dad and tried to explain to him what the families I see have gone through, in contrast to the experiences his family has had this past one hundred years — well, he would get angry and hit his fist on the table and say to me: look, where there's a will there's a way. And that's the point, for him that has always been true. Like everyone else in this world, his source of knowledge is his own experience. It would be easy for me, I suppose, to dismiss him, but I don't think it would be

fair — even though I realize that a lot of the welfare rules and proce-
dures, awful as they are, have come about in response to the feelings
that millions and millions of people like my father have. Does anyone
doubt that the majority of the country's people talk the way he does?"

She can go on only so long in that direction. Soon she feels the
tug of her clients, her families, her friends. Soon *their* voices are in her
mind, clamoring for recognition, craving a word, many words: "I don't
know how to talk with my dad, but I do believe from the very bottom
of my heart that he is blind to some terribly important facts. I wish
some of the people I go to see could sit in his living room and tell him
about their lives. I wish they could say: Mr. Howe, you don't know
what it has been like for a lot of people in America. You just don't. We
don't have anything against you personally. We can't expect you to go
and visit all over and take an interest in everyone else's problems. It's
just that we *do* have our problems, and believe us, they are *not* yours
and they aren't necessarily solved the way you've solved yours.

"I know that my father is never going to hear someone in the
ghetto talk like that to him. It takes time to explain what others have
to face, more time than anyone has got, I sometimes believe! I myself
sometimes have to be convinced! On a rough day, in each home, I hear
complaints and more complaints, and requests and more requests, and
threats — more than you would ever imagine. I'll be tired and all I can
do is say to myself: wait until you get home; a glass of sherry or a gin
and tonic, and you'll be feeling better. Instead, I'm in the last or next-
to-last apartment, and someone raises her voice at me and tells me I'm
not doing enough, I'm not providing enough money, and it's *my* fault,
mine, because I have to ask a supervisor for permission, or I have to fill
out a request and hope — that is *all* I can do — the right decision will
be made back at the office. Suddenly I hear myself saying: enough! I've
had enough of it. Suddenly I picture myself quitting and going to work
in a school, in a hospital, in an office — anyplace where I'm not under
this kind of cross fire. And I'll admit it, if I get *really* annoyed, and I'm
completely exhausted, my voice gets sharp with the people. Then I
obey the letter of the law and get out fast — because I'm tempted to
tell them to shut up and stop swearing and stop cursing and leave me
alone and *go out and work.*

"I've never said something like that to a person, but I know at
times they can read my mood if not my exact thoughts. And I'm one of
the young, so-called activist welfare workers. I'm one of the protesters.
I've even picketed our own headquarters! I've signed dozens of

protests. I've called our regulations inhuman, unfair, condescending, arbitrary — you name it! I've refused to ask some of those insulting, demeaning questions. I've written letters to my congressman and senator. I've written to the governor. I've joined new organizations. And I honestly believe that, day in and day out, I do pretty well with the people I visit. It's just that the whole system is an impossible one, and the people who need welfare are in an impossible series of binds. So, when I come to see them, and they have me right there and available and ready to listen and not push them around and not scream at them and not threaten them, they just let it all out on me, the anger they feel toward the landlord, or the city's garbage department, or the whole social and economic system in America, actually — and if they don't use the words we do, they come close enough. They pull themselves together and say it's not me, they know, but 'everything.' If I ask them what they mean by 'everything,' they let me know — that everything is 'the way things are run' or 'the way people are allowed to treat other people.' And I prefer their way of speaking to the hazy, indirect talk I used to hear from my professors of social work. Some of *them* are as afraid as the people in the ghettos. I guess we've all got our bosses to worry about, me included."

She certainly does have a boss to worry about. Every day "special situations" come up, emergencies that compel families already living marginally to cry for help. She hears the cries, but others approve or disapprove the requests for money subsequently made. And rather typically, she refuses to do to her supervisors what at times she feels being done to her. That is to say, she tries to understand them, too. She tries to remember that the laws prevent even the most compassionate and evenhanded official from doing what he knows ought to be done. She tries to remember that there simply is not enough money to go around. Sometimes, no doubt about it, bureaucratic blindness or inertia or duplicity is at work, but by and large Janet Howe cannot successfully turn the welfare department into the devil she every once in a while openly wishes it were: "We have some fools in that office; and even worse, there are some cold and mean people, who are everything the families say they are. But the fools are a minority, a small one at that. It's so easy to turn the welfare office into the problem, rather than a symptom of the problem. I can't tell you how much I wish the whole problem *was* the welfare department! Then, a change in personnel would be all we'd need. But if you came to our office and spent a lot of time talking with people there, from the top man down, you'd find on the whole a superior group of people. They bend and twist those laws and regulations — which for the most part the state legislature has made — in an effort to help individual families.

"I can honestly say that some people in the welfare department are the biggest lawbreakers in the state. Every day they enter into collusion with the client in order to help people through a bad time. As I've said, we have our share of incredibly insensitive and tightfisted people, but they do not dominate the department, and among the younger employees they are nonexistent. The laws direct us to do only so much, and no more, with certain families and not with others. Even if new federal laws were enacted, we'll still not have the money these people need: they are more than simply poor, remember; they have been living for years and years under conditions that make their problems not only serious but very, very costly. I mean, they had rheumatic fever but they never were treated for it in Alabama or Georgia, and now they're up here and their hearts are badly damaged, and they need not only careful medical evaluations and treatment but help at home because they can't do things, lift things, catch their breath, all that. They can't get to the hospital easily, because for them to go up and down stairs is dangerous, sometimes impossible. They need expensive medication. They need special diets. People don't realize what a welfare department in a northern city has to face: we're supposed to heal and repair each day the damage that hundreds of years of history have paved the way for. We're the ones who see the end result of poor nutrition and diseases never once treated and poor sanitation and all the rest — not to mention the psychological damage."

She will not stop with generalities. She has uppermost on her mind the specific illnesses and hardships with which many families contend, and in any conversation about that abstraction called her "work" she is more than ready to bring up those specifics, to talk about everything from tuberculosis to malnutrition to rat bites to parasitic infestations to alcoholism. Alternatively, she will talk about the high rents the poor often have to pay — for the most miserable of places, or the poor service they get in garbage removal or police protection. "Everyone talks about the police and their attitude toward ghetto people," and then, that said, she pauses as if to say that she too has also talked about it. When she is ready to resume her line of reasoning she becomes openly ironic, even sarcastic: "I'm sure a lot of the people I see wish the police were around more — and would do a better job of being policemen — rather than be on the payroll of the racketeers who prey upon the people in the ghetto. We could start a

second complete welfare service on the amount of money that is illegally made around here: prostitution, drugs, gambling. And, of course,
there are payoffs all the way up and down. The landlords are always
slipping money to city inspectors and the police. No one comes
around and really checks into the violations of the law, not unless one
of the newspapers runs an exposé, or the people really organize and
make a lot of noise. It's very discouraging to me, and even more so to
the people who have to live in those tenements. People on the outside
always think of a slum or a ghetto as a place where nothing much is
happening, where poor people live and sometimes riot because they're
unsatisfied. But the ghetto is also a place where storekeepers charge
outrageous prices they'd never be able to force upon middle-class customers, who can drive from place to place and speak out and raise
their voices. In the ghetto there is a network of crime that makes a
few black men rich and keeps plenty of policemen and fire inspectors
and plumbing and heating and building inspectors happy with extra
dollars.

"That's why I have to laugh when I hear people talk as if the police drive up and down ghetto streets looking for trouble and trying to
push people around. And I have to laugh when I hear talk about the
white oppressors, the outsiders, who are always bleeding ghetto
people. Some of the police are bullies, yes, and of course the ghetto is
a product of our society, so if we had different values and priorities the
ghetto might be a lot better place for people to live in. But I really
wonder whether many who talk about these problems have ever put
one foot into a ghetto, or done more than walked through — or driven
through! — on some afternoon. The people I see, black people mainly,
are exploited every day by other blacks. The kids I know grow up
among black pimps, black addicts, black pushers, black prostitutes,
and black salesmen who cheat their customers, sell them worthless insurance, and gouge them with prices far higher than they should be.
Whites own some of the stores, but blacks also own a good number of
them, and I've not found them angels and public benefactors, those
black real estate men and property owners and storekeepers. That's a
joke, the idea that a man's skin color makes him more honest or compassionate. Tell that to the people in the ghetto who know! And listen
to them talk about the payoffs that a black policeman can take just as
easily as a white one does. I learned that from the people I visit. They'll
sit me down and tell me to forget all my nice, liberal ideas. They don't
say it that way, but the message is clear.

"One tough old grandmother — you would think she is the sweetest, most innocent thing alive until you heard her speak — told me to 'stop dreaming and face the facts.' What facts, I asked her. 'Sister, around here it's kill or be killed, and that goes for black and white and tan and pink and green and yellow and any other color you can think up.' I wasn't convinced then, because I was just starting out, but now she wouldn't have to say that again to me. I've met too many black hoodlums, robbing and stealing from little children or weak and frightened old women, to settle for the notion that it's all a matter of white racists and what *they* do. I've even seen some landlords — everyone can jump on them so easily! — try to keep their buildings in good repair and make sure the trash is carried off and the alleys are swept regularly and the halls kept clean and reasonably well lighted, only to find mailboxes forced open, even ripped out of the walls, and banisters kicked and broken and windows or screens smashed and destroyed and half-full barrels deliberately overturned. It isn't easy to talk about all of that. I hope you've heard black people on the subject; many of them know only too well how their own people, their immediate neighbors, can terrorize a whole block. One of the worst parts of my job is hearing *those* facts, learning how *really* awful it can be *among* the poor — and not only because we continue to deny them entry to 'our' schools or colleges or jobs or neighborhoods."

Maybe she should have *known* such things, she hastens to say. She did take courses. She did read widely. She always has kept her eyes open, and in addition she has had her father's warnings. Still, she went into social work, and particularly welfare work, because she believed that by and large the poor are victims, even if not necessarily saintly victims. Now she knows that she was silly and naïve, at best, when she failed to consider the real price poor people have to pay for such sustained weakness: their susceptibility to all kinds of sad and terrible "temptations," if that is the right word; their vulnerability, which makes them easily tricked and used and abused; their sense of futility, which so frequently unnerves them, undoes them, prods them to turn on themselves vengefully. Now she dwells on such issues so exhaustively that she feels she has ironically come full circle and in so doing lost a good deal of her effectiveness as a welfare worker: "There comes a point in this kind of work when you see too much, perhaps. All the wretched 'facts of life' come upon you with such a wallop — well, you become terribly discouraged. I am. Tomorrow I may not be, but today I am — discouraged and about ready to quit. Welfare, anyway, is not the answer. Many of the people on welfare have somehow lost respect for themselves, not for the reasons my father would say, but for other reasons. They are sick, disabled, fearful, brutalized — and therefore able to be brutal themselves. They are dazed and confused.

"I saw a mother today: she has had one illegitimate child after another. She comes from the South, near Augusta, Georgia, I believe; she came up here as a child and promptly lost her mother and was sent from relative to relative and then to a foster home; soon the street became her home. By the time she was ten she'd been 'around' so much that if she came from a rich family and they wanted to shower her with affection and concern and put her in psychoanalysis and do everything else they could, she would still require, as we put it in our jargon, 'a major rehabilitative effort,' and she would still have a 'guarded prognosis.' Meanwhile, she stayed in those tenements, one day after the other, and was tossed around and beaten up and plied with booze and pills. And still, *and still*, she fought to keep her children and make a home for them. And I swear, within the limits of her knowledge and experience and resources, she does well, damn well. She feeds those kids and tries hard to clothe them well. And she takes them to church. She has her lapses. She buys a bottle. She lets a man come and get her pregnant, which means she forgets the pills I got for her — without my superior's approval and yes, with my own money. She wanted those pills, desperately did. But she forgot. There it is. We've 'forgotten' about those people for a long time, and now they've got the habit of forgetting. I give up."

She doesn't really give up, though. The next time I see her she is full of talk, full of concern about another family, another mother, another set of problems — and quietly hopeful that somehow, in some way, at some time, she and her kind will be put thoroughly and completely out of business. That is what she says all the time: the faster there are no welfare workers like herself, the better it will be; provided, of course, the people she sees have their own resources to call upon, have a sense of their own power, have an unmistakable sense of self-sufficiency and self-respect — all of which are transmitted to children and need no boosters from weekly visitors who work for "the city" and who like Janet Howe want to scream, cry, and tear out their hair.

My Buildings

He is puzzled by the accusations he has heard only in recent years. He claims he is troubled by what he considers to be an impossible predicament. He is convinced that the worst is yet to come, and he is persuaded that whatever happens he will lose. The aging but sharply observant and skeptical man can only fall back again and again upon sentences which seem to be at once an affirmation of his faith and a warning to anyone inclined to doubt his intentions or his will: "They are my buildings. If they are not mine, whose are they? I paid for them, and I've tried to keep them up. I'll stop owning them when I sell them, and only then — period."

He insists repeatedly that he is no "operator," no "speculator" out to milk property dry, then abandon it. He is fifty-five years old and for thirty years has owned buildings all over the city, *all over* and not just in a black neighborhood. He started buying buildings in 1940 when the depression still lingered and when he had exactly five thousand dollars to his name — and that from his grandfather's life insurance. He had graduated from high school, had not gone to college because his parents had no money to send him and because he had no interest in reading books and writing papers and taking examinations. He was always active, he now says, and always willing to do the unconventional, to take risks and then stand firm. He feels, then, that his life has had a certain reassuring continuity and consistency. It is the times, the times that are out of joint.

Under stress a man may look back and try to make sense of his life, to know just what it is he is fighting for and against. Certainly a man who talks like the man I am now writing about is trying hard to gird himself and say that he stands *here*, and by God, he will not surrender: "Why should I? Why should I walk away from buildings I've put my whole life into? If I'm supposed to do that, then everyone who owns anything in this country will soon be in the same spot I'm in. Someone with a big, loud mouth will come up and say: hand it over, brother. Then the television boys will do their usual one-sided documentary, exposing the owner as no good and heartless and fat and rich and mean, and the next thing you'll see is a few pickets, and then a bigger demonstration, and then the poor owner feels like he's committed the crime of the century. And what is the crime? The crime is that he's owned something, he's had the colossal nerve in the United States of America to take some of his money and buy something and keep it and try to make a profit out of it! That's what we've come to these days — you have to defend yourself for being a businessman and for trying to make a living. And if you do make a halfway decent living, then you're exploiting the poor and squeezing them dry and you're a Nazi and a white colonialist and a murderer.

"I'm tired of it! I ask myself every now and then why I stay, why I keep coming here and trying to keep my property in good shape and trying to have a reasonable talk with my tenants. I'm no illiterate, you know. I read the papers and the magazines; I read what all those smart-aleck writers say. I know that I'm supposed to be plundering my property. Even though I keep my buildings looking good and say hello to the tenants and hear them say hello back to me — I'm still supposed to be a plunderer. A lot of guys I grew up with and went to school with had money behind them, so they went to college. They live 'cleaner' lives, I guess. One is a lawyer, and he makes his money because other people have got themselves into trouble. No one calls *him* an exploiter or a plunderer. Another one is a doctor; he makes his money because other people are sick and dying. Half the time he can't do a thing for them: they either get better on their own or they die or they keep on moaning and groaning because they *want* to be sick. But no one thinks the doctor is exploiting anyone or plundering. I've been to his office: they come in and leave every five minutes, and they pay him ten dollars in cash, a lot of them, and God knows how much of that money gets declared on the income tax forms. But he's a *doctor*, a pillar of the community. And I just own 'slum property.'

"My kids, or at least one of them, is ashamed of me. He's in college, and he says he won't tell his friends where some of my property is. He'll only tell them about the stores in the suburban plaza. I told him he'd better stop telling *me* things — like what he doesn't want to tell friends. I told him that I'm no crook and I'm no thief and I'm no drug addict and I'm no traitor to my country, and I'm sick and tired of hearing about slum landlords, slum landlords from a bunch of hypocrites! Everyone who has money in this country is an 'exploiter,' if you want to look at the world that way; and the more money a person has, or has inherited, the bigger an exploiter he is. But a guy like me, who goes out and works and tries to keep his property going and visits it and talks with his tenants and listens to their complaints, he's the scapegoat. Every doctor or lawyer with money can sneer at me, and every son of a guy with money can call me a name instead of looking at how his own father made money.

"I'm not saying I do everything my tenants want me to do. I'd have to be a multimillionaire to keep them happy. They're unhappy people, you know. When a person is unhappy, he complains. When a person is out of work, and he's just sitting there, and who knows if he's married to the woman or not, or how many men she sleeps with — then that guy will tell you how bad everything is. I know it's bad for

them; they don't have to tell me. I'm no bigot. I've always liked the colored people — excuse me, the *black* people. I was talking with them
and going into their homes and on a first-name basis with them before
this whole civil rights movement got going. In 1950 — how do you
like that! — I was given a scroll by one of the Negro churches. They
said I was a trusted friend. I've given money to that church for over
twenty-five years. 'If only all white people were like you': I've heard
those words for twenty-five years, too — for thirty years. But no, those
people are just Uncle Toms, I'm supposed to believe, or else they were
lying to me, just trying to please me, fool me — I don't know *what*
they were supposed to be doing, because every day I hear a new theory
about the Negro, and every day he's called by a different name."

The man owns many buildings in a black section of a large northern city, some of which are indeed to any middle-class eye old and
crowded tenements, in need of various kinds of repair, and some of
which, old though they be, are well kept up and relatively uncrowded.
In other words, the man has as tenants both large families and modest-
sized families. One need be no social scientist to see that on one street
the families are black, but generally headed by men who have steady
jobs that yield at least halfway decent wages, whereas on another
street welfare workers can be seen knocking on most of the doors in
his buildings. He claims that as a landlord he is actually "impartial," so
far as his comparative "attitude" toward his better-off tenants and his
poorer tenants goes. He claims that all along he has tried to do everything that each of his nine buildings inhabited by black people requires. He claims that he has working for him a full-time plumber and
steam fitter and a full-time carpenter, and a more-or-less full-time
electrician, and they spend a good deal more of their time in those
nine buildings than they do in the apartment buildings and stores he
owns elsewhere — that is, in white, middle-class neighborhoods. And
finally, he wants to emphasize his personal approach to his work, his
effort to go out and see things for himself and instruct his employees
quite openly and directly on what he wants done.

Those employees, by the way, include four black janitors, who
care for the nine buildings which he sometimes collectively refers to as
his "headache." Yet, he will not deny that he makes a certain profit out
of that headache, and he has as reward not only the solace of money
but a sense of pride in achievement which he feels his daily behavior
somehow demonstrates: "I've got respect for myself, and that's one
reason I don't sell those buildings. I could have sold them numerous
times, and at a profit. I don't sell property, though. I buy property and

I hold on to it. I make my living by being a landlord. I'm not a speculator. I bought those buildings a long time ago, when Negroes were
there, but also some white people. The whites moved out a year or two
later. They just wouldn't live with Negroes, not that close to them. I remember being angry at them. One of them asked me why I don't sell
the building he lived in and was just leaving. I asked why. He said,
'You know.' I said, 'No, I *don't* know.' Then he gave me a long look and
he said, 'Look, it's not me, it's my wife. She says they're not clean.' I
said, 'Do you believe her?' He said no, and what's more, she didn't
really believe herself. He said they were really moving out because
they just didn't think it was 'natural' for white people to live 'surrounded' by Negroes. Well, I told him I thanked him for being honest,
and I could understand his feelings. I told him I didn't live with them,
and I wouldn't, for the same reason: I believe you're always happier
with your own people. But I had nothing against Negroes, I told him
that, and I was going to stay right where I was, so far as owning those
buildings was concerned.

"Two banks had offered to buy the building from me, and I felt
like this: if the buildings are fully rented and they net a good profit,
not a huge one, but over ten thousand dollars clear, which is part of
my income, and a good return on an investment, then why should I
turn that kind of investment over to a bank? Or to a big real estate
firm? That's the way I thought. Sure, I could have made a fast pile of
money, but then it would either go to the government or I'd have had
to reinvest it. And those buildings are good investments."

He is, then, proud that he bought the apartment houses and
proud that he did not sell them. He is proud that he did not become
panicky and flee at the sight of more and more blacks. And he is proud
that he has maintained a steady, satisfying kind of acquaintance with
dozens of black people, who do indeed, in the course of various discussions, affirm their friendship for him — or at the least, their toleration of him. "He's a fine man," one tenant says. "He's no worse than
anyone else, black or white," another more guarded tenant says.
"What can you expect? He's the landlord. If he was black, he'd be no
better. I know worse landlords who *are* black," a third and more cynical or begrudging tenant observes. When he arrives at a building he is
greeted cordially and often offered a cup of coffee — although that holds
mostly for his better-off tenants. Sometimes he collects the rent from
them. Often his agent comes and does so. None of his black tenants
mails money to his office, a contrast with the way his white, middle-
income tenants choose to do things. Yet, he has no illusions; he knows

that even though things *seem* relatively quiet, there is a lot of tension in the air, and he may well one day be in serious trouble, if not face to face with what he calls "a business catastrophe." So he lashes out. He becomes angry. He anticipates criticism, then replies to it. One gets the feeling that he somehow gains a sense of control over an unpredictable destiny by arguing out things with himself. And anyway, in time he will become hurt in some way, he knows that — which is why he believes that the best thing to do is prepare himself: "I know I'll have trouble. Maybe they'll burn one of my buildings down. I hate to think about it, and yet I've got to. I'd be like an ostrich with its head in the sand if I didn't.

"Who will suffer if that should happen? It's so stupid! I'll collect on my fire insurance, but what about the tenants? Of course, arsonists and hoodlums and petty thieves and crazy revolutionaries never care about people. They do what their wild impulses tell them to do. They aren't sincere, kind people who want to help their fellowman. They're exhibitionists. That's what they are. And they're willing to have others suffer so that they can say: look at the fire I set; I'm a *militant;* I'm a *leader*. It's always the poor and the innocent who pay for the theatrical types!

"I know exactly what the militants say about me. And it's a bundle of lies. They exaggerate. They exaggerate the money I make, and they ignore the costs I have: the money I have to spend on upkeep and maintenance, the taxes I pay, and all the rest — insurance, water bills, mortgage payments. I don't own the buildings outright. You should see the interest the bank gets out of me every month. But the public has no interest in all that. They just say: those landlords collect all that money and stick it in their pockets. If you try to explain to them what a landlord has to do, what his bills are like and what the risks are that he takes, they say you're crying false tears. There's no point in even trying to argue.

"The one thing that bothers me most is that the really crooked and dishonest landlords, and the cheapest, tightest, most inhuman owners of property are the ones who never get blamed by anyone, black or white. It's someone like me, who *comes* here, who is visible — he's the one attacked. Who can insult someone never, never seen? Who can figure out who owns some of those buildings? I'll tell you who owns them: banks who have foreclosed mortgages on deadbeats or crooks — guys who took all they could from a building and never paid the bills, so the bank had to come and take the building away, while the guy disappears or claims he's broke or something like that.

The other kind of owners are the large real estate companies. They are huge, impersonal firms. No one knows who is in charge of the buildings. There's an agent who collects the rent, and every once in a while someone comes to fix a leak. But it takes a team of lawyers to figure out who it is — what collection of guys or what individual — owns most of the apartment houses around mine. The Negroes don't know. How could they? In a way, they're right when they talk about the big banks being the landlords. The banks *are* the mortgagees in a lot of cases. Or there are a series of 'trusts' and 'corporations' and 'companies,' with all kinds of 'officers' that a tenant will never see, and the buildings are 'owned' by them: the so-and-so trust, you know, and all that. If you did track them all down, the leading investors in the banks and the officers of the real estate trusts and companies, guess what you'd find. You'd find big, prominent families. You'd find the same people who invest in stocks and bonds and everything else. You'd find the most respectable and honored names. Some of them probably have no idea they're 'slum landlords.' Some of them just give their money over to a man or a company 'for investment.' But some are quite aware; they know they own huge blocks of property in the ghetto, and they know that the management company in charge of the property is 'doing as well as can be expected.'

"It's a laugh! It's so hypocritical! I'll bet some of those people give to the NAACP and the Urban League. I'll bet some of them are on the boards of those organizations. In fact, I know that's the case here in this city. I know a man who's on the board of a bank that owns some of the worst property in this neighborhood, and at the same time he's on the board of all kinds of Negro organizations. He's considered a 'friend' of the Negro community. He's a big lawyer. He's a nice man. He's probably never stopped and checked into the various real estate holdings of his bank. Why should he? He's a busy man, everyone says. He's got so much on his mind. He's so generous with his time and money. He wants the colored people to have a better life. Meanwhile, I pick up the bank's reports and whose name do I see on the board of trustees, and who is a stockholder or something like that in the bank — a big depositor, you can be sure? Who gets his interest from the money the bank makes out of its properties in the ghetto? Well, that man of course, and many others — when you come right down to it, thousands of people who would never consider themselves property owners as such. Their hands are clean. They don't know where their money comes from. They feel morally superior. They probably look down on me a little. I'm grubby. That's me: a grubby slum landlord.

"I'd like to tell those holier-than-thou types what I have to do. I'd like to tell them what some of my worst tenants do to my property. Better, I'd like them to come and see. They'd see things done to walls and stairs and mailboxes: dirty words scrawled everywhere, locks broken, screens slashed, windows constantly pushed in, garbage just thrown out the window as if I was there, ready and waiting with my arms wide open. What is a landlord supposed to do? I spend thousands of dollars every year — you heard me, *thousands* of dollars — in order to fix up the damage that those 'poor, underprivileged' Negro kids do. It's part of my expense. I have to figure on that when I anticipate my costs. The police laugh at me when I call them. And I laugh at them. What can they do? We'd have to have a million police in some of our cities if we were going to stop these gangs. They come with paint and smear the walls. They break bottles, one after the other, until the alleys and streets are covered with *layers* of glass. I try to sweep up after them. I mean, I ask my janitors to do so, and they try, they really try. They are hardworking men — like I said, Negro. You should hear what *they* say about their own people. I never dare speak like that, even to my own kids — *especially* to my kids.

"I once asked my son to come and talk with those men, but he said no. He said they worked for me, and so they said what I wanted them to say. I said OK, OK, have it your way. But you're wrong, so completely wrong I'd like to laugh, but I end up almost in tears. Why is it that a boy like mine, in college, prelaw, gets an idea in his head and then doesn't try to find out whether it's right or wrong? I see him reading books about 'logic' and 'reason' and all that, and I say to him: before you call your father an exploiter, and his janitors paid dupes, please come and look around and ask some questions. But no. He's willing to insult those janitors, never mind me — and believe only what he thinks is right. He doesn't even want to test out his beliefs. I guess he's afraid that if he did, life wouldn't be so clear-cut — I'd say black and white, but I'm not trying to be funny. This is no laughing matter, the way a person believes only what he wants to believe, and doesn't bother with the facts."

The facts — more than anything else he stresses the importance of facts: the money he makes, the money he spends, the rents he collects, the cost of maintenance he has to put up with. Like the policeman he calls but knows cannot really help him, like the fireman he has also had to call (so far only for "minor" blazes, mischief done by children or accidents in particular apartments), and like the welfare workers who come to see his tenants regularly, he claims to know things about black people that others do not know. He thinks of himself as the outsider who is also the insider, the white man who really has his eyes on the black man, the heavily scorned person who is really the knowing and courageous person. Again and again he wants that last point made: others talk, but he sees; others use rhetoric, but he takes part in a neighborhood's "action." He uses that word, action. He considers himself a restless, active man, and he says that he is glad he has to take risks, test his willpower and perseverance against the growing danger and uncertainty his work provides.

One thing I must know: he is not afraid. And I do know that. True, somewhere "underneath" or "way down" he is scared and ashamed and guilty and all the rest, as many of us are for one set of reasons or other. But in his everyday life I am quite convinced he knows little fear. He walks those streets, streets in a sense he partially owns, and for all the world he seems almost carelessly casual and untroubled. He likes to whistle, which can always prompt from someone like me the clever observation that at some "level" of his mind he is indeed whistling, whistling in the dark — quite literally so, because he is at large among the darkskinned people who pay him so significant a part of their income. But one of those darkskinned tenants, on welfare and capable of intense anger at white people, finds that landlord no real menace and even laughs at him — with scorn yes, but genuine appreciation of sorts: "He's always smiling, and he'll whistle you a tune if you ask him to. So help me, he will. Now, how can you hate a man like that? I hate him on the first of the month when that Uncle Tom of his comes around for the rent; but when he drives up here, whistling and worrying about a leak in a pipe and pointing out something to his plumber and worrying if the plumber is going to cheat him good by stretching the job out — well, I have to smile and say: the poor guy, he's running scared, too, like the rest of us. I'll save my gun for the bigger cats."

So it is that those two have their moments of agreement, that landlord and his tenant. Only moments, however. Each of them can attack the other, and do so with words and phrases which make one wonder whether there is any hope that somehow this country will keep itself reasonably intact. And yet, and yet; I can only add the "and yet," the qualification those two human beings and others like them require from me — because again, for a moment here and there, and sometimes even longer, they think and talk almost alike, which may never mean a thing, or may one day mean quite a lot.

White Northerners

What Have We Done?

When the black children first came to the school her nine-year-old boy and seven-year-old girl attend, she spoke as if she faced something far more awful than a "crisis." I thought, listening to her, that the apocalypse might be finally at hand. She spoke about how ineffective her opposition was doomed to be: "People don't listen to someone like me. I went to our club at the church, and we all said that: no one is going to care about us. The only people that get themselves heard on television are the colored people. They stand on the street and threaten everyone and tell their people to burn down the city, and I have to see that on my television station. And our newspaper listens to any colored man, no matter what crazy thing he says, just because he's colored. But do the ordinary white people ever get any space in the paper? The answer is no."

She says she is that, an ordinary white person; she used to be "just ordinary," but now she emphasizes that she is white. For three years her children have gone to school with some black children who are bussed several miles, so no longer does she feel that the world is coming to an end. But she does continue to have her serious misgivings — about black people in general, and the ways in which one hundred black fellow students affect her children. Nor is she a peculiar or especially disturbed or anxious person. It so happens that I have met, week in and week out, for several years with her and thirteen other mothers like her; they all belong to a community whose men work in factories, work in offices, work as civil servants of one kind or another. The homes are two-family homes, with an occasional single-family one. The streets in the neighborhood are clean and lined with trees, with cars, with street lamps and with carefully tended lawns. To this woman and her friends that street means a lot: it is a quiet and respectable street, I am told by them, and it is near a church, near a school, near a drugstore, near a supermarket, near a busline, near a bank, near a hardware store, near "everything you want and need," is the way it is put. And now everything seems in jeopardy; even with the first scare over, the mothers continue to be fearful.

The mother of the boy and girl speaks her fears passionately and with bitterness: "What have we done, I ask you? Do you know that the city is not only letting these total strangers come over here, but some of them don't go home in the bus, as they should, but just stay around? I wouldn't want my children sent to a strange part of town when there is a neighborhood school for them to attend. All I hear is that in the colored sections the schools are very old and crowded. Well, they are old here, and they're full here. With these colored kids, there isn't a single seat vacant. The difference is that we teach our children to be respectful of property, even if it *is* old, and with the colored people, it's a different story. My son says they are a restless bunch of kids. They are always moving around, and they give everything wear and tear. The colored boy next to him sits there and his leg is jiggling all day, up and down. And he wears sneakers to school, and in recess all he does is run and jump and try every piece of equipment they have out there in the yard. My son says he thinks the kid has ants in his pants, and he's always breaking his pencil and dropping his eraser, and he opens and closes that desk of his a hundred times a day. Now I ask you, what is wrong? I've watched them getting off the bus, and they're just not like our children, and no one, no doctors and no college professors and no politicians, can tell me anything different."

Perhaps she is angry at me, I think. She *is* angry at me, I later decide. In the beginning I tried to listen and occasionally respond — but only to restate her own remarks. After a while I realized that she also wanted to discuss things with me. She asked me frankly for my thoughts, and I offered them, in as respectful and quiet a manner as I could. I have never looked on it as my role to educate that "group" of mothers or get "therapeutic" with them or "change" them; they agreed to meet and keep me informed about things going on in the neighborhood and I agreed to speak up (when they asked me to do so) and tell them what I had seen elsewhere and what I believed I was learning in the course of my work. We always talked rather informally, and I certainly did get a continuing sense of what was happening in the school as well as in their lives. Yet, I am a doctor and from a university. From time to time I have made it clear that I felt close to those political leaders who wanted to make changes, plenty of them, rather than congratulate all of us on how big and rich and mighty we are. So, when the mother talked about "doctors" I wondered out loud whether I had become a stand-in for all the other "bureaucrats and social planners" who were "messing things up," in the words of that same mother who mentioned doctors and college professors.

No, the mothers said, I was wrong. They implied that I was really going mad a little, or at the very least I was just too self-conscious, too worried, too taken up with noticing everything and giving everything so much importance, so much significance. They did not offer me any "interpretations" of my implied "interpretation" — that I was becoming a living representative, as it were, of white, upper-middle-class liberals — but they did say some moving and instructive things. To call upon our same mother again: "No, no. I'll tell you what *is* bothering us. We have been told that we are prejudiced and that we should be taught how to be unprejudiced. Someone in the school department wants us to go and hear a psychologist. He's supposed to clear our minds of bigotry. I went to my minister, because it was his idea, I heard. I told him to mind his own damn business. I think the church should leave us alone when it comes to some of these problems. I get sick, watching the ministers marching in the street, demonstrating, and taking sides against their own government and their own people. There are times when I think our minister cares more about the colored people than he does about us, members of his own parish. I didn't say it to him, but my husband did. He said we don't want any movies and any college people telling us our minds are sick, and we don't want to be told we're bigots and all that, because the fact is that we're *not*; we're not prejudiced at all.

"I wish I could say it the way he did. When he gets excited, he really knows how to talk. He's not afraid. I am; I'll have to admit it. I hear those sermons about *prejudice* and *bigotry,* and I feel as if I've been a bad girl, and I should be punished. Then I go to visit the school, and the teachers, a lot of them, are on our side; but the school department and the governor and the mayor or someone send those psychologists to give us a talking-to — there's so-and-so, and he's connected with around ten universities, they say when they introduce him to us, and he's supposed to make us think differently, I guess. And my God, you can't pick up the paper and you can't turn on the television without reading something about the poor colored people and all their troubles and seeing a documentary on how they're all nice, and they've been punished by us — me! — all these years, and we owe it to them, we owe *everything* to them. I've never been bad to any colored person. I don't know them. But America is racist, they tell you. I'll tell you what I believe: I believe there is an effort on the part of some to make people like us, the ordinary white people of the country, feel as if we're criminals and get an inferiority complex, you might say."

I told her that I certainly hoped I wouldn't say anything that would add to the already large stock of accusations she had just mentioned. I told her that I believe one accusation after another does little to help people see things more clearly; on the contrary, one gets defiant or moody or disgusted not only with oneself but the brazen nerve of others, who display very little good sense (not to mention generosity or breadth of understanding) when they push people further and further into a corner — to the point that they can only yield and hate themselves for doing so, or strike out in what is felt to be self-defense.

She interrupted me to say that each person has a right to be heard, and not any "one group." I told her I certainly agreed, but I said I believed there are indeed people ready to respond to people like her, including some of our very highest and most influential leaders. Well, yes, she did not feel entirely without support and understanding. Nevertheless, she felt increasingly put-upon these days, and she wanted me and the others in that room to hear the sources of her discontent: "Everywhere you turn, there's a poster or a commercial on television that says the colored people are like other people, and we should have them next door, and we should apologize because we had them as slaves, and it goes on and on. On my mother's side my grandparents moved down here from Canada; on my father's side they were farm people in Maine. They never had any slaves. They were working people, and so were my parents, and so am I. What is all this business about racism, racism? Am I supposed to spend my whole life thinking about the colored, the colored, the colored? I never gave them a thought at all, one way or the other, until the last few years, and now I'm told I'm a racist, and I'm trying to kill off all of them, and a lot of other nonsense.

"I believe that every single person is fine, no matter what his color or the church he goes to, so long as he doesn't bother other people and cause a lot of trouble. I'm not against colored people. I've never had anything to do with them, one way or the other. The same goes for my husband. He works for the milk company. He delivers milk. He gets up at five o'clock in the morning. He comes home dead tired. He never sees colored people, and he doesn't have a thing in the world against them. All we want is peace and quiet. We bought the house, and we'll be paying for it the rest of our lives. We'd be crazy if we said we'd like colored people to move in here, and then we'd have a house that was worthless, but we'd still have to keep up the mortgage payments. Do the people who write those editorials, do they think we ought to let this whole neighborhood be a colored neighborhood? Should I stay here if the colored move in and surround me? Is it wrong for me to want to live near people like myself, and near my husband's cousins, two of them?

"It seems to me that the people who do the most talking on this subject have a lot of money, and they can live wherever they want. Even our minister, his house goes with the church. He can change churches, if worst comes to worst. And the church, that's been a great disappointment to us, the way the church has behaved lately. All my life I've gone to church. My uncle is a minister, himself; he's a Methodist. He was the bookish one in my father's family. I've been in many churches and heard many sermons since I was a child. It's only in the last few years that these churches have gone crazy over the colored, and they're also against the government more than they're for it. We still have the American flag in our church, but I really wonder whether one day I'll come and it'll be there no more. My uncle says you can't just suddenly switch on people and expect them to go along so easy, and he's right. I was brought up to expect a minister to give you support and lift up your spirits, not to tear into you and make you feel so low and bad that — well, that you don't want to go back next Sunday and hear it again, how you have these prejudices, and the colored people are suffering, and white people don't give them a chance.

"Who gave my husband a chance? He made a chance for himself. He works so hard that I worry for him. He even does carpentry on the side. We've got to meet those bills. I was trained as a nurse, and I have been putting in some hours at the hospital or on private cases since the kids are in school. Now, all of a sudden, our kids have these strangers in school with them. I don't know what the colored kids are actually learning here that's so much better than what they could be learning where they live, in their own schools. The teacher told us it's not the same. Before, everybody was relaxed. Now if kids fight, like they always do, and one is colored and the other is white, there's no telling what will happen. You might have one of those colored parents phoning the principal; or worse than that, some snotty white minister or college student will come and say he's over here 'on behalf of' the colored people. My boy says that a lot of the time he forgets about the colored kids even being there, and my girl says they're a nuisance, but they don't bother her, and they mostly just keep to themselves. Well, they could keep to themselves much better if they'd stay where they live.

"I'm sure they are going to try to move in here. They'll hop, skip, and jump their way toward us, inch by inch they will. I have a cousin in Connecticut, and it happened to them — the first thing it was children brought in to the school, and the next thing it was houses they wanted, the colored. It's got to the point that you have to look ahead and try to figure out if you're safe for one year or five years or what. I tell my husband: we should sell the house while we can get a good price, and then rent someplace. That way, you can get away fast. It's terrible when you're in America and you have to think that way. I suppose if we had more money and could afford to live way out there in one of those plush suburbs, we'd be all right. No colored person can afford to live with the rich, and that's why the rich can afford to give us all those sermons on how they favor integration and they believe in treating everyone equal. I believe in treating everyone equal, too. It's just that no one's fighting for my rights, only me. The colored have the papers and the television behind them, and the professors and the college students and a lot of the politicians and a lot of rich people who like to *help* the poor out but make sure they're far enough away from them — and from people like us, too."

Am I to point out to her the various inconsistencies she has expressed, and pursue her and pursue her until she agrees that through her opinions runs a streak of obstinate unreason? Am I to listen as best I can, and see how worried and fearful she is, how hard she fights for what she has, how nervous she is about what the future holds, how confused she is by events which move along rather fast — events for which she was never prepared by the schools she attended or indeed the churches she went to or even the particular newspapers she read? As she points out, the churches and newspapers have only recently begun to speak out so loud and clear on certain issues. And anyway, she doesn't read a lot of magazines and books, or "analyze" events and take "positions" with respect to them. But she and her hardworking and not enormously well-paid husband and their young children live with and are involved in and worry about those events — to the point that what we call "events" or "issues" she calls "the biggest danger we have ever faced."

I have been pressed to make my observations and comments, and maybe they will have their place and their value. But that woman and others next door and across the street and "over on the avenue" and "down near the square" all continue to feel apprehensive and ignored, even, in cloudy moments, betrayed by ministers and newspaper editors and others who "change their tune and expect everyone else to come running along." As I hear in those meetings we have, "people have their limits" and "you can ask only so much of people." I hear that last statement rather often, and sometimes when I am driving home I say to myself that I have seen people change a lot, an incredible amount, but I have to add that when people don't want to change so much as hold their own, they will let anyone who has other wishes for them know exactly what they think.

Laura

Laura was seven when her school became the subject of considerable controversy. "Seven is a good age," Laura told me when she was seven years, eleven months and five days old. She wasn't sure what it would be like after her birthday, after she turned eight, but she did make a point of letting me know that she hoped the third grade might prove to be "easier" than the second. I asked her to write out her own prescription, tell me exactly what she would want in the way of improvement, exactly how things might get "easier," if she could have an important say. Word for word, I said: "If you could have your way, how would you make sure the third grade would really turn out to be easier?" She replied with a long silence. Eventually she raised her head a little, darted with her eyes toward my face, then quickly turned her head away and spoke. She spoke as if to an audience, as if she was making a public statement, as if her mother's words had finally achieved a certain power over her that could no longer be stayed. Indeed, she spoke like her mother, and the words she used were her mother's: "If the school went back to normal, and they left, the colored kids, we would have it good again — no trouble."

Laura is the only daughter and youngest child of a man who works as a foreman in a factory and a woman who on occasion, now that Laura is in school, works for a secretarial pool. The mother describes her work and her family this way: "I have two sons, and they're growing up fast. John is twelve, and he's becoming a real man. Ted is ten. He has a lot of friends, and I don't see him much, what with school and his baseball or football after school. Laura is our favorite I guess, being a girl. Her dad adores her, and I must admit, after two boys, I was glad to have a girl. They're easier to bring up, I believe. Even now Laura helps me take care of the house. I try to make some extra money by doing typing. There's a company that takes in work, and they call me up and I go there and type a few hours, I'd say three times a week. Laura is very good at taking care of herself. She dusts and she loves to use that vacuum cleaner. I'll come home and she'll tell me she's 'done' the living room, and when she says she has, she means it. Our next-door neighbor keeps an eye on her if I'm not around when she comes home from school."

All of that sounds pleasant and not very remarkable. But when she used the word "school" she came to the end of one train of thought and began another. The word "school" started this off: "This past year has been awful, and there were days when I really wondered if I should ever be away when Laura comes home. We had a nice school, with no trouble at all there, and then the next thing we all knew, the school wasn't normal any more. It was a different place, because the colored said they wanted to come over, and our school officials tried to stop them but failed. Now, all we have is trouble."

Later on she would qualify that observation. Less pressed by her own anger and rhetoric, she could almost casually acknowledge that things had not been "all bad," that from day to day Laura had not witnessed "racial trouble," that maybe over the long run "a few colored" in the school would be all right — but no more than a few, she hastens to add. Nevertheless, Laura has gone through a difficult time in school, that she knows — and that she finds unforgivable: "I'll never forget what a year that child had; it's a shame when a child can't even have a quiet time in the second grade. I shudder to think of what it'll be like in this country when she gets up to high-school age."

Laura herself had all along been quite able to talk about what she saw and heard during that eventful year: "They brought them over in a bus, and some of the mothers were there, right in front of the building, and they were trying to get the colored people to go back home. But they didn't. There were the police there, a lot of them. One of the police was the head, and he kept on telling the other police what to do. They had to take the colored kids into the school, the police did. My mother didn't go there. She wasn't one of the mothers standing there. She said she agreed with the mothers, but she couldn't bring herself to stand in the street with a sign, but maybe she should have, she says.

"Now the colored kids come every day, and there's no policeman around. We have some trouble sometimes. The teacher has to tell them that she can't understand what they're saying. They must go home and tell their parents what the teacher says, because a man came to the school, he's a lawyer, and he complained to the principal that there's prejudice. That's happened maybe three times, I think. I hear the colored kids talk, so I know all about what's going on.

"I like some of the colored kids, and some I don't like. They are like us; they look different, but after a while I forget that they're colored. There's one of them, he's a big kid, and a lot of the boys are scared of him. He pushed two kids, two white kids, and they fell down and had to go see a doctor. Then the teacher said there wasn't going to be any more of that, and we're not animals, and this isn't a zoo. So, then the kid stuck out his tongue at the teacher, the colored kid did, and then the teacher told the kid to get out of the room and stay in the hall until she called him back in. Well, a little while later she did, but he was all gone, and do you know: he's never returned to us. The teacher told my friend's mother that she was very glad, because he was really tough, that boy, and he was always looking for trouble."

Laura, like her mother, wants to observe rather than take part in things. She has managed to keep her distance from the six black children in her room; that is, she has not fought with them, as some children have, nor has she played with them, as other children have. She has two friends, Mark and Sally, and together they keep themselves busy during those recess times and lunchtimes, when there is indeed a chance to talk a lot and have fun with other children. "I was told by my mother," Laura once reminded me, "that it's best to stay out of people's way if you don't know them, and the colored kids come from another part of the city, and there's none of them living where we live."

Does she think those children would want to live near her? Does she think they like being at school with her? And in general, what does she make of them? How are they doing, now that she has had a chance to watch every day for a number of months? Always the first answer, rather naturally, is a noncommittal "all right I guess" or "I don't know" or "maybe" or "pretty good." But Laura likes to talk, again like her mother, and so she can be depended upon to amplify her terse characterizations. What she needs to do is hear yet another question, because the second inquiry tells her that the listener knows she has some ideas and wants to hear them and, indeed, would be disappointed if he did not hear them. Then comes the story or two, the expression of amusement, the question of her own to ask, the statement of doubt or the admission of error or the declaration of pleasure or the inscrutable remark which is elaborated upon and unraveled and made quite clear, all by the girl herself.

"They've been OK, pretty good, the colored kids," Laura told me one day after school. I decided that after six months of talking with her I could get a little pushy with my questions, so I asked, "How good?" She was properly confused. Did I want a grade for them, some exact evaluation? How is she supposed to know "how good?" She sat in her chair and puzzled over my question until I decided I had been dumb, and I had better pull myself together and demonstrate more intelligence and tact to the young lady — who must have been thinking, so I thought later, that it was not her place to make quantitative judgments about her classmates. (And what is wrong, anyway, with that man? How can he possibly believe that a question like his can be answered?) In any event, I next asked Laura whether she could think of some good moments she's had in class and some not-so-good ones — hoping thereby to bypass for a while our previous discussion of her "colored" classmates. We certainly hadn't always talked about racial issues, and now was a time to speak more broadly about school and home, I felt. Laura at times wanted very much to discuss how things were going with the school's new students, and at other times — *this* time, I believed — wanted no part of such a discussion.

"Most of the time it's good in school," she said right off. She seemed pleased to have, at last, something she could dig into and expand upon: "We all play, and then the teacher tells us to hush, and then we do. The best time comes later, after we've done our work, and we have juice and cookies. She lets us get up and walk around and talk — but no games and no fooling around, and we have to keep our voices low. Janice is one of the colored girls, and she always goes across the room to see her friend Henrietta. They won't leave the room without each other. The teacher asked them one day if they were related, and they said no, but they live near each other."

She had on her own moved the discussion toward one that had to do with the "adjustment," as some would have it, of "colored" children like Janice and Henrietta; so with only the slightest prodding from me I could hear her sharp and sharply worded observations: "They seem scared. That's what I think. They don't talk to you unless you talk to them. Sometimes they do, I guess. But mostly, Janice and Henrietta and the others stick together. When they forget, they'll break up and play with us. If the teacher tries to get them to scatter, they obey her. The teacher says, 'Now I want all of you to scatter and meet new people!' She's kidding us, but she means it. She gives us a talk sometimes about not sticking with only one person at recess.

"There's a boy in our room who is very nice. He's colored, but he dresses very good. He wears a bow tie every day. I asked him if he knew how to make the knot. I told him I said to my daddy one morning when he put on a bow tie that we have Jerry at school, and he has a bow tie on all the time. Daddy told me to ask Jerry if he had a real knot that he made himself, and he probably didn't, Daddy thought. I asked Jerry and he said yes, he did. The teacher heard him, and she said, 'Jerry, that's not a knot you made yourself, is it?' Then Jerry said it wasn't, and he showed me he could pull the tie and it would snap back, because there was an elastic, and he just put it around his neck, like an elastic band, and it looked like my daddy's tie, only Daddy stands before the mirror and it takes him too much time, because he has to have the tie 'just right,' my mother says, and it's not easy to do.

"I try to stay out of trouble. Jerry fights with some of the boys. He's strong. The other day he said one kid called him a nigger. He went and told the teacher. The teacher told both of them they should stop fighting and she didn't want any noise. She wanted them to shut up and stay shut up, she said. Then Jerry talked anyway; he turned and talked with his friend Richey. Richey is colored, too. The teacher sent them both out of the room. But she must have been afraid they would go and leave like the big colored boy did after she put him out in the hall, because no sooner were they out than she called them back in — and they came. They didn't cause any more trouble that day. She kept on walking up and down the aisles, and when she came to their desks, she stopped and looked at what they were doing. She told them they were doing OK. She had her ruler in her hand. We know she means business when she walks around with that ruler. She'll tap you on the shoulder if she likes what you're doing, and if she doesn't, she tells you what's wrong. The colored kids are scared of her, I believe. I've heard them say so. They call her Miss Whitey. Her name is Miss Cunningham, but they still say Miss Whitey. My mother says they're rude if they do that. I told her that if you're colored, you notice the skin color of the white person. I think the teacher notices their color, too — and that's why they call her Miss Whitey. If she's against them, they become against her."

Shortly after that conversation, Laura drew for me a picture of her school. It was one of some twelve pictures of that school she has done for me in the course of the four years (as of the time I write this) I have known her. Sometimes when we have nothing much to talk about, or indeed sometimes when we have all too much to discuss — a particular incident at school may have aroused the girl's imagination — I suggest that we both sit down and use the crayons or paints I carry around with me. I rarely have to suggest a subject for Laura, though she often tells me to do a particular sketch: a home, a college building, a doctor's office, an airplane, a dog, her school building or the school building my children go to, among others. I do the best I can, and as Laura tells me often enough, so does she.

This time she worked extra long on her picture, done carefully with crayons. Meanwhile, I did my work. I was asked by her to do a picture of a tennis racket. I had a few weeks earlier told her, when she asked me, that my favorite sport was tennis. She pointedly had let me know that her brothers liked baseball and football, and that they don't play tennis at all, and that her father doesn't, and that she wasn't even sure she knew how one plays the game. I had told her that when I was her brothers' age I, too, played baseball a lot and not tennis, but now I love to play tennis. I had explained the game to her. She wanted to know where the game is played and how one learns, and I told her that there are indoor courts and outdoor courts, and that I knew a good tennis player, who was about halfway between her age and mine, a college student, and he was right at that time doing a great job at making me a better player, and perhaps someday she would be able to meet a teacher like him and learn how to play.

Now, a few weeks later, she wanted that racket drawn, and I tried my best. Meanwhile, she did her best. When I asked her about what was happening, as I often did when clearly something *was* happening in the picture, she said this: "It's a school day, so we're all in the building. The only ones outside are Janice and Henrietta. They think they'd rather stay in the yard and talk than come in. But the teacher will go get them. Maybe they should stay at home, if they like to talk so much. But I guess you can't be at home all the time. I guess they should stay here, and then when they get home there will be plenty of time for fun."

So it goes for Laura — and for Janice and Henrietta. The two girls have stayed — and not done so badly, after all. Laura continues to take note of them; they are special in her mind, two close "colored" friends who quite obviously rely upon one another and have demonstrated to Laura and others their pluck, their determination, their ability to keep on coming to that building. As Laura has noted, they could probably have a better time elsewhere, but again, they "can't be at home all the time." I later asked Laura whether she in fact thought Janice and Henrietta desired to stay home rather than come to the school they are now attending. "No," she answered immediately. "I think they really do want to come to our school. They say it's *their* school, too, and I think it's right they say that. I'm not for more and more colored kids coming here, because pretty soon we wouldn't have any room, the white kids wouldn't. But if they send over Janice and Henrietta each year, and some of the others, I think we'd all feel good, because it's like our teacher says: there is every different kind of person in the world, and if you don't get to meet them all, you're not going to know what they're like. The teacher told us she thought she was learning herself, now that we have new people coming from different places in the city, and we should, too — we should learn, too. My mother said the best thing is to let everyone be polite toward everyone, and we try to do it."

From all I have seen they indeed are polite; girls like Laura and Janice, or Laura and Henrietta are not very friendly to each other and not unfriendly. They keep a certain distance, yet talk in an open and cordial and familiar way. At times as I talk with Laura or with Janice or with Henrietta, I think that for all the world the year could be 1962 or 1963 — and I am back in the South, talking with young southern white children and young southern black children, who likewise gradually learned to get along, to stay somewhat apart but also move step by step by step toward some familiarity, some capacity for mutual recognition and acceptance.

In the Places Where the Mountains Are Gone

Work and No Work

The states of Illinois and Ohio are familiar to him. He also knows the southern part of Michigan. Breathitt County, Kentucky, is where he's from, though, and like so many others, he gets back to Kentucky a few times a year, mostly on holidays. He is six feet three and muscular and blondish; his face is prematurely lined. He has gray eyes. His arms and legs are long. I believe a lot of people would think of President Lincoln when they saw him: the angular features, the heavy eyebrows, the untamed hair, the heavy, sad look on the face. In Chicago he talks about his mountain life ahead — after he strikes it

rich. There is a pleasant glow to him when he speaks about that future, but the glow fades fast. One believes in his self-knowledge without his having to put his despair into words. Though he cannot give
his "realistic perceptions" the brutal force of language, no sensitive observer would need him to construct a wordy analysis of "the muck of
life" he feels himself struggling through.

He tries hard to get through that life, as hard as any "realistic" observer could ever expect him to try. Yes, he has a huge appetite for beer
and whiskey, which are supposed to push people into a "dream world"
or bring on "depression," if not a "manic" attack. Here he is, though,
sober as can be and utterly "oriented" and thoroughly clearheaded —
two days after he has lost a job, an hour after he tried to find another
job: "The trouble with me is that I've got my body here, and it's willing
to work, and I've got my head, and it tells me to go to work, and I can
take care of a horse and goats and chickens and I can grow crops, but
I'm not good for a single thing up here, except what they call 'day labor.' When they run out of day labor, that's the end of me. In Breathitt
County I couldn't make a single penny. There was no work at all; and
that's why we've all come up here to Chicago: we thought we'd go get
work, and then we could buy our kids shoes and our women would
have shoes, too. But you get up here, and there's work one day and no
work the next, then work again, then no work. How long can a man
stand it? I try to talk to myself. I try to tell myself that this is a good
country, and I've not seen the end of my life yet, and one of these days
a man like me, who's strong and willing, will be able to go into a place
and say: here I am, and all I want to do is give you every ounce of energy I've got, and do anything I can, and all I want back is a fair wage,
enough to give my woman some money to buy food and my children
the clothes they need, so they won't go cutting their feet all the time
and shivering come winter.

"I wish I could go back to Breathitt County. If only I could get
work there! Up here I can at least tell my wife to say I've deserted her,
and she'll get money from the city. But I don't picture myself doing
that. I couldn't swallow my pride that way; nor would my wife ever be
able to say something like that. She says she tried to say it, just to herself, and she broke down and cried and cried, to the point that my little girl, Mary Elizabeth, thought she was crying because something
bad happened to me, and when she told her mother what she thought,
of course her mother broke down even more, and I think the child was
really scared quite bad.

"I don't know what is going to become of us. There was a time that I thought God would take care of us. I used to hear my mother pray, even when she wasn't in church, and what she said was this: it's hard, living on that patch of land by the creek, but if God had any other ideas for us, He'd let us know. Well, how long can a man put up with that way of thinking about the world? I tried — until I found myself cussing at the Lord so hard I figured He'd rather I stopped relying on Him at all than saying yes, I'm waiting for you, but then giving Him a piece of my mind when nothing ever happened. I really had to leave Breathitt County. What was there for me to do? Nothing, is the answer. And how many of us brothers could live off that one little farm we have? I was glad to go. I thought I'd do well in Cincinnati, but there wasn't work there. A minister told me to try Chicago. He said this is a bigger city and there's more work up here.

"It sure is a bigger city. I hear on the radio: Chicago, Chicago, a wonderful town; that's a song. I never want to sing it. I'd like to know who wrote the words. He never talked to us who are here from the hills; I know that. Like my wife said when she heard the song: wonderful for those who have it good, and terrible for those who have it bad. Bad as it is here, we have to stay. We've tried Dayton, and we've tried Detroit. I've had jobs for a week or two, and I've tried to save a few dollars each time, and when I heard I might get a permanent job in Detroit, I took us all over there. But they're not making cars the way they used to. Things are slow, so I couldn't find a job. Thank God for the church missions. They help you eat, and they try to get work for you. But when I saw that there was less work in Detroit than Chicago I took us all back to Chicago. Thank the Almighty Lord for my car; and if I didn't teach myself a long time ago, in Breathitt County, how to make an engine go, I do believe we would have ended up in some ditch by some road, and we never would have gotten out. We would have sat there and waited for God to say: OK, come on up here, because you people are really stranded now."

He goes on to tell how he's had that 1959 Dodge for years, how his older brother and he bought it together with money they both got when they came out of the Army, how his brother reenlisted and is still in the service. Now the brother has a new car, while he drives the old Dodge and cares for it and tries to keep it running, because he may have to move on to another city or he may want to go home. And anyway, the one thing he really looks at and feels proud about, feels to be *his*, is that car. Memories, too, go with the car: in it he and his wife and four children left Breathitt County; in it they drove up Route 75 to Cincinnati, crossed the state of Ohio, headed for Chicago, went over to Michigan, returned to Illinois; and of course in it they all go back there to Kentucky "oh so many times a year, whenever it's a good time."

What does he mean by those few words? Is he nostalgic, incurably and ruinously so? (There is a touch of the skeptical moralist in the listener because he wonders whether the man's remark might just possibly "give away" something that explains his trouble finding or keeping a job.) Does he really get tired of the work he finds, leave it, go home, then come back homesick as well as on the look again for employment? I fear a question like that last one is too readily asked by someone who knows something, but not enough, of what actually goes on when many mountaineers try to find work in cities like Chicago. All one need do is go to certain bars in that city, or in Dayton or Cleveland or Detroit, and listen to the men dreaming about the next trip home and talking bitterly and sadly about the disappointments they have met in the city — and the conclusion seems obvious: their hearts are elsewhere, so that they never really stick with whatever possibilities or opportunities may be forthcoming; indeed, after a while they either return once and for all to the mountains of Kentucky and West Virginia, or they live in limbo, not quite settled in the city, but not quite back home either.

All well and good, such explanations; and I suppose one can add the observation that many mountaineers are "naïve" and "gullible" and easily persuaded to accept almost anyone's promises. And of course mountaineers are also poorly educated people, unsuited for most skilled jobs, and by their "cultural tradition" prone to "passivity" and other "traits" that a big, booming, buzzing, business world can do little with except exploit in its own relentless, unthinking, and rather automatic manner. Meanwhile, there is a man's life, his personal experiences, his history as a particular human being, and his narrative history, too — which, as it emerges, gives the listener a thing or two to think about before he accounts for everything in a life: "When I was a boy I'd ask my dad what I'd be doing when I was his age, and he said that most likely I'd be doing what he was doing, trying to stay alive by squeezing what he could out of the land. But there was just so far we could go on a few acres of land. And there were more and more of us hungry for food, too! I hated to leave Breathitt County, but let me tell you something right now: I was also *glad* to leave. I recall saying to my dad: if I can find work up there, I'll be the happiest man that ever lived. He said: son, I know how you feel.

"Since then I've been looking. I've been looking for work, and I guess looking for happiness. I'll never be happy until I find a job and it lasts; and the way things look, that means I'll never be happy. The first thing I found out in Cincinnati was this: if you have only your strong arms, it's no good. They want you to be a carpenter or a plumber or an electrician. I can build a house, but I didn't have the references they wanted. I've never been an apprentice to anyone, excepting Dad. And the last few years they've been cutting down on construction in the cities, so even if I was a certified electrician, something like that, I might have trouble finding work. I take jobs washing dishes and floors and all that. I've tried to hold on to each job, but no luck. Once the owner said he didn't like a white man doing that kind of work; it was for colored, he said. He said I was being too careful with my work, and I took too much time. Another time they got a machine and didn't need the three of us with the mop and pail. I almost had a job a few times elevator-operating, but they seem to like the colored for that, too. They always complain, the colored, but the way I see it, white people want the colored in a lot of jobs. The people at the employment agency kept on telling us that white people like us, from the hills, don't stand much of a chance in Cincinnati, because some jobs are reserved for the colored, and there are so many of us white people coming in. I had a job washing cars, but it was the same story there; the man said I cleaned each car like it was my own, and that's no good. He said I should go back to Kentucky because I was too good a person for the city; so I told him I would, if he'd only tell me how I could find a job there. He shook his head and said he didn't know.

"In the beginning we were all in one room, the children and my wife and me; and Cincinnati is a hot, sticky city in the summer. We fought for air all day, and at night we were so tired we gave up; I would fall asleep and it was bad, because the last thing I'd think was: maybe I'll never wake up, and *then* I'll be happy. I decided to go farther north. I heard it would be cooler, and besides, I kept hearing we'd have a better chance to find work in Chicago. Well, I heard right and I heard wrong. In Chicago we get it hot and sticky, too — come summer. It's true there are plenty of temporary jobs here, but none that I can keep and hold on to. I get up at four in the morning and I go and try to find something. They'll take me for day labor, like I say, but they tell me right to my face that I'm not an educated man, with a degree from a high school and all that — and with a lot of jobs the people will tell you they have to hire the colored, or else the government will get after them, and all that. It's no good. The factories take people who've got friends and relatives, and now it's slow for the factories anyway;

they're laying off, a lot of them, not hiring. Things have been getting worse the last couple of years, and here it is, 1970, and there's no sign of the country having jobs for a man like me.

"The ministers try to help us out. They have missions. They have people looking out for us. They try to find work for us. They do all they know how. There are some good people in this world, I'll say that: young students and some people that work with the churches. Thank God for their help. They've given us food and helped us find a place to live. We go over to a place they have and we meet other people, and they're just like us: they can't really go back, because you can go for a year and not see a dollar bill up there in the hollows, and they hate it here, but at least there's day labor, so we're not starving.

"I've done so many jobs. I've cleaned places and helped people move and done some raking or shoveling, and I've had some good jobs before Christmas, loading and unloading and keeping stock moving in the warehouses. I wish Christmas came once a month and not just once a year. Between all the part-time work and the busy seasons in the fall and the spring, and with the help we get from people up here, we manage to keep going, and I'm grateful, I really am. I'm sure my kids eat better up here, for all the uncertainty we have from day to day. It's no joy living in these old buildings; there are too many people around, and the halls are as bad as can be — pitch-black, and holes in the stairs. My boy tripped and fell and his arm was broken. My wife tripped and fell and she was bruised and it hurt bad. We all crawl and scurry upstairs like we are frightened squirrels. We stop and go. When we've made it to the top we're safe for one more day!

"I have my beer. Sometimes I have a shot or two of whiskey. I'll tell you why: maybe I've been taken out in a truck to do some moving, and I've been lifting all day, and now I'm through with work and my arms are sore and my hands are red and my back hurts real bad, but I'm home at last. It's been hot all day, and we've been stuffed into that dark truck as if we were pieces of furniture, too. I didn't eat anything, because I get a stomachache when I eat fast and then go right back to lifting. I'd sooner not eat and just work right through. Then the truck finally gets us back to the agency, and they check us out and give us about two-thirds of what we make — the rest goes to them — and then I've got my money. I'm hungry. I'm parched. I'm tired. I'm thinking: what will I do tomorrow? I'm thinking: if I was back in Breathitt County, what would I be doing? The boys say, 'Let's stop and have a beer.' I say, 'Yes.' I think to myself, 'I shouldn't have a beer; I shouldn't have two beers.' But a man has to relax a little. I feel tired enough; if I didn't stop and listen to the music and nurse along my beer, I think I'd explode. I feel like dry powder near a fire, come five or six o'clock in the afternoon. And when you've been going since four or five in the morning, you're ready for a rest.

"We all sit around and talk about the old country, that's what some of us call it, back in Kentucky. We talk about going back, until you'd almost think we *are* back, to hear us. I'll close my eyes sometimes in the bar, and by God I can be right up that creek — sitting there, deciding whether I should go hunting or go visit my cousin Jim. He was killed in Korea, you know. If I keep my eyes closed too long, someone has to nudge me, because I fall asleep. It's in between being awake and falling asleep that I like the best. I'm not really in Chicago and I'm not dead to the world. I'm in the woods, or up one of the hills, or I'm in that store, with some of my 'Chicago dollar bills,' Mrs. Perkins who runs the store calls them. When I come there and pay her for something with cash she says that right off.

"I do, I certainly do, look forward to going back on visits. It's a lot of driving, but we arrange to go when it's really slow up here and I wouldn't be missing any jobs I might otherwise get. We go on holidays, too. We drive through the night. We drive and drive. The old car holds out. I can fix almost anything, if I can get the parts. I try to keep good tires, all four of them. Here in the city as long as I know there's that car outside, waiting on us to tell it where to go, I'm not too unhappy. I can always go back, I say to myself. But I never do, except when it's a good time. A man has to dream, and I do. I see myself finding a real, lasting job, and then I save up money, and we go back to Breathitt County, and I buy the store from Mrs. Perkins. She's getting on. She's over seventy. She would sell, but there's no one to buy. She has no children. She doesn't trust her kin. She'd sell to a stranger first, I believe. But how could I run a store? I'd know everyone, and I'd trust them for the money, because they wouldn't have any. Soon, I'd be owing to the people that supply me, and I'd have to close the store down. She's tough, and she can scare people. It's not in me to be like that. So, like I say, it's a dream I get now and then.

"Up here I can rest on Sundays. I try to find work on Saturdays, if there is any. If there isn't I come back and sleep a little and have a beer and sit and talk with some of the neighbors. I'll throw a ball with one of my boys. I'll watch the television, and that puts me to sleep again. There sure is a lot of talking that goes on in this country. No matter what hour it is, there's someone talking away on the television. And the news, they keep telling you the news, and how bad it is for the

country. I don't understand why America is always having trouble on
its hands. If we're the strongest, we should be winning all the time, not
having everyone talk back to us. But what the country takes is what I
have to take: people say bad things to you, unfriendly things. They'll
say you have no education, and you haven't the right way of talking,
and you're too careful, and you spend too many minutes trying to be
perfect — they say the same thing all the time. Then they'll tell you
they've driven through the mountains of Kentucky and West Virginia,
and they thought it was pretty there, and they want to know if there
wasn't *something* that I couldn't find back there. I tell them no, there
just isn't. They don't understand, though. They think jobs are around,
if you really look. They think we're lazy, or something, and we didn't
have the brains to stay in school, and we're running away from some
crime, you know, or we've done a bad deed — otherwise we'd be back
there.

"There's no use explaining things to people. They believe what
they want to believe. They want to think ill of us; it's easier for them to
do that than think there's something wrong with Chicago. One man
told me that; he said Chicago is his hometown, just like Breathitt
County is mine, and he always thought that anyone who comes here
can find a good job for himself and settle in, and he's sorry I haven't
found what I was looking for up here, but maybe I'm a special case, he
said. I told him he could think so if he wanted, but the truth is that I'm
like my friends and my kin — we have some kin up here, too. I told
him to go check us all out, but he said he had a lot of other things to
do, and I said I wished I was as lucky as he is."

Actually, he does feel lucky at times, because he remembers
worse hardships than those Chicago presents. He knows that he is up
in Chicago because there he can obtain work — even though it is in-
termittent and not highly paid; but still it is work, and the result is
money, food, clothes, and a place to live. To a man who used to go for
days and weeks without seeing a single dollar bill, such a state of affairs is not a disaster. And for such a man the world was never expected to be an ideal place, or a place without substantial pain. The
years in cities like Chicago can only remind a man that if he has it
rough, so do others; and if many have a relatively good life, then no
one is without tribulations. Here, for instance, is what might be called
a philosophical statement, an exercise in reflection and introspection:
"I never thought I'd find Heaven up here. I've been asked whether I'm
disappointed. Are you disappointed, a minister asked us one day. I
said, 'Hell, no.' I shouldn't have sworn, but I forget myself. Of course,

I *am* disappointed; I won't say I'm not. I'd like to be making a regular living. I'd like my kids to be able to say their dad has a job, and his work is something that has a *name* to it. In school they ask them what I do, and they don't know how to answer. I don't blame the kids. They get to feeling sorry about themselves. I tell them not to worry, we'll be fine, but they'll worry anyway. One of my boys asked me if we were on relief. I said no. He said a kid had told him that all of the hillbillies are feeding off the welfare department. I told him to go ask the kid to come home, and I'll straighten him out. I wouldn't hurt the kid. I wouldn't lift my voice at him. I'd just tell him he's mistaken, and I'm sorry he is.

"I'll be walking, and I say to myself: there's something wrong in America, and I wish the government would make the country better. I'll be on the truck, coming back from work, and I see people all dressed up in their suits, you know, and driving good cars, new ones, and even so they look to be in real bad shape. I look at their faces and I say, 'Oh, it's not a good day, is it!' They glare at each other. On the road they use their horns at each other, and they go cutting into each other. If my dad ever saw me use a horn, he'd stop me from driving. He said a horn is for real bad-mannered people. And I've never used my steering wheel the way they do up here. They mean to kill, the way they cut out of line, then cut back in. Then they all catch up with each other, because lights make them stop and go and there's no figuring them out, no matter how clever you try to be.

"There's a lot of good about the city of Chicago. I'm not one of these people who always say bad things. I'm not ungrateful. I saw a television program a few months back. They told me at work to be sure and see it. They said it was about the hillbillies. I felt like telling them to go to Hell, but they're foremen, and they pay you, and it's not worth it, fighting. You never change anyone's mind when you fight. But I remembered what they said, and I watched the program. They had some nice people there — talking and speaking their minds — but there was too much bellyaching, if you ask me. Just because it's not easy for us, that's no reason to keep on complaining and asking for more of everything. I want more work; I could use more money, but I'll be damned if I want someone else I don't know to turn on a television set and see me there saying that it's all bad up here in Chicago. The truth is it's bad everywhere, if you're not making any money.

"If I had money, I'd drive back home. But if I was born here and never knew anything else, I guess I'd be driving all over those big, super-highways, just like the people here do, and cutting in and out, and stepping on the gas with all my might just to move ahead a few feet, and cussing at the next guy because he won't move out of the way — when it doesn't make any difference, because ahead of me is someone else, and then someone else, and then someone else. The way I see it, a city is like a forest, only the people are trees and bushes, and they're all over, and you learn to live with them. I'll be walking down the street, and I see people cutting into each other, like they do in their cars, and they run and bump into the next fellow, and they push someone else to one side. They're just trying to make a path for themselves, I guess. I'll be thinking to myself that it's like in the hills, when I want to be in a meadow but I'm in the woods, and I get caught by a bush, you know, or I nearly trip over a fallen branch, and I say: I've got to keep pushing through here, even if the path gives way and it's hot and the bugs are all over me and I get scratched and I'm afraid I'll lose my bearings. If you want to hunt, you have to push into the woods. No animal is going to stand out there in the meadow and say: here I am, and there's nothing to hide me, or protect me, and go ahead, enjoy yourself walking through the grass, and I'll be standing and waiting on you to come across me and lift your gun and fire. Like I say, if you want to hunt you have to make your way through the woods, and if you want to get someplace in Chicago you've got to force yourself through the crowds.

"I'm not as God-fearing as I guess I ought to be. When I was a boy my mother taught me I might have to wander for a long time before I found my God. I always thought that would be after I died, and not before I go to my grave. We've been doing our share of wandering since we left home, and there may be more ahead. I should pray harder when I'm in church. Maybe God is signaling us. Maybe He wants us to go someplace else. But Chicago is the best we can do, I believe. I told my wife the other day that if there's to be more wandering, like the minister says, it'll probably come later, when we've departed this earth. We're alive here in this city, and if a man can say he's kept his family alive, I don't believe he ought to be too bitter, you know. I moved with my wife and children because there just wasn't another thing to do, except throw ourselves on the mercy of the county officials, and they would have laughed and told me my family is no friend of theirs, and why don't I leave right away, before I'm carried into jail. I have a friend who keeps on saying that these cities are like the Hell you would hear the ministers back home talking about, but I look him in the eye and I say, 'You're here, aren't you?' Then I say, 'I'm going back home in a month or so, and you can squeeze in with us. Would you like to go? Would you like a one-way trip for free back to Kentucky?' He'll show a big grin then and say no, and then I say that I feel like he does all the time, but you can't let yourself forget why you're up here. My wife is the one who reminds me, and I keep her words in my head. A woman can make a man stop and think."

He likes to stop and think. He likes to talk and reminisce. But most of all he likes to keep busy. If he can't find work, he walks and goes to a bar and talks, and he goes to a "center" and sips free coffee, and he goes to his car and looks at it and checks on the motor and makes sure it sounds right and runs right and looks to be responsive and ready to go and able to last the journey. More and more, though, he doubts there will be any more long journeys. Trips, there will always be trips back to Breathitt County; but his children will grow up in Chicago, and it may even be that he and wife will die there, rather than in Breathitt County. He has to accept such a likelihood, come to live with it and find it not unbearable. He has to see in the coming years hardship and struggle, but also a life to be lived, day after day and concretely. The alternative is endless dreaming about a distant and unlikely future in which the prodigal son returns home in triumph. "I'll stay here; I'll stay here and work here and die here." He says that after he has put in a long day's work and has a beer or two in him and has had a thought or two about the old days "back home" and now has to pick himself up from the chair and walk out into the streets, Chicago's streets, and make his way "back home" — to his family in a nearby building.

Sally

Ten years is a decade, I was told by Sally three days after she became a decade old. In Chicago a child learns things like that, Sally also hastened to tell me. I asked her whether there was something special about Chicago that enabled her teachers to be so fine — because, after all, Sally was always telling me how "very good" these teachers are, and how "poor" (she was sure) her teachers were back home. Not that she can really remember that one year of school she had in the little school near Burning Springs, Clay County, Kentucky. As we talk I find her constantly struggling to forget the past, or else happening to forget it, or else pretending to forget it — then all of a sudden remembering it with a vengeance.

I fear I had better explain my language and my various qualifications. Sally likes to think of herself as a native of Chicago, even though she knows full well that she was not born in the city. About three years ago her teacher asked the class who was *not* born in Chicago. More than half the children in the class raised their hands, Sally told her mother later — but Sally didn't. She said at the time that she didn't know why the teacher would want to ask such a question, since it seemed "stupid." Her mother told her she was right: "I said to Sally that there are a lot of poking, prying people up here in this city. They want to know everything. They're worse than the sheriff and his people in Clay County, that's what I believe."

More recently, Sally likes to joke with her younger sister, tell her that they were both born in Chicago, and they will one day go to New York City, which is even bigger and "more of a city" than Chicago. Sally hears her teacher talk about New York or Los Angeles, and then tells her sister Anne what has been said — but, again, she confuses her sister by mixing in with all sorts of facts and descriptions the remark that Chicago is their birthplace, when Anne knows otherwise. Is there something wrong with Sally? I mean, is she at the very least becoming swept up with her own fantasies? Is something even more ominous at work? Does she, in fact, know where she was born; and, if so, does she have a very good reason for amusing herself and perhaps her sister with her story?

I have no intention of turning little Sally into a psychiatric patient. Her "problem" is that she is a very imaginative girl who likes to march up before the class and tell them stories. When she was in the second grade, and not long in Chicago, her teacher asked various children, including her, to come up front and talk for a minute or two about anything the child wished to share with other children. Sally apparently obliged. She said that she had been born in Chicago, then moved to Kentucky for a while, then returned. She said that her father loved to drive bulldozers and once owned a mine, but now had given up on that and instead had brought his wife and children to the Windy City, as Chicago is called. Then she sat down — amid applause. Later, she came home and told her mother what had happened, what she had said, and her mother laughed and laughed, and her usually taciturn father also laughed. So, Sally decided, one gathers, to keep on amusing her parents, keep on trying to make them laugh — and she has succeeded.

Her mother can give a chronology: "Sally has become better and better with her jokes and her stories. She makes us laugh more than anyone. Her dad comes home and he is tired and he doesn't feel any too good. His heart is poor, you know. He always asks for Sally. She comes and laughs at him. She says, 'You're no owner of Kentucky horses.' She says, 'You're no owner of coal mines.' She tells him he'd better go wash up fast, or else she'll *begin* to believe he might be a plain old workingman, just as he says he is. Sometimes she talks like one of her teachers, I guess — I've never met any of them. She tells her dad that she has big hopes for him, but he'd better go and put on the best clothes he has and try to speak the best possible words he can think up. So, her father laughs and laughs and goes and scrubs his face and hands and puts on another shirt, and if he'll have another beer in him before he gets home, and he's not too tired, he'll take up with the girl. I mean, he'll come away from the sink and announce that he had a good day inspecting his mines, and they really are producing. Then he'll tell her that he decided to ride a bulldozer or two, just so he could show the men how good he was, and how good *they* ought to be. She comes right back at him and tells him she still wonders about all those horses he owns. I guess the teacher told the class that Kentucky is known for all its fast-running horses. Well, her daddy says he rode two or three of them in the morning and turned them over to one of his 'men.' Sally says she wants to ride a horse someday, she really does — and then I get a little frightened for the child, because I'm her mother, and I can look in her eyes and see the tears she's fighting back and see what's in the back of her head: she is wishing with all her might that she *could* be riding a horse, and be out in some pastureland and not here in this neighborhood. I'll have to agree with her, but I never could say so. I think it would break the girl's heart to hear *me* say that it's too bad we're not back home — only with some money, enough money so we could own a horse and not be hungry all the time."

Sally can also turn her attention toward others. Yes, she is partial to her father, but she is also close to her mother, and the mother depends on the child for the same kind of affectionate reassurance the father often gets upon his return home. If the mother can describe what goes on between father and daughter, the father can describe what his wife and child say to each other at certain moments: "They're like on a television program, that's how I'd describe them when they get to talking and laughing. Sally tells her mother that she's going to Washington, D.C., and when she gets there she'll send a postcard back home. Then my wife asks the girl what kind of postcard, and Sally says it will be of the White House, and she will say on the card that she's visited the place and talked with the President. Then her mother asks her what she'll tell the President when she gets to see him. Well, damned if that little girl hasn't got a long story figured out in her mind. I don't know where she gets those ideas from, but she sounds like the old union men I knew back home, some of the time she does — and great storytellers they were! Then at other times she just seems funny, like a comedian, you know. Maybe she will get herself a job one day on television; they have a lot of nice ladies talking and letting you know all kinds of things when you turn on to listen to them.

"Sally will say she wants the President to know that we're the best people in the world. She tells her mother to get ready, because the postcard is going to be a huge one, and there will be a big, long message on it, with the White House for a picture on the other side, like I said. Sally says she'd write like this: Dear Mother, I'm here in Washington, and I saw him, the President, and he's a nice man, but he hasn't come to Kentucky to visit our people there, and he hasn't seen us in Chicago. We're doing fine in Chicago, but we need help. He should make sure everyone in Chicago has a job, or else there will be trouble. I told him so. I told him he's got a nice house, and there are nice buildings in Chicago, too. So, we should have a nice place to live.

"She has a new message each time, and her mother surely does laugh. She tells Sally that she started talking the day she was born, and she's never stopped and never will. I have to say that the girl is a puzzler to me sometimes; she's got a very strong imagination, our minister said, and her teacher back home said the same thing after the first day the child spent in school. When we left for Chicago the teacher said we should tell Sally's teachers up here that Sally was the best storyteller in the mountains. We never have met any of Sally's teachers, what with city living being as it is, but I think they know, they know about Sally. We got a note last year that said our daughter might turn out to be an actress one day. I told my wife: she'd make a lot of money, a lot of it, and we'd have our problems over that — spending the money. The truth is that Sally has a good sharp ear, that's all. She can listen to me or her mother or a kid she's playing with or a teacher, and then what she does is come home and start talking like she's heard the person talk, imitating the person. I believe I could do the same, but I'm too shy. My brother, he'll get a drink or two in him, and he starts picking away on that guitar of his, and soon he'll stop and tell one story after another, and he has everyone laughing so hard they're pleading with him to stop, but when he does, they plead for just one more story, please. The thing that gets to them is the way he'll take off after other people; he uses their voices, and he makes you think that it's them, and not him, who's the one talking. Now, Sally has been with him, and I told her mother: it's catching, like a sickness can be, except that I'd rather make people laugh than get them sick. Sally caught her uncle's storytelling gift, the minister told me, after I said she'd sit on his knee and listen to him.

"Sally's uncle, my brother, is dying. He should be up here in Chicago. They'd fix him if we took him to a hospital. He can't see a doctor back home. He's got no money. They only care for money, most doctors do. They have all that talk about helping people out, but if they don't get those dollar bills, they say, 'Sorry, mister, I'm too busy for you.' Sally says we should bring my brother up here, and she'd go with him to the hospital and between the two of them all the doctors would be laughing, and they'd become a friend to him and cure him. She's always seeing the good side, that girl is. I tell her, she was born in the middle of the day. I remember. The sun was out all the way. I think the result is that she's a very happy child, and she likes to make everyone else happy."

Does the girl get carried away with herself? Does she know the difference between fact and fantasy, between the stories she tells and the actual, day-to-day life she lives? Is she "basically depressed" or seriously fearful and anxious — all of which she "denies," or "projects" onto the people in her stories? Is there something "bizarre" about her behavior, something seriously "hysterical" or "prepsychotic" — and on and on? I have to emphasize that Sally has not been sent to a child-guidance clinic or any other kind of clinic by her teachers or her family's minister. Nor does she make people nervous or apprehensive or worried for her or about her. Nor is she out of touch with what psychiatrists call "reality." She knows exactly who she is and where she lives and what her prospects are. Perhaps she knows all that a little more acutely and vividly than the rest of us, who spend a good deal of our own time using psychological mechanisms like "denial" — to protect ourselves, for example, from thinking "too much" (or at all) about the fate of people like Sally and her family, including her uncle, whom I have met, who worked in a mine for twenty years, who was fired without a pension and now is dying of pneumoconiosis, so-called black lung disease. The coal dust is choking the man to death, but still he struggles not only for a breath, but a chance to entertain, make people laugh, keep his own spirits up. As for Sally, she also is struggling with the darker side of life — and she also tries to push aside her

worries, many of them quite real, or "objectively based," as I sometimes hear it put in conferences.

Here, drawn together from many conversations — because, of
course, children of ten, even those natural-born talkers and entertain-
ers like Sally, don't go on at such lengths without interruption — is
the sober and undramatic side of the girl, the side, I suppose, that
would reassure one like me, who always has to consider how "appropriate" various forms of "behavior" are, and how "well-integrated" or
"pathological" a child's "defenses" are, and how successfully the child
is moving along up some "developmental scale," which means how
"normal" the child can be considered — perhaps *judged* is the word: "I
don't believe everything I tell my friends, no I don't. My daddy told me
once that we don't have to sit and stare and feel glum all the time. He
said I should never lose my smiling face, so I try to smile, and if I tell
him a story, then he smiles. I've seen my daddy cry. He hasn't the
money we need. He tries to work, but the jobs close down, and he has
to look again. He has a bad arm from working in the mine. But at least
he can breathe OK. My uncle, he tries so hard to breathe you just sit
there and hold your breath and hope he'll catch *his*.

"When I grow up I'd like to live in a nice, big home. I'd have a lot
of food in the kitchen, and anyone who wanted food could just knock
on the door, and I'd ask them to come in, and I'd tell them they should
eat all they want, because it's no good to be hungry. I'd give people
work to do. They could work on the house to make it look nice. My
daddy had a job cleaning out a place; they had torn down a building,
and they were going to build a new one. Daddy helped get all the
wood and pipes and bricks into trucks. It's too bad they won't let him
do work on the new building, then he'd make a lot of money, he says.
He can build anything, I think. He says he can. But he's not in the
union. All they let him do is clean up and load the trucks.

"I don't think I'll ever live in a mansion, no. The teacher showed
us some pictures of big homes, and she asked which we liked best. I
said I'd like to go and see them, and then I'd decide on my choice. The
teacher said that was what she expected me to say. She said I was always wishing I'd get a peek at the rich people. I didn't answer her, but
I was almost going to say that a peek would be all I'd ever get, I know
for sure. Daddy said that's right, and so did my mother. It doesn't seem
fair that only a few people have houses like that, big ones with a garden all around. If we had a garden, we could play on the grass. I think
my uncle could breathe better if he lived in one of those houses.

"I wish we'd go back to the mountains. I like my teacher and my friends, but I think we'd all be happier in the mountains. My daddy says if only we had a little money, he wouldn't stay here one minute. I tell my friends I was born here, but I'm fooling them. I'm from Kentucky. Maybe I'll live there when I get older. I told a boy that I was going to Washington and to New York, and he believed me — until someone told him I was fooling. I don't think I'd like going so far away from home. My mother says that if you don't know a politician, there's no reason to go visit Washington. All the politicians from all over the country live in Washington, because it's the capital. Daddy says the politicians get the money that's collected in taxes, and they fight over who is to keep the money. He says that no one in Washington or any other place sees that people up the hollows get much of anything.

"If I had one wish, and no more, I know what I'd wish. I'd wish my uncle got better. Then, if I could have another wish, I'd wish that my father found a good job. He says it's in Kentucky that he'd really like to be working — so, I'd wish he had a job back in Kentucky. Then, if I still could wish things, I'd ask for a new dress and some shoes and a doll and a pair of roller skates. I'd ask for a bicycle. They are expensive. They cost more than a man can make in a week, even up here in Chicago. Of course, if you live up the hollow, there's no need for a bike. Even a car can only go halfway up the hill; that's how it is if you live in a hollow.

"The saddest thing I see is when my mother has to go shopping, and she's afraid she hasn't the money she needs, and she starts crying. I try to make her stop. I come near and tell her something funny. If I can't make her smile, I keep on trying. I make up a new story, one she's never heard, and she pretends she's not listening, and her head is still down, and she's sniffling and wiping her eyes, but I know she's heard me. Yes sir, I know by the way she turns a little to me, and I can see her face, and there's a smile beginning on it. When I finish, she takes me round and says, 'God bless you,' and I can see she's more smiling than anything else. The tears are mostly gone."

I am not sure that the description Sally offers of what goes on between her and her mother doesn't apply quite exactly to what goes on between Sally and some of her friends, whom she so ambitiously and warmly and generously entertains. For that matter, I am not so sure that Sally doesn't do her share for her teachers, too. They also get weary and discouraged — and as I try to show in a long section of this book devoted to schools, a classroom can be a scene of great sadness, and therefore present a child like Sally with a particularly strong challenge. And so, when I went to see Sally's fifth grade teacher I got from her the following response: "She's a lovely child. Her mind fairly races along. No, I have never felt her to be particularly troubled. I suppose all my children here in this school are in a bit of trouble. They come from poor families. Their parents would much rather be back in Kentucky, up those mountains, than here in this big, sprawling city. They all get confused, the parents do, and the children naturally try to help them out. We forget sometimes how much a child like Sally can do to comfort her mother. Sally is a born nurse, that's my opinion of her. Miss Florence Nightingale, that's Sally. I've called her that. She looks embarrassed, but she loves me for giving her such a nice, long, impressive name. I told her that Florence Nightingale was a nurse who helped soldiers who got hurt in war. Sally said her father had been in the war, the Korean War I believe, and he'd been in the mine union and fought with the bosses — the bosses of the union, I'm quite sure, as much as the bosses of the coal mine. They're all corrupt, you know — labor and industry both. It's people like Sally's parents, and us, the schoolteachers, who get caught in the middle.

"Anyway, when Sally once told me that her father had been in fights, I told her that we never stop fighting, one way or another, until we die. After I'd said that, I bit my lip. I thought to myself: she's ten years old and too young to hear that kind of talk. But she knew exactly what I had meant. I'm afraid that she's probably heard much worse at home. She said, 'I know. My daddy says he has to fight all the time.' I asked her what she meant — as if I didn't know! — and she told me how he has a bad arm, but he goes out every day and uses it and uses his good one, too; he shovels and rakes and lifts things and pushes things and moves things, and then he comes home dead tired, but glad to have the dollar bills. I felt my eyes filling up, so I turned away from the child. That was all she had to see. She's a bright little one. She doesn't miss anything. I think a lot of my children are like that. They live close to much suffering, so they keep their eyes wide open. True, some of them close their eyes and keep them shut tight for the same reason — they've seen so much, and they don't want to expose themselves to one more thing. But a girl like Sally is too smart; she's going to keep on noticing all the troubles in her world, and then she's going to do her level best to heal as much as she can. The first day in this room, she asked if she could bring her daddy over to plaster the walls and get rid of the cracks. I was taken aback, and then I thought to myself: there's a girl who's trying, really trying!

"I was saying — I was saying I almost broke down and cried before the child. I turned away, and there she was running up to me and telling me that her daddy was a funny, funny man, and when he got started on one of his real funny stories, she knew the clock would go around and around until at least a whole hour was gone. Then she told me how her father knows more songs to play on his guitar than anyone she's met, and how he makes faces at her, and she makes faces back. By that time I'd forgotten everything sad I'd heard. The child is so full of life that she makes you want to take her aside and ask her how she does it, become so charming and vivacious. I believe some children are born that way, and their parents have a godsend when they get such a child. I just cannot imagine Sally's mother or father becoming *too* sad, not with a girl like her around. She's like a soldier. She stands guard over people so they don't sink too low, so they keep their morale as high as possible. And she is not a mixed-up little girl. She's not constantly worrying over something. I've seen children worry about their parents and worry about the entire neighborhood they live in. They may also try to cheer their parents up, but they never do — because they're not very cheerful themselves. With a child like Sally — she's not the only child I know who's so sensitive and thoughtful — the good humor in her soul, the lighthearted quality she has, simply comes across and lifts up a person's spirits.

"Don't ask me where she gets those qualities. I told you I thought one either has them or doesn't. I think children are born different. Some are going to live, and some are going to die. I believe that. Some look sickly from the first day, and some look as if they're ready to leap into a boxing ring and start fighting. I'm no mother, but my sister has had four children, and I've been working with children and meeting their mothers and talking with them for twenty years now — so I think I know a little. When I get my new class each year, I look at the boys and girls, and in a few minutes I've moved from face to face, and I can almost count the children with spark in them and the ones who have given up. That's what I'll catch myself thinking with a child. She's *alive,* or she's *given up.* Sally will never give up. She's like her ancestors. They were tough people; they battled their way into those hills, and they've managed to stay there despite all the suffering they've had to face. I've taught all sorts of children, not only children from Appalachia, and I do believe there's a special sadness some Appalachian children feel — and a special liveliness and strength they have. In a girl like Sally I think I see both of those qualities; she's very wise, the way a tired and old and disillusioned grandmother can be, but she's also as sprightly and gay and lovable as the young and vigorous child she certainly is."

I was told more, all of it essentially the same thing: Sally is a somewhat extraordinary girl, but then every year there are to be found a few children like her because, in the teacher's words, "that's the way the human race is." Sally herself admires a boy who is not in her room but is in her school and her grade; her reasons for admiring him and considering him special and extraordinary tell a good deal about her: "Tim is always trying to run fast and hit the ball as far as he can. He says he could climb up every mountain in Kentucky if he could only have the time. He says he wants to be a pilot, and then he would fly over the mountains and find the tallest one. He would land the plane in a valley, and he would go climb right to the very top. Then he would go down and help get his grandfather to the top, because his grandfather is very sick, and he says that before he dies he'd like to go up the tallest mountain in Kentucky and sit there and look. Afterwards, he could die happy. I told Tim I'd like to go with them. We could see for miles and miles, in all directions. Tim says here in the city you can't see anyplace, just a few houses ahead of you, and the streets have big trucks, so you can't even see across to the other side a lot of the time."

She goes on to describe Tim as an active, bright boy and she admires him because he is very much able to manage things in Chicago, but at the same time he has not forgotten the mountains and their importance. And Sally, who can blithely deny being born in those same mountains, how can she so admire Tim for talking so much about Kentucky and its hills and rivers and fields and animals and creeks and hollows and small towns and winding dirt roads and ponds and lakes and flowers and animals and fish and single-track railroad lines and small bridges one can casually walk over — right down the middle and with no fear of traffic? Sally is not in the least worried by the apparent incongruities some fastidious grown-up has noticed and seen fit (had the gall) to mention: "I like to get some of my friends real mad at me. Almost everyone in my room was born in Kentucky or maybe West Virginia, my daddy says, or if they weren't, they just barely made it to Chicago. My mother says a lot of people from the mountains have been here for a long time, so they could have been born in Chicago, a lot of the kids in my room, but their mothers usually have gone home to be with their families when they found out they were going to have a baby. In my room most of the kids admit they were born in Kentucky. No one wants to be born in Chicago. This is no city to be born in! So, I go and say I was born here, and they all laugh and say you never can tell what Sally will come up with."

She can actually go back and forth about Chicago: the city is awful, noisy, too big, or the city is full of secrets and mysteries and nice, nice people. There is her schoolteacher; there is her best girl friend; there is Tim; there is the janitor, who is kin of hers, and is very much taken with Sally. "I guess I haven't made up my mind," Sally says, speaking about Chicago and Appalachia and urban living and the rural life and her future: "Sometimes I think one way, and sometimes the other. Sometimes I think I'd like to live in a new apartment building right here in this city, on the top floor; other times I want to be back with my uncle and grandmother in Kentucky. I know my daddy's heart is there; he says so. I know the same is true of my mother — she stays here because we all have to stay here, she says. And she doesn't agree that we should go back home to Kentucky all the time. My mother says if she was going to have another baby, she'd be glad to go into a hospital right here. When my daddy worked in the mines they had money, so we were all born in the hospital, and my mother had a doctor when she needed one. But after he got laid off they didn't have any money at all, and my mother lost two babies soon after they got born."

For Sally, life goes like that: one measures advantages and disadvantages; one sees the good and the bad; one doesn't quite know; one tries hard to find and then emphasize the enjoyable and amusing side of life; one does what a person can to keep going, to be animated and of a sunny disposition; and all in all one manages, even at ten, to inspire in young friends and older parents or teachers a certain "gladness" about life. That is the word Sally's mother uses to describe her child's influence upon her particular world: "The child gives us a little gladness when we sorely need it." The mother said that and moved her long, thin, bony fingers toward the child; quickly the fingers worked their way up the child's short arm and reached her shoulder and clasped it; then the child rocked a little, in response to her mother's pressure to do just that; and the child smiled, obviously delighted to be having such a good, close time. And the mother smiled, too.

Those Places
They Call Schools

P eople like me visit a large number of schools, talk with the principals and assistant principals and teachers and children, then leave and soon have our say: this school had some interesting things going inside it; that one was awful; the children over here are learning practically nothing; the children over there may be picking some things up in the classroom, but the price — psychological, emotional, spiritual if you will — they pay for the achievements is much too high.

Meanwhile, the children keep on going to school. Sometimes we learn what they think: their poems or compositions are published; their words, spoken under a particular set of circumstances are reported. Their "attitudes" are elicited and are analyzed and are declared to be statistically significant so far as one or another "variable" goes, and are then summarized and written up and discussed. For all the effort that goes into those studies, and for all we find out from them, I am not sure we don't miss a lot, miss a lot that we want to know and need to know. I realize from my own work how much I miss — how the drawings I ask children to do, because I have in mind certain things, often disappoint me, simply because a few moments earlier or later I hear something or see something that reminds me once again how ambiguous and inconsistent and contradictory and ironic and frustratingly, delightfully unpredictable the human mind can be. So, I have to place those drawings and paintings alongside other "data": the observations I've made of the way children play, the talk I come upon, the things that are done (or indeed not done) in the natural course of a child's life — a part of which, it happens, I'm going around to witness.

Yet, I also have to give those drawings or the words I hear spoken an authority all their own, not subject to all the qualifications and interpretations and explanations and translations that in this age have made any statement, however clear-cut, direct, and to the point, something to be deciphered only by a certified oracle. I think one of the children I am soon to quote put the matter very well when he took me to task this way: "I don't know if I meant anything — except what I said. I listened to what you asked, and then I thought to myself that he wants a straight answer, so I'll give it to him, and then I thought of what I thought, and then I tried to tell you."

Perhaps at this point I had best simply describe what I did and when — the "method of research." I selected for study schools in thirteen cities, located in every section of this country: the Atlantic seaboard, the Midwest, the upper South, the far West. The cities (large, medium-sized, or small) were chosen because they have, or claim to have, schools which are making some headway, some substantial progress with — well, the boys and girls are called any number of names: "ghetto children," or "culturally disadvantaged children," or "poor achievers," and many other euphemisms. The point was not to document once again how awful it can be in school for ghetto children, or how frustrated and finally enraged many of our teachers have become. Rather, I hoped to discover what hope there is, and to compare one kind of effort against another, and thereby see which educational achievements seem to offer most promise for children, for teachers, for principals.

So, I traveled the country, and I took the schools at their word, letting their claims determine which ones I studied. If a school declared or even tentatively suggested that it was *doing* something, then I asked if I could come and see and listen and learn what I could about what can be done to make better students out of apathetic or distrustful or merely indifferent or dazed ghetto children; about what changes have to take place — academic, institutional, psychological — if children are to learn more than they have and remember more of what they learn; about how those changes, when made, actually affect children, and others, too — since teachers and administrators may also change, may also feel themselves on the one hand more useful, or perhaps on the other disappointed or even betrayed, to use a word not at all out of keeping with the depth of feeling I eventually encountered. Throughout, I hoped to learn whether something was actually happening in schools said to be places of improvement, of reform and uplift. I looked at everything in the school that might make teachers teach better and expect more of their pupils, or make children feel better about themselves, their studies, their destiny. I tried to take into account for each school its past history; its present policies; its architecture; its facilities; its curriculum; its personnel and their background, their training, their reasons for being there and not elsewhere;

and most intangible but very real, its "tone" — a product, immediately, of a particular principal and set of teachers and group of children, and even the climate of opinion that characterizes a given region, a state, a city, a neighborhood, then a street, a school, a classroom, eventually emerging in a teacher who teaches in a certain way, and across the room, a child who responds to it all in a certain way.

Though I interviewed a wide range of children — black and white, from rich and middle-class and poor homes — I was chiefly interested, first, in the educational difficulties that face poor children (and their teachers), and, second, in progress made, however minute, rather than yet another examination of how bad things are. In three cities the schools were clearly in ghettos, were almost totally made up of black children, though in each instance the faculties contained both white and black teachers. In five cities a bussing program was in operation — bringing black children, and even on occasion, white children from relatively poor districts to schools set in the middle of well-to-do neighborhoods. In the remaining five cases, whether by deliberate design (districting and redistricting) or by fate (mixed neighborhoods or adjacent ones) children of both races and varied "socioeconomic levels" studied side by side.

I found among teachers three consistent sets of attitudes and expectations; and I found among children three consistent views of themselves, their position in the world, their future. Moreover, in most instances, what the teachers predicted and deemed possible for the children about what life in the long run would bring them, about what schooling meant and will mean to them, had come true. The children had already, even at, say, six or seven, acceded to their teachers' judgments about themselves, about what would happen to them, sooner or later.

Ghetto Schools

East Park

Two separate municipalities combine to form this small northeastern community of twenty-four thousand. Before 1966 each ran its own elementary and junior high schools, although one high school served them both. The smaller of the two towns integrated early and easily: in 1948 all kindergarten through fifth grade pupils were assigned to one elementary school and all sixth through eighth grade pupils were assigned to one "middle" school. The larger town could not find so simple a solution. Since it had only one middle school, integration was guaranteed on that level; but the four elementary schools served neighborhoods of varying racial makeup, and the townspeople were reluctant to bus children to relieve racial imbalance. In 1966 the two municipalities decided to put all students under the control of a single, elected board. The board immediately faced the touchy problem of bussing children, and despite opposition, favored bussing. Today fifty-one hundred students attend the town's schools; nine percent are black. There are four elementary schools, one middle school, and one high school. Elementary pupils are bussed daily to assure balanced enrollments.

Sometimes true wisdom takes the form of doubt, confusion, uncertainty. East Park's superintendent of schools is a young, vigorous, exceptionally well-educated man who has the intelligence to speak clearly and directly, without resort to the jargon that all too many schools of education have borrowed from the social sciences and pressed upon thousands of students. I did not have to ask many questions before he was able — pointedly and exactly — to state the purposes of this study: "You want to know what our teachers *want* for our children, what they have in mind as possible and probable when they enter the classroom and look at those children, mostly white and well-to-do, but some black and far from well-to-do. We've been wondering that, too. We've been wondering whether something doesn't happen almost right off between the teacher and the children. It's hard to put what I mean in words. I guess you have to talk about an 'atmosphere' or a 'climate,' or, if you're an experimental psychologist, perhaps you could say that 'cues' are given back and forth. The teacher comes in and says something or does something, or doesn't say something or doesn't do something — and pretty soon the children have her sized up: what she likes and dislikes; what she thinks about all sorts of things; what she thinks her job is like; how she expects them to behave and learn and get along together in the classroom. And the teacher — she's doing her own sizing up: this kid over here said something 'bright,' and that one over there looks 'dumb' or 'stupid,' and it'll be a long, hard struggle with some of 'those' over there, and this group right here, near the window, they all seem eager and smart and ready to learn. In a month, maybe a week, and I sometimes think in a day or two, the children and their teachers have it all decided about each other — who's who and what's what and how the whole year will go. It's all frightening, and we don't like to think about what it all means."

Yet, in fact, he *was* thinking about what "it all means." In his town black and white children have gone to school with one another for years, but the academic and social problems persist, and he had no desire to let the school system he headed relax and enjoy a certain national distinction that had come its way. In his words: "We moved the bodies together years ago, and we thought that would solve our problems; then we started worrying about the curriculum, and we thought some changes in that would solve the problem. Now we realize that we have to go way back to the most fundamental thing in all education: the teacher. If he or she can't teach certain children, then no matter what else we have here in this town — well, it's just not enough."

He and his deputies regularly meet with the school principals, and they meet with their teachers. They all talk about life in the South, life in the ghetto, life in East Park — for themselves and for poor children, almost all in this case black. They feel it important that they understand various social, political, and historical matters before they ask their schoolchildren to do so. In one meeting I heard a principal talk about an "undertow" that exists in every school — one that is "either positive or negative." Later, I visited his school and spent several days there talking to him and his teachers and a number of children. What did he mean by "positive or negative undertow"? What did he think could and could not be done by the schools, in contrast, that is, to the home, the business world, or the voting booth? How did his teachers see things going with the slow learners, the "difficult black children," to use an expression I had heard him use — sardonically.

"Well, that's the problem. As I said at the meeting, when a teacher talks about 'difficult children' she's in trouble and so am I as the principal — because she's lumping together a lot of girls and boys; I know she is. In a way, you know, a lot of our teachers, in a progressive school system like this, have learned too much sociology and psychology, or maybe learned to use what they've learned in a very self-defeating way. They read and read and take extra courses on Negro History or whatever, and then they take all the phrases they've picked up and do the same thing with them that supposedly ignorant people do with blunter words — discount, discredit, and even slyly insult black people. It's not easy to say something like that, but I see it happening, I hear it happening, all the time. I have some teachers in this school who obviously like clean, quiet, well-dressed, and obedient children who do just as they're told. They don't even like the more active and 'wild' — their word — white child, no matter how intelligent he is, and no matter how 'important' his father is. They are a little aloof and self-contained themselves, the teachers, and they don't take to children who are 'fresh' or 'undisciplined' or 'unpredictable.' If that kind of boy or girl is white, and if they *do* manage to make some kind of peace with him or her, they'll call the child 'zany' or 'zestful' — but in need of 'control.' If the child is black, and they're honest with themselves, they'll say they don't like him; if not, they're liable to fall back on a lot of lingo — he's 'immature,' and he comes from a 'culture of poverty,' and he's 'disruptive,' and he's one more 'difficult black child.' That's why we have to meet a lot, all of us, and I have to say — what I've just now said to you."

One of his teachers seems not to hear his message. She refuses to attend many of his meetings and is frank to say that she "looks for excuses." Yet she has an astonishing record of success with those "difficult black children" — something her principal and vice-principal both know. In the words of the vice-principal: "If all our teachers were like her, we wouldn't have to have those meetings. She's considered an oddball, and she is — but for other reasons than those who call her that realize. They think she's brusque and outspoken — and, of course, she's from the South. Actually she's odd because she really makes those kids work, and sometimes she makes them do more — come out of themselves is the way I'd put it."

So, she skips the meetings, but in class somehow gets "slow" children to speed up. I watched and watched her (and them). I asked her how she did it, realizing all the while that she was not disposed to put the whole business into a few phrases. But she did: "I'm a kind of intense person, emotional you might say. A lot of these kids, they come from families like that — where the mothers shout and scream and cry; you know, let out their feelings. I don't do that, but I let the kids know how I'm feeling. I lean on them, you might say — and I let them lean on me. I don't ever want them to think they can't come up and hold to me, or have me hold to them. And I *look* at them — eyeball to eyeball. I tell them what I want and tell them that they're going to do it, and no nonsense, no messing around. I've lived with colored people all my life, you know. In the South they're no strangers to us. We may not have treated them as our equals, but we lived with them, right beside them and sometimes closer than that. Up here, they don't know the Negro. They don't know where he comes from and how he *is* — in his mind, I guess you'd say it. They don't know how they talk and think and — everything.

"You know what I do. I say, 'Hey, there,' and I say, 'Come on now, y'all go and get that done, and I mean now, or I'll paddle the life out of you.' I'd be ashamed to have some of our teachers hear that — they might call me mixed-up, some of them might. They do, I know. But I'm trying to make these kids feel at home so they can get with it! I talk about the South — many of them have relatives there. I talk about music, *their* music. I show them I'm not afraid of what *they* know, what *they* can do well: music and art and athletics. I show them I know about their history, their speech, their everything, I hope — and they catch on. Oh, it's not even all that deliberate. It sounds it, now that I'm talking, but the truth is that I feel close to a lot of those children, and I guess they pick that up. Then, they also pick up that I want them to move on, get ahead in the world. I tell them that. I say it right out loud. I say are you going to mess around and amount to nothing, or are you going to take notice and get your work done and *be* somebody?

"They want to be somebody, too. They want to read. They're hungrier for education than most teachers realize. We should change our teachers, that's what I sometimes think. We should recruit different kinds of *people* to be teachers. It's what you feel that counts, not only what you've learned in education school — I never went to one, thank God. I might have been ruined for life. I'd be afraid of my shadow — and afraid of theirs, I'll tell you. I'd be afraid to speak up, to give it back to them when they're messing things up, to let them know I'm alive and they're alive and we're going to make something out of it. I'm so tired of all this introspection, this analysis, analysis. You get to the point you watch yourself breathing in the classroom — and of course you get nowhere. The kids can spot that — spot that nervousness, the self-consciousness that takes over. It's terrible, I think. I like to teach. I like these children. I want them to learn, and they get the message. I believe it's as simple as that. Yes sir, I do."

Whether things are as "simple" as she would have them or not, she does indeed reach her children. They study hard, and by everyone's acknowledgment (even those she annoys and antagonizes) she "gets results." Her children speak of her with pleasure and warmth and a proper bit of awe: "She makes you work. She wants you to work, and she'll not stop until she wins you over to her way. She's real friendly, though, at the same time."

To one of her black children she is "the best kind of person because she won't settle for less than everything. That's what she says, and she makes you believe it yourself. One day she asked me what I wanted to be, and I said I didn't know. Then she said, 'What do you mean, you don't know?' Then I said I was sorry, and I did know: I wanted to be a — a teacher. Then she leaned down, and she looked right at me and said, 'I know you're saying that because you haven't really thought of what you're going to be, and you should.' And then she said I had a good kind of mind to be a lawyer — because I was always figuring out the puzzles and asking questions and things like that. So maybe I will be one."

I asked him to paint a picture of her (Figure 25), and to paint one of any other teacher he knew (Figure 26) — and, if he wanted, to tell me how they were alike or different. He would indeed make a good lawyer. He talked as he painted, and he outlined his case rather insistently — in paints and words. I noticed during my stay in that school that his ideas and feelings — about that teacher and about other teachers — were shared by many children.

West Park

This west-coast city has perhaps led the nation in an effort to desegregate its public schools. In the fall of 1968 it became the first city of more than one hundred thousand residents to achieve total desegregation. Some northern cities have closed ghetto schools and bussed black children to schools in other parts of the city or to those in the suburbs, but only this city has combined that sort of bussing with the bussing of white children to former ghetto schools. School officials had to fight hard to do so; board members had to face a special "recall" election when they introduced their initial plan; but they did, and won.

The city has a population of about one hundred twenty thousand: seventy percent white, twenty-five percent black, and five percent Oriental. Many retired people have made it their home, and since they usually have no children of school age, the school population, sixteen thousand, is small for a community of its size. Among the students, fifty percent are white, forty-one percent are black, and nine percent are Oriental. Local chapters of national black organizations — CORE, NAACP, and others — are numerous, articulate, and active. They started desegregation as early as 1958, though not until 1964 did anything tangible result. That year school board members decided to desegregate the city's three junior high schools. They changed one to a ninth grade school, essentially an annex to the nearby high school, and they had seventh and eighth graders use the other two. In 1968 they were ready to desegregate the fourteen elementary schools. This has required bussing thirty-five hundred of eighty-nine hundred pupils daily and takes a considerable slice from the budget, but local citizens have complied with little fuss. Besides, the federal government pays almost half the fare. So, today the entire system is desegregated, down to individual classrooms.

Unquestionably the city of West Park wants to do more than most cities even dream to be either possible or desirable: "We want to do *everything* — everything that has to be done so that black children and white children can go to school together, learn, and learn from one another. That's our purpose, and we spend long hours trying to achieve it." He is a forceful superintendent, no stranger to social struggle. He is surrounded by equally stubborn and bold deputy superintendents and associates of various kinds. He wants, in his words, "more than the appearance of change." He wants "real change," which he defines as "a mixture of academic improvement and psychological transformation." What sort of psychological transformation? "Well, a child's sense that others who are different matter very much, and a child's sense about himself — that he can do a lot, a lot more than he once may have thought possible." Then comes the elaboration: "I'm talking about white children as well as black ones. A lot of black children don't think they can live easy with books, and a lot of white children are afraid of something else — any world except the one they know and own. I'm not sure which fear is worse, but I believe we can help *all* our schoolchildren feel less afraid and more sure of themselves and the world — and of us, as a matter of fact, the teachers and principals and officials in the school system."

So it is intended in West Park's schools, at least at the top. What happens to such intentions as they work their way down the ladder — as commands struggle for obedience, as programs encounter daily events, as outlines seek to become action? The principal of an elementary school gave me some answers to that kind of question. He told me that he was in charge of a "completely and carefully integrated school," and that "every day we see things happen here, important and worthwhile things. We've tried to do away with 'tracks' and 'grouping,' at least the kind that separate children by race or class or even achievement. We try to mix children and teach them not only how to read and write, but live with one another — the rich with the poor, the quick with the slow, the confident with the fearful. I don't mean to sound pious, though. It's not just a matter of being 'good' or 'democratic.' We've seen how children learn from one another and become better students as well as better citizens. And it doesn't only go one way. I mean, I've seen bright white kids from well-to-do homes learn a lot, a real lot from some of our slower kids that came here from what is in comparison a ghetto. I hope you'll ask the children about that — about what they've learned from one another. They might end up telling you what they've *learned*, period!"

I talked to the children with that in mind — did so before I spent time with their teachers — and found the principal's suggestion a very good one indeed. A rather properly dressed white girl had this to say: "My mother was going to take us out of this school, me and my brother. She said she was in favor of integration, but we're very good at school, and we need a school that can keep up with us, she said. My brother, he has an IQ that's so high he's in the genius range, the lady told my mother. But my father said we should stay for a year and see how everything goes; then if we're wasting our time here, we could always go to another school, because there are some real good private ones around.

"I can't say I've made real close friends with any of the Negro kids, but a couple of them, yes; we're pretty good friends. Last week I went over to one girl's house with her. She invited me, and my mother was real worried. When I told her I was invited, she said no, how could I possibly go over there. I said, 'You could drive me, Mum,' and she didn't say anything — except that she'd talk it over with my father when he came home. I don't know what they decided, but later the next day my mother said OK, I could go, and she would drive me, and she'd come and pick me up in a half hour or so. I think it was my dad who told her to stretch it to an hour, though.

"I had a real good time. Sally, she seemed real different in her home. She wasn't so quiet. She was telling me this and that and — everything. She showed me around and had me meet her friends, and she took me to the store, and I met some people there, and she played me some of her records, and I had a good time. She has four brothers, and they think she's the best person that ever lived. They'll do anything for her. They all seem real close together, her and her brothers and her baby sister. They don't have the things we do, they sure don't, but they're real good to each other. I told my mother that on the way home, and she said that's right, because they're poor, and they have to stick together or they won't have anything at all left. But I told her — I told her they *liked* sticking together."

Could she draw a picture or two of her home (Figure 27), and perhaps one or more of her friend's home (Figure 28)? Yes, she could, but before she did and as she did she wanted to say one more thing: "If you go visiting, you see a lot you'd never know about. Now when I see Sally come into school, I know where she's coming from, and it isn't as if she was just Sally, and from nowhere that I've ever seen."

Her teacher had some similar thoughts. Like most of her students and their parents she was also "in favor of integration," but has had her doubts, too. She saw, every day she saw and struggled with, "the great disparities between ghetto children and middle-class children." She remarked, on the favorable side, how obliging and cooperative many black children are, compared to some of the provocative, snobbish, and self-centered children who at nine or ten already know they have inherited the earth: "You hear a lot about the noise that ghetto children make in class, and how unruly they are, fresh and combative. I wonder how many articles have been written about our spiteful, spoiled suburban children, who *also* cause us pain in the classroom." Yet there are, finally, those academic problems: "There is no doubt that the black children we get here are a real challenge to us. At first I tried hard to ignore all differences and simply teach, teach them hard so they would catch up with the rest of us. Then, for a while, I'll have to admit, I became very discouraged. I began to believe that it wasn't hopeless, but it certainly would take time — more time than we have in an elementary school, or maybe any school. But one day I decided to visit several black parents in their homes — they'd asked me several times — and it was the best decision I've ever made as a teacher, yes sir. I saw where those children live — but it wasn't only bad news that I found. I realized how *many selves* there are in one person. The children were different in their own neighborhood. Now they could show *me* things, explain things to *me*. They talked more, were more alive and alert. They seemed friendlier, more trusting. Oh, they were shy and scared, too, but they did something with their shyness and fear — because they felt able to. After all, they could entertain and teach me!

"When I spoke with their parents I realized that we had to do more of this, more visiting back and forth. The black children come home and say things that are picked up and distorted by parents who are as cut off from our school as they are from the rest of the middle-class world. The result is the children's fear increases tenfold in the mother's mind. She becomes angry and resentful. An incident here or there becomes something much larger — and there's no way to talk about it, certainly not in a large, public, formal P.T.A. meeting. In those private conferences with each parent that we have — well, they're held on our home ground, and they can be pretty brief and formal, too. Somehow we've got to bring these families and our family, the school family, nearer. I did it to some extent that day, and I've continued to do it ever since. I think it has made a difference. I *know* it has; the black children come toward me in a more open and direct way. They don't mind being pushed and prodded. They know I'm doing it *for* them, not *to* them. I've seen how smart they are — and smart they can be, in a way, at acting dumb! They know how to frustrate teachers. They know how to be polite, then rude, then nasty. If they see that I'm convinced they're hopeless or worse, they act accordingly. If they see me giving them a lot of excuses, they give them right back to me, plenty of excuses. But once I asked one of them to do something and he said, 'No one ever asked me to do that before.' Then I knew I was at last getting someplace. At last I'd had the sense to tell that child that he *had* to do something, that he was *going* to do something. He had seen that I knew he could do a lot more than seemed to be the case. The reason I felt he could was I'd been to his home and seen what he could do there — take care of his sister and help his mother and deal with the storekeepers and all the rest, even help out at a cafeteria."

She did indeed seem to know her children and get them to respond to her. "Oh, yes, yes you can" were words she used — unselfconsciously and with feeling — over and over again as I sat in the back of her class and watched things move along. The children heard her and seemed to believe her. They tried one more time, and often they succeeded. And then — well, she promised to call up their mothers and fathers and *tell* them they'd succeeded, or, if there was no phone at home, go visit them and tell them the same thing in person. "Why should we only call parents when there's trouble?" she asked me. I had no answer to that.

Mixed Schools

Upstate City

According to the 1960 census 216,038 people live in this northeastern city; six percent are black. In 1959 the city's median family income for whites was $3,308, and $2,566 for blacks. There are many major industries in the city, and electronic and industrial machine industries alone employ over a quarter of the labor force. More than eighty percent of the black population lives in a small "ghetto" area in the center of the city.

About thirty thousand pupils attend the city's schools; twenty percent are black. In May of 1962, CORE picketed the school board and organized a one-day boycott of a highly segregated elementary school. This provoked some response: meetings, confessions, promises. But in 1962–63 fifty-eight percent of all black elementary-school children attended two of the city's thirty-three elementary schools, and most of the other thirty-one were solidly white. Since then school officials have made various efforts to elim-

inate segregation and improve the education given to black children. They have closed "ghetto" schools and bussed black children to predominantly white schools. They have redrawn district lines to correct racial imbalance; they have transformed "ghetto" schools into special, experimental ones — open and attractive to applicants from all over the city. They have also recommended that schools be no more than thirty percent black and no less than ten percent, and they have started a voluntary *transfer program and paid for bussing to help implement their recommendations. Still, segregation persists in certain schools.*

The principal in the elementary school I visited has a quiet, old-fashioned charm. She admits to feeling "behind the times," but in fact has very much tried to keep up with them. She has tried very hard to keep the size of the school's classes down. To do so she has brought in aides, helpers, and part-time teachers. To do so she has worked long hours, read everything about "the disadvantaged child" she could get her hands on, and by her count, attended fourteen institutes devoted to "teaching the deprived." She considers herself a fighter, a veteran of all sorts of battles, not all of them won: "I'll be honest. The city isn't much interested in some of these matters, not really interested. Some are, a lot of those who live near this school, but you lose a lot when you can't fall back on your own superiors, on the school system as a whole. Sometimes I go to meetings downtown and the others there — they look at me as some sort of curiosity. 'Are you *still* trying?' one of the assistant superintendents says to me almost every time. I know he means well, but it doesn't help my morale. And every once in a while I begin to ask *myself* that question."

Most of the time, though, she pours her heart and soul into her school. She is proud that when the city was plagued with riots, her school was ignored. Black people live near the school but traditionally used to go to another one, in the heart of the city's ghetto. Now, through a combination of a bussing program and a change in school-district lines, her school is integrated, and considered "progressive" and "experimental" by school officials. Much of that reputation is due to the principal's efforts — aided by those of some white, professional people whose children make up a large percentage of the school's population. Integration brought troubles, but the principal and her assistant made a series of responses to those troubles: "I had always been interested in retarded children. Amid all our very bright and able children we get some slow ones — who make their eager, intelligent parents feel very frustrated. I know how stubborn such children can be — and how much they can be persuaded to learn, if only we reach them and convince them that there is a *point* to learning. So often they've already learned something — about themselves. They've learned that they're "slow" or "retarded" and that they can't do this or that or whatever. No wonder they're afraid of school, or they become angry and agitated here. I found that teachers who really liked slow children, and believed in them, in what they *might* do, they *could* do, did in fact do wonders. If the teacher feels she can succeed, if she says to you, 'I love the work,' if her face shows her real interest and concern — then the children feel it and respond to her and learn from her. I know that. Of course the entire school system rarely encourages such teachers. Bureaucracies don't usually encourage much of anything — ideas, people, a philosophy. Bureaucracies just exist, I'm afraid. When I was developing my program with retarded children I never went to the bureaucrats. I went to the parents of those children. I invited them to come to the school. I called them 'aides.' I had them all over, learning with their children and learning what their children could learn and — just learning. You'd be surprised at the difference it made. They'd go home and feel better about their boy or girl, and at school they'd help our teachers."

Her teachers need help. They admit to feeling troubled, uncertain, even in despair: "I feel confused. A lot of the time I feel worse than that. I think it's just hopeless. I used to come to my classes full of enthusiasm and pleasure. Now it's different. You never know what new kind of trouble will face you each day. We still have our bright, ambitious children, but we also have these new children — and their whole way of looking at things is different, totally different. I try. Lord knows, every day I try. If it weren't for our principal I'd probably have given up a long time ago. But almost every day she gives us a pep talk, and I take an oath with myself to keep on trying. The trouble is they just don't seem to want to learn — mainly the Negro children. They look bored, or they start getting spiteful, or they turn on the other kids. I don't mean *all* of them, no, but enough to make every day a new source of worry, real worry for us teachers."

She and others in the school cause some of the children to worry, also. One black child in her class, the brightest in fact, the source of least worry to her teacher, spoke these words: "It's a joke here a lot of the time, because they keep telling you they want to help you, but they're all out for their own kind, the white, if you ask me. She keeps giving us those talks on how everyone is created equal and all that, but she's trying to convince herself, that's what I think. She thinks we're dumb, and we need all the help we can get — that's how she's always saying it, 'all the help you can get.' How about her? She could stand some help, too. She gets annoyed at us, and then she tells us we should just keep quiet and behave ourselves until lunchtime. One time we went down to get lunch and she was with us and she saw the woman throwing the food at us and shouting and I heard her say to her friend: 'How can we expect the children to behave, when they treat them like this in the cafeteria?' And her friend, she said they were Negroes, the people in the serving line, and that's what we're used to at home — getting bad treatment, I guess. If I was bigger and out of this school for good, I would have said something. But I didn't. I went home and told my mother, though — and she said that's the way it can go, and you have to close your ears a lot of the time, and your eyes. That's right."

His friend also closes his eyes and ears: "I don't pay that much attention to a lot of things around here. A lot of the kids, they've got so much they don't know what to do with all they've got. I can tell. I listen in. They'll be talking about this thing they have and that thing. So I just pretend I don't hear, and I think to myself that I could take most any of them and knock him flat down, if it came to anything. The teacher, she'll be giving you these lectures on how we should all be friends and like that (Figure 29). But they keep on pressing you down, and trying to get you to talk like them and act like them. You know what I mean? They're unhappy because we don't speak like them, and they want us to cut it out and step along the way they do, but as I see it, we've got our own lives to live. That's what my daddy says all the time — 'Don't you let them give you the idea it's all their ball game, and we have to play according to their rules.' That's what he says, but I'm not sure he's right."

A white student isn't sure either. He comes from a very liberal home. His father and mother "favor civil rights." He has been told again and again that black children and white children are "all the same" and "learn just as well as each other, if only given a chance." So he thinks and so he speaks. Yet he also says other things: "The way it looks, the Negro kids, they're just not prepared like we are. They don't speak up, and the teacher can't understand them a lot of the time (Figure 30). She'll lean over and tell them to say it again, only this time go slower. But they're already talking slow. I think she does understand, but she wants them to speak like us — that's what my dad said — and they can't right off. It'll take a long time — maybe our grandchildren, my mother says. A lot of the time I think the Negro kids would like to be like us and speak the same way and have the same things, but they won't admit it, and they get mad if you say so. The principal, she's trying to make everything go smooth — but she can't do it all alone, and my father says she's fighting a losing battle because of the riots, and the white people, they're just fed up now and won't stand for much more trouble. I asked one Negro kid if he thought integration would continue, and he said he never thought about it one way or the other. But his friend said he hoped not, and he wanted to know what I thought, and I said I was in favor of it, but we had a long road to go yet. My parents say it will take years."

Capital City

Seventy thousand people live in this New England suburban community. Almost thirteen thousand children attend its public schools; until 1966, fewer than twenty-five were black. That year local citizens agreed to accept eighty black students from schools in the nearby city, where the population is one hundred sixty-five thousand and over half the schoolchildren are black. In the city the median income is $6,000; it is twice that in the suburb. City children were taken from schools where the black population exceeded eighty-five percent of the total student body and were assigned to suburban classrooms with vacancies. Most were elementary-school children, though some junior and senior high school students found places. Officials studied the experiment with care and great thoroughness, finally deeming it "successful." Today the program operates on a somewhat larger scale.

"I have to say to you that I never would have dreamed a few years ago that something like this would happen, that I'd be standing out here in front of this school and watching Negro children come here from the city. Sometimes I wonder what they think as they get off that bus and go in the building and go to school."

So he thought — and he certainly knows children, if not black children, quite well. For two decades he has worked with children in a small town near Capital City, first as a teacher, then as assistant principal, and finally as principal. He speaks forcefully, even brusquely, in a way that an older man can sometimes get away with — indeed, in doing so even gain a bit by being considered a man who is "kind underneath." What does he think of the bussing program? What does he think about the black children, about possibilities that they may possess — as pupils and students and future citizens? Does he have any thoughts about how they think of themselves, about their view of what the future holds? How do particular teachers influence the kind and amount of learning that their pupils acquire? The questions are put forth with unusual speed and candor because he seems to invite that kind of pointed, direct conversation. He has strong opinions, he says almost immediately, and he is quite willing to make them known: "I was against this in the beginning, like a lot of people who are now willing to give it all they've got. I'd be fooling you if I told you I said, 'Bring them all out here!' What ran through my mind was — well, 'how can this possibly work?' I kept on asking myself that, but the town didn't want to wait and think. They said they wanted to *do* something — and sometimes I think they didn't care *what,* so long as they felt less guilty. One mother came to see me and practically got hysterical. She kept on saying that we'd done bad things for three hundred years, the white people, and we had to start making amends. After about ten or fifteen minutes of that I told her to stop, please. I asked her what *she* had done to any Negro — she or anyone she knows. Well, of course, the answer is nothing. Then I asked her why she was getting so *emotional* and putting the whole thing on a personal basis. She said she didn't know what I was talking about. So, I said that the way she talked, anyone who had reservations about this bussing program or anything else having to do with Negroes — he's just no good. They call you every name in the book. Talk about 'tolerance' — have the liberals ever looked at their own intolerance? I wonder."

He went on in that vein, and then had the courage and honesty to go further: "I frankly don't believe this is the answer. It will only work for a handful anyway, and it's hard on everyone, the Negro kids and our own. I believe Negro kids need a kind of schooling we just don't offer here — because our children are different. The Negro child brought out here needs discipline, firmness, and patience from teachers. I don't believe they take easily to the kind of freewheeling and imaginative atmosphere we encourage here for our children. Yes, they are stimulated by things here, and some of them have done very well indeed. But some of them have had a very difficult time here, and so have we — with them. They have trouble academically, then they become angry and even violent. Rather than face their own inadequacies, they start striking out, provoking people — teachers and children alike — so that they can have someone to blame other than themselves. It's a very sorry business, and I frankly don't know how to solve it. One thing, too: I know I'm blunt, and I know some other principal will talk a lot differently to you. But they're all facing the same problems I am, even if they put the whole thing in different words. One of my friends in the next town over — they have the same program we do — keeps talking about 'stages' and 'understanding' and 'working out the tensions in time.' It'll take a long time. I think the Negro children know that better than we do, much better. We can fool ourselves, but not them."

One of his teachers disagrees with him. She has heard him say that black children are for all practical academic purposes "different" — which he did indeed say to me — and she has even challenged him at a staff meeting: "One good thing about him is that he can say outrageous things but not hold a grudge against you for disagreeing. He even likes arguments. I do believe the Negro children respect him, too. He is gruff and stern, but he's very personable with them, and they feel that and look up to him. I suppose he's a lot better than the smooth-talking types who smile all the time and say the 'right' liberal things — but really don't like the Negro children one bit. We have some of those, you know.

"The thing that bothers me, though, is that because of our principal's attitude we're not doing all we could, not by a long shot. Actually, I shouldn't say that. Sometimes I think his attitude is good. He makes us stop and think about what *we* think. He makes us question the conventional wisdom, I guess you'd put it. He dares to say a lot that some of us think but are afraid to say. The trouble is that *he* misses a lot, too. He doesn't see the positive side, the slow changes in the attitudes of both our white and black children. He doesn't see how white children from suburban homes learn things from these black children, and how the black children learn — oh, they learn a lot. They learn academic things, and they learn to feel some of the hope that our kids feel. It's hard to put your finger on hope, but if you have it you've got the most important thing in the world, and if you don't, you're in real trouble. I think our black children are doing quite beautifully, for all their troubles here. *They* tell me they're learning better, and I *know* they are, most of them. Bussing is no panacea, I admit that, but something has to be done, to begin with. In the long run maybe we'll have a more metropolitan kind of school system; towns like this one and the cities will join together. We either do that or we tell black people they can have their America, and we'll have ours out here. Our children look to us for signs, too — signs to tell them we believe one thing or another. There are times I think we teachers should be graded. We should pass or flunk, depending on how our children do. I've had some Negro children who would confirm every one of our principal's opinions — and yet I've said to myself that they're going to do better, they're just going to. And it's not the class size or the equipment that *made* them do better. I hesitate to say it, but it was probably me, me and some of the children I enlisted to help me. I called them in, five of them, my best — not my smartest, my *best* — and I said we had to work together and help some of our new students, and yes, we had to let them help us. I didn't know exactly how to put it to the children, and maybe I was condescending — I realize that now. But I wanted something to happen between all the kids, not only between me and the Negro children. So, I told some white children I wanted them to work with the black children: show them around the school and the town, and tell them things, and *be told* things. I had the class divide itself up, so that one child could tell a story to another and be graded — for *interest,* for the power in the story, not grammar. It's not easy to tell you all this, but I think it worked; the children caught on to one another, that's how I'd put it. No matter what their parents thought, or the principal, or after a while maybe even me, they proved they could do things side by side and be teachers, almost as much as I am, I sometimes believe."

One of the white children she mentioned was even more vague, if just as touching to hear: "They're all right. That's what we discovered. And they said we are, too. They told us they wanted to grow up and buy some land out here and build themselves a huge, big house, and we could all go swimming together in the summer. They said they might want to go to high school and get their diploma, and go to college and pick up one there, the same. They said it was fun a lot of the time where they lived, but a lot of the time it wasn't, either. I didn't dare ask what was the matter, and my mother said they probably wouldn't have said, and I did right to keep quiet and mind my own business and try to be friendly. She said a lot of people who live near us, they have a lot of trouble, too."

The black children generally felt glad to be at the school, glad to be "on the inside," one of them phrased it (Figures 31 and 32). He went on: "I don't like everything here, and some of the kids and the teachers, too — they turn you off. But I've made some good friends, and they have a lot of nice things here: it's better in the building, and they give you better food, and they really try to make you learn your lessons. Back at the old school, all they wanted was that we keep quiet and don't make any trouble and sit still. They told us we'd never amount to anything, anyway, and they weren't going to let us cause them any pain. So, if you squeaked your chair, they looked at you as if you'd gone and killed someone, and they were going to kill you back. Here, they're better to you. I believe I'll stay with it, and maybe get myself one of these fat jobs like my friends, their fathers have got. It's getting easier for us; that's what my mother said. So it's worth the ride on the bus, I believe."

Committed Schools

West City

This northern California city has a population of three hundred seventy thousand; about thirty-five percent is black, and about five percent is Mexican-American. The unemployment rate among blacks ranges from fifteen to twenty percent, and dissatisfaction with the squalor and uncertainty of daily living has turned many blacks toward militant leaders, who have considerable power in this community. Fearing "another Watts," the federal government has anxiously responded with aid, studies, "pilot programs" — and with some success; but the sad, explosive mixture of apathy and rage still infects the air and casts a shadow on the city's future.

The majority of schoolchildren are blacks. Schools, like the neighborhoods they serve, are pretty thoroughly segregated. Officials have tried only a small number of "experimental" bussing programs.

He was in many respects the kindest, most sensitive principal I met: a black man, a man capable of firmness and kindness both, a man very much respected by the white parents he met and spoke with every day. (Their children make up over half of his school.) He was born in the South, but brought to West City as a child: "My parents came here to escape. I think they were smart enough to know that there's no escaping the South in some of those northern cities in the East, but the West, maybe there it would be different. They were wrong, of course. This city, West City — well, we're known all over the country for our racial troubles. It's a hard thing to say, but sometimes I wonder whether the long trip across the country was worth it. We're not segregated like we used to be in Alabama, but a lot of my people came here penniless, dazed, confused, at a loss to know what to do. And their children, they don't have much going for them at home. When they come to school they're hungry and weak, and a lot of them, they're sad — sadder than anyone really knows, I'm afraid."

He knows how sad those children are. He also knows how much hope those same children have: "They're already suspicious, a lot of them, but they're looking for something better, too — something better than what they see all around them outside of school. The way I see it, we can try to offer them a little here in this building. We can try to show them other people — me, my secretary, the teachers, the nurse, the doctor, the people who come to help with speech problems. We can try to show them how we take care of ourselves, how we appear and act and talk and all the rest. It may be a long way from here to some of those tenements, even if they're nearby in distance, but we can try to bring things closer together, at least a *little* closer together, in the child's mind. That's what I want to do, as well as see the children learn how to read or count or whatever. But it's not any easier for me, I'll tell you, than for them. They have their problems, the children, and I have mine, too — plenty of them."

He does indeed have his problems. As a principal he feels lonely and embattled. His is in many respects a "showcase" school, one of the city's best, the city's only "really integrated" school. By "integrated" he means something quite specific: "I don't mean bodies whose skin color varies. I mean children from different backgrounds *learning* from each other. I also mean parents learning, too. I try to get the black parents to put pressure on me, to demand things from me, to go downtown and tell the school board they're not happy with what I'm doing, because I don't have enough to offer their children. It's not easy to do — to get them going and to take the risk to myself of getting them going. But I must, as I see it. Our white parents feel that there's a *point* to school, that there's a good reason to keep their eyes on what we're doing here. Many of the black parents aren't at all sure. In fact, they either *know* things are hopeless — and tell you why — or they *feel* things are hopeless, no matter what I say, no matter what they say to themselves. That's pretty bad, isn't it? And that kind of attitude gets across to children very quickly. One black girl was sent down here for being fresh to her teacher, swearing at her when she tried to be helpful. I asked her why she'd done that, and she didn't pause a second before she gave me her answer: 'There's only room for one of us who's black. The rest of us, we have to live different from you. That's what my uncle said. He said school won't get you far, and there's only room for a few black people up top. They'll never let us have our own schools, unless we build our own, and we haven't got the money.' That's about what she said, and you can imagine what she really heard at home. Why *should* she study, if that's what she believes, if that's what she's told every other day of her life, now that she's growing up and finding out about things?"

Children like that child move about, too; from school to school they go, as their families wander within the confines of the ghetto. Children like that child or her brothers don't want to be secretaries, teachers, nurses, professional men, or even big-name sports heroes. A teacher told me how those children think: "They don't really have anything in mind about the future, not when they first come here. They're not accustomed to thinking about the future, about next year and five years from now. With them it's minute to minute. One of the things they learn here, I know, is how to plan ahead, think ahead, and *antici-pate* things — I mean, count on them as well as wish for them. They learn that from some of our better-off children as well as us."

It is not easy for those children to learn, though. So I was told by the principal and by all his teachers. The school has a reputation for being "a good apple in a basket full of pretty bad ones." The school's white children come from rather liberal homes, and as a result, this state of affairs, described by one teacher, is what holds: "The white parents have kept their children here, and as a matter of fact, kept *themselves* here, in this neighborhood. In the beginning they did so with a good deal of fear, but out of principle. Now they're not afraid, and they realize that. *They've* gone through something: *they've* learned something. I know I have. I've learned what black children have learned before they ever step foot in a school. I've learned to redefine the word 'learn.' That's how I'd put it. Many black children learn all the time, but don't learn in the schoolrooms. It's not only that they aren't 'motivated,' as we say it. There's something else: they come here afraid. Sometimes the fear is obvious, but sometimes it takes other forms — boasting, gloating, noisiness, insolence, belligerence, silence you cannot penetrate, a sullen look that never leaves the child's face, or in one case I just thought of, a half smile, a half scowl, really, that haunted me for weeks. I thought the boy was disturbed and needed to see a psychiatrist. But one day I asked him to stay after school, and I just held my breath and *told* him — how he looked to me and what *I* thought that *he* thought. Then he straightened up and smiled, really smiled, and said one word: 'Yes.' He wasn't yessing me, either. He *meant* yes. After that he started doing better in class. There were no miracles, but he paid attention and asked for my help and improved — improved and improved and improved. I'd like a lot of other teachers to hear about him — but I'm sorry I can't prove exactly how it all happened. I only know that he was a troublesome, distant child, and then at long last he and I came to an understanding with one another, and then his work in class improved a hundredfold."

The young boy she talked about is quiet but constantly on the watch. His eyes follow his observer around the room. His eyes never stay anyplace for too long. His eyes are open but not exactly trusting. "I like it here," he says, "but you don't stay here after the sixth grade. So I won't be here after that." His family moved from Mississippi all across the country, and since then have done a good deal of moving about — from tenement to tenement in West City. It is "no picnic" moving a lot, and "no picnic" going to school — though he does indeed, with no prompting, describe his teacher as a "good lady." He drew a picture of himself (Figure 33), and of himself twenty or thirty years from now. When he had done that he wanted to know whether I had asked any *teachers* to do drawings — of, say, a pupil like him. No, I hadn't. As a matter of fact I had never thought to do so. Why? Well, actually for no reason — except that often grown-ups talk easily whereas children may prefer to keep quiet, but draw and sketch and paint their ideas and feelings. Maybe so, but still it would be a good idea to ask this one teacher to draw this one picture of this one person — him. I complied with his request, and his teacher complied with my request, but insisted that she keep the drawing she did. She said she was not very good at drawing, which is precisely what her young pupil said, too, as he did his work with the crayons — drawing a picture of his teacher (Figure 34).

Central City

Civil rights groups pressed long and hard to obtain improvements for the black poor in this city, one of the largest in the Middle West, which contains a vast and populous black ghetto, one of the largest in the country. They asked for better housing, for better streets, for playgrounds and parks, and for better schools. They also asked for school desegregation and eventual integration, which very few of the city's schools have.

A third of the city is black, as are over half the schoolchildren, but only three blacks, and until recently only two, represent them on the eleven-man school board. Eighty percent of the schools are "segregated," with a student body at least ninety percent black or white. Even the twenty percent labeled "integrated" are not quite that: many of them are simply changing from white to black, as blacks move into a neighborhood and whites leave it for the suburbs, ending such "integration" quickly. Most black teachers and administrators end up in nearly all-black schools, segregated like their pupils. Of seventeen black principals, sixteen run such schools. These schools are more often overcrowded, understaffed, and ill-equipped than white schools; for instance, they average thirty-four pupils per class compared to twenty-nine in white schools.

"We are trying everything, everything we can find, everything we can come across, to help these kids." Again and again that theme made its appearance in conversations held with deputy superintendents and assistant deputy superintendents — and in fact a whole array of administrators and educators and social scientists, all working on Central City's educational problems. What is "everything"? After visits to several elementary schools "everything" comes to a strong emphasis on relatively small classes (wherever possible) and "intensive" teaching through the use of "new and imaginative curricula." In one school the principal talked and talked and talked: "I've got a lot to say, because we're trying to do a lot; though how much we *are* doing, I'll admit, is debatable. We've brought in more teachers, and we've been provided with special services for difficult children. We have a speech therapist, a psychologist, and the doctor spends twice as much time with us as before. We've been holding a series of conferences for our teachers, and we've really tried to get the community involved. I was told a few weeks ago by a young man — he went to school here — that if ever a riot broke out, our building would be spared. I'm not so sure. We've got some of the best reading materials in the country here for our children. What we're attempting to do is saturate the children, saturate them with pictures, books, movies, everything audio-visual we can get our hands on. They've been deprived of that, and need it, a lot of it, if they're going to make it in our society.

"And we also hope to get the parents more motivated, because without their help, it's hard to turn these kids on. They come in here sometimes looking as though they'd been working all day in a factory or someplace. They don't have good clothes, many of them don't. More important, they haven't had breakfast, we've discovered, or at least a good number of them haven't, or if they have, the breakfast can't be considered adequate. I really believe that one thing we should do that might help our children a tremendous amount would be provide nutritional education for their mothers. I know we're a school, not a service center for the neighborhood, but when a child hasn't had anything nourishing for breakfast, and maybe something not very healthy the night before for supper, he's not going to be alert and responsive during the day. Sometimes I go through the school and see those lovely pictures we have posted on the walls — of glasses full of milk and big oranges and pineapples and grapefruit and eggs and bacon and children brushing their teeth — and I feel we either have to make those pictures more a part of the lives of our children here, or take them down from our walls and put up something that really speaks to these kids and doesn't make them laugh or get angry. Yes, they do get angry and outspoken, too — more so than an outsider can believe possible, considering that they're seven or eight, that age. Every time we try to do something for them they get fresh and nasty instead of grateful. It's hard for some of my teachers to take. The parents are like that, too — in fact it's the parents who say things, and the children of course, repeat what they hear at home.

"The other day one child, he must be nine, or maybe ten, told one of our best teachers that we were all wasting our time and trying to patch up a broken-down mess when a whole new thing has to be built — words to that effect. I asked the teacher what she said in reply. She hesitated for a while, I gather — she did with *me,* too — and then told the kid he was right, basically. You know what the kid said? He said that he knew she'd say that, because she was their favorite teacher, and that was why, because she saw things the same way they do. And that kid is slow in reading! The same teacher told me a few weeks ago that the whole business of learning and teaching in this school has to be reexamined. 'Some of the brightest kids, clever as can be, just don't *want* to learn. They mock learning.' That's what she said, and she's right. Not all of our kids are like that, but enough to make us tear our hair out. And get this: Negro teachers, black teachers, have no more success with them than we do, no more. It's not only a race issue; it's a class issue. Many of these children have learned from their parents that there's no hope, that if you have hope — hope about getting ahead in the system is what I mean — you're a fool, a real jerk. The kids come here and live out that conviction — that school is a jail, a place of temporary confinement, a place where the white world rubs the black boy's history into his face.

"If you question some of our kids closely you'll hear that, hear their embarrassment at the little heritage they have, at the poverty of their homes — *cultural* poverty as well as the economic kind — and their sense of futility. Oh, they're smart about *their* world, but to them ours is way off, and meaningless. And under the present circumstances — well, there isn't much I can do to persuade those kids that they're wrong. They know how a lot of people in this city feel about them. They know they're not wanted. They know who runs things here — and they also know what some of our leading *school* officials have said in the past. I'll be honest with you: it's only because we've had a change up top that I can talk as openly with you as this. What happens at the top gets right to the bottom. We feel every vibration. But there's only so much that even the best school system in the world can accomplish when it has to contend with the things that go on in this neighborhood, and the things that each of these children live with all the time — before school and after school and on weekends and vacations, and for their entire lives, I'm afraid."

The children did indeed respond to the "close" kind of questioning he urged. They spoke more directly, openly, and brusquely than others did in many other cities visited in the course of this study. They seemed almost waiting for a half-interested ear: "The teachers, they want you to read, but I've got a lot to tell you, mister, and you won't be able to read what it is, because no one writes books that talk the way we do, I'm sure of that. The teachers, they keep on telling you tomorrow it'll get better, and then the day after it'll get even better than better, but they're not even kidding themselves — we know that. You can see them driving in here from where they live, and they have that look on their faces when they park their cars, and they lock their doors and check them, and then they come into the building, and you can tell they're worried. My dad, he says he's worried, just like them. He can't get a job, and someone came and stole our TV. The lock on the door didn't mean anything. They just picked it as easy as that. They have to lock the school doors here. I don't blame them, but then they drive away and we're here all the time, and that's the difference."

"Me?" said another boy. "Me, I'm going to get myself some kind of a deal just as soon as I can. I don't want to be like my dad. You know what his trouble is? He thinks if you sit back and try to be a good guy, that it'll pay off one day. That's what's wrong with him. The other day he said I should be a doctor, like the guy who gave him medicine in the hospital, and he was black. That's right, there are some, like the teacher says, doctors and lawyers and all that. But that's just a few, and around here there aren't many who can go and become someone like that. You have to have someone backing you, yes sir. The teacher says if you just read and like that, you'll get ahead, but my dad says you can read every book there is, and they'll still step on you and keep you out if they can. I'd like to read, though, I would. I'd like to read faster than anyone, and I hope someday I will. And I hope I can have a car, and someone could drive it for me, and I'd be sitting back there and reading! Boy, would that be a deal! A big Cadillac, and me in the back seat with a book!"

His friend is much less dramatic: "The way I see it, there's not much you can do in school but try to get through it, and when you do, hope for the best so far as a job goes. I'd like to have one, a job, when I get through with school, but I'm not sure I'll be able to — to get one. So, I'm just trying to learn all I can here, yes sir, I am. The teacher, once she said she knew how we felt, that it was hard for us people. And we all said — we all said amen to that. Yes, we did. Then she said it was too bad the school and the buildings around here weren't as nice as in other places, and we said amen to that, too." A little later he drew "the school and the buildings around here." Some buildings were crossed out with a brown X, and the sky was brown rather than blue.

Vitality and Violence, Life and Death

If we would only stop and think, we would realize that children are the world's great skeptics. More than anything else they are seekers. What do they seek? When do they start seeking? And why should their quest be of concern to us as *citizens*, rather than parents? To answer questions like that we have to break down the separations we usually make between the home and the neighborhood, between the nursery and the marketplace, between the living room and the courthouse or voting booth. Each child of two or three is already well on his way to becoming a fascinating and unique mixture of follower and leader, fighter and peacemaker, activist, negotiator, arbitrator, recluse. It is on streets and alleys, in backyards and playgrounds, that children learn what can properly be called the politics of the classroom. There, we as parents and teachers, and they as future citizens, come to terms with one another more decisively than we may care to realize. "There, children learn to cooperate with one another, to respect one another; or to use and abuse one another. There, children are encouraged to respect older people but feel free to disagree with them as a right, indeed a human obligation; or there, children learn obedience at all costs — fearful obedience, unquestioning obedience.

There, children learn to share their intelligence or to exploit it for themselves and themselves alone. They learn to master themselves, or to beat upon the nearest available neighbor.

In a sense, then, before children even start school they have begun to acquire what philosophers call a "world view," and what psychologists call an "inner sense" — a sense of themselves as worthwhile or as thoroughly expendable. They have learned that food is around when they want it; or, possibly, that food is simply not to be had. They have learned that the winter brings warm coats and jackets, sleds and toboggans, plenty of blankets and plenty of hot chocolate and hot soup; or they have learned that in winter the rats do go in hiding, but only because the ice and cold of the outside has come inside — to add frostbite and shivers to the hunger that exists in any season.

Children learn other things, too. They learn that their parents work, or that they can't find work. They learn that their mother feels reasonably happy and contented, or that she is really up against it, and afraid from day to day of one or another danger. They learn that their fathers bring home no money, or barely enough money, or so much money that they don't know what to do with it all. They learn that their fathers feel like failures or, to some extent, feel successful. They learn that they don't have a father, or they do have one but he dare not come home if the "welfare lady" is around. They learn, in short, just about everything economists or political scientists talk about.

I suppose it could be said that children learn both the joys and hazards of existence — and no region or class or race has a monopoly on either joy or hazard. The politically and socially weak often produce desperately ambitious children, as history proves. In contrast, well-to-do parents have more than occasionally tried to figure out why their children lack all ambition and even spirit. In the ghetto small children learn to negotiate their ways through dark, broken-down buildings and incredibly dangerous streets. And in our well-to-do suburban communities parents worry because their children seem confused or bored or unwilling to take on or negotiate anything. It is no great discovery that life is ironic, but it can be a tragedy for parents and for a country when the ironies begin to pile up — and in the wrong direction.

One day we may realize that, above all, human beings need a purpose. We are born; we live; we die. It is only a moment we are here, and the mystery and ambiguity of life are always about us, ready in a second to confuse and surprise and frighten us. As children grow they start bombarding us with questions, and we nervously try to comply with answers. Often we are made nervous not because the questions are silly, or absurd, or even unanswerable, but because for a second, in a flash, we have been brought up short. Years of lame excuses, sad rationalizations, and whistling in the dark suddenly are ended by a child's innocent, humiliating curiosity. Why do people kill one another? Why do we live this way and other children that way? Why is it that on television you keep on hearing that people have headaches and stomachaches? And why are they so nervous? What is it, being nervous? Can't we clean up the smoke in the air, the way we clean up the house? Why is the river so dirty? What would you really *like* to be doing, Dad? Why do you say one thing outside the house and something else when we're alone? Is it true, Mother, that we're in trouble, and the world might get all blown up? Why should they make me cram all those facts inside my head and then keep testing me to see if I know how to take tests? I mean, why don't they let me think and say what I think? The teacher says it's so I can get into college someday. She says you have to start early. And when I ask her why, she says so I can be successful. But I want to know why — why be successful if someone can't think for himself or have his own say.

So, the questions keep coming at us. There are brief questions that children of four or five share with philosophers of all time. And there are larger questions, asked by ten- or twelve- or fourteen-year-old boys and girls who are trying their hardest to make sense of all sorts of puzzling and often enough senseless conditions. What are we to do in the face of such trouble — trouble for us as American citizens as well as parents? We can always shrug our shoulders and tell our children to hush, to go off and play. And they listen, too. They hear and sense our silence, our annoyance, our resigned indifference. Often enough they do not dispute us for too long. They do as we suggest, as we urge. They leave us and go out to play. And there, on those carefully tended lawns, or in those alleys littered with debris and vermin, they begin to become *us*. All too often they begin to fight and squabble, hate and retaliate. All too often they stop asking questions and come up with instant, dogmatic answers which they try to force down everyone's throat. Confronted with something new, different, and challenging, they hunch their shoulders and narrow their eyes. Why should they exert themselves, flex themselves, take a risk, make a dare?

Yet, America was founded by people who said no to others and yes to themselves, by mothers and fathers who were willing — more than willing, even anxious and determined — to expose their children to danger, to trouble, to exile itself in order that they might live not more comfortably, but *free*.

Eventually we may persuade and even compel our boys and girls to stop asking, stop thinking, stop wondering. But the price is high — on them as human beings and on us as a nation. Simply put, the price is *the death of the heart* — the title of Elizabeth Bowen's novel, in which a young girl slowly becomes disenchanted with a comfortable but hypocritical world. Her passions seemed futile to her because she judged others unworthy of them. And, of course, she came to feel herself unworthy, too. We cannot feel good about ourselves if we have learned to shut out or distrust others. And to do that, to live peacefully and respectfully with others, we need a certain kind of moral order, a certain kind of social order and political order. It is, therefore, no step at all from the nursery to a city hall, a state capital, or the halls of Congress. Children live in particular nations, and nations have particular climates of opinion and stand for particular goals.

A child's passion for excellence, for justice, can be killed at home, or in a school, or even, in fact, by public officials. By the same token, those passions can be encouraged, nourished, and most important of all, given coherent, visible expression in the daily life of a child's nation. A child who sees excellence and justice all around him will not need to learn about such virtues. He will know them in the sure, quiet, unostentatious way that reflects a living, continuous kind of knowledge. Our children desperately need that kind of knowledge, that kind of familiarity with excellence and justice.

All this has to be said before the so-called slum child or ghetto child is singled out for discussion. Children of the ghetto are first children, the particular children who have to learn things no school will ever credit them with learning. If all children learn about the place where they live and what they can reasonably expect of life, ghetto children do so rather precociously.

How is it done? Are six-year-olds taught the ghetto's facts of life by their parents? Do elementary schools brief them on how to fend off large, insolent rats, or how to deal with the mosquitoes and flies that enter windows unprotected by screens? Do those children learn in Sunday School about narcotics and prostitution and alcoholism so that when they walk to a nearby store (and pay higher prices for food than the rest of us do) they can recognize, be unafraid of, and maneuver their way around the drunks and pimps and streetwalkers who frequent certain ghetto streets?

I can vouch for the old-fashioned kind of morality that large numbers of ghetto children are exposed to. Again and again I have wished some of our most conservative citizens could hear the things I hear, see the things I see. I am not now referring to the wretchedness and hunger and squalor, but to the almost desperate (alas, often enough mindless) puritanism to be found among very poor mothers and fathers. We picture them as "loose," immoral, thoughtless, those parents — as lazy, as spendthrifts. We say they don't know how to control themselves, work, save, plan for the future, sacrifice today for tomorrow. And yes, so many of them are wayward, have *come to be* wayward.

But what about the beginning, the first years in our urban or rural slums? Were all those children born criminals? Were they *told* to be criminals by their parents? Is there perhaps some *lumpenproletariat* ideology, some ethic this nation's Mexican-Americans and Negroes and Indians and Appalachian whites have all conspired to believe in? Do they all tell their children to ignore school, loaf around, violate laws, cause trouble, take part in riots, appear disorderly or sullen or apathetic? Is the "welfare road" (as one ghetto resident describes his fate) chosen cynically and opportunistically by able-bodied men and women who simply don't want to work?

I have no universally applicable answers to those questions, but my observations lead me to believe that ghetto children are treated, if anything, more strictly and punitively than their middle-class counterparts. They are shouted at more. They are beaten more. They are trusted less. They are preached at more. They are given more specific and rigid rules to follow — and less leeway in the following. At the age of four or five they often are quiet, all too accepting and accommodating and fearful in the presence of their elders, particularly their mothers. When they first come to school they are ready to be still, to take it on the chin, and indeed be sternly rebuked — whipped, pinched, screamed at — if they dare go astray. Slowly, however, in the words of one teacher I have interviewed — a woman who has worked in a ghetto school for fifteen years — "the whole thing comes apart."

What "thing" comes apart? "Well, everything," she replies, and then spells it all out: "They're told to obey, obey, obey. Their mothers scream at them all day long, and beat them at the drop of a hat. Not all of them, but a lot. They're tired, those mothers, tired and desperate. So they suffer and the kids suffer. And the worst of it is that they keep on telling those kids to shape up, be good and all that, and then they'll get ahead and be rewarded, by God and their country. Imagine that! It would be funny if it weren't so tragic.

"And finally those kids get the score, you know. They see that this school, it's a detention center. They see that we don't care, that we've given up caring. All we want is silence, quiet, just like their mothers; that's all they want, a moment's peace. So, we tell them to 'mind their manners,' and they get the point. They know we're running a 'holding operation' here, a delay, a period of time between their childhood and their grown-up years which, let me tell you, come when they're about ten or twelve, when they start *doing* what they've *learned about* at six or seven: how to live in the ghetto and stay alive.

"So, that's about the story. They 'get wise,' as they put it. Oh, I've heard them say it, exactly those words, a million times these past years. They realize that every word they've heard preached at them is silly, foolish, not to the point. They realize that their mothers shout the American dream at them but are themselves, in their very lives, living proof of some terrible nightmare. They realize 'it's no use,' as we hear them say. And so they get stubborn and difficult and 'recalcitrant,' we call it. And they wait and wait and wait until the streets claim them, and the courts and the jails and the insane asylums and the hospitals, and pretty soon, death. But, you know, by that time, they've been dead a long time — deep inside."

Her "deep inside" is in the heart, the soul. And we who live, and die only late in life never quite can "understand." We keep on wondering why, for God's sake, they "behave" like that. But can the living *ever* understand the dead?

Vitality in Ghetto Children

When I read about ghetto children in psychiatric journals and educational reviews — not to mention the public press — I do not recognize the boys and girls I meet and observe every day. From the psychiatric quarter I hear about the mental illness that plagues the poor (though none of us has noticed psychiatrists — or any other kind of doctors — rushing in large numbers to practice in Harlem, Watts, or Chicago's South Side). I read about how apathetic or unruly ghetto children are: the "culturally disadvantaged," the blacks and Puerto Ricans, the surly, suspicious, "deprived" whites who come from Appalachia to northern cities, or the older southern immigrants who still live in the slums. One report mentions the "poor impulse controls" of lower-class black children; another, the "personality defects" of slum boys who, at five or six, are destined to be "sociopaths," delinquents, or worse. The picture is bleak: untended or brutalized children threaten teachers, assault one another, violate school regulations or city ordinances, and in general show themselves bound for a life of crime, indolence, or madness.

Educators confirm what their brother social scientists have noted: ghetto children do not take to school; they are nasty — or plain lazy. I wish they at least were frankly described that way. Instead one has to wrestle with the impossible jargon of educational psychologists who talk about "motivational deficits" or "lowered achievement goals" or "self-esteem impairment." We are told that slum schools must be "enriched" with programs to suit children who live in a vast cultural wasteland. Machines, books, audiovisual equipment, special "curricula," smaller classes, trips to museums, contacts with suburban children, with trees and hillsides — the ghetto child needs all of that and more. He needs personal "guidance." He could benefit from knowing a VISTA volunteer or a college student who wants to be a tutor or a housewife from the other side of town who wants to give poor children the things her own children take for granted.

Though some of those assertions are obviously correct, their cumulative implication is misleading and unfair. It is about time the lives of ghetto children were seen as something more than a tangle of psychopathology and flawed performances in school. Children in the ghetto do need help, but not the kind that stems from an endless, condescending recital of their troubles and failures — and often ignores or caricatures the strength, intelligence, and considerable ingenuity they do possess.

As I have already indicated, for a long time I, too, looked only for the harm inflicted on the boys and girls who grow up on the wrong side of the tracks. I found plenty to point to. Yet, while I was busy documenting such conditions I failed to see the other side of the picture. Determined to record every bit of pathology I could find, I failed to ask myself what makes for survival in the poor; indeed, sometimes for more than that — for a resourcefulness and vitality that some of us in the therapy-prone suburbs might at least want to ponder, if not envy.

My dilemma was not too different from the one that many civil-rights workers — particularly the white middle-class kind — have come to recognize. In 1964, when by the hundreds we went south to Mississippi, the emphasis was on setting free a cruelly oppressed people. Again and again the black man's plight was analyzed, his suffering emphasized. We had come to put an end to it all, to fight with the weak against the strong. At that time a writer like Ralph Ellison — who for years has insisted upon the rich culture that Negroes have created for themselves — was summarily dismissed by "liberators" who could not imagine they had a lot to learn from the victimized rural blacks of the South.

However, one by one we had to face the ironies in our apparently clear-cut situation. "It's not so easy, the longer you stay down here," said one northern student who had been living with a black family for a few months. "They're poor and beaten down. They can't talk right, and they can't write at all. There aren't any pictures on their walls, and the cabins they live in — you wouldn't even use them for a summer hideaway. They're scared out of their minds when a cop comes near them, like in a police state. But something starts happening to the way you think, because you like the people, the poor, downtrodden Negro, and the more time you spend with him the more you begin to admire him, and even wish your own family were more like his."

"If I talk like that up in Cambridge," he went on, "they'll tell me how romantic I am, how naïve. They'll say it's fine for me to talk — with my white skin and my father's bank account and my ability to leave any minute I want. I know, because a few months ago if I heard someone like me talking about 'the dignity' and 'real character' and 'integrity' of the people down here, I would tell them to get their kicks some other way, not by going native with the people who live the way they do because they have no other choice. And most of all, I would tell them to go ask the sharecropper in the Delta if he wants to stay the way he is, with his 'dignity' and 'integrity,' or get what the rest of us have, the cars and clothes and washing machines and everything else.

"It's a fact that a lot of the people we've met down here are stronger than we ever assumed. And a lot of them really do treat their children in a different way than we do — and sometimes it's for the better. The kids are close. They sleep together and help one another. They don't go off by themselves, the way we do. They're respectful to their parents, and to grown-ups, and very good to one another. They have a real warmth and humor and a natural kind of directness or honesty — I don't know what to call it, but I see every one of us noticing it, and I hear them all trying to describe it, even the hard-nosed social science types. They're ashamed at what they see; they don't want to be troubled by finding anything 'good' in people they came to save from everything 'bad.'"

The longer we talked in our all-night "soul sessions," the more we found ourselves in agreement. We had shared similar experiences and found them surprising and worth considering. I think more than anything else we felt chastened by the sight of our own arrogance. Late one night, a black man who lived nearby spoke up, confirming our feelings. "The people who help us, we're grateful to them," he said, "but I wish they wouldn't keep on telling us how sorry they are for us, how bad we have it. And I wish their eyes wouldn't pop out every time they stay with us and see we're not crying all day long and running wild or something. The other day a white fellow, he said how wonderful my home is, and how good we eat and get along together, and how impressed he was by it all. And I was sure glad, but I wanted to take him aside and say, 'Ain't you nice, but don't be giving us that kind of compliment, because it shows on you what you don't know about us.'"

Of course people under stress can develop special strengths, while security tends to make one soft, though no one in his right mind can *recommend* hardship or suffering as a way of life, nor justify slavery, segregation, or poverty because they sometimes produce strong, stubborn people. The issue is one of justice — and not only to the black man. The black man deserves to be seen for who he is and what he has become. If giving him his due — as a citizen and longtime victim of all sorts of exploitation — requires first calling him destroyed, "sick," a psychological cripple, or a moral menace, then perhaps we should recognize our own political bankruptcy. If psychological or sociological labels are to be pinned on the black man, then those who do so might at least be careful to mention the enormous, perplexing issues that plague the white suburban middle class: a high divorce rate, juvenile crime, political indifference or inertia to match any rural black man's, psychiatric clinics and child-guidance centers filled to the brim and with waiting lists so long that some are called only after two or three years, greed and competitiveness that worried teachers see in the youngest boys and girls and accept wearily as a manifestation of the "system."

There are, to be fair, some observers who have consistently remarked on the considerable energy and "life" they see in slum children. They have seen openness, humor, real and winning vitality. Many ghetto children I know have a flesh and blood loyalty to one another, a disarming code of honor, a sharp, critical eye for the fake and pretentious, a delightful capacity to laugh, yell, shout, sing, congratulate themselves, and tickle others. Their language is often strong and expressive, their drawings full of action, feeling, and even searing social criticism.

One thing is certain, though: ghetto childhood tends to be short and swift. Those fast-moving, animated children quickly grow old rather than grow up, and begin to show signs of the resignation accurately described by writer after writer. At twelve or thirteen these children feel that schools lead nowhere, that there will be jobs for only a few, that ahead lies only the prospect of an increasingly futile and bitter struggle to hang on to such health, possessions, and shelters as they have.

"They are alive, and you bet they are, and then they go off and quit," said one mother, summing it up for me. "I can tell it by their walk and how they look. They slow down and get so tired in their face, real tired. And they get all full of hate, and they look cross at you, as if I cheated them when I brought them into the world. I have seven, and two of them have gone that way, and to be honest, I expect my every child to have it happen — like it did to me. I just gave up when I was about fourteen or so. And what brings us back to life is having the kids and keeping them with us for a while, away from the outside and everything bad. But there comes a day when they ask you why it's like it is for us, and all you can do is shrug your shoulders, or sometimes you scream. But they know already, and they're just asking for the record. And it doesn't take but a few months to see that they're no longer kids, and they've lost all the hope and the life you tried to give them."

The vitality of each new child restores at least the possibility of hope in a parent, and so life in the ghetto persists in seeking after purpose and coherence. Mothers tell their children to do this or not to do that — even as they hold their breath in fear and doubt. Meanwhile, many of us comfortably on the outside hide our shame by listing the reasons we can't change things in our society, or by making the people who need those changes utterly dull and deteriorated.

Though we may console ourselves with some of the programs we offer the poor, others are not only condescending and self-defeating, but they overlook the very real assets and interests of ghetto children. It has never occurred to some of the welfare workers, educators, or Head Start teachers I have met that "their" programs and policies bore, amuse, or enrage children from the slums.

Consider, for example, one ghetto family I visit twice a week. They are on welfare. Two children were in a Head Start program for a summer. An older son took part in an "enrichment" program. A teen-aged cousin has been in the Job Corps. At school the children are told by their teachers what they already know, that their school is "inadequate." The building is old, the corridors are packed with many more students than they were intended for, and the teachers are disciplinarians at most. The head of this family is a woman not much over thirty who regularly calls herself "old." Once she added that she was also "sick," and I immediately took notice, expecting to hear about an ache or pain I could diagnose. But she went on to say that she was "tired of everything they try to do to help us. They send us those welfare checks, and with them comes that lady who peeks around every corner here and gives me those long lectures on how I should do everything — like her, of course. I want to tell her to go charge around and become a spy, or one of those preachers who can find sin in a clean handkerchief.

"Then they take my kids to the Head Start thing, and the first thing I hear is the boys' fingernails are dirty, and they don't eat the proper food, and they don't use the right words, and the words they do use, no one can make them out. It's just like that with the other kids. They try to take them to those museums and places, and tell them how sorry life is here at home and in the neighborhood, and how they are no good, and something has to be done to make them better — make them like the rich ones, I guess.

"But the worst is that they just make you feel no good at all. They tell you they want to help you, but if you ask me they want to make you into *them* and leave you without a cent of yourself left to hang on to. I keep on asking them, why don't they fix the country up so that people can work, instead of patching up with this and that and giving us a few dollars — to keep us from starving right to death? Why don't they get out of here and let us be, and have our lives?"

I can think of many things that could be done to take advantage of what that mother already has. The city might help her take part in a school she felt was hers, was sensitive to her feelings, her experiences, her desires — as indeed schools are in many other communities. There is work in her neighborhood, in her building, that she and her family might want to do, might be paid to do. Her children might be encouraged to use the strong and familiar idiom they know. Why should they learn the stilted talk of people who continue to scorn them? They might be appreciated for their own dress, their own customs, their own interests and energies — their *style*. They might read books that picture them, their lives and their adventures. Perhaps, then, some perennial "observers" would be surprised. With work, with money, with self-respect that is not slyly thwarted or denied outright by every "public" agency, the poor might eventually turn out to be very much like — us.

Violence in Ghetto Children

When I worked as a child psychiatrist in a children's hospital, I spent most of my time with middle-class children whose parents very often seemed earnest and sensitive; certainly they were worried about their children, at times excessively so. The boys and girls, for their part, were usually quiet and controlled. They were suffering from "school phobias" or the various fears and anxieties that have been described by a generation of psychiatrists. If they were disobedient and loud, usually it was a specific form of disobedience I saw, a very particular noisiness I heard, all responding to something they dreaded or dared not to look at. In a sense, then, the unruliness I noticed only confirmed my impression of a general restraint (emotional tidiness, I suppose it could be called) that middle-class children by the time they are two or three years old are likely to have acquired, never to lose.

Yes, there are the usual signs of aggressive tendencies in the "latency years" (the years preceding puberty when sexual urges are quiescent) — the bold and even nasty games, the play seems involuntarily brutish. But a long look often reveals how curiously formal, even restrained, the unruliness of these children actually is. Despite all the "drives" one hears psychologists and psychiatrists talk about — the surges of desire, spite, and hate that continuously press upon the child's mind and in dreams or daytime fantasies gain control of it — the fact remains that by the time middle-class American children first reach school, at age five or six, they are remarkably in control of themselves. As a result, when the violence in such children erupts in a psychiatrist's office during a session of drawing or in the midst of a game played by the psychiatrist and the child, it is almost a caricature of violence — violence so safe, so exaggerated, so camouflaged, and so quarantined that the very word seems inappropriate.

We in psychiatry are often accused of seeing only the drab and morbid side of human nature. If it would be any comfort to people, I suppose we could easily make partial amends for that morbid bias by letting it be known how overwhelmingly law-abiding a certain kind of middle-class man is: if he is vindictive, he is likely to be so toward himself. Psychiatrists spend most of their time helping people take a look at violence removed far enough from their own recognition to be, in effect, somebody else's property. If in time the patient, whether child or adult, owns up to what he secretly or temporarily senses, he will be in greater, not less, control of himself. Thus, I remember treating a ten-year-old boy who drew wild and vicious scenes, filled with fire and death or at least an injury or two. When I wanted to know about what was going on, he let me know the score rather quickly by pointing to the people in his pictures and saying, "I don't know; you'd have to ask them."

Not everyone in America is brought up to disown violence so consistently that its very presence in his own drawings can be adroitly (that is, innocently) denied. As I have worked with children in both southern rural slums and northern "ghettos," I have come to appreciate how useless it is to think of, or judge, the growth and development of the children of the depressed poor in the same way I ordinarily view the development of middle-class children. It is, as one boy in a Boston ghetto recently reminded me, "a different ball game when you're out in left field, instead of in there pitching."

If we consider what a child of the slums goes through, from birth on, and if we keep a special eye on what in his experience may make him "violent," even at the age of seven or eight, we may well gain, rather than lose, respect for the upbringing he receives. To begin, I have seen how much childbearing means to poor women: it is the only thing *they* can do, and do creatively. It is the one chance they have to show themselves and others that there is hope in this world, as well as the next. By pointing this out, I am not arguing against keeping families to a sensible size, nor overlooking the impulsive, dreary background that is also commonly associated with pregnancies among the poor, whether in or out of wedlock. I am simply saying to others what a mother once felt she had to let me know: "They all tell us to cut down on the kids, cut down on the kids, because you can't keep up with them as it is, and even a few is too much if you're on welfare for life, the way we have to be, like it or not. I try to cut down, and I want to, but it's not so easy. You have to watch your step all the time, and we can't afford the pills they have for the others.

"Anyway, it's the one time in my life I really feel like I'm *somebody,* like I'm doing something. People come around and expect me to feel ashamed of myself, like I've done something wrong, and I'm adding to crime on the streets — that's all you hear these days, *our* crime, not anyone else's — but, instead, I feel proud of myself, like I can at least make a baby, and maybe he'll have it better than us — who knows? — though I doubt it."

Another time she spoke the following words, and for some reason I felt the need to arrange the words this way.

Both Ways

> *They say no, no, no*
> *No more kids*
> *The welfare worker*
> *She tells you you're*
> *   overpopulating the world*
> *   and something has to be done*
> *But right now one of the few*
> *   times I feel good*
> *   is when I'm pregnant*
> *And I can feel I'm getting somewhere*
> *At least then I am*
> *Because I'm making something grow*
> *And not seeing everything die around me*
> *   like all the time it does in the street*

> *I'll tell you*

> *They want to give me the pill and stop the kids*
> *And I'm willing for the most part*
> *But I wish I could take care*
> *   of all the kids I could have*
> *And then I'd want plenty of them*
> *Or maybe I wouldn't*
> *I wouldn't have to be pregnant*
> *   to feel some hope about things*

> *I don't know*
> *You can look at it both ways, I guess.*

If we want to help that woman keep her family small, I hope we also want to give her what she needs to feel like the somebody she still desires to be. I know her children, and already I have seen them readying themselves for what their mother herself calls "the goddam street." Each one of those children has been held and breast-fed in ways I think some middle-class mothers might have cause to envy. Though the flat is cold and rat-infested, there is real and continuing warmth between that mother and her babies. "Symbiotic," some of my colleagues — who have a name for everything — might call the relationship of that mother and her children; it is also a bond that unites the fearful and hungry against the inevitable day when the home has to yield to the outside.

Slum children do not always go unprepared when that time comes. As I indicated earlier in this chapter, the chances are these children receive specific and brutal instruction about the "realities" of life at the age of two, three, or four — so that when they emerge from the home the police, the hoods, the addicts, the drunks are already familiar. The disappointments in the schools or on playgrounds are already expected. The mother I have already quoted has also testified to the morality and lawfulness she tries to inspire in her children: "I don't know how to do it. I don't know how to keep my kids from getting stained and ruined by everything outside. I keep them close to me, and sometimes I feel like everything will be OK, because they know how much I want for it to be, and they'll go make it be, the way I thought I could. But after a while they want to go out. You know how a kid is when he's three or four, and he wants to *move*, no matter where, so long as he keeps going. And where can he move in here? So I let them go, and I stop and say a prayer every morning and ask for them to be saved, but I have to say it, I'm not expecting my prayers to be answered, not around here. And when the kids come back upstairs, I give them a look, if I have the time, to see what's on their face, and what they've learned that'll make a mess of everything I try to teach. And I can tell — I can tell from day to day what's getting into them. You know what it is? It's the devil, and he tells them to give up, because there's no other choice, not around here there isn't."

She is a churchgoing woman, as are many of her neighbors. I have found that she knows her Bible better than me or my neighbors, and in fact she doubtless puts more store in prophetic, messianic Christianity than most Americans do. When her children start walking and talking, she starts teaching them rules and fears — enough of both to satisfy anyone who is worried about the decline of "morality" in America. At least in that home, and others like it I have visited, children are not allowed free rein. Instead, they are told to obey, and they are swiftly slapped or punched if they falter.

Over the years I have learned how loyal slum families can be to America's ethic of "rugged individualism." Children are taught through the ubiquitous television to seek after all the products of our proud technology: the cars that can speed faster than any law allows, the records and clothes whose worth can only be seasonal, the bright and shiny places to frequent, the showy, gadget-filled places that not only shelter people but also make statements about their power, influence, and bank accounts. At five and six years old, ghetto children in today's America share through television a world quite similar to the one known by their wealthy age-mates. I find it almost unnerving when I see drawings from a child not yet old enough to attend school that show the appetites and yearnings our advertisers are able to arouse. Precisely what do such children do with such wishes and fantasies, besides spell them out on paper for someone like me?

When a child of six or seven from the ghetto encounters the politics of the street or the school yard, he brings along both the sensual and the fearfully moral experience he has had at home. Slum children live at close quarters to their parents and their brothers or sisters. They are often allowed to be very much on their own, very free and active, yet they are also punished with a vengeance when distracted or forlorn parents suddenly find an issue forced, a confrontation inevitable. They face an ironic mixture of indulgence and fierce curtailment.

Such children come to school prepared to be active, vigorous, perhaps much more outgoing on an average than middle-class children. But they are quick to lose patience, sulk, feel wrong and wronged and cheated by a world they have already learned to be impossible, uncertain, and contradictory. Here are the words of an elementary-school teacher who has worked in a northern ghetto for three years and still feels able to talk about the experience with hope as well as bitterness: "They're hard to take, these kids, because they're not what you think when you first come, but they're not what you'd like for them to be, either. I don't mean what I *used* to like for them to be, but what I want for them now. They're fast and clever and full of life. That was the hardest thing for me to realize — that a boy or girl in the ghetto isn't a hopeless case, or someone who is already a delinquent when he comes into the first grade. The misconceptions we have in the suburbs are fantastic, really, as I think back — and remember what I used to think myself.

"I expected to find children who had given up, and were on the way to fail, or to take dope, or something like that. Instead it was in a lot of ways a breath of fresh air, talking with them and teaching them. They were friendlier than suburban children, and they got along better with one another. I didn't have to spend half the year trying to encourage the children to be less competitive with one another. We don't call middle-class children 'culturally deprived,' but sometimes I wonder. They're so nervous and worried about everything they say — what it will mean, or what it will cost them, or how it will be interpreted. That's what they've learned at home, and that's why a lot of them are tense kids and, even worse, stale kids, with frowns on their faces at ages six or seven.

"Not a lot of the kids I teach now. They're lively and active, so active I don't know how to keep up with them. They're not active learners, at least learners of the knowledge I'm trying to sell them, but they're active and they learn a lot about the world, about one another. In fact, one of the big adjustments I've had to make is realizing that these kids learn a lot from one another. They are smart about things my kids will never understand. They just don't think school is worth a damn. To them it's part of a big outside world that has a grip on them and won't let them get anyplace, no matter how hard they try. So what's the use, they ask themselves. The answer is that there isn't any use — so they go right on marking time in class until they can get out.

"We teachers then figure they're stupid, or they're hopelessly tough and 'delinquent,' or their homes are so bad they'll always be 'antisocial' or 'incorrigible.' I've found that when they're playing and don't know I'm looking they are different kids — spontaneous, shrewd, very smart, and perceptive. Then we go back into the classroom, and it's as though a dense fog has settled in on all of us. They give me a dazed look, or a stubborn, uncooperative one, and they just don't do anything, unless forced to — by being pushed and shoved and made to fear the authority they know I have."

We have compared notes many times, this teacher and I. One child we both know is a boy of eight who does very poor work in school. He is a belligerent child, a troublemaker. I see him in his home because his brother is going to a predominantly white suburban school, one of the very few children in the neighborhood who does. Their mother, living on public assistance with six children and no husband, has her hands full. She finds her "difficult child" smarter than her "model" one, the boy I watch riding a bus that takes him away from the ghetto.

The teacher and I agree, the "difficult boy" is a smart boy, but an impatient, agile, and provocative boy. He is headed for trouble, but as I talk with him I find *myself* in trouble. I have asked him to draw pictures — of himself, of his school, of his home, of anything he wishes. I get from him devastating portrayals: schools that look like jails, teachers whose faces show scorn or drowsiness, streets and homes that are as awful to see on paper as they are in real life, "outsiders" whose power and mercenary hostility are all too obvious and, everywhere, the police, looking for trouble, creating trouble, checking up, hauling people to court, calling them names, getting ready to hurt them, assault them, jail them, and beat them up — even though they are children.

Once I asked the boy whether he *really* thought the police would hurt someone his age. He said: "To the cops, everyone around here is a little bad boy, no matter how old he is or how many grandchildren he has around." At moments like that my psychiatric, categorical mind finds itself stunned and for a change ready to grant that boy and others like him freedom from the various diagnostic, explanatory, or predictive schemes people like me learn so well and find to be (in our world) so useful.

Welfare workers, in the pictures ghetto children draw, stand near the police like dogs, with huge piercing eyes, ears that seem as twisted as they are oversize, and mouths either noticeably absent or present as thin lines enclosing prominent and decidedly pointed and ragged teeth. To ghetto children, as to their parents, the welfare worker is the policeman's handmaiden, and together they come, as one child put it, "to keep us in line or send us away."

I have listened to public welfare workers and their "clients" talk, and I recognize the impossible situation they both face, the worker often as insulted by the rules and regulations as the family he visits. I often compare the relationship between the workers and their clients with one that develops in psychotherapy, as for a while powerful forces pull both doctor and patient backward in time toward those early years when parents check up on children, trying to keep them on the right side of a "line" that constantly puzzles the child and perhaps also the parent more than she or he realizes.

One welfare worker recently summarized the situation for me: "They behave like evasive kids, always trying to avoid getting caught for this or that. And me, I'm like a child myself, only an older one — always trying to take care of my poor brothers and sisters, but also trying to get them in trouble or find them in trouble, so I can squeal on them."

I find in some of the children that worker sees a vitality, an exuberance, that reminds me often of the fatally ill I once treated on hospital wards: for a long time they appear flushed with life, even beautiful, only to die. I remember hearing from a distinguished physician who supervised a few of us who were interns: "they're fighting the battle of tuberculosis, and they're going to lose, but not without a brilliant flash of energy. It's a shame we can't intervene, right at the critical moment, and help them win."

IV
Eskimos, Chicanos, Indians

Once and Still the Frontier

T he American West still seems endless, untouched, even unknown. The West's land is not the land of the South; it is not a
clearly defined mixture of plantations, farms, and copper-red
earth covered, mostly, by piney woods. The West's land is not the land
of the Appalachian highlands; it is not hollows, for the most part easily walked in a few hours, or valleys that are all to narrowly crowded
by hills that may be tough and austere, but are rarely uninviting or unyielding. The West's land is certainly not the open land left in the East,
conservation land, small national parks or so-called rural land —
meaning, rather commonly, the space between cities that planners expect, eventually, to become more and more settled, to become, successively, "countryside," "developed land," then part of a town, a suburb,
even a city. The West's land is not even the land of much of the Midwest: large, formidable cities like Chicago, St. Louis, or Omaha, hardly
distinguishable from those in the East; highly developed agriculture —
one farm after another, a productive network of family farms, or, in
recent years, enormous agribusinesses whose wheat, corn, and cattle
spread predictably over the vast flatlands, interrupted by rail lines,
rivers, strategically placed towns.

Not that the West doesn't possess with its enormousness, its diversity of weather, land, and people, elements that dominate or characterize other regions of the United States. In the Southwest one can
find cotton growing, if not antebellum homes; coal being mined, if not
a "hollow-culture" that goes back a century or two; and cities like Los
Angeles, San Francisco, Albuquerque, or Denver, which manage to offer and suffer from all that other cities elsewhere in the nation boast
and complain of. To be more specific, the West, like the South, is migrant workers, living a life of virtual peonage, if not slavery. The West
is widespread, racially connected poverty. The West is, like Appalachia, coal companies and utility companies, intent on taking what
is there, no matter the devastation visited on the land, not to mention

on the lives of many thousands of people. The West, like the North-east, is cities with smog, the bewilderment of families newly arrived from farms, the guarded sovereignty of suburbs, each nervously look-ing at others nearby, and all in mortal fear of something called, these days, "the inner city."

But the West is also itself, much more than the sum of resemblances to other regions. To a degree every region is, among other things, a state of mind. Self-conscious plantation owners of Mississippi's delta or Boston brahmins are not the only Americans who proudly identify themselves by region. Even migrant farm workers, as rootless a people as one can find in the United States (except, perhaps, for some corpo-ration executives) find it important to place themselves, locate them-selves not only geographically but by race, religion, occupation, or, in the case of Chicanos, national ancestry. In Florida, among Spanish-speaking migrants, one hears talk of "Mexican-Americans from Texas," talk of how "different" they are — from those who once were them-selves Mexican-Americans. Now they have become, at the very least, residents of Florida, if not Southerners. One Florida migrant with such a history makes plain what he has gone through and why he makes a distinction between his past and present situation: "Here it's no Valley; there's no Mexico across the river. When I was in Texas I could always cross over the border and become a Mexican, even if it was for a few hours. We worked for the Anglos, but they were only a few, and they would respect one of us, if he became a businessman and made money. Here we're like the colored; we have to watch our step. Here it's the South. I keep telling my children to be careful — there's no place to go, except to jail. They tried to send us to jail in Texas too; but we could usually slip away before they came. There's a lot more room in Texas than around here."

He goes on to spell out the particular social, economic, and racial problems he has encountered in the ten years he has spent as part of the so-called eastern migrant stream — one of thousands from Texas who have made Florida their base (November through May) if not their home. But as he does so he talks about space, room, a boundary, a river, a nation (Mexico) beyond; that is, he talks very much like those who once employed him, ordered him around, threatened him with the very expulsion from America he both wanted and dreaded. Eventually he expelled himself — from Texas but not America. He heard that he could make more money in Florida. He went east rather than south, where his heart would have taken him, or west, where others like him, not to mention many millions of Anglos (as he calls them), have sought a better life. And, at times, when he is not utterly exhausted or preoccupied with harvesting crops or moving himself and his family to them, he even has what might be called nostalgic reveries in which the Rio Grande Valley figures prominently, for all the economic exploitation and political repression that he experienced there. The memories have to do with people, past events, or experiences; but there is, as the social scientists put it, a context that is broader — as far-reaching, spacious, and immense, maybe, as the Texas land he crossed so many times in his young life: "I'll be working my way up from Florida, through Georgia and South Carolina and North Carolina, and I'll look around, and I'll say to my wife that we're not in the Valley, or anywhere else in Texas. The other day I thought of Amarillo; I don't know why. We'd go through there every year, on our way to Colorado, for the beets."

He stops, changes the subject. He has no interest in imagining Texas, with its dry and lonely panhandle, to be the New Jerusalem. He knows why he left the Valley, why he never sees Amarillo anymore, why he is quite willing to go in and out of Carolina towns without too much annoyance. But he does feel the relative congestion of the East and his own situation as an outsider. The black man is, after all, a Southerner, a natural part of a region's human landscape; hurt and betrayed and badly put upon still, but always there — thoroughly integrated, it can be said, into a once-segregated society. The Chicano receives looks or glances, hears remarks that expose the feeling of white and black alike: that man, his family, his people — they belong elsewhere. And he can only agree: "If I ever got some money saved, I'd leave. I'd go back to Texas. I wish one of my boys could get a job in the Valley and stay there — a job in a grocery store. I have a cousin who runs one, but he can't hire everyone who is related to him. He'd be even poorer than he is. He'd be broke. The market is a small one. Even our Chicano people now go to supermarkets. When I was a boy the Anglos didn't even want us to buy in their stores. All that has changed. The Anglos here aren't the same as the Anglos in Texas. I used to hate the Anglos in Texas, but here they're worse. One foreman told us that his boss doesn't like 'the Spaniards' picking his crops! But he has no choice. The foreman said he hoped I didn't mind being called a Spaniard. I said no; I said I loved being called a Spaniard. I'm a Spaniard from Texas!"

For him and for hundreds of thousands of his people, both in the state and separated from it, Texas is a rather special expanse of land: the rich, dark alluvial soil of the Rio Grande Valley, the hill country to the north of San Antonio, and, not least, the great high plains, known as the Staked Plains or, in Spanish, *Llano Estocado,* of which the panhandle and the west Texas area that abuts New Mexico are a part. The Valley is, of course, for many Chicanos "home," a row of counties that stand like dominoes against the long, winding, somewhat depleted Rio Grande as it works its way toward the Gulf of Mexico. San Benito, Texas, is where the Florida migrant already quoted originally came from — at least so far as the American part of his heritage is concerned. It is a town near the gulf and near the river, a town surrounded by large farms, on which all sorts of fruits and vegetables grow. The climate is semitropical — warm and humid almost all year around. Not only crops flourish; in winter large numbers of ducks, geese, and a variety of birds come and stay until spring: egrets, cranes, spoonbills, herons, and ibises. Not too far inland are doves, quail, pigeons, and the wondrous mockingbird, the officially adopted state bird of Texas. The gulf is, of course, full of shrimp, red snapper, flounder, and mackerel. Chicanos go to San Antonio to visit relatives and friends in the city; they also, like the Anglos, go to the gulf to fish, though they do not have much equipment or boats.

Working westward up the Rio Grande, the communities yield to one another, and within them the towns — a strange assortment of Anglo and Spanish names: Cameron County, with towns like Rio Hondo and Harlingen, as well as San Benito, and to the south, Brownsville; Hidalgo County, where much of the interviewing for this book was done, with towns like Edinburg, Pharr, and McAllen — balanced by La Joya, San Juan, and Donna; and on up to Starr County, Zapata, Webb, Maverick, Val Verde, Terrell, Brewster, Presidio, and Jeff Davis (a wedge of it barely touching the river), and finally, Culberson (another wedge directed toward the Rio Grande), Hudspeth, El Paso. The point is that these are evidences of cultural intimacy, for all the tensions between those who speak Spanish and those who speak the Texan kind of English. The Chicanos who live in, say, Hidalgo County know people in the other counties along the river, and they know what is going on where: a good Anglo sheriff in one place, a bad one elsewhere; a relatively decent grower or foreman, as opposed to a mean and spiteful one.

The land in Hidalgo County and other counties up and down the river is unrelievedly flat — so flat that one looks with gratitude to palm trees and some tall, pliant pines. Tropical flowers are everywhere — wild sometimes, along the roads, or in carefully tended abundance in the gardens one sees in both Anglo and Chicano sections of the villages and towns. There is oil in the northern parts of some of the Rio Grande Valley's counties, but the nearer one comes to the river itself, the more lush and developed is the agricultural land. Cattle and sheep graze casually, but there is nothing easygoing about the planting, tending, and harvesting of crops — which are especially abundant in the warm winter, when the nation to the north is seized by cold and snow. Apparently endless fields of cotton, corn, tomatoes, cucumbers, lettuce, and beets can be found on the same farm, often subdivided by individual crop into separate worlds, each with its own foreman and "trained" crew of harvesters.

A particular Chicano family may, for example, specialize in cutting lettuce or celery, as opposed to picking tomatoes or cucumbers. There are machines, astonishing in their size and complexity — the dinosaurs of agribusiness. But human labor is still needed — cheap, more precise, more "reliable," one hears: no sudden breakdown of a piece of equipment that may cost tens of thousands of dollars to repair. Cantaloupe and watermelon also abound, and citrus fruits — enormous orchards devoted to oranges, grapefruit, tangerines. If one favors the slightly exotic, by ordinary American standards, there are papaya and banana trees. And there are flower farms — as well as acreage given over to peppers or black-eyed peas. In the words of one grower: "We are rich here with a good climate — warm, sunny, and plenty of rain. And we have all of Mexico nearby to help us; the Mexicans need the work, and they do a good job. Of course, there are exceptions. But to me the reason we have such good crops is that we have the right people to work here as well as the right kind of weather."

He merges the two, field hands and climate, for his reasons; Chicanos do so too — a response to the kind of lives they live. The strong, rarely absent sun, "Mexico's sun" one hears it called sometimes, starts the day for thousands of Chicanos, many of whom have never heard an alarm clock go off. Once awake, the first question has to do with the weather: is it clear, cloudy, rainy, or (in winter) has a freeze, uncommon but deadly dangerous, settled upon the citrus? Soon enough the men and women (and very often, the children) are on their way to the land — *their* land once upon a time, as they often remind one another. The Rio Grande Valley was, in fact, first settled by Europeans in the middle of the eighteenth century at the initiative of the Spanish government of Mexico. Indians had been probing Spanish territory, and the French, who controlled what is now Louisiana, had expansionist designs. To protect its claims, Spain sent its Conquistadores up to and across the Rio Grande, with instructions to clear the land and begin settlements. The province of Nuevo Sontoneer was established, headed initially by Count José de Escondón. Large grants of land were given to certain families, the descendants of whom still live in the various counties of the Valley. These families began to work the land; they brought with them Indians, introduced cattle, sheep, goats, and, not least, agriculture. Corn, beans, and squash were the first crops.

When Mexico broke away from Spain the Valley became part of the Mexican province of Tamaulipas. In 1836, when Texas broke free of Mexico, the Valley was declared part of Texas — by the Anglos, who did not, however, make any immediate effort to move south. Until 1849, when the United States troops moved to enforce their claim to all land north of the Rio Grande, there were virtually no Anglos in the Valley. American children, Anglo or Chicano, are usually told what happened in 1847: Mexico was decisively beaten after President Polk instructed General Winfield Scott to take the war into the heart of "enemy country." After Veracruz and Mexico City itself were occupied, the government of Mexico was willing to cede all territory north of the Rio Grande to the United States — the treaty of Guadalupe Hidalgo. Mexican citizens were permitted to choose between remaining where they were and becoming Americans or moving south and starting a new life. Most stayed.

In the latter part of the nineteenth century, as middle-class (professional men, storekeepers, landowners) Spanish-speaking people in the Valley will tell an outsider, a trek of Anglos began, bent on farming, mostly. Land was cheap and plentiful. Often the Anglos were single men, and they often married Spanish-speaking women. The crops were bountiful, and there was a minimum of friction between the Anglos and the old Spanish families. Significantly, the Spanish-speaking people were then proud of their heritage and quite able to absorb Anglos socially and culturally. The daughters of the old Spanish families who married Anglos did so across the border, on Mexican soil and under the sanction of the Catholic Church. Many Texans, accordingly, had Mexican marriage certificates and, even more confusing, their children had Mexican birth certificates because the Spanish families sought out the superior medical care then available in the towns south of the Rio Grande.

In the last three decades of the nineteenth century the number of Anglos markedly increased, and the social and cultural equilibrium of the Valley was upset. Crude and greedy land speculators arrived, buying cheap, selling dear. There were always takers — men who wanted to dig in, try to make a living out of the obviously fertile land. Yet no one was going to get all that rich in the Valley, however good its soil and weather, unless transportation north to the rest of the country improved. Throughout the nineteenth century the Valley was approached by steamboat up the Rio Grande or on horse (stagecoach) through the various cattle trails that had been forged. In the first decade of the twentieth century a railroad connection was at last established, and with it, the possibility of enormously profitable agricultural production. Land speculation increased; a fever of buying and selling swept the Valley. Soon thousands of Mexicans were being brought in by Anglo landowners to clear the land, irrigate it, plant and tend and harvest its crops. A once-picturesque region, inhabited by old, aristocratic Spanish-speaking gentry and poorer Mexican laborers of mostly Indian ancestry, gave way to a bustling, Anglo-run, highly developed agricultural economy. And the Spanish cultural domination ended; the Valley became — socially as well as economically and politically — very much part of Texas and the rest of the United States.

Cheap, compliant labor turned into an obsession with newly rich Anglo growers. Mexico had for a long time been poor; in the first decades of the twentieth century, it was also plagued by a series of revolutions, with their attendant disorganizing influence on the people, thousands of whom crossed the Rio Grande. Better, they thought, the arrogant, demanding Anglos, who at least paid *something,* however little, than the chaos and near starvation that went with constant civil strife in Mexico. And the Anglos were not full of apprehension or self-recrimination, never mind the guilt a bad conscience can generate. They were eager to keep wages low. They had come to a sleepy, relaxed, casual valley, owned largely by a few wealthy Spanish-speaking families and populated by a larger (but overall, not very large) number of other Spanish-speaking people. In a few decades they had turned the place around, making of its land a rich breadbasket — one of the most valuable in the nation. Now the cactus and mesquite were virtually gone. Now the quaint burros and smiling, hesitant people had lost control to strong, assertive, active, and industrious landowners, anxious to make the most of a region beginning to be known (in the 1920s and 1930s) as the Magic Valley.

With the crops came other initiatives: canneries, cotton gins, packing plants, transportation centers, stores that sold machinery, fertilizers, farm equipment of all kinds. At times one can look around Texas and feel oneself to be in Mississippi's delta or in south Georgia or central Alabama: cotton or vegetables as far as one can see, interrupted only by irrigation ditches and, occasionally, a tree-lined road or some railroad tracks; or maybe the squat, flimsily constructed but constantly busy packing plant — a wooden or tin shell to protect dozens and dozens of workers from the sun, as they sort out fruit and vegetables all day long, and sometimes by night too. They pack up boxes or crates full of produce, which are loaded and dispatched by truck or train to the rest of us, who have learned to expect fresh or frozen fruit and vegetables all year.

The "magic" of the Valley is, of course, a wondrous combination of ample sun and water that makes already good land produce so abundantly. The contrast with much of New Mexico's land is rather apparent to Chicano migrants who have had yearly occasion to move from the Valley north and west in search of work. There is not all that much rain in the Valley; the river itself supplies the water, except during the wet season, midwinter, when more than enough falls and gets soaked in. But during the spring and summer it can be dry, almost semiarid, for weeks on end. When Chicano field hands first came across the border in large numbers a few decades ago, they camped out. There were, at best, old shacks to house them; they crammed into small rooms, empty save for a mattress or two, maybe an old, rickety chair — as if the buildings too were going to be packed, sealed, and sent off somewhere. "Wetbacks" the people were called, Mexicans illegally in this country: *mojados.* Soon enough they found *el patrón,* and from then on his needs became their obligation — work in the fields from sunup to sundown.

In the summer, though, when the sun is too hot and the Valley's land rests for a few months, the Chicanos move hundreds, thousands of miles north in search of work. They cross Texas, moving steadily uphill with their old cars, and eventually (those headed for the West Coast) reach New Mexico. In west Texas and in eastern New Mexico (referred to as Little Texas) they cross space that is limitless and uninhabited, striking in its rugged, unpredictable appearance. They wonder, on their return to the Valley in the autumn, whether they could ever find a halfway useful or comfortable place for themselves, as Indians have, as other Spanish-speaking people have, in the area near Albuquerque. In a curious way the new interstate highway system has given them a sense of security and confidence; they remember with mixed awe and apprehension the old, narrower roads that brought the traveler closer to the plains, the desert, the mountains, the buttes and mesas and canyons, the highlands and scrubby pine and cactus lowlands that make up the state that has their ancestral home as part of its name. Best to keep moving; in Colorado, or farther north and west, in Oregon and Washington, there is work. New Mexico, as one migrant keeps saying, is "a place you see in dreams; it's strange — like the Indians."

The western sky: immense, boundless, infinite, it seems, while under it. And if one is leaving Texas, moving higher, steadily higher, closer all the time to that sky, the ascent does indeed become unnerving, mystifying. Ahead are grasslands that end in a strange rise of the land — a high table, as it were, awaiting visitors. "God must be there," Chicano children have said with mixed curiosity, surprise, and apprehension. Suddenly tumbleweed comes rushing toward the road, dry and withered almost, yet at the same time round and bouncy and endlessly responsive to the wind. "A skeleton of a plant," a young Chicano child comments; he enjoys his observation, but his mother tells him not to speak like that: "You mention a skeleton and you flirt with Death."

Death is indeed very much present: land that has long since given up hope for moisture; or mountains once boiling with volcanic gases and liquids but now extinct; or arroyos, gulleys, ditches that even desert lizards seem to have shunned. Suddenly, though, deeper into New Mexico, there is a strange shift; the land seems kinder, softer. A few aspens assert themselves — thin, tentative, huddled together against the still, dry, bleak, windswept landscape. How have they managed to grow, to stay alive, to remain standing? A young child, for the first time (at five) conscious (to a degree) of the natural world outside of his immediate environment — that of a car, a family on the move — lifts his finger and points and counts: five of those aspen trees, so fragile and isolated to anyone who comes from a woody region, but here a surprise, if not a miracle. The questions begin: how come their presence, and how come no more? His mother shrugs but has an answer: there will be more ahead. They have been a sign, those trees, one of many signs the traveler comes to anticipate in New Mexico. The state offers an extraordinarily mysterious journey that begs and defies comprehension.

No one really knows when the Pueblo Indians of New Mexico first made their journey across New Mexico's high plateaus, cut by deep canyons or interrupted by various ranges of mountains. The Spanish came about 1540, and there is no doubt that Pueblo settlements like Cochiti, north of Albuquerque and south of Santa Fe, had then been in existence at least several centuries. Archeological studies, incomplete but continuing, date some Pueblo pottery as far back as

1050, and perhaps before that. Coronado's expedition wandered widely across central and northern New Mexico, as well as Arizona, and to the east to Texas and Oklahoma. The Pueblos were approached, surveyed, conquered — without any real opposition. The Pueblos showed a willingness to make token gestures toward a Christian God so long as they were allowed to have simultaneous concourse with the various spirits of their own faith.

For a while the Spaniards were too busy hunting for gold, following the course of rivers, and in general sizing up a beautiful, dramatic, inviting landscape to come down hard upon the Indians. But in time the demand was made: go along religiously as well as economically and politically. By 1582 the Pueblos of the Rio Grande Valley were part of an amorphous expanse of land called New Mexico. Before then the term *Nueva Andalucía* had been used. From 1597 onward the territory that included the Rio Grande pueblos was colonized in earnest. Spanish settlers, as opposed to roving bands of explorers or soldiers, arrived; soon churches were built, Santa Fe was founded (1610), and Indians were being converted rather zealously. (By 1624 there were 34,000 Christian Indians.) In 1680 the Pueblos revolted, fought hard and successfully against the Spanish, compelled them to retreat south. But by 1696 the conquerors returned, this time in even larger numbers. They had never completely gone away, of course. They raided pueblos from time to time, burning property and killing people, or taking them away as slaves. Eventually superior force won its victory, and the Pueblos were, in turn, required to help subdue other Indian tribes, the Navahos and the Apaches.

The Hopis, however, were never really reconquered by the Spanish, who had initially stormed the Hopi villages, located in territory that is now northern Arizona, during the early period of exploration (1540). The Hopis had made an effort to defend themselves the first time around, but when overwhelmed, became friendly and generous. The Spanish did not quite know what to make of a people who presented gifts to those storming a village with guns. When the Spanish came back to the Rio Grande pueblos, they continued to engage with, plot against, and try to overcome the wandering Navahos and Apaches, but they kept their distance from the Hopis. It had been the Hopis who had first shown the Spanish explorers the apparently limitless Grand Canyon, which failed to assuage their disappointment at not finding gold and silver but had struck them with awe for a few moments, at least. It was to be the Anglos of the United States, in the nineteenth century, who would gain decisive political control of the Hopis and all other Indian tribes.

The area of land called New Mexico, including present-day Arizona, was for a few decades part of the Mexican republic, which had been granted independence from Spain in 1821. The Spanish rulers had not wanted some 20,000 of their own people and the 10,000 Indians under their control to have any dealings with the Anglos, who were constantly probing the Southwest. But under Mexican rule trade began to flourish. Santa Fe became the terminus for goods brought by the Anglos — and sold profitably indeed. Other Anglos, from Texas, regarded such successful economic activity as an invitation for conquest. In 1841, and again in 1843, Texans tried to take over New Mexico, but failed. Soon thereafter Texas joined the United States, and an American army, under the command of Colonel Stephen Kearny, took over New Mexico. In 1850 Congress formally set up the territory of New Mexico, and by 1863 had given that territory the size of the present state by splitting off the western half as Arizona, the northern half as Colorado.

During the second half of the nineteenth century, railroads entered the Southwest; with them came an increasing trek of white men from the Midwest and the East. The Indians were gradually "quieted," as it was put then — and not sent to the best land by any means. Texans crossed into New Mexico with their herds of cattle. Mining and agriculture (enabled by irrigation) began to be developed. By 1880 the Atchison, Topeka and Santa Fe Railway had reached Albuquerque, which had been founded in 1706, but grew rapidly only in the latter decades of the nineteenth century. In 1912 New Mexico was admitted to the union, followed (in the same year) by Arizona. The rest is contemporary history — motels, interstate highways, air force bases, nuclear testing stations, atomic research laboratories, and, not far away, Indians on reservations and Spanish-speaking people near villages or on farms or within the barrios of Albuquerque.

For those people New Mexico is something else, not measurable by economists, physicists, or engineers. For an Indian child or a Spanish-speaking child, New Mexico is aspens turning yellow in early autumn — a gradually unfolding blanket that covers the Sangre de Cristo mountains. New Mexico is sandstone formations in all their strange, eroded, suggestive diversity. New Mexico is a sea of gypsum, of white sand that seems infinite and utterly lifeless. New Mexico is also for such children a field of primroses, a mesa followed by another, a quick storm subsiding and so allowing everything to be lit up again: the cottonwoods, the low adobe houses, the coats of the grazing horses. "See the yellow," one hears a child shout as the sun penetrates the clouds, reasserting a rather common hegemony; and the eyes of the six-year-old girl race from place to place: trees aflame, the sky a furnace, cacti suddenly in bloom, and the side of a building a strange, alive mixture of yellow, orange, red, brown, which together, on blinking, become a blazing fire.

The girl asks: "Will the sun burn them up?" She has in mind that adobe house, so solid looking, so comforting to its inhabitants, so much a part of the landscape. She also has in mind her horse, brown with white spots, but of a different color at certain moments of the late afternoon, after a rainstorm, and under a weakening, reflective sun: chestnut brown, an outsider might say, thinking of a yellow-red hue of low brilliance, but to the girl's eye something else. She can't quite find words for what she is thinking, or so she says. But in fact she can get across exactly what she believes to be the case: "The horse has been under the sun all day. She stands there dozing. I worry that she is hot, that she will get sick. But no, she doesn't want the help of the shed. The flies are in the shed. The sun drives the flies away. The horse is happy. The horse likes the air; the horse's feet like the ground; the horse's coat is full of the day's sun."

Her father, an Indian who moves back and forth, back and forth, from an Albuquerque office building, which he helps keep clean, to a Pueblo reservation north of the city, where he lives, has spoken many times of the sun's "spirit" and the earth's "spirit." The child sees one of those spirits in her horse's coat, as it appears on a particular afternoon, and takes note in her own way of the influence exerted by a particular region's weather and terrain on the everyday life of a people. In the girl's words: "The horse may get tired in the middle of the day; the sun is too hot for her. But she waits, and soon the air is cooler, and she is ready to gallop for miles. That's how we feel, too. I wait for the end of the afternoon; then I know I'll feel better. My mother always tells us come inside and rest in the first part of the afternoon, and go outside later. She will thank the sun for warming us and later she will tell us that the air is cool and the ground is cooling off, and we can go play. We pick up rocks and throw them into the shade. They feel better after they have landed. They are glad to have the cool air on them."

The air — warm or cool; for her it is something more than a condition of weather. There is a glow to the air, a promise. She is comforted by it, even as outsiders, unlike her in dozens of ways, find themselves immediately struck by something intangible yet recognizable — the extraordinary visual character of the air: thin, dry, clear. In our eastern cities, in California, or in the Midwest, even on a sunny, cloudless day, the air is not what it is in New Mexico. A layer of low-altitude air that is relatively heavy with humidity hangs over most of us; we have learned to live with a certain haze in the air, not to mention the additional and more blatant murkiness that environmental pollution prompts in the atmosphere. But in New Mexico one has moved high up; one is among mountains or on an elevated plateau. And one has come upon increasing dryness, too, apart from the altitude. The result is a crispness of vision, even on hot days, and even after a rainfall. The hazy, somewhat softened, even blurred vision of the coastal plains or the prairie gives way to a clear, bright, almost harsh, sometimes blinding field of view. Air that an outsider has come to regard as transparent suddenly becomes translucent — so sharp, so clean, so light that one feels in a new world or possessed of new eyes.

Scientists know why; the air has lost one-fourth of its weight, as compared, say, to the coastal flatlands of adjoining Texas. The air, too, is low in oxygen, in carbon dioxide, but higher in hydrogen. It is an air that has, to a degree, lost its capacity to refract or diffuse the light. It is an air that seems to bring objects almost too close; they assert themselves strongly, even harshly. But when one is on a hill and looking at the countryside many miles away, it is an air that lends itself to mystery, especially in the evening, when the stars and any speck of man-made light fairly glow before the observer, as if, against all laws of nature, hundreds, thousands, even millions, of miles have been deprived of their meaning, and one need only reach out and touch something in the sky, or nearer at hand, a town's, a house's, a car's lights. Those lights are sharp, pointed, immediate, forceful; there is none of the soft glow one is grateful for when up a mountain or a tall building in other parts of the country. The "big sky" of New Mexico or Arizona is not only a matter of view; it is a striking freshness and immediacy of vision that seem almost God-given — the result, at the very least, of a complicated series of natural coincidences.

Nor is it only the eyes that have to accommodate themselves to a new physical, if not psychological and spiritual, reality. In the late afternoon the sun suddenly vanishes. Warm updrafts leave the earth, go higher and higher, produce clouds as if the sky were ground upon which a whole city was to be built. The result: thunderheads that dispatch bolts of lightning in all directions, followed by a rumble of noise and those brief, scattered, soft showers that settle dust, surprise and awake cactus plants, delight people who regard a full-fledged rain as an unusual event indeed. Indians laugh at the short-lived, noisy outbursts, call them "male rains" — full of pomp and circumstance but little substance. They rejoice at great length when they are visited by the longer, quieter, wonderfully sustained and soaking "female rains." Then it is that a mother tells her child: "The sky spirits want us to have water; they want to feed us. They are mother-spirits. Usually it is men-spirits, quarreling or telling each other off." So much, at least at this point, for the relationship between culture and sexual imagery, not to mention between a region and the psychological development of those who live in it — that is, have to make sense of its weather, its terrain, its physical and biological conditions.

It is an almost timeless environment — endless sky, strangely empty land, and everywhere volcanic spires, reminders of agitation and energy long since spent. It is a gentle, almost unnervingly arresting environment — views that bring life to contemporary clichés: vista, panorama. It is also a harsh, mean, forbidding, ungenerous environment — a violent one too: a summer's flash flood tears through the land, sweeps across arroyos, spills itself wastefully, only to be hungrily absorbed by the land, evaporated by the sun's beating warmth. A child can point to a moment's mud and silt and say: "In just a second there will be dust, and the same old cracks on the soil." It is as if life's rhythms are brutally condensed — ashes to ashes before the comprehending eyes of a boy or a girl. Those children are sometimes casual with a physical world that may excite, surprise, delight a visitor; at other times they can turn quite serious, become preoccupied with the strange mixture of action and stillness they see and feel around them.

The great silence, the solemn loneliness, the provocative suggestion of a surreal and ghostlike world, are balanced by warm, lively winds, by the continuing side-by-side presence of the two oldest cultures in this nation, and by the earthy concreteness of adobe houses, which have themselves become (as they were meant to) part of the natural landscape rather than buildings thrust upon it. No wonder some Indian children talk about home and mean by it a field of cactus, or a tree on a particular hill, or an expanse of semiarid grassland, as much as a building or a street with a group of buildings on it. No wonder some Chicano migrants can pass through New Mexico, on their way from the Rio Grande Valley of Texas to the crops that need harvesting in the mountain states or those of the Pacific Northwest, and tell their children that not only Indians are nearby, but the Lord Himself — and the Devil. The Chicanos may sometimes mean, with respect to the latter, a state highway patrolman; but they also have in mind a God-given terrain — of a kind that strikes them as *too much*: ordinary proportion and symmetry have given way to a supernatural intervention. "It is just too much," a mother dutifully says each year as she looks at the land north of Santa Fe. Her child remembers the description, oft-repeated, from last year's trek and observes: "Sometimes I think my mother thinks everything is 'too much'; she cries a lot. But she is right about this place. I asked the priest if there is some place where Jesus Christ comes and visits the earth every once in a while. The priest said that may happen; maybe He comes to the valley, in Texas. But I don't think so. Why would He want to come there? Here, yes; I can understand why God would want to visit New Mexico."

Up in Alaska there are Eskimo children of his age, eleven, who regard the world similarly. They have been converted to Christianity, and they believe all too strongly and concretely in an immanent God. He is the God of ice and snow, of a whiteness that is unrelenting, all-encompassing, transcendent. When told by teachers or ministers that some children on this planet never have seen ice or snow, an Eskimo child smiles in disbelief. When asked whether he might want to live elsewhere, in a warm or tropical climate, the same child again smiles: "There is no such place." Like everyone else, he has some utterly rock-bottom assumptions. One of them is that the earth is always covered by some snow, some ice; even in the summer the sun can achieve only a partial victory. And as if to point out that he has the evidence nearby, if not directly in hand, the boy points silently at a distant mountain, one of dozens that stand far away — a perpetual horizon of nameless, snow-covered peaks.

The boy's ancestors came to Alaska, saw its land and presumably mountains, hundreds, maybe thousands, of years ago. Eskimos are light yellowish-brown in color. Their faces are broad, their cheekbones high, their eyes black, their noses flat. They resemble in physical appearance the people of northern Asia: China, Mongolia, Siberia. Archaeological and ethnological research connects Eskimos to the Lake Baikal culture of Siberia. Radiocarbon dating indicates that several hundred years before Christ walked the earth, perhaps as much as a thousand years before His birth, Asian families arrived on Alaska's shores and built settlements there. They were a stolid, enduring, patient, lively people. In the face of severe, limiting, sometimes crushing weather they somehow managed to persist. They built crude sod houses out of a frame of driftwood timber and for walls used packed ice: the igloo, now extinct, replaced by today's small frame houses. In the summer they once constructed the tupek out of animal skins; now they use canvas tents manufactured in distant factories. They fished and hunted: the seal, the walrus, the sea lion, the whale. Those who ventured inland, following the course of rivers, encountered the caribou, an additional source of food. And there were berries and roots, in apparently endless proliferation during the short-lived but exuberant summers.

For transportation the men and women relied upon dogs, the legendary huskies who may well have come to North America with the first Eskimos. Sleds were fashioned. Kayaks were built, extraordinarily light and serviceable — an extension, in a way, of those who used them, who were (and are) a people of quick reflexes, sharp vision, and obvious manual dexterity. Decades ago they fashioned the umiak — an elaborately constructed large open boat made of skins and used for hunting and transport. The motorboat has replaced the umiak, but old Eskimos still remember it, not only with nostalgia but pride: a distinct engineering and aesthetic achievement. Ivory carving is another justly famous accomplishment — and, alas, mostly a source of nostalgia rather than everyday self-respect. Some Eskimos, as well as Aleuts and Indians, have also in the past done first-rate basketry. In this century, increasingly, commercial fisheries have commanded the time and dedication of Eskimo men and women and, not rarely, older children. Oil prospecting, and more recently, the building of the controversial trans-Alaska pipeline, as well as (during the 1940s and 1950s) military construction and maintenance, have also been a source of Eskimo employment.

Alaska's modern, recorded history, and with it, a chronology of Eskimo life, goes back to the early eighteenth century. Russian explorers, traders, colonial expansionists had been pushing steadily eastward; eventually the rivers and valleys of Siberia ended: the Pacific. Peter the Great asked Vitus Jonassen Bering (after whom the Bering Sea is named) to find out if Siberia was linked to the continent of North America. Bering, Danish-born, a man of vision and enterprise, made two voyages; on the second one he explored Alaska's southern coast extensively, not to mention a number of islands, including the one now called Bering Island, on which he died of hunger and scurvy in 1741. But some whom he commanded survived and brought back to Russia the pelts of the sea otter. The result: a new demand for fur, a new surge of exploration, hunting, trapping in Alaska.

Eskimo and Aleut settlers grew to fear the Russian trappers and traders, the first in a succession of outsiders who would arrive with all sorts of demands: food, shelter, goods and services, and, not least, the favors of all available women. In essence, the "natives" were exploited, killed outright, or enslaved. The Russians were followed by the Spanish, the English, the French, and finally, in 1788, the Americans — on the ship *Columbia,* under Captain Robert Gray, a citizen of the newly formed United States, and on another ship, the *Lady Washington,* under Captain John Kendrick. But Russia ruled Alaska in the eighteenth and the first half of the nineteenth century — Russian America, it was called. A number of Russian governors encouraged an active shipbuilding industry, as well as various smaller industries and foundries, sawmills, machine shops. Church bells, for instance, were made in Alaska and sent south to the Spanish missions in California. Agriculture was attempted, but unsuccessfully; the growing season was too short in the southern part of Alaska and obviously nonexistent in the far north.

For a time the Russians contented themselves with intensive explorations of Alaskan territory, but in the early years of the nineteenth century they penetrated as far south as present-day San Francisco and even to the Hawaiian Islands. Yet Russia was only peripherally interested in its North American territory. Its czars and, through them, various governors did indeed issue various ukases, forbidding to other nations "the pursuit of commerce, whaling and fishery, and all other industry, within an area extending from Bering Strait south to 51° of north latitude on the American coast" (1821). Even so, American and British ships were everywhere, it seemed; and they would not be deterred by the wishes of the St. Petersburg court. With the outbreak of the Crimean War in 1854, Russia was even less able to enforce its will in North America. Soon the imperial government was entertaining thoughts of disposal; and in 1857 the Russian ambassador to the United States suggested as much to this country's officials. The Civil War interrupted negotiations, which were begun in 1859. In 1867, however, William H. Seward, our secretary of state, put his signature to a bill of sale — his well known "Folly": Alaska for the sum of $7,200,000.

The Russians left, American troops entered. Until 1877 the War Department ran the territory of Alaska. When Indian uprisings in the West became serious, prompting a need for all available troops, the soldiers left Alaska, and the Treasury Department, with its revenue collectors (whose boats were the precursors of the coast guard), maintained law and order. In 1880 gold was discovered in Juneau. From then on the Eskimos and all other "natives" became relentlessly, hopelessly entangled with one wave after another of settlers or mere visitors from the United States: gold prospectors and, later, miners come to work at the large copper deposits uncovered from 1898 onward; missionaries, who to this day try to convert heathens, educate children, provide medical services, and, sometimes, argue strongly on behalf of the rights of the economically poor and socially vulnerable; federal officials of one kind or another, including, of course, those from the Bureau of Indian Affairs, charged with providing for the "health, education and welfare" of "native" people; and a motley assortment of others — homesteaders, the owners of fishing boats, engineers and surveyors, bush pilots, dreamers in self-imposed exile from the ways (and pressures) of contemporary urban, industrial life, naturalists, and tourists. Many of those people have stayed, become Alaskans; indeed, Eskimos and their distant kin, the Aleuts and the Athapaskan Indians, are now decisively outnumbered by the rising tide of newcomers from "the lower forty-eight," as the rest of the United States, apart from Hawaii, is often called by Alaskans, among them Eskimo children.

The word *Alaska* is derived from the Eskimo *Alakshak,* which refers to *the mainland.* Eskimo children, even those who live far up a river, hence a long journey inland by snowmobile or motorboat, are ever conscious of the ocean. Often they regard the ice and snow around them as, ultimately, the ocean's property, spread over the land by a prodigal (and fierce) nature. The "mainland" for them is the earth immediately under them; the ocean is everything else — as far-reaching and infinite, they believe, as the sky. For Eskimo children who live, say, on the Aleutian Islands, land seems an especially fragile and, for many months, a nonexistent element. Feet walk on ice or snow. Rain pours or snow falls all the time, it seems — over 250 days of the year, on average. Fog is an almost constant companion. The water is insistent, noisy, sometimes threatening and savage. Children wonder whether the sea will claim the islands — even the mainland. And children who live in the coastal settlements watch the ice floes move closer in the short-lived interval between summer and full-fledged winter, see the snow accumulate higher and higher around the houses, occasionally wonder whether the "mainland" won't itself become absorbed into a giant ice floe and get carried deep into the Arctic Ocean.

The children actually know better; they are taught in school how enormous Alaska is — one-fifth the size of the entire United States of America: 986,400 square miles, or almost four hundred million acres, stretching over fifty-eight degrees of longitude and no fewer than four time zones. The children are also taught that there is a lifetime of exploration waiting for any of them who wants to stay in this largest of American states, a nation within (or more exactly, outside of) a nation. It is still a quiet, sparsely settled land — about three hundred thousand people, or only .51 person per square mile. In summer, when outsiders naturally find it easiest to visit, much of the state seems deceptively warm, approachable, hospitable. The surface of the permafrost begins to melt, though below the surface, silt and sand and gravel and rock remain as hard, as cold as ever. The tundra — a seemingly endless plain, bereft of large trees — suddenly is no longer brown and dead-looking. Flowers appear, the purple mountain saxifrage or the array of white flowers: *Dryas integrifolia* — or to Eskimo children, "summer snow flowers"; also the bright yellow glacier avens — "the little sun" to some Eskimo children — and the wind flowers (*Anemone parviflora*) with their touch of blue under the white petals. Grass is everywhere, and shrubs. A carpet of mosses and lichens covers land that just a week earlier seemed hopelessly inert.

The tundra gives way to the sea, which is also stirring — cracks in the ice, currents and eddies that are encouraging to those who want to see the ocean set free again, but dangerous to navigate. The icebergs melt gradually — mountains to hills to mounds to an underwater existence; some icebergs, of course, never yield to any sun, as if the Arctic Ocean will only go so far in acknowledging summer. The tundra also gives way to higher country, and to forests: hemlock, spruce, cedar, mixed occasionally with birch and even balsam poplar. There are, too, stretches of less imposing willows, and even they fall off, at points, to shrubs. Berries of various kinds are available, and the grass can be lush, rank, deep green, and triumphant. The combination of heavy rains and long-lived sun, the arrival of swarms of mosquitoes and flies, the constant sound of birds, whistling, crying, croaking, chirping — it all goes to suggest a miraculous, definitive transformation: from a freezing, white death to a tropical jungle's brimming exotic life.

And the animal life confirms the impression. While the steady passage of geese, ducks, and shore birds masks the suddenly open sky, bear, moose, and elk stir, run, seek yet another summer's assertive activity. Great herds of caribou range the Arctic slope, go south, penetrate the woods. And less obvious and awesome, the smaller ones go about their business: fox, sable, ermine, wolverine, mink, land otter, beaver, muskrat — animals whose names evoke visions of fur coats in millions of city people thousands of miles away, people for whom Alaska is also a suggestive name — of igloos that don't exist anymore, of Eskimos who fight long and not always successful battles with giant polar bears or whales. There are polar bears, of course, though it is more often the white man from far away who wants to hunt them and has to be carefully kept in bounds. There are also whales, and they are indeed caught, if less commonly than salmon and halibut.

Mostly, these days, there are village stores with frozen foods, no less, as well as candy galore, soft drinks, and canned goods. And snowmobiles and motorboats; their noise competes with the gentler call of the geese to one another, as flocks of them work their way in stately regiment across the sky. Not that birds don't, under some circumstances, make their own urgent, shrill, even frantic sounds. Near open water, near hundreds of Alaska's ponds, inlets, lakes, male and female phalaropes, for instance, skirt, plunge, jump, flutter, and all the while create a frenzy of sound and motion as they seek one another out, make their claims, adjustments, rebuffs, assaults — the prelude to a new generation. "Do airplanes have babies?" an Eskimo child of four once asked — so accustomed was she to the shrill but important noise of other flying objects, nature's, and to her mother's explanations: mating, then offspring. Why not those planes, too — those larger, even noisier, birds? And even more precisely: why not a link of propeller to propeller — and later, the emergence of a smaller plane out of the belly of one of the planes, whence at other times come mail, packages, and those who carry them?

Soon enough the endless days give way to the dominant and then utterly victorious night. The sky is no longer light blue, has turned black-blue. The stars offer all the hope there is. The birds scurry away, or leave well in advance, an orderly, proud, at times mocking retreat: let man stay where he is; we will have no part of these long, grim, devastating winters. Sometimes the dancing, sparkling, streaming lights of aurora borealis, the northern lights, appear — wild and strange electricity showing a huddled, snowbound people that all is not lost, that there is action, movement, dazzle even, at the least promising and most fearful time of the year. And the silence, the firm, solemn, eerie silence; young Eskimo children pay homage to it, ask their parents, with a touch of desperation to their curiosity, why the snow is so noiseless as it falls. The parents have no explanation, only the reassurance that below and above the ground there is indeed life; and if one is careful to listen, some sounds as proof.

The fox is as agile and evasive as ever through the winter. The snowy owl watches, glides or swoops magnificently, finds its rodents. And fish do not flee heavy snows, thick ice, treacherous glacial movements of a sea, a slope, a whole world of frozen restlessness. Nor, it has to be added, do the Eskimos, who for generations have gone down to the ocean, to the rivers and streams, the wide expanse of a delta, or the marshes and swamps, all so tightly covered by winter, to match wits with the Arctic, with "life," with the fish running underneath and, not least, with themselves, because when the temperature is some fifty degrees below zero, the winds cut across the tundra, and the snow seems to have become not part of a fall, but an expression of a permanent condition, then even Eskimos, with all the strength of a heritage, can experience a moment of doubt, of apprehension.

It is, as Eskimo children are often taught in school, the frontier that they are part of, and must in various ways learn to live with and, to a degree, master. Even with airplanes and snowmobiles and motorboats, there are days on end of danger, uncertainty, isolation. In New Mexico, too, or in the Rio Grande Valley of Texas, where the weather is so different, the frontier is still either right there or not so far off: the edge of things; the spaces that seem to know no limit; the aloneness that is not the result of self-judgment or worse, self-punishment, but nature's quite natural resistance to any creature's easy domination. Miles of the Rio Grande's loam separate people and towns; miles of New Mexico's hill country keep one Pueblo reservation from another; miles of the tundra, and storm upon storm, make one Eskimo settlement utterly removed from others, even in this age of planes and wireless. "Once it was the frontier here," an Indian child in northern New Mexico says; then he adds, sure of himself in spite of contemporary technology, "it is still the frontier."

So it still is — where he lives, where Eskimo children live, where Chicano children live in various parts of the Southwest; not the old frontier, not the frontier of savage battles, new railroad tracks, smoke-producing trains, daily shoot-outs, anarchic gold prospecting — and anarchic drinking, fighting, stealing; not the frontier of frequent homestead rushes, though in Alaska they do occur occasionally; and not the frontier of boastful ignorance or dark, even murderous escape from God knows what, God knows where; but as the child says, still a frontier where it once was one — comparatively and substantively.

The land has yet to be fully conquered or fully settled. The immense sky is still available, not blocked or shut off by man's various constructions. The woods or rivers or desert or mountains are often untamed, or if brought under control, under surveillance, only somewhat frequented. There are fewer people than are to be found in the settled regions of America; and among those men and women who do live "out there," closer to the earth, farther than all others from our cities and suburbs, there is a responsiveness to that fact, that state of affairs, that state of being, that mixture of physical fact, social circumstance, tradition, memory, and mood: the badlands (once); the hinterlands; the Far Northwest, Southwest, or West still the frontier — and homeland for hundreds of thousands of Eskimo, Indian, Chicano children.

Eskimo Children

Custodian of a Spirit

Wind, strong and uninterrupted, hits the old man, pushes the girl of five backward. She holds her grandfather's hand tighter. He wants to reassure her; he points to the river, as if to say: it is only a matter of yards, so let us keep going. They reach their destination in a few moments, stand silently at the water's edge. They seem oblivious to the mud that moves quickly to cover their boots. The wind, which had fought them so hard, now seems to let up a little. As the old man has told his granddaughter several times, they have reached one of the sources of wind, the river. The girl looks closely at the ice. She points with her right hand, smiles, says quietly: "Many cracks." The old man smiles back and nods his head. The girl does not say a word more, nor does the man move, for about ten minutes. Then he squeezes the child's hand, pulls his feet out of the mud, turns around. She follows suit, and soon they are on their way back, hurried along just a bit by the wind that now is a friend.

They continue their silence. The man looks straight ahead. The girl tends to look downward, except when she suddenly lifts her head all the way up — to catch a glimpse of her grandfather's face. He quickly responds each time she does so — he seems to sense her glance toward him rather than see it; he smiles at her, lifts his chin noticeably, using it to point ahead: we will soon be under cover. When they have reached the top of a gentle incline, they both turn around and look again at the river; it is April, the ice is beginning to break, they are excited and pleased to have taken this particular walk. The old man at last begins to talk with the child; he tells her that the wind is coming in from the ocean, sweeps up the river, leaves it for the banks on either side, takes a lurch upward to get on top of the slope, even as they have done so, rushes through the village and out across the tundra. The wind is not an enemy, though; the wind is part of life, he tells the girl, who is listening carefully to his every word. She moves her head emphatically up and down as he talks, not necessarily following a particular thought but indicating a sort of general acceptance of his authority and good judgment. When he has finished his mixture of description and explanation, she stops indicating her assent and says one word: "Home?"

Soon they are there, slowly unburdening themselves of their coats, hats, gloves, boots. The man watches the child as he takes his outdoor clothes off but makes no move to help her. She is agile, fast; she is done before he is. He is quite pleased, pats her back, smiles, goes back to his boots, which he makes no effort to clean, simply pulls off — a bit of a struggle — and puts them down beside the door on an old, torn brown bag. The two of them are cold, but they make no effort to warm themselves near the stove. They sit down on chairs that face one another and for the first time since they prepared to leave the house about an hour earlier, look at each other intently and with a certain persistence: a full minute. The silence is broken by the grandfather; he tells the girl that she is a good companion, a sturdy walker, and that she has taken her grandmother's place in a ritual he has performed for years and years, since he was a young boy himself, having learned to do so by walking with his grandfather: the walk to the river to catch a glimpse of the ice beginning to break.

The girl had, of course, walked to the river many times that winter; she had gone with her father, with her older brothers, with her grandfather — to fish, to watch the snowmobiles move on the ice, or simply to meet other children and play. But this was a special walk, and she had been honored to be asked. Her grandmother had died the year the girl was born. At the age of five she knew a lot about her family; most especially she knew that her grandparents had been quite close and that her birth, coming as it did three months after her grandmother died, had meant a lot to her grandfather. In fact, he once told her — she was maybe three or three and a half — that her grandmother's spirit may well have moved into her. He had no proof; he simply had a feeling, and he wanted the little girl to know. Not that he made too much of such a conviction; he avoided seeming portentous when he made his announcement (the girl's mother tells me), and he has since then avoided going out of his way to mention it. Still, upon occasion he has reminded his granddaughter that she resembles her mother's mother and that when one of them left, the other arrived. And so doing, he has given the child a special sense of herself. She watches him more carefully, with more regard, than his other grandchildren do. She asks her mother about *her* mother more often than her brothers and her older sister do. She asks, too, about "the time before" — her way of referring to her grandmother's span of life. She knows that when her grandmother was five or six, snowmobiles were not in existence, nor were airplanes commonplace in Alaska. Now they cross the sky every few days and land weekly on the ground near her village. She knows there was no electricity a few decades ago. She also remembers that her mother and her grandfather both have remarked that her grandmother died glad she had lived when she had and had not been born much later — in the girl's words, "these days."

The girl is glad to be alive now. Her name is Betty, but she had decided she likes Betsy better. She has been called that by a schoolteacher, a white man who lives in the village and has come to know her rather well, even though she is not yet six, hence not old enough for school. The teacher has told Betsy's parents that they have a smart and likable daughter — all very pleasant to hear. The parents say thank you over and over again, sometimes reminding the teacher of his observation with respect to their daughter so that they can, once more, express their appreciation. The parents also remind Betsy of the judgment that has been made about her, and she delights in hearing the outsider's prophecy. She connects his analysis with her grandfather's attitude toward her: if she is indeed a continuation, so to speak, of her grandmother, then she naturally would possess some of the old woman's intelligence, wit, and common sense, all of which she was reputed to have in abundance. She has heard about the old lady: "She was tired a long time before she went away from us. My mother said

one day she woke up, and her mother was calling her. My mother
went to her, and her mother told her that before the sun set, she would
be gone from us. My mother believed her mother; and she did go away
just as she said she would. It was early spring, so the sun set a few
hours later. Everyone said that our village would be in trouble, because no one was smarter than my grandmother, and no one knew
how to fix things and settle arguments better than she did. But my
grandfather disagreed with people; he said that he knew that his wife
would stay with us and people would remember her; and then he decided that she passed me as she was going away: I was coming here,
and she smiled at me — that's what he says he's sure happened."

There is just a touch of uncertainty, maybe confusion, in Betsy's
voice as she makes that assertion. She has tried to learn exactly what
her grandfather believes happened when his wife died and his granddaughter was born. But the man waves off her questions, not brusquely
or angrily, but with a gentle vagueness she finds it impossible to get
beyond. If not he, then his daughter, the girl's mother: what does she
know, and, just as important, what does she believe? But the mother is
even less helpful; she tells Betsy that she knows nothing — that it is
the grandfather who must be asked. If he has no more to tell, then that
is that. But the girl has herself to turn to; she has a lively, imaginative,
speculative mind, and she calls upon it to answer questions others
shirk altogether or respond to, it seems, unsatisfactorily: "I think I
know how I got to meet my grandmother. She was being carried away
by the wind, and suddenly the wind stopped. Everything was still.
Then I was born, and she had a chance to breathe her breath into me,
and then the wind came up again, and she was gone. I saw my uncle
lean over his son, and he kept breathing into him, but my cousin died
anyway. My father said that sometimes it helps, when you see someone who isn't breathing, to breathe for him. A teacher at the school,
who used to be a nurse, taught us all to do that kind of breathing."

Someday, Betsy thinks, she might become a teacher. She looks
forward to school; she will join her older sisters and brother. They are
not all that enthusiastic about the time they put in as pupils, but that
is a mistake on their part, she knows. Her grandmother had told her
mother to encourage all her children to go to school. The Americans
from "the states" would be coming in increasing numbers to Alaska
during the next few years, and the Eskimos had best be ready for the
influx. The mother repeats to all the children what she was told, but
Betsy listens most attentively. Her older sister, aged nine, reprimands
her, tells her that she needn't be a slave to their dead grandmother's

every word. Betsy denies being a slave to anyone or anything. Besides, who or what is a slave? The older girl talks about black people and their fate as Americans in the eighteenth and nineteenth centuries. Betsy is neither interested nor impressed: "I'm not a slave. I don't want to go to school because my grandmother wanted me to go. I want to go because *I* want to go. I'm only a slave to myself! Don't tell me any more about slaves."

She turns away abruptly. She goes to the window; how are the dogs? She looks at them, decides out loud that they don't need food at that moment, but keeps looking at them. Meanwhile, the sound of a snowmobile can be heard, and she listens carefully. Betsy turns to her mother, who is frying cut-up potatoes, with Spam to follow, and asks whether (and if so, when) they will get one of those snowmobiles. The mother says no. She says they are expensive, and only the rich people in the village can afford them. But there are a lot of rich people, the child retorts, with a mixture of annoyance, envy, and incredulity. Not so, the mother insists. Anyway, the machines make so much noise that a handful of them dominates everyone's hearing and, maybe, thinking. They are an exaggerated presence. The girl is not persuaded. She mentions four children she knows whose parents own snowmobiles. The mother casually mentions ten or twelve whose parents don't and then, both teasing the child and making a sensible, generous suggestion, tells her to go ask her various friends for a ride; surely their parents will oblige. Betsy is both grateful and quite stubbornly aware of her mother's ironic, if not sardonic, proposal. She does not underestimate the hospitality of others, but she wants something for herself. She conveys her feelings by apparently changing the subject, by asking a question rather than making any further comment, and by shifting the discussion to a different level of abstraction, arguably a more pointed one: "How do you get rich in the village?" She seems ready to wait patiently for hours after that request for information, but when her mother does not immediately respond, and indeed appears lost in thought — will the potatoes burn, or will she ever be able to tell the child how a few prosper while others are lucky to get through the winter alive? — another effort, this one more personally directed, is made: "Will we ever be rich?"

That is enough for the mother. She hits the stove with her spatula and tells the girl to go clean up. The girl does not often hear such a demand, and she knows to obey quickly. The mother is smiling at her, but the eyes above the smile are hard and glaring, and Betsy does not speak another word or prompt any further injunction. She moves directly toward her bed, an old iron military cot, and with her hand brushes crumbs from the sheetless mattress, arranges the blanket neatly, dusts off the small pillow, and then with her cupped palms gathers what has fallen on the floor and carries it to a basket near the stove. As the old crumbs, a couple of lollipop sticks, and an empty orange soda-pop bottle get thrown in, the mother remarks, in a soft voice, that the rich have learned to take good care of themselves, to be tidy and prompt. The girl now does a philosophical about-face; she says she hopes her parents never become rich and that she would give away her money if she had a lot. Then she has a second thought: "I'd buy everyone in the village a snowmobile, even the smallest baby. Then no one would have one while other people didn't. It's not bad to have a lot of money; but it's bad to have it while other people don't have it."

Betsy has heard that point of view expressed many times by her grandfather, and by her mother and father, too. When the mother hears her daughter speak so, it is as if a threatening war had been replaced by a pact of friendship and mutual support. The child finishes her chores; the mother moves close to her, helps her straighten out the particular corner of the room that she has responsibility for, pats her lightly and with obvious tenderness on the back. Betsy had thought of going outside before, but now, acknowledging her own shift of mood, announces that she will stay in and try being of help, if she can, to her mother. As the girl helps cut up some fish, which will be fried in deep fat, the mother responds to questions about the history of the Eskimo people. Betsy wants to know how long they have been in the village, and how long they have had snowmobiles in the village, and how long they have been visited by airplanes once a week. The questions continue, are answered briefly, factually. They are both general and specific, have to do with matters of faith and conviction or with technology, both primitive and highly developed. Motorboats interest the girl, but so do rowboats and kayaks.

Eventually there is silence. Betsy decides to draw a landscape (Figure 35). She makes no effort to look outside and remind herself what there is to see, nor does she close her eyes first — a gesture some children make, as if to summon up for themselves what they want to represent. She simply sets to work, quickly and forthrightly. She makes the sky first, a light blue, lighter than the sky other American children make. She omits the sun altogether. She works on a river, setting it off with the thinnest of black lines. The ice is breaking, she observes. Consequently, blue water interrupts the snow. The white crayon is used most, and she worries that it fails to evoke the visual reality around her. So she abandons the picture when it is done for another attempt. She decides to let the white paper *be* her accomplished landscape, except for a few interventions with blue for the sake of the sky. That does not work either; she decides to abandon hope of picturing the tundra and nearby river. Instead Betsy turns her attention to a nearby hill, whose pine trees offer a limited relief from the endless white, flat land she had been trying to evoke. She is ever so delicate with the trees; they are each fragile, yet obviously strong and flexible: they survive the winter, as she remarks when she is done (Figure 36). She is told that she can use black paper, cover it with white — a visitor's suggestion, a "technique" explained. She shakes her head. She will have no part of that idea.

Betsy's mother smiles, admits she will never be an art connoisseur, but is appreciative of her child's ability. The girl asks the mother if she has ever drawn a picture. No, she hasn't. Has her grandfather? The mother says she is always reluctant to answer for him, but she is sure he hasn't. The girl decides to try her hand at a snowmobile. She has just heard the noise of one, and she is sure it is going down toward the river. As she works, using a black crayon for the machine, her mother looks outside: some birds, no doubt just returned from their winter stay to the south. Betsy does not get up to catch a glimpse, but she does turn her attention away from the machine to the portrayal of a sky. Soon it is filled with birds, each one small but in their sum a virtual blanket. The snowmobile is eventually completed; it was going to be small, anyway, but now, in comparison to the birds, it seems quite insignificant (Figure 37). As a matter of fact, the mother remarks that the machine looks like a fallen bird. Yes, that is not such a bad idea, Betsy muses: "The snowmobile is like a bird that wants to fly, but can't, so all it can do is make a lot of noise and try to go faster, faster, but it never takes off. Why don't the white men who make planes give wings to their snowmobiles?" She pauses only briefly before she comes up with a reply to her own question: "A snowmobile isn't a plane; they're different." As she looks at her picture, she decides to pursue, almost as in a reverie, the subject of differences. "An Eskimo is not a white man. The teacher told my brother that we're all like animals; we were once animals. But then we became people. My grandfather said the white man comes from one place, and we come from another, even if now Alaska has a lot of white people. When my grandfather was a boy, he said he didn't see too many white people; and *his* grandfather had told him there were no white people around most of his life — only at the end. The teacher told my brother that today girls are the same as boys. My father laughed, and my grandfather did. But my mother said she knew what the teacher was saying!"

Her mother at first says nothing in response; she is putting on her outdoor clothes to go get some more fish, kept frozen in a small cabin removed from the main house. As she leaves she tells her daughter that Eskimos have seen their whole world change in recent years, and there is, no doubt, more to come — more people, more machines, more alterations in customs, habits, beliefs. The birds somehow survive, despite the continuing turmoil beneath them; and the fish still are to be found, for all the motorboats that have made the river far from the quiet place it used to be in the summer; so, Eskimos will also manage to survive. The girl is unhappy with a certain fatalism she detects in her mother. She has heard the same attitude expressed by her grandfather: stand firm, and somehow we will stay around, and the generations will follow one another. Betsy has other ideas; she is convinced that the snowmobile and the motorboats, if given even further reign — if owned by more people — would make Eskimo life better, easier, more pleasant. The mother will hold her ears when one of the snowmobiles goes by; Betsy listens to the noise quite eagerly.

Not that she is infatuated with the machines or allows their presence to change her overall sense of perspective. While she draws, she thinks: the machine is no match for the natural world in all its threatening, awesome, and occasionally quite beckoning presence. The machine is a help, even as the dogs are. The dogs, those Arctic huskies that are almost taken for granted by her and the other children of the village, are still (as her grandfather has often reminded her) the mainstays of village life. For a machine even to be compared with the dog is, in itself, noteworthy. But the child knows enough not to get hypnotized and fooled by Western industrialism. More planes might mean faster mail, a more varied and plentiful diet — assuming the continued willingness of the state and federal government to provide a subsistence economy with welfare checks, food stamps, surplus commodities. More planes might mean a greater intimacy with the outside world, something intangible, yet quite real to an Eskimo child: "We would see a lot of white people; there'd be more movies brought in, and we'd hear more news." But there is no likelihood, Betsy knows, that machines will overcome the long Arctic winter. She has seen dogs penetrate the coldest weather. She has seen machines rendered useless by weather she herself considers, at the very least, unsurprising. The dogs are utterly essential; without them life seems unimaginable. The motor-driven boats, the snowmobiles, and the airplanes belong to another world — one that has steadily encroached upon her existence but not one she wants to see replace the essence of Eskimo life.

Is there still such an "essence" that a child like her can confidently and persistently know — even put into words? In her own way she both asks and answers that question: "I think I will paint a picture. It is better to use paint than crayons; I've decided that if you want to show how we look, especially in winter, then it's best to use the paint set." She ambitiously undertakes a study of the village in midwinter, well before the weather begins to moderate. She ignores the sky, even the snow and ice, at first; she uses black and a touch of green to indicate the houses of the village, some nearby trees, a store, and a school. Then she surrounds all she has done with white — flat stretches of it, hills of it, flakes of it. There is no sky. There is no sun or, for that matter, moon (Figure 38). When she is finished she recalls what her father once told his family: "He has a cousin who went to live in the city, a long way from here. Then he left Alaska; he went to the lower forty-eight. He was in the army, I think. They sent him to a school down there. When he came back he said he knew how other people live: they look at the sun, but we look at the ice and the clouds. My father wasn't too happy with his cousin. He said we look for the sun, too. Now that the weather is getting warmer, we will see more and more of the sun. My father says that the Eskimos are like our dog: we know how to live here. The white man, he comes here and then he leaves."

But Betsy knows that white men, too, have remained in various parts of Alaska. They may not, by and large, live in small villages, under the circumstances she takes for granted. They may come, dig in, dig the earth out (for gold, for other minerals, for oil), and then leave. They may retreat to southern cities as often as possible — to hotels and motels, to buildings that are large and made of brick or concrete. But for limited periods of time even some of those people have endured the Arctic at its most oppressive; and there are some white people, she knows, who have done so for years at a time. Her grandfather and her father have told her about one such family. She speaks of them as if she knows them, though she has never met them: "They came to our village. They asked our people if they could join us. We said yes. They get their mail here. They buy at our store. They come to our meetings. When the ice melts, we always look for their boat. My grandfather asked them once if they would like to live closer to the village, instead of upstream and away. No, they wouldn't, they told him. He said he is sure that they have the spirit of our people living in them. He said maybe they are Eskimos who look white, just like there are some of our people who look like Eskimos, but they have the white man's spirit in them."

Betsy is halted by her own, vivid remark. She considers, silently, what she has said, resumes in a minute or so: "One of those Eskimos with a white man's spirit came from our village. He was married to my grandfather's sister. He took her, and they went to the big city: Fairbanks. He works for the government; he has something to do with the planes that bring us mail and food. He came back here two years ago; I don't remember him, but my mother says he was not very nice. He kept on telling all of us how dirty we are, and how clean we should try to be. He didn't even like our new school. He said we are not good at school; and it didn't look neat, the way it should — and he told people he'd talk to the important people he knows in the city. My father told my grandfather not to be so unhappy with his sister and her husband. Finally, my grandfather could smile; he told my father that he woke up in the night, and he realized what was wrong: his sister had married a white man; she'd married a man who thought he was an Eskimo when he was a boy, but pretty soon, when he was older, he turned out to be white. Or maybe he'd been taken over by some white spirit."

Young Leader

There is a twelve-year-old boy who also likes to talk to the pilot who comes to the village. John is a boy whom others of his age, even those a year or two older, regard as a leader. He talks to the minister like an equal. He challenges him on matters political, theological, philosophical. He asks him if God favors white people over Eskimos. He asks him if God likes the Bureau of Indian Affairs and the schools it sponsors. He asks him if God is on the side of the storekeeper, who makes the most money in the village, or on the side of the elderly people who have nothing to their name. The minister rallies to the defense of the poor, the weak, the vulnerable. But the boy is not easily persuaded to let up his scrutiny. What is the church like in the lower forty-eight? He wonders that aloud at one meeting, after a series of Kodachromes show the Eskimo children some stunning pictures of the California seacoast, as well as interesting, attractive San Francisco. The minister acknowledges openly that the Christian Church, in its various expressions, forms, structures, has betrayed Christ over the centuries. He tries hard to explain himself and his own purpose — to serve a number of villages in a particular section of Alaska.

Later, in his own home, John both defends the minister and continues his critical appraisal: "He's a good person. We all like him. He wants the Eskimos to live better. He argues with our schoolteachers. I've heard them; it is fun to listen while white people argue! The teachers didn't realize for a long time that my friend and I were listening; when they did, they stopped. I don't blame them. When my mother gets angry at my father, she says nothing until they can be alone. She doesn't want everyone to know how much pepper she can have on her tongue. Later I told the minister that I'd heard all he'd said, and I was on his side. He was glad I was. But I told him that he should go talk to other ministers, not to the schoolteachers in our village. He should tell the rich, white people that it's wrong, the way the Eskimos are pushed around. We don't have much to say about how we're going to live — even the teachers admitted to him that he was right when he said that."

John goes on; he repeats much of what he had heard the minister himself say. But the boy and the boy's father and grandfather have said the same things many times. The minister is, however, a white man — and to hear such self-criticism from white people is not an everyday experience for Eskimos, the boy knows. He says *that*, too — indirectly but with unmistakable emphasis. For the boy, white people are powerful, hard to speak to, a source of confusion. They introduced, on the one hand, snowmobiles, airplanes, frozen foods, electricity, welfare checks; on the other hand, alcohol, drugs, jails, schools where children learn to look down on themselves, other schools located hundreds, even thousands, of miles away, to which children are arbitrarily sent. The particular village this boy belongs to has banned alcohol, but there is another, larger, village nearer the ocean where alcohol is plentiful — along with work during the summer season at a commercial fishery, where the river's salmon are cleaned, cut, salted, and packed — to be sent "down there," as the boy refers to the lower forty-eight.

The boy has heard his grandfather complain endlessly about white people and what their presence means; the boy both agrees with and takes issue with his grandfather: "The white people are everywhere, so I guess we can't expect them to stay away from here. The minister showed us a map; all the places where America has air force bases were marked; they're all over the world. Air force planes land down the river; they never come to our landing strip, though, because it's too small. The big pipeline, carrying the oil, won't come near us; but I have a cousin who lives near where it will run, and he's waiting to watch the machines come in to dig. They've come to his village and talked to the people. I'm in favor of the pipeline, I think; the Eskimo people will get some money. My grandfather says that money is like liquor — you end up waiting for the checks, just like you end up drinking every day. My father doesn't drink anymore. But he used to, and my grandfather doesn't forget. He told my father that if he didn't stop drinking, then he'd have a funeral to go to — his father's! My grandfather was going to kill himself! That stopped my father, and then he went around the village, asking people to join him in getting rid of liquor. We have a vote; the people from the state government came — and we won: no liquor is sold here. Men go and buy it in other villages; they bring it home and we can hear them getting drunk. But at least you can't just walk to the store and spend your money there on whiskey, instead of food. The store owner wanted to pay each person who voted five dollars so that they would say yes, we should have the whiskey here. And he is an Eskimo! I keep reminding my grandfather of that, and he turns away. My father said to stop reminding the old man. My mother said not to stop, because if I remind someone else I remind myself! A lot of Eskimos drink when they get to be fifteen or so, and there's nothing to do."

John stops talking. He looks at an empty whiskey bottle his father insists upon keeping on a table near his bed — a reminder to him of the bad times he used to have. His wife has repeatedly objected. She would have thrown the bottle out a long time ago. But the man has his reasons, and his son has heard them being turned into the basis of an argument: "My father took me once with him; we were going to catch salmon, then get them ready for drying. We started setting up the racks, then we got our nets ready. Before we went out on the boat, Father told me how glad he is to get up in the morning and be without a sore head and a sore stomach. He told me how he used to feel when he'd been drinking; he felt terrible. But he couldn't stop. He'd t morning he'd try. But each morning he'd end up taking then another. He'd hold the bottle to his lips. He never When my mother offered him a glass, he broke it. He could wait long enough to find a glass and pour th he could keep himself from taking the whiskey. H bottle and drank from it, or he kept away from th my mother from throwing the bottle out. V and threw the dishes and pots around, an

"My mother would tell us, in fror

alone. My grandfather said that my father had fallen under the power of the white people, and that one day he would 'break out and be free.' My father smiled when my mother told us that. My father was drunk, but he said she was right! When he did break out, he said he was sure that he'd never have another drink. My mother wasn't so sure, but my grandfather told her not to worry. He had gone with my father to get firewood, and my father told him that he would *never* drink again. My father hadn't said that before; he refused to promise because he didn't want to break his promise. He's never made a promise that he couldn't keep. Now he talks to men who still drink; they smuggle in bottles, and you can walk by their houses in the summertime, and you can hear by the way they're talking that they're drinking a lot. My father tells me to go home, and he walks right into the house of a man who is drinking and he starts talking about how sick he used to be, and how sick he gets now, just thinking of the past. Then he'll tell the man *not* to stop until he is really ready to stop.

"The man's wife will get very upset; one wife told my mother that my father must be getting five dollars from the owners of the store where the men get their whiskey. My mother was very upset, but the woman was only teasing her. The wives wish my father would be a better preacher. I asked the minister why he doesn't help my father become a better preacher! The minister said that preachers don't stop people from drinking. I told my mother what he'd said, and she shook her head and said that you can't let a man drink and drink. But I think she knows now that the minister is right. She tells the wives of men drinking that you should try to stop a man from drinking, but if he won't stop, no matter what you say or try to do, then you should sit down and even lift the bottle for him, if his hands and arms are shaky. Then pray the day will come that he learns to say no. If you get him to promise every day to stop and he doesn't, then he'll be a man who can't keep his promise, and he'll drink because he'll want to forget that he made promises and couldn't live up to them.

"When my father and I went to catch salmon, and he talked with me about the drinking he used to do, he told me that when he was very sick, and when he thought he wouldn't live very long, he promised himself that he wouldn't say he'd stop until he was ready to stop. told me that when you promise someone you'll do something — or another person — then you are saying the most important in the world: I will. He said never begin with those two you know you'll be able to do what you say. When he de- grandfather and my mother and all of us that he'd stop drinking, he took the bottle off the floor — it was half-full — and put it on the table and said he'd never again take a drink. And he hasn't. Then my mother picked up the bottle, and she was going to empty it and throw it away, but he said no, she must never touch the bottle. He wanted it to stay near him! A few days later, he emptied the bottle, but he's never going to throw it out. He says it reminds him of the promise he made. My mother doesn't understand why he needs to be reminded, but she never argues with him. I think I understand. He told me; he said that the bottle on the table is the bottle he beat. He said he fought with the whiskey in the bottle, and he won over it. He said it's like going out with a gun, and there are a hundred white men, and they have their guns, and they have their fast planes, but he is the only Eskimo, and he just tells them that they can kill him, but they can't take him a prisoner and put him in their jails, so he'll just stand there, and let them go ahead and do what they want, but if they try to touch him, he'll shoot himself. They don't know what to do. They just stand still. The white men only know how to fight, not how to stay away from fights."

John isn't so certain, it turns out, that he would want to be faced with the challenge his father described. He is a tough, combative boy — or so his teachers describe him. They consider him unusually assertive, as Eskimo children go. As teachers, of course, they welcome such a trend; they have come to the village — whites from the lower forty-eight — to be themselves an "outside influence," to bring change. The boy agrees with them; he refers to them as "white people" and is sure that they will one day leave — having taught Eskimo children a lot about places they have never heard of and will never see. He disputes the emphasis they place on themselves, the high regard they have for their "influence." He considers his forcefulness to be a quite traditional trait, acquired from his grandfather, who is one of the most respected men in the village and, for that matter, other villages.

The grandfather is well known to many Eskimos, as the boy makes clear — and not only to boast about a man he is proud of: "The teachers ask me why everyone looks up to my grandfather. I tell them I don't know. My grandfather said I give the right answer! One teacher said he had an explanation. He is an Indian, and he wants to stay here for a long time. He told the other teachers that my grandfather is a leader and that's why everyone pays attention to him. The teachers asked why my grandfather is a leader; the Indian answered: why is anyone a leader? I told my grandfather and he laughed. He said he'd be glad to talk with the Indian teacher I like, but they haven't talked much. They say hello when they meet, but my grandfather has not been feeling too good, and he does not want to talk with strangers. He believes that he's alive for a reason; each day he tries to do what he believes he's here to do. He says he'll die when there's no longer any reason for him to be here. He helps my father get wood. He helps my mother with the fish; she says he's better at cooking than she ever was. He takes me out for a walk and teaches me how to find wild birds' eggs and how to collect moss. He knows how to keep warm, and he tells me and my sister and my brother how to keep warm. He makes sure I know how to put the moss in my boots when it is very cold. He told me that he hopes he stays alive until he has taught my youngest brother how to take care of himself. Then my grandfather will leave us.

"My mother says he almost died a few years ago — and many times he's been sick, and people have given up, and told themselves that he's soon not going to be here. But he stays with us, and it's because he wants to make sure we hear every story he knows! Everyone believes that he knows more about the village than anyone else. Even faraway people will say that if you want to know anything about our village, go ask my grandfather. He will sit down and explain how the village was built, and why his grandparents built our house here, and not further up the river. He should have been a teacher — that's what my favorite teacher, the Indian, said. My father said: your grandfather *is* a teacher. But when I told my grandfather what the teacher said, he didn't get annoyed. He said he can remember when the government built the school, and when they brought in the first teachers from outside, and how hard it was to persuade the people to send their children there every day."

The boy admires the old man's pride, his tact, his unwillingness to take any statement or controversy personally. He remembers once when younger going for a walk with his grandfather, hearing him talk about the snow, the ice, the long sunless winters. The boy wanted to know why — why are other parts of the world warmer, easier to live in? The old man had no answer for a long time; he told the boy he would like to think about the question. Finally he told the boy that there was no point asking whys, only a need to get through that day, then the next, and all those that follow, until the end comes. The boy was not at all satisfied; he wanted to know whether his grandfather had ever thought of trying to live elsewhere. The grandfather said no. The boy asked *another* why — why not? The grandfather suddenly turned the tables on his grandson: why was he asking all those whys? The boy didn't know how to answer. He said he didn't know; he was, quite simply, curious. The grandfather replied that he didn't know, either, why he couldn't come up with satisfactory explanations; perhaps it was because, quite simply, he *wasn't* curious. But the boy knew how eager his grandfather was to search out eggs, find geese, hunt seals, go fishing, scan the skies, spot the first crack in the ice, watch the sun rise or set, discover some good thick moss that he could cut, dry, and use to pad shoes, and thereby keep his grandchildren warm. Why did such a vigorous, independent, thoughtful man refuse to allow himself the ruminative, speculative moments the boy felt prone to?

The old man never would answer such a question, but John had his own way of finding out what he wanted to know: "I asked my mother and she said I was being foolish, because when you are born in a place, you have to live there, and no one knows why one place is different from another, so I'd better stop wasting my time asking. My father said he'd wondered, too; but he said he was told by his mother that it was once hot here all winter, then it got cold, and one day it might get hot again. My grandmother told my father that there was a big fight long ago between a white bear and a brown bear, and the white bear won, and that was when the snow came to our land. She heard stories like that when she was a girl, but she didn't really believe them, and she was happy to see that my father didn't either. She told him that the winds bring bad weather, but they can change and bring good weather. I asked my grandfather if he'd let me tell him what I believed; and he said yes, he'd much rather listen to me than talk. So, I told him about the winds — that I'd heard they cause the snow and ice, and if they changed, there would be different weather here. And he said I was right, and that was the secret he hadn't told me — about the winds."

Not that the grandfather went any further. John remembers asking about the winds: where do they come from, and why are they so harsh, and when will they let up, go elsewhere, try hurling their force on other regions of the earth? Whereupon the old man told the boy something he has never forgotten: "He told me that I had better stop asking him questions like that, because no one knows the answers to them — even the white man, and he thinks he knows the answer to every question." The boy has heard words to that effect over and over again; he has, upon occasion, repeated them to the one teacher (the Indian) he trusts. The teacher listens respectfully but disagrees; he tells the boy that there are causes, effects, reasons, explanations. The boy smiles, nods his head, says nothing. As he compares in his mind his grandfather's way of regarding the world and his teacher's, he decides to make a drawing. A blast of wind has reminded him of what he has heard at home about Arctic weather; he decides to show the tundra under siege — a fierce, snow-bearing wind sweeping across the land. He announces that the first snow is the one that he finds most exciting, so he will attempt to show how it appears to him, as he thinks about the early autumn months when suddenly, overnight it seems, summer turns into winter.

He draws the tundra with great care and obvious affection. He works hard on the grass. With a mischievous look, he sketches a nest, full of eggs. He tells his mother that he has drawn some eggs, and they are not far from the village. She laughs. It is an old source of tension as well as humor between them. The boy is supposed to keep an eye out for eggs, and sometimes he comes home, after an extensive search, claiming that none are to be found. His mother then goes out and, invariably, stumbles upon a nest of eggs even before undertaking the pursuit formally. As the boy tells of his mother's sharp vision, her successes, in contrast to his failures, he decides to put aside the larger drawing and do another one: more eggs. He makes them big, spotted; he puts them in a bed of grass, then works at the tundra — flat and without trees or shrubs. He loves to go find eggs, loves to bring them home, loves to eat them. He had learned at school that children elsewhere merely have to open a door to find a dozen or so eggs before them. But he has also been told that they are chickens' eggs — and far less attractive to look at, and of a different taste.

John would not like that kind of life, he says firmly, as he puts his drawing aside — unfinished. He also seems uninterested in working on the previous, more ambitious, one. The soft, easy life of other Americans interests him; he has heard it remarked upon, criticized by his father and mother, his elderly grandfather: "They have told me that we will no longer be Eskimos if we have all our food here at home, and have forgotten how to go out and find food for ourselves. That is how the white people live, and that is how some of our own people have begun living — in the cities of Alaska. My friend's uncle lives in Nome. He went to visit his uncle and his aunt and his cousins. He said that they have a television set, a refrigerator, a snowmobile, a motorcycle. They have a stove that is electric. They have a motorboat. They are talking of moving to Fairbanks because they'd like to own a car, and they say in Nome you can't go too far with a car. My uncle was in the air force, and now he works for the government. He may get a job from an oil company. Then he'd go north by himself and send all the money home. My father says that his brother is ruined. He keeps telling my father to come visit him. He lives in Nome too. He sends us letters. He says it's too bad we don't have telephones in our village. My father says that when we have telephones and television, it will be time for us to leave. He won't go see his brother anymore. And his brother won't come see us. But they write to each other. My grand-father says that when he dies, the two brothers will stop being brothers. My brothers and I will never let that happen to us."

John has immediate second thoughts: maybe, one day, he will travel, and will like a certain country, and will want to stay there, and so will lose contact with his family. He would never want to live else-where in *Alaska,* but the teachers have showed him and his classmates pictures taken from the *National Geographic,* and he has to admit that some of them have whetted his appetite. He especially responds to the tropics, to stories about and pictures of the Amazon, the African jun-gle, the Pacific islands. What is it like to live under a hot sun, to be able to dress so lightly, to fight sweat and mosquitoes rather than chills and frostbite? He has a slight idea; summer comes to the Arctic too — however briefly. It is never an unbearable summer — to outsiders, like pilots, teachers, government officials, the white people who visit vil-lages like his. But for him warm weather can be strange, unsettling, even unnerving, and he knows quite clearly some of the reasons why: "The sun never leaves us, and we keep telling ourselves that we should enjoy it while it's with us, but after a while we get so tired. We are tired because we can't sleep too well when it's light all the time, and we are tired because we have been doing too many things and for-getting to go to sleep."

He muses out loud about the tropics; he wonders whether he would be especially vulnerable, were he to go there on a visit. He has seen white people come to Alaska and become sick, weary, constantly fearful: can anyone possibly survive a particular storm, never mind an entire season of winter — a half-year of temperatures at or well below zero, and of heavy snows, relentless winds? Just after he observes that he would probably learn how to live with one hundred degrees, day in and day out, he reminds himself that he ought to finish his aban-doned, large drawing of a windy, winter storm. White people have learned to survive Alaska's winters, he comments as he picks up his drawing again. He contemplates it, seems ready to work at it, then puts it firmly aside. He will start all over again, and this time he will finish what he starts. He reaches for the largest piece of paper avail-able, reaches for paints instead of crayons, and works long, hard, silently. The result is an astonishing painting — really something in the abstract expressionist vein: thick white upon thin white, streaks of black, lines of white and black, and nothing else (Figure 39).

John is apologetic, yet determined as he tries to indicate what he hoped to accomplish: "The wind comes from the mountains or from the sea; we get winds from both directions. We sit here and my grandfather laughs when we ask what it is like outside and go look through the window. He says that we'll never see anything standing in the house and looking; the only way is to go outside and look — or else close our eyes and stop talking and listen and picture the snow up in the air, speeding across our village like airplanes, millions of them, only even faster than they go. I remember closing my eyes, and besides the wind, that shouts at us, and never loses its voice, I could feel the snow touching my face, and I tried counting the flakes, but I gave up: too many. Once I asked my grandfather what would happen if all the flakes came together, because there were so many of them. He said it is a mystery — how the air can hold so many flakes; but perhaps that is what the wind is for: to keep the flakes away from each other until they fall on the ground. Sometimes when I see a heavy snowstorm coming, I joke; I tell my grandfather that the snowflakes are coming *together,* and it's *all white* out there, it's falling big *pieces* of snow. He smiles and says he hopes so! I think he'll like this picture, even if we haven't had *that* much snow. I guess I could have done better, but the picture shows what the wind would do if it was so strong it made snow come down in big lumps."

Snow and the wind that carries it are apparently taken for granted by him but are really a continuing source of wonder and awe. John has been taken down the river to the sea over and over again, yet the sight of giant icebergs still captivates him. He would like to go exploring on them. He would like to watch them break up, yield slowly to the spring. But they never yield completely, as he keeps reminding himself, almost with pride: "The teachers tell us that in a lot of places the snow doesn't last too long. When I was younger, I used to tell my mother, when we came back from a trip to the ocean, that I was worried that the icebergs might melt during the summer, and there would be only the water to see. My mother would laugh and repeat my words: *only* the water! She loves to walk to the edge of the river. She loves to walk on the shore, near the ocean. She collects stones or shells, and brings them home and keeps them in a box. She says she doesn't care about the ice; she is glad, I think, when it leaves the harbor and goes further and further back. But I like the ice, and when it is far away, I tell my father that I hope to come back later, when I can see no water, only the ice and snow."

He has heard from his grandfather stories of his ancestors, who used to live by the ocean and only recently (the generation of his grandfather's father) moved inland. He has been told of expeditions through dangerous waters, of ice floes that shift, appear suddenly, disappear strangely, only to return so that lives are threatened or lost. He makes no pretense of concealing the excitement he feels when such accounts or stories are told: "My grandfather remembers being in his father's boat; they were coming in after fishing, when suddenly the wind came upon them, and it brought the ice from different directions, and they were cut off, so they couldn't land. They stopped rowing. They thought they'd be crushed to death, but there was a narrow channel still open, and my grandfather can remember his father saying that they should keep moving, and follow the channel. They could have been crushed to death at any moment. But they didn't become scared; they used their arms and they talked to the ice, and the ice never cut them off all the way, so they got to shore. I don't believe that the ice heard anything they said, but if they didn't keep moving, they could have been killed."

John is excited as well as impressed; they were skilled, able people, his ancestors, they faced natural elements more strenuously than he will probably ever have to. He and his friends have heard the stories, though, and have attempted in play to re-create the moments. They build walls of snow, the bigger the better, and imagine themselves navigators, with their lives at stake against the whims and excesses of ice floes. When their parents or grandparents have a moment, the children ask for new stories, or the repetition of familiar stories: struggles against the elements, including floating ice. And sometimes a picture makes a statement about the sea, about those floes, about Arctic life in all its savage or fragile beauty. The boy particularly treasures one painting he did at school (Figure 40). His teachers questioned him closely when he submitted it to them: had he seen ice floes that enormous, or was he making something up on the basis of hearsay? No, he was making up nothing; he had gone to a village near the sea, stayed with an old great-aunt, his grandfather's sister, seen exactly what he had tried to represent. One teacher had told him that he made the ice floes seem like skyscrapers in a city like New York. He had looked at pictures of American cities, heard about the tall buildings in them, but he had never realized that they were *really* tall. He had estimated them to be, maybe, as tall as a water tower he'd seen in one seacoast town, or the tower on top of a small airline terminal building he'd seen at the edge of that town, but he had never thought any building could rise to the height reached by massive floes.

He paraphrases his grandfather's memories as he looks at the painting he did for his teachers, took home and showed to his parents, and then put aside, against the advice of his teachers, who wanted him to hang up the picture at home — after he had refused to let them do so at school: "My grandfather remembers when he saw a picture in a church school of the ice in the harbor of the village where his father and his grandfather had been born. It was a photograph, I think. He went home and told his parents; they did not want to go and see the picture. They told him that as long as they had eyes, they would go look at the harbor. The white people would rather look at a picture than anything else. They go to movies, and they have television, and they have cameras. All the white people we see have cameras; and in school the teachers tell us about movies and television, and they get movies and programs flown in here to show us. My grandfather tells me to sit down and close my eyes, while he closes his. He sees the ice in the harbor, and he tells me what is happening — the wind is beginning to move the ice, and everyone is trying to take his boat back to the shore as fast as possible. I tell him what I see — the ice is moving in, but there is no one fishing and no boats are out, and he and I are standing and watching the ice. The sun makes some of the ice so bright I can't look too long. So, I open my eyes — and I'm back in our house again!"

When John says that, he stops talking. He looks outside. He lifts his eyes upward, scans the sky: the poor, weak, short-lived sun. The boy has imagined himself to be an ice floe, the wind, the river, a salmon running it, but never the sun. He pities the sun, even the summer sun, that brings the tundra to life so poignantly: "The sun must get cold. The teacher told us that the sun is so hot it would melt anything, but it doesn't look very hot. My mother used to tell us that she can feel the sun shivering, and the moon, too. The sun goes south, just like the birds. My sister sees the birds going, and she calls to them, and tells them not to forget the sun. When my friends and I told the teacher what we thought about the sun, she was very upset. She told us that we had to learn the truth, that the earth goes around the sun, and it doesn't run away, and it's always very hot, even when it doesn't melt our snow and ice. They must be right. They told my older sister that *we* make up stories, but *they* tell the truth! I'd like to go see other

places, where the sun is hot; then I'd know they're right. In the summer it gets warm here, and it's hard to believe that the winter will ever
come back. But before long the birds are flying away; they know. I
wish the teachers would invite our parents and grandparents to
school, and explain to them what they know. My father says the teachers are right, but they wouldn't be much help if they had to leave school
and work with us. They would walk on top of a lot of eggs; they would
plant flowers in the summer and hope to see them bloom in the winter."

Such sarcasm, such episodes of bitterness and scorn, are relatively infrequent and, it seems, self-limiting. The boy likes to go to the
village store sometimes; there to sit and say nothing at all, only watch
intently and listen, as the teachers, among others, gather close to a
wood-burning stove and talk, eat, drink, even doze in public. A father
or grandfather offers stories about the past, information about the tundra, the nearby river, or the ocean, at once dangerous and inviting.
The schoolteachers, or the visiting pilot and a passenger or two, offer
stories about the outside world, the lower forty-eight. The white people
are more relaxed in the store. The winters bring everyone in the village
together. The teachers sing, drink, avoid self-important pronouncements. The children are endlessly fascinated by the difference — by
what they hear in the store as opposed to what they hear in school.

A Modern Girl

Eskimo girls are not without their own moments of boredom, irritability, dissatisfaction with themselves and their life. One girl in a
small Arctic village has just turned thirteen; Mary sympathizes with
those who yearn for the old days and ways, but she is not about to
turn her back on today's "progress." She is an expert on rock music,
has a stereo set, wonders when she will get to a city, dance in a dance
hall. She has finished school, does little to keep herself busy, resents
the fact that her father is, by Eskimo standards, rather well-to-do —
but can offer her only a limited version of the future she would like for
herself. If some of the village's more proper, conventional people find
her self-centered, even insolent, she has some thoughts about them,
among others: "My father worked with the white people; he helped
them build the airstrip, and he was the one who showed them where
to build the school. He can fix the generator, if anyone can. Other
people are jealous of him; and they turn on my mother and me, just

because we like to wear clothes that aren't like their clothes. There are some old women in this village who are very mean. They spend all their time exchanging gossip; and when there isn't any to tell, they make some up.

"On our radio I heard that in places like California, women are living different; they aren't bowing before men, and taking orders all day from them. I'd like to go to California. Or maybe the gossiping women of this village, all of them, should go there! My father heard that my mother and I are 'friends' of the pilot — that he comes here on an extra trip every week, just to 'visit' us! Of course, everyone can see and hear that plane landing — so if he came in secret he'd have to be quite a pilot; he'd have to be like Superman in the comic books! When he *does* come he is greeted by the whole village, and he's never out of everyone's sight. But the women sit and sew and say that he's my mother's 'special friend,' and that when he gets tired of her, he turns to me! That shows what is going on here in this village: nothing! I wish the pilot would go 'visit' those old ladies and do something for them! They are worse than the minister and the priest put together! They are always calling me a 'modern girl' — and then they sneer!"

Mary cannot bear hypocrisy, and she is convinced that next to some of the gossipy village women, the most two-faced people in all of Alaska, maybe the entire world, are the pair of ministers who come to her village on weekly visits and who have long been objects of her derision. Often she wonders why in the world those men even want to visit the village. But she has figured out the reason and is most adamant when she comes forth with it: "They don't like their own people, so they leave them and come up here to be with us. I heard one of the ministers say that white people are 'plundering' Alaska; but he's up here, talking us into believing that he knows what's best to believe in. And he'll call you a bad person, and tell you about Hell. How does he know there's such a place? My mother says he's never been there, and no one has who's alive, so it's all up in his head, that there's Hell and Heaven. The ministers both expect to be in Heaven one of these days; I'll be glad to be in the other place, if that's how God will divide people up.

"I don't want to hear one sermon after another forever. Anyway, I'll bet they did something wrong, before they ever decided to come up here. They keep talking about the Eskimos they haven't converted, and how they want to convert them; but I think they ought to go back to the cities they come from and stay there, and stop telling us that it's wrong to drink and wrong to swear and wrong to do anything, except go and pray in their churches. The older minister asked me last summer where I got the dress I was wearing. I told him I ordered it in the Sears catalogue; but he looked very unhappy with me, and I was almost in a fight with him. But I was younger then; I was a little scared. If he dared say something like that to me again, I might pick up a rifle and aim it at him and tell him to go radio Kotzebue for that pilot who flies him in here!"

Mary doesn't really ever intend to talk like that to the minister or to any other grown-up; at least she can't imagine herself doing so. She recognizes the difference, even in someone as relatively outspoken as herself, between a thought and the actuality of words uttered — meant to be heard, taken quite seriously. But she is not really joking, either; nor is she being fresh and sassy — without taking the risks of putting herself on the line, so to speak. She has dared tell her teachers what she thinks, knowing full well that she has accepted their invitation to say candidly what is on her mind, but at the same time risked offending them. They have wondered aloud why she is so adamantly interested in urban life, why she seems so anxious to join what one teacher quite explicitly called "the rock culture."

She immediately challenged the teacher to describe that "culture," and the description given prompted a rather strong response: "I told her she was not right about me. I decided to say what I was thinking. Most of the time I don't. *All* the time the others in class don't! I know I'm sounding conceited; that's what my best friend said to me. She said I think so much of myself that I make the teachers feel uncomfortable — and her, too. We had a fight. I tried to explain to her why I say what I say. But she was too upset to listen; she said I shouldn't talk to people like I do — especially to white visitors who come here to teach us. But that's what I told the teachers; I said it's not right for people like them to come here to this village and talk to us the way they do. They think they're acting like Eskimos; they think they're saying what our parents say, and what we'll say to our children when we're parents. But they're wrong. Is it wrong for me to tell a teacher she's wrong — or he's wrong? My friend says yes; she says that you should stay quiet and smile and try to agree with what you've heard. I say that it's wrong to pretend to agree when you don't. But maybe my friend *does* agree! She says she agrees with the teacher when the teacher talks, and when I talk, she begins to agree with me! My friend says *I* should be a teacher!

"All I said was that I thought the teacher was trying to sound like an Eskimo; I mean she was talking like she *thought* an Eskimo talks, or like she thought we all *should* talk. Even my grandfather doesn't talk like that. He likes the electricity the white people brought to our village; and he likes to listen to my stereo; and he likes to go on a ride in a snowmobile. He says that if he was only younger he'd learn how to ride a motorcycle himself! He wasn't kidding me, either! The teachers are white and they come here from Chicago (one of them does) and New York (another one), and last year we had a teacher here from Portland, Oregon. They all say the same things to us; they tell us that we're good, but the white people are ruining us, because they're bringing in movies and radios and motorcycles and snowmobiles and potato chips and bubble gum, and we're getting lazy, and we no longer have our own 'culture.'

"Don't ask me what that word means: *culture.* I asked the teacher, and she explained, and I still couldn't figure out what she was telling us. So I asked again. That was my first mistake. My friend says I was being mean by asking, but I swear I didn't understand the explanation. I asked my friend what *she* thought 'culture' means, and she said she wasn't the teacher, and she couldn't talk like the teacher! Oh, did I laugh at that answer! Then I told her *she* was conceited because she was so proud of what she'd said! All I'd wanted, anyway, was an explanation from the teacher that all of us in the room could understand, and take home to our parents and give to them. What's so great about living in an igloo, and not having a store where you can get food in the middle of the winter, when it's fifty below and the wind is getting ready to carry the whole village into the ocean? What's so great about living here, when there's no doctor or nurse who can be flown in, with the medicine they bring?

"My younger brother would have died if they hadn't brought in a nurse, and she gave him penicillin, and he lived. I agree with the teachers about some things. The ministers don't belong here, and they don't really respect us. They ought to close down the church here and leave us alone. We don't need their sermons. But my grandfather disagrees; he says there was a lot of fighting, a lot of bad trouble here in the village *before* the white man came, and it was the church people who tried to make us get along better here, and he thinks they succeeded. He remembers that the old minister, who lived here for a long time, would go and talk with one family, and then with another, and he'd turn enemies into friends! He was a kind man, my grandfather says, and he brought food to people all the time, even people who never wanted to listen to his sermons, or go near his little church."

Mary is taken aback by her own capacity to emphasize ironies and inconsistencies. She laughs at herself, declares herself to be a touch mad. Her friend, in fact, has warned her that she will become the village eccentric if she doesn't watch out. She wonders out loud why she doesn't just go along, yield to her teachers, to the many neighbors and their children who retreat in embarrassment and dismay from her unashamed militancy, her willingness to speak out, on issues and dilemmas others are content to ignore or tolerate. She holds on tenaciously to a lively interest in the outside world, is determined to visit places most of her friends or classmates have no interest in seeing, can be self-deprecating as well as sardonic: "I heard one teacher call another one a busybody. I'm a busybody. I'm always watching what's going on; if I lived in a city, I'd have to stop because there are so many people. But here I can keep my eye on everyone! There's not much else to do here! A lot of my friends agree with me; they'd like to go live in the city for a while. They wish they had as many records as I do; they bring theirs over, and we play them and play them, until my mother says she can't let us go on, because she feels like walking away from the house and never coming back.

"That's what her uncle did; I guess he was her great-uncle. He was old, and he was sick. One day he got up and he was in pain. My mother tried to help him. She made him tea, and she gave him some bread and jam. He turned away from her food. He said he wanted to go out; he was sure that the cold air would make him feel better. He got dressed and went out. He never came back. Later that day we all went looking for him, and we found him up the river. He'd found a small tree, and he'd sat down under it and died. When we brought him back everyone was sad because he had always been a good person. One of the teachers said we should have told her, so she could get a doctor here. But the old man would never have let a doctor look at him. He told my mother that the day would come when he'd go out and lie down and die, and he did. My mother told the teacher what her uncle had said and done; the teacher thought it was 'beautiful.' My mother admitted to me later that she felt like laughing at the teacher but didn't. I would have laughed. It's stupid to say our uncle did something 'beautiful.' He wasn't painting a picture. He was dying, and he knew it. But maybe the teacher didn't mean bad. I guess she likes Eskimos."

The person she feels closest to is not her best friend, or either of her parents, but a younger brother, aged nine, who has severe nearsightedness, complicated by astigmatism, and who has relied upon her heavily in the past for vision — literal and figurative. The boy had no glasses for a long time. His parents accepted his near-blindness as something fated. His sister urged her parents repeatedly to go talk with the state officials when they came by, as they do often enough for one administrative reason or another. Finally she took the boy herself, telling their parents that they were simply going out to play. She stood with him at the airstrip, waited for the plane to appear and land, and went right up to the pilot, who stood watching and smoking while the mail and various supplies were being unloaded. Did he know when someone from Fairbanks, someone who could help her brother, would be flying in next? What was the boy's problem? His eyes — he can't see well. When he is five or six, the teachers will pick up the trouble and get it corrected, won't they? But that is in the future, and there is so much the boy can't do right now! Oh, all right! He told her to be standing exactly where she was, with her brother beside her, one week to the day, the hour.

They obliged. With the pilot this time came a doctor, who had agreed to change his schedule of visits to the various Eskimo villages. He did not only come for the boy, but the boy was seen first, at the school, where his vision could be tested. The child was measured for glasses; he has worn them, mostly, ever since. On very cold days, however, or wet days, or snowy days, they become a hindrance; they fog up in response to changes in temperature, become themselves wet and snow-covered, hence a barrier rather than an aid. And the boy has not always been able to get his glasses fixed; they become loose, bent, eventually useless. Mary describes what happens in the winter, when the planes throughout Alaska have a hard time responding to the most routine and urgent of village requirements: "My brother says to me that he likes my eyes better than the glasses. He says he is glad it's winter, and he'll be on his own — or sticking close to me and my eyes! I take him with me when I go to the store, and I read the labels on the cans and packages I buy there, and I tell him what I can see in the sky — a lot of stars or only clouds. And we play a game we call *Wish*. In the game he makes me guess what he's wishing — that he could be someplace, or that he could have something. If I guess right, it's my turn; if I'm wrong, he tells me. He's easy to play with; he always has the same wishes — that he could see better, or go out and catch a seal or a whale. He's afraid that because of his eyes, he may not be able to do a lot of hunting or fishing.

"A lot of people here need glasses, but they don't want to get them. A friend of my mother's asked me if everyone in the city wore glasses, and I said I didn't think so. I don't like questions like that; they are stupid. I keep telling my brother that the day will come when we'll fly out of here, and it won't be to Kotzebue, except to change planes. We'll go in a jet, and we'll visit a city in Washington, or Oregon, or California — those are the three states that face the Pacific Ocean, like Alaska does. When we're down in the lower forty-eight they'll fix my brother's eyes so he won't even have to wear glasses. A teacher told me they can put something in his eyes, a very small piece of glass, and he'll be able to see the way other people do. Then we could go look around; and we could buy some records. We'd have some money saved up. You can only order certain records in the catalogue.

"My mother says she's worried that all I'll ever do is listen to my records, but I tell her I'd like to get a job in some city, maybe working in a store where they sell records! The pilot told me I could get the records cheaper that way. And I could get myself a new stereo. It would cost a lot, but if you choose a set that isn't too expensive, and you get it even cheaper, because you work at the store, then you've done pretty good. If I brought the set back here — had it sent back on the plane — I'd have a lot of visitors. Even kids who think I'm strange because I want to leave here tell me they'd like to have more records and a big stereo. They'd all come over here, and they'd not only listen; they'd want to know what my brother and I saw down there in the lower forty-eight. We'd tell them. I'd let my brother do most of the talking because he'd be real excited, telling the kids what *he* saw."

She smiles at herself — a little critically, a little indulgently. She suspects it would be hard, after all, for her to keep quiet for long, even though her brother would have so much to tell. When she was much younger, maybe four or five, her grandfather told her that she talked too much; he was sure, accordingly, she would be a great favorite with the white schoolteachers when she started the first grade. But he had not realized how much the particular teachers in that village school admire what they keep calling "traditional Eskimo culture." A child who likes to talk a lot, and who, even at five or six, was intrigued with the shortwave radio because it made available "dance music" and news of other villages, distant cities, and countries would hardly be the traditional Eskimo child.

Mary rather soon discovered that her interests were not those of her first-grade teacher. When the teacher tried to point out how strong and proud the Eskimo people are, this one pupil of hers observed that children who lived in other parts of America were lucky. The teacher asked why. The child remembers well her answer — and the consequences: "I spoke quite loud, and she was surprised. I told her that I wouldn't mind living near a city in the United States of America where there was a Sears Roebuck store. She asked me why, and I told her why. I told her my mother sits with us and lets us look through the catalogue; and we point at the pictures we like, and she tells us how much money we'd need, and then we keep looking. The teacher said there was so much around us up here that we could look at, and we don't have to pay any money, just go and look — so why think the pictures in the Sears catalogue are so good? I didn't answer her back, not then; I was too young to know what to say. I did tell my mother what had happened between the teacher and me, and my mother told me not to tell the teacher what *I* think but to find out what *she* thinks.

"That is what my parents and my grandfather and my aunts and uncles have kept telling me, all the time: that I shouldn't speak my mind to the white people; instead, I should ask them what they believe and what they want, and be friendly with them. But it's hard for me to pretend I like a person if I don't really like her! Anyway, the white people who come up here aren't the only white people in the world, and if the pilot is right, the white people we see are different from the white people in the lower forty-eight. Once the teachers decided to come and talk with my mother and father; they decided that I was different from everyone else! They asked my mother if she was happy with the school — was I learning a lot? She said yes, she was happy and I was. She said she was glad all of her children were learning to read and write, and she hoped we went as far as possible in school. The teacher thanked her, and I remember my mother offering her tea; we had teabags. The teacher said we certainly had everything! My mother didn't know what she meant at first. She looked to my father. I think he knew, but he only smiled and asked the teacher if she wanted some sugar in the tea. The teacher said no. We gave her cookies, too; but she didn't want any.

"Later, when I was older, I could figure out what had happened. The teacher didn't expect us to serve tea and cookies; I guess she'd only recently come up here to Alaska, and she thought we had completely different food than the kind white people eat. In the past we lived on what we could catch in the water, or find on the land. But it's different now. She had seen the store, I guess, but hadn't gone visiting us yet. It's strange: some of the teachers don't really want us to live the way we do. They want us to be even poorer than we are! My grandfather says a lot of white people who come here would like to see us living in igloos. He jokes; he says he's going to build an igloo, and go live in it, and then he'll be the teachers' hero. I'm not sure he would know *how* to build one! Maybe he would. My grandfather sometimes says he doesn't know how to do anything, except fish, and dry out the fish, and eat; but other times he tells us long stories about the things he used to do when he was younger. Then I wish the teachers were here to listen. They'd really love him, because of what he says."

Chicano Children

In Texas: Carmen

The head is fixed in position, tilted slightly downward. The feet are slightly apart, and they do not move. The forearms are held tightly behind the back, the hands clasped. The eyes look straight ahead, as if focused on infinity. The only discernible movement in the body is an occasional blink; the force of a shock, it prompts in others a glance, raised eyebrows, a shift of vision. Suddenly the silence is broken: "You may go." No more and no less than those words; again and again, over the days, the weeks and months, the father uses the expression — permission for his sons and his daughters to leave, to resume whatever activity had been interrupted. And always, before the departure, there is a brief acknowledgment of gratitude: "Thank you, Papa" — three words in exchange for three words. With that accomplished, the head becomes unlocked, the eyes move to the door, and, finally, in a burst of movement that defies anatomical specification, the body comes alive, and in seconds has disappeared. Then it is the father's turn; he has been standing still himself, a mirror image, save for his eyes, of the child. As the child leaves, the father's eyes hold fast to the moving body; when it is out of sight, his gaze for the first time searches out the long view that a window offers. "A child who goes without discipline becomes an animal." Then there is a brief pause, followed by an important qualification: "No, I do not let my animals go wild. They must watch themselves too. We all must." He throws a quick glance at the mirror, pulls back, checks the clock unnecessarily ("I don't need to be reminded of the time; I have a machine that keeps good time in my brain"), and is on his way.

As he leaves the house he catches up with the child he has just reprimanded; they exchange greetings as if they had not seen one another for quite some time. The father quickens his step when he sees his nine-year-old son, is at the boy's side in a few seconds, stands there for an additional few seconds with his right hand on the child's left shoulder. The man says nothing. The child says nothing. They simply stare at one another, and a squeeze of the hand is acknowledged by a slight responsive turn of the boy's body — toward his father. They show smiles simultaneously. They break away from each other at the same time — the father in the direction of the street, the son toward the house. When the son is out of sight, the father again permits himself a few words: "He is a good boy. He behaves himself. God smiles on us through a child's eyes."

And the observation leads to a qualifying afterthought: "They are the eyes of a boy; they seem wild with greed sometimes. But that is as it must be. I must help him see what is right and what is wrong. Otherwise he will turn out to be a man blinded by his passions. A father does his best. A father is the law. A mother is love. A father's love is important too, but it cannot be given as fully as a mother's. My own father taught me how to grow up, and now it is my turn to teach my children. When I become too strict, my wife speaks up. She knows how to make her point without stirring anger in me. She begins telling me how much she respected my father, and she reminds me how gentle he could be with her — and with us, his children. She has made her point. I tell myself not to forget her words, and sometimes they will come to me as I am telling one of the boys to behave better."

He claims not to need such reminders when he is disciplining his daughters. They are different, girls; he dares anyone to tell him otherwise. As if someone might be near at hand who would indeed try to make such a case, he launches into a justification of his opinion, summoning in exquisite balance personal experience and a theoretical position he readily admits having been brought up to maintain: "One of my daughters is ten; she was never in much trouble. She is now so grown-up — it is hard to believe that she is but a year older than her brother, or two years younger than her older brother." He stops at that point to reflect and, it turns out, gather some ammunition: "My wife feels that I am partial to the girls. When I ask her if she knows any father who is more just than I am, she is quick to say no, I am a man, and there is no other reason for the way I act. She then tells me that she is quite sure that she favors our sons.

"I think she is wrong. I have a strict code; I was educated by both my mother and father to look upon myself as someone God uses. He uses all of us, I know — why else would He place us here for a few years of His time? I try to keep my eyes open; when I see a child of mine saying something wrong, making a mistake, I speak up. I don't enjoy what I have to do; it is my job as a father to be alert to my children, and I try to do what I am supposed to do as successfully as I can. I will admit that I have some prejudices. Who doesn't? I wanted all boys — and all girls. Does that sound crazy? If so, I know why; I am hopelessly divided in my loyalties. My sons, they are me — I know no other way to say it. My daughters, they are not only mine; they belong to others — to the men they will marry, to the children they will bring into this world, to our people: Mexican-Americans, they call us, the Anglos whose state this Texas is, whose country this United States is."

He stops again; it is as if he has slipped into a slightly awkward grammatical construction to give himself time to think, as well as place his emphasis on a certain political and economic set of circumstances. He does not, however, allow the United States to thwart him, at least on this occasion. Even if he were a citizen of Mexico, of Spain, he is convinced that he would have the same ideas about children and their upbringing. The church transcends all nationalities and races, he reminds himself; and too, there is a certain common sense that is part of one's nature — a biological given, he takes pains to point out: "I am not very good with words, and anyway, I know some things that I can't put into words. I try; my wife and I start talking about our children — and soon, about ourselves when we were children. We try to say what we think, but it is hard. A man is not a woman. A boy is not a girl. A father is not a mother. A child is a boy or a girl. A boy has it in him to stretch his arms, to run when his sister would be content to walk. A girl wants to hold on to her doll. Let the brothers throw away the sticks they have just turned into slingshots — an hour or two of time spent; a girl will keep faith in every single toy she receives — or makes for herself. The boy will marry; he will learn to keep faith too. But his mind will wander, and there is no stopping it. My wife doesn't even admit that I am telling her the truth when I say that *my* mind wanders, not just any man's. It is not within her power of imagination to under-

stand what I am struggling to explain to her. I always end up shrugging my shoulders. There is more to life than she and I can discuss.
That is what life ends up being — silences that mean a lot."

One of them, several minutes long; and a body's stillness; then his
voice chords again: "I keep saying that I can't find words for my
thoughts. That is what happens to me; I'm sorry. The priest has told
me that Christ Himself knew when to give up — hold His tongue and
pray to our Lord without saying anything. It is very strange: I will talk
too much with my daughters and not enough with my sons. I stop myself sometimes, when I am alone, and ask why. I never come up with
the answer. Once I turned to my wife: why the difference? I wanted to
find out why a man is a different person with his wife, his sons, his
daughters. My wife suggested that I go ask our children — take them
into my confidence and let them teach me. I did not like her suggestion. To tell the truth, I was angry."

He becomes angry remembering his anger. He flushes. He turns
restive. For a man who can be so immobile he suddenly seems to have
the jitters. He will never turn his children into "witnesses." Children
are not meant to talk about the rights and wrongs of the world; that is
for parents to do. Children must learn to behave — must master in
their daily activity the kind of moral tact and ethical discrimination he
as a Catholic parent strives to convey, day after day: "It would be terrible for a child of mine to be asked what he thinks of his father, what
she thinks of her mother. The boys, the girls, mine or anyone else's —
they all would wonder what has happened to us, that we have no trust
in our own beliefs. A father needs his standards. My wife is not so sure
of our standards. Are we perhaps wrong, she wonders? I tell her no,
but she keeps on questioning herself and sometimes even me, though
I don't want to give the impression that we are unhappy together or
that she is rude to me. I have my suspicions that often she has discussions with the children that I do not want to know about or hear. It is
best sometimes to ignore what, in any case, one cannot change."

A nod of his head, as if to say he agrees with himself; then a wink
of his right eye — and the right forefinger directed toward the outside.
There his wife is hanging some clothes. The sun is strong over the Rio
Grande Valley of Texas, so it will only be a few hours until the clothes
are being removed and taken back inside. They are mostly children's
clothes. "And why not?" the mother asks, as she looks at the large
number of shirts, pants, dresses, and socks she has put on display, as
the wind comes and goes. She knows her brief question has come out

of nowhere, has meaning only for her. She explains herself, apologizes: "I sometimes think that I am a slave to washing these clothes. I am always collecting them from the floor and scrubbing them on the board, the same one my mother used. It is a miracle that the board still exists, and that my knuckles have not become jelly or powder. But then I catch myself; I ask myself *why not* — that is what must be done if children are to look halfway clean. We are poor, but we take good care of ourselves — the best we know how and can afford to. I never went to school, but my parents taught me how to live a decent, God-fearing life. Can many of the rich Anglo landowners say as much for themselves?"

She is surprised by what has come out of her mouth. Her husband, she is certain, would not at all like hearing such talk. He has often cautioned her to stay away from political remarks. Who knows what lackeys of which Anglo county official or grower might be near at hand? The priest, too, has advised silence; there is no point, he has preached, trying to fight the guns of the Texas Rangers — and their well-known willingness to use them. Best to obey God's commandments and trust in His will — which, one is told, "will be done," if not now or indeed within the foreseeable future, then when "time" is exposed as a mere construct of mortal man. None of that is too abstract a way of regarding Catholic theology for this mother; she has her own way of indicating the breadth of her vision — as it fastens upon eternity or the utterly concrete and immediate issue of children and their laundry: "I think of God often; I talk with Him often; He is with me, I believe. But I know that I have no right to expect more of Him than anyone else. We all make our mistakes, and He has to judge us. That will happen in the very distant future, I know. I throw my hands in the air; I give up wondering when that future will come. Not in anyone's lifetime. I am certain that a thousand years from now we will be no closer to that future. I told that to my husband one day, and he laughed: 'You are invading the priest's land,' he said. So I told the priest what I believe, and tell my children — about the time when we all will be saved or damned. He said God alone knows when — it could be tomorrow or thousands and thousands of years from now. I told the priest I was sure it wouldn't be tomorrow, and he looked annoyed with me at first, then he broke out into a laugh. I said that the only thing I was certain tomorrow would bring is washing — more clothes to scrub and soak and put out to dry.

"Once I had a dream; I was dead, and a shadow — instead of myself, here, with this body to house my soul. Suddenly I started to laugh, in the middle of the dream. I realized that I was still alive, only dressed up in bed sheets, like those on the clothesline the wind has just been whipping. I woke up and I was amused with myself; but I was also frightened. I told my husband the dream, and he waved me aside: 'Don't make more trouble for yourself; we already have enough.' I was afraid to confide in the priest. I told my oldest child; she is thirteen, and I can open my heart to her, and she to me. She asked if she was anywhere to be seen in the dream, and I said no, not to my memory. She was disappointed. She said that God was probably whispering to me, when I was asleep; He was telling me that if I did a good job every day, I'd be all right. I didn't understand what the child was saying — oh, she is no longer a child, I know it. Then my younger daughter, who is only ten, mind you, spoke up: 'I hope the sheet you were wearing was clean — not a single spot on it.' Then I understood myself better; my little girl had revealed my mind to me!"

The girl is not so little, her mother realizes. The girl is watchful, active, helpful, if at times a touch morose. She is given to solitary walks; they worry her parents. Why should someone ten years old want to leave her family and her friends for the sake of paths that lead to the wide, cultivated fields? The mother will not talk with the girl about this habit of hers. Even a child of ten is entitled to her own preferences, her willfulness; even a girl: "My husband worries. Let the girl be like everyone else. She *is*, of course — most of the time. Occasionally she wants to go off, be alone. Is that so bad, such a terrible wish? I envy her the good sense she has. She avoids arguments and fights with the other children that way. To be honest, I think I was the one who taught her, a year ago, to leave a scene of noise and trouble. She listened to me; she took me seriously when I gave her a suggestion. For doing so, her father frowns upon her, and to her face calls her strange. But she will not easily break; no, that child has a mind of her own. At times I think to myself: she has a man's spirit in a girl's body. Maybe she will be unhappy later on. Maybe she will try not to let a man be the boss. But if her husband tells her never to leave on long walks by herself — then there will be a struggle; and I guess she will know to surrender."

She slumps in the chair; mention of surrender, even if the word came from her own lips, has surprised her and weakened her. She admits to periods of sadness: a woman's life is hard. Not that she wants to compete with her husband; his life is hard too. Once he was a field hand; now he drives a pickup truck for a grower. Wages are slim. Anglo authority and power are a constant, unforgettable presence. And he is sick, that burly, forceful, hardworking man she married sixteen years ago. He gets severe headaches; often, inexplicably, has fits of hiccups and vomiting and shortness of breath. Neither of them has ever seen a doctor for any complaint. Their children were delivered by a midwife. They pray when they feel ill — and go on as best they can. For the man it is a matter of work that starts at six in the morning and ends around seven at night. For the woman there are children, always requiring her attention.

The woman who has suddenly appeared tired and worn is not one for self-pity — or invidious comparisons. Her troubles are neither heavier nor lighter than her husband's, she is quick to insist; they are different troubles. The ten-year-old daughter is a somewhat special person though; it has been upsetting to contemplate the child's present characteristics or her likely fate in the years to come: "I wonder whether she will be as contented as the rest. She is too smart, I sometimes think. But the teachers don't agree. They have told me, year after year, that she is like all the others in her class, no better and no worse. But how are they to know the truth about the children before them? They have no use for us anyway: Anglo teachers. I return the sentiment. My husband tells me that it is just as well the children meet Anglo teachers in school who are unfriendly; then our sons and daughters will be prepared for the world. I think that is what my ten-year-old girl isn't ready to accept now — the life she will have to face later on.

"My husband wants me to be tougher with the child. I hold my ground though. His word is law; I believe it should be. But a mother has her own way of enforcing the law! I tell him to be patient, and the child will come around; she will get tamed. She is a bit of a wild horse. But even a wild horse needs to learn to watch her step — or soon someone will tame her. Our children belong to this world; they learn about what it offers them — each differently. I would not have it any other way. My husband is less patient. He sees the child standing up for herself, walking off to be alone and collect herself, and he worries that she will get in trouble — at school now or later on when she goes shopping in town by herself. Someone will tell her to step aside; someone will call her a name — one of the Anglos — and she will glare and speak back, or she will run off. The police cars, with their lights and sirens, will catch up with her in no time, of course; her father knows that. Well, so do I — but I am ready to take a chance: the girl will catch on, as I did, as her older sister already has, as one must."

She is now feeling stronger; determination lightens the burden of a resignation that never quite leaves her. She wants to talk about herself; she wants to explain why it is that she is quite content that all the difficulties she has to count on will never leave her, at least while she is on this earth. She insists upon her essential good humor: a willingness to smile when things are at their worst — a quality she is certain she obtained from her own mother. But to her own surprise she finds herself making a more general kind of comment: "Women are not born to fight the world, as men do. Women are born to suffer. We must stand back and remind ourselves that there are others, whose daily needs require attention — so there is no time to become bitter. I think my husband is afraid that if our girl becomes too much of a fighter, then she will not only get in trouble herself, but her children will suffer even more than the children of our people have to suffer, and that will be sad. I repeat myself: a woman has to suffer. To bear a child, to give birth to it, to know in one's heart what is ahead for it, to hear it cry and not have enough food for it, or good clothes, to think about what it will hear in school — memories of one's own past: that is to suffer.

"There are times when I wish I was a man. I have a dream: I am my husband, and I find some wild horses and tame them, and I give one to each of the children, even the smallest. And then, miraculously, they can all ride safely, and they do — no saddles, only us and the swift animals. We all ride off — away, away from this terrible Texas and the Anglos; back to Mexico. We find a village, and the horses graze, and we build a house, and we live quietly, and that is the end of the dream. I tell it to my husband each time I wake up and remember what I have been dreaming — always the same. He is annoyed. He thinks I am silly for repeating and repeating myself during the night. But what can I do? I have fallen asleep, and the rest is up to the Holy Ghost. I am quite sure that it is the Holy Ghost that puts things into our minds when we are lying on our beds at night. And there is one thing I don't like to mention to my husband; I did once, and he has never forgotten: in the dream we lose him, the children and I, as we are riding on the horses. He is with us for a while, but all of a sudden I look around, and he is nowhere to be found. My ten-year-old daughter goes looking for him, but no luck. She seems glad, and I ask her why. She says that we can have a good time on our own. Later we can go find her father. He will show up, she is sure. That's the part of the dream it isn't easy for me to think about."

Her ten-year-old daughter has the name Carmen, and loves it. She was told once that she is indeed a Carmen — by an Anglo school-teacher who wasn't being all that complimentary: "She told me that I was like a woman in an opera, flirting with all the boys. I wasn't doing that; I was just playing with them." She doesn't tell of her disagreement with shame; she was not upset by the teacher's criticism. In fact, she wishes one day to see the opera that bears her name. Meanwhile there is school to finish, and a daily life to live: "I don't like school. The teachers don't like school, either. They look at us in the morning as if it's our fault that they have to show up. But they need the money, like everyone else. I heard one telling another that if she only could find another job, she'd take it, because we're no good, the Mexicans. The principal calls us Mexican-*Americans* in assembly. But he's not very friendly either."

She is a thin, active girl. When she stops speaking she is ready for some other kind of activity. She flexes her thumb, waits a couple of seconds, unbends it. She moves her feet about as she sits. She looks at her dress, examines closely the pattern on it, then stares at the window: what is happening outside? When she is given a wish, any wish she might possibly come up with, there is no period of anguished hesitation: "I'd ask for a horse. I'd have it and ride it. I'd stop school and care for her. It would be a mare, like the one my father used to ride. Now he drives a car." Her father rounds up not cattle but men; he makes sure that Chicano farmhands stay together and work on certain specified stretches of land. He is always afraid of losing his job, and his daughter Carmen knows exactly why: "My Papa is not cruel enough. He does not frighten the men to death. That is the only way to make them obey, but he won't be an Anglo's bad man. So, he's afraid he might be fired."

The girl looks around. Her mother is outside with the chickens, and so not able to help explain what her father does all day. Carmen can't understand how anyone would ever be unhappy with him, even the men he has to keep in line: "My father is a good man. He loses his temper only when it is right that he get mad. I have earned his temper a few times; I have disobeyed him. He has let me know that he won't be fooled. He can tell when we are not doing as we should; he says he can tell by my face whether I have been good or bad. I try to practice in the mirror: how to smile, even when I don't feel very happy. But my mother says that the truth comes out, through our eyes, whether we want it out or not."

Carmen closes her eyes briefly, then opens them wide and stares at a mirror across the room. She acknowledges shyly that if no one were there, she would examine her brown eyes with the greatest of care — an occasional indulgence that affords pleasure. Talking about her appearance has made her self-conscious; she moves her glance from a table to a picture of Jesus, to the mirror again, and finally, to her own legs, her knees: "I fell down a year ago, and split my right knee open. The blood would not stop coming out. I thought I would never walk again. My father got very upset with me when I told him that. He was standing there, shouting at my mother to press harder with the cloth, and I said she was hurting me, and please to stop. He said no, continue; then he shouted that I had better start learning right away about pain. My mother said no, it was the wrong time for me to have a lesson. My father did not like to hear her disagree with him. He picked up my brother's slingshot and threw it at the door. He said my mother and I are alike, and I will be a spoiled wife to some man, if they don't tame me. I thought he was going to hit me; I even thought he was going to hit my mother. But she ignored him; she kept the pressure on my knee, and she told me to help her in putting both my hands on the cloth, and then she put her hands on top of mine: four hands — and they won out over the blood."

With the mention of blood, she touches her knee, pulls the skin over it tight. The scar is still there, a tribute to her body's ability to heal — and without the aid of stitches, which other children, of different background, would unquestionably have received. She begins to talk of the future. Will she again fall down and hurt herself? What would happen if she had broken a bone, as indeed her father had thought was the case? How much blood is there in the body — more than the amount needed to fill a Coke bottle? Two such bottles? She is sure, as a matter of fact, that she lost one bottleful at the time of that accident. As for the subject of fractured bones she recalls an incident: her brother had hurt his arm so badly that he screamed incessantly for a whole day and through the following night. Finally the father took him to the Anglo boss, the foreman, who in turn had driven the child to a hospital ten miles away. The arm was put in a cast, and eventually the boy had to return for the cast to be removed. Carmen had wanted desperately to go with him, to see the inside of a hospital, to watch the cast being put on. On television she has seen nurses taking care of patients, and imagined herself one day as a nurse. Outspoken child that she is, she once asked her teacher if she might study subjects that would help her become a nurse. The teacher was surprised and annoyed: no, not then, and not next year, and actually, never. Nursing requires a high school diploma, and Carmen was told she would soon enough be dropping out of school, just as others of her kind do all the time.

She was not really made angry by that prophecy, even as, upon describing what took place, she does not stop and ask for reassurance by looking hurt, or through a self-pitying remark. She brusquely slaps her knee, as if to show how strong it has become, gets up, and announces that she doesn't like school, may stop going, but would stay and stay — for years, if necessary — were she actually to decide to become a nurse. No Anglo teacher is going to tell *her* about what the future does or does not hold in store. When her father makes his predictions she takes exception, even if, out of fear, she doesn't speak up. She tells her mother later and in confidence what has crossed her mind. The mother advises caution — but, significantly, does not chastise the girl or give her the impression that she has thought something wrong: "My mother says that you have to keep quiet about a lot of things, or else there will be trouble. She says even at home you mustn't say everything that you think of saying. I ask her why, but she shakes her head and says she won't explain anything to me; I'll just find out. I know what she is thinking. She is thinking that if you're not Anglo, you'd better be careful. You can't be too careful, she tells us. But my older sister says you can't just give in, all the time give in; the Anglos take, and we stand by, but if we fought them, *they'd* have to watch their step too. My father heard us talking one day about Anglos, and he didn't say a word; he just stared at us, and we could tell that we had better go out and play. I hope my brothers grow up to fight the Anglos. I'd like to fight them too. I don't think my mother should always put her hand to her mouth and tell us to be seen and not heard."

She has been speaking rather more softly than usual; and now that she has made her strong opinion public, she has some misgivings. Perhaps there are indeed reasons for her and others like her to learn to live with silence. Are not her parents older and wiser? Have they not gone through years of living, and thereby obtained a certain kind of education? Is it not presumptuous of her to challenge them so? Even now, as a grown man and a grown woman, her father and mother defer in dozens of ways to their own parents. And if Carmen's parents are cautious and easily made apprehensive, her grandparents, she knows full well, are thoroughly circumspect, and never in any doubt about their fate, if not destiny: "My grandmother tells us that when she was young, and my mother a little girl, the Anglos wouldn't let us walk on the sidewalk. My grandmother has a lot of bad memories. I tell her that the world is getting better, but she doesn't believe me. I tell her that we should call ourselves Chicanos and stand up to the Anglos. She tells my mother that I have the Devil in me, and there will be a lot of trouble if we don't get rid of the Devil. She wants the priest to stand over me and ask God to help drive the Devil out of me! My sister and I just laugh to ourselves; but we look very serious when our grandmother is nearby. She would be upset if we didn't agree with everything she says."

How about her mother — does she also regard Carmen's rising political consciousness and activism as the work of the Devil? The girl is emphatically sure of the answer: no. There is a difference between the generations, Carmen is quick to point out. The state of Texas is still no great welcoming friend, but its customs and laws have changed over the years. Carmen is, of course, brief in the comparisons she makes, but pointed too. She summons imagery that is connected to her daily experience: "Once we hid behind the trees; now we walk out in the open." She knows that there are many exceptions to the observation she has made. She knows, too, that even in her own family, among her sisters and brothers, there are different hopes, worries, doubts. Her older sister has given up on the United States, would like to return to Mexico and spend her life there — no matter how terrible the poverty. Then there is Carmen's older brother; at twelve he is anxious to leave Texas for a northern city, the larger the better — perhaps Chicago. He is aware of the risks — idleness in a strange, cold environment; but he believes that in far-off cities there is a different America: "He thinks it is better to leave and try to find a place where people are so busy, they don't worry what you look like."

Carmen tells her mother upon occasion that she can't help it, she isn't as proud of her appearance as she'd like to be. She half wonders whether there isn't a way for her to look different. One day she spends more time looking at herself than she feels comfortable acknowledging; the next day she denies herself any self-confrontation through the mirror. She notices the way various Anglo or Chicano women do their hair, dress, walk, talk. She wonders how she will look and act later on, when she is herself a wife and mother. Then she refers to those arbiters of all taste, the Anglos: "If you look like an Anglo, you'll be treated better by the teachers. There's one girl, her father is an Anglo, and her mother one of us; she's light, and in school we keep hearing how smart she is and how she has the best manners of anyone. Then some kids want to beat her up later, after school." She is not one to want to do that; she senses the envy, the rivalry generated in herself and others. She becomes sad rather than angry or resentful. In a picture she made one afternoon, an hour or so after she had come home from school, she draws her school, and beside it, her teacher — whom she dislikes, but also holds in a certain awe. Near her is the half-Anglo classmate, and quite a bit farther away is the artist, Carmen, who isn't hiding behind the trees she has placed in a noticeable clump, stretching to the edge of the paper, but who at least has available the option of that refuge (Figure 41).

When Carmen draws pictures of herself away from school (at home, out in a field, near a road) she seems less demure — or apprehensive, depending upon the interpreter's point of view. (She herself insists that she is "just watching" in the school scene.) Gone is her stiffness, shyness, and relative inconsequence. Now she is at the center of the viewer's (and her own) attention. Her eyes are more in proportion to the rest of her face and, similarly, her head is made to fit her torso, not be dominated by it. Moreover she is quite willing to talk about what she has drawn: "It's just me; that's who it is in the picture. I'm going to play, but I've stopped to rest, because I was eating a piece of bread and jelly, and I wanted to get the jelly off my fingers before I met my friends. We might go to the fort we built. It's strong, and we are making it bigger" (Figure 42).

There is such a fort — a rather sturdy place, made of tree trunks and branches and other pieces of wood, along with some sun-baked mud. Boys and girls alike use the place, and if some of the girls want to pretend to be good, compliant housewives, Carmen has other notions of what she ought to do: "I like to be like my mother; if I had a lot of dolls, I'd bring them to the fort. But a girl can fight too. I tell the boys, when they choose sides, that they're crazy not to take some of us girls and use us to fight. It's better to win than to have half your people sitting there, praying and sweeping the floor." Does she, in fact, pray or clean house when she is in the fort? Do her girl friends do so, even if she chooses to go with the boys? In "real life," she points out, mothers stay at home and tend to their traditional duties, but at the fort even the least outspoken or forceful of her friends end up joining the boys in the various contests and struggles that take place — all of which prompts a moment of reflection and analysis: "It's my mother who says that a girl shouldn't get herself into trouble outside the house. It's not our business, she tells us. But even my father will disagree; usually he is the one who laughs when my mother speaks up, but when he's feeling very bad himself he turns to her and tells her that maybe if she and all her friends would stand up and fight, maybe if the *women* spoke up, then the rich Anglos would back down. Isn't that a great idea! But he does not really mean what he says. He reminds us later that he was joking."

She takes him seriously, however. She smiles, claps her hands, pretends to be in possession of a gun: bang, bang, about ten times — and a few dead Anglos. She quickly apologizes: she did that once in front of her parents, and they were quite disapproving — her father, it turned out, more than her mother. He had told her that women don't go shooting guns; and that, actually, if he walked around with a rifle, there would soon enough be trouble to pay. She elaborates on her father's words: "He said that Anglos have guns, and we must never forget that. He said that when our people have tried to fight the Anglos, we have lost. I asked him why, but he said I should stop asking my questions, because they bother him, and if I don't know the answers to them by now, then I'm in big trouble. Later my mother told me that there's no use trying to figure out the world because only God can do that. I asked if Anglos ever wondered how they got to be the bosses over us, and she said no, they have their inheritance, and they're too busy enjoying it to ask questions. Then she asked me if I'd be worried and ask questions if I was on top, and others were below me, and I had the guns and they didn't. I wasn't sure. I said I hoped I would."

A long silence; she looks steadily at a clump of trees, then her eyes shift to her own feet. She notices that her shoes have yet again become untied, and she hastens to do them up. She looks at her knee, feels the scar, then decides that she would once more welcome a chance to draw. But she has a change of heart; it is the paints she desires to use. She chooses the largest kind of paper available and sets to work. She appears to know exactly what she wants to portray. She speaks only briefly and intermittently — for example, to express her annoyance with the relative slowness of painting, as opposed to drawing, when one can use the crayon without the need to keep dipping it in water. When she is finished she is not especially anxious to display her work, a contrast with other times, when she quite eagerly holds up for inspection what she has accomplished. She gives the painting one lingering silence, then announces that she has a chore to do for her mother and will be back in a few minutes.

The paper has been almost completely covered, mostly with a vast blue sky (Figure 43). There is no sun, however — unusual for her. Birds are all over, rather broad winged and with prominent beaks. They hover over a stretch of land that lacks houses, trees, flowers; only one person is there — standing, or rather leaning against a pole. She is looking skyward and has her right arm raised. At first one notices how many birds are above; eventually it becomes clear that they are mostly at the edges of the sky rather than right over the lone woman in the picture. When Carmen returns she needs no encouragement for a remark or two about her work: "That is someone who is trying to decide whether she'll stay where she is, or go someplace else. The teacher told us that in Texas, a long time ago, people would come and find some land, and they'd claim it for themselves, and they'd fight, if anyone came and tried to move in. No one has come yet, and she's trying to decide: should she begin to build a house, or should she go get some food, and prepare it over a fire? But there are some vultures, and she has to scare them off first, and she does."

Why are the vultures there? Carmen is not sure; she thinks that vultures are "almost anywhere." But vultures or no vultures, she is convinced that a Chicano who wants to stake out land and build on it is in for a fight of one kind or another. Perhaps those birds aren't even vultures, she adds; perhaps they are hawks. She has heard her father talk about hawks with great admiration; they can manage such a long, smooth glide, and they seem to rule over all the terrain below them. Maybe there are some Anglos nearby; they have not yet appeared, but they will, and the woman in the painting will have to settle with them. How would she do so? Without a moment's hesitation, the answer is forthcoming: "I didn't put the rifle there, but she has one, and she'd have to use it. There's no other way. She'd have to shoot the Anglos or shoot the vultures, if they didn't take a hint. She would do so; she would defend herself if she had to." Is there anyone she might call upon for help? Nobody right there; but Carmen is not willing to leave the woman all alone forever. There is a husband, but he has gone into town to buy some food; and he will no doubt go to the hardware store and purchase a hammer and some nails, so that the two of them would be able to put up a house. Meanwhile he has left his wife to defend their new-found land, and she will do so effectively — let there be no question about that.

Two days later Carmen has come home from school and is full of rage; a teacher asked her when she was going to change her dress, and she had felt embarrassed. She wants to talk about the incident, but she also feels that her pride is at stake — to discuss what she went through, even with her parents, never mind anyone else, would be to empha-

size the sense of weakness and humiliation she felt. Her mother had
tried to talk with her as soon as she mentioned the encounter with the
teacher, but no luck: "Carmen didn't want to say anything — except
to let me know what happened. When I tried to make her feel better,
she became quite angry — with me! Sometimes it is best to let the
dust settle, then come back and try to be of help." But Carmen did not
really agree with that line of reasoning. Carmen has all along felt that
her mother and her father are inclined to be excessively comforting,
let too much dust settle. Three hours after she returned from school
and had her brief discussion with her mother, she was no more anxious than ever for reassurance, for affectionate support — but she did
quite explicitly and knowingly decide to use crayons as a means of
getting something off her chest: "I'd like to draw a picture of that
teacher."

She is quick and rigorous as she picks up the various crayons and
makes the figure she has in mind (Figure 44). She spends a good deal
of time with the woman's dress and also with her face. Suddenly she
leaves the woman to start another person. For a while it is not clear
whether it will be a man or a woman; it turns out to be a child, a girl.
She is holding on to a rake and seems to be doing some gardening.
There is grass and even a flower or two at her side. A thin, blue sky
looks down upon the two figures, a modest sun. Just as the picture
seems completed, Carmen reminds herself that she had an addition to
make. She adds one rather large, black bird. Then she begins putting
away the crayons.

A minute or two goes by; she has nothing to say. She seems curiously calm — no movement of her hands or legs or her head. She is
staring at the wall — or so it seems. Suddenly she springs to life. She
stands up, crosses the room, takes hold of a picture on a table — her
father in an army uniform. A few seconds later she releases her grip on
the picture, begins to talk: "My father fought in the war; it was in Korea. He was shot. They sent him to Japan. They got him better, and he
came back here. My brothers always ask him why he didn't keep his
gun. He says because — because it wasn't his, it was the army's. He
says he'd get shot again if he tried to escape with army property. My
brother says he should have put the gun under his coat and walked
away. I don't agree. They would have caught him. Once my sister and
I decided to ask him if we could save up our pennies and try to buy a
gun. We said we'd leave school and help him with the crops. We'll
soon be doing that anyway. Never, he said, never. He won't have us
working in the fields if he can help it, and he won't have us buying a

gun. His brother has gone to El Paso, and he works in a factory. Another brother and sister are in San Antonio. Maybe he will also go to a city. I would like that. My brothers say that in a city you can laugh at a teacher if she puts on airs. Here you have to keep your mouth shut.

"The sheriff drives by the school every day on his way to the fields. He makes sure all the Chicanos know he's nearby! My father has to give him a cup of coffee; that is his job. I wish my father could steal the sheriff's gun. I'd like to draw a picture — and show the sheriff and the teachers in jail and my father standing outside, and he'd have the keys on a chain around his neck and two guns, one on each side, and he'd be talking with the sheriff and the teachers, and he'd give them a cup of coffee, but that would be all they'd get for their lunch, and for supper they could have what they give our people in jail — stale bread and dirty water. My cousin is a brave man; he tried to work for the union people, and they arrested him and they beat him up and threw him in a cell and kept him there for a week, and when he came out he was half himself and no more, and my mother said she went to confession and told the priest that she wanted to go kill the sheriff, but the priest said she mustn't have thoughts like that, and besides, she'd never get very far because they'd catch her and throw *her* in jail and never let her out, until they decided to hang her. My cousin left, and he's in Chicago. He doesn't like it there — no work. But he's afraid to come back here. My father says you're a fool to fight people who have all the guns. But there must be a way you can stand up and fight that sheriff and his people. I'd like to learn a way. My mother and father don't want to hear us talk like that; but our cousin told us a lot, before they arrested him, and he said he hoped we never forgot what he was telling us."

There is just so long that she can sustain that kind of grave, reflective, and combative mood. She decides to put on her radio; it is small, not very strong on pickup, inexpensive. She loves to play it when she goes to bed and when she wakes up. She listens to a local, Anglo station — music and more music, mostly rock, interrupted by commercials and brief episodes of news. If she had a better radio, she would be able to pick up Mexican stations, or Spanish-speaking ones located in San Antonio or El Paso. She would like a record player and some Spanish music to play — but that is a dream for the future. Right now she can live rather comfortably with Anglo music and Anglo voices: "I've wondered if I'll ever get to see a radio station. The people who play the records sound nice; I wish they taught school. Some Anglo people are real friendly. They are the good ones. There are plenty

of bad ones; not one of our teachers is any good. My cousin told us he
hated Anglo schoolteachers, and I agree with him. My father doesn't
like us saying bad things against schoolteachers. He says that the only
way we can get ahead is to stay in school. My sister and I whisper to
each other: No! My mother says we must not dare speak back to our
father. I wouldn't dare! But even he will shout that many times he is
afraid to say what he really believes. Sometimes my friends and I want
to go and get some guns and dare the Anglos to try anything, just dare
them."

Carmen's attention returns to the Anglo voices on the radio. They
are, she is sure, people who themselves don't like much of what their
own people do. The same goes for the people she watches on television, the people who take part in serials or read the news or tell about
the weather. They come across, to her at least, as reasonably fair-minded,
thoughtful men and women. She is certain that they are not the sheriff's kind of person: "I've seen him. I've seen his men. They are very
bad. You can look at them and see how mean they are. They snicker,
but they don't smile. God must have been asleep when they were born.
They must be the Devil our priest always talks about. They must be related to the disciple who betrayed Jesus Christ. I saw one of them, the
deputy sheriff, coming out of one of the Anglo churches — our Lord
must have seen him too. I asked the priest how such a man could be
allowed in a church. He said that the nails on Christ's hands and his
feet — they are still there, and they will always be there, until
everyone is judged by God."

She has become more philosophical or theological than she cares
to be. She laughs and says that she sounds like the priest himself.
She envies him for all the answers he seems to have. There are times,
she acknowledges, when she feels quite uncertain, even confused. She
wonders why God allows so much injustice in the world — and why
those who inflict the injustice manage to show up so confidently,
faithfully at church. Her cousin often remarked on that irony, to say
the least — the source of scandal, one might say. He would scoff at all
churches, his own Catholic Church included. For Carmen, however,
as for her mother, it is sad to think of his estrangement from the sacra-
ments. Carmen's mother has often remarked upon the high price of rebellion — not only imprisonment, but bitterness, self-laceration, and
a kind of unrelenting despair. The girl has her own way of trying to
take account of the turmoil, exploitation, and meanness she is often
witness to: "My father says you can't bang your head against a stone
wall without causing a lot of blood to flow. My mother says that if you

try to climb a mountain, and it's too high, you either give up and come down, or you die from cold — because you get so tired, you are no good anymore, and your head stops working right. I'd like to go up to Chicago, where my cousin is. Maybe I could live there. Maybe I'd find a job there. There's a horse I see a lot; she is brown, and very fast. I've watched her galloping. She belongs to one of the growers, to his girl. I would take her if I was going to leave. I would ride her north! They'd never catch me! I could find a place to keep her in Chicago; someone would have a barn there. Maybe we all could move up there one of these days. I asked my mother once, and she said no. I guess my parents will never leave; they'll stay, and we will. My cousin isn't very happy up there, my aunt says, but he hasn't given up hope."

She is going to add a few more thoughts, but she abruptly stops herself, and also stops the radio, which has been on, at a subdued level, while she has been speaking. It is time for her to help her mother with the supper. She and her older sister like doing that; at times they prepare virtually the entire meal, while their mother sews and watches closely. But upon second thought, there are a few minutes left — time to do a final drawing. It is to be of the sheriff; she knows that, and indeed has been preparing herself for the occasion: "I've wondered what I could do to show him up; he is our enemy, and I would like to make sure he comes out that way when I draw him." She takes the paper and makes a pretense of covering it with black, while in fact leaving it empty. Then she settles down: a big face, a circle at first, followed by the details of his features. The eyes, she points out, are very large, because he is always looking, looking — for any trouble he can find. When he finds none, he makes some up. The ears come next, also large. He is a busybody, an attentive troublemaker. Moreover, he knows whom to seek out — and whose orders to follow. Hadn't her cousin pointed out that the sheriff never does anything without first going to the big growers and asking them what they want done? A man who is under someone else's orders has to have good-sized ears and a willingness to use them well.

Finally she offers her subject a nose and a mouth, the latter with large, pumpkin-like teeth. This is the sheriff who is constantly poking around, on the hunt for "trouble" — any sign of unrest among the "Mexican-American field hands," as the local Anglo paper refers to various neighbors and relatives of Carmen's. This is also a sheriff who is big, fat, and quite content with himself. The result: a large stomach to go with a large, open, toothy mouth — and for good luck, as well as for the sake of accuracy, a beefy pair of arms and legs. And that is that:

no land, grass, sky, trees, flowers — only the big, powerful man. And a few final reflections: "I hope my children are all like my cousin. I probably won't go to Chicago. I'll stay here with my sister, and we'll be as close as my mother and my cousin's mother are. My aunt says that she is proud of her son, even if he can't get a job in Chicago. At least he stood up and looked the Anglos right in the eye. If I had one son, and he did that, I'd feel I had done a good job. If I had five or six children, girls and boys, and they *all* did that, I'd feel as if I was a great success in life."

A Barrio Game

Her cousins aren't doing so well in San Antonio. Francesca wants very much for them to be prospering, and unashamedly she acknowledges why: there would be hope for her too. But they have exchanged one form of hard life for another, as the uncle, Antonio, who insisted that they leave willingly admits: "Up here, no sheriff rides up and down checking on you; it is different. We are left alone — so long as we stay to ourselves. The police don't want to come here if they can help it. The storekeeper calls them when he is robbed, and they take half the day to show up. When they do, they give the storekeeper a lot of trouble. They threaten to close his place down because it's a fire hazard, they say. The poor man, he ends up pleading to be left alone. He'd rather be robbed than threatened by the police! He slips them a few dollars, and they go! That's justice in the city! I walk the streets here and wonder why I ever left the Valley. My brother was right. He is always right. I thought I'd show him what I knew, but I'm afraid that I didn't know very much!"

He pauses, seems about to resume, then indicates by his lowered head that he has nothing more to say. He has been in San Antonio for a year and has not found a job that lasts. He worked for three months as a short-order cook, but the restaurant closed. He has applied for many other full-time jobs, only to be turned down. He has resisted welfare with vehemence, turning instead to the church. He gets odd jobs that enable his family at least to eat. If only there were some large farms near San Antonio; then he could work at harvesting crops but live in the city, where (he feels) his children are getting a better education than they would have received in the Rio Grande Valley. He takes exquisite care of the house he rents. He weeds the lawn, hovers over the flowers, frets about a semitropical vine. When he can find no more work to do around the house, he volunteers to help the priests at the church; their garden needs the kind of affection he has for grass and plants. His wife will soon work; when their baby son becomes a toddler, she will try to become a maid. Then, at least, there will be a steady if small income.

The barrio where they live is, of course, not near the well-to-do section of the city, but there are buses, and she will be glad to take them, even if she will have to be away from early in the morning to rather late in the afternoon: "I wish I could find a good job," says Antonio. "I don't want my wife to work. She doesn't want to take care of anyone else's house. She wants to take care of us. But there is no choice. She will be glad to find work, and we can only hope that she finds a boss who is a good person. The Anglo women can be mean and spoiled and selfish. The Anglos have too much for their own good. My neighbor's wife works for a lawyer's wife. She is a big Anglo woman; she eats cake all day long. She goes to a bakery and buys a cake — after her husband has left for work — and she eats it up before he comes home. Once she caught my neighbor's wife eating a piece after telling her to eat anything, *anything at all*. The Anglo woman went crazy. She screamed and told my neighbor's wife that she was fired, and she had to go home right away. Then she changed her mind and said that she should stay, only she must never tell the lawyer about his wife's habit.

"The poor Anglos — they have more than they know what to do with. But ask them to give up a dollar for one of us, and they are ready to fight at the Alamo again! That lawyer's wife, she is always telling my neighbor's wife how lazy and spoiled the poor are. If the poor really wanted work, she says, they'd go find it. Instead, the poor demand welfare checks, and sit back and cash them and eat to their heart's desire. She is swallowing a big piece of her cake when she talks like that! Then she goes to the bathroom, gets a diet pill, and announces that she's going to lose fifty pounds in the next month. An hour later, another slice of cake goes down to her stomach. I am sure that she could swallow all my children, and there would be plenty of room for them to breathe and move around. I remember my oldest son coming home with a story he'd heard at school — a big whale had swallowed some people, and he had been tickled, and he coughed or sneezed them up, and they swam away. The Anglo woman must have a stomach that big, to listen to my neighbor's wife. But the fat Anglo lady has gone away now, to a resort in Arizona. She will come back thin, she says. She has already ordered dozens of new dresses. Our neighbor is sure it won't be good; the lady will hide food in Arizona. The lady buys crackers and eats them in front of her husband, but she knows where the cake is. He has his own life; he has a girlfriend. So he doesn't care. That is the rich for you up here in the city! I miss our grower and his foreman; they are tough people to work for, and when they get mad, you are in real trouble. But I think they are more honest. The Anglos up here, even the lawyers and businessmen — the priest tells us that they are all scared of each other, and they don't trust each other out of their sight. And I came here to improve myself!"

But Antonio is sure that he will do just that — hence his refusal even to consider (seriously, at least) a return to his former home. There are some people in the barrio who have fairly good jobs, by his standards. And no doubt about it, the city offers a certain privacy, a certain sense of remove from the immediate and overwhelmingly assertive political and economic authority of the Rio Grande Valley. Nor does he forget what he left "down there," though to his own surprise, at times, he manages to come up with nostalgia: "I wake up in the morning, sometimes, and I say to myself that this is no place to be. But before I am ready to go back to the Valley, I stop and remember. I remember the foreman with his guns. I remember the grower, driving up to us, and spitting, always spitting, while he leaned on his car and watched us picking his tomatoes. Then he'd whisper something to the foreman and go drive off — while the foreman stayed and started blowing his whistle and shouting at us: harder, harder, pull in more, pull in more. My back would be almost broken, and my hands covered with blisters, and I'd be covered with sweat, but they'd want more, and if they didn't get it — well, they'd get us. Some men would go back and forth, from the farms to the jail. They'd call them drunk, whether they'd had a beer in them or not. You learn to work as hard as you can; it's better than being inside, behind bars. But the weather is better down in the Valley than up here; not so rainy, and warmer. And you had more room; your children could go and play, and you didn't worry so much that a truck might come and run them down."

His children do indeed find life different. His oldest son is ten; he had stopped going to school at age eight, when he was in the second grade. A teacher had told his parents that he was very slow, that he was, in fact, retarded, and that he would never really learn very much. She had suggested to the parents that the boy leave school, go work with them in the fields. That way, she observed, the boy would learn how to do something useful, would make money, and would be a source of help to others. In school, it seems, he was noisy, overactive, and uncooperative. When the family came to San Antonio the mother took the boy, Luis, to the priest, who in turn took him to a school, where he was enrolled in a special class for older children who have not yet learned how to read or write. Luis began to do well in that class, and his parents were told that he was, actually, a rather bright boy, who had a lot of interesting things to say about the world around him. He was an *expressive* child, and they liked hearing that very much. So did Luis: "Once my mother called me to her. She was sewing. She said she wanted to talk to me. She said the teachers think I'm smart. I told her the truth. I told her I don't like the teachers. I'd rather not go back to school. It's a waste of time — repeating the capital of Texas after the teacher, and the capital of the United States, and the other countries. My friend, my new friend up here, he wants to be a pilot. I wouldn't mind being a pilot. But I'd rather be the chief of police, right here in San Antonio. Then I could give orders to the police. I could tell them to leave us alone here and go bother other people. I could send them down to the Valley, and they'd outnumber the sheriff there and beat him up. He belongs in jail.

"I won't ever be the chief of police. And you can't send the police from here to the Valley. My father always pours cold water on my ideas. He tells me I'd be lucky if I got a job selling in a store, or working in a factory. The chances are, I'll be standing in line for the welfare checks. Or my wife will. I don't want to get married for a long time. I'd like to meet a girl who is smart, and she can get a good job. If you work as a maid for a rich family, and they're good people, then they will help you out — they'll get you a job, if you ask them. That's what I've heard. There's a friend I've met, he's twelve, and he said you're better off looking for a rich Anglo family that needs the grass cut and the garden weeded and dug up than you are sitting in school listening to those teachers tell you how stupid you are."

Luis is, again, not stupid; and he has not been called stupid by his San Antonio teachers. Quite the contrary; they have tried very hard to encourage him about his academic future. A Spanish-speaking woman has given him a battery of tests and found him "superior." Nor does Luis talk as cynically to his teachers as he does at home. His father is quite cynical, and with good reason; he has had serious trouble keeping his head above water in San Antonio. The boy hears his father, repeats what he has heard. He is the first one to acknowledge how much he admires his father — despite all the hardships the father has had to face and has not succeeded in overcoming. Luis has only one criticism he feels willing to state: he regards his father as too kind toward his natural enemies. Luis has asked his father how he would behave toward Anglos if he had all the money and power they have. The father said he would be very kind — he would follow the example of Jesus and love people he knew to be, in a way, his enemies. Luis was quite upset; he told his father that he felt that the Anglos deserved less. The father said nothing. The boy prodded him. The father became angry, said *basta!* no more talk about a fantasy rather than a real possibility. Luis nodded, left for the street, his friends, a game of war.

Those games of war take place every day: us against them, Chicanos against Anglos, the barrio against other barrios, the Chicanos of Texas against the people of Mexico — but most often, Spanish-speaking boys against imaginary Anglo boys. If only the latter were there in the flesh, then there would be a time: "We'd go after them. We'd even give them a head start: let them make the first move. We'd dare them. We'd trick them. We'd surround them. They'd have to surrender. If they refused, we'd move in. They'd be all through, all through. They wouldn't know what happened to them. Even if we went to fight on their streets, even then we'd win. The reason Anglos are on top — it's because they tricked people, and shot them, and did everything dishonest. That was our mistake. We gave in too easily. We weren't tough with them. My father says we should love the people who spit on us, but my friends say that's the trouble, a lot of people like the Indians trusted the Anglos too much, and it did them no good. They lost everything. That's what the Anglo teachers don't like to tell you. They admit that the Indians lost most of their land, but they tell you it was only right because there wouldn't be the America we have if the Indians had been allowed to sit there and do nothing. One teacher kept telling about 'the trouble with the Indians' and 'the trouble with us,' my people: we sit back and do nothing, while the Anglo, he's always building up the country, and now it's the strongest, richest, best country in the whole world. I guess that's true. I don't like to hear the teachers talk like that, though. They seem to be saying that they're good and we're bad."

He returns to the imaginary game, the large-scale struggle between mortal adversaries that he and his friends play. They picture themselves older, and with guns. They picture themselves in downtown San Antonio. They meet the chief of police, walking down the street. They stop him, ask him to come talk with them. He says no. As he begins to reach for his gun, they surround him, tell him that he either comes with them into their car or he dies immediately. He complies. They drive away, keep driving to a deserted area, stop the car, get out, begin to talk. The police chief cannot understand why they are troubled. He keeps begging that he be let loose. They tell him that the police are unfair to their people; in their own language they list many grievances: a high rate of unemployment; poor jobs; insulting school-teachers; streets that are unpaved; whole neighborhoods denied adequate sanitation and drinking water. The chief is indifferent; he simply wants his freedom. He makes a final demand: let me go, or there will be a high price to pay. They tell him they are quite ready to die, and will not be intimidated. He realizes they are serious. He begins to agree with them. He tells them that they have a point, several points. He tells them that they are right, that he regrets not acknowledging so earlier, that he intends to repent his ways. He will hire many more of their people; he will try to bring about various changes in the way justice is done in San Antonio. He will, in short, be a friend of theirs and will enlist other friends.

The particular words used may vary, but the drama that Luis and his neighborhood pals go through again and again remains quite constant: "We play 'police chief,' that's the best game. One of us becomes the chief, and the rest of us have got to capture him, then persuade him to join up with us. If you're the police chief, you have to fight back, but after a while you begin to see that you've been wrong, and the guys who have captured you are right. They've got to argue you down, but you aren't dumb, and you're not completely bad, so they get to you after a while, and then you make your promises to them, and that's the end. We used to have the chief escape sometimes, but mostly we don't anymore because you've got to convince him to change sides, and the more he escapes, the harder it will be, and we don't want him to escape. Why should we let him? There are a lot of us; he's only one. If we let him trick us and get away, the teachers would say: You see, you guys are lazy, and you're not quick enough; you're dumb, compared to the Anglos. That's what they say in school, and they give us a smile, and look at the clock: how much more time until we can leave and get out of here and go over to our side of town, where the smart Anglos live?"

Occasionally Luis doesn't want to think about that game. The same holds for his friends of nine or ten or eleven. They are a band of boys who now and then favor what they call "the real thing." They leave the barrio and work their way toward downtown. They walk, or they persuade an older brother or sister, rarely a parent or aunt or uncle or grandparent, to give them money for a bus ride. When they arrive at their destination, they are excited, curious, active, happy. They move fast; they stare intently at a store window, abruptly become bored, move on. They especially are drawn to stores that display men's clothing, musical instruments, posters advertising travel abroad. They are also taken with various automobiles they find parked. They can gaze in windows for two or three hours straight, or examine car after car. They show no apparent desire to enter any store, even the one whose display holds their attention the longest. Finally they decide to go home: they will be missed, and will be punished, unless they appear at such-and-such a time.

On the way home they begin to think of games they might play later on that day or the next. They will, for instance, break into a bank, leave with a lot of money and a policeman as hostage. He, too, will be won over to their side and will help them escape to Mexico, where they all will live in comfort, joy, and self-respect for the rest of their lives. Or, less ambitiously, they will venture into a music shop, convince the owner that they are truly extraordinary musicians, come home with drums, a banjo, a clarinet, a harmonica, some records, and a hi-fi set. Their families will rejoice — especially when told that those objects were gifts and not stolen. Or maybe they will go into a clothing store, be promised jobs when they get older: salesmen. With the jobs, of course, go a wardrobe: suits, jackets, and slacks, shoes and socks. Everyone they know will envy them! They will move elsewhere — but return to visit their families. They might even get similar jobs for their brothers, cousins, good friends.

There are other times, however, when they all become moody, distracted, sullen, resentful, and exceedingly quiet. On the way home they speak monosyllabically, if at all. Once, on such a day, Luis said not a word from the moment he got on the bus in downtown San Antonio until the moment, a half-hour later, he got off another bus — back in the barrio. It was then that he muttered, to no one in particular: "It's not fair." One of his friends asked him *what* wasn't fair. Luis shook his head, and could only say: "Everything." No one felt it necessary to ask that he be more specific.

Indian Children

Pueblo Children
on the Boundary Line

In a pueblo between Albuquerque and Santa Fe, Rose, a girl of nine, talks to herself. From a distance her mother watches and smiles. Overhead a small, single-engine plane slowly approaches. At first it is a silent object in the sky, a welcome addition to exceedingly sparse terrain. But gradually the plane becomes something immediate, noisy, commanding, intrusive, distracting. Rose does not hesitate to register her disapproval, her outright annoyance. She gestures impatiently; she waves off the plane rather than waving at it. Almost simultaneously her mother also expresses how she feels: a frown upon her upraised face. Soon the plane recedes from view, and the girl resumes talking; the mother's face again shows a smile.

Ten minutes go by. The mother withdraws. She has chores to do. Rose keeps talking sporadically to herself; a minute or so of words, a couple of minutes of attentive silence. The girl's sister appears; she has been playing elsewhere but has become bored and curious: where is Rose? Sally, aged eight, picks up a stone and throws it. The stone lands where it was meant to — near, but safely not-too-near, the older sister. Rose acknowledges the kind intent, but appears upset — as if Sally is an airplane that has been moving along the land, preparing for a long takeoff, and now has chosen this spot, of all places, from which to lift up toward the sky. Soon Sally finds out why Rose has looked so impassive, surly even. An injured jay, able to hop, skip, jump, but not to fly away, has been chirping nervously, incessantly around Rose — neither leaving her altogether nor coming close enough to warrant a rescuing grab.

Rose wants to feed and care for the bird. She has been intermittently talking, singing an improvised song, standing rather still, hoping that the bird would get the message: here is someone friendly but not pushy — someone without ulterior motives. Rose's mother has been delighted that her daughter can feel such concern, can demonstrate restraint, such a continuing and respectful sense of control. When Sally learns — rather quickly, in fact, and without any instructions — what has been going on, she too takes her position and tries to be, at the very least, an impassive, earnestly neutral figure. For several minutes longer they split roles — the older sister actively beckoning, the younger one almost transfixed.

Finally the scrub jay is enough won over to stand still and be silent — at a distance. The three of them now form a triangle. For another few minutes there is not a movement, not a sound. Then, Rose gently signals Sally with her right forefinger to edge over. Gradually, step by step, with periods of stillness in between, the younger sister moves toward the older one. When they are together they say not a word; they stand still, then slowly sit down. The bird is by now interested in them. It does not move away. It stares at them, and they at it. An impasse, it seems. But the bird relents, moves toward the girls, and soon is busy eating. Rose has been furtively surrounding herself with small amounts of grain, and the bird could not resist. Finally, Rose swoops and catches hold of the bird. With great skill she seems to persuade it — most likely by the assurance her hands convey — that she is up to good rather than harm. The bird has not frozen in the girl's hands and does not make a lot of noise — but rather, nibbles some food that is offered.

Like a skilled but tender and respectful surgeon, Rose examines the bird; it continues to be strangely compliant, quiet. The girl talks to the bird, reassures it, tells her younger sister what the problem is: a damaged wing, most likely. They must go home, the two of them, and find a place for their newfound friend. The girls walk silently toward their house. They are ordinarily capable of, prone to, continuous chatter. But they worry that their talk would frighten the bird. When they reach their house they have second thoughts. Without saying a word, Rose starts to make a detour, and Sally not only follows but registers a knowing look: what will their mother say if she sees them entering the house with the bird but with no resting place prepared for it? Soon they are ready for their mother's possible objections; they have some of their pony's hay, are fashioning a nest, and smiling at the bird — and, with a certain satisfaction, at themselves.

Their mother, who had gone inside to prepare food before the bird was caught, stops cooking and joins their silent company. She motions with her head toward a corner of the room; the girls go there so that they can attend to the nest. The mother examines the bird, lingers attentively with the wing, thereby concurring in the diagnosis her daughters have made, and walks over to them. In a minute or two the bird is in the nest, with some water and grain nearby, and the mother and her daughters are outside the house, their eyes eagerly searching the sky: is there another bird up there circling, circling in vain? Satisfied that such is not the case, the three feel free to resume the rhythm of their lives. The mother has her cooking to complete, her washing to do. Rose and Sally want to help her, but she says no, they have been very helpful to the bird, and now ought to play.

Sally spies her cousin and runs to say hello. Rose is feeling a little reflective and nostalgic: "My father told me once that his uncle used to ask him a question: 'Do you know whether the sheep were put here for us to use, or whether we were put here to be of help to them?' My father would kill a coyote, then he would think of his uncle's question, and if one of us was with him, he'd ask the question again. I would say that I didn't know, and my father would always say that I was right, and he hoped I never answered any other way. Last year a coyote killed one of our sheep, and we killed a coyote later, and my father said it was probably the same one, though he wasn't sure. Then I asked him about the coyote: Why is he here? My father said he didn't know, but he was glad I was asking. Then when I was in school I decided to ask the teacher. She said it was a foolish question. She said that coyotes are a nuisance; they kill our sheep, and they should be shot on sight. She said animals are for us to use; that's what the Bible says. Then she told the class that sometimes the Indians worry too much about animals and birds and plants; and if you keep on worrying all the time, you'll never build a country, like the white people did here in America. When I came home and told my mother what the teacher said, she was very sad. She told me to feel sorry for the white people and for that teacher of theirs. She said there's nothing we can do to change the way white people think, but we at least can shake our heads and think to ourselves that coyotes aren't always as bad as we may think they are when we see a dead sheep. She told me to tell my father what I told her, the story of the teacher, when he comes home later in the day. I did, and he looked very serious, and he thought to himself; finally, he called me over and he told me that long ago our land was a young sheep, and then the white people came, and they built the country up, like the teacher said, and now we are living in a pool of the sheep's blood."

She looks upward, notices a large puffy cumulus cloud racing across the sky, predicts that it will narrowly miss the sun, is proven right, feels pleased with herself. When she was younger her father and an older cousin would stand with her and watch intently as the sun struggled to break through a cloud. Sometimes they would venture predictions: yes or no. She would always say maybe, until one day her father with some seriousness, and a touch of disapproval, indicated that henceforth she ought to stop hedging and risk a choice. She remembers how afraid she was to do so. She remembers her cousin trying to let her know the basis for his decisions — the size and thickness of the cloud, the speed of its movement, the heat of the day. She has never really taken those various considerations into mind as she makes her predictions, at least consciously, but she has made a lot of them, and apparently with a good deal of success: "I look at the cloud, and I may decide right away that nothing, not even the sun, will break through. So I say no. Or I may be unsure; then I say yes. I'm never really positive, but if I'm doubtful, that means the sun will probably shine through to us. I worry about the broken clouds — all the pieces scattered. My grandfather heard me asking my mother if it is painful. He said no, there is no pain, there are no good-byes. The small clouds are on their own, and they just keep moving."

She decides to draw the sun, the sky, a cloud (Figure 45). She starts with the cloud rather than, as white or black or Chicano children almost invariably do, with the sun or the sky. She works very carefully with a pencil; she is anxious to convey a mixture of fragility and strong presence. When she is satisfied with what she has done, she takes a black crayon and goes over the pencil lines ever so gently. Then she is ready for the other crayons. But the sky, too, is a demanding task for her. Unlike American children of different ancestry, who tend to draw skies quickly, often as an afterthought, she works slowly, painstakingly. She muses aloud as she works her way across the paper: "I hope I am being fair. The sky never stops watching over us, and I want to show my appreciation." As for the sun, it is, as she often observes, "the mother of the earth." She uses a pencil first, slowly makes one circle after another, until she produces a size that strikes her as right. She wants the sun to be prominent, but not too prominent.

Why that struggle — the circular lines put down, then erased in favor of another broader arc, or smaller one? She is quite sure of what she has in mind, and why: "If you look at the sun when it is trying to break through a cloud, but so far hasn't, you wonder how it will ever break through *any* cloud. But if you look at the sun on a clear day, you might be blinded. The sun is the most important part of our world, but you could forget about that and never remind yourself — if it wasn't for your mother or your father. Once I brought a picture home from school. I was just learning how to draw, and I drew our house and the tree next to it. My father saw the picture and he didn't like it. He called me over, and said that something was missing. I didn't know what to say. I looked carefully, and then I noticed that I'd left out one of the windows to our house. He became even more upset. He told me that he didn't care whether I had any windows in the small house, or whether I drew the house so that it looked like one of the big houses rich Anglos have in the city. It was the sun I'd left out! How could I do that, he kept asking. I stood there and wished I had crayons like those the teacher gives us to use, so that I could do something right away to make the picture look good to him.

"I told him that I'd like to go buy some crayons, but I didn't have the money. He asked me why I wanted to do that. I told him what I was thinking. He didn't like me at all for saying that I wanted to please *him!* He was even angrier. He said that I owed it to the *sun,* not to him, to be more careful. We owe the sun our lives, and so does everyone else — he kept saying that every day for a week or two, until I could tell when he was going to mention the sun, by the look on his face, and I started saying what he was about to say before he opened his mouth. Then he decided that I had learned my lesson; and he was right, because I've never since drawn any picture without first wondering where I should put the sun, and how big it should be, and whether I should have the sky clear or cloudy."

When Rose has sketched the right outline for the sun, she is ready for her crayons. She does not quickly apply yellow, then go on to something else, as most other children from other parts of the country are likely to do. She works slowly, deliberately — with the same care some children give to pictures they draw of themselves or friends. When she is through with the yellow crayon, she takes the orange one, and gently touches the sun with the darker color. Still not completely satisfied, she uses a touch of red. Then she hesitates, considers whether she wants to do any more with the picture, and decides that she is indeed through: "I will call this picture 'The Sky'; it is my favorite subject. It is my mother's and my father's favorite. My uncle likes me to draw the ground; he says I should show where the sun's light falls. But that's what I'll do in another picture. I would rather draw two than one!"

She is quick to prove herself a person of her word. She takes another piece of paper and picks up a brown crayon, as if ready to proceed, but looks at that paper's emptiness for a minute or two, a rather long time for a child of nine — especially one who has a clear idea in her mind of what she intends to draw. When she does begin she again shows herself different from many other American children. She starts her view of the ground from well below its surface. In fact, she begins by outlining a rabbit's burrow. Then she uses a heavy application of brown to illustrate some worms. The sandy earth is made light brown. She is very careful with the roots of plants and small brush, which she indicates with strokes of her black crayon. The above plant life also gets close attention. As she works along she reflects: "If this was the desert, it would be different. We're at the edge of the desert here. We're near enough to the Rio Grande, so there is a good water bed. I went with my father to Arizona a year ago, and there I saw the true desert. Even here we have cacti, and to someone from the city, who has never been to the southern part of New Mexico or Arizona, this looks like the desert. Our teachers at school say it is semidesert. My father said that before the white man is through with his tricks, all the rivers will flow to the cities, where the white people live, and on the reservations we will have no water at all. But the teachers say no, the government in Washington wants to be fair. The teachers work for the government, and they are sure they know what it's going to do. My father says he knows the history of our people, and it's not the same history they teach us in school."

As she concludes her drawing (Figure 46), she makes remarks about the land she has pictured, and she freely acknowledges their source: "My mother used to punish me. She would see me kicking the earth, or pulling up some brush, and she'd tell me to stop. We'd complain that we were just playing, but she didn't accept our excuses. Once I brought some water out, and I was making mud-bread, I called it. She didn't like that idea too much. She said I should be more careful. She told me to go in the house and think about what I could do that was better. I told her I didn't know why it was so bad for us to make forts or cook food — with the mud we made by bringing water to the outside earth. She said it was the *way* we were playing; she had been watching us, and we were digging in one place, then another, leaving ditches and holes, and not bothering to fix up what we'd done to the land after we were through. Instead, we started a new game further down the path. She told us we were acting like white people. She told us that a lot of Indians learn to act like white people. They learn in school, and they learn in their jobs. She said we'd better watch out.

"Then my father came home, and he told us off. He was upset with my brother. He told my brother that he's thirteen, and he should have stopped us, instead of going along and helping us. My brother had an old tire from a car, and he'd put water in it, and was making it go round and round, up and down the path. My father made him return the tire to the car. My brother said the car was just a pile of junk; it had been left by some white man near the reservation. My father said the white man had been very successful; he not only spoiled the land, and got rid of something he had no use for anymore, but he managed to spoil *us*, too!"

She stops abruptly. She looks out at the path that leads from her house and takes in her hands another piece of paper, as if she were about to make yet another drawing, this time of that path. But no, she puts the paper down. She has remembered her father's remark. She has, she acknowledges, spoiled nearby land upon occasion — the path, for example. If left to her inclination and that of her brother or her sisters, the path would be even more rutted than it is. But she has learned. She has been told repeatedly that even if Indians are weak and vulnerable, with respect to the white man, they are a thoughtful and intelligent people, who treat with respect what they do own, what they have left. And what they own is, actually, not theirs. Rose is careful to distinguish between her own sense of property and the lessons she learns at school: "We are here, and we will stay. But a day may come when we leave. A day may come when the white people have to leave too. That might be in the future. My brother once asked a teacher if she thought America would change — if the white people would always be here. The teacher thought he meant that someone would attack the country and drive all the white people away. She asked my brother if that's what he meant, and when he said no, she decided that he was asking her a 'stupid question,' that's what she told him. She said there are over two hundred million people in the United States, and most of them are white, and they'll just stay here, and the country is changing all the time, because it's a free country, but that didn't mean it's in any danger of disappearing.

"My brother decided not to argue with her. He came home and told us that all he was trying to say was this: there was an ice age, and a tropical age, and there were the dinosaurs, and then they disappeared; and it could happen that people would disappear, too. And he was trying to tell her what our father always says: that the white man keeps on winning victories, but he may lose the war. He may end up turning his land into a big pile of junk. He spoils everything he touches, our father says — including us, the Indians! So it's our fault;

we've become like the white man. That's what my father wants all of us to remember — that we should fight the white man right here, in our house and outside, on our land, by being different from him."

On the other hand, her father was pleased to be given an old television set by a white man he knew. The man was going to throw it out and asked her father whether he wanted it. Yes, of course, he did. The set works well; it has a small screen, however. Rose cannot fail to wonder about that set — and the pleasure her father and mother get out of it. Not that she, too, doesn't like very much to sit and watch one program after another. But it has been her teachers, the whites who are at the school run by the Bureau of Indian Affairs (BIA), who denounce most television sets — in the same vein she hears her father speak of other gadgets. Once she talked with her brother Tom about the apparent incongruity. Ought they not talk with their father? No, the boy said; if they were going to anyone, and he recommended against it, they should approach their uncle, their mother's brother, because he is more outspoken and tends to influence their father. Moreover, he knows white people quite well. He worked for a time in Albuquerque for the Bureau of Indian Affairs; he was a clerk, a person who ran errands, and later he was in charge of a pool of cars. Now he works for the state of New Mexico; he helps maintain and protect a series of irrigation ditches and helps with plans to develop the state's roads.

Rose speaks of the uncle with a certain awe: "He has been around. He knows the state of New Mexico like I know the front and back of our house, like I know the lines on my palms. That is what he tells us; he shows us the lines on *his* palms, and says he knows the roads just as well! When we decided to ask him what he thought of the television set, we were a little worried. He might think we had no right to ask any questions of him. He might send us back to our parents. He might become angry. He can give someone a look, and he doesn't have to say a word afterwards. Once we saw him walk away from a friend. They were talking, and suddenly our uncle turned and walked away. His friend followed, and tried to say something, but our uncle wouldn't recognize him. He just kept on walking. He had his head fixed; he wouldn't turn it to the right or to the left — only straight ahead. I felt sorry for the friend, but our mother said the man must have offended our uncle in some way, because he's very polite, except when he feels you've bothered him with a stupid question or said something that doesn't make any sense at all, and then he feels that you've insulted him, and the only thing he can do to let you know what's happened is to walk away. According to our mother, he is trying to teach the other person to be wiser."

She stops to think. She wonders out loud whether the person so confronted actually learns the lesson. She has, on several occasions, brought up that question with her parents; they have answered guardedly; maybe no, in some cases, but certainly yes in others — and one must be grateful for the latter. Rose is often told that there is good news and bad news every day, that one has a choice: emphasize the one or the other. She has not by any means been told to laugh away the most obvious worries. The point is to add one's energy to the more hopeful side of things. She recalls her mother's advice: "Our uncle told our mother to take us outside and show us the land; part of it is without grass or bush, and the rocks are broken and crumbled; part of it is good for grazing. The sheep don't stop when they find land that is no good for them; they keep looking until they come upon the good land, and then they eat. When our mother told us that, my brother Tom said that we aren't sheep because we keep thinking about what has happened before. My mother told us to go tell our uncle that! We were afraid to! But she made us do it. So when he came to see us, we asked him if we could talk with him, and he said yes, and we did.

"He told Tom that he was right, we aren't sheep. But he said we must eat too; and if we trouble ourselves all the time with thoughts of regret, and more regret, then we won't have time to find food for ourselves. And then he said it; he said that the white people think sheep are dumb, all animals are dumb, and even a lot of people are dumb — the people they have conquered. But sheep know how to find food, and they do the best they can. At least they leave the land alone that doesn't offer them food; and they leave other animals alone. The white man won't leave anyone alone, and he'll take land that is no good, and before he's through with it, there's even more trouble. The white man could learn from a sheep because he thinks he's made things better, and they're actually worse, while at least the sheep doesn't add to the world's troubles, and doesn't pretend he's better or smarter than he is."

She is not quite sure of the value of her uncle's, her mother's comparison. Her father and her mother and her uncle stress the hypocrisy white people are capable of, but she and her brother Tom, who is thirteen, have seen their own people deceive or exploit one another — and have heard their parents or uncle call attention to that fact. Moreover, sheep can be willful and destructive as well as innocent. Rose calls upon her brother's observations: "Once Tom and I went to see our uncle, and he was very angry at white people. He said they have hurt us Indians a lot. Then he said they don't think for themselves. They are like sheep. Tom was going to remind our uncle that he once said sheep are better than white people. But we were both afraid to speak. On our way home Tom said that when he is bigger, he will argue with our uncle, even if it means trouble, and even if our mother and father are upset.

"Tom likes the teacher he has this year. The teacher tells Tom he is smart, and he should stay in school, and he should go to college later on. Tom says Indians can be unfair to white people; Tom says some of them even lie to each other, and steal from each other. And didn't they do that before the white man ever came here! The Navahos and the Pueblos fought hard all the time. The Hopis and the Navahos also fought hard, and they still do. The white man didn't bring us *all* our troubles. Tom says we should be fair. He tells our mother a little of what he thinks, but she says he should keep his ideas to himself, or else he'll get into trouble with our father and our uncle, and the spirits of our grandfathers, both of them, will be made restless, and they will come to visit Tom.

"Our mother says that she knows when she has said or done something wrong; she gets upset, and she walks up and down, and she can't stop walking, for an hour she can't, and that's because the spirit of her mother or her father has heard what she said or found out what she did, and is unhappy with her, and she can feel the unhappy spirit inside, and she has to walk and say to herself that she will not repeat her mistake if she can help it. Then the spirits leave her, and she can go back to cooking, or something else she was doing. Tom wouldn't say it to our mother, but he told me that he's never had any spirit visit him, and he doesn't think any spirit ever will visit him. When you die, you say good-bye. The teachers say there aren't any spirits. If you know you've done wrong, then you try to say to yourself that it won't happen again, if you can help it. That's what the teachers tell us in school — to try to learn from the mistakes you make and not worry about spirits."

Rose cannot let it go at that, however. The teachers, too, make mistakes — spirits or no spirits. And then, even more explicitly in defense of her people, she reminds herself out loud that there are crimes and crimes, that Indians have never been quite as successful at dominating others as white people have. Her brother has acknowledged that also; like her, he can go only so far as a critic of his own people. On her own, Rose has come up with a theory about the difference between white people and her own people. The former, she believes, are fast-moving, restless, all too worried about themselves and what the future has in store for them. She watches the white teachers in school, watches white people when she goes to Albuquerque, watches them when they get out of their cars near the reservation, to look around. They can't stay still; they walk faster and talk faster than Indians, or so she believes.

She is willing to express what she feels with crayons; she is willing to sketch a white man she knows, who works for the federal government, and an Indian she knows who does the same. They often come to the reservation together, and Rose is convinced that if she were blind, she could still identify the one as opposed to the other. She draws the white man first (Figure 47). She explains why: "If I draw the Indian first, I won't want to draw the white man. It's best to draw your favorite picture last. You can look forward to doing it." She has no interest in putting the white man on the ground, or in showing a sky or the sun or clouds over him. She starts with his feet rather than his face, a rather unusual point of departure. She works her way rather rapidly up to his knees, his hips, his chest. Finally his face begins to take form. She gives him wide eyes but no ears. His arms are added at the very end, and they are quite long, simian, really. The last touch is the mouth, which she says out loud that she has forgotten. It is wide open, teeth bared.

As for the Indian, she needs another sheet of paper for him, even though there is plenty of room on the one she has just used, and even though when she sees the two men they are almost invariably together — "inspectors," she calls them, "from the bureau" (Figure 48). The Indian is done from top to bottom — his face first, and it is a contrast with the white man's: hair quite slicked down, ears rather substantial, eyes mere slits, mouth firmly closed, head turned slightly down. The neck is shorter than the white man's, the torso thinner, a touch smaller, the legs and feet also thinner and also smaller. When she is through with the body, she prepares to stop drawing. She begins to gather her crayons together and puts the two drawings side by side as if to look at what she has accomplished. Suddenly she has an afterthought. She decides to put ground under the Indian. In fact, she ends up locating him on a slight incline, barren but with some desert grass nearby. No sky over him, no sun. As for the white man, she feels no inclination, it seems, to do anything further about him. The Indian is put on top of him, and the crayons on top of both of them.

But they are not so easy to put out of one's mind. Rose remembers the last time the two men visited the reservation: "They were curious about our water supply. They did some tests, I think. They had test tubes, like in school; they were going to send the water to a laboratory. The white man always smiles at us; he smiles too much. He likes to pat us on the head. He told the Indian that we are good children. My brother filled up a bag of water; he wanted to throw it at them. My mother said he mustn't. An Indian can get into trouble with the government. The Anglos say it is our land, our law; but they run everything. The Indian man is the one who knocks on the door; he's the one who asks if he can come in. But it's the white man who carries the notebook and he drives the car. My brother said if he was older, he'd pull the Indian to the side and ask him if he knows how to drive. If he said he couldn't, I'd tell him my father would be glad to give him lessons. Tom says the teacher told him at school that the only way that white people will ever get to look up to Indian people as equals — well, according to the teacher, the only way is for us to *prove* we're equal. Tom and Sally and I will prove we're equal when we're older. It will be hard though. My mother says the Pueblos have to walk on a boundary line — one foot on the white man's land and one foot on our land. You shouldn't go too far in either direction. You can get into trouble."

Keeping an Eye on the White Man

Another student of the teacher Tom quotes so often is less impressed with what he hears — and less inclined to worry about boundary lines. Sam is Tom's second cousin; he is also Tom's age, give or take a few months. He won't tell Tom his birthday; or rather, he likes to move his birthday around, one day claiming to be Tom's junior, the next his senior. He has his mother's sanction for such evasiveness or forgetfulness; she long ago told him that she isn't quite sure herself of his birthday and doesn't especially want to be, either. Sam can be defiantly her champion in that regard: "I don't care if I'm twelve or thirteen today. It's all right to keep track of the years, but why bother with the month and the days? My grandfather says it is the white man's madness, birthdays and wedding anniversaries and the candles on the cakes. He says he doesn't know when he was born or how old he is and he's tired of being asked by white people. They look at the lines on his face.

They ask him his birthday. He smiles and says nothing. He tells us that once he was a child, and then he became a man, and then he became a husband, and then a father, and now he has us grandchildren, and two of his grandchildren have their children, and he is old, and he will die one day. He says it is only white people who spend most of their time calling themselves twelve, thirteen, fourteen, or sixty, seventy, eighty.

"Once he took me on a walk, and we walked very far, out to the mesa, and then to another mesa. We talked a lot. He kept pointing out birds to me, hawks, eagles. He showed me where snakes hide. He told me about the rocks, which ones are soft and which ones are hard, and how to tell without picking them up. He remembers when the bureau came and when they built the school. He told me about his grandfather, and how they would walk together on the reservation, and how his grandfather would be with white people: he would look at them and not say anything, but if he had to talk, he would think to himself first how to say what was on his mind in the fewest words.

"I told my grandfather that in school the teachers want you to talk a lot if you're giving an oral composition. He smiled. He said I was right; you can't make anyone's life the guide for your own. He said that he knows many ways to walk to the mesa, and it's up to both of us, when we're walking, to decide which way is the best one. But he said one thing I must never do is stop every other minute and ask myself — how far have I gone, and how far do I have to go? All the signs on all the roads, telling you that there are twenty miles between here and there, and a few minutes later, eighteen miles — all those signs are the white man's, and they are his way of stopping himself all the time, to ask how old he is and how far he's gone and how much he has to go until he gets to — the next sign!"

Sam laughs. He can recall the impatience and scorn in his grandfather's voice as he talked about birthdays and road markers. He can recall the smile that came over the old man's face. There are times when Sam worries that his grandfather belongs to another age — that his strong convictions are hopelessly outmoded. But there are other moments when the boy realizes that he has been brought up short by the old man — and that it is all to the good: "My grandfather is from the past; he belongs there. When he grew up there weren't any automobiles. No one thought of traveling from home to work (over thirty miles) in a half an hour; you couldn't move like that. Those signs just let you know how fast you're going. But he makes you stop and think. It's true, people aren't like they used to be. He wishes they were. But if you're young, you don't have his memories. When I go see him, he tells me what happened in the First World War and the Second World War. He sounds like the teacher, when she reads from her history book. He's talking, a lot of the time, about white people who aren't alive. The white people today aren't the same as the white people were fifty years ago. The Indians aren't the same, either.

"I'd like to have a car, and if it could go real fast, I'd really be glad. And if I was driving along, I'd want to know how many miles I'd just traveled, and how many more until I hit Albuquerque. My grandfather doesn't drive, so he laughs at the signs. And he makes me laugh too — because when I walk with him I see what he means: it's nice, like he says — just using our feet and not worrying about the state police or the traffic signs or lights. He walks half the day, then he rests. He worries that we don't walk as much, his grandchildren. My father says it's the same with birthdays — in the old days you didn't have to worry about when you were born, the day or the year; but now it's different because the teachers and the government people, they all have to know, and the reason is that it's the law. The government has to know when you're old enough to go in the army, or when you've reached the age you can collect money because you're too old to work."

He has been quite serious, but suddenly he smiles. His grandfather has again come to mind: such a proud, strong man — and so wise, so kind. A few seconds later the boy is less relaxed. His grandfather is intransigent, irreconcilable, pointedly scornful of "progress." He reveres the old man, indicates that his words also mean a lot to many on the reservation — but that many others are all too caught up with the white man's world. He begins to draw a picture of his grandfather. As he draws, he tries to give voice to the old man's, to his own, ideas about contemporary life on the Pueblo reservations of New Mexico. He was prompted, as he indicates, by his desire to do justice to an old man's apparently frail, yet ever so lithe, strong, and certainly well-practiced legs: "I can't do it. If I was the best artist in New Mexico I still couldn't do it — draw his legs right. If you look at them they seem ready to fold under him, and never carry him anyplace. But he stands up and starts moving, and it's a miracle. He talks to his legs, especially when he is getting started. He thanks them for all the carrying they've done. Once I asked him: For how long? He said he doesn't know. And what difference does it make? I laughed. I said I know, I know. He joked with me. He said he didn't know if he was seventy-five or eighty — so he couldn't tell me how long his legs have been going! He said he has never kept track of his age.

"My uncle's legs have moods; one day they feel bad, and they don't want to leave the bed. The next day they are full of life. They want to keep going, even when he says no, he is ready to stop. That is when there is a war going on, between his legs and his chest. He coughs, so he wants to rest; but he can feel the itch in his feet. He sits down and holds his feet and talks to them, and then they quiet down, and he is smiling again.

"My uncle tells me that I should learn to do what I want to do, and think what I want to think, and not be taken in by the white man. I say yes, yes; but he gives me a look, and tells me that he knows that I am young and he is old, and I don't agree with him. When I tell him no, I do, he laughs and says I must stand up to him and say what *I* believe. Then I do. I try to argue. I repeat what I've heard others say. He listens. He says yes, yes. I think I've won him over. But no, he is following me, but not agreeing. He is saying yes to let me know that he sees exactly what I'm telling him. But he's heard it all before. And he has the answers. If you give in to the white man, then you are not yourself any more — that's his reply to me. I don't understand; so he goes on. I'm *still* not convinced. Finally, I'll say it: we have been conquered — a long time ago. Then he'll smile some more and give me his long speech.

"He'll say yes and no; we were conquered, that's right, but we can still fight for ourselves, and the best way to fight is to stay away from the white man's habits. Once you start counting time like him, and miles like him, and coins like him, then you've been trapped, you're beaten. At least we can live according to our own beliefs on the reservations. The white man has cornered us but not trapped us. There's a big difference, he says. Even my father agrees — and he will defend the white man sometimes. I'll be driving with my father, and he'll want to know what time it is, or how many miles to Santa Fe, and I smile, and then he does too because he knows that I'm thinking of my grandfather and what he would say, and suddenly my father is thinking of his father too."

Sam says that he knows one thing for sure: he will never live to be as old as his grandfather, nor will he be as strong as his grandfather — physically or mentally. Any effort to cast doubt on that conviction is regarded as meaningless and ignorant reassurance. Hasn't Sam's father said essentially the same thing — about himself, of all people: that he is soft, that he has been "corrupted" by the white man? Sam remembers those words, "soft" and "corrupted," as he draws his grandfather's face: strong features, lines and more lines, large and knowing eyes. As for the arms, so strikingly stretched, the boy offers an explanation: "He loves to call the land ours; he says it *is* ours, and no one will take it away, not while he is alive. If white men come from Albuquerque to invade us, he will walk in front of their cars or trucks. They will have to kill him. When I try to say that I'm sure no white man wants to touch our reservation, he says that may be true today, but tomorrow might bring different news. Then he will laugh and say that I am the wise old one and he is the small child; he says that every time we talk about the white man. No, I try to tell him, but he shows me why. He holds his arms out wide and says the land *is* ours, and the white man can't take it away from us, even if he drives up and down every road, with his trucks, and even if he sends his planes to cover us like a big cloud, and even if he hoists his flag over every building on the reservation. I'm right, he tells me: there is nothing to be afraid of. He bends over and picks up some of the soil, and says that it's inside him, not just there, beneath us. And soon he expects to die, and then he'll watch over the reservation, and no white man will dare try to bother us."

It is hard to argue with that line of reasoning. The boy has been told that he is right, but he isn't sure that he is being considered right for the right reason. The boy puts aside the drawing — puts aside his grandfather, it seems. The boy even admits that upon occasion he has thought of joining the white man's army and traveling all over the world. He would, as a matter of fact, prefer the navy or the air force. He has watched old movies and followed serials on television, and taken a liking to the planes and boats used in World War II. Might there be some of them left? Might he get to travel on an old destroyer across an ocean, or fly across America on an air force plane? As for the new jets, to be a pilot and fly them, one requires a college education, he has been told. He will never get that far in school, never be a pilot. There may be other air force jobs available, but he doubts he would be found suitable for them. As for the navy, why should it accept someone like him — an Indian who knows nothing about the water?

He wonders out loud about other Indians. Have any of them been in the navy, the air force? If so, as pilots, as members of a submarine crew, or in less interesting and attractive positions? Suddenly he turns on his own train of thought; it is foolish for him to think of going into the air force or the army, and for precisely the reasons his grandfather would suggest: "My grandfather knows many Pueblo Indians who have left the reservation and gone into the city to live. He knows men who have gone into the army, and men who have even tried to leave the country, and live in Canada — anyplace to leave here and try to get work and make some money. But they come back. They are not happy away from home. If a place is your home, you never will stop missing it. Our ancestors, they call for us, wherever we go. My uncle says he can feel the pull; he will wake up, and he will be thinking of his mother or his father, and he gets out of bed because his mother always wanted him to get up as soon as he's awake, and he checks on the horse and the dog and cat, because his father always said: Animals before people! When we're walking, he passes a tree or a shed, or the store, and he lowers his head, and I'll think he's talking to himself, but he isn't. He says it's the spirit of his mother or his father — inside him.

"My father and mother are a little like my grandfather. They talk to people who have died. My father gets angry with himself; he says that he has made a lot of mistakes, and he is sorry, and when I see no one nearby, I know it's his mother he's talking to, and his mother's brother. The teachers tell us we've got to forget a lot of the beliefs our people have, but we don't agree. We keep quiet. We say yes, but cross our fingers — that way we are really saying no. I don't think I could stay away from my people for too long. I don't talk to my ancestors, but my grandfather's voice — I do hear it a lot of the time, when I'm wondering what to do. He taught me how to ride his horse, and he taught me how to care for the chickens, and build a shelter for our dog, so the sun doesn't beat on him all the time. They used to have horses in the army, but no longer. I guess an Indian belongs on land, not the sea or the air, if he's going to be in the military. There are Indians at the air force base in Albuquerque, I believe. They are janitors."

That observation stops him short. He stares out the window — up at the sky. It is a clear, sunny day in April, not too warm, a bit breezy. He has never been out of the state of New Mexico, and only rarely has he ventured to cities like Santa Fe or Albuquerque. His father is a janitor, not at an air force base, but another property of the federal government, a Bureau of Indian Affairs school. And his father considers himself lucky indeed to have that job, any job. Sam has five uncles, two on his father's side and three on his mother's, who are without work and have been for several years. Sam breaks his silence by making reference to one of his uncles, his father's younger brother; he wanted to join the air force, dreamed of being a pilot, or a navigator, watched any television program that had to do with aircraft, got as far as a recruiting station and a medical examination, was told he had tuberculosis, spent two years in a sanatorium, almost died, managed to recover, has never been able to find any permanent job, drinks excessively, tells his nephew Sam that he ought to go to Denver or California, and try to find work and lose himself among white people, but has also told the boy it is impossible to do that, and so he may one day be in the same predicament as his uncles are and will be for "all the years to come."

The boy repeats the phrase when talking about the sky he has been silently gazing at: "Up there it is always the same. For all the years to come there will be the sky. When it gets very cloudy, I wonder how deep the clouds are, and I think that maybe they have won their battle with the sun and will keep it from us every day. But soon there is only the blue, and the sun and the moon and the stars. My mother is sure that the stars talk to each other. When they flicker and twinkle, she says they are gossiping. My father says no, we will never know the secrets of the heavens. I told them what we learn in school; and when the white men went up to the moon, I told them that one day there would be landings on other places up there, but my mother said that the white men landed here, in New Mexico, too, but they didn't really know what to look for. My father said that some white people are good, and they mean well, but they don't live in the same world we do; they go driving through their world, and we're walking through our world on tiptoe! That's what his father told him when he saw the first automobile come to our reservation. His father knew that a million more would follow (that was the number he predicted) because the white man does everything big."

He has averted his eyes from the sky toward the road, but now he again stops talking and again regards the big sky. He decides to draw a picture of that sky (Figure 49). He works carefully and without feeling the need to say anything. Soon he has covered a large piece of paper with blue. He uses his yellow crayon cautiously, subtly. He will have no part of conventional yellow circles with radiating spokes — the white man's sun his schoolteachers have portrayed and handed out in their illustrated storybooks. He infiltrates the blue with the yellow, manages to give the light he has evoked a somewhat vague, ill-defined appearance. He is offering an impression, a suggestion of what he senses going on above him. A child who has never heard of French Impressionist painters, or their predecessor, the Englishman J. M. W. Turner, struggles hard, and knowingly, to escape the tyranny of form. As he turns to a black crayon, holds it poised, he decides to clarify his intentions: "I wish I could see a cloud when it is born. We used to watch chickens being born, and my uncle would say that trees are born and clouds, too, and once, a long time ago, the sun and the earth, they were born; but we can't just go out and see things like that happening. My grandfather used to tell my father that everything has a life; the sun will die, and when that happens there will be other suns being born. Everything comes and everything goes. The years to come are the only things that stay; they aren't the white man's years, though; they are just light and dark in the world."

He acknowledges his deep sense of awe at the mysteries of being — of time and space, of beginning and end, of life in its various manifestations. He approaches the paper with the black crayon; it has been suspended from its task for a while. Just before the crayon touches the paper the boy tightens his hold, moves his hand in a circular fashion over the drawing — as if wielding an instrument. Suddenly he stops his hand, he moves the crayon from a slanted to an upright position and lets it touch the paper gently, then firmly: a black dot. He makes another, another. He talks freely about what he has in mind to create: "I'd like to show the start of some clouds. A cloud must be very small in the beginning. There must be a place in the sky where (if you could only be near there) you could watch clouds begin to form. They told us in school that clouds are moisture; but my mother said that clouds are *clouds,* not moisture. There is moisture in clouds, I guess you can say that. The reason I'd like to go up in a plane someday is that I'd like to see the clouds from the other side, and I'd like to see rain falling from them, and I'd like to see how they bump into each other, and become bigger or smaller or disappear."

He is done. His last gesture is a determined, brisk move of the palm of his drawing hand over the picture — as if to insist that he wants things blurred rather than precise. Then a new drawing (Figure 50); possessed of a new surge of energy and enthusiasm, he decides to take on the night.

Sam is a great one for the evening. His mother loves that time — after supper. She asks her children to go outside and sit with her. She asks them to be quiet. She asks them to look at a particular segment of the sky. There is no apparent method in her nightly inclination to scan the stars. She simply follows her whim — one night that spot over there, the next night another spot somewhere else. The moon comes first though — at night, as well as in the drawing. The mother and her children smile at it, or lament its absence — in which case, however, they always remind themselves of the near future: a full moon will come sooner or later. The mother often tells her children what she calls "sun-moon stories," which she heard from her mother and grand-mother.

Sam tells his favorite story of the evening while he wields his crayons: "Once it was a very cloudy day, and my mother saw the sun trying to break through, but it never succeeded. Then it rained. Then it stopped raining, but still no sun. Finally evening came, and no moon, either. Early the next morning everyone woke up, because there was much thunder, lightning. It was one of the worst hailstorms we'd ever had: large stones all over the Valley and up the Sandia Mountains. By the time my mother got out of bed, my grandmother had made cereal, and was singing away. My mother asked her why she was singing so much. She didn't like the question at all. She said she always sings in the morning. But my grandfather said that some morn-ings she hardly sings, or doesn't sing. And he said she'd never sung as much as that morning! My grandmother smiled and said she wasn't going to argue. 'You are the listeners,' she said, 'and so you must be right.' Then she said that she'd jumped out of the bed, with the first strike of thunder and lightning, and that she'd been watching the rain and later the hail fall, and that all of a sudden the sky cleared, just be-fore sunrise — and there was the moon. And a few minutes later the first light came over the sky, beyond the mesa: the sun slowly rising.

"She said the hailstones sparkled in the early morning sun, and she went out and picked them up and looked at them in her hand. Then she noticed the shadow of the full moon, and she decided that she would ask the moon and the sun what had happened. She made herself coffee, and she brought a chair outside, and put it right in front of the house, and she sat and drank her coffee and looked up at the sky. That's when she decided the sun and moon had been fighting, and they'd been chasing each other, and finally they stopped, and threw stones at each other; but only for a while. The sun decided to stop, and the moon said yes, it was time to stop, and they made up, and the next thing everyone knew, the sky was as clear as it could be, and the sun was warming the earth up, and the moon could hardly wait for the evening, when it would come out a full moon, and all around it would be the stars. That evening the moon was low, and there were more stars than anyone had ever seen, and even the white men, the Anglos, stopped on the road, at the high point to the north of the reservation, and got out of their cars and looked at the sky. My mother thinks the hail might have been small stars that fell. The moon and the sun used the stars to fight each other. When they made up, the stars celebrated; they were brighter than they'd been before."

He has no memory of the actual evening, for he was a baby of two or three. When he asks his mother whether he *ought* to remember the event, she says he *does*. She tells him that once in school they showed the children a picture of a microscope, whereupon he came home and said that he wished he could put a hailstone under the microscope because thereby he would be learning more about the fights that go on up in the sky. Sam doesn't remember *that* either; he does, however, remember quite well the various times, more recently, that his mother and father have sat down with him and his brothers and sisters and talked about the sun and the moon, the clouds and the rain, the hailstones and thunder and lightning — and about the mesa, toward which they look so often and about which they think and wonder and talk. The boy wants to finish his drawing of the sky. He works intently. He falls silent. His moon is very much like his sun, indistinct yet luminous. His stars are glowing, anything but remote from the viewer. His sky is dark yet inviting, intriguing. He takes the unusual step of mixing paints and crayons — a splash of white paint to give a phosphorescent quality to the evening clouds, which (he patiently explains) have caught a moonbeam, hence their virtual sparkle in the night sky. A splash of blue to lighten the darkness — a promise, maybe, of the coming morning. He acknowledges that he is glad to be finishing this particular drawing. It is not easy to do an evening sky; he is sure he gets too easily and too much distracted by his family's strong and continuing interest in what happens (and what might be happening) in the world above them.

But that difficulty, that "problem," is nothing, he is quite willing to assert, compared to the challenge of drawing the mesa. For Sam, and for other Indian children who live near him, this mesa is both nothing and everything. It is a mere elevation of land — as his teachers have time and again reminded the boys and girls in their classrooms. It is no rarity; mesas are a fairly constant feature of the southwestern landscape. It is also, however, a distant place that one might reach, given the energy and will, but which one is by no means anxious simply to use or enjoy (for games and rest). The mesa, actually, is something to *see*; it is also something that literally enables vision — and most broadly, a certain perspective.

Sam struggles hard to say what he wants to say, no more and no less. He is anxious to indicate where physical appearance ends, psychological significance begins. He is anxious to indicate the challenge that the mesa as an artistic object presents to him and to his crayons and paints. And as he speaks, he makes clear, also, his conviction that those crayons and those paints are not inert. "I remember my father took us to the mesa. He said he didn't want us to go there all the time, but he wanted to show us that we *could* go there. So we did. When we got halfway there I told my father that it wasn't the same mesa we'd been looking at; and he said that was true. And when we got all the way there, it wasn't a mesa at all. I mean, it was, but it wasn't. When we were on the mesa, we looked at our reservation. It seemed different — almost as if we were in the sky, looking down at the earth. You start thinking when you are on the mesa. You don't talk. You look. I was glad to be there, but I was glad to leave. I was glad to get back home; then I looked out, and there it was, the same mesa we'd always had. My grandfather used to talk to the mesa; he'd say that when he woke up and he didn't feel too good, he'd sit down and keep looking out toward the mesa, and he'd ask it for some of its strength, and after a while he'd begin to feel better.

"I hope the crayons know that they're doing an important job; and the paints, too. They can be a help; sometimes I feel they do all the work! In school, my little sister says she doesn't like to draw at all. But at home it's different. She says that when the crayons are here in the house, they're our crayons, and they do the right thing. But in school you're doing something for the white man, and the crayons are his. My grandfather used to tell us not to bring home a lot of rocks from the mesa. That's a white man's trick, he kept reminding us — to take things and move them around and dig up everything and change the whole world around, and soon nothing is the way it was meant to be."

Sam has been working carefully with brown, green, and gray, trying hard with crayons to evoke the arid semidesert of north-central New Mexico. As he approaches the mesa itself, he stops talking and switches to paint. He does not, interestingly enough, look at the mesa while he paints it. He had glanced at it repeatedly while on his way to it, so to speak, but now he gazes intently at the image that is slowly, stroke by stroke, emerging in front of him. Only when done does he sit back for a moment and look outside. It is good that he does; he realizes that he has by no means completed the job. The paints are again mobilized, this time for the sky, which becomes an extension of the mesa. When he is satisfied with his work, he puts it aside. His sister had wanted the picture, but he says no, it belongs to no one and everyone. He will leave it on the table, and there it will be the family's.

He wishes he could go and visit cousins of his who live to the north in another pueblo. They have a rich choice of mesas; they have mountains too; but his cousins are near the Rio Grande at its full, stormy, swift best. Farther south (where Sam lives) the river becomes weak, tired, dissipated, a ghost of itself.

As the boy talks about his cousins, he provocatively evokes the meaning to himself of the land about him: "I like to sleep outside, even when it's cold. I don't like ever to sleep with the windows closed. My father says that when you cut yourself off, all the way, from the outside world, you are headed for trouble. Most white people live in buildings, and they don't care if they ever leave them. Even our teachers tell us that the Indians have always liked the land. Well, the white man likes the land, too; he wants to own all he can get. Our land is good; even if we don't grow much, it is good land. But my relatives have better land to walk on. My father tells his sister: You had better watch out, you'll lose what you've got. Some Anglo will come there, and he will wave dollar bills under your nose, and say take them, and if you say you won't, he will smile and go to some judge, or call up the people in Washington, D.C., and the next thing you know, you'll be pushed back into a smaller reservation, and they'll be telling you that you shouldn't worry because the United States takes care of the Indians. My aunt laughs; she says that the Pueblos know how to take care of themselves, and the days of the white man are numbered, anyway. That's the way my cousins talk, too; they say we will be here as long as it is meant for us to be — as long as we are sent here by our ancestors to stay awhile, then return to them. But the white man, he could get into bad trouble, and he'd be gone. The Anglos could destroy themselves with their bombs. That's a good reason for us to stay away from them — or at least to keep an eye on them. Sometimes I like them, but then I remind myself that I should watch every white man I see very carefully! My cousins have a lot of hiding places up north. We could get there in an hour."

Hopi Girl

In a Hopi settlement in northern Arizona a mother stares at the sky, nods toward a cloud, turns her back on the sun, bends down toward her daughter, who is one year old and learning how to talk. As the mother does so, her older daughter, aged nine, also leans forward. The older daughter reassures the infant as she steps, falters, sits down, crawls, lifts herself up, moves more confidently, but alas, falls down, now a little hurt. The infant cries, softly but persistently. The mother looks down with a kind and not alarmed look, as if to say: this, too, shall pass, and the worst thing I can do is become too preoccupied with the quite natural and inevitable effort on the part of yet another child of mine to stand and move on her own. But she does smile, tilt her head ever so gently toward the baby. The older child, whose name is Miriam, begins to sing words of encouragement to her sister: "You will go / nothing will stop you / soon you will be tired / of walking, walking."

The words and music turn out to be Miriam's. She has heard her mother and grandmother, her aunts and older cousins sing songs — brief, unspectacular, not especially melodic messages, chanted with a rise and fall of the voice that indicate an earnest, lyrical conviction on the part of the speaker: I will speak to you, and you will hear, and we will join hands spiritually, *be*. Yet Miriam may in truth have no such intent. The girl's continuing encouragement to her little sister conveys some very concrete suggestions, as well as what anthropologists call "a world view." When, for example, the baby gets up to walk, Miriam kneels down, blocks the probable point of departure and line of travel, looks into the child's eyes, holds out two arms parallel to the ground, though without touching the child: they are there, to be called upon, leaned upon, if need be. Miriam begins to sing, then speak: "Do not run / do not run before you walk / do not walk / do not walk before you stand / When you stand / you will be one of us / the Hopis. That is for *you*, little one. Just look about. Just move with your eyes. You can go far with them. Later you can use your feet; rest them now. They will get strong, and they will hold you and carry you — until you leave us here. See my arm; if you try to walk, and feel like falling, hold on to it. Hold on to both arms. I will help. I will stay with you. Don't worry. The day will come that you are running with me, and after me, and away from me; and the day will come that you will be standing here, right here, and you will have a baby at your feet, and you will be singing to it and talking to it and you will tell it that you were once here too — crawling and trying to walk. To walk is for us what to fly is for that bird."

She stops to point toward the sky. The baby has watched her, listened intently, even if unable to understand the specific words. The baby has remained still for a few minutes. Now the baby lifts her head upward, tries to capture with her eyes the moving bird — but no luck.

The eyes, too — the head, for that matter — are not ready. The baby sits down, at the same time lowers its head. The older girl sits down, also begins to look at the ground. She spies a small, flat stone, picks it up, feels it in her hands, holds it tightly between her palms, moves the palms toward the baby's face, holds them transfixed, almost as if in prayer, in front of the little girl, and suddenly: "Here you are! This is one of many; this is a Hopi stone. Do you see the lines on it? Someone made them. I do not know who it was, but they are here to remind us that before us there were others."

Again she pushes the stone toward the baby. Finally, she places it in the baby's hands and sits quietly to the side while she enjoys what white people would call a toy. But for Miriam the stone is no toy. She wants her sister to learn something about the land that she is trying so hard to walk on. While the mother continues to say nothing, the older daughter gets up and surveys the immediate vicinity for other stones. She finds them, including a rather sizable rock, and gathers them before her sister. She begins to point them out to the little one and talks for a few minutes about the wind, the rain, and time — how large rocks erode or get broken up over the centuries. She does not speak as an authoritative scientist or naturalist but rather as a philosopher: "These stones may have come from a mountain; we do not know. They are here for us, and we will leave them for others. I used to ask our mother if I could take them into the house and save them. I liked them. No, she told me; they are for you, here. They were for others before you, and they will be for others after you. Now it is your turn. I am glad I did not take them away when I was younger."

As Miriam makes her pronouncements, utters her prophecies, comes up with observations or interpretations, the baby leans slightly forward, reaches out with her hands, picks up the stones, holds them up high, drops them — one after the other. Then the last, big one — she puts both hands on it, apparently wise enough to know that an obstacle confronts her. No luck, though. She decides to push. What she cannot lift she can indeed cause to tumble over. She is delighted. She smiles *at* the rock, then looks toward her mother and older sister for approval. They nod their heads but say not a word. The baby seems to take their silence as a cue: if they do not resume their singing and conversational companionship, she had better find some momentum within herself. And she does; she crawls, begins to stand, succeeds in her effort, sets out, moves away from the two older people, and walks, walks.

Not a sound from the mother and Miriam; they pretend indifference, preoccupation with other interests. When the baby decides to turn around and announce to them, standing up, her triumph, they seem involved in another scene: the sheep grazing a mile or two down the hill. The baby feels free of them. She changes her direction, walks off at an angle to her previous course — in the direction of the sheep. She is walking at an incline and, one would think, is taking an unnecessary risk. But she does exceedingly well. She walks thirteen steps, abruptly stops, then decides to confront her mother and sister once again. Now they are quite willing to respond; they smile, they stand up, they say "good, good," but they do not move toward her. Miriam breaks the impasse by pointing to a rock that rests on the ground between them, and the baby dutifully and respectfully moves toward it, leans over, falls down, quickly stands up — with the rock in her right hand. She moves her other hand toward it, forms a cup with both hands, cradles the rock, peers at it, then throws it — her body swaying — in the direction of the other rocks. As her mother and sister look at this addition to the small collection, she moves toward them and stops only when she is right beside them. All of a sudden she sits down, right on top of the stones.

The baby's mother and older sister are delighted; they clap their hands and virtually exclaim to the world beyond them — as if a thousand people were waiting nearby to hear — the news that a little girl has claimed her heritage. The mother says: "She has made them hers, and they will be hers. She belongs to us, and we belong to her." Miriam says, far less grandly, but with no lack of serious appreciation: "She is beginning to understand. Soon she'll be walking all over, and she'll know the best places to stop and rest."

One such place is where they are, on top of a gentle but barren hill, at the edge of a virtual desert. All around them the land, their Hopi land, stretches. After a few minutes the mother decides to intervene directly for the first time. The mother draws close to the baby, fondles her, then gently lifts her up. The baby is glad to be standing again, smiles, looks up at the mother. But she wants the baby to look elsewhere, and she conveys her wishes patiently, quietly; she looks with her own eyes not at the baby, but out toward the rising hills, and she points in that direction with her forefinger. Soon the baby's eyes leave the mother's face; soon those eyes scan, a bit unsteadily, to be sure, the Hopi reservation. The mother, as if it were bedtime and a lullaby were in order, recites, with a slight singsong inflection to her voice, a series of reassuring predictions: "You will walk from here to there, to the highest of those hills / You will walk to that tree down the road / You will sit under that tree and say thank you, tree, for the love you give to the Hopi people / You will run so fast that the sun will draw sweat from you / You will find the valley and the water / Then you will not be a baby, but a *Hopi.*"

Miriam nods with each assertion, moves her eyes across the land slowly, deliberately, thoughtfully. She looks at the solitary tree longest. She watches the sky, follows a cloud across it. She sees some Hopi men walking in the distance, smiles at them. She seems ready to point them out to her infant sister but apparently has second thoughts. She points them out instead to her mother, who shows no great interest. The mother has only one more sight to urge upon her younger daughter, and it is a rather subtle one, which seems beyond the grasp of a one-year-old child: "The sun is breaking through the cloud; it is light over there, and darker here. Shadows don't always last. The sun. The sun." The baby does not look at the sun, but the mother is nevertheless pleased; she has made her point. Miriam reinforces it by cautiously moving her sister's face in the direction of the sky, and more precisely, the part of the sky the sun occupies at the time. The baby quickly wants to look away and, of course, is allowed to. But a moment later, on her own, she is bending her neck, peering over the heads of Miriam and her mother toward the sky.

They leave shortly thereafter. Miriam holds her sister for a while, then without saying a word hands her to their mother. The baby is hungry and is given the mother's breast. Miriam smiles as the baby works away, stopping occasionally for rest or to burp. Back at the house Miriam is delighted to tell her older and younger brother's that their sister is getting to know the reservation and even laying claim to some of its stones and rocks. They pass the baby around, each of them holding her, cradling her, congratulating her on her new acquaintance with their reservation. Soon the baby yawns, is put down to sleep. The children scatter — the boys to run and vie with other boys (who can throw farther? who can jump higher?) and Miriam to her mother's side: clothes to wash, food to cook.

An hour later Miriam has some spare time; she is in the kitchen, and has just taken a Lorna Doone cookie. She sits munching at it very slowly and starts a drawing. She will draw the entire reservation! It is easy! She scratches the paper lightly with the brown crayon, then with the blue one, and makes only slightly more restrained gestures with the green one. She is done! An afterthought, however; she picks up the yellow crayon and draws no sun, but rather scratches the entire picture with that crayon too. The result — a sun-drenched version of the Hopi reservation, as seen from the hill where the baby had just been (Figure 51).

She attempts another drawing. She loves a nearby valley, tightly held in by red and brown clay hills. She sketches those hills — is now quite concrete with her crayons. She is especially interested in a solitary clump of grass and a small tree in its midst — on the side of one hill. She works at the tree with painstaking care, then moves on: the sun, the sky. When she is done (Figure 52) she has a few remarks to make about the scene: "I am waiting for the day I can take my sister to the valley, and we can sit on a rock there and look up at the tree and be near the grass. My brothers like to stand on the rock and jump; I like to sit on it and listen. Almost always a few stones come tumbling down the side of the hill — our ancestors running about! I don't hear them speak words, but I know they are there, and they love the tree; it is the place where they can rest. There may be an underground river nearby. My father says no, but my older brother says the teacher told him that for the tree and the grass to grow, there has to be water, and there's not enough for grass to grow on any other part of the hill, so maybe there's a well there, if there isn't the river.

"My father laughs: what do the teachers know? He's always saying that. He says the teachers sometimes have come in here from far away; they want to be of help to us, and they don't know how to understand us when we tell them no, we don't need their help. My father says that once people came here because they thought there was gold. They looked and looked. They looked very hard near the tree; they were going to cut it down. They were sure that there might be some gold underneath the trunk. Our people came and stood next to them and prayed that they would stop trying to hurt the land. They said they'd kill us if we didn't stop bothering them. Our people said they would stand there, even if they were killed. They wouldn't leave. They were ready to join their ancestors. The white people kept looking, but they didn't find anything. They were going to cut down the tree, just to make our people feel bad; but one white man got scared because the wind started blowing very hard, and the sun hid behind a cloud, and then hail began to fall; it was getting toward winter. So they left fast. My grandmother will tell us the story when the moon is full, and then we go out with her and say her prayer to the tree: 'Stand there / Bend toward us / Your green reminds us of the brown / Your height makes us know our size / Your shadows whisper to us / We are Hopis / We are Hopis.'"

She has memorized the words and sings them to no particular tune, only with the slightest of inflections. She has been told at school that she is a bright girl, but her parents are not all that impressed. They wonder what difference the schooling will make in her life — and they express their doubts to her. She speaks of what she has heard with an air of authority: "My mother says that at school we learn a lot, but what we learn doesn't help us here on the reservation. The teachers want some of us to leave and try to live someplace else, in a city maybe. My father says this reservation of ours is the whole world, and he never wants to leave it; he never wants to go live in another world. Last week I went with him; he was leading the sheep to a field where there is grass. We came to the big rock; it suddenly is there, when you turn the corner of the path. The rock looks like three fingers pointing up to the sky.

"My father told me again the story his grandmother used to tell him — about three Hopi men a long time ago. They were very good friends, but they didn't help others, only themselves. They left their families, and they met some white people, and they joined up with them. They all looked for gold, I think. The three Hopis stopped being Hopis. They became lost; they belonged nowhere. They went to the West, on their way to California. They got into trouble; they were caught stealing. They never got to California. They turned around, and came back to us, the Hopi people, and asked to be taken in. Our ancestors said no, we shouldn't do it. But the three men begged, and their mothers were still alive, and they came, and they asked the other Hopis to be good, and to take the three men back. There was a vote, and most Hopis said yes. But before the men could come to a ceremony and be welcomed back, they died. Then someone said that the bodies should be taken to the Three Fingers Rock, and the bodies would rest there, and they would be among us, and we would not forget them. And we haven't. My father says at night you can hear sand falling down from each of the fingers, and it's the spirits of the three men, moving up there. When some of our Hopis have gone away, they go to the Three Fingers Rock right away when they come back, and the three Hopis up there welcome the travelers back. My uncle went to Phoenix, Arizona, then to New Mexico, and when he came back he went to the Rock, and he said he thought he heard some noise up there, so he asked out loud if the three Hopis were there, and just then the wind rose, and it didn't stop for a long time."

She uses crayons to convey that rock and the surrounding land: a few trees, some sagebrush, a path. As she puts the colors brown, red, and orange on the paper, she makes clear her sense of inadequacy: no one, she is sure, can really draw or paint that towering, mysterious, somewhat frightening rock as it really is — because it changes its appearance so often. She apologizes for her attempt. She stops painting, drawing, talking. She looks at the Rock. It is late in the afternoon; the Rock glows from a distance as it catches the setting sun's rays. Some Hopi children have gone rushing to their parents, uncles, aunts, grandparents to tell them that the Rock is on fire. All who hear go to a place that affords a view and watch silently — until, as Miriam's mother puts it, "the night will put out the fire." In a few days there will be the sight of the Rock lit up by the moon — an eerie luminous color that has prompted various legends. The one Miriam likes to tell has to do with the three men. They express the regret they feel for wandering so far and for abandoning in their minds the conviction that they were and wanted to be Hopis. The glow of the Rock is the result of the intensity of their sadness, their self-accusations, their fervently spoken remorse.

In broad daylight and under the sun's unremitting intensity, the Rock seems to glow with the heat. At times the Rock seems to have captured the sun itself; the Hopis shun looking at it lest their eyes be hurt. Stories have been made to go with that brightness: the three buried Hopis, still greedy for gold, have set a trap for the sun, convinced that it is the prize of prizes — full of gold, blazing yellow rays. But they succeed only in scorching themselves; the sun, of course, escapes. And finally, there are the shadows that clouds bring. Miriam is not sure that she likes the Rock at that time. She has been told that for the Rock, as for people, shade offers relief from the scorching sun. But she worries that the three Hopis who dwell there may well feel cold, shut out from the world, condemned to something akin to the white man's hell.

She is not too talkative about such matters, but enough so to reveal the awe she and other Hopi children accord that rock: "My mother says I worry too much about the Rock, and the three men; but she says she is glad that I do. Some Hopis have tried to forget about the Rock; they laugh and say we make too much of the place. But why is it there, and why does it change its look so often? I don't know how to paint it. My father asked me why I bother. I said that we have a Hopi teacher, and he says that we should try to close our eyes and think of the Rock, then draw it or paint it — and that's a way of going there on a visit. I've gone there in the morning, in the middle of the day, and at night. The

Rock looks different at different times. The three Hopis are like everyone else; they have moods. My mother tells us to look very closely because each time the Rock looks different. I like to look from far away: the three fingers practically touch the sky. Once we were far, *far* away, and the sun was going down, and the sky was red, all over it was red, and the Rock was a shadow, and it looked as if, any minute, the shadow would go away — it would disappear into the sky, and there would be nothing for us to find if we went near except some tumbleweed. Tumbleweed will run away from you, or it will bother you, if you've been doing anything wrong. My mother says tumbleweed is the wind's hand; if the tumbleweed comes after you and hits you, that means some spirit is telling you something and you've done wrong; but if you're walking and the tumbleweed gets out of your way, then you've been doing good, and you deserve an easy walk."

V
Privileged Ones

Comfortable, Comfortable Places

Dramatic and secluded; old, historic, and architecturally interesting; large and with good grounds; private and palatial; beautifully restored; big, interesting, high up and with an uninterrupted view: so the descriptions go, phrases meant to lift a person's eyebrows, make a person get the point, the facts of money, prestige, position as they come to bear on something called "the real estate market." In the South, the house may be an old plantation manor, made modern, with cool air pouring through tastefully decorated rooms; or an imitation of such a building, designed by an architect and furnished by an interior decorator; or a rambling, nondescript brick or wooden home, contemporary but not conspicuously or outlandishly so; or a self-consciously Tudor home, with wings and maybe a turret; or, far less common and an obvious object of admiration and envy, an antebellum home with an interesting history.

In Appalachia, the home is quite often a heavy brick presence, likely as not with white columns that prompt, or are supposed to, reveries of the Southern landed gentry. The house may be tucked away on the side of a hill, quite visible from the road; or one may have to drive and drive, in seemingly concentric circles, until all of a sudden it is there — two, maybe three, floors, several large cars, and not much in the way of lawns or gardens, because the woods are immediately nearby and not easily pushed aside. In West Virginia or eastern Kentucky, if the home is located in a town or a city it may be of wood, and less imposing. Out toward the western part of Kentucky, of course, one is no longer in Appalachia, though a number of families that own mines in the eastern counties have taken themselves to "bluegrass" country, to horse farms: gentle hills, rich growing land, an established tradition of leisure — and, through riding or racing, fierce competition. And in the northern part of West Virginia one also leaves Appalachia, approaches Pittsburgh — with it, the Northeast and its cities, near which lie the well-to-do or wealthy suburbs.

In the suburbs and beyond — of Pittsburgh and Philadelphia, of Boston and Hartford, of New York City and Washington, D.C., of Wilmington, Delaware, and Cleveland: towns, townships, villages, stations, even crossings, anything to make it clear that one does not live in the city, that one is outside or away, *well* outside or *well* away, as it is so often put — the houses vary: imitation English castles; French provincial; nineteenth-century American; contemporary one-levels in the tradition of Gropius or Neutra. Sometimes the setting is formal, sometimes one is in view of a farm — animals, rail fences, pasture land, a barn, maybe a shed or two, a flower garden, and, more recently, a few rows of vegetables. Sometimes there is a swimming pool. Sometimes there is a tennis court. Sometimes there is a greenhouse, attached to the house or on its own. Sometimes the house stands on a hill, affords a view for miles around. Sometimes particular trees stand close guard; and beyond them, thick brush and more trees, a jumble of them: no view but complete privacy. Sometimes there is a paved road leading from a street up to the house's entrance. Sometimes the road is a dusty path, or a trail — the casual countrified scene, prized and jealously guarded. Sometimes the property, as it may be called, is clearly marked. Sometimes no one but the owner seems to know where the "land" ends and someone else's begins, though upon occasion there may be a marker, a fence, a road, a natural boundary like a stream. Sometimes the house is within sight of another house or two or is on a street of large homes surrounded by ample land. Sometimes the house is acres away from the nearest "neighbor." Sometimes life is immediately apparent as one comes near: a barking dog (or two, or three); a watchful cat; children's toys, bicycles, their sandbox — or their pony chewing relentlessly on the grass — a station wagon, another car, still another car. Sometimes there is an eerie silence, and no evidence of anyone — just a long driveway that leads to a home, which seems formidably closed up, even the garage doors tightly closed, and everything neat and tidy, even the flower garden.

The trees matter; so do the grass and the shrubbery. These are not houses in a row, with patches of new grass, fledgling trees, and a bush or two. These are homes that are surrounded by spacious lawns and announced by tall, sturdy trees. Hedges are common, are carefully arranged. The grass is fine yet thick — years of cultivation. And not rarely there is water — a sprinkler system, a nearby pond, a brook running through the land. There are also quite likely wild birds who are fed food, given drink. If the people in the house are their friends and observers, squirrels are their constant competitors. The bird feed-ers are ingeniously constructed and placed, but squirrels are quick, clever, and, it seems, able to get anywhere. And there are chipmunks, and garden snakes, and colonies of ants, and, in many cases, pheasants — a semirural landscape that particular boys and girls talk about, draw or paint, discuss with a visitor.

Out West, in Texas or in New Mexico, the homes are ranches, big sprawling ones, many rooms in many wings. In the Rio Grande Valley the material may be wood, painted white; in New Mexico it's adobe. The land is wet and fertile throughout the southern part of Texas, so tropical and semitropical flowers and trees adorn estates or ranches — acres of land given over to horse trails, gardens, large swimming pools, even landing strips for private airplanes. In New Mexico the large adobe houses abut cacti, corrals, and often stunning views: across a valley, over toward mountains miles and miles away. And the horses: they are not part of a "hunt" club, not exquisitely combed; they are just there, grazing or waiting to be used — and by boys or men as well as girls or women: Western style riding, sometimes bareback. And the cattle. They have to wander far over the stingy land for food — and in the clutch, must be fed grain by quite well-to-do owners, who don't worry too much about costs, about profits and losses. And the dogs. Often three or four of them run about — after horses, around the house, up the trails on a scent. Signs announce to anyone who chances to come near that at a certain point a ranch begins — belonging to so-and-so and stretching maybe as far as the eye can see and then some.

Who are the people who live in all those homes, who own all that land — or acreage, as it is sometimes put with just the slightest of commercial implications? How is one to characterize them, region by region? As rich? As wealthy? As well-to-do? As members of the upper middle class? As affluent or prosperous or well-off, well-off indeed? As advantaged or privileged? The words are plentiful, and there are plenty of numbers to go with them. Clearly the issue is money, and with it social position, and, rather commonly, political leverage. The homes belong to people who have a lot of money, are "successful." They are plantation owners, bankers, stockbrokers, business or corporation executives, lawyers, doctors, architects, strip mine operators. They are politicians whose salaries for "public service" only begin to indicate the extent of their resources. They are ranchers and growers. They are entrepreneurs of one sort or another. They are those lucky enough to inherit substantial sums of money. They are sometimes men or women successful in the arts. They are people considered to be "on top," or "the bosses," or very, very "lucky." They are people who, in the middle

1970s, make, say, forty or fifty thousand dollars a year, and up. Some growers in the Rio Grande Valley are many times millionaires, as are mine owners in Appalachia or plantation owners in Louisiana or Mississippi. In cities of the North or Midwest, certain business or professional men bring home seventy-five or a hundred thousand dollars a year — and look up to others who make twice that and therefore are judged and called "better off."

Inside the homes all those dollars have done their work — tastefully or insistently or at times quite gaudily. A formal, nineteenth-century spirit dominates the plantation South — by no means inhabited only by cotton growers, because professional and business men want homes that look like antebellum homes and in some instances have bought "the real thing" and restored it. Mahogany furniture, often heavy, is found in living rooms and dining rooms: solid breakfronts; grand pianos; long and wide eating tables with heavy silver candlesticks; captain's tables; end tables or casual tables on which one finds books that belong to hunters or fishermen — pictures of birds, fish, wildlife; writing tables or desks that boast a gardening lady's books — the flowers of a region beautifully illustrated. Air conditioning is everywhere — entire houses, rather than a room or two. There are exceptions, though — stubborn holdouts: a family in, say, Mountain Brook, Alabama, that won't, under any conditions, let "good, warm Southern air" be turned into "Yankee weather." Not silly, eccentric people but a distinguished lawyer and his wife who genuinely like summer weather, however hot and humid, and who don't want to surrender themselves to "artificial air."

Cars are everywhere, too; a car for the husband and a car for the wife, a car for each child over sixteen, and often a car that belongs to a maid, to a cook, to a man who "helps" with the garden. The "help" is all black, of course, in the South, and sometimes in the North, too. In the South the swimming pool can be an almost all-year-round center of family life. The pools are lit, are heated. They are guarded by columns of mosquito repellent — steel poles on top of which burn mysterious chemicals that only some people worry about as pollutants. There are many chairs and a table or two — the former bright-colored, the latter usually with a glass top. There is a phone nearby — in a few instances a phone that is mysteriously, miraculously free of wires or cords. There are electrical outlets, television sets, phonographs, radios, rotisseries, toasters, small refrigerators — a kitchen outside the house's kitchen, all arranged decorously and without clutter.

In Appalachia the pools are more modest; often they are nonexistent. The furniture is likely to be new — North Carolina-made imitations of antiques. Not always, however; it depends on who has made what money, when, and how. Rather often, simple mountain furniture — part of the region's arts and crafts tradition — gets shunted aside in favor of massive, imposing couches and stereo sets or televisions encased in giant mahogany or cherry cabinets. Cadillacs predominate; Rolls Royces are not unknown. The driveways are occasionally something to see: lights, spaced at intervals, that blaze at night and a certain sweep that goes beyond any requirements of convenience. The garages can be enormous; inside are large cars, motorized lawn mowers, snowplows, diggers or cultivators — a warehouse of mechanized equipment. And near the house, often, a flagpole, used daily. And large television antennae, able to pick up distant signals. And, maybe, a boy's aerial for a high-powered shortwave radio or a police radio. And motorbikes; they are fun, and "children" of eleven, say, use them a lot, indifferent to any law that might urge otherwise.

There is, of course, other wealth in Appalachia — older, self-consciously understated, Southern in affiliation, or, if near Pittsburgh, quite Eastern in many respects. In those homes, as in Southern homes catalogues are often to be found on the desks of wives and husbands, mothers and fathers: for clothes, for jams, jellies, fruits, cakes; for hunting or fishing equipment; for toys; for books or records. And clippings, coupons, advertisements — cut out of magazines like *The New Yorker*: promises of goods and services, bearers of symbolic assurance, reinforcements of a family's sense of itself, reminders for anyone around that there is a national culture (material, at least) for the upper middle class and wealthy people of this country. Guns are part of that culture; especially in the rural South and in Appalachia those guns assert themselves: on walls, in corners of rooms, in closets, or even outside, in barns or garages — sometimes almost as numerous as the tennis rackets and golf clubs.

Golf: a game, but for many a way of life. Some homes are regarded as especially convenient, because near a golf course. The weekends become a marathon of golf, interrupted by a meal or two. The mood of particular parents varies with their "game," with their scores. And endless discussions are devoted to experiences in one way or another connected to the sport. Families travel with a certain golf course in mind. Clothing is often geared to what is worn on the links. And to move toward a less sociological and more psychological, even existential, vein, some well-to-do men and women openly acknowledge that without golf life for them would be unbearable, even hard to imagine.

For others, tennis has the same function — not only a game, a means of exercise, but virtually an organizing principle. Social lives depend on who is playing against whom, when and where. Couples meet other couples. Wives play in the morning, as soon as their husbands and children have left, or right after a housekeeper arrives to care for a preschool child or indeed an infant. On Monday, husbands talk about the sets they played during the weekend; and the memories hold those busy, important men together, so some say, until the next weekend — that is, the ones who are too busy for weekday tennis, increasingly played on indoor courts. The fear of coronary heart disease adds a certain determination to the game, when the opponents are middle-aged professional and business men — who, however, also worry out loud about the competitive intensity they feel as they serve, lob, smash the balls. Will they, on that latter count, be right back where they started, candidates for a sudden and possibly fatal heart attack?

People who make enough money to live a privileged life, socially and economically, spend a considerable amount of time and money making sure that they are near the water. Summer homes are for many of them an utter necessity: Cape Cod, certain stretches of Long Island, Maine, the New Jersey and Delaware coasts, the Carolina beaches, the whole state of Florida, the Gulf Coast, the beaches of the Caribbean islands, Mexico, or the Pacific states. Or lakes: Michigan and Wisconsin, New Hampshire and Vermont, the Northwest and into Canada. Or the Portuguese and Spanish and French resorts, or the islands of the South Seas, not to mention Hawaii. Many families try one place, then another, out of genuine curiosity, out of a desire to taste different pleasures, or out of a nervous sense of what is fashionable — or strictly out-of-bounds. Other families are quite content to stay with a permanent second home, and pour into it years of lavish devotion: a whole new set of furniture and electrical gadgets; boats of various kinds; snorkeling equipment; a tennis court sometimes; often a movie camera and screen — for rainy days; a special library (old favorites and recently published books); and almost always a sampling of records that usually get played more than those in the "other" house and that have a broad family appeal. Needless to say, a group of families may stay together, winter and summer — move from one upper-income community to another one near an ocean, lake, or mountain. In other cases, a whole new world of friends and acquaintances awaits a particular family.

There are third homes, too; in order to ski, and avoid the crowds or disappointments associated with motels, families purchase condominiums near a particular ski resort, or own their own lodges. In the upper three New England states, in Colorado and northern New Mexico, and Idaho and Utah and northern California, and recently in the mountains of western North Carolina and Tennessee, a winter social and even cultural life centered around the "slopes" has developed and steadily grown. Shops, moviehouses, even educational programs cluster near ski tows; so do an assortment of restaurants and bars. Private planes struggle to land amid winter weather that closes small airports; the alternative, going to a particular city's jet field, annoys the passengers, who would like ideally a lot of snow on the ground, but in any case clear weather for landing, for the departure of Lear jets or more old-fashioned prop jets. Sometimes a family is torn: to ski at Christmas or to go to the Caribbean, or Mexico, or Rio de Janeiro, or the warm and fine beaches of Uruguay? Sometimes both desires are appeased — a week in Switzerland, a week in the Caribbean, where a number of well-to-do Americans keep winter homes. The two seasons most likely spent entirely at home (the main home) are spring and fall, though spring skiing or a last fling or two in the autumn at a summer home are by no means unusual. And there is always a fishing trip, a hunting weekend in the autumn or the spring: a cabin up some chain of mountains or in the middle of woods or near a stream — a place where commonly a man and his friends go, leaving behind wives and children, or a place where an entire family goes a few times a year for yet another change of scene and a sustained effort with guns or rods.

Garages are but one part of a chain of secondary buildings: a shed for bikes and lawn mowers and lawn furniture; a place where barrels are kept; a barn, with horses, hay, grain, saddles; and sometimes yet another building for chickens, maybe a rabbit, maybe some ducks. All that on acres of land *not* considered a farm, but rather a home in a certain village or town, out of which every day men and women travel to cities (by car, by train) in order to work, to shop, to dine, to attend a concert, the theater, a movie. Hunt clubs or, more informally, weekly hunts pursued through woods delightfully untouched except for the paths themselves, or across rolling meadow lands, are an important part of the social life of certain families: the so-called horse country of Virginia, New Jersey, or Massachusetts.

In the Southwest and West horses have until recently been part of a culture's mythology as well as the common man's unpretentious but lively and even passionate enjoyment: the rodeo, the fair, the horse show. In Texas, New Mexico, and Arizona boys and girls alike learn to ride, and not only the more well-to-do. The latter, however, are able to indulge their interests in many ways: ranches with many different kinds of horses and ponies; large stables, and individuals to care for them; trails and paths and grazing land; vans to move horses, employees to do the driving, even as they have filled and refilled water pails or containers for grain, and pitched in hay, and shoveled out manure, and spread out shavings on well-put-together wooden floors or on cement ones or, sometimes, the Western earth. For some children and their parents the care of horses as well as the riding of them becomes one of the most important tasks of each day. The "animals" get fed before people do. Even if there are caretakers, and handymen, the children may well go out first thing, talk to their horses, feed them, fill up their water buckets, even groom them a little. Then comes breakfast and "horse talk."

On weekends there are rides, races, or a lot of care: the shoes, the coat, the mane, all in need of work. And a talk with the veterinarian. And a discussion: to go here or there by van on such and such weekend? Some Western ranches are justly famous — beautiful horses, immaculately cared for and trained, ridden on stunning paths that lead up hills, across streams, into valleys or prairies a feast for the eyes. In the East all sorts of social tensions and rivalries get worked at or worked out when horses are mounted in particular places on certain mornings. As with golf, there are clubs and clubs, hunts and hunts, horses and horses, stables and stables. Much has been made of Little League baseball — its searing effect on working- or middle-class children, who fight hard to win; so hard, some claim, that any loss becomes a devastating psychological experience and any victory an exercise in arrogant self-congratulation, accompanied, alas, by a haunting apprehension of future defeat. But among certain quite well-off children the performance at a show or on a hunt can be an occasion for fear, self-doubt, and fierce rivalry. Even a successful morning of dressage can end with tears — the gnawing conviction that one ought *be* better, *do* better, *appear* better.

Sailing, for children of well-off families, also generates strong competitive demands. The relationship between such families and boats in general is at once apparent: canoes alongside garages of winter homes; sailboats anchored within sight of summer homes; motorboats kept in garages attached to lake-front cottages; and, among the wealthy, yachts of palatial size and equipment. Children take sailing lessons as well as tennis lessons, enter races or regattas, learn every trick they can to pull out front and stay there. Some of those who sail detest motor-driven boats as a noisy, vulgar presence and as the toys of the *nouveaux riches*. In the inland parts of the country Sailfishes or canoes share less socially conscious company with the fast-moving motorboats. Out West, canoes have their own special place — traditionally and symbolically the pioneer's means of navigating swift, treacherous rivers.

A number of children whose parents are quite well-to-do also take an interest in flying and parachuting; a father owns a plane or works in a company that does. Such a family flies privately, perhaps, more than on commercial planes. In the New England states the family finds its way to airports that serve the needs of small planes. There, a spirit of camaraderie exists: families whose planes the same mechanics care for; people who recognize in a way of travel yet another sign of what might be called the apartness that goes with wealth. Among the very rich, there is a pilot, whose work is analogous to a chauffeur's. Among the modestly affluent the husband has learned to pilot the plane and, these days, the wife, too. They may well fly from one of their homes to another — or to visit friends a few hundred miles away for a weekend. And not rarely their children, as they become older, have their eyes on flying lessons and on parachuting.

In the "main home" or "winter home" of such families one sees constant photographic reminders of how diverse life can be, given the money and the will: framed pictures of other houses, or of parents and children riding horses, sailing boats, playing with tennis rackets or golf clubs. Other pictures show tourists in strange lands or about to board planes, disembark from them. There are always new lands, continents to visit. Old, worn Persian carpets are valued, among other reasons, precisely because they give just the slightest impression of shabby gentility to homes owned by people determined to indicate how casual and relaxed they have become with their considerable wealth. In other homes one finds magnificent new Oriental rugs — lush Bokharas, sometimes placed on top of wall-to-wall carpeting, the latter especially prominent in the newer homes of upper-middle-class Southern and Midwestern families. In some homes prayer rugs or Navaho or Pueblo rugs hang on the walls. In some homes the rugs are changed by the season. At times a woman may replace one Oriental rug in mid-winter with another: a pleasant change of scene for her and the rest of the family.

The antique market depends heavily on the aspiring tastes of people who regard chairs, tables, clocks, and pictures as important aesthetic objects — and a means of self-definition, self-assertion. Antique shows, auctions, or benefits can be important social occasions. The acquisition of a particular painting, or some piece of Oriental art — jade, a bowl, a tea service — or of a fine old desk becomes, at least for a while, an event in a family's life. The furniture in a young child's room may be old, valuable, rare — or quite new and decidedly ingenious, interesting. Sometimes there are mixtures: a nineteenth-century Windsor chair, resplendent yet fragile, next to a two-level bunk bed, equipped with a ladder, attached lights, pull-out sideboards, and decorated with a patchwork quilt that may have been sewn a hundred years ago and that cost almost as much as the bed itself. Across the spacious room stands a disarmingly "common" roll-top desk, once the unpretentious property of nineteenth-century or early twentieth-century burghers, but now relatively rare to find, as children know and say, echoing their parents' words. The desk is against the wall and not far from a window. The walls of children's rooms in upper-income homes are a vivid contrast indeed to the bare and forsaken surfaces within the homes of not only poor but also working-class people. A child sitting at the roll-top desk can lift his or her head and look at attractively decorated wallpaper, at framed photographs, a painting, curtains that nicely set off the room's windows. The curtains offer their own view — in fact, the room is a room of views, each somehow tastefully connected to the others. And beyond there is the land, there are the trees; everything, it seems, contributes to a child's sense of place, privacy, property, stability. And beyond too there are others, waiting in readiness to serve, to work, to make things as easy as possible.

Many of those "others" work in stores that sell "provisions" as well as regular American food, stores that may take great pains to distinguish themselves from supermarkets. Even supermarkets, for all their uniformity, make exceptions, feature special kinds of meat, canned foods, preserves, bread, fruit, and vegetables. The steaks are the best. Lobsters are available, sometimes flown hundreds of miles. Jams and jellies are English as well as American, or indeed French, Swedish, Spanish. Spices and condiments abound; so does the very best of fruit, plentifully available out of season. In many towns or villages there is a cozy "country store," which despite its name carries all that is convenient and contemporary in packaged food along with various nostalgic offerings — candy in buckets or individually weighed and wrapped; meat specially ordered and cooked; a rotisserie that never seems to stop from morning until evening — indeed, a store that keeps open virtually every day of the year and offers to cater food as well as sell it from the shelf.

Such a store serves a community of people who may not at all take to the notion of large-scale suburban shopping malls. Yes, if need be, one drives a car to those malls, enjoys what they incontestably have to offer, but they are best located elsewhere. The drugstore in a well-to-do village or town may be deliberately old-fashioned in appearance. The hardware store carries feed for animals. The post office is small and informal. The bank is designed not to stand out prominently. There is often a bookstore, a record store. And maybe there is a pleasant restaurant that responds at various times of the day to quite different customers. A point is being made, though no one has ever got up and made it publicly — and, maybe, few have ever done so in private: the people hereabout want to keep the neighborhood where they shop cozy, informal, even intimate. It is as if a minority of Americans had decided that they want to remove themselves, to a degree only, from the twentieth-century commercial actuality of their country and return to the business spirit of another age.

The men, women, and children who come to those stores often do so in what other Americans might call "farm clothes," if not worn-out rags: dungarees, battered khakis, tennis shoes that rarely look white, sweaters with a hole or two in them or at the least well-worn, shirts with sleeves rolled up and not so thoroughly tucked in. Not always, of course; not every successful businessman or lawyer or doctor has the desire to drive a conspicuously old car or wear clothes a garbage collector or factory worker would refuse ever to put on. Nor do the well-to-do always go shopping with little or no money and, at times, no credit cards, either. But in all parts of the country one does see among a significant number of such men and women just those habits and preferences — as if one must act like a nearly indigent farmer, who has barely enough standing in a particular village to secure the necessities of life.

There are men and women worth hundreds of thousands of dollars, maybe millions of them, who make it a habit not to carry money when they go "down" to a nearby group of stores and make various purchases. They look at a man or woman near a cash register, smile, exchange greetings, and walk out, their arms full of costly items. In some instances even a milk shake for a child gets charged, but never in such a way that the boy or girl sees or hears anything to prove that such a transaction has in fact taken place. Usually the parent doesn't even have to nod, or look in someone's eyes, let alone suggest the need for payment. Rather, the owner of the store or an employee in it has learned how to be utterly discreet, never do or say anything that so much as implies acknowledgment of a sale, and talk instead about that old reliable, the weather. If something more serious comes up, especially of a political nature, there may well be a smile, and a brilliantly relaxed kind of noncommittal acknowledgment: indeed, indeed, the times are strange and vexing — on that we *all* can agree! Meanwhile, the children are there — walking in and out of such stores, hearing words exchanged, noticing who says what to whom, observing their parents' several cars get filled up, yet never at all observing the gas get paid for, watching their parents take money out of a bank, but not often seeing their parents bring money into the bank.

The very rich have family compounds, but so do merely quite well-off families — many acres, on which may live several families in several homes, none of which is visible to the others. Sometimes among the wealthy there is the large house of a child's grandparents, even great-grandparents; then, farther up the road, a "cottage" or two — substantial, even magnificent, homes in their own right, but offspring of sorts to the "main house." In the "cottages" live a child's parents, uncles and aunts, cousins. If the original tract of land is large enough to accommodate those families in adequate seclusion, they may decide to deed some land to a village for "conservation," in the interests of "ecology," or maybe, recreation. Thus the "character" of many such villages in the East or the South and even in the far West changes more slowly than would otherwise be the case. From the air one sees a cluster of homes, or maybe only one or two, then stretches of woods, streams, meadows, marshes, hills. Or one sees a series of full-fledged farms — belonging to so-called gentlemen farmers, who work in cities and maybe have apartments in them but return nightly or on weekends, at least part of the year, to a cattle farm, or a produce growing one, or both, which an employee (or two, or three, or more) keeps going.

Small private schools are very much part of the landscape. In the beginning it is a nursery, maybe in the basement of an Episcopal church, or maybe in the home of a person who is not rich at all but has earned the confidence and respect of those who are, and wants very much to work with their children. The nursery teacher's home may be nearer the center of the village or town — and smaller, though in keeping with the architectural tradition of the surrounding country-side. The children are transported there as much by housekeepers as by parents, and by the age of four are spending not rarely more than a morning away from home. The school may have a special "orientation" — Montessori, for instance. There are relatively few children, compared to the number of adults who work with them. For older children there are the "country day schools" — dozens of them by that name all over this country, and not dissimilar, be they in New Mexico, Texas, Alabama, West Virginia, or on the Atlantic Seaboard. Those schools, too, enjoy an architectural affinity to the prevailing mode of the neighborhood served. They may be quite well endowed, supported not only by tuition but various fund-raising social events. It is in those schools (their playing fields, their classrooms and eating halls) that a small but important number of American children begin to live, for a few hours at least, with others of their own kind, and begin also to get some sense of what the rest of the nation is like. Often the teachers in those schools are the first adults to give the children sustained, clear expression of their own views — in contrast to the fearful or ingratiating agreement of shopkeepers.

Many upper-income families, however, live in cities and even in the summer prefer travel to Europe, Asia, the Pacific islands, to a country or seaside life. They live in luxury apartments, occasionally in hotels, or in old town houses — on Boston's Beacon Hill, on the East Side of New York, in the Garden District of New Orleans, in the Georgetown district of Washington, D.C., on the Near North Side of Chicago, on Nob Hill in San Francisco, right smack in the middle of downtown Los Angeles, or on Canyon Road, Sante Fe. Those are all well-known neighborhoods, and of course, some of the people who live in them also have country places, Caribbean retreats, ski lodges. But a substantial number of quite privileged parents prefer to live and bring up their children in the city, even shunning at times the actual ownership of a house or an apartment. Young boys and girls who live such a life can be seen walking in city parks, often accompanied by a governess. They can be seen riding bicycles on sidewalks or using swings or playing in sandboxes, again under the watchful eyes of a parent or a housekeeper. They may live in penthouses that have their own gardens and areas for play. They may live in a town house that has a small, open courtyard, also convenient for the activity of children. Some practically never play outside; instead, they spend time in rooms set up for the vigorous, uninhibited energy of the young. Often such children get to know museums, restaurants, department stores. They learn how to dress more formally, restrain themselves in public, be watchful, careful; they do so because for them life is more "public," is more connected to the demands of others — and yes, because of the dangers city life presents. A child learns, at five or six, about taxicabs, waiters who expect to be tipped, policemen, elevator operators — not to mention an elevator that requires those who use it to push the right button, or else. And then there are the doormen, who befriend children, keep an eye on them for brief, and sometimes not so brief, periods — and who, for some boys and girls, become important friends, allies, and teachers.

Those same children may well learn, even at nursery school age, that they possess passports, that they have Social Security cards, that an income accrues to them by the year. The passports enable travel; and some boys and girls know certain foreign places as well as their native city — to the point that in kindergarten or before they talk about various experiences abroad, often more extensive by far than those of their teachers. The schools are often, to outward appearances, homes very much like those many wealthy families own — town houses made into nurseries or elementary schools. The children walk to school or are driven — by cab, by a chauffeur, in a car pool. Some parents want their boys and girls to learn as much as possible about urban living and so encourage them as they get older to take the bus, the streetcar, the subway. Other parents want no part of that life for anyone in their family. Even servants arrive and leave by cab. Occasionally limousines are called into service, driven by chauffeurs hired for the day: a trip to visit someone in the far suburbs or to an airport. Some families keep a car and a chauffeur all year round, however little they are used.

Children learn to amuse and be amused by servants, and also learn to make do in apartment houses or old, restored town houses. They run races up and down stairs, go on expeditions to the boiler room, open and close doors meant to receive trash, learn to make friends with policemen or janitors, develop a keen sense of the dangers as well as the opportunities city life offers. The foyer to a distinguished apartment house can become a virtual playroom, with the doorman (he may be one of several) a casual and inventive overseer. The network of servants in such buildings — maids, cooks, chauffeurs, and those who keep the heat going, the entrances secure — is for children a source of friendship, assistance, and, not rarely, fear or intimidation. A boy may ask who is on duty at some particular station, knowing that if it is one person the morning or afternoon will be fun, if another then best to think of some other way to pass time. And even in the city, time can be spent ice skating, horseback riding, learning to distinguish between various kinds of birds, even fishing. And there is a zoo or an aquarium. There are plays for children and concerts for them, special magic shows, tours, and lectures, in sum: "everything," according to one eight-year-old girl who lives in an apartment house on Lake Shore Drive, Chicago.

Her words provide a useful way of describing and summarizing the way other children of quite well-off parents live, however removed from the cosmopolitan life of America's "second city," or for that matter, its first city, its third city. "Comfortable, comfortable places," she once said, referring to her parents' enormous duplex apartment, a ski lodge they maintain in Aspen, Colorado, and a lovely old New England clapboard home by the ocean toward the end of Cape Cod. She was not bragging; she knew a pleasurable, cozy, even luxurious life when she saw one (*had* one) and was not at all uncomfortable describing its many, consistent comforts. She happened to be sitting on a large sofa as she offered her observation. She touched a nearby pillow, also rather large, then moved it a bit closer to herself. The pillow had many colors, was soft, blended in nicely with the couch's covers yet maintained its own authority. In a rather uncharacteristic burst of proprietary assertiveness, the girl said: "I'd like to keep this pillow for my own house, when I'm grown up."

Children like her have a lot to keep in mind, look after, and, sometimes, feel attached to. At the same time, they may often be overwhelmed with toys, gadgets, presents; and they may wonder why it is that their rooms keep on being redecorated, or whether their family ever stays in one house longer than a year or so. Even within a given home there may be more rooms than a child knows how to make sense of, or come to terms with — at least when he or she is seven or eight. As a result, parts of an apartment or a home become foreign territory, virtually — to be kept at a distance, or entered only with caution and perhaps in the company of a servant or a parent. The same may hold for the surrounding countryside — land that children know to be the property of their parents, but prefer to keep clear of. Better to stay inside; and inside, better to enjoy the "comfortable, comfortable places" — a particular room or two.

There is just so much a child's mind can easily absorb and feel at ease with. Children can be as acquisitive as anyone else, but they prefer to stake out territorial limits, and they also have a stubborn habit of clinging to the familiar, however old and even useless it has become. So it is that children whose parents are wealthy indeed insist upon holding on to a tattered security blanket, a certain pair of worn pants, a dress that no longer really fits. They come home from school, from a walk or a game outside, from lunch with their parents in a restaurant, and they announce that the living room is theirs — but the sitting room or the dining room or the library is utterly out of bounds. After a vacation spent in the South or halfway up a mountain or on another continent they are especially determined to establish their own sovereignty and indicate thereby the limits of their (contemporary) possessiveness.

These are children, after all, who have to contend with, as well as enjoy, enormous couches, pillows virtually as big as chairs, rugs that were once meant to be in palaces of the Middle East, dining room tables bigger than the rooms many American children share with brothers or sisters, and, always, the importance and fragility of objects: a vase, a dish, a tray, a painting or lithograph or pencil sketch, a lamp. A boy or girl who is just beginning to figure out a dependable rhythm of activity and restraint for himself or herself has to stop and wonder how much of a "comfortable, comfortable world" he or she dares include in various journeys or forays through the house. And how much of that world can the young child even comprehend? Sometimes, in a brave, maybe desperate, attempt to bring everything around under control, a child will enumerate (for the benefit of a teacher or a friend) all that is his or hers, all that goes to make up what an observer might call the "setting," the background against which a life is carried on. Large trees get mixed up with globes built into tables; a pond is linked in sequence with a library of thousands of books; a Queen Anne desk shares company with a new motorboat that goes so fast the child's father, no stranger to speed, has begun to have second thoughts about the safety of those who go aboard with him.

Finally, the child may grow weary, abandon the spoken catalogue, and, think of one part of his or her life that means *everything*: a snake that can be reliably seen in a certain stretch of mixed grass and shrubbery along the driveway; a pair of pheasants who come every morning to the lawn and appear remarkably relaxed as they find food; a dog or a cat or a pony or a pet bird; a friend who lives near a summer home, or the son or daughter of a Caribbean cook or maid; a visit to an amusement park — a visit that, for the child, meant more than dozens of toys, some virtually untouched since they arrived; or a country remembered above all others — Ireland or England, France or Switzerland. Posters that commemorate those voyages are often found in the rooms of such children — elements of fantasy and pleasure, evocations of what was seen, heard, and enjoyed, and, not least, reminders of what the child confidently, realistically expects to see yet again. No preliminary sketch of the physical "ground-being" (as both Heidegger and Tillich put it) of upper-middle-class life, or of the habits of the rich, ought to fail to mention travel as a strong influence on a select number of children.

Not that the parents of those children necessarily live uprooted lives; some do, but others have a firm sense of belonging to a particular region and, within it, a given town, village, or city; and those men and women usually try hard to give their children a similar sense of themselves. Boys and girls, when born, get silver cups, engraved with their names and birthdays. Children are shown family insignia, "trees," lines of descent. If a parent's picture appears in the newspaper, a clipping is put on a child's bulletin board, even if he or she is not yet old enough to read the words. Banners that fathers had in college rooms appear in the rooms of their children, as do banners handed down from grandparents or great-grandparents.

The child can look at himself or herself as a baby, or as a toddler, or when first going to school, because there are usually many photographs that commemorate moments or events in his or her life. Indeed, there may be photographs that commemorate similar events in the lives of parents and grandparents. Diaries and family letters of ancestors may well have been kept, or published for the general public, or privately printed. An old family home or family compound, long since gone, nevertheless lives in the child's mind through a photograph. In contrast, of course, are those families that have quite a lot of money but few links to the land or to a region's history, or indeed, so far as their loyalties or memories go, to preceding generations. But even children in those families are often taught reasons to feel proud of themselves and, just as well, to feel grateful for what their parents may have done on their own, against great odds and with considerable self-sacrifice.

These children learn to live with *choices*: more clothes, a wider range of food, a greater number of games and toys, than other boys and girls may ever be able to imagine. They learn to grow fond of, or resolutely ignore, dolls and more dolls, large dollhouses and all sorts of utensils and furniture to go in them, enough Lego sets to build yet another house for the adults in the family. They learn to take for granted enormous playrooms filled to the brim with trains, helicopters, boats, punching bags, Monopoly sets, Ping-Pong tables, miniature tea sets, stoves, sinks, dining sets. They learn to assume instruction — not only at school, but at home — for tennis, for swimming, for dancing, for horse riding. And they learn often enough to feel competent at those sports, in control of themselves while playing them, and, not least, able to move smoothly from one to the other, rather than driven to excel. It is as if, for many such children, the various outdoor sports are like suits of clothing, to be put on, enjoyed, then casually slipped off.

Something else many of these children learn: the newspapers, the radio, the television do not offer news merely about "others," but rather about neighbors, friends, acquaintances of one's parents — or about issues one's parents take seriously, talk about, sometimes get quite involved in. These are children who have discovered that the "news," that events, may well be affected, if not crucially molded, by their parents as individuals or by their parents as members of a particular segment of society. Similarly, parental authority wielded in the world is matched by parental authority exerted at home. Servants are told to do things, are called in, are rung in, are given instructions, or, indeed, replaced summarily. In a way those servants, by whatever name or names they get called, are for these American children a microcosm of the larger world as they will experience it. They are people who provide convenience and comfort. They are people who, by and large, aim to please. Not all of them "live in"; there are cleaning women, delivery people, caretakers, town inspectors, plumbers and carpenters and electricians, carriers of telegrams, of flowers, of special delivery letters. Far more than their parents, the children observe the coming and going, the backdoor bustle, the front-door activity of the "staff": teas, cocktail parties, receptions, or just an ordinary meal.

It is a mixed world, a world in which social classes come together, work alongside one another, in ironic ways — a lawyer come to draw up a will or give advice on a business arrangement, being served coffee by a maid, both of them awaiting a child's father, while the child bounces a ball, walks in and out of the room, and decides to ask that he also be given something to drink. It is a world others watch with envy and with curiosity, with awe, with anger, bitterness, resentment. It is a world of decisions — purchases to be made, bids to be offered or taken up, places to go, people to see. It is a world, rather often, of action, of talk believed by the talkers to have meaning and importance, of schedules or timetables. It is a world responsive, of course, in its own way to the cycles of birth and death, to the seasons, to engagements and marriages, to children and their vicissitudes and triumphs. It is a world in motion — yet, at times, one utterly still: a child in a garden, surrounded by the silence acres of lawn or woods can provide. It is a world of excitement and achievement and eventually inescapably, disaster, tragedy, failure. It is an intensely private world that suddenly can become vulnerable to the notice of others. It is, obviously, a world of money and power — a twentieth-century American version of both. And it is a world in which children grow up, come to terms with their ample surroundings, take to them gladly, deal with them anxiously, and show themselves boys and girls who have their own special circumstances to master — a particular way of life to understand and become part of.

The Children

Defender of
the Garden District

New Orleans has some fine old homes, especially those that belong to the historic Garden District. Some of the children who live in them take for granted what others come from near and far to see: lovely columns, or an especially attractive portico, or trees and shrubbery and flowers (the azaleas, the wisteria), which adorn buildings quite appropriately called mansions. But for James, a twelve-year-old resident of the city, those mansions are of endless interest, as are the city's cemeteries, one of the most beautiful of which is not far from his home, in the center of the Garden District. The boy has for a long while hoped to be an architect. His own home has been turned modern on the inside, with every effort made to preserve the exterior. He had become (at the age of six) a good friend of the carpenters, electricians, plumbers, and painters who worked on the various rooms and from time to time came back to check on things or do an additional job.

The boy's father is a cotton broker, a man of substantial, inherited wealth. The boy's mother is an artist whose landscapes have become well known to many residents of the Garden District; she has had several showings in one of the city's art galleries. A number of the landscapes — the bayou country of southern Louisiana — adorn the walls of the artist's home and the nearby homes of her friends. Some paintings, as the boy is proud to announce, have gone to "complete strangers," who have paid "hundreds of dollars." He adds right away that his mother has given the money to charity. Asked what kind of charity, he is quite knowledgeable and forthcoming: "She has a lot of charities, but her favorite is hospitals. She likes to give money to them, and she said that if she didn't have her studio and the pictures she makes, then she'd go and do volunteer work in one of the hospitals. She feels sorry for people who get sick, and she's told us that she wanted to be a nurse when she was a girl, but her mother wouldn't hear of it."

James can walk down one of the Garden District streets and tell which home is the oldest, which home has been recently renovated or restored, which home belongs to what family. He ignores a few homes, sometimes with barely concealed disdain; a "new" family has moved in, he has heard, and he doesn't know (or can't quite remember) their name. But for a year or so he has been more interested in cemeteries than homes; he loves to walk through the former, read what is said about the dead on the aboveground mausoleums. He is not, however, morbid or eccentric. He also likes old watches; he has inherited a family collection, begun by his grandfather, and it is a source of constant fascination to the boy. He is an only son; he points out quite self-consciously and with a touch of boasting that he is also "the last male heir." He is, in fact, referring to his father's family; there are several male heirs on his mother's side, cousins of his whom he sees rather often, because they too live in the Garden District. His father's people have also lived in the Garden District of New Orleans for a long time — though in northern Louisiana there is a family plantation, and in Bay St. Louis, Mississippi, there are several summer "cottages" (rather large oceanfront homes) that belong to his parents and his two uncles.

He is sometimes money-conscious. When he talks about the watches his father and he jointly own and treasure, he makes mention of the hundreds of thousands of dollars the collection is worth. When he points out a home he especially likes, he remembers what he has heard his father say about the value of the place. When he talks about a friend of his, he is apt to call attention to the friend's parents as well — who they *are*, what kind of work the father does, what kind of family the mother comes from. He is not, however, overly preoccupied with "society," not compared to others he plays with or goes to school with. He lives in a city whose upper-income people are quite conscious of where they stand in relationship to each other. The morning newspaper, the *Times-Picayune,* often devotes page after page to social announcements: teas, coffees, lunches, suppers — honoring people, celebrating occasions, and so on. The boy can echo his parents' mixture of delight and chagrin as they go through the pages of the newspaper over breakfast: "My mother usually starts. She tells my father that he should turn from the news to the society page and learn all about what is happening to our friends and our neighbors. Dad doesn't turn; he asks her to tell him. She does, and then they're both unhappy because a lot of the time there's a conflict. They can't be in two places at the same time. They don't like to go out *too* much. They have to pick and choose. My father has a bad back, and my mother tells him never to tell *anyone* that it's better. She writes her 'regrets' notes, and she likes to mention Dad's back pain! Sometimes they both agree that they're going to try to accept every invitation they can, because they like to go out. But Dad gets tired; and my mother says that even now, after all these years, she's still a little shy with people, and so she likes to be at home at least *some* of the time!"

He is not being especially ironic and certainly not sarcastic when he talks that way about his mother. If anything, he is expressing sympathy for her, and more than a little understanding of how she feels. He is himself rather shy. He has no close friends, has never had any. He doesn't like to talk very much with those of his own age, though he is considerably more open with older people. His maternal grandfather calls him an "extrovert," but James disowns the description a little contemptuously. He is not all that close to the old man, who has (the boy believes) confused his polite conversation made in the presence of elders with a genuine desire to be with people. James says he is "most happy" when he is looking at his watch collection; in second place he puts playing tennis with his father — provided they go afterward to lunch at a certain private club whose food the boy especially likes. They don't often go there; it is a treat and they prepare for the moment a week or more in advance. There is, first of all, an announcement of a kind: "My father will tell me that next week we can go have lunch." When they go alone, it is always to the club; so the boy has been promised something quite appealing, by his standards. It is upon those occasions that he talks about "important subjects"; his father, he says, is his "best friend," and he likes very much talking with him. He also likes going with him to buy clothes — another "time" (the boy calls it) they have together. When Brooks Brothers comes to New Orleans, James and his father, also James, go to the hotel where the clothing representatives are staying, and get fitted.

The boy wants to go to Princeton; his father and his grandfather and his great-grandfather went there. He does not want to go to Tulane. He says unfriendly things about the college, and thereby irritates classmates of his in the private secondary school he attends. He criticizes the college's buildings, maintains that the courses there aren't "so good." His source: his father. When the boy is asked whether there aren't good reasons for some of his family's neighbors to send their children to Tulane, he says yes, there are. He doesn't know them, but again, he has heard his father speak: "My Dad says it's a city university and it has to serve a lot of people, and the classes are probably bigger than they should be. A lot of people here in New Orleans would die for Tulane. It's a good school. It's got a good reputation. But I'd rather go to Princeton. You keep up what your ancestors started. My great-grandfather went to Princeton, but he got in some trouble there. He never graduated. I think he fought with a Yankee. That's what my father always tells me. My mother says it may not be the whole truth, but it sounds good — it's a good story! Dad doesn't like her talking that way. Now women can go to Princeton. Dad was against the idea, but he says it had to happen. My grandfather graduated with high honors; he was a lawyer, and he invested in cotton, and he started a brokerage house, too — three professions, my Dad always says. And besides, my grandfather bought a lot of land in northern Louisiana and he invested in the railroads, and we can go free on them, even now. I think he was a director of the Louisville & Nashville — but who wants to ride on the railroads, the way they are now? I used to have a set, trains going in all directions, a whole room of trains, but I lost interest. Now I like to go out to the airport to meet my Dad when he comes back from a trip: all the jets to see."

James likes to draw planes, mostly large jets, but some smaller ones too, and, rarely, some older planes which he's only seen pictured. When he was younger, eight or nine, he favored struggle — aerial dogfights, formations headed toward formations. But more recently he has abandoned military aircraft for the commercial kind. He sketches 707s, 747s, DC10s, puts Delta or Eastern or United labels on the fuselages. As he does so he recalls the various flights he has taken — to Atlanta, to Nashville, to New York, to Mexico, to Brazil, to Europe. And he talks about the advantages of comfortable, first-class travel: "My mother said she didn't know how people travel tourist, especially on the long flights across the ocean or up to New York. You can't relax when you are sitting in a narrow seat and there's someone on each side of you. My father's friends, two of them, have their own planes, Lear jets. We've gone with them to Washington, and to Birmingham. I'd like to be a pilot, but I wouldn't want to fly commercial. I'd like to have my own plane, and then if I read the *National Geographic* and there was a city I wanted to see, or a country, I'd just pick up the phone and tell them at the field to get the plane checked out, because I'm coming over soon and I'd like to leave as soon as possible. I'd call up my friends, and the next thing you'd know, we'd be up in the air and headed north over Lake Pontchartrain or south over the Mississippi River. When you're over the clouds, you feel you're on your way. My father has promised that when I'm old enough to take driving lessons, I'll be given flying lessons too, if I still want them. I know I will. I think I'd rather fly than drive. There are too many cars on the road, too many madmen speeding in cars that shouldn't even be allowed to move out of a garage. I once dreamed up an idea: special roads for people who have real good cars and really know how to drive and can afford to pay — first-class roads, they could be called, like the first-class section of an airplane."

He remembers one evening when no amount of money in the world could separate him and his parents from hundreds of other travelers, many of whom he still quite vividly remembers: "I've never seen so many people inside a building. We came into the New York airport from London, and we were the last plane to land — a bad snowstorm. We were supposed to go into the city for a couple of days, but we decided to go right to New Orleans. We couldn't. We just sat there. All these people were sitting there, too. My mother got nervous. She was afraid we'd be robbed. My father says it was one of the worst times he's ever had." He doesn't easily bring up what specifically bothered his parents and himself. He talks about a "bad storm," a "long delay." Finally, he refers to "the crowd," and to "some of the people in the crowd." Then he describes his mother's fears — not only that she'd be held up, but that for some reason violence would break out, a riot would take place, there would be (she was utterly convinced) trouble and more trouble.

The boy volunteered to draw a picture of the waiting room at Kennedy Airport. He thought it would be rather a challenge to recall and evoke that scene through crayons. But he could not really get himself going. He stared at the paper, started to draw, stopped; in the end, he abandoned the project. He decided to draw, instead, particular individuals whom he still could remember — people who belonged to what he calls the "mob" at Kennedy that stormy evening. He contemplates drawing a man in a wheelchair first. That man seemed lost, helpless. The boy had wanted to go help, offer to push the chair — but no, his parents told him to sit with them, not go anywhere or talk with anyone. James decides not to draw the man. The next possible subject is a Texan, the boy was sure — a man headed for Houston and wearing a "cowboy hat." He had come up to them, asked a question or two, been politely denied satisfactory answers. Again, the boy had wanted to be of assistance. Might he go ask a policeman he saw walking in a certain direction? No, he should not, said his father. The boy had seen how much luggage the Texan had, and merely tried to lend a hand, but his parents had by then become quite annoyed. The mother spoke to the father; the father took the boy aside and told him that he must sit down and stop "getting involved with a lot of strangers."

James begins work on the Texan. He draws him quite tall, gives the hat obvious emphasis. The man's hands are made large, his feet also oversize. The mouth is open, toothy. The boy gets curiously agitated as he tries to complete the drawing. He seems satisfied at last, ready to turn to other matters, when suddenly he crosses the effort out with two strokes of a black crayon (Figure 53). It is not that he is artistically too critical of himself: "I can't do a good job on any of those people I saw that night. I think I remember them, but I forget them while I'm trying to draw them. I guess I didn't get as good a look at those people as I thought, because if I had, I know I could do good pictures of them. Maybe I obeyed my mother. I remember she told me to close my eyes and think pleasant thoughts. I kept opening my eyes and peeking, but maybe I didn't peek very much."

He has learned over the years to do as his mother suggests — and with less and less desire on his part to peek. Waiting with his father for a cab downtown, he sees someone or something, feels uncomfortable amid the jostle and hustle of the situation, and immediately his eyes close and he thinks, invariably, of his room at home or the inside of his father's club. He is not so much afraid as amused by his ability to spare himself unpleasantness, to create for himself a feeling of well-being: "My mother was right; if you're having trouble or you don't like the people around you, then you can get rid of them. All you have to do is think of some other place! My father says I'm lucky. He can't close his eyes, except when he goes to sleep. He says it can be dangerous, anyway. If you just stand there on the street, with your eyes closed, someone will think you're blind and come up and try to steal from you. The other day I went Christmas shopping with Dad, and I was holding the packages and waiting for him to pay for them. I guess I must have closed my eyes again, because he took hold of my shoulder and said I should pay attention and not 'be in a dream,' or else I'd end up with nothing in my arms, and some colored kid would have a real good Christmas! Or it could be a white kid too!"

His father had in his remarks mentioned only a "colored kid," but the boy wanted to be less specific. He has, in fact, remembered his father's social and racial views quite well and is insistently loyal to them. The father has worried about the impoverished condition of black people, expressed repeated concern for their lot. The father has also denounced the Klan in no uncertain terms — and other "redneck" social groups or activities. Not far from the Garden District live working-class whites (in the city's so-called Irish Channel district); and also not far away are clusters of black people — servants, many of them, to families like his. James has been driven through those neighborhoods, has heard opinions expressed about the people there, and has heard their lives connected to his — as it is and as it will be: "My father says I'll have to learn how to live with the colored, the Negro people, and I'll have to live with the rednecks. We have a lot of rednecks in Louisiana. They can cause trouble. They vote for someone who gets them excited. A lot of people don't know how to keep their tempers, and they go shouting in the streets. The rednecks hate the colored, and the colored hate the rednecks. My mother says she'd rather be with the rednecks, but my father says he trusts the colored more.

"We used to have a governess, she was French — from Paris, not New Orleans. She taught me to speak French. She didn't like a lot of the white people in the city. My father would agree with her, then my mother got angry. She said — she says she'll always say — white is white and black is black. The reason my mother let the governess go was that I was old enough to be in school all day; but my mother says she would have let her go anyway, because she was more interested in the colored and their troubles than taking care of me. I think she even joined the colored — the NAACP, my father said. She used to tell me that it was not the fault of the colored that they are poor; we made them be, the whites. I told my father, and he told her to stop talking to me about the races, and concentrate on the French language. So she did. But Daddy agrees with her; he says there's good and bad in every kind, and he says sometimes the worst kind are the rednecks.

But both parents make references to "the colored" as pickpockets, thieves; it is the boy who corrects them, reminds them of their own past observations. Neither parent argues with the boy. They are both impressed with what they call their son's "sensitivity." He is not, however, "a bleeding heart," they reassure themselves. He has heard himself openly talked about, heard his mother worry, right to his face, that he would get "too worried" about blacks and their struggles. And he has heard his father reassure the mother, remind her that children go through "stages." James doesn't know what a "stage" really is, but he knows what his father means — that for a while, but only for a while, it is all right that he worry a little more than his parents do about blacks or working-class whites or, indeed, the Indians.

The last have intrigued him for a long time — ever since he saw some of them being rounded up in a movie and heard his governess say that "it wasn't only the Negroes." He can still hear her repeating those words to him, to herself, to the one friend she had in New Orleans, whom she'd call on the phone, the boy listening in all the while. The governess read to him books that gave a chronicle of the fate of various Indian tribes, and James's parents did not object. But when, James, at six, talked of *becoming* an Indian and fighting on their side against "the white man," the mother began to ask around: did any of her friends know of a housekeeper who would be "good" with a boy like James or, even better, a "girl" from Europe who was here, didn't want to go back, and might enjoy a not too demanding job? The father called in the governess and told her stop talking to the boy about Indians. By that time the governess was ready to quit, her employers ready to fire her, and James quite ready to abandon all interest in this nation's racial or ethnic minorities. Still, the parents noticed after she was long gone that their son continued to worry over blacks who begged in the street or whites who cussed out blacks. When at eleven James was still applauding the Indians in the Westerns he saw, the parents lost their capacity for detached silence, and spoke out: the Indians were as cruel or brutal in their own way as the white man, and it's not fair to take sides.

The boy has learned that message; says it is a "prejudice" when a person takes sides with one party in a struggle and forgets about the viewpoint or experiences of the other side. But there are times when he abandons the various messages he has heard and plays all-out war. He mobilizes his considerable army of soldiers, tanks, airplanes, and shoots at the enemy. He includes in the enemy blacks, whites, Indians. He declares himself a general defending his territory — one of his father's plantations. His troops have been hired; he isn't calling upon friends or neighbors. They are contemporary Hessians, those men he controls and launches against what he calls "the Americans." Then he explains: "I could be the descendant of a French prince; he came here to Louisiana and then France left, but he held out, and no one noticed, until one day the census people came and spotted the plantation and they started asking a lot of questions. Then the government agents said they wanted us to give up, and let them own the plantation, and we could work for them! That's when I decided to fight! I said *never,* and I hired the troops, and they fought and won."

He goes through the motions — the arrangement and rearrangement of his troops. He pretends that guns are going off, makes noises for the sake of realism, abruptly ends the encounter. He declares himself, thereafter, "a kind prince"; he will not take advantage of those he has vanquished. But he will keep some of "the enemy" on his plantation. They will work the fields, produce good crops, look after the main house, and in return get "all the food they want." Of course they won't be eating his kind of food. They like french fries and sausages and Kool-Aid and candy; he has learned to like grapefruit, cut oranges, fortified cereal, lots of vegetables, and steak from which the fat has been trimmed. He has pecan pie or vanilla ice cream occasionally, but not every day. He takes vitamin pills year round. He uses Vitamin C in winter, as soon as anyone in the house begins to suffer the flu or a cold. He never eats chocolate; takes only a Life Saver occasionally. He used to like popcorn, but now finds it "too salty"; however, he is willing to supply "them," his various employees, with all the popcorn they desire.

It comes to that — the use of a blanket "them" in his story or fable or imaginary game; and also in his "real life," the expression he and many other children use for the day-to-day activity which a boy of his age has learned to take for granted. When he becomes more "realistic," more "grown up," he sees himself as a businessman, an architect who designs and builds shopping centers, a lawyer, a man who buys and sells land in Central America or crops from there. He talks of choosing one of those pursuits, or maybe trying all of them. He talks of becoming an experienced scuba diver. Every year the family goes to Mexico or the Caribbean after Christmas Day — to "unwind." His mother, he knows, has a case of the "nerves." She tires easily, takes to her bed for no discernible reason. She becomes demanding, more critical of the boy than usual. The father intervenes, reassures the child, tells him that time will soon enough bring a change in the mother's "spirits." The father goes further sometimes, insists that the country is going "mad" — so no wonder his wife wants virtually to lock herself up. The boy has heard talk of "therapy," of a possible "rest home," of too many pills. But always, it seems, as things are getting alarming, the mother inexplicably and to everyone's surprise "snaps out of it," an expression the father uses when talking to his son. And when the son wants to know how she has managed to become so much better, so soon, the father gives his reply: willpower.

The boy is told often that he, too, has obligations, must not stumble, has within himself an exacting conscience. There is a time, James knows, for fun and games, for strolls through cemeteries or mock games of a historical and military nature; but there are also times for intensely serious "business." He spells out the demands he has learned to place upon himself: "I'd like to know about the stock market. You can't inherit money and just forget about it. My father goes over the financial pages with me. He points out what's been happening to our money. I have to tell him whether we've lost or gained — the total. He bought me a little calculator, a pocket one, made in Japan. It's great fun, but it's very important business. If you have money, you have to know how to keep it, or you're in big trouble. I have my animals to take care of. I have a dog and I have three white mice. I used to have a snake, but my mother didn't want it around. The maid can't touch my mice, and only I feed the dog and take her for a walk. I have my homework, and that's *very* important. You have to have good marks to get into Princeton. Daddy says he was lucky. When he was young he could just know he'd go there. If I do my work, I will. But I've got to do my work."

He does indeed apply himself. He goes to a first-rate bilingual (English and French) private school, where, as he puts it, "all the kids are from homes like mine." What does he mean by that? He replies tersely at first: "They live in the Garden District." He thinks of an exception or two; then, prompted to explain who the students are and why they have come to his school, he goes into a description of the school's purposes. "There are some other schools that prepare you for college. But we have French as well as English. Some parents drive their children a long way to get them here. I'm lucky, I can walk. We have a colored girl in the school. She doesn't pay tuition, I hear. If you have a few kids different from yourself, then you learn from them. The colored girl — her father is a professor at a college, I think. There's a boy who is Chinese. I don't know how the Chinese got here in Louisiana. My Daddy says they're all over, and they came a long time ago. I think this boy is the son of a businessman who owns a motel. But mostly the kids are regular, and I know a lot of them well, because they live nearby or their parents know my parents."

When he does his homework he likes to stop after a bout of concentration and look out the window. He will see someone standing or walking and quickly do a sketch of the person. He will doodle, then put a big circle around the doodles, then throw them out. He will pick up a board with nails driven into it and arrange elastics around the nails, to make up various patterns. He will look at a map of the world, and wonder where he will go in the course of his life. He expects firmly and without qualification to visit every single continent before he is twenty-one. His father has told him so, because the father also wants to get to see every continent — before *he* reaches the age of forty-five. Left to be seen are Australia, Africa, and Asia; but the boy knows that "it only would take two trips at the most" for the goal he and his father have set. Once in a while he doodles like a geographer; he sketches North and South America, or Africa. He puts in a river or two, makes note, through dots, of certain cities he happens to think of, then abandons the diversion for a mathematics assignment or a composition he is struggling to write. He has trouble writing; he is quite fussy about language — is constantly asking his mother or his father about the meanings of various words or looking them up in the dictionary. Though he talks well, he finds it hard to write about his personal thoughts or ideas.

Nor is the boy unaware of the possible reasons he has for holding back, for struggling hard to achieve a more impersonal essay than an English teacher may have in mind as desirable. "My father says that once you've put something down on paper, you're committed to it. When you're committed, you're really on the line — you can't just forget about the whole business. My father once wrote a letter to the newspaper; he said that he was against the colored people going to our schools, but the law is the law, and if the judge said they had to go, then we should all obey the judge. Well, we had to disconnect the phone, and we got letters from people saying they were going to kill us. We were scared. The police came, and they looked at the letters. They had a police car near the house for a few days. My father hired a detective to watch the house. My mother drove me the two blocks to school. When it was all over, my father said there was one lesson to learn: if you have an opinion, keep it to yourself. My mother said she didn't agree, because if no one expressed any opinions, it would be like living in a dictatorship. But Daddy said that he wasn't against *speaking* your opinion; he just thinks that there are a lot of no-good people around, and they are ignorant, and they are violent, and if they don't like what they hear from a person, they're as likely to try to hurt him, or even kill him, as not. So, the best thing to do is stay out of their way — the mob."

That word "mob" has interested him for some time. In one of his doodles he drew a mob, a lot of people pressed again one another, their bodies not distinguishable, their faces small and sometimes twisted. He used shading to connect faces, or stray hands and legs and torsos — a rather powerful sketch, actually (Figure 54). And he didn't throw it out as he often has done. He gave it a title, "The Mob," and put it on his bulletin board. He has read about mobs in history books — the mobs that turned the French Revolution into an orgy of killing, with the innocent suffering as much as the guilty. He has heard his father talk about "mob rule," the danger in a democracy. He has seen a mob, too; the frenzied white men and women who heckled black children of his own age when they tried to enter previously all-white schools. For days, weeks, months, that mob persisted, aided and abetted by a city's indifference, a state's defiance of federal laws, and, for a long time, a national government's (in 1960, under President Eisenhower) reluctance to move quickly or effectively. James was taken by his parents to the scene of the riots and mob formation, will never forget what he saw and heard — from the mob, and from his parents, as they drove away and reflected upon what they had seen: "The women were calling the colored girls bad names. The men were threatening the girls. A lot of people had posters, telling the girls to stay away and never come near the school. The police were just standing there, and my father said he thought the police were joking with the mob, and encouraging them, instead of telling them to cut it out. When the girls were gone — inside the school building — the mob stayed and they cheered and shouted and said they'd be back in the morning. On the way home my father said that there's a great danger in a country like ours that mobs will take over, because there are a lot of ignorant people, and they listen to ignorant politicians, and the next thing you know, there's a lot of trouble. My mother said she never wanted to see that neighborhood again. My father said he agreed, but mobs can move into any neighborhood, even ours."

He was younger then; the words above, spoken five years later, have to do with memories that still linger. A city's turmoil became for a rich and prominent family the basis of an emotional series of discussions which the child did not so easily shake off. The father took the boy back, just the two of them. They never left the car, but they saw once again the hate and threatening violence. Afterwards, the father repeated to his son certain philosophical premises, which the boy in subsequent years has fashioned into a way of looking at the city of New Orleans, the state of Louisiana, the United States of America.

When he had completed his drawing of a mob scene, and drawn a circle around it, he pinned the paper to the cork of his "message to myself center," as he calls the bulletin board, and began to talk about his views: "If that mob broke through the circle, we'd all be in trouble. My father says there's always that danger. When we go downtown to his club, the people you meet on the streets and coming out of the stores — a lot of them look as if they might join a mob if something got them upset. They push and shove; Dad says they're already half a mob — the way they act when they go into the department stores. Even in the good restaurants you'll meet people who push when they're standing in line, and they make a lot of noise, and they could cause trouble, if they weren't in a good mood. That's why the city has to have policemen who know how to keep control, and that's why the state has its own police, and the government has the troops, and there's the National Guard.

"My father was a colonel in the army. He says a strong army is important. If we didn't have the army, the Russians would invade us. And there'd be mobs all over, and the country wouldn't be the same. A lot of people don't believe in obeying the law. They want to steal and rob; or they want to hit someone; or they want to march up and down on the streets and scare people. If the police don't stop mobs from forming, then the city begins to fall apart. We almost had the whole city of New Orleans become a huge mob a few years ago, and it could happen again."

He draws a picture of a policeman, makes him tan, burly, wide-eyed. He provides the man with a billy club in one hand, a gun in the other. The reason: he has just seen a thief and is going to take after him, catch him, apprehend him. The officer has another gun in a holster. He has a large badge on his chest. James shows no interest in turning the portrait of the man into a street scene. He does not provide, either, a sky or any ground for the officer to stand on (Figure 55). He explains the reason he doesn't want to show an actual chase: "I've seen the police, and I talk a lot with one policeman who stands near our school, but I've never seen any thieves, so I don't know what they look like. I've asked my father if he has ever seen a thief, and he said no — but then he changed his mind and said he's probably seen thousands of them, but not when they're actually stealing something, or being chased by the police." And anyway, he wouldn't want to draw a thief even if he had caught a glimpse of one. He prefers to draw pictures of friends or allies rather than enemies.

There was a time when he himself thought about becoming a policeman. He mentioned his idea to his parents, and was not actively discouraged. His father knows the chief of the New Orleans police, and so the boy was brought to headquarters and shown around; he met a number of officers, got a ride in a cruiser, and even saw a few rookies being given training. When a year or so passed, and James was still talking about the glories of a policeman's life and his own intention of sharing in those glories later on, the mother began to have second thoughts and to speak them. She was sure there were other boys who would grow up to be quite satisfactory policemen; James had "better things to do." The boy couldn't imagine what they were. The mother came up with a few suggestions: law, business, or the boy's long-standing interest in architecture. But James would not budge; he was going to be a policeman. He remembers telling his mother that "there is no work more important than a police officer's"; and he remembers telling her who told him so: his father.

And it was the father who carefully remained loyal to his earlier pronouncements. He told the boy that he agreed — the police do indeed "hold everything together." He bought him two children's books that try to tell boys and girls about the working lives of the police. He allowed the boy to watch television programs that featured the activities of the police. And gradually he began to tell the boy how the police in turn need others to help *them* — prosecuting attorneys, judges who are not "soft" but utterly determined to "protect the public," and, not least, "ordinary citizens," who will back the police, if need be, against their enemies. The boy learned, with respect to "enemies," that the police not only have to hunt down criminals but to deal with the attacks of all sorts of "dangerous people." Who? The father has been both vague and precise. He has referred to "lawless people," and to mobs, of course; also to the Ku Klux Klan, but no less to "civil rights agitators."

Eventually James began to lose interest in the police — so far as a career for himself was concerned. At eleven he had even decided that the police had failed to curb various "mobs"; they therefore may be part of the nation's problem. He has wondered out loud repeatedly why Princeton University doesn't train police officers — who would, he is sure, be much more competent and effective than many now on the force. His father has agreed but tried to explain to the boy what is meant by the expression "division of labor." The boy tries hard and with considerable success to explain the concept: "Some people are good at being carpenters and some people are good at being architects. The carpenter doesn't know what to do in a house that is being built unless the architect makes his plans, a blueprint, and shows the carpenter what has to be done. That's division of labor. Princeton University is where you learn to be an architect, or a lawyer. If you want to be a carpenter, then you don't go to Princeton. You can learn that in a high school or from a carpenter who will teach you. The policeman is like a carpenter; he doesn't need to go to college. If you went up to a policeman — to most New Orleans cops — and asked them if they would have liked to go to Princeton, they'd think you were some nut trying to be funny. They wouldn't even know, a lot of them about Princeton; it's too far away. And my father says they don't like Tulane, and that's right here in our city."

The mob he saw as a child is the mob he thinks about when he stresses the importance of the police to New Orleans. When a Tulane professor criticized the city's police for being heavy-handed in the way they dealt with blacks or poor people regardless of race, the boy rallied to the defense of the police — after hearing his father do likewise. At such moments James stakes out an interesting position. He condemns Tulane, condemns the people of both races who complain against the police, declares himself only too anxious to leave the city and attend Princeton when the time comes. But he will come back, and then, he hopes, the police will be at his side protecting the Garden District, he says bluntly and unashamedly, from the people who "want to take away what we own here." His father has said as much: "Dad says that when people want to cut down on the number of police we have, and cripple them with rules and regulations, it's because those people don't want the city protected. Once the police are gone, the mobs will start marching, and they'll come here and break into the homes. We'll lose all we've got."

James has heard his mother argue time and again that the family ought to sell their city home, go live upstate on their plantation year around — or, alternatively, take an apartment, in which they would be "less exposed." The father has said no, he will not budge; he insists that once fear obtains that degree of leverage over the lives of people, they won't know when to stop running. He wants to stand and fight. He has several guns in the home, two rifles and a handgun. He does target practice on weekends, when he and his family do indeed go to their plantation or their oceanside home in Mississippi. His son has also learned how to shoot, possesses a lightweight rifle, enjoys using it in the woods of northern Louisiana.

Upon occasion James has thought up a rather spirited if harrowing scenario of what might prompt him to aim a weapon and pull its trigger inside the New Orleans house. In a picture drawn at the age of ten he showed himself at the window of his Garden District home, with his newly acquired gun. The street outside was filled with another of his "mobs," and the assault was obviously directed toward his family's property. The house seems vulnerable indeed, not the sturdy, even imposing, building he sometimes draws — as if the mob had already won part of its objective simply by putting in an appearance. The boy is prepared to fight to ward off the enemy. The mother, the boy explained later, is in the kitchen preparing for the necessity of flight — cooking food, filling up a thermos or two, packing a suitcase. There is a lot of smoke coming out of the chimney, more than one expects, since the home is in New Orleans, not known for its cold weather. The sky is cloudy; no sun is shown (Figure 56). The boy explains the smoke — and much more: "I think my mother would probably be burning some family papers. My father says we shouldn't keep anything important at home. But my mother doesn't like to go back and forth to the bank. She keeps her papers in her desk. She's told us that if a robber wants to find out how much stocks she inherited from her father, that's all right. But if a mob tried to break in, I'll bet my mother wouldn't want them poking into her papers!"

A year later, as he talked yet another time about the police and a recent news story of a robbery in a Garden District home, James began to speak of envy — his envy. If only he were "one of those poor colored kids" he had seen five years earlier, walking past a mob into school; then he wouldn't be worried about thieves and robbers and mobs and the destruction of his home. It is an anxious and fearful life, the one he has inherited from his parents — or so he was beginning to believe. Better to be poor; one has little or nothing to lose! Nevertheless, he had no choice but to do the best he could under the circumstances — try to gird himself for future hazards, stresses, times of outright danger, if not disaster.

"I know that I've got a lot of advantages," he announced a week before turning twelve. "But it's not all easy for us, here in the Garden District," he went on. And he knew exactly why: "The more you have, the more people want what you have. My Dad says he wakes up, and he's dreamed that he's been robbed and lost his watch, his wallet, his key chain, and even the coins in his pocket. I've had the same dream:

a kid came — he was white, I believe, but he could be colored — and he took away my model planes and my Tonka toys. My father said it was just me saying I was too old for those toys. I told him I disagreed. I said a lot of kids want my toys, just like a lot of grown-ups want his wallet! He said I was right. Then my mother asked him again if we couldn't please move away to the country. And he said no. And she wouldn't talk to us anymore. She asked to be excused, and she rang and had her breakfast brought upstairs to her bedroom. And she wasn't too nice later on, either. She was working on her plants until a minute before supper, and then she said she didn't feel too good, so she was going to skip eating. But Dad went upstairs, and persuaded her to come down, and the cook had made a good supper — her favorite red snapper — and we forgot about the trouble. It's always around the corner, though — the trouble that comes when one of our neighbors tells us that someone tried to break in; and then mother gets upset. She's had three locks put on all our doors. And we have an alarm that's supposed to be the best. Dad says he'd hire a private detective to watch the house at night, if it would make mother feel better; but he says it's crazy to do that now, and if he ever really has to do it, then he *will* sell the house and we'll leave the whole United States, not just New Orleans, because by that time there will be mobs in the small towns, too!"

The boy is sure that there are some poor children, black and white, who will never grow up to be greedy, lawbreaking, violent people. He recalls quite vividly the dignity of "the colored kids" who started school desegregation. He recalls the "nice" children of his parents' servants — boys and girls whom he has, however, seen only occasionally, because their mothers or fathers are not prone to bring them to work. He wishes there were more like "them" — those children of his family's maid and laundress and gardener and handyman, who also serves as a butler at formal parties: "They are polite. They look at you with real respect in their eyes. I told my cousin that the colored kids are the equal of their parents. My cousin is going to Princeton next year. He said the colored up North aren't as nice as they are down here. My Dad says the children of our servants would naturally be good, but some other colored kids in New Orleans aren't so good. My mother says she's never met a bad colored kid from the country; the city makes the colored greedy and they lose their manners and they get in trouble with the law. I asked her about the children we've met, the children of our servants, and she said they're special.

"We go to their houses every Christmas; my father was brought up to do that. On Christmas Day we bring gifts to the servants before we open up our own presents. We've been going for years. I was once given a long lecture, because my father said I was rude when we went to the servants' homes. I didn't ask after them, and I didn't try to make conversation with them. I guess I just stood there. I must have been about six. I remember it was when those colored kids were having all the trouble with the mobs. The next year I was much better. I got so friendly with one colored boy, our maid's son, that I asked him to come over and play with my Lego. He said he'd like to, but his mother said no. My father said he'd try to get us together one day, the colored boy and me; but afterwards, in the car, I got another lecture. I realize now that I was too young to realize how to behave. It was a bad thing to do, because it really embarrassed the maid's whole family, and the boy must have felt bad. My father was sure that the maid gave her son a whipping. She talks a lot about whipping her children when they don't behave. I asked my father if he wouldn't turn around, please, and let me go back in the house and apologize, and ask the maid to leave her son alone. But my Dad said no, if we tried that there'd be even more trouble, and they'd all be in a real scared state over there, and they wouldn't know what to say or do. So, we drove on, and I realized then and there how careful you've got to be when you're talking with colored people, and it's our responsibility."

The word "responsibility" is one he has learned to use with increasing frequency. When he was six years old, and his parents were upset by the racial struggle and near chaos facing New Orleans, there was a lot of talk in front of him about "responsibility." When the boy was taken to see the mob in action, his father told him afterward, day after day, that it was the "responsibility" of families like theirs to fight for "law and order," to resist "mob rule," to prevent "violence" from spreading — to the point that the city becomes "a jungle." The boy still links together in his mind those various words or phrases. He talks about a safari his cousin went on; then goes on to remark upon how "violent" the jungle is and how hard it must have been for the white men who explored Africa to come to terms with the various tribes, as well as the animals. So with our own settlers, who came West against the opposition of Indians, some of them violent. His uncle worked for a while in Latin America as an executive of a major American corporation and has told James and his father a number of times how "primitive" the people are in countries like Brazil, Colombia, Venezuela, and how much "responsibility" an American company incurs as it tries to "raise the standard of living," "stay in business," and "make a reasonable profit."

James has heard, and will not forget, that there are a lot of people in this country who have never been within a thousand miles of "a jungle" or "an underdeveloped nation" and have no idea what the people of such places are like — but who are against all American companies on principle, and "make a lot of noise" to that effect here and abroad. The same holds nearer at home, the boy knows, at the age of eleven. He is worried about his nation's future: "My uncle told us that he tried to get the people near the jungle of Colombia to be clean and to take medicines, so they wouldn't be tired and they wouldn't feel so bad, and they could work better and live better. But they suspected him, and they were very superstitious. They need a lot of education, and that takes years. That's why the colored in our country should go into the same schools as whites do; then the colored will begin to learn a lot more than they once did, and they will be better off. The trouble is, a lot of white people aren't too good either. You'd think white people would know better, but they don't. It depends on who the white person is. The same with the colored: my father says there are some very smart colored people, and they're more civilized than the white. Dad told Mother he wouldn't mind going to lunch at his club with a colored man, if he was the president of a colored university, or a doctor, a surgeon. There's supposed to be a very good colored surgeon in Nashville, my mother heard someone say. She says she's never been convinced the colored should go to school with whites; she says they should civilize themselves, like the surgeon did, and stay away from the rednecks. Dad says *they're* the *most* uncivilized — worse than any colored are.

"My father went to a meeting; he talked with judges and he met the chief of police, and he said they all agreed that America is in trouble. By the time I grow up New Orleans might need an army to keep the peace. The colored have become more violent. They're not as polite as they used to be, except for our servants and some people like them. The rednecks are looking for fights with the colored. My father says we've got to do all we can to be umpires; it's our responsibility. My uncle says that he used to think he was crazy for going to South America and trying to live there, but now he's sorry he's become vice-president and lives here, because it's safer in the jungle than in downtown New Orleans; and it's getting worse here, and you can't be sure that even in your own neighborhood you're safe. People want the government to take everything away from the people who have earned it, and they want a lot of things for nothing, so it's like the jungle, with everyone trying to beat out everyone else — only in the jungle, when you come there from this country, and you have your bulldozers and rifles, and you bring food and medicine for the natives, then you can make them work, and they live better than ever before, and it's pretty safe down there. Up here it's getting more and more dangerous. My uncle says he's glad he's lived most of his life; the way it's going in America, everyone will soon be nervous about being robbed. But my father says I shouldn't pay any attention to talk like that, because there's always going to be *some* trouble, and if you read the diaries of my grandfather and my great-grandfather, they were in a lot of trouble too, but they didn't retreat, and they knew how to live up to their responsibilities, and they did right well, so it's not all so bad."

No, indeed; he has wonderful times throughout the year. He goes north to the family's plantation on weekends; there he fishes, learns to shoot and hunt, swims in a pool that is heated (hence usable all year), goes horse riding, learns to play tennis. In addition to family travel abroad, there are other trips, too; James occasionally goes skiing in Colorado with his parents on long winter weekends, missing a day or so of school, or goes to the family's home on the Gulf Coast, where he has learned to sail. In fact, as he has noted often, the family's "main home" (his expression) seems like a stopping place: a place among places — all very reassuring, actually, for people who have increasing doubts about city life, however privileged it be.

But the city at least offers the excellent private school he attends, and the teachers there are quite accommodating as well as serious-minded and demanding. "They expect us to miss school," he observes. As a result, they keep high standards, get a lot of work done with each child when he or she is in attendance, and assign a lot of homework to someone going away with his or her parents. The headmaster has even told the children that absences are not all that detrimental, so long as the student really takes advantage of the time spent in school: "He said he knows our families are living busy lives, and have a lot to do, and places they have to go, so he doesn't get upset when our mothers or fathers write letters saying we're going to be out for a couple of days, or even a week. He says that we're all from good homes, and our parents have gone to college, and they're successful, and they want us to be successful, so they'll keep us working and make sure we don't lose out if we miss school. My father does keep me working, too; no matter where we go on a weekend, he makes sure I have my books with me, and either he or my mother go over the work. My spelling has never been very good, and my father is always asking me to spell words. We'll be driving, and he'll say: 'James, how do you spell "restaurant"?' Then I do, and then my mother says to him: 'You must be hungry!' I think I've learned how to spell from my father more than from my teachers. They say you have to keep practicing, and my father makes sure I do. Even at breakfast, he'll look up from his paper and ask me a word. When we're skiing or way over in Europe, he remembers to 'give me a word.' He'll stop what he's been doing and say: 'James, let me give you another word.' I tell him okay, I'm ready."

James looks forward to the future — when he will be the father and a child of his will be asked how to spell. He assumes he will have a son; he bears the number III after his name, and he wishes that one day the number IV will appear after the name of a newborn baby in the family. The family will persist, he is sure; it has for centuries — through wars, revolutions, natural and man-made disasters. Maybe there will be a strategic retreat: the abandonment of New Orleans, even of Louisiana. But the father has said that this will not be necessary. In the event of a disaster, however, there are always the mountains of east Tennessee or of Colorado.

The son is reassured as he contemplates the safety of the mountains, but he hopes never to leave New Orleans. He remarks upon the affection he feels for his Garden District home, predicts that his own children will love going there and visiting his old room. He might, one day, have a house nearby, well placed in the District, and so his parents and his future wife and their children would be quite *intime,* as his mother puts it. And maybe "the colored" and "the rednecks" by then would be the ones to have left New Orleans. After all, as his parents keep mentioning, cities are expensive places to live in. James has wondered why the poorer people don't move out, find cheaper places to live. His father has explained that people stay in the city because they can get work more easily there than in the small towns or the country. But the father has also mentioned repeatedly that the unemployment rate is high in New Orleans, so the boy has felt puzzled.

He has asked what the poor who can't find work do. He was told that "a lot of them don't do anything, they just loaf around." James suggested that they might eventually get tired of "loafing around" in the city. They might pick themselves up and go back to places like northern Louisiana or the Mississippi Delta. At least they will be able to hunt and fish — and so eat rather well. In the small towns or the countryside they'd feel better, live better, and if they got into trouble, they'd know the sheriff, and he'd give them a second chance and keep a friendly eye on them. The father heard the boy out, said nothing for a while, then decided that his son was a social prophet, a young person of hope and wisdom. When he acknowledged as much out loud, the boy smiled, asked his father if he was "just fooling" or "trying to be nice." No, the man was quite serious. Well, if that is the case, won't the Garden District soon be as safe at night as the homes his parents owned elsewhere? The father shook his head, told his son that it may take decades for his prediction to come true — for the poor and potentially troublesome ones to be gone from New Orleans. Meanwhile, they had to gird themselves for more trouble, rather than less. The son asked when he might own a pistol as well as a beginner's rifle. Soon, he was told. The boy left for his room, where he looked at a gun catalogue and made a selection, which he showed to his father, who said yes, one day the two of them would go make the purchase.

When James has recalled the mob scene he saw at the age of six, he has wondered repeatedly whether the parents of the black children had guns at home, or on them as they walked with their children — "just in case." The father used to say each time that he doubted very much "any colored person would pull a gun on a white mob." But more recently he has changed his mind. The city has seen crowds of blacks stand up and assert themselves rather forcefully, so the father is quite sure that never again will he or his son see what they once saw — terrorized children and parents heckled mercilessly, with no apparent inclination to fight back. The boy goes a step further, speculates that blacks have been secretly "practicing," hiding guns and using them to aim at targets, on the assumption that one day there might be an awful confrontation. He would fight to death to defend his home, his neighborhood, and has imagined himself doing so. Blacks would, too. That is the bottom line, he is sure — defense of one's place of residence against mob assault.

Grandchild of a Mine Owner

Four daughters, and each so different; everyone comes up with words to that effect. The mother is delighted with her girls, the father has long since given up being annoyed that he has no "heir," a word he once summoned with a certain bitterness and now uses casually — such as when he reminds his wife that the girls will marry someday and maybe provide a grandson or two. But that is all in the future. Right now the oldest girl, Marjorie, is a mere twelve. She has an eleven-year-old sister, a seven-year-old sister, and a five-year-old sister, who cheerfully announces, often, that after her "they gave up." Their father is quite willing to tell them all his theory of why they have no brother. Their generation, he has informed them several times, is the first one in the family that lacks male offspring. There has to be a reason, and the father wonders whether it is the move to Charleston (West Virginia) that accounts for, in his phrase, the "chain of girls."

The father first heard the theory proposed by his father, a mine owner who likes to visit Charleston, but prefers to live in Mingo County, where he owns several mines. The grandfather is not a "first-generation owner," as he refers to some newly rich mountain men who have recently (in the 1970s) made a lot of money stripping the land mercilessly, or going after second- or third-rate coal in hazardous seams — anything to find the stuff and send it on to a newly profitable market. No, the grandfather of "those four Charleston girls," as he playfully calls them upon occasion, was himself born "pretty well-off." *His* father owned a store, a small mine, and, late in life, an automobile agency. The grandfather went to West Virginia University in Morgantown and thought of going to law school, living in Charleston, as his son eventually did.

But there were family investments and interests to be looked after, and as the grandfather has pointed out, it was a good thing he did go back home after college: "We're not one of America's richest families, by any means, but we're quite well-off, and by the standards of West Virginia, of Appalachia, we're wealthy. I guess we're wealthy by national standards; we have several million salted away — it's no secret. But we've worked for the money. I'm no fly-by-night strip miner. I've never wanted to squeeze profits, just make them! I try to be a responsible man, and I try to think of my son and my grandchildren. My people have been in this state for many generations, and I hope the family never leaves. I didn't mind my son becoming a lawyer and leaving Mingo County. If I'd done that, we wouldn't have the money we all have now. My father was born dirt-poor, a subsistence farmer the census people would call him, from up a hollow. But he came down from that hollow and he borrowed money and he bought land and there was coal under it and he just kept on making money and investing it. I had about a hundred thousand dollars to play with when he died, a lot of money in the nineteen-thirties. I didn't gamble and I didn't drink, and I knew how to take risks — *good* risks; so I made a lot more than a hundred thousand dollars. The times got good, especially during the Second World War and afterwards. We needed coal, and I had it to sell. Also, I spotted IBM and Xerox and Polaroid, companies like those, right at the beginning; I put my money in them. I bet on free enterprise!

"Things haven't been so good in the nineteen-seventies. I'll tell you, I've pulled a little out of the stock market, and put my money back in land, where it all started — our family's rise from poverty, you could call it. My son says I should forget about making money. He says we've got enough — plenty, as a matter of fact — and the best thing to do is keep it in good securities and enjoy ourselves. But that's him; I'm me. You don't change an old dog; he's younger, and he's different. Up there in Charleston they live a fancier life, and they don't want to be caught *crawling* for money, the way we do out here. But I've never had to compromise my principles; maybe my father did — if he did, he never told me. I'll bet my son doesn't even mention the word 'money' to his girls."

He is correct. The son is a prominent West Virginia lawyer, a member of several corporate boards, an influential stockholder in a number of local companies — and of course not without substantial shares in national companies. But he doesn't like to talk about such matters, nor does his wife, the daughter of a West Virginia bank president. Their daughter Marjorie wrote a composition for her sixth-grade teacher about the future, and never indicated how she'd be able to do all the things mentioned. The girl wrote about ballet lessons, a trip around the world, a spell in Holland, where she would learn about various cheeses and wear wooden shoes, a year or two on a ranch out West, with several horses to ride. Marjorie's teacher surprised the girl with this comment: "A very nice paper, full of interesting plans. But do you have the money for all this?" The teacher was being a bit facetious, but Marjorie did not respond with a smile. She was confused, upset. She came home and showed the paper to her mother and father, then with a touch of anxiety, asked them whether in fact the teacher was suggesting that there wasn't enough money in the family to support the aspirations of the children? The girl's mother contributed to at least an hour or two of apprehension and uncertainty by saying she didn't "know anything about money," and so "Daddy will explain everything later." That evening Marjorie's Dad told her not to worry, there was "enough money" so that she could go ahead and "have her dreams."

But the father had no desire to sit down and talk at any length with his daughter about money. She remembers a somewhat awkward, even tense time of it: "Daddy said I shouldn't be thinking about money, because there are more important things in the world. He said the teacher was just pulling my leg. If she wasn't, he'd get her fired. He asked me about the horse riding, and I told him I was doing real good; the jumping was getting better and better. Then he asked me if I wanted more allowance. I said no, a dollar and a half a week was still enough. I don't even spend that, a lot of weeks. He told me it's a good idea to learn how to save, and if I wanted, he'd open up an account for me in the bank and I could put away some of my allowance. He said if I put a lot of the allowance away, he might add some of his own money to my account, 'a matching amount.' Then we started talking about my room, and how it should be neater, and it wasn't fair to expect the maid to clean up after us all the time. I told him that when I grow up and I have my own house, I would like to have a maid, but it *was* 'good discipline' for us girls to know how to clean our own rooms. I asked him if I'd be able to afford a maid. That's when he got annoyed with me. He slapped his knee and said it was getting time for me to go up to bed, because I had school the next day and a ballet lesson afterwards. I told him I was just trying to ask a question, but he wouldn't answer. He said he didn't like all this talk of money, and I should keep my room neat — and he might go talk with my teacher so she wouldn't make another comment like the one she did about money on the composition I wrote. Then I said good-night."

Marjorie didn't let the matter drop, though. She tried to have a talk with her mother. She told her mother that she thought that Daddy had been upset by the questions she put to him. The mother said yes, that was true. Her father had said later that night (to his wife) that he hoped none of his daughters became "money conscious," because it's "not at all nice for a girl to be like that." When the mother had finished telling her daughter what the father had said, the girl immediately asked this: "If I was a boy, then would Daddy want me not to be asking him a lot of questions about money?" The mother didn't answer right off, but she did say, finally, that "it makes no difference, boy or girl; it's wrong to have your mind dwelling on money." Marjorie gave in, said she didn't really care about money; she had just become curious as a result of her teacher's remark.

But the girl was not convinced by her own words; she had, anyway, asked her mother several times how much money her father made each year. The mother had said she didn't know, and the girl was persuaded that was so: "My mother told me that if our lives depended on it, she couldn't tell someone how much money Daddy makes, because she doesn't know — and she doesn't really want to know. I told her I didn't want to know; it's just that you hear kids talking, and they'll say my father owns this, and my father makes that, and then you begin wondering — what does *my* father do? My father is a lawyer, I know. In our social studies class the teacher asked us to put down in the papers we wrote what our fathers did and what we would like to do when we grow up. We were writing about the state of West Virginia, and the teacher told us a lot about the state, and she told us that it was coal that is our biggest asset. She said that if any of us come from families that make money from coal, we should write that down too. I didn't think I should write down that we made money from coal, because Daddy is a lawyer. I started worrying later, though — because my grandfather owns some mines. But that's his money, and not Daddy's, I think. Anyway, I said Daddy is a lawyer, and I'd like to be part of a ballet company.

"I don't think I could be a leading ballerina, like I once wanted to be. The ballet teacher says I don't concentrate enough and work hard enough. She said you have to be *possessed*. I asked her what she meant, and she laughed and said if I knew then I'd be a future ballerina! I didn't know what she was talking about, so she explained to me that there are very few good ballerinas in the whole world, and to be one you have to give your whole life to dancing, and that's too much for most people to give — even for her, and she's a good ballet dancer. That's right; I'd like to do other things as well. But I would like to dance in a ballet company, for a year or two, maybe. My mother says I might change my mind later, but if I didn't, she'd back me up. She says my father might not like the idea of ballet as an *occupation* — that he'd rather I take ballet lessons, but do something else: go to college, I guess. Maybe that's what I'll do, go to college. But the ballet teacher says that you can't work part-time for a ballet company. So, if I want to be part of a company, I'll have to postpone college."

Marjorie does rather well at ballet; she is the most committed of her friends. Her mother has taken her to New York City three times to attend the ballet there and also go shopping. They stay at the Plaza, dine at various French restaurants, go shopping in Bergdorf Goodman's and Saks Fifth Avenue. Marjorie was ten when she first went; at eleven she went twice; and she has her mother's promise of an annual visit. The mother went to Vassar and knows New York City well. She also believes in taking each child off alone, as the particular girl gets old enough, and since Marjorie loves ballet and New York City is where ballet is most commonly available, it is there her mother takes her.

Marjorie is quick to point out how flexible and versatile her mother is. For example, Susan, the daughter a year younger than Marjorie, loves the outdoors, is an excellent horse rider, has already won several prizes in shows, and loves as well to go on long hikes with a friend or two, even camp out. The girls take a bare minimum of food, have learned to cook outdoors, make do without matches, find safe and relatively comfortable places to sleep. Susan and her mother go on "overnights" alone, setting out from a "camp" the family has about an hour out of Charleston and wandering through paths, up hills, along a stream or two, and then back. Marjorie has no such interests or inclinations; she likes to ride, but "for pleasure," not "to compete"; and she prefers the city to the country. The family lives outside Charleston, actually; the girls don't get into the city all that much. Even their mother stays away except for certain evenings — a play, a concert. When Marjorie talks of the city, she has in mind not Charleston, West Virginia, but New York City, or Pittsburgh, or Washington, D.C. Her father has taken the family repeatedly to the last two cities; he has board meetings, and while he attends them, his wife and daughters (and a maid, who comes along to help out) "have a good time," as Marjorie sees it. They go shopping. They go to the movies. They visit museums. They eat in elegant restaurants. They romp through fine hotels, and especially enjoy room service.

How can Susan have any doubt that such a life is the very best one imaginable? Marjorie asks that question often — but answers, she knows, only for herself. She and Susan have always disagreed, have fought constantly, have entirely different hopes and plans, or so one tells the other on many occasions. When Marjorie was nine she drew a picture of herself, another of her sister. Marjorie's self-portrait shows a limber-legged ballerina in a conventional pose — one leg up, the other only barely touching the floor. She is smiling, has light blue eyes that are open, stretches her arms upward to the ceiling of what turns out to be a stage when the drawing is done (Figure 57). As for Susan, she is shown under a cluster of trees, and near some bushes, holding a horse by the reins. She is looking down at the ground, and the viewer doesn't actually get a direct look at the girl's face. Rain is falling, the rider and her horse have stopped for a moment to take cover (Figure 58).

Marjorie was willing to make more distinctions than those she acknowledged and portrayed in her drawings: "My sister says she hates fancy clothes, and she doesn't like to get dressed up at all, even for church. My mother has to insist. Sometimes she talks back to Mom, and then Daddy steps in. I like to get new dresses. I like my ballet clothes, and I go with Mom when she buys her clothes, and she buys some for me. Susie won't go. Mother has to order clothes for Susie, and get our sewing lady to fix them up. The lady comes once a week. She does the laundry, and she sews. My mother was taught to sew, but she doesn't like to do it. She says she won't even teach me, because she can tell that I'm going to be like her; but Susie is a great friend of the sewing lady, and Susie says *she* wouldn't mind being a sewing lady herself! She would work one day a week, then ride her horse or go camping on the other days! We had a talk at the supper table once. Susie told Daddy of her plan, and he laughed and said she'd change her mind when she got older — because she'd never make enough, with one day of sewing, to live the rest of the week and be able to pay her bills. She told Daddy that she wouldn't be spending much, just enough for snacks, and she'd camp out a lot. Daddy asked her where she'd *live,* and she said here at home, of course. Then he laughed again and told her that he *hoped* she did, because if she didn't, she'd be in real trouble, trying to get by.

"Susie didn't like what Daddy said. She told him she could camp out all week, even in the winter. Then Daddy started listing all the expenses she'd run up, and he asked her about the worst winter days, or the summer days, with the mosquitoes. She didn't give in. She argued with Daddy until he got angry, and he told her to stop talking because she didn't know what she was talking about. That's when Susie had her temper; she told Daddy she didn't want to live the way we do. He asked her what she meant, and she said 'like rich people.' He turned to Mother and asked her where Susie got the idea we're rich. Mother said she never talks with us about money. I spoke up; I told Daddy that Mom was telling the truth. Susie said we were all playing pretend, the way she would when she was five or six. She turned to me and told me I was rich, and she said she was, and she said everyone in the family was. My father said he was glad our younger sisters had eaten and were being put in bed. He told Mother that Susie and I should eat with them for a while, until we knew what to say at the table and what not to say.

"I started to cry. I hadn't said anything, really. Mother defended me. She told Dad that it wasn't fair to blame *both* Susie and me, when it was Susie who was doing the talking. Then Susie said she couldn't see what she'd done that was so wrong. Daddy decided to give us a lecture. He said we might as well understand who we are and why we live the way we do. He told us about his grandfather and his father, and how they worked hard, and how they didn't work so we would just sit around and do nothing. He said he sets his alarm for six in the morning and he likes to read over his work for a half an hour before he comes down for breakfast. He eats little in the morning, just fruit, toast, and coffee — because he wants to be in 'top shape' for the office. He said he didn't *have* to work. He said he could just sit at home and watch television and read the newspaper. Then he wouldn't be doing anything for anyone else, only living like a lazy person does. He said he could play golf all day. But if he did, it wouldn't be any better than watching the television set. He said we had to learn the difference between a hobby and work. It's a hobby to go for a walk, or ride on one of our horses, but it's work when you have a job, and you go every day to the office."

There was much more to the lecture, but the girl didn't hear any more; she complained of a headache, a stomachache, a sore throat — all three! — and left, followed by her mother. Her father stayed with her sister, and they apparently kept on talking for a half hour or so, Marjorie learned the next morning. Not that she had any clearer idea, then, what her father meant when he talked about their collective "responsibility" as a family to provide "leadership." She knew when she was in the first grade that her father was an important person in Charleston, West Virginia. He was on the school's board of trustees, and her teachers obviously deferred to him when he came to visit the classroom. During one recess period she was overheard by the teacher telling another child that her Daddy was a lawyer; the teacher added, "a prominent lawyer." Marjorie didn't know exactly what "prominent" meant; at the supper table that evening she asked — and heard about the "responsibilities" that go with prominence.

When she was seven she drew prominence, so to speak; she made a painting of an office building, made it quite tall, and placed her father on top of the building. He was almost as tall as the building, and his head quite literally touched the sky. The sun seemed like a neighbor of his. The earth appeared as a distant object, perhaps of little concern, because the father's head was turned upward (Figure 59). The girl's explanation for that posture was quite direct: "Daddy likes to listen to the wind. There's a lot of wind on top of tall buildings. He's probably thinking while the wind blows. Daddy likes to climb up hills and mountains. He says he thinks better, when he's climbed to the top of a hill, and he can see for miles, and the wind is strong, and he's away from all the things he has to do down below."

Five years later, at twelve, she still had only a vague sense of what those "things" were; but she could take comfort in the fact that her mother was not all that sure, either, of the man's various obligations: "My mother tells me that a woman shouldn't be poking into a man's business, and the same goes vice versa. She said that when they got married, she and Daddy made a pact, and she recommends that I make one, too, with my husband, when I get married: stay out of each other's hair, but try to be of help, when there's need for help."

But Marjorie knows that her father belongs to various committees, is a trustee of various institutions. She has heard him talking on the phone, recognizes the influence he wields, the authority in his voice. She has heard him talking to her mother, heard the latter express her unqualified confidence in his ability to "get things done." She has seen his picture in the newspaper repeatedly, and watched her mother clip the articles, paste them in a scrapbook, which the family upon occasion looks at together. And she has thought of her own future: what kind of man will she marry?

She said at nine that she couldn't possibly imagine the man. She said at eleven that she couldn't be "too exact," but she did have some ideas. She is partial to blond men, for instance; and would like to marry a tall man. Unashamedly she indicates the connection between her father's appearance (tall, sandy hair) and her own preferences. But she has some reservations, too; she doesn't want her future husband to be as "busy" as her father is. He has too many duties — burdens, really. He gets too many requests, has to take far too many phone calls, must deal with a heavy correspondence. He himself has sometimes wondered out loud how he manages to do all he does. His oldest daughter wonders whether she might one day meet a "farmer," fall in love with him, whatever her prejudices in favor of the city. At least, if that should happen, she would know what her mother refers to, wistfully, as "peace and quiet." But she doubts such an outcome is in store for her. She will "probably" marry a lawyer, she suspects, or "maybe" a businessman. Her best friend is the daughter of a surgeon, and he is also an enormously overworked man. Marjorie has emphatically crossed surgeons off her list of prospective successful suitors. She would be "too lonely," like her friend's mother.

Since she was in the third grade Marjorie has been described as an imaginative and expressive child, who has a knack of describing what she thinks and feels in vivid and strong language. When some forty miners were killed in a serious disaster north of Charleston, the girl was saddened and prompted to become reflective in her sixth-grade English composition class. The title of her brief essay was "Dying Underground," and it went as follows: "I read in the paper that forty miners died the other day. They were digging coal, and suddenly there was an explosion. On television the man said the miners must have been killed right away. I wondered what the men thought when they heard the explosion, and they knew they were going to die. They must have thought of their wives and their children. They must have prayed to God. They must have said good-bye to each other. They must have thought that it's not fair, for people to die like that. I hope the coal company gives the families of the men a lot of money. They deserve it. I hope we don't have more explosions like that one. We should have more mine safety, like the newspaper said. A lot of people are poor. They have hard jobs. They suffer. Sometimes they even die. Then the rest of us feel sorry for them. We should worry about them when they're alive."

For that effort she got an "excellent," though her teacher wrote this comment on the paper: "You must understand, Marjorie, that explosions are accidents, and sometimes there's nothing anyone can do to prevent an accident." The girl brought the composition home, and of course, her mother and father read her words, and her teacher's words, with great interest. The mother hugged her daughter, told her she was a "good Christian," and said she hoped the compassion expressed so eloquently would last the child's lifetime. The father said he loved his daughter's "sincerity," and agreed with her about the miners — the sadness of their death; but he also agreed with the teacher. "The fact is," the father reminded his daughter, "miners often cause a mine disaster, because they are careless; they don't pay attention to the safety rules."

The girl remembered her father's analysis and felt even more troubled. A day or two afterward she brought up the subject again; she asked her father whether it wasn't true that "it's very dangerous down the mines, and no matter how careful you are, there can be an explosion." He replied by asking his daughter why she was "still talking" about the accident. The girl was silent for a while, but did come up with an answer: "The newspapers and television are still talking about the disaster, too, so it's hard to forget." Her father agreed, but became rather stern, as the girl remembered: "He told me that the newspapers can make a lot of mistakes, and I shouldn't believe everything I read in them. Mother said she was sure I didn't. Then Daddy explained what really happened in the coal mine; and he knows, because he's on the board of directors, and the president of the company got his job because Daddy recommended him. The president says he's been told that one of the miners must have done something wrong. Daddy says everyone feels sorry for the miners who died, but if one of them caused the accident, then he's the one to blame, and not the company.

"On television they're always criticizing the company and in the newspapers, too; that's what Daddy decided — and that's why he called up the owner of the paper, and he told him that it wasn't fair, the way the reporters were writing their stories. The publisher told Daddy that he'd call him back, but first he wanted to investigate. And Daddy had an answer for him; he told the publisher that he'd send over a file, with all the facts, right away. The publisher said thank you, but he didn't need the file. My father thinks the publisher is afraid of the editor, and doesn't run his own business the way he should. It would be like someone working in my father's office, one of his law clerks, telling my father what to say, and my father going along, and not ever disagreeing.

"We have a man who comes and works in the garden. He planted some roses and my mother didn't like them, but she wasn't going to say anything, because she knew how hard the man had worked, and he told her the roses would last for a long time, and they are a good color to have. When my father heard my mother tell my sister and me about the roses, he got very upset. He was in the hall, but he came into my mother's sewing room, and he said that we had to have one thing settled in our house — that the servants were taking orders from us, and not telling us what to do. He said that Mother should fire the gardener right on the spot, when he starts telling her what to do, and the same goes for the maid — or anyone else. I was upset, and so was my sister. He left right away, and we thought he was mad at us, but mother said no, he wasn't. She said he had to go to an important meeting — and it was about the mine disaster, she was sure. That's when I asked her if Daddy was right in what he said — that the miners could be the ones who caused the disaster. She said she didn't know. She told me and my sister that our father is a lawyer, and he is honest, and he'd never tell a lie, and if he believed something, it was because he had the proof. So I said he was probably right. When I said that, she said I shouldn't say *probably*, I should say *definitely*. I did. My sister asked her about the gardener, and she said she'd try to be tougher, but it wasn't in her nature to be like Daddy. I told her *she* could be right, and Daddy wrong — because, like the teacher says, *everyone* makes a mistake sometime. Mother said she can't remember when Daddy had ever made one!"

The roses attracted Marjorie's interest after that episode. She looked them over carefully, came to be fond of them. She had been interested in flowers and plants for several years; she kept several cacti in her room, and a month or so before the gardener had made so bold as to take the initiative with certain rose bushes, he had obtained for Marjorie three quite lovely plants, or so she had judged them. Did her father have quite another opinion? She was afraid to ask. She was afraid even to ask her mother. But the maid also loved plants. Why not ask her? She could innocently enough ask her father what he thought of his daughter Marjorie's plants. The maid did ask the girl's father, and reported back that he had indeed noticed them and pronounced them quite lovely. Shortly thereafter the father brought the subject up at the dinner table, told Marjorie how very much he liked her room, how pleased he was to see the care she gave to it, and how particularly fond he was of her three plants. Then he turned to the mother — saying nothing, but smiling and nodding, as if to send her a compliment, also: the one who, no doubt, selected the three plants and gave them to the girl. The mother said that she did agree with her husband's judgment, but in all fairness had to admit that it was the gardener who had selected the plants and given them to Marjorie. A moment of nervous silence, then a smile from the father, a relaxation of everyone's apprehension, and a statement from the man at the head of the table: "I think we are all becoming the gardener's protégés. I must sign up myself!"

A month later Marjorie used paints to indicate her approval of the lush late summer garden outside the house. She was especially drawn to the roses, but also to some enormous and beautifully arranged sunflowers — a stunning column of them, astride rows of vegetables. They were so "lucky," she reminded herself, to have a gardener of such skill and devotion. He grew beautiful flowers all year around (the mother had a hothouse, attached to the stable) and he also had an exceptional way with lettuce, tomatoes, carrots, and squash, which wandered and flowered and intrigued Marjorie by their independent ways. The gardener also helped out with the horses — kept an eye on "everything outdoors."

Marjorie tried hard to do justice to the beauty the gardener had made possible near her home, but worried that she was not a good enough artist. She was especially anxious to make the sunflowers the commanding presence they were for her. Each one received her closest

attention. And she topped them off, so to speak, with the sky's sun —
in her words, "the sunflower that makes all other sunflowers grow."
She decided at the last minute to put the gardener in the painting, but
abruptly changed her mind: best to leave people out of it. As she put
the painting aside (Figure 60), she gave herself some credit, but was
still humbled by her self-acknowledged inadequacies. If only she
could become even a half-competent amateur artist one day! But she
has no gift in that direction — unlike two of her sisters. Yet, she loved
to look at the flowers outside the house, and she could at least learn to
grow them, care for them, keep them reasonably healthy and attractive. Now she had a thought: the ground, the earth that nourished the
gardener's flowers, her family's flowers, the earth she had rather
quickly suggested with a few strokes of brown paint, was the very
same earth, not too far away, that men dug and cut into — miners in
search of coal.

She began to wonder out loud about coal: "There might be coal
right under our house; if we dug up the garden and kept digging, we
might find coal. I've never seen a coal mine. I asked my father, after
the forty men died in the disaster, if he would take me to a coal
mine — a safe one! — so that I could see the coal being dug and carried up. My father said no, there are more important things for me to
see. I asked him if he'd ever gone down a mine, and he said no. He said
there are a lot of things he hasn't done. He didn't want us in a mine, he
told me, and I shouldn't ask anymore! I did ask my mother, the next
day; I was sure she could just take us to some mine, and they'd show
us how it works. But she said no, you can't just drive up to a mine and
expect the miners to stop work and become your guides! My mother
gave me a talk — on how I was growing up and ought to be more con-
siderate and think of others. She was right! They work hard down in
mines, and they don't want people staring at them and asking them a
lot of questions. I'll bet my grandfather could show me a lot of mines,
down where he lives. But maybe he wouldn't. Mother says it's the same
there; he has to hire very strong men to do the work, and they
wouldn't like to be bothered by me and my sisters! And we'd be staring at them, and it wouldn't be polite, and you can't just go and see
anything you want to see.

"The mines are off limits to everyone except the people who
work in them. What if someone older went down there, and he lit a
cigarette? There'd be an explosion! You have to be trained not to do a
lot of things you might be tempted to do — if you're going to work in
the mines. It's like being in an airplane; you don't smoke, if you're

older, when they tell you not to smoke. I told my mother that I wouldn't smoke, anyway, but she said there might be other mistakes I could make, and so I still couldn't go visit a mine. She didn't know what the mistakes might be; maybe I would kick over a lamp, and then a fire would get going."

Marjorie has, however, seen pictures of a mine — of miners, at least, at work in West Virginia. The occasion: a social studies course — a book in it meant to "bring life in the United States closer to the young reader." Marjorie asked the teacher where in the state the mine shown is. The teacher said she didn't know. Marjorie thought of asking the teacher how the class might find out, might go visit the mine, but she did not. Another child did, a boy she didn't know well — "only his name." What had the teacher said? She said no, it would not be possible. The boy had asked why, only to be ignored. The class had to "move on." Marjorie started paying attention to the boy; his name, Miles, began to interest her. She knew no one but him with that name. She had never said anything to him, not even hello. He sat on the other side of the room — "and besides, he's a boy." But a day or so after the incident mentioned, Marjorie approached Miles and asked him if he'd ever visited any mine, anywhere. He said no. Had she? She said no. Would *she* like to do so, also? Yes — and she liked hearing him say that he would. The boy confided in her: his uncle was the vice-president of a coal company. It was located in Alabama, however, and the boy had never gone to the state, let alone a mine within the state. The girl told *him* something, in exchange: her grandfather owned several mines, and they were located right in West Virginia. But she had never been to a mine, either. She had been to her grandfather's home; she had gone fishing with him, and had taken walks with him, but she had not even seen his office. As for the mines, her own father had not seen "one of Granddaddy's mines." She wasn't even sure that Granddaddy himself had actually gone down any of his mines. She had asked her father that question; he had said "probably." Miles and she decided that "it must be very dangerous to go where the miners go" and for that reason "no one really wants to go there."

But the two of them could not quite forget that for some people there is no choice: "Miles said he saw the people on television, the families of the men who got killed, and he asked his father if there wasn't some way to prevent mines from having explosions inside them. His father said no, there are always accidents. I told Miles that my father said the same thing. My father said the miners can cause the trouble, and it's not fair that everyone gets mad at the owners of the company. Miles said that was the way his father looked at the trouble, too. We both said it was no good — that all those miners should die.

"I once thought I would like to try being a miner for a few weeks. I didn't tell anyone except my sister, and we both told our mother, and she just laughed. My sister Susie really wouldn't mind marrying a miner one day; that's what she told me the other day! She said she'd like to live way out on a farm, and if there was a mine nearby, and her husband worked in it, she would like the idea of him working hard and coming home covered with coal dust. She would have a hot shower ready to go, and she'd cook him food they'd grown themselves. I don't think I'll ever meet a miner or a miner's son. I told Susie I don't think she will either. I asked Miles if he thought he would, and he said no, that he wouldn't. If my father had to go down the mines every day, I'd be plenty worried. If my husband was the one, I'd be worried. If I knew a miner, I'd worry about him.

"My mother said the other day that anyone can get into an accident. Look at the number of automobile accidents every year. But it's worse being a miner — more dangerous. Mother said I'm making a mountain out of a molehill, but I told her I'm glad Daddy doesn't work in a mine. She said Daddy carries a lot of burdens on his shoulders; he has worries, and he's always in a rush, because of the cases he has in court and the meetings he has to go to. Even so, he doesn't have to worry that there will be a spark, and it will make some gases explode, and that will be the end. Miles said he told his father that he didn't want to have a job even near a mine; he'd rather be in a submarine than down a mine. Miles says we're both lucky. He wants to learn how to ski and go live in Switzerland; his uncle goes there every year to ski. Miles says if you go all the way over every year, you might as well live there."

Marjorie's family has a summer home in the Adirondacks and regularly rents a home on the West Coast of Florida, near Venice, for two weeks every February. Marjorie likes those two homes a lot, but wishes there were yet another one, a permanent apartment in New York City. A classmate of hers speaks of such a place — the property of a law firm that does a lot of litigation in New York, and in West Virginia for companies located in New York. The companies are coal companies, and the lawyers in Charleston go back and forth, mostly getting instructions in New York and carrying out agreed-upon efforts "back home." Marjorie has asked her father why his firm doesn't rent such an apartment. She has been told that his particular firm handles other "accounts"— railroads, utilities, various wholesale distribution outlets. Those companies don't all have offices in New York City.

The firm does not, surprisingly, handle her grandfather's legal problems. The girl is not sure why, but knows what she has heard and been told: "My father wasn't supposed to live here. He was supposed to stay home in Mingo County and help my grandfather — be his lawyer. He would become the boss himself when my grandfather got too old or else died. But my father didn't want to go back. He kept stalling after he got out of law school. He met my mother, and she didn't want to go back with him. I think she once wanted to be an actress. She wanted to live in New York City. She made a compromise with my father: if he agreed not to go back to Mingo County, she would agree to give up the idea of going to New York. She asked him for a long time to take a job in a law firm up there, and he almost did. But he was afraid of the big city, my mother thinks. She says she's glad, now. She says she wouldn't have wanted to bring us up in a big city. But she likes to go up there on visits. My father says he wouldn't rent an apartment in New York, even if he had to spend half of every week in the city — not when he can go to the Plaza, and they know him there, and he and my mother have a much better time in the hotel than they would in an apartment, and it all gets written off as expenses."

The question of income taxes prompts from Marjorie a thought about money: "Some have a lot, and some have none, and it's not right that people should have none." Her father strongly believes in private charities, as opposed to government-sponsored welfare programs of various kinds. He proudly tells his wife and children that he tithes himself, as his father and grandfather did before him: 10 percent of his gross income goes to assorted causes — the Presbyterian Church, the United Fund, a program directed at "problem children." After the mine disaster Marjorie wondered out loud at the supper table whether her parents would be sending any money to the survivors of the men killed. She was told the answer immediately and abruptly: no. She did not ask her father why. The next day, characteristically, she turned to her mother for information. The mother was rather terse herself. She told the girl that it is her father's "decision" where the charity money goes. The girl was insistent: why not try to help such obvious victims? The mother again called upon her husband's authority and his rights: it is his money, and he has every justification to spend it as he pleases. What might she want to do with the money, if he gave her the chance to spend it as she pleased? The mother could not come up with an answer. She would have to "do some thinking." The child asked if, in the course of her reflections, she might, just might, consider the survivors of the dead miners possible candidates for charity. The mother said yes, they were possible beneficiaries.

But the mother never gave any money to the survivors of that particular mine accident, or to any miners, or to their families. And Marjorie learned her mother's reasons — learned over a period of a year or so to stop being interested in such people and their difficulties. When Marjorie turned thirteen her grandfather became gravely ill, was flown to Charleston in a private plane, became a patient in a hospital there, was operated upon, and almost died. When he had recovered enough to begin contemplating his future, Marjorie asked him whether he would go back to Mingo County and resume his work, which was to keep an eye on several quite profitable businesses there. No, he would not. He was tired of "the smell of coal," he told his granddaughter. He was tired of workers making demands and "outsiders" coming into the county, seeking him out, and also making demands — of him. He wanted rest and "peace" during his final months.

But he did not want to live with his son: "My grandfather told me there would be fights between him and Daddy if they both lived under the same roof. Daddy was supposed to stay in Mingo County, but he didn't. My grandfather is going to sell the mines he owns down there. He can't leave them to my father, and there's no one else in the family either who wants to run them. I have an aunt in Pittsburgh, and she is married to a stockbroker, and they don't want to leave Pittsburgh. I have another aunt in Beckley, West Virginia, and her husband owns a shopping center, I think, and they like living where they are. Like my grandfather says: there's no one to take over. Anyway, there's a lot of trouble now in the coal fields. It's no joke owning a mine. Some of the owners have to hire bodyguards. There's a lot of violence. My grandfather says on some days he feels like he's just sitting and waiting for the union men to come and get him. He practices shooting his guns, and he keeps them near him. He has an alarm that can detect anyone even coming *near* the house, and he has a rifle right beside his bed. He's a light sleeper. The doctor told him that's another reason for him to stay in Charleston; he won't sleep well at home, and he'll get weak. But my grandfather says he'd really like to face down some of the union organizers and show them how he can shoot to kill."

Marjorie would hate to see that kind of confrontation. She has told that to her grandfather, and he has not argued with her. He has, rather, told her that she is a "girl," and that he can understand how she would abhor "gun-shooting." Still, she must know "the facts of life"; and he has supplied them to her — long statements about the "rights of mine operators" and the "violence" that the miners have been visiting upon West Virginia in the name of "progress." For him it has been a painful decade; yet he is no quitter and only regrets that someone in his family isn't prepared to take a continuing stand against "them," the United Mine Workers and their various "sympathizers," not to mention the "agitators."

His granddaughter had begun to lose interest in drawings by the time she was thirteen, but she did initiate one out of a certain frustration she felt when asking questions of him: "I love him," she would say, "but he is a hard man to pin down." She had in mind the various questions she'd asked of him: for instance, what do the miners look like when they come out of his mines? What do they say to him when he talks with them — or indeed, has he ever talked with *them,* as opposed to the union officials who are their representatives? Marjorie drew a picture of him standing upright and ready for action, his gun at his side. His eyes were wide and attentive, his ears large and meant to be alert. He was, she pointed out, "just waiting," but he was also fully prepared to "raise the gun and shoot." The gun is rather large, almost his size — in real life, a half inch or so under six feet. And beyond him stretch, somewhat shapeless, the surging masses, it would appear, bent on having their say, getting a number of concessions he was unwilling to make. In the background are smoke, shadowy buildings, a chimney or two, a gray, bleak sky with no sun. When the young lady had finished her drawing (Figure 61) she gave it a final look, pushed it aside, spoke one sentence: "Too bad for Granddaddy and too bad for those miners."

Then she turned her attention elsewhere, began to wonder whether her grandfather would accompany her parents, herself, her sisters, to Colonial Williamsburg in Virginia. Her father had to attend a meeting being held there, and he thought it would be a fine occasion for the entire family to go away and glimpse an earlier America, "when life was simpler." She rather suspected her grandfather would jump at the chance to take this particular trip, would enjoy it enormously, would get on very well in Williamsburg with his family and with everyone else, and might even, she added at the very end, insist upon "paying for everyone, even Daddy." There would be a fight over that matter, but the girl had no fear that a gun would be used. Her father would yield, she was sure. Her father liked to stand up to his father, but she was sure that "on money" there wouldn't be "trouble" — because several times she had overheard her parents talking about the money to be left them by the grandfather, and both her mother and her father seemed quite anxious to get the money, rather than keeping it at a remove for the sake of their independence. And as she said: "You can't blame them." She even went further. She insisted that there wasn't anyone she knew who would blame them.

Withdrawal

High up in an office building the boy stands with his father and listens to a political analysis of a city's turmoil. Black and white children are being bused, black and white parents are up in arms, violence has repeatedly taken place, and the boy's father has been dismayed, saddened. The boy has wondered why. The father has tried to explain. Then they enjoy the view. It is part of a ritual they have — looking out the window, picking one part of the view for discussion (a building, a neighborhood, the river, one of several parks, a particular street) and then, when the conversation is over, just staring for a moment. The boy is proud of the view, proud of his father, proud of what he has learned from his father. The boy wishes his father were mayor of the city, governor of the state. Then, there might be less trouble. But his father is no politician, the boy knows. And that is the trouble with the United States of America: the power wielded by politicians — as opposed to men like his father or, for that matter, women like his mother.

A day or so later, the newspapers carried a letter the boy's father had written, urging "reason" and compliance with the federal judge's school desegregation order. The boy had asked for an extra newspaper; he, too, wanted a copy of the letter to keep. The next day, in school, he wrote his own brief statement as an impromptu composition: "If white people and black people were friends, we would have a better country. I think that there's nothing bad about going to school in a bus. It's good that we have black kids in our school."

He was then nine. His is "a liberal, progressive school," the boy's mother says. His name is Gordon. He has always been a bright, committed, forthcoming student. He has rarely descended to B work, yet is not especially bookish. He laughs easily, is good at sports, is called "a natural leader" by his teachers. He likes to give oral compositions, has been speaking up in class rather vigorously since the first grade. The school he attends is a private urban school just outside Boston. Children of doctors, lawyers, businessmen, and professors go there; but so do poor children, a substantial number from the ghetto. Gordon has made a point of befriending those children, has long been encouraged to do so by his parents. When busing got under way in Boston Gordon not only joined his father in supporting the idea but offered to be bused himself. His parents said no. His father, a scientist and college professor, emphasized the importance of staying in a good school — one which was, besides, integrated. His mother, of a quite wealthy family, insisted that he owed it to the black students in the school he was attending to stay and speak or write on their behalf. The boy agreed to remain, but was not able to still the voice of his conscience. He wrote a brief comment for his school's student newspaper: "I believe it is not fair that if you have money, you can go to a private school, and not be bused. Only the white kids who are poor and don't like blacks go on the bus. No wonder there is a lot of trouble in Boston's schools. We should try to help, but I don't know how. Any suggestions?"

He received none. He went about his business, tried to push Boston's torment out of his mind, but could not: "If I was eleven or twelve, I'd just tell my mother and father that I was quitting the school I'm going to, and taking a bus over to any school in Boston I got sent to. They might not like what I'd want to do, but they would let me go ahead. My sister is thirteen, and she tells my parents what she's going to do, and they disagree with her, but they don't stop her. She told me yesterday that if I got really upset, and stood my ground, they'd give in. I asked her how she gets upset! She said it's easy — just get upset! So, I tried. I told Dad at supper that I wasn't happy at school and I wanted to leave. He asked me what I meant. I told him I just wasn't happy there. He asked why. I said for a lot of reasons. He said to name one. I didn't. I said I just wanted to leave and go to a public school in Boston. Then he guessed my reason. He said I wanted to be of help.

"But he wouldn't let me leave. He said no, definitely no. My mother said that if I could persuade them, then I could do what I want, but I had to be a good lawyer! I tried. I told them what I'd written for the school newsletter. I told them why I thought I should be bused to a black school. I told them what a black kid told me in school; he said that he felt like a traitor, because he was going to a fancy private school, while other kids on his street were going on the bus into Hyde Park and South Boston and places like that. He said I should be bused and so should he, because we both live in Boston.

Then my mother interrupted and wanted to know what difference it would make if two extra children got bused. I said I didn't know. My father said I'm going to a good school and I have black friends there, and he wouldn't take me out, even if I did the best job of arguing in the world! That's when he and Mom had an argument. She said that if I really wanted to leave school and go to a public school, they should at least discuss it, and leave the door open. My Dad said I wasn't old enough to decide where I was going to school. He said later, *later* I could. My mother said he was *dictating* to me. He said he was just being my *father.* That's when my mother turned to me and asked me what *I* thought. I didn't know what to say! My sister said I should speak up, but I couldn't find any words. I kept quiet. My father said: 'That settles it.' If I knew how to persuade them, I think they would have let me switch schools."

Gordon was enough like his sister to stay concerned with the problem of busing for a long time. He continued to alert his fellow students and his teachers to the vexing moral question, as he saw it, of who was being bused and who was not. At the age of ten he drew a picture of a bus, filled with black children, approaching a school, in front of which stood some white children (Figure 62). The whites seem large, strong, unfriendly. One has a club in hand. The blacks are mere faces, peering out of windows. The boy has left half the windows empty. He had a reason for doing so: "I should be on the bus. Other white kids should be there, too. It's not fair that the blacks are being bused and the whites mostly aren't. I'd like to be bused, but I won't be. It's no fun going in a car pool — the same old people! I told my mother that yesterday, and she laughed. She said she could understand why I feel like I do, but I have to remember that someone else's problems are not always mine; there's a limit to how many fights we can get into. I said that I agreed, but this was *my* fight. She smiled and said she was glad. She told me to tell Dad that I was still in the ring fighting! I did — at suppertime. He said he was proud of me!

"Dad believes Boston is full of racists, and it's getting worse rather than better, and the whole country is laughing at the city. Even at our school there are kids who say that the blacks aren't as smart as the whites, and they need special help, and it's all right to have them in our school, but they're not the same as we are. I got into a fight with a kid who said that last week. He thinks he's so nice and tolerant, but he doesn't really like black kids. When I told my father, he said that was a good reason for me to be right where I am — so I could argue with the kids who are going to be racists later on, if they're not told to stop talking like they do."

He more than fulfilled his father's expectations. At eleven Gordon was a forceful, incisive spokesman for integration, if necessary through busing. He was also worried about other problems; he wrote a composition denouncing our high military budget, our willingness to support certain dictators, our failure to align ourselves more dramatically and enthusiastically with the world's poorer (mostly African and Asian) nations. The essay was given first prize for the best seventh-grade written exercise. Gordon had supporters among his classmates, but there were those who found him rather more sure of himself than they liked. Gordon was not inhibited by disapproval. He actually enjoyed it. He enjoyed being regarded as a person of strong, uncompromising opinion, as a well-informed boy who didn't hesitate to speak out, even to the point of criticizing his own situation. Who else in the school had called himself "wrong" for not being on a school bus every morning, on his way to a public school in a black section of Boston? Who else had acknowledged that his parents, as quite well-to-do people, had "good reasons" to want to keep the status quo, or modify it only so much? Who else brought in suggested reading about Cuba and China — books and articles that Gordon's older sister had found interesting and valuable and which she recommended to him?

At the age of twelve Gordon even mentioned a desire to go to both Cuba and China. Why? Because he felt those nations to be "the wave of the future." He wanted to see countries where "poverty has been wiped out." He wanted to meet Castro and Mao, because he believed both of them to be "great men." He thought that each was like our Abraham Lincoln, the one president he really liked a lot. His father would ask Gordon what he thought Castro ought to do, or this country ought to do with respect to Cuba. The boy would take a position and argue it out over supper. The father would press hard, take issue with the son, point out one or another issue the boy had overlooked. The mother would eventually ask both of them to stop, to get on with the meal, or turn to lighter, less abrasive conversation. When Gordon indicated that he really did want to go to Cuba, rather than a summer camp he'd been attending since the age of eight, his father expressed approval. Why not? The boy would learn a lot, and begin to see how other people live, other governments operate. The mother became nervous: wasn't the boy too young? But she, too, assented; and both parents tried hard to learn if there was some way for their son's wish to come true. There wasn't. Instead he went to the Southwest, stayed with a Navaho family on an exchange program, toured Arizona and New Mexico, came back full of affection for another region of America and full of concern for the Indians he had stayed with and come to know somewhat.

At school he wrote one composition after another about the poverty he saw, the consequent demoralization of a once-proud people. His teachers were quite pleased with him — both for going to the Southwest and for coming back even more troubled than before about others, less fortunate. At the end of a composition the author was told that if only there were more people like him, this would be a better country. But Gordon was not so willing to be thus complimented. He wondered out loud at supper what difference his teacher's attitude toward him made to the Navaho Indians. Ought he not, in a few years, go out West, live there all the time, work hard on behalf of the Indians? Ought he not to ask his father to send money, a lot of it, to the Indians? Why should he, one twelve-year-old boy, have "almost a hundred thousand dollars, maybe more," put away in his name for his future use, while thousands of Indian children of his age are penniless and always will be, things being as they are?

His father supplied answers to those questions, and Gordon listened carefully but not always in agreement: "My father says we've done a lot of harm to the Indians, and he agrees with me, it's been bad that we haven't tried to make up for our mistakes. But it's got to be the government that will change everything. Even if my family gave all its money to the Indians, they wouldn't be much better off than they are now. I think that if everyone who worries about the Indians really started trying to help them, it would make a difference. It's not right that I become a good guy in school, just because I say the right words about 'the poor Indians.' That's what our social studies teacher keeps on telling us — that we've got to realize how bad everything is for 'the poor Indians.' I agree, it *is* bad for them; but we're not helping them by saying so all the time!

"When I asked my mother if she'd mind if I went out West next summer again, she said I was getting 'overinvolved' with the Indians. Her friend — her roommate at college — used to be a psychiatric social worker before she got married, and she was the one who put it in my mother's head that I was 'overinvolved.' My mother told me what she thought, and I got very angry. Then she told me, the next day — after she'd called up her friend, I'm sure — that I *was* overinvolved, and the proof was that I'd become so angry! Isn't that wild! I told my

Dad, and he agreed with me; he said that Mom is really upset because I'm only twelve (I'm almost thirteen!) and she is worried that I'm talking like some college student who wants to be a revolutionary. I told Dad that isn't true. I don't want to get into any trouble. But if a lot of people don't try to help out the Indians, and the black people too, then it won't do any good for just me to go and sacrifice. I laughed at her, I guess, when she kept on telling me I was 'overinvolved.' She just walked out of the room; and later she told Dad that she was upset with me. I guess that's why he spoke to me. Maybe next summer I'll go back to my old camp as a junior counselor. I think the director told my Dad I could be a junior counselor if I wanted."

Gordon did become a junior counselor. He turned thirteen that summer, and he began to hear his voice crack and deepen and see new hair appear on his body. He had always loved swimming, loved playing in the sand, loved the sight and sound of the ocean as well as swimming in it. He began to lose some of the intensity of commitment he had felt a year earlier to the Indians. He decided that he really wouldn't be happy living in the Southwest; the ocean is too far away. A lake or two would not suffice. Might he go away to some school located at the edge of the Maine shore? Might he become a sailor one day? How about marine biology for a career? He had an uncle who worked as a marine biologist at Woods Hole, Massachusetts, and perhaps that was the best possible occupation for a boy of thirteen whose parents got obviously nervous when future enlistment in the navy or merchant marine was mentioned.

When he was through with his eight weeks of working in a summer camp, Gordon went to Woods Hole, became familiar with the various ways his uncle pursued his work. He went out on a boat, from which he went underwater in a special cage. He examined specimens from the sea that were under study. He talked with his uncle about the future: what to study, where, and with how much hope or certainty of becoming a first-rate scientist? In the autumn Gordon stopped writing about politics for a while, devoted himself almost exclusively to essays on the ocean. He did not, however, lose a strong social conscience. He announced to his teachers (in one essay) and to his parents many times over the dining table that he was going to try to help the Indians and other impoverished people "in a real serious way" one day; he was going to learn how to take organic matter from the sea and make cheap food for the world's hungry masses.

Let others indulge in empty talk; Gordon was going to be the best kind of idealist and activist — a practical, competent, knowing man who could come up with something of obvious worth: "I'd like to be helpful to others. My mother and father tell me that if you have a lot, then you have to give back to others who don't have anything. That's why I study hard, I guess — so that I'll be able to become a scientist maybe, and then I can really be of help. I might end up being a doctor. I have an uncle who's a surgeon; he does research. I have another uncle who is a doctor; he delivers babies and he does research too. He's my mother's twin. He always tells me that a lot of children never should be born, because they're going to live a bad life. It would be nice if they could all be born, and then have plenty of food. If only we could discover some cheap food that everyone could eat; then no one would starve to death. I wouldn't want to be born poor."

In school, when Gordon was twelve, he had written the following composition: "We are the privileged ones; we have been born lucky, and we'll probably die old and still pretty lucky. We have parents who have plenty of money. They love us, and when we want something they say yes, and they go and get us what we want. That's being lucky. I wish that others were as privileged as we are. I wish everyone in the world had enough food and a good home. My father says that when you're poor, you feel like two cents. There are many people in this world who feel that way, even in our country. If I thought I could help a lot of those people out, then I'd feel a lot better. Then I'd really be lucky. Then I'd really be privileged. Right now, the trouble with a lot of my friends, and with me, is that we are so lucky, we don't even know how lucky we are. I asked my parents if there wasn't a plan we could discover that would help all the kids all over the world who don't have the good luck we do. My parents said they wished we could, but they couldn't think of any plan like that. I can't think of one, either. I hope one day there will be a plan."

He did, of course, think of such a plan — the application of marine biology to problems of nutrition. But when Gordon was almost fourteen, he became disillusioned with that idea and inclined to return to his parents' faith — that political and economic changes might ultimately affect the lives of the poor. He took a new interest in history and in civics, and he asked his mother and father more and more questions about "the government" and how it works. He went with them to the state capital and to Washington, D.C. They visited his congressman and both his senators. He watched the Supreme Court, the Senate, got to see a room in the White House. When he came back he was full of information, but also inclined to wonder even more about his country and how it is run and for whom.

Gordon wrote another composition for his English teacher, and in it he repeated old preoccupations but imbued them with new doubts: "I went to Washington, D.C. I saw a lot of places. I realized that our government has many parts to it. You can't help thinking how beautiful the buildings are there, but you worry about all the American people who never get to Washington, and don't care, because all they do care about is getting enough food to eat. My father said that the government supposedly belongs to everyone in the country, but when you come right down to it, a lot of people don't know how the government works. All over Washington there are lobbyists, and *they* are the ones who know how the government works.

"I asked our congressman if he thought Thomas Jefferson and James Madison ever dreamed there would be so many lobbyists in Washington, and I didn't get a good answer. The congressman said: 'There weren't any lobbyists then.' But my father said there probably were, only they didn't get called by that name. The congressman wasn't happy to hear my father say that! He said that any citizen has the right to come to the Capital and *petition* — that's what a democracy is. We didn't answer him back, but later my Dad and I laughed: a lot of people don't have the fare to get to Washington, and no one would pay any attention to them if they did. But if you've got influence and money, everyone listens to you. That's one lesson I learned in Washington — that there are a lot of interesting places to see, and a lot of lobbyists, too."

Gordon added other comments later on, when talking to his friends. He emphasized the physical beauty of the city, the pleasure he had in riding the Senate railway, and the awesome majesty of the Supreme Court in session. But he kept referring to lobbyists as well. And he wondered what he himself might do, when older, to influence the government. His parents suggested that he could best be of service to his country by choosing an honorable profession and becoming a kind and generous husband, father, neighbor. The boy was not so sure. He talked of writing a letter a day to his congressman and of persuading friends to do likewise. When he read of the Children's Crusade in a history book he asked his eighth-grade teacher whether she thought such a crusade (on behalf of America's poor) would work in this country in this century. The answer was no. His parents also said no. By the end of his eighth-grade year the boy had also decided no. He was "into" marine biology again, but keeping an eye on the front page of the newspaper. When he read in a social studies class about the civil rights movement of the 1960s, he remarked in class that it would be "nice" if one day his generation could become involved in such an effort. His teacher agreed; later, his parents did. But none of them, including the boy, could imagine what such a future effort might be like.

A week before he turned fourteen Gordon suddenly became cynical in a school report he had written on Woodrow Wilson's presidency: "It does not pay to become idealistic. You try hard, but you get misunderstood and destroyed. That is the lesson of Woodrow Wilson's life." His teacher thought Gordon "too pessimistic"; his parents told him he would "change his mind" and realize one day "how many chances there always are" for people to express their idealism forcefully and to great effect: "They tell me to cheer up, and they say that I'm *only* thirteen, or I'm *only* fourteen, and in a few years I'll see what they mean. But I hear my parents talk about things, and I know what they believe in their hearts. They say things to me they only half believe! I say things to my friends I only half believe! The teachers say things to us they only half believe! We say things to the teachers we only half believe! My mother used to tell me that you can't say a lot of things out loud. Now I know what she meant: you don't even admit to yourself a lot of things. My father says you've got to compromise in this world. I used to think he was wrong. I hate to believe it's true, and I wish it wasn't true. I wish everyone was more honest, but you can't be.

"I'm a teenager, my parents keep telling me. I'm supposed to be 'idealistic' because I'm a teenager! Then I'll grow up, and that'll be the end of my idealism! Then I'll become 'practical!'"

After he spoke that last sentence he looked at an old drawing of his, which he had kept on a bulletin board (Figure 63). He drew the picture when he was twelve and first developing a strong interest in the sea, in the life within it. A boat is anchored in the ocean. Divers have gone under water. Some machinery will soon follow them. The sea stretches indefinitely in one direction; in the other is the mainland: people, trees, a wharf, a building or two. A person stands on the ship; he is made big, out of proportion even to the size of the ship, let alone the people on the land, who are huddled together in discrete bunches. The artist knew what he intended — a portrait of the artist as sailor, scientist, explorer, and, not least, man removed from others, privileged to have his own activity, while they cling to each other and do nothing, get nowhere. When he had finished the picture the boy had tersely expressed his sadness: if only others had his opportunities, but they haven't and won't.

Two years later Gordon repeats himself, decides he doesn't want the picture near him anymore. After all, he observes with a smile, the boat must have long since pulled up its anchor and gone someplace else. Nor is there any point in drawing such pictures. He has tired of autobiographical writing. He has come to respect more and more those scientists who withdraw from the world's distractions, carve out an exceedingly circumscribed domain for themselves and work it to the fullest. He knows one such biologist who claims never to read the paper, never even to watch the news on television. Why should anyone become acquainted with, agitated by, events over which he or she has utterly no control? It is a question the boy, the youth, asks himself more and more often.

Rich in the Barrio

The girl was named Joan after an Anglo woman who had befriended the baby's mother. At the time Joan was born her parents lived in a barrio of San Antonio. Their house was small, only two bedrooms. Joan was the third child; she has an older brother and an older sister. Their father now owns a store in the barrio. He also owns a number of houses, some vacant land, and a small office building in which a Chicano doctor, two Chicano lawyers, and a Chicano dentist have offices. Joan's mother is the daughter of the dentist; she is a tall, dark, quite composed woman, known to many as "the silent one." She measures her words carefully, speaks slowly and quietly. She prefers to talk in English, though her husband will often not oblige; he is comfortable talking Spanish, and besides, he has to speak it all day with his customers. They are the poor of San Antonio, many of them migrant farm workers who have worked their way to the city from the Rio Grande Valley, in hope of bettering themselves, only to find jobs relatively scarce, and those available menial and poor-paying. To such people Joan's father is an authority, an established figure in the community, a rich and important man, an intermediary with the white world.

When Joan was four her father had a rather large ranch house built for his family on some vacant land he owned. He spared no expense. A year later, when the last of the decorating was done, the last of the important furniture purchased and moved in, Joan was clearly pleased with the result: "My Daddy told us that he was only going to ask us to move once, and so he made the house very big, and he told Mamma that he would have the best that money can buy, and then we would enjoy our life in the new home. Each of us has a room; our parents have the biggest bedroom. They have a huge color television in it; but we can come and sit on their bed and watch. There is another color television in the living room, but Mamma doesn't want us in there all the time, because the furniture costs a lot of money, and she wants to keep the room looking very nice, for company. My older brother broke a dish in there, and we weren't allowed back for a long time. Now, we can go in the room — if we ask her first. The kids I play with say we have the nicest house in San Antonio. My father says maybe it's the nicest in the barrio; he says the Anglos have bigger homes. They have more money than we do. They are the bosses, my father says. His friend, the priest, came over, and he said the same thing, that the Anglos are the bosses. The only Anglos we see are the people downtown; we go shopping with Mamma, and see them."

A year later Joan was seeing other Anglos — the nuns and lay teachers in a private, parochial school she was sent to. It was about then she began to wish that she could one day become a singer, and appear on television. Joan had a good voice, was taking piano and singing lessons, was described by her father as "ambitious." Even at six and seven she talked about going to Hollywood or New York, carving out a career for herself — so that she might, on a Saturday night, appear on the Lawrence Welk Show. Her brother was bored by that program, and her father agreed. But Joan had her mother's support: Lawrence Welk featured attractive young women, who sang "nice songs" and looked "very pretty" on the television screen. They must live, Joan was sure, quite interesting lives. One of her teachers, as a matter of fact, had left Texas for a stay in New York City, and told the class, from time to time, how "different" it was in the East, and especially in New York City.

Joan listened intently, came home and implored her parents to go to New York City on the next vacation. The parents said yes — someday; but not right away. After all, the girl had not really seen much of San Antonio, let alone other Texas cities, like Houston or Dallas. Her father's younger brother is in Chicago, trying hard to make it on his own, and admittedly not doing too well — but writing proud, stoic letters, full of praise for the city's tall buildings and fast, cosmopolitan life. All right, Joan would settle for Chicago, for a visit to her uncle, who sounds like a real swinger, a happy-go-lucky man who is not afraid of the Anglo world, but rather seeks to be part of it. If she went to Chicago, she was convinced, she would come home different. She would look different. She would be ready, then, for another trip — to New York City. And she would have so much to tell her teachers at school, she kept reminding her parents — as if to make it easier for them to say *yes* (an educational trip, after all!) rather than their predictable *maybe later.*

When she was eight she drew a picture of herself in front of her home (Figure 64). She stood rather stiff (she actually had a rather relaxed, casual carriage), her arms straight down and close to her sides, her feet firmly together. She gave herself thin lips, small eyes, a small nose, and very little, black hair — a flat-top of sorts. She wore the black dress required by the nuns. In back of her loomed, it seemed, her home: in her mind, apparently, as enormous and imposing as it was to other Chicano children of the barrio — "the rich one's house." The roof virtually touched the sky. The sun was nearby, but without a face, only rays. As a background Joan supplied other homes of the barrio — cramped, huddled, nondescript, a blur of poverty. On her comparatively spacious lawn she put her beloved black hound dog. The animal had more freedom to roam than the dozens and dozens of people who live in the houses shown. There is a fence around her home, and it is shown in the picture. No one from the cramped, swollen barrio can use that lawn unless invited.

Joan has known for years that she is granting a privilege when she invites a friend over, as she indicated when she commented on her own picture shortly after drawing it: "I have two girl friends, and they love to come here, because we can run all over the lawn, and we have the swings and the slide and the sandbox and the pool. Daddy says he's going to build a real pool; then we can throw away the plastic one. My friends say they don't care; they like the pool we have. They joke with me; they say I live in a park! When we drive by the old house, where I was born, I can't believe that we once lived there. I don't remember living there. If I had to live there, I guess it was best to spend the first three or four years there, when you're not doing much anyway. I've asked Mamma why we lived there, and she says that I'm talking spoiled, because the old house is a lot nicer than most houses our people have in San Antonio — or in Chicago. I picture my uncle living in a house like the one we have now, but my mother says I'm all wrong there!

"My Daddy says we moved to our new house because he made

the money we needed to buy it. He says money is very important. He says I'd better watch out; if I leave here and go to New York City, when I grow up, I might not be able to make the money I'd need, and then there would be real trouble. He says he'd fly up there and take me home. He thinks my uncle will soon come back from Chicago. Our people don't like the cold North, the bad winters. My father says we can have all the dreams we want about Chicago and New York, but it's not in our blood to live there and be happy, the way we are in San Antonio. My mother will agree with him some of the time. She says that we should look around us, right here in San Antonio, and see all the poor people here. This city isn't so good to our people either."

She stops, she wonders whether there is anymore to say. She puts the drawing aside. She looks out the window: another hot, humid day. She is glad that her room is air-conditioned, that all the bedrooms are. Her father has talked of air-conditioning the entire house. She remembers those remarks, makes a few of her own about him and her mother and her brother and sister and herself: "We are lucky, I guess. That's what everyone says. I don't like to hear my mother and father keep reminding me that I am lucky, but they are right, I know. I wish we lived in New York. I wish I could go see television programs, and take music lessons from the best people. Maybe I'll never leave San Antonio. When my mother gets angry with me for not cleaning up my room, she tells me that she's going to send me back to the Rio Grande Valley; I have an uncle there too — well, three uncles, I think. They work on farms. They pick crops. My mother says if I was down there, I'd be doing the same thing already.

"Once she got really mad; my room was a mess, and she told me to clean it up, and I forgot to. She came into her bedroom, and I was watching TV, and she started screaming that I belong down in the Valley. My friend was there with me. She said that when we get older we should both leave our homes and go there, to the Valley. I don't think we'd like it there. The nuns try to scare us. They tell us in school that we'll burn in hell if we don't watch out. That's what my mother says about the Valley — that it's hot, and there's no air conditioning in the houses. Kids go to work at five in the morning to pick the crops, and they come home late, at six or seven at night, and they're all worn out. Maybe my friend and I *will* go there in a year or two. Then we can send postcards home, like my uncle does from Chicago. Who knows — we might end up liking the Valley, and staying there for the rest of our lives!"

It is a passing thought, or speculation: she has no real intention of going down to the Valley nor does her mother plan to send her there, even on a brief, punitive visit. By the time Joan was twelve she had forsaken her New York plans, but very much wanted to go up North, to Chicago. She wanted a career in radio or television. She had been told for years that she had "a good voice"; now she wanted to use it as an announcer or a newscaster, rather than a singer. Joan watched with interest, approval, and a certain envy a woman reporting the news on a local television station. She was Anglo, and Joan had begun to believe that only Anglos could obtain the kind of jobs she had in mind for herself. She had also begun to worry about how she looked. At one point she even talked of becoming a nun — on the theory that nuns don't have to be beautiful, and she saw herself as unattractive, if not ugly.

Soon, however, that ambition faded. The girl became increasingly interested in her father's business. Wasn't there a way she could work for him? She asked him that repeatedly, and he scratched his head, and shook his head, and said no, there was only room for his son and three nephews, and maybe not all of them. Besides, in a few years she would have other ideas in mind — marriage and motherhood. Joan was not so sure; she resented being told exactly how her life ought to unfold. She resented, too, being given one dress after another, along with bracelets, a watch and then another, fancier watch, some necklaces and hair braids and an endless number of shoes. She took to wearing her jeans all the time — or as much of the time as she could. She was now delighted with her school uniform — its somber simplicity pleased her immensely. She felt torn between her desire to dress up (in the future) and talk before the television cameras, and her desire to be utterly casual (right then and there) and lounge around the house, watching television.

She also felt torn between various "lessons" she had heard from her parents: "I can't win. My mother tells me I should study hard. Then I do. Then she says I shouldn't study too hard, because boys do that, and I should try to be 'lighter.' I ask her how, and she says I shouldn't ask her, because I already know the answer, and I'm only being stubborn. My father says I'm not supposed to be interested in his business. Then he catches me sitting in the house watching television, and it's nice outside, and he gets very angry, and asks me why I don't go outside. Then I tell him there is nothing for me to do outside, and he gets very angry. He pulls me! When we get outside he points to the

pool, and to my bike, and to the grass. He says I can swim; I can go on
a bike ride; I can cut the grass. I said it was for my brother to cut the
grass! He exploded. He told me I would get no allowance for a month.
I was glad. All I do is put the bills in my wallet, and it gets fatter and
fatter! When my father is in a different mood, he won't even let us
spend our own allowance. He buys us what we want, and tells us the
allowance is for the extras. But a lot of times, I can't think up anything
extra that I want, and so I get richer all the time!

"Maybe a few years from now I'll have so much money I can go
and invest it somehow and start making a lot of money, like my father
did. I could buy some land; he says that land is the best thing to buy,
because it always goes up, up. Once he gets going on the subject of
land, and the money you can make from owning it, he doesn't care
what he was telling you before. He will sit down with us and explain
why he bought the land in this place, and this place, and this place. I
wish he owned the land where the television station is. Then maybe
he could get me a job on one of the television programs, when I'm bigger. But he says there's a lot of land that only the Anglos own. They sell
it to each other. They wouldn't let a Mexican own the land, even if he
had a lot of money, and was ready to pay anything they wanted."

She will switch from one ethnic or racial self-description to another, depending on the subject of discussion. She knew that Anglos
often referred to her people in a derogatory way as "Mexicans." She
herself can unselfconsciously assume Anglo attitudes and words
toward her own kind as if she were one of "them." She can also be
more evenhanded, can talk in a rather neutral tone about "the Mexican-
American streets" in San Antonio, as contrasted to the Anglo ones. She
can also become fiercely proud of her own ("Chicano") people. At
twelve or thirteen she frightens her parents with her declarations of
solidarity — and enmity: "I don't like to hear my father talk about the
Anglo bankers. He admires them. He says he is sure that they like him.
Well, why shouldn't they be nice to him and like him? They make a lot
of money off him! First he makes money; then he borrows more money
from the Anglos; then he makes more money, and so do they! No wonder they smile at him and pat him on the back, when he comes to
them and tells them that he is going to build some stores or some office buildings or some houses. I wish some of our own people had as
much money as the Anglos do; then we could go to a Chicano bank
and borrow money from Chicanos, and then Chicanos would be helping each other. The Anglos don't like us; they do business with my father, but he is just another 'Mexican' to them. He told me that himself

a long time ago, and I remember. But when I remind him, he gets angry with me and tells me I should stop talking like a man who is running for mayor of San Antonio!

"I wish I could be mayor! I wish a Chicano got elected mayor; then our people would be better off. The nuns told us that would be good too; and they are Anglos. One nun told us that it's already been too long that the Anglos have run Texas. Once Texas belonged to us, the Chicanos. Now, we are under the Anglos; they are over us. I asked my father the other day, when we were all joking and he was in a very good mood, if he would give me enough money to run for mayor of San Antonio. He laughed. He said he would; yes, he would. He asked me how much money I thought I'd need. I said, maybe five hundred dollars. He said I'd need hundreds and hundreds of *thousands* of dollars! Even he couldn't give me that much! He has a lot of money, but my mother has always told us that when a Mexican-American has a lot of money, it is one thing — you're still in the barrio, even if you're rich. When an Anglo has a lot of money, that's another story. We can lose our money overnight. The Anglos can put the squeeze on us. It's their country."

Toward the end of the eighth grade, when Joan was a few months short of fourteen, she "settled down," as her parents described it. She didn't by any means become, in the mother's words, a "dream girl." She played her hi-fi set louder and louder; her choice of music (acid rock) confused and enraged her parents. Her dress continued to be casual, or provocatively disheveled. She was no better at taking care of her room. She turned sour and petulant inexplicably and remained so for hours, even days. But she indicated to her parents a desire to stay in San Antonio, to go to college, to take there "a business course," and to become, at least for a while, a "business secretary." Her father was delighted. Maybe Joan could, after all, join his business. He had a part-time secretary already; he had for some time felt the need of someone to keep track of his various obligations and commitments, as well as the bills he sent out and received, the payments he had to make and expected to arrive. Why not entrust such important and mostly quite confidential matters to someone in the family?

He and Joan talked about such a prospect with increasing intimacy and relish. The nuns soon heard from her of the plan, and supported it. The father gradually laid bare to his daughter much of his financial situation. On the weekends, especially, he would take her aside for an hour or so, explain what he owned, how he had acquired it, and what he hoped to do in the future with it: hold on, make improvements, sell at the first opportunity, sell eventually. He also showed her how to use an adding machine he kept in his study at home; and he explained to her what he does with the profits he makes — stock investments, insurance, savings accounts. "There is not a *lot* of money," he kept telling her. "The Anglos can wipe me out in a moment," he kept telling her. "The Anglos hold my fate in their hands," he kept telling her — because he believed in "expanding" rather than "standing still," and so he would rather (and constantly did) borrow money to enlarge one or another part of his business.

Every once in a while the girl would suggest to her father that he stop in his tracks, even change direction: give some of his money away to the poor, to the Church, to an orphanage next door to some property he owns. He was not resentful. He even promised at times to remember them when making his will, or rather, revising it. But he did warn his daughter that later on, when she was "all grown up," and so "no longer a trusting child," she would have "different ideas" about what he ought do with his money — while alive or in anticipation of death. If he were "really rich," he told the girl, he would indeed leave large sums to charity. For that matter, if he knew that she would, years in the future, marry a Mexican-American man who himself was quite well-off, then he would perhaps contemplate giving her share, at the very least, of his estate to charity. But he rather believed she would not want him to do that. And when he asked her what she thought, she said yes, he was right, she would "probably" want to receive and hold on to her inheritance. She did hope to have children someday, and her father had quite successfully convinced her that a lot of money is required if they are to live well.

Entitlement

The poor both are and are not all alike. On the one hand they struggle against the same odds — hunger and malnutrition in the worst instances, or a marginal life that poses constant threats. Yet Eskimos do not regard their poverty in the same way that

Appalachian yeomen do, or Chicanos in Texas or southern California. In the four sections that have preceded this one I have tried to show how the common social and economic vulnerability of the poor does not make for a uniform pattern of child rearing. Historical precedents, cultural experiences, religious convictions exert their influence on parents and children, make boys and girls differ in all sorts of respects, depending on where they live and who their parents are. The same holds for the well-to-do or the rich. It won't do to talk of *the* affluent ones in America (never mind the world!). It won't do to say that in our upper-middle-class suburbs, or among our wealthy, one observes clear-cut, consistent psychological or cultural characteristics. Even in relatively homogeneous suburbs, there are substantial differences in home life, in values taught, hobbies encouraged, beliefs advocated or virtually instilled.

But there are indeed distinct groups among the well-off — equivalent in their way to the various kinds of poor people. It is the obligation of someone who wants to know how children make sense of their lives — agricultural migrancy, Indian reservation life in the Southwest, the upper-income life of large homes amid ample acreage in rich towns or in wealthy urban enclaves — to document as faithfully as possible the way the common heritage of money and power affects the assumptions of individual boys and girls. Each child, however, is also influenced by certain social, racial, cultural, or religious traditions, or thoroughly idiosyncratic ones — a given *family's* tastes, sentiments, ideals, say. The issue is "class"; but the issue is not only "class."

Many of the influences, even some of the more idiosyncratic ones, that distinguish some children from others are themselves subject to side influences — a "rebound effect," one rather prosperous Illinois Mormon called it. He was anxious for me to know (just as he could not forget) that there was only so much his faith could resist. He took pains, constantly, to tell his children that he was not like his father; that he was not like his brother either, who lives in Salt Lake City and works for a bank. To live near Chicago and be a doctor, to be a Mormon living in a highly secular upper-middle-class world, was to be an exile. He felt stronger in his faith, but also weaker; he felt like his neighbors in many ways, but unlike them in critically important preferences and articles of faith.

What binds together a Mormon banker in Utah with his brother, or other coreligionists in Illinois or Massachusetts? What distinguishes such people, one from the other? Old New Orleans upper-class families are not in certain respects like families who live in, say,

Wellesley Hills, Massachusetts, or Haverford, Pennsylvania, or up the hills outside San Antonio. There *are* resemblances, based on class, occupation, religion, common experiences, expectations, ideas conveyed to children. And yet, again, there are distinctions, shades of feeling and thinking, emphases of one sort or another — even within those families and well-to-do neighborhoods.

I use the word "entitlement" to describe what, perhaps, all quite well-off American families transmit to their children — an important psychological common denominator, I believe: an emotional expression, really, of those familiar, class-bound prerogatives, money and power. The word was given to me, amid much soul-searching, by the rather rich parents of a child I began to talk with almost two decades ago, in 1959. I have watched those parents become grandparents, seen what they described as "the responsibilities of entitlement" get handed down to a new generation. When the father, a lawyer and stockbroker from a prominent and quietly influential family, referred to the "entitlement" his children were growing up with, he had in mind a social rather than a psychological phenomenon: the various juries or committees that select the Mardi Gras participants in New Orleans' annual parade and celebration. He knew that his daughter was "entitled" to be invited here, to attend a dance there, to feel part of a carefully limited and sometimes self-important social scene.

He wanted, however, to go beyond that social fact; he wanted his children to feel obligated by how fortunate they were, and would no doubt always be, all things being equal — or unequal! He talked about what he had received from his parents and what he would give to his children, "automatically, without any thought," and what they too would pass on. The father was careful to distinguish between the social entitlement and "something else," a "something else" he couldn't quite define but knew he had to try to evoke if he were to be psychologically candid: "Our children have a good life ahead of them; and I think they know it now. I think they did when they were three or four, too. It's *entitlement,* that's what I call it. My wife didn't know what I was talking about when I first used the word. She thought it had something to do with our ancestry! Maybe it does! I don't mean to be snide. I just think our children grow up taking a lot for granted, and it can be good that they do, and it can be bad. It's like anything else; it all depends. I mean, you can have spoiled brats for children, or you can have kids who want to share what they have. I don't mean give away all their money! I mean be responsible, and try to live up to their ideals, and not just sit around wondering which island in the Caribbean to visit this year, and where to go next summer to get away from the heat and humidity here in New Orleans."

At the time he said no more. It was 1960, and I was interested mainly in what his son and his daughter thought about black children — and about the violence then being inflicted on a few black children brave enough and stubborn enough to walk past mobs into two elementary schools. But as months became years, I came back to that word "entitlement," especially because it was one I had heard years earlier, in Boston, when I was receiving my training in child psychiatry. "Narcissistic entitlement" was the phrase I had been taught to be familiar with, to use occasionally when speaking of a particular kind of "disturbed" child. The term could be used in place of more conventional, blunter ones that everyone else uses from time to time: a smug, self-satisfied child; or a child who thinks he (or she) owns the world, or will one day; or a self-centered child who expects a lot from just about everyone.

I recall a boy of eight I was treating in Boston, before I went South; my supervisor, a child psychoanalyst who had worked with a similar child for three years, and anticipated, alas, another year or two, at least, of thrice weekly office visits, told me that I was being naïvely hopeful, and a touch simpleminded, when I remarked upon the curiosity of the boy, his evident willingness to ask me questions about all sorts of persons, places, things — and so his capacity for engagement with the world around him. Yes, she pointed out, there was indeed a measure of that, but it was best that *we* ask questions about the nature of *his* questions. As we did, they all came back to him — to quite specific experiences he had gone through and wanted to talk about. And he had told me that, actually; he never asked a question out of intellectual interest — rather, in his words, "because I like to know what might happen next to me."

It is hard to describe the special fearfulness and sadness such a child struggles with. He was not the "ordinary" child; he was quite troubled. And I suppose the parents of such children (even if those mothers and fathers have other, relatively solid children, psychologically speaking) must be disqualified as "normal" or "average." They may be like anyone else on the street; may be rather knowing, psychiatrically — able to sense something "wrong" with a child's "behavior" and go do something about it by seeking out a doctor. But the analyst-supervisor I was myself "seeing" once a week was convinced that there was a "special narcissism," she called it, that a certain kind of parent offers a child: "Narcissism is something we all struggle with; but some people have more of it than others, and some children come from homes that have so much that all the money and possessions, all the rugs and furniture and toys and vacations and savings accounts and insurance policies come crashing on the child's head. There is a shift from narcissism to narcissistic entitlement."

I wasn't sure exactly what she meant, or how the "shift" she had mentioned did indeed take place. I know, because she is someone I still discuss psychoanalytic theory with, that she was not sure herself what the exact dimensions were of that childhood journey. But she knew even then, before there were "fields" like "social psychiatry" or "community psychiatry," that at some point a family's psychology and psychopathology engage with its social and economic life; and that when a migrant child or a ghetto child has to contend with narcissism, it will take on a certain flavor (narcissistic despair, for instance); whereas for a child who lives in a big house and whose parents have a lot and want to give a lot to their offspring, "narcissistic entitlement" may well be a possibility. The child withdraws not only into himself or herself but, by extension, into a certain world of objects, habits, and rituals — the comfortable world of a room, a home, a way of life. The child has much, but wants and expects more — only to feel no great gratitude, but a desire for yet more: an inheritance the world is expected to provide. One's parents will oblige, as intermediaries. And if underneath there lie apprehension and gloom and, not least, a strain of gnawing worthlessness, that is of no matter to many children whose "narcissistic entitlement" becomes what psychoanalytic theorists refer to as a "character trait," rather than a "symptom" that prompts a visit to a doctor. That is, the child is regarded by everyone, psychiatrists included, as "normal," as "all right," or different, but not all *that* different. One doesn't send every cocksure, greedy, self-centered child to a child psychiatrist.

In many other well-to-do homes I've visited, parents have known in their bones what child psychiatrists think and wonder as they talk with their children. Will a certain child get too much — so much that he or she runs the danger of turning away from life, forsaking people for a life of passionate involvement with objects? Less ominously, might a mild tendency in that direction become especially evident when things get tough, psychologically, for one reason or another? Will the child be willing to reach for people, and get along with them, but always with certain limits on the involvement? Often when children are four, five, and six, parents who have felt able to offer them virtually anything begin to pull back, in concern if not outright horror. A son not only has become increasingly demanding or petulant; even when he is quiet he seems to be sitting on a throne of sorts — expecting things to happen, wondering with annoyance why they don't, reassuring himself that they will, or, if they haven't, shrugging his shoulders and waiting for the next event.

It was just such an impasse — not dramatic, but quite definite and worrisome — that prompted that New Orleans father to use the word "entitlement." He had himself been born to wealth, as will future generations of his family be, unless the American economic system changes drastically. But he was worried about what a lot of money can do to a person's "personality"; he uses that word as a layman, but he knows exactly what he has in mind. It isn't so much a matter of spoiling or indulging children; he is willing to let that happen, "within limits." But he knew precisely what those limits were: when the child begins to let his or her situation, the life that he or she lives, "go to the head." It is then that children begin "to act as if they have royal blood in them." And conservative though he is, for him each generation has to prove itself — not necessarily by finding new worlds to conquer or by becoming extraordinarily successful. He has wanted his children to show an interest in the world, to reach out and touch others, to develop their own initiatives, however circumscribed, undramatic, and conventional. It is those kinds of initiative he naturally finds appealing. He is rather satisfied with the life he was born to. He finds each day to be pleasant, interesting, and by his lights, quite useful. He has, however, worried at times that his children were taking *too* much for granted. When his young daughter, during a Mardi Gras season, kept *assuming* she could one day receive this honor and that honor — indeed, become a Mardi Gras queen — he realized that his notion of "entitlement" was not quite hers. *Noblesse oblige* requires a gesture toward others. Had a parent sensed the danger of what my supervisor referred to as a "shift" from "entitlement" to "narcissistic entitlement"?

He would not be the only parent to express such a concern to me in the course of my work. In homes where mothers and fathers profess no explicit reformist persuasions (to say the least!) they nevertheless worry about what happens to children who grow up surrounded by just about everything they want, virtually, on demand. And if much of the apprehension is conventional — that the child will become "spoiled" — there is an element of uneasiness that runs deeper. The parents may begin to regard spoiled behavior as but a symptom: "I don't mind if my children become a little spoiled. That's bound to happen. I worry that they will think that everything is coming to them; that they will grow up with the idea that if they're frustrated, or if they want something, then all they have to do is say a few words, and they'll have what they asked for. When they're like that, they've gone from spoiled to spoiled rotten — and beyond, to some state I don't even know how to describe."

When children are two and three they become increasingly conscious of what belongs to whom. They also become, usually, more and more willing and able to leave themselves behind, so to speak — reach out for objects as well as individuals. They develop their first friends, their first interests or regular and cherished activities. They learn too, most of them, a variety of restraints and frustrations. They must gain control of their bodies, manage without diapers, remember to empty their bladders before going to bed, and get up at night and do likewise in the bathroom rather than on the sheet and mattress. They must learn not to touch hot stoves; not to leave refrigerator doors open; not to spill things, break things, step on things; not to intrude on what belongs to others; not to confuse their prerogatives or possessions with the rights and property of parents, brothers and sisters, friends. At three and four, children from homes like those in New Orleans' Garden District have often started nursery school, have also started making visits to other homes or receiving visitors at their own homes. There are toys to share, games to play, a sandbox or a lawn or indeed a swimming pool or a paddock with its animals. All children have to struggle with themselves for the strength to offer as well as take, or to yield with tact and even a touch of gratitude what has been loaned rather than made an outright gift.

But for some children, a relative handful of the world's, such obligations and struggles are muted. Obviously it is possible for parents to have a lot of money yet avoid bringing up their children in such a way that they feel like members of a royal family. Yet even parents determined not to spoil their children often recognize what might be called the existential (as opposed to strictly psychological) aspects of their situation, and that of their children. A father may begin rather early on lecturing his children about the meaning of money; a mother may do her share by saying no, even when yes is so easy to say — but the child may well sense eventually what the parents know quite well: the difference between a voluntary posture and an utterly necessary one.

Such a child, by the age of five or six, has very definite notions of what is possible, even if not always permitted; possible because there is plenty of money that can be spent. That child, in conversation and without embarrassment or the kind of reticence and secretiveness that comes later, may reveal a substantial knowledge of economic affairs. A six-year-old girl in New Orleans knew that she would at twenty-one inherit a half a million dollars. She also knew that her father "only" gave her twenty-five cents a week — whereas some friends of hers received as much as a dollar. She was vexed; she asked her parents why they were so "strict." One friend had even used the word "stingy" for the parents. The father, in a matter-of-fact way, pointed out to the daughter that she did, after all, get "anything she really wants." Why, then, the need for an extravagant allowance? The girl was won over, told her friends thereafter that it was no matter to her whether she even received an allowance; the important point was the future and what it had to offer. The friends then checked back with their parents, who were rather alarmed — that such young children were talking so freely and openly about family financial matters.

As a result the girl learned from her friends that she had disclosed what ought to be kept firmly under wraps. She decided on the basis of such declarations that her friends may well be "comfortable," but they are not as rich as her parents are or as she will one day be. They in turn explained to her that she had gone beyond the bounds of available evidence. The friends may simply have been told to keep quiet about their family's monetary status — a good idea, the girl was reminded by her parents. The girl agreed, but was not really prepared at the time to follow such advice. She had heard her parents talk with *their* parents about money matters and had been told that it is best that she, too, gradually understand what her financial situation is and will be. That being the case, she wondered out loud why it wasn't appropriate for her to share what she had learned about her future prospects with those she considered good friends. Her parents could only repeat their conviction that certain matters are quite definitely and properly kept within the confines of the family.

Such conversations between young children and their parents help consolidate in boys and girls a conviction of present and future affluence. It obviously never occurs to these children that they won't have food at some point in the near or distant future. Nor do they ever really lack for anything. There are differences in amount, and lectures and sermons may accompany parental acts of generosity. But admonitions don't modify the quite shrewd appraisal children make of what they are heir to, and don't at all diminish the sense of entitlement.

With none of the other American children I have worked with have I heard such a continuous and strong emphasis put on the "self." In fact, other children rarely if ever think about themselves in the way children of well-to-do and rich parents do — with insistence, regularity, and, not least, out of a learned sense of obligation. These privileged ones are children who live in homes with many mirrors. They have mirrors in their rooms, large mirrors in adjoining bathrooms. When they were three or four they were taught to use them; taught to wash their faces, brush their teeth, comb their hair. Personal appearance matters and becomes a central objective for such children. A boy of eight expresses his rebelliousness by clinging to sloppy clothes, but leaves the house every day for school in a neat and well-fitted uniform. A good number of these children wear them — shirts or sweaters with a school's name and / or insignia on them. Even when the child relaxes, comes home, and changes into "old" clothes, there is an air of decisiveness about the act — and certainly, the issue is one of choice: to wear *this,* or *that;* to look a particular way, in keeping with a particular mood, time of day, event.

The issue also is that of the "self" — its display, its possibilities, its cultivation and development, even the repeated use of the word. A ten-year-old boy who lives in the outermost part of Westchester County made this very clear. I had originally met him because his parents, both lawyers, were active in the civil rights movement. His father, a patrician Yankee, very much endorsed the students who went South in the early 1960s and, nearer to home, worked on behalf of integrated schools up North. His own children, however, attended private schools — a source of anguish to both the father and the son, who do not lend themselves easily to a description that only emphasizes the hypocritical element in their lives.

The boy knew that he also *would* be (as opposed to wanted to be!) a lawyer. He was quick to perceive and acknowledge his situation, and as he did so he brought himself (his "self") right into the discussion: "I don't want to tell other kids what to do. I told my father I should be going to the public schools myself. Then I could say anything. Then I could ask why we don't have black kids with us in school. But you have to try to do what's best for your *own* life, even if you can't speak up for the black people. When I'm grown up, I'll be like my father; I'll help the black people all I can. It's this way: first you build *yourself* up. You learn all you can. Later, you can *give of yourself.* That's what Dad says: you can't help others until you've learned to help *yourself.* It's not that you're being selfish. People say you're self-ish, if you're going to a private school and your parents have a lot of money. We had a maid here, and she wasn't right in the head. She lost her temper and told Daddy that he's a phony, and he's out for *himself* and no one else, and the same goes for my sister and me. Then she quit. Daddy tried to get her to talk with us, but she wouldn't. She said that's all we ever do — talk, talk. I told Daddy she was contradicting herself; because she told me a few weeks ago that I'm always doing something, and I should sit down and talk with her. But I didn't know what to say to her! I think she got angry with me because I was put-ting on my skis for cross-country skiing, and she said I had too much, that was my problem. I asked her where the regular skis were, and she said she wouldn't tell me, even if she knew! It's too bad, what hap-pened to her.

"I feel sorry for her, though. Like my sister said, it's no fun to be a maid! The poor woman doesn't look very good. She weighs too much. She's only forty, my mother thinks, but she looks as if she's sixty, and is sick. She should take better care of herself. She said my sister and I make big messes in the bathroom. But that's because we *use* the bath-room! And her breath — God, it's terrible. She isn't as clean as she should be. My mother wanted to get her some deodorant, but we were afraid she'd just blow up at us. But she did anyway. So it didn't make any difference! Like my Dad said, it's too bad about her; she didn't know how to take care of herself and now she's thrown away this job, and she told my mother last year that it was the best one she'd ever had, so she's her own worst enemy. I wonder what she'll think when she looks at herself in the mirror and tries to figure out what to do next."

He was no budding egotist. If anything, he was less self-centered, at ten, than many other children of his community or others like it. He was willing to think about, at least, others less fortunate than himself — the maid, and black people in general. True, he would of-ten repeat uncritically his father's words, or a version of them. But he was trying to respond to his father's wishes and beliefs as well as his words. It was impossible for him, no matter how compassionate his nature, to conceive of life as others live it — the maid, and yes, mil-lions of children his age, who don't look in the mirror very often and may not even own one; who don't worry about what is worn, and how one looks, and what is said and how one sounds, and what is done (in the bathroom) and how one smells.

Sometimes minor details of a life tell more than larger attitudes spoken and duly recorded by outside observers. A boy's fingernails, for instance; or his sister's skin — in each instance, a reflection of much more. Here is the boy from Westchester County, at eleven, talking about the new pair of scissors he has received from his father: "I like them. I didn't want my mother to clip my fingernails any longer. I'd rather take care of myself! I'll be shaving soon. I look forward to that! I've watched my father a lot. He showed me how to use the scissors and end up with nails that aren't too short and aren't too long. There's a kid in my class, he lets his nails get longer and longer and there's a lot of dirt under them, and you wonder how long they'll get, and then all of a sudden, one day, you notice that they've been cut off. His parents have got a divorce, and they have a maid taking care of him and his kid brother, and she runs the house and there's no one supervising her. You have to tell the help what to do, because if you don't, they forget and they don't live up to your standards, and they're acting as if they were back in their own homes."

So it happens — a boy's developing sense of himself as against a collective, amorphous "them." It is a "sense" that has both sociological and psychological dimensions to it. The former are perhaps more painful to spell out but also more readily apparent. The boy has learned that in the ghetto people live who don't use his parents' kind of judgment, and don't, either, have the same personal habits or concerns. The boy's sister has a similar kind of knowledge. At twelve she could be quite pointed: "We've had a couple of maids, and they don't know why I use my mother's Vaseline lotion on my arms and hands — and in winter on my face, too. They say I've got a wonderful complexion; but I don't think they know how to look real carefully at my skin — or their own either. Maybe they don't have the time. But I see them taking a 'break,' and what do they do? They go put on a prize show in the morning or a 'story' in the afternoon. I don't know how they can stand looking at that stuff! I've got a lot of chores. We're not spoiled here! I have to clean out the stalls and brush the horses carefully before we go riding. I have to pick up my room. My mother told me when I was real little, before I was even old enough to go to school, that she wasn't going to have me sitting and looking at television while the maid was straightening out my room. The same goes for outside the house; we have a gardener, but he's not allowed to come into the barn and help us with the animals.

"We had one maid, and she said we spent more time with the animals than she does with her children. I felt sad when she told me that. She has no understanding of what an animal needs. She was the one who was always telling me I was beautiful, and so I didn't need any lotion on my skin. I wanted to give her the lotion. She needs it. Her skin is in terrible shape. It's so dried and cracked. My mother says you can be poor and still know how to take care of yourself. It's not the money; it's the attitude you have toward yourself. If our maid stopped buying a lot of candy and potato chips, she could afford to get herself some skin lotion. And she wouldn't be so fat!"

A child has learned to distinguish between her own inclinations or preferences and those of another person — a whole category of people. This girl was, at the time, not quite an adolescent; for years, however, she had been prepared for that time, for adulthood as well — prepared by parents who not only wanted her to know how to use skin lotions, or choose "tasteful" lipstick, or shun anything but "natural" fingernail polish, or learn how to care for her hair and wash it, and pay attention to the scalp as well. Those parents wanted her to give an enormous amount of attention to *herself* — to her thoughts, which she has been taught are worthy of being spoken, and to her body, which is going to be, one day, "attractive." So she has been told by several maids — far too emphatically to suit the taste of her parents. They prefer a more understated, indirect approach. They remind the girl that she looks like her grandmother ("a handsome lady") or her aunt ("who was quite beautiful"). They let her know how graceful she is as a young dancing student, how agile and accomplished a rider she has become, how fast and accurate a game of tennis she has developed, even at her age. They smile at pictures of her smiling, applaud her once again when watching home movies. Her picture is on the mantel over the living room fireplace, on her father's desk, on her mother's desk, and is on her own desk, for that matter.

When she was six and seven she asked a lot of questions about herself. They were answered patiently, thoughtfully, and often with enthusiastic pride — a contrast indeed with many poor children, whose parents are tired, embittered, sad, or all too resigned to their fate, and hardly able to boast about the circumstances of life. The girl's questions occur to all children, rich or poor — are the banal inquiries we never quite stop asking ourselves: who am I, why am I here, whence do I come, and where am I going — the continuing preoccupations of philosophers, novelists, and painters. Children prefer the painter's approach. They sometimes don't pay much attention to the answers to their questions. After all too verbal family meals they retire to a desk or table, draw pictures meant to suggest what life is and will be about. When the girl mentioned above wonders who she is or has questions about her future, she picks up crayons and draws herself with care and affection — on a horse, in a garden, high up in a tower, surveying the countryside.

In doing so she draws upon her concrete, day-to-day experiences. She also uses those experiences in order to suggest something larger about her particular life. Especially noteworthy is the care she and others like her take with themselves as they draw. So often poor children treat themselves cursorily; they quickly sketch a rather unflattering self-portrait. Sometimes they are unwilling to complete what they have begun — as if they are unsure of life itself. A migrant child once told me in a matter-of-fact way that he had no expectation of living beyond twenty. He was simply a child who knew the score. The children of doctors and lawyers and business executives have learned the score too. The girl mentioned above spends a half hour drawing herself, moves her eyes toward a mirror every once in a while to check on how she actually does look, and is eventually quite proud of what she has drawn. She also spends long periods of time looking at old photographs — of herself, her parents, her grandparents. Such observations and bits of anecdotal family history have become consolidated in the girl's mind. She regards herself — though she has learned to be affectingly modest — as a rather attractive person. No wonder she once posed herself, in a picture, beside a giant sunflower. She was in no way overshadowed by the flower; if anything, it adorned her own luminous presence.

When that girl became ill with chicken pox the anguish of her mental state was noticeable and instructive. She wanted to scratch the many lesions on her face and arms but was told, of course, by her parents that she must not. She heeded their advice. In the beginning she did scratch one pustule midway on her upper right arm. Her mother became quite upset. Before the mother could say a word, the child spoke up, acknowledged her awareness of the future implications of her deed. She had lost control, and she would suffer. Her description of that talk and of her later, more successful, bout with the disease, has struck me as a classic of sorts: "I don't want to look ugly. If I had scratched my face, like I did my right arm, I'd look a mess for life. I knew that. But I had *such* a bad case! The doctor said it was one of the worst he'd seen in the last few years. He told me he had seen even worse than mine, and I was sort of disappointed. I figured that I'd like to go through the biggest challenge, and come out on top!

"After a day or two, I began to wonder if I'd be able to survive! I got very weepy. I began to wonder whether I'd done anything wrong — to deserve this punishment. I couldn't look myself in the mirror. I didn't want to wash at all. I felt so dirty and horrible looking. I asked my brother and my parents not to look at me! My brother tried to kid me out of my mood. He came in with his Polaroid camera and said he'd take a picture of me, and I could keep it, and when I was over the disease, I could just laugh! Instead I started crying, right in front of him. He apologized.

"The worst part of the chicken pox was the waiting and the trying to keep control. My mother sat with me, and my Dad did too, when he got home. On the worst day, he offered to stay with me and not go to his office. I said no, I'd be all right. But he decided to stay anyway. He just sat there and read to me. We watched some television — the news and a cooking class. We talked a little. Dad kept telling me I was great, and not to worry; he was sure I was going to have a wonderful life, because I've got everything going for me. I told him 'not the chicken pox,' when he said that. But he just laughed and told me that the chicken pox would soon be a bad memory, and I'd forget about it completely in a couple of months. I'm not sure I ever will, though. I have this scar on my arm, and I'll always have it. My mother says no one will notice; but I do! She got angry the other day. She said I was worrying too much. But I've seen her worry a lot too. If a dress doesn't fit her, she sends it right back. She's always either on a diet or coming off one, or getting ready to go on one again. We have scales in every bathroom, and one in her bedroom. I told her I don't need to weigh myself and my brother doesn't; but she wants us to get in the habit, so we'll know later when to start being careful about food. She tells the maid to give us cookies only when she's not around; she doesn't want to be tempted. And her hair — well, that's 'a whole subject,' as my Daddy says. When he was with me that day, I asked him why Mom worries so much about her hair, and dyes it. Who cares if there's some gray in her hair! But Dad said that gray hair for Mom is like the chicken pox for me. I could see what he meant, but it's not exactly the same."

She did not for long insist upon the difference; she went along with her father's comparison. She did so not reluctantly, but with the detachment that goes with complete recovery — a feeling of remove from what was once painful. Her mother has always been regarded as a rather lovely woman; the girl was prepared to emphasize that fact in her mind, and associate her own present and future appearance with her mother's deserved reputation. The girl was also prepared to acknowledge quite candidly what a relatively severe case of a basically benign disease could do to her thoughts about herself: "I began to worry whether I really was as pretty as everyone had been saying. It was a mood; I'm over it now. I do have a few bad memories. Dad says they'll go. I hope so. I look at myself in the mirror and I'll suddenly be afraid that the chicken pox is coming back. I get scared. It's silly. I know I'm never going to get the chicken pox again!

"I wish I hadn't scratched that one place. It's such a small scar. But it gives me nightmares! I woke up the other night and my parents were in my room. I guess I'd been crying or shouting. In the morning my mother said I'd half-awakened, and I'd told them that a cat had been chasing me, and scratched me, and I was afraid there'd be a scar. I wonder a lot about the man I'll marry. Will he have brown hair or blond hair or black hair? My mother asked me if it makes any difference; I told her I like brown hair and green eyes, and I hope he'll be tall and thin. I wouldn't even want to go out once with a man who was overweight!"

This is no petty, superficial, half-witted, or empty-headed girl. She has gone to very good private schools — each of which has high academic standards and expectations. She can be serious, thoughtful, and idealistic — that is, worried about others less fortunate and hopeful that they somehow get to live better lives. As a child she can hardly be expected to come up with solutions for the world's various problems, but some of those problems do at times weigh upon her. Yet she can, all of a sudden, move from writing a composition about "world hunger" to discussing with her mother the virtues of various cosmetics or the appropriateness of certain dresses for one or another social occasion. She can also, rather disarmingly, stop thinking about "the troubles in America" her teacher has asked the class to write about, because her parakeet needs food or water, her two gerbils require new bedding, her alarm clock has to be set, her desk is cluttered and ought be straightened out, or her phone has rung. She has a room with its own demands and requirements, with a bureau mirror and one on the back of the door, a full-length mirror. Sometimes she gets tired of thinking of arithmetic problems and social problems, and spelling problems, of coming up with ideas meant to straighten out society.

It is important that a privileged child's normal sense of "entitlement" be distinguished not only from pathological narcissism, but from the more common phenomenon known as being "spoiled." It is a matter of degree; "spoiled" children are self-centered all right, petulant and demanding — but not saddled with the grandiose illusions (or delusions) clinicians have in mind when using the phrase "narcissistic entitlement." The rich, the "well-to-do" are all too commonly charged with producing spoiled children. Yet one sees spoiled children everywhere, among the very poor as well as the inordinately rich. A child can be spoiled by a mother's attitude. What the child is "given" can be called excessive instinctual leeway or, in everyday words, however politicized in recent years, "permissive indulgence." I remember a migrant mother who knew precisely and uncannily what she was doing "wrong" — knew, indeed, to call it all "wrong." She told me one day that she had given birth to a particular child with more pain than usual and had been in lower spirits than ever before in her life during the first months of that child's life. When the baby began to notice the mother and the world, start crawling and separating himself from her, she felt a fierce desire within herself, expressed with unforgettable intensity, "to let that boy have anything he wants, anything he can lay his hands on." She was careful, for all her lack of education and her troubled spirits, to qualify herself. She moved quickly, immediately, from "anything he wants" to "anything he can lay his hands on." She knew that in the first or second year of life the child would have all he could do to reach and hold on to what he wanted.

But soon enough a child begins to see things that others have; on a rented, only half-working television set the migrant child saw a lot, and looked around the room and realized a lot. His was no blessed life! He continued, however, to want to take what little he could get. And of course children (or adults) can want things that are psychological in lieu of what is "material." They can become demanding, possessive, insistent, if allowed to be. They can compete with others for attention, push hard against others who try to assert themselves. They can make every effort to obtain center stage at all times. The migrant mother developed, deep within her hurt and sad self, a pride about her child and his stubborn, indulged, expropriative, loud-mouthed, and at times impossibly egotistical behavior.

He was the child who would shout and scream and swagger, shake his fists, really, at the wretched world he had been born to. No matter that such behavior, whether allowed or even encouraged, is hardly a guarantee of a future rise to success. On the contrary, a child of migrant parents who acts like that one is headed, quite likely, for future trouble. The mother knew that too. She knew that migrants are virtually peons; that they submit to endless demands and manipulations. Perhaps one of her children would be so "spoiled" that he would be utterly incapable of becoming a migrant or lasting as one for very long. She answered along those lines when her husband asked her why she doesn't spank the "spoiled one" as she does the other children.

He in turn mentioned the grim likelihood that the boy would not indeed last as a migrant. He would instead end up in jail — or soon dead. All right, better a last stand, the mother replied. But she knew that really there was no point to such a hope; it would never even come to that, because the boy would either learn to mind his manners, and submit to the only life he would most likely ever know, or go down not in defiant resistance but through the slow attrition of cheap wine and harmless side-of-the-road braggadocio — the "maladjusted" migrant who works inefficiently, goes to the bars before and after work, dies in a car accident or drowns drunk in one of the hundreds of irrigation canals that crisscross the agricultural counties of Florida, where this particular family spent its winters.

The parallel with spoiled children of upper-income families is not so farfetched. In one of the first such families I came to know there was a girl who was described by both parents as "spoiled." At the time, I fear, I was ready to pronounce every child in New Orleans' Garden District spoiled.

Nevertheless, I soon began to realize that it wouldn't do to call one set of children spoiled, by virtue of their social and economic background — as against another set of children who were obviously less privileged. Though one meets among the poor any number of spoiled children, one also meets among the rich restrained, disciplined children; sometimes, even, boys and girls who have learned to be self-critical, even ascetic — anything but "spoiled" in the conventional sense of the word. True, one can find a touch and more of arrogance in those apparently Spartan boys and girls, who seem quite anxious to deny themselves all sorts of apparently accessible privileges. But one also finds in these children a consistent willingness to place serious and not always pleasant burdens on themselves. They often struck me, as I came to their homes fresh from visits with much poorer age-mates, as remarkably *less* spoiled: not so much whining or crying; fewer demands for candy or other sweets; even sometimes a relative indifference to toys, a disregard of television — so often demanded by the children I was seeing across the city, on the other side of the tracks.

Those children from prominent families appeared, even at the age of four or five, to put their energies in the service of "constructive" play or "useful" activities. They had begun to learn at two and three how important it was for them to do "right" as against "wrong"; to build rather than destroy; to concentrate their energies, devote them to particular tasks, which were to be finished rather than started and abandoned. They had, in some instances, even learned to take care of their own rooms — keep them neat, pick up after themselves, be conscious of what belongs where. Maids came to help, or lived with the family, but sometimes a particular boy or girl, as young as five or six, was a taskmaster to the maid rather than, certainly, a helpless or indulged child. And sometimes the maid herself became astonished by the example set by such children — and became their strong admirer.

A New Orleans black woman said to me in 1961: "I don't know how to figure out these rich, white kids. They're something! I used to think, before I took a job with this family, that the only difference between a rich kid and a poor kid is that the rich kid knows he has a lot of money and he grows up and he becomes spoiled rotten. That's what my mother told me; she took care of a white girl, and the girl was an only child, and her father owned a department store in McComb, Mississippi, and that girl thought she was God's special creature. My mother used to come home and tell us about the 'little princess'; but she turned out to be no good. She was so pampered she couldn't do a thing for herself. All she knew how to do was order people around. It's different with these two children here in New Orleans. I've never seen such a boy and such a girl. They think they're the best ones who ever lived — like that girl in McComb — but they don't behave like her. They're never asking me to do much of anything. They even ask if *they* can help *me!* They tell me that they want to know how to do everything. The girl says she wants to learn how to run the washing machine and the dishwasher. She says she wants to learn all my secret recipes. She says she'd like to give the best parties in the Garden District when she grows up, and she'd like to be able to give them without anyone's help. She says I could serve the food, but she would like to make it. The boy says he's going to be a lawyer and a banker, so he wants to know how much everything costs. He doesn't want to waste anything. He'll see me throw something away, and he wants to know why. I wish my own kids were like him!

"I wish my kids weren't so lazy; they don't care what's going on;

they just want to play and play, and they waste a lot of food, and they break the toys I get them real fast. I even told my children I wish they could learn from these two children here. But these children here are special, and don't they know it! That's what being rich is: you know you're different from most people. These two kids are even more special, because they act as if they're going to be tops in everything, and they're pleased as can be with themselves, because there is nothing they can't do, and there's nothing they can't get, and there's nothing they can't win, and they're always showing off what they can do, and then before you can tell them how good they are, they're telling the same thing to themselves. It's confusing! They're not spoiled one bit, but oh, they have a high opinion of themselves!

"And I'll have to admit, there are times when I have the same high opinion of them! I'll look at them, and I'll say that they could be dropped on an island in the middle of a big ocean, and they'd know what to do, and if they didn't have anyone around to be pleased with them, they'd be all right because they'd be pleased with themselves! And it wouldn't take them long to know where to go and what to do on that island, because they are just so sure of themselves and so full of themselves that they always have their chins up, and they're happy, and they know where they're going, and they know what's ahead — that everything will come out fine in the end. When you have that kind of spirit in you, then you'll always get out of any jam you're in, and you'll always end up on top, because that's where you started, and that's where you believe you're going to end up, and if it's in your mind that it is like that, and it's *going* to be like that, and if you're willing to work hard, like these kids are, and if you're careful about everything, like they are, then you just *can't* lose, and don't these kids know it, I'll tell you!"

Actually the children she speaks of aren't as confident of themselves as she thinks, though she certainly has accurately conveyed their appearance. The kind of children she knows so well are extraordinarily privileged by virtue of background and money, are also intelligent and of attractive appearance; but those children have demons that occasionally urge them on, and their nature is not always easy to divine. Boys and girls may seem without anxiety or self-doubt at, say, eight or nine. Yet, there are moments of hesitation, if not apprehension. An eleven-year-old boy from a prominent and quite brilliant Massachusetts family (three generations of first-rate lawyers) told his teachers in an autobiographical composition about the vicissitudes of "entitlement": "I don't always do everything right. I'd like to be able to say I don't make any mistakes, but I do, and when I do, I feel bad. My father and mother say that if you train yourself, you can be right *almost* 100% of the time. Even they make mistakes, though. I like to be first in sports. I like to beat my brothers at skiing. But I don't always go down the slopes as fast as I could and I sometimes fall down. Last year I broke my leg. That was the first time I'd ever gone to a hospital and stayed there. It was my mother who reminded me that I'd been in the hospital for a week just after I was born! I'd forgotten! I was saying that I'd *never* been in the hospital overnight, and she corrected me.

"My great-grandfather is eighty-four, and he's in the best of health. It worries me that I have bad sinus trouble a lot of times after I get flu. I'd hate to be sick when I'm older. There's too much to do; if you get sick, you can't do much of anything, except stay home and rest. When I get a bad cold, I feel disappointed in myself. I don't think it's right to be easy on yourself. If you are, then you slip back, and you don't get a lot of the rewards in life. If you really work for the rewards, you'll get them."

His teachers have often given him that kind of platitude. In the fourth grade, for instance, his teacher had written on the blackboard (and kept it there for weeks): "Those who want something badly enough get it, provided they are willing to wait and work." The boy has been brought up to believe that it will be like that for him. He knows that others are not so lucky, but he hasn't really met those "others," and they don't cross his mind. What does occur to him sometimes is the need for constant exertion, lest he fail to "measure up." The expression is a family one, used repeatedly. No matter how difficult a task, no matter how frustrating it is for others, one "measures up" when one does it well. One "measures up" when one tries hard, succeeds. One measures up because one *must*. No allowance is made for any possible lack of ability or endowment. The assumption is that one has been "given a lot" (another family expression) and so a "return" is obligatory if justice is to be done. If one slackens or stumbles, one ought take oneself to task. The emphasis is on a quick and efficient moment of scrutiny followed by "a fast pickup," yet another admonitory injunction handed down.

Such counsel is not as callous or psychologically insensitive as it may sound — or even as it may have been *intended* to sound. The child who hears it gets briefly upset, but "a fast pickup" does indeed take place quite often. Again, it is a matter of feeling "entitled." A child who has been told repeatedly that all he or she needs to do is try hard does not feel inclined to allow himself or herself much skeptical self-examination. The point is to feel *entitled* — then act upon that feeling. The boy whose composition was just quoted from wrote again, apparently about his younger (aged five) brother: "I was watching my brother from my bedroom window. He was climbing up the fence we built for our corral. He got to the top, and then he just stood there and waved and shouted. No one was there. He was talking to himself. He was very happy. Then he would fall. He would be upset for a few seconds, but he would climb right back up again. Then he would be even happier! He was entitled to be happy. It is his fence, and he has learned to climb it, and stay up, and balance himself."

The little brother was indeed happy on top of the fence. He would talk to himself with obvious pleasure — tell nameless, invisible people that they are stupid and inadequate because, unlike him, they are unable to climb the fence and stay there and enjoy themselves. Yes, he was obviously talking to himself. He was also speaking to an earlier version of himself, to the boy of four who had wanted to climb that fence, wanted to get on top, and, just as important, stay there and enjoy the experience. Once he had succeeded, he enjoyed his new-found competence. He would practically never be curbed, humiliated, denied interesting or engaging occasions because of the "reality" of the world around him. Quite the contrary; there would be one inviting adventure after another over the months and years. One day, as a matter of fact, he ran across the field after he had shown himself able to climb a particular fence with ease — in search of a taller, slightly more precarious fence on the other side of the corral. And when that climb was "nothing" and the position of balance a giant bore, he predicted quite casually that he would never see a fence that he couldn't rather quickly master. His father did not want the boy to be completely unrealistic, however. To whistle in the dark, to assume that one can always triumph, is to be vulnerable — the weakness of the overconfident. One ought to have a great deal of drive and ambition, a conviction that the world will eventually be made to oblige — but only after a substantial effort.

It is absurd to say that all children whose parents make a certain amount of money or work at certain occupations, or live in a certain neighborhood, possess an attitude of mind (and an attitude toward the world) that might be sensibly tucked into the generalization referred to here as "entitlement." More than once I have insisted that each individual has his or her unique way of pulling together the various elements of mental life. I have wanted, however, to suggest a common manner of response toward life among children of a certain class and background. I realize that the particular word "entitlement" has complicated psychoanalytic implications or, for some, pejorative social or political implications, or indeed, for others, quite defensible and justifiable implications. For the children I have worked with, however, the word is simply a description of a certain actuality. There are both social and psychological dimensions to that actuality, and deep down these children know them rather well.

I have in mind especially the son of a powerful Florida grower. When the child was five he kept using the words "I'm entitled to." His parents were much annoyed. The father did not want his son using such a peremptory, self-important, demanding expression. He began interrupting the boy, telling him that he was not "entitled" to *anything,* that he must ask for what he wanted, and be grateful when he got it. The boy kept asking why, why. The father kept explaining — a litany of oughts and musts. The boy in turn fell back upon his considerable intelligence and powers of observation. He reminded his father of his own words: "If you earn something, you are entitled to keep it." Had not the boy "earned" the right to make his various requests — by trying to be "good" or "quiet"? Had not the father told him on a number of occasions that he was "coming along nicely," that he was "making his parents proud"?

The boy spoke up for himself in fits and starts, but he got his message across, because his father eventually settled for an ironic statement: "A boy who stands up for himself like that boy has — well, he's entitled to say every once in a while, that he's *entitled* to something!" It must be rather obvious — it was to the grower, for all his lack of interest in the plight of the hundreds of impoverished migrants who worked his land so long and hard — that not every father can be grateful for his son's outspokenness, his young son's assumption that he was entitled to political freedom, social equality, economic privilege.

What Profit Under the Sun?

All the children I have been writing about in this series are try-ing to come to terms with what one child born to great wealth in New Orleans referred to as her "one and only chance," by which she meant nothing less than her life. She will never be a latter-day Marx or Kierkegaard. She is today well on her way to being a mem-ber of upper-crust, conservative New Orleans society, a perfect foil for a person like me, I suppose: the preoccupation with dinner parties, flowers, dances, and clothes, not to mention a suitable suitor. She has read nothing I have written, as far as I know, since I met her almost two decades ago. She reads very little, actually, except the New Orleans *Times Picayune* and a news weekly or two, which she only "browses through" at that. She has read her share of textbooks in school, but they don't "attract" her, she is frank to say. She is, it's not unfair to say, a vain, self-centered, flighty person who cares not a whit for her fellow man or woman, unless they be part of a small circle of relatives, friends, neighbors: her kind.

Yet, when she was eight she had a habit that puzzled, worried her parents, short time that it lasted — a few months in a girl's long years of childhood. She would, as her mother put it, "sit and stare." In fact, the girl liked looking out the window of her parents' Garden District mansion. Across the street was one of those striking (and to visitors, hauntingly unique) New Orleans cemeteries — the graves, the elabo-rate and various tombs, all above ground. The tombs cast shadows, and in the early evening or morning the girl would notice them. She wondered about who "those people" were, the departed. She won-dered what kind of lives they had lived, what they could tell her now about those lives. Maybe what she was making, in retrospect, a feeble and ultimately futile effort to avoid coming to was herself. She was really struggling hard for a few seconds of detachment, perspective, humor about the world she was part of. She would smile when she looked out and caught sight of an especially ornate, imposing, as-sertive monument of stone. She would, in her own way, meditate about life's meaning.

But, alas, she told her parents what she liked to do in an occasional "off moment." They were hardly reassured. They were quizzical
the first time; annoyed the second; admonitory the third; worried the
fourth; and ready to consult a doctor the fifth — those "off moments"
indeed! They did call a doctor; he urged intelligent restraint, and his
advice proved correct. Not that there was actually restraint. The girl
was implicitly and sometimes directly told to get on with it — life. She
was, her parents decided, "a little too introverted." She had best be
made "busy." They knew the enemy — inwardness. They knew the
point of life: the headlong rush; the ferris wheel at the age of six, the
assembly dance at the age of sixteen; the full calendar; the school
choir, everyone beautifully, expensively, similarly dressed; the clock
that keeps moving; the dream that is promptly forgotten; the sigh before retiring that registers satisfaction and congratulation — no wasted
time. No wasted time. No time heavy on one's hands. No time to spare.
No time left. In no time, no time at all — world without end.

The girl felt the push. It took her a little time to stop being part of
some bad time her parents were convinced she must be having — else
why the "funny time" she was for a while reported having. So the
mother put it: "She still has a funny time up in her room, looking at
that cemetery. She tells us she talks with the people in the tombs! I
was horrified. She smiles. I thought at first she was teasing me. I guess
she's all right. She's just growing up. All children do a few crazy things
before they get sensible." She was right; just about all children do have
their strange, wondrous, luminous, brooding, magical, redemptive
moments. The girl described hers in a way Clarence John Laughlin,
mystical and messianic photographer of her native city, would likely
find helpful to remember as he stalks the light and shadows, the memories and bizarre actualities of a place, a time: "I don't think there's
anyone there, across the street, inside the cemetery. I just like to look
at the place. I used to walk in there with my grandmother. I was little,
and she was still alive. She told me she had lived a nice long life, and
she had been happy, and she was ready to leave us, whenever God decided she had been with us long enough. She would be glad to go. One
day we found her asleep, and it was late in the morning for her — nine
o'clock. She was dead. My mother said there was no need to call the
doctor, but we had to. I never saw her. I wanted to go in the room, but
they wouldn't let me. I tried to sneak in, but they said no.

"The maid said they should let me in. The maid almost convinced
my mother. I heard them arguing. I never heard the maid speak back
to my mother like that. But my mother won. The maid came out cry-

ing. She wasn't upset because of my grandmother. The tears were for me. The maid wanted me to say good-bye to someone, but I never could. They didn't bury my grandmother in that cemetery across the street. I'd hoped they would. She and I had always been close — 'real tight,' she said. If they had buried her across the street, we'd still be 'real tight.' But there isn't any room left, my mother says. I don't think that's exactly right. The maid says it's exactly wrong! The maid says she's done some listening, and she knows what's true — that my mother didn't want someone in the family buried there so near to us.

"Some of the time, when I look across the street, I might be wishing my grandmother was buried there. A lot of the time I just wonder who someone was — someone who's inside one of the little buildings. And I wonder if a long time from now there will be a girl like me, and she will be sitting, maybe, right in my room, and she will be looking at the cemetery, and I'll be there, and she'll be wondering about me! If I want, I can be buried there. The maid told me so. I guess I have a lot of time to make up my mind! It's funny, looking at a cemetery. It's funny playing there. We play there, some of us. It makes people nervous when we do; but they let us. You wonder if there are ghosts. I know there aren't, but I wonder. You hear a sound, and you think someone might be talking to you. Even with the window closed, and you're inside the house, you'll hear a noise, and you wonder. It'll be the dog, in the next room, shaking himself. But you wonder."

She stopped all that wondering within a few months. She had gone through her worrisome time, had "recovered." So the mother had it: "Thank God, she's better. She's recovered from her interest in cemeteries." An "interest"? Or was it, perhaps, a brief spell of release, of openness, of escape from Kierkegaard's, Walker Percy's "everydayness"? And maybe a dialectal moment or two — such as Thomas de Quincey, with Clarence John Laughlin approving, once described: "When one feels/oneself sleeping alone, / utterly divided from all call / or hearing of friends, / doors open that should be / shut, or unlocked that / should be triply secured, / the very walls gave, barriers / swallowed up by unknown / abysses, nothing around one / but frail curtains, and / a world of illimitable night, / whisperings at a distance, / correspondence going on / between darkness and darkness, / like one's deep calling to / another, and the dreamer's / own heart the center from / which the whole network of this / unimaginable chaos radiates . . ."

As for that child's maid, she was, as the girl's mother often said, and as the girl would grow up to say herself, "not always in control, the way she should be." So much for psychiatry, its normative judgments, and the uses to which they are put. Nevertheless, the maid surely deserves a little space, if not equal billing; she deserves to speak on behalf of herself, and maybe a lot of other maids. This book could, of course, go on and on; maids could speak about children, and so could cooks, and grocers, and druggists, and tennis instructors, and hockey coaches, and camp owners.

But this particular New Orleans maid, let free for a few lines, will help us as we come toward the end, here — because she has never lost sight, really, of "the end of things," as she has repeatedly put it: "I look at these folks, and my heart goes out to them. They feel sorry for me. I know they do. I hear them talking. But I feel sorry for *them*. Mind you, I feel sorry for myself, too. I'm not fooling myself! It's no good being Mr. Charlie's maid. It's no good working in the white man's kitchen and cleaning up after him, and getting his few dollars, his pat on the back — and because of the pat you're supposed to act like you've seen God's face, at last you have, and He's smiling down on you. But who is Mr. Charlie? My Momma told me who he is; he's a sad one, that's who he is. They're all right, these people here. I've worked for them for fifteen years. I'll stay with them, most likely, until they carry me out, and that'll be the end of things. My Momma told me: remember that you're put here only for a few seconds of God's time, and He's testing you. He doesn't want answers, though. He wants you to know how to ask the right questions. If you learn how to do that, then you'll do all right when you meet Him, and He's there looking you over. You have to tell Him that you've learned how to question yourself, and when you show Him what you know, He'll smile on you. God's smile, that's the sunshine. God's worries, that's the night. We have to face the night. We have to face the end of things.

"These people here, they've got all that money, and all this big house, and another one out in the country, and still they won't let that little girl just be herself. She's eight or nine, and she's got an independent spirit in her, but they're determined to get rid of it, and they will, let me tell you, and soon. The girl asks me a lot of questions. That's good. She looks out on that cemetery and she starts to wondering about things. That's good. She wonders about life, and what it's about, and what the end of things will be. That's good. But she's stopping now. That's what they want: no looking, no staring, no peeking at life. No questions; they don't want questions. They go to a church a couple of times a year, Christmas and Easter, and no one asks them any questions there. No one asks them questions anyplace they go. The people who are gone, who live across the street there in the cemetery, inside those tombs — they know what's important, they've discovered what's important, they've reached their destination. I'm poor, but at least I know that I should ask myself every day: where's your destination, and are you going there, or are you getting sidetracked? A lot of days I wish I was them; I wish I was rich like them. Then I ask myself: would you be any different? I don't know the answer. I mean, it's like the minister keeps saying to us in church: 'Who knows whether he's going to be a wise man or a fool?' And then he'll remind us that 'all is vanity.' And he'll remind us that 'there's no profit under the sun.' I wonder if there is any. I wonder a lot if there's any profit under the sun. I read the Bible and I wonder. I'll ask myself one day, and I'll ask the next day, and I'll just decide not to be too sure; just keep on asking."

Best to let that black woman have the last word. Like that child, the maid meditates, wonders, takes notice, keeps her eyes and ears open, knows to think about "the end of things," and never stops praying. She prays that she be able to keep her mind and heart and soul, as she always says it, "open to God." She wants to know whether she is a wise person or a fool. She wants to know whether she will always be able to believe that "wisdom excels folly," and "light excels darkness." She knows the ambiguities of life — even of words like "light" and "darkness." She can talk of "light folks" and "dark folks." She can talk of the rich who are light — and yet succumb to vanity; and the poor who are dark — and yet *also* succumb to vanity.

I said I would give the black woman the last word, but I had best take a certain "responsibility" upon myself. *The* answer is a prelude to many further questions. I placed it at the end of the first volume of this series — a sentence James Agee wrote as he sweated and struggled for the words of a language. Hope against hope. And despair all the time a threat, a temptation. Those Alabama tenant farmers, amid their wretchedness and worse, gave him, finally, this victory: "All that each person is, and experiences, and shall never experience, in body and mind, all these things are differing expressions of himself and of one root, and are identical: and not one of these things nor one of these persons is ever quite to be duplicated, nor replaced, nor has it ever quite had precedent; but each is a new and incommunicably tender life, wounded in every breath and almost as hardly killed as easily wounded: sustaining, for a while, without defense, the enormous assaults of the universe." To have been presented that statement is to be privileged. We are "privileged ones" by virtue of that possession, allowed us by a certain grace. It is a start — Agee's message, and our struggle to prove him right. The rest is life: particular human beings — and those questions from Ecclesiastes that one American black woman, under the Louisiana sun, the American sun, will not ever, it seems, stop asking.

Index